Lecture Notes in Computer Science　9451

Commenced Publication in 1973
Founding and Former Series Editors:
Gerhard Goos, Juris Hartmanis, and Jan van Leeuwen

Editorial Board

More information about this series at http://www.springer.com/series/7410

Man-Ho Au · Atsuko Miyaji (Eds.)

Provable Security

9th International Conference, ProvSec 2015
Kanazawa, Japan, November 24–26, 2015
Proceedings

 Springer

Editors
Man-Ho Au
The Hong Kong Polytechnic University
Hong Kong
SAR China

Atsuko Miyaji
Japan Advanced Institute of Science
   and Technology
Ishikawa
Japan

ISSN 0302-9743   ISSN 1611-3349   (electronic)
Lecture Notes in Computer Science
ISBN 978-3-319-26058-7   ISBN 978-3-319-26059-4   (eBook)
DOI 10.1007/978-3-319-26059-4

Library of Congress Control Number: 2015952774

LNCS Sublibrary: SL4 – Security and Cryptology

Springer Cham Heidelberg New York Dordrecht London

Printed on acid-free paper

Springer International Publishing AG Switzerland is part of Springer Science+Business Media
(www.springer.com)

Preface

The 9th International Conference on Provable Security (ProvSec 2015) was held in Kanazawa, November 24–26, 2015. The previous ProvSec series were successfully held in Wollongong, Australia (2007), Shanghai, China (2008), Guangzhou, China (2009), Malacca, Malaysia (2010), Xi'an, China (2011), Chengdu, China (2012), Malacca, Malaysia (2013) and Hong Kong, China (2014). This was the first ProvSec held in Japan.

The main goal of ProvSec as a conference is to promote research on all aspects of provable security for cryptographic primitives or protocols, including but not limited to the following areas: asymmetric provably secure cryptography; cryptographic primitives; lattice-based cryptography and security reductions, leakage-resilient cryptography, pairing-based provably secure cryptography; privacy and anonymity technologies; provable secure block ciphers and hash functions; secure cryptographic protocols and applications; security notions, approaches, and paradigms; and steganography and steganalysis. This year we received 60 submissions from 23 different countries. Each submission was reviewed by at least three, and on average four, Program Committee members. Papers submitted by Program Committee members received at least four, and on the average 4.4, reviews. The committee decided to accept 19 regular papers and seven short papers. The broad range of areas covered by the high-quality accepted papers in the current edition attests to the fulfillment of that goal.

The program included three invited talks, given by Prof. Sanjam Garg (University of California, Berkeley) titled "New Advances in Secure RAM Computation," Prof. Phillip Rogaway (University of California, Davis) titled "Advances in Authenticated Encryption," and Prof. Serge Vaudenay (École Polytechnique Fédérale de Lausanne) titled "On Privacy for RFID".

The decision on the best paper award was based on a vote among the Program Committee members. The best paper award was conferred upon the paper "From Stateful Hardware to Resettable Hardware Using Symmetric Assumptions" authored by Nico Döttling, Daniel Kraschewski, Jörn Müller-Quade, and Tobias Nilges. In addition, the Program Committee selected the best student paper. To be eligible for selection, the primary author of the paper has to be a full-time student who gives a presentation at the conference. The winner was Bei Liang from the University of Chinese Academy of Sciences, Beijing, China, for the paper "Constrained Verifiable Random Functions from Indistinguishability Obfuscation."

We are very grateful to our supporters and sponsors. The conference was co-organized by the Information-technology Promotion Agency, Japan (IPA) and Japan Advanced Institute of Science and Technology (JAIST), it was supported by the Technical Committee on Information and Communication System Security (ICSS), IEICE, Japan, the Technical Committee on Information Security (ISEC), IEICE, Japan, and the Special Interest Group on Computer Security (CSEC) of IPSJ, Japan, and was co-sponsored by Mitsubishi Electric, National Institute of Information and

Communications Technology (NICT), Support Center for Advanced Telecommunications Technology Research (SCAT), and Nippon Telegraph and Telephone Corporation (NTT).

We would like to thank the authors for submitting their papers to the conference. The selection of the papers was a challenging and dedicated task, and we are deeply grateful to the 35 Program Committee members and the external reviewers for their reviews and discussions. We would also like to thank EasyChair for providing a user-friendly interface for us to manage all submissions and proceedings files. Finally, we would like to thank the general chair, Dr. Tatsuaki Okamoto, and we the members of the local Organizing Committee.

September 2015   Man-Ho Au
                                                                 Atsuko Miyaji

Provsec 2015
The 9th International Conference
on Provable Security

Jointly organized by

Information-technology Promotion Agency, Japan (IPA)
and
Japan Advanced Institute of Science and Technology (JAIST).

General Chair

Tatsuaki Okamoto NTT, Japan

Program Co-chairs

Man Ho Au Hong Kong Polytechnic University, SAR China
Atsuko Miyaji Osaka University/JAIST, Japan

Program Committee

Michel Abdalla	École normale supérieure, France
Elena Andreeva	KU Leuven, Belgium
Joonsang Baek	Khalifa University of Science, Technology and Research, UAE
Olivier Blazy	Université de Limoges, France
Carlo Blundo	University of Salerno, Italy
Colin Boyd	Norwegian University of Science and Technology, Norway
Mike Burmester	Florida State University, USA
Liqun Chen	Hewlett-Packard Laboratories, UK
Chen-Mou Cheng	Kyushu University, Japan
Céline Chevalier	Université Panthéon-Assas, France
Yvo Desmedt	The University of Texas at Dallas, USA and UCL, UK
Alexandre Duc	École polytechnique fédérale de Lausanne, Switzerland
Eiichiro Fujisaki	NTT, Japan
David Galindo	Scytl Secure Electronic Voting, Spain
Swee-Huay Heng	Multimedia University, Malaysia
Xinyi Huang	Fujian Normal University, China
Aniket Kate	Saarland University, Germany
Kwangjo Kim	KAIST, Korea
Miroslaw Kutyłowski	Wrocław University of Technology, Poland
Alptekin Küpçü	Koç University, Turkey
Joseph Liu	Monash University, Australia
Subhamoy Maitra	Indian Statistical Institute, India

Mark Manulis	University of Surrey, UK
Mitsuru Matsui	Mitsubishi Electric Corporation, Japan
Ali Miri	Ryerson University, Canada
Tarik Moataz	Colorado State University, USA
Jonghwan Park	Sangmyung University, Korea
Josef Pieprzyk	Queensland University of Technology, Australia
Willy Susilo	University of Wollongong, Australia
Mehdi Tibouchi	NTT, Japan
Damien Vergnaud	École normale supérieure, France
Cong Wang	City University of Hong Kong, Hong Kong, SAR China
Shouhuai Xu	University of Texas at San Antonio, USA
Bo-Yin Yang	Academia Sinica, Taiwan
Fangguo Zhang	Sun Yat-sen University, China

Steering Committee

Feng Bao	Huawei, Singapore
Xavier Boyen	Queensland University of Technology, Australia
Joseph K. Liu	Monash University, Australia
Yi Mu	University of Wollongong, Australia
Josef Pieprzyk	Queensland University of Technology, Australia
Willy Susilo	University of Wollongong, Australia

Organizing Committee

Local Arrangements Co-chairs

Kazumasa Omote	JAIST, Japan
Shoichi Hirose	University of Fukui, Japan
Kenji Yasunaga	Kanazawa University, Japan
Yuji Suga	IIJ, Japan
Jiageng Chen	JAIST, Japan

Finance Co-chairs

Takato Hirano	Mitsubishi Electric, Japan
Masaki Fujikawa	ALSOK, Japan
Yuichi Futa	JAIST, Japan

Publicity Co-chairs

Takeshi Chikazawa	IPA, Japan
Ryo Kikuchi	NTT, Japan
Tsuyoshi Takagi	Kyushu University, Japan
Naoto Yanai	Osaka University, Japan

Liaison Co-chairs

Toru Nakamura	KDDI Labs, Japan
Toru Nakanishi	Hiroshima University, Japan
Seonghan Shin	AIST, Japan

System Co-chairs

Atsuo Inomata	NAIST, Japan
Akira Kanaoka	Toho University, Japan
Toshihiro Yamauchi	Okayama University, Japan
Masaaki Shirase	Future University Hakodate, Japan

Publication Co-chairs

Isao Echizen	NII, Japan
Keita Emura	NICT, Japan
Satoru Tanaka	JAIST, Japan

Registration Co-chairs

Hideyuki Miyake	Toshiba, Japan
Dai Watanabe	Hitachi, Japan
Chunhua Su	JAIST, Japan

External Reviewers

Aminanto, Muhamad Erza
Arriaga, Afonso
Azzurra Marson, Giorgia
Behnia, Rouzbeh
Blasco Moreno, Pol
Bogos, Sonia
Chen, Rongmao
Choi, Rakyong
Ciampi, Michele
Condition, Merge
De Caro, Angelo
Eom, Ji Eun
Etemad, Mohammad
Faust, Sebastian
Fuchsbauer, Georg
Golebiewski, Zbigniew
Han, Jinguang
Hanzlik, Lucjan
Hassanzadeh, Yahya
Hirano, Takato
Iovino, Vincenzo

Kakvi, Saqib A.
Kawai, Yutaka
Kim, Hakju
Kim, Hyoseung
Kim, Jong Hyun
Kiyoshima, Susumu
Kluczniak, Kamil
Kuchta, Veronika
Kuo, Po-Chun
Lai, Junzuo
Langlois, Adeline
Lauks-Dutka, Anna
Li, Huige
Liang, Kaitai
Liu, Jianghua
Matsuo, Shinichiro
Naito, Yusuke
Nakasho, Kazuhisa
Onete, Cristina
Park, Seung Hwan
Peters, Thomas

Poettering, Bertram
Rafols, Carla
Siniscalchi, Luisa
Slowik, Marcin
Sugawara, Takeshi
Sung, Jaechul
Taheri, Sanaz
Takashima, Katsuyuki
Tan, Syhyuan
Tang, Jiayong
Vaudenay, Serge

Vivek, Srinivas
Vizár, Damian
Wang, Ding
Wodo, Wojciech
Wu, Wei
Xagawa, Keita
Xie, Shaohao
Yau, Wei-Chuan
Yu, Yu
Zhang, Huang
Zhang, Yuexin

Invited Talks

Advances in Authenticated Encryption

Phillip Rogaway

Department of Computer Science, University of California, Davis, USA
rogaway@cs.ucdavis.edu

Abstract. Authenticated encryption (AE) is a rare topic for so effectively bringing provable-security to cryptographic practice. I'll describe some recent advances in the AE, placing the ideas in their historical context. In particular, I'll look at *robust* AE and why it was developed, and I'll describe a recent notion for *online* AE, and why it was developed. I'll give a modern account of *generic composition*. Finally, I'll talk a bit about the CAESAR competition, which drew 57 AE submissions.

New Advances in Secure RAM Computation

Sanjam Garg

University of California, Berkeley, USA
sanjamg@berkeley.edu

Abstract. Customarily secure computation techniques are devised for circuits. Securing random access machine (RAM) programs using these approaches requires the conversion of the RAM program to a circuit, which can be prohibitive for various applications. For example, this conversion implies an exponential slowdown for binary search. State-of-the-art direct constructions for securing RAM programs suffer from inefficiencies such as large round-complexity or non-black-box use of underlying cryptographic primitives. In this talk we describe techniques for overcoming these barriers.

(Based on joint works with Steve Lu, Peihan Miao, Payman Mohassel, Omkant Pandey, Charalampos Papamanthou, Antigoni Polychroniadou, Rafail Ostrovsky, and Alessandra Scafuro.)

On Privacy for RFID

Serge Vaudenay

EPFL
CH-1015 Lausanne, Switzerland
http://lasec.epfl.ch

Abstract. Many wearable devices identify themselves in a pervasive way. But at the same time, people want to remain anonymous. Modeling anonymity and unlinkability in identification protocols is a delicate issue. In this paper, we revisit the privacy model from Asiacrypt 2007. We show how to achieve forward-privacy (in the V07 sense) using an IND-CCA secure cryptosystem with the PKC protocol. We review the impossibility result of strong privacy and the model extension from CANS 2012 to reach strong privacy (in the OV12 sense) using the PKC protocol with plaintext awareness. We also discuss on the simplified model from ESORICS 2011 and achieve strong-privacy (in the HPVP11 sense) using IND-CCA security only. Finally, we apply these results to add privacy protection in distance bounding protocols.

Contents

Encryption and Identification

Privacy and Cloud

Leakage-Resilient Cryptography and Lattice Cryptography

Signature and Broadcast Encryption

Invited Paper

On Privacy for RFID

Serge Vaudenay[✉]

EPFL, 1015 Lausanne, Switzerland
serge.vaudenay@epfl.ch
http://lasec.epfl.ch

Abstract. Many wearable devices identify themselves in a pervasive
way. But at the same time, people want to remain anonymous. Modeling
anonymity and unlinkability in identification protocols is a delicate issue.
In this paper, we revisit the privacy model from Asiacrypt 2007. We show
how to achieve forward-privacy (in the V07 sense) using an IND-CCA
secure cryptosystem with the PKC protocol. We review the impossibility result of strong privacy and the model extension from CANS 2012
to reach strong privacy (in the OV12 sense) using the PKC protocol
with plaintext awareness. We also discuss on the simplified model from
ESORICS 2011 and achieve strong-privacy (in the HPVP11 sense) using
IND-CCA security only. Finally, we apply these results to add privacy
protection in distance bounding protocols.

1 Introduction

People wear more and more passive RFID devices, from identity documents or
credit cards to smart socks[1]. These devices typically identify with a traceable
ID number to whichever device trying to scan them. Clearly, this opens oppor-
tunities for malicious people to tracing people based on their ID or to check how
frequently they changed their socks.

Concretely, an RFID system defines a set of legitimate tags, readers, and a
communication protocol between a tag and a reader. Sometimes, the protocol
may also require the reader to communicate with a centralized (authority) server.
The input of the tag consists of an internal state (which may contain a certificate
and a tag-specific secret key). The private output of the tag may be a new state
(for stateful protocols). The input of the reader may contain a root certificate or
a database of the secret keys of legitimate tags. The private output of the reader
is the ID of the tag. So, the purpose of the RFID protocol is to *identify* the tag
to the reader. At the same time, the identification must be secure (i.e., it must
authenticate the tag). A typical secondary issue is that the protocol must keep
privacy. I.e., no adversary could infer any non-trivial information about the ID
of the tag from the protocol.

A typical example is the GSM protocol: a GSM phone holding a SIM card
identifies for the first time to the network cell in clear using its IMSI number. This

---

[1] which tell when they stinks so that we can wash them and also how to pair them
again after washing.

© Springer International Publishing Switzerland 2015
M.-H. Au and A. Miyaji (Eds.): ProvSec 2015, LNCS 9451, pp. 3–20, 2015.
DOI: 10.1007/978-3-319-26059-4_1

tells the cell to which home network the SIM card belongs and how to get means to open a secure communication channel with it. Once this is done, the cell gives a pseudonym TMSI to the phone which will be used for the next identification. The TMSI is renewed through the secure channel as often as required. Security is based on symmetric cryptography. Privacy is clearly ineffective for the first connection. Furthermore, active attacks can break the synchronization between a phone and the cell, forcing the phone to identify in clear again. So, privacy protection is very weak in this case.

One difficult task when defining privacy is to model the capabilities of the adversary and his goal. In the early days of secure RFID protocols, some simple protocols were proposed with privacy protection [19,30,45]. These protocols assumed the adversary could not *corrupt* legitimate tags to get their internal state. A step further was made by the Ohkubo-Suzuki-Kinoshita protocol (OSK) [32,33] (see also [17,34]) to model *forward privacy*, i.e., such that uncorrupted tags running the protocol could not be identified in the future after they become corrupted. An early model for RFID privacy was proposed by Avoine-Dysli-Oechslin [2,3]. Their, the adversary chooses two tags; one of them is drawn at random and they must guess which one after interacting with this tag and the reader concurrently. The model was later refined by Juels and Weis [25] by telling the adversary when the reader succeeds to identify a legitimate tag. This information, which is the *result* of the protocol, models a side-channel information that the adversary could exploit.

The most complete privacy model (called the V07 model herein) appeared at Asiacrypt 2007 [39]. It is based on simulation. Essentially, the adversary plays with tags and readers concurrently. He specifies the distribution following which tags are drawn. His goal is to infer some information about identities, but the information must be non-trivial in the sense that it cannot be inferred by simulating the protocol messages. The V07 model defines a 2×4-matrix of privacy levels, depending on whether the adversary has access to the result of the protocol (which are called *narrow* and *wide* adversaries), and depending on how corruption is feasible. With no corruption, we have a *weak* adversary. With corruption which can only happen at the end of the game, we have a *forward* adversary (to address forward privacy). With corruption which destroy tags (i.e., the adversary can no longer play with a corrupted tag), we have a *destructive* adversary. With corruption which happens with no such restriction, we have a *strong* adversary. In [39], a secure RFID protocol protecting both narrow-strong and wide-forward privacy was constructed based on a chosen-ciphertext-secure (IND-CCA) cryptosystem. This protocol based on a cryptosystem is called PKC herein. It was further shown that wide-weak privacy was achievable with just a pseudorandom function (PRF).

In [39], it was proven that an RFID protocol could not offer at the same time wide-destructive and narrow-strong privacy. In particular, wide-strong privacy is impossible. The impossibility result was however quite technical, more showing that the privacy definition was overly restrictive than showing a concrete impossibility result. This made Ng *et al.* [31] propose the notion of *wise* adversary, i.e., an adversary who does not ask questions for which he knows the answer. The definition from [31] was not formal enough to be usable, but this made Ouafi and Vaudenay [35] to refine the V07 model by letting the simulator know the input of the adversary (so, know what answer the adversary expects). This model is called the OV12 model herein. Then, they have shown that the PKC protocol is wide-strong-private when the cryptosystem is further plaintext-aware (PA).

Finally, Hermans *et al.* [23] proposed another privacy model (called the HPVP11 model herein) in which the game uses a left-or-right oracle and corruption is not made on anonymous tags. Surprisingly, this makes the notion of "trivial information" obtained by adversaries easy to specify and allows to get rid of the simulation. In addition, the PKC model is shown to be wide-strong private in the HPVP11 sense with only IND-CCA (and not PA) security as an assumption. This makes the model much more easy to use. However, it was shown in [35] that the OV12 model is strictly stronger that the HPVP11 model in the sense that we can construct a protocol being HPVP11-wide-strong-private but not OV12-wide-strong-private. However, the proof that the protocol is not OV12-private does not yield any convincing real privacy threat. So, the definitions of the OV12 model may be too restrictive and the HPVP11 notion of wide-strong privacy may certainly be enough.

With distance bounding (DB) protocols, the tag wants to prove its proximity to the reader. There are symmetric DB protocols in which the tag and the reader share a secret and public-key DB protocols in which the tag (and sometimes the reader) has a public/private key pair to authenticate. Modeling security for DB protocols is not easy.

The first complete security models and provably secure protocols were independently proposed by Boureanu *et al.* [8–12] and by Fischlin and Onete [18,20]. None of these protocols were optimal but by combining both ideas we obtain the DBopt protocols [7,26]. In these protocols, the tag and the reader must share a symmetric secret.

Regarding public-key DB protocols, the DBopt model was adapted for public-key DB in [41–43]. Not many public-key DB protocols exist. We list them in Table 1 with the known proven security/insecurity results (see [42,43] for details). The table includes *Man-in-the-Middle* security (MiM), *Distance Fraud* (DF), *Distance Hijacking* (DH), *Collusion Fraud* (CF), *wide-Privacy* (Privacy), and *wide-Strong Privacy* (Strong Privacy). Note that DBPK-Log [15] is broken [4]. As we can see, only the HPO protocol and privDB [24,42] provide some form of privacy. HPO [24] relies on ad-hoc assumptions. Futhermore, it does not provide wide-strong privacy (as shown in [44]). So far, only privDB [42] provides wide-strong privacy. We added in the table the eProProx protocol which is proposed in this paper. It extends ProProx by providing wide-strong privacy.

2   The V07 Model and the OV12 Extension

We describe here the V07 model [39] and the OV12 extension [35], as presented in [40]. The V07 model [39] from Asiacrypt 2007 follows up some joint work during

Table 1. Existing public-key distance bounding protocols

protocol	MiM	DF	DH	CF	Privacy	Strong privacy
Brands-Chaum [14]	secure	secure	insecure	insecure	insecure	insecure
DBPK-Log [15]		insecure		insecure	insecure	insecure
HPO [24]	secure	secure		insecure	secure	insecure
GOR [21]	secure	secure	insecure	insecure	insecure	insecure
privDB [42]	secure	secure	secure	insecure	secure	secure
ProProx [43]	secure	secure	secure	secure	insecure	insecure
eProProx (this paper)	secure	secure	secure	secure	secure	secure

the MSc Thesis of Bocchetti [6]. The results were also announced in [38]. For completeness, we also indicate that some extension with reader authentication was proposed in [36] ... but with a few incorrect results as shown by Armknecht et al. [1].

The V07 model considers a multiparty setting with a malicious adversary and several concurrent honest tags and honest readers which can be activated by the adversary. All readers are assumed to be front ends of a secure server which contains a database. The communication from readers to the central database is assumed to be secure. Although all tags are honest, some belong to the system (these tags are sometimes called *legitimate*) and some do not. The adversary can initiate the creation of new tags (in the system or not). He controls the communications to every participants. Furthermore, the access to random tags in practice is modelled by having the adversary being able to draw anonymous tags with a chosen probability distribution.

RFID system. More concretely, there is an algorithm

$$\mathsf{SetupReader} \to (K_S, K_P)$$

producing a key pair. The key K_S is secret. It can be used by readers. The key K_P is public and used to create tags. Indeed, there is an algorithm

$$\mathsf{SetupTag}_{K_P}(\mathsf{ID}) \to (\mathsf{data}, S)$$

producing an initial state S for the tag and some data so that the entry (ID, data) is inserted into the database when the tag is meant to belong to the system. In addition to SetupReader and SetupTag, an RFID system specifies an interactive protocol between a tag and a reader. The tag has as input its current state S and as output a value S' which becomes the new state of the tag. The reader has as input K_S and as output some value out. If out $= \perp$, we say that the identification failed. Otherwise, out shall corresponds to the ID of the tag.

Game. In a game, after SetupReader was run, the adversary receives K_P and can access to an oracle

$$\mathsf{CreateTag}(\mathsf{ID}, b)$$

which runs $\mathsf{SetupTag}_{K_P}(\mathsf{ID}) \to (\mathsf{data}, S)$. Additionally, if $b = 1$, the oracle inserts $(\mathsf{ID}, \mathsf{data})$ into the database. So, $b = 1$ means that the tag will be recognized as belonging to the system but $b = 0$ can be used to create "foreign tags".

The adversary can also access to the

$$\mathsf{DrawTag}(D) \to (\mathsf{vtag}_1, b_1, \ldots, \mathsf{vtag}_n, b_n)$$

with a chosen distribution. This oracle draws a vector $(\mathsf{ID}_1, \ldots, \mathsf{ID}_n)$ following the chosen distribution D. If any tag ID_i is already drawn or was not created, the oracle returns $\bot$. Otherwise, it defines some fresh random identifiers vtag_i and sets b_i to 1 if and only if ID_i belongs to the system. Additionally, the oracle adds the matching $\mathsf{vtag}_i \leftrightarrow \mathsf{ID}_i$ in a private table $\mathcal{T}$. So, the adversary can draw anonymous tags with a chosen distribution and can see which tag belongs to the system. This assumption is realistic as practical tags often leak their version, manufacturer, and other information from which we can deduce what type of tag it is. Clearly, the drawing oracle is such that a drawn tag cannot be drawn again. However, the adversary can call a

$$\mathsf{Free}(\mathsf{vtag})$$

oracle to free the anonymous tag vtag so that it can be drawn again.

As discussed in [35, 36], the oracle Free must reset the temporary memory of the anonymous tag before releasing it. This is in order to present protocol sessions to span through several anonymous tag instances.

The adversary can call a

$$\mathsf{Launch} \to \pi$$

oracle which initiates a new reader session which can be called by the identifier π.

The adversary can send messages to a launched reader π or to a drawn tag vtag as long as it has not be freed. He can call

$$\mathsf{SendReader}(m, \pi) \to m'$$

to send m to π and obtain the response m' (if any). If the reader initiates the interactive protocol and π did not start yet, m is empty. If π was not launched or if the protocol terminated on the session π, nothing is returned. He can call

$$\mathsf{SendTag}(m, \mathsf{vtag}) \to m'$$

to send m to vtag and obtain the response m' (if any). If the tag initiates the interactive protocol and vtag did not start yet, m is empty. If vtag was not drawn, or was freed, or if the protocol terminated on vtag, nothing is returned. A new session may start with vtag by calling $\mathsf{SendTag}$ again.

The adversary may use a

$$\mathsf{Result}(\pi) \to x$$

oracle which tells whether the reader protocol succeeded to identify a tag on session π. (So, $x = 0$ or 1.) If the adversary is *narrow*, this oracle cannot be used. If the adversary is *wide*, no restriction applies on using this oracle.

Finally, the adversary may use a

$$\mathsf{Corrupt}(\mathsf{vtag}) \to S$$

oracle which returns the current state of the anonymous tag vtag. As vtag can only be accessed between the time it is drawn and the time it is freed, the oracle returns nothing at any other time. If the adversary is *weak*, this oracle cannot be used. If the adversary is *forward*, only further Corrupt queries can be made after this oracle call but no other oracle can be used. If the adversary is *strong*, no restriction applies on corruption.

Matching conversation. We say that two participants have a *matching conversation* at a given time if the sequence of incoming/outgoing messages that they have seen match and are well interleaved. I.e., if the protocol transcript seen by one participant is of form

$$(t_1, \mathsf{in}_1, \mathsf{out}_1), (t_2, \mathsf{in}_2, \mathsf{out}_2), \dots (t_n, \mathsf{in}_n, \mathsf{out}_n),$$

or (when the participant initiates the protocol)

$$(t_1, \bot, \mathsf{out}_1), (t_2, \mathsf{in}_2, \mathsf{out}_2), \dots (t_n, \mathsf{in}_n, \mathsf{out}_n),$$

with $t_1 < \cdots < t_n$ (meaning that at time t_i, the participant received in_i and sent out_i), then the protocol transcript seen by the other participant must be

$$(t'_1, \bot, \mathsf{in}_1), (t'_2, \mathsf{out}_1, \mathsf{in}_2), \dots (t'_n, \mathsf{out}_{n-1}, \mathsf{in}_n),$$

or

$$(t'_2, \mathsf{out}_1, \mathsf{in}_2), \dots (t'_n, \mathsf{out}_{n-1}, \mathsf{in}_n),$$

respectively, for some $t'_1, \dots, t'_n$ such that $t'_1 < t_1 < t'_2 < \cdots < t_{n-1} < t'_n < t_n$ (meaning that at time t'_i, the participant received out_{i-1} and sent in_i).

Correct system. The protocol is *correct* if for any game, whenever there is a matching conversation between some vtag and some π, if vtag was drawn by DrawTag with the bit b, then, except with negligible probability, the output of π is $\mathsf{out} = \bot$ if $b = 0$ and $\mathsf{out} = \mathcal{T}(\mathsf{vtag})$ if $b = 1$.

Secure system. An RFID system is *secure* if for any game, except with negligible probability, for all π which produced $\mathsf{out} = \mathsf{ID} \neq \bot$, there must exist vtag such that $\mathcal{T}(\mathsf{vtag}) = \mathsf{ID}$ and either vtag has a matching conversation with π or vtag was corrupted.

Privacy. In the privacy game, the adversary $\mathcal{A}$ plays with the oracle. When done, he receives the table $\mathcal{T}$ and produces a binary output. To identify the trivial ways to output 1, we use a simulator based on a *blinder* B. A blinder sees all oracle queries of the adversary (but cannot see the table $\mathcal{T}$) and simulates the responses of the Launch, SendReader, SendTag, and Result oracles to $\mathcal{A}$. When

$\mathcal{A}$ interacts with the blinded oracles (instead of the oracles directly), we denote it by $\mathcal{A}^B$. A trivial way for $\mathcal{A}$ to output 1 is such that there exists B such that $\mathcal{A}^B$ outputs 1 with nearly the same probability as $\mathcal{A}$. Intuitively, it means that $\mathcal{A}$ learns nothing new from the protocol messages, as he could simulate them by himself. A protocol is P-private if for any adversary $\mathcal{A}$ in the class P, there exists a blinder B such that $\mathcal{A}$ and $\mathcal{A}^B$ produce the same output except with negligible probability. As an example of class P, we can consider all wide-strong adversaries.

Impossibility of wide-strong privacy in the V07 model. To prove the impossibility of wide-strong privacy by contradiction, we essentially have to make the adversary play against the blinder. Let us assume that the protocol provides wide-strong privacy. We consider a first game in which the adversary creates a legitimate tag ID_1, draws ID_1, and corrupts it to get its state S_1. Then, he runs on its own $\mathsf{SetupTag}_{K_P}(\mathsf{ID}_0) \to S_0$. Now, the adversary can simulate either tag ID_0 or tag ID_1 using their state. So, he can flip a coin b, launch a reader session π and simulate ID_b to π using S_b. Finally, the adversary calls $\mathsf{Result}(\pi)$ and gives it as an output. Clearly, correctness imposes that the result of π is b. Due to privacy, there must exist a blinder B such that from the states of the two tags S_0 and S_1 and the messages from the tag ID_b, then B can guess b. This means that we can make a second game in which we create two tags in the system, corrupt both of them to get their states S_0 and S_1, then draw one at random and play with, and use B to infer which tag was drawn. This would identify the tag, but there is no blinder to do so. So, there is a contradiction. The crucial point in this argument is that the adversary in the first game knows which tag he simulates and makes the Result guess it. So, a blinder must simulate this guess.

V07 vs OV12. A big difference between the V07 and OV12 models is that in OV12, the blinder can use the view of the adversary as input. So, he can simulate the internal computations of the adversary and somehow "read his thoughts". This is an essential technique used with plaintext awareness (PA). Essentially, whenever the adversary issues a ciphertext, we can use a plaintext extractor on the view of the adversary to see what was encrypted. With the previous impossibility result in the V07 model, we can see that now, in the first game, the blinder could now read the bit b from the thoughts of the adversary and no longer need to guess it from the states and messages. So, the argument of impossibility does not hold in the OV12 model.

There are also tricky issues about the $\mathsf{DrawTag}$ oracle when the number n of tags to be drawn is not logarithmic. For instance, if n is linear, the vector spans in a set of exponential size. So, the representation of the input distribution D can be large. In [35], it is specified that D is submitted in the form of an efficient sampling algorithm Samp. It is required that D must additionally be *inverse-samplable*, i.e., there exists an efficient algorithm Samp^{-1} such that $(\rho, \mathsf{Samp}(\rho))$ and $(\mathsf{Samp}^{-1}(x), x)$ are indistinguishable. (This is always the case when n is logarithmic.) Furthermore, [35] requires that there exists a simulator S such that the pair $(\mathsf{View}_{\mathcal{A}}, \mathcal{T})$ consisting of the view of the adversary and the table $\mathcal{T}$

is indistinguishable from the pair $(\mathsf{View}_{\mathcal{A}}, S(\mathsf{View}_{\mathcal{A}}))$. This is used to reconstruct some possible random coins which are used in the privacy game so that we can feed the plaintext extractor of the PA game (see [35]).

PKC protocol. The PKC RFID system is pretty simple. First, SetupReader sets up a key pair (sk, pk) using Gen for a public-key cryptosystem $(\mathsf{Gen}, \mathsf{Enc_{pk}}, \mathsf{Dec_{sk}})$. We have $K_S = \mathsf{sk}$ and $K_P = \mathsf{pk}$. Then, SetupTag picks a random K_{ID} and sets up the state $S = (\mathsf{pk}, \mathsf{ID}, K_{\mathsf{ID}})$ and data $= K_{\mathsf{ID}}$ to be inserted in the database. Then, in the identification protocol, the reader selects a nonce N, sends it to the tag. The tag then encrypts his ID, his key K_{ID} and the nonce N and sends the ciphertext to the reader. The reader can then decrypt, check that the nonce is correct, and that $(\mathsf{ID}, K_{\mathsf{ID}})$ is in the database.

A variant based on a PRF avoids using a database: we add a generation of a secret K_M for a PRF by SetupReader (so $K_S = (\mathsf{sk}, K_M)$) and use $K_{\mathsf{ID}} = \mathsf{PRF}_{K_M}(\mathsf{ID})$.

In [39], it was proven that if the cryptosystem is IND-CCA secure then the PKC protocol is correct, secure, wide-forward private, and narrow-strong private in the V07 model. In [35], it was proven that if the cryptosystem is further PA (in the PA1+ sense [16] or the PA2 sense [5]), then the PKC protocol is wide-strong private in the OV12 model.

IND-CCA security is necessary for the security of PKC. Clearly, it is essential that the cryptosystem is IND-CCA secure: without non-malleability, we could loose security by forging the ciphertext of a legitimate tag. For instance, given a secure cryptosystem (Gen, E, D), defining a malleable yet IND-CPA secure cryptosystem $\mathsf{Enc_{pk}}(\mathsf{ID}\|K_{\mathsf{ID}}\|N) = E_{\mathsf{pk}}(\mathsf{ID}\|K_{\mathsf{ID}})\|E_{\mathsf{pk}}(N)$ would allow to take $\mathsf{Enc_{pk}}(\mathsf{ID}\|K_{\mathsf{ID}})$ as a reusable credential to be use with any fresh nonce. Hence, we could impersonate a legitimate tag.

IND-CCA security is insufficient for the wide-strong privacy of PKC in the OV12 sense. In [35], it was further proven that IND-CCA security was not sufficient to achieve wide-strong privacy. To prove this, the authors essentially construct a cryptosystem which is IND-CCA secure but not PA. More concretely, if (G^0, E^0, D^0) is an IND-CCA cryptosystem and if (G^1, E^1, D^1) is a homomorphic IND-CPA cryptosystem over the message space $\{0, 1\}$ such as the Goldwasser-Micali cryptosystem [22], we define

$$\mathsf{Gen} \rightarrow ((\mathsf{sk}_0, \mathsf{sk}_1), (\mathsf{pk}_0, \mathsf{pk}_1, z)) \quad \text{for} \quad \begin{cases} G^0 \rightarrow (\mathsf{sk}_0, \mathsf{pk}_0) \\ G^1 \rightarrow (\mathsf{sk}_1, \mathsf{pk}_1) \\ \xi \in_U \{0, 1\} \\ z = E^1_{\mathsf{pk}_1}(\xi) \end{cases}$$

(note that ξ is discarded and never used again) and

$$\mathsf{Enc}_{(\mathsf{pk}_0, \mathsf{pk}_1), z}(m_1 \cdots m_n) = E^0_{\mathsf{pk}_0}(E^1_{\mathsf{pk}_1}(m_1)\| \cdots \|E^1_{\mathsf{pk}_1}(m_n))$$

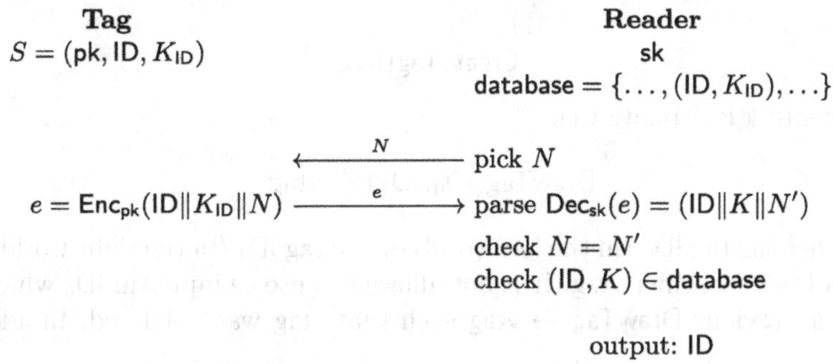

$$\text{Tag} \qquad\qquad\qquad\qquad \textbf{Reader}$$

$$S = (\mathsf{pk}, \mathsf{ID}, K_{\mathsf{ID}}) \qquad\qquad\qquad\qquad \mathsf{sk}$$

$$\text{database} = \{\ldots, (\mathsf{ID}, K_{\mathsf{ID}}), \ldots\}$$

$$\xleftarrow{\quad N \quad} \text{pick } N$$

$$e = \mathsf{Enc_{pk}}(\mathsf{ID}\|K_{\mathsf{ID}}\|N) \xrightarrow{\quad e \quad} \text{parse } \mathsf{Dec_{sk}}(e) = (\mathsf{ID}\|K\|N')$$

$$\text{check } N = N'$$

$$\text{check } (\mathsf{ID}, K) \in \text{database}$$

$$\text{output: ID}$$

Fig. 1. The PKC protocol based on a cryptosystem Enc/Dec.

where the m_i are bits. We can show that $(\mathsf{Gen}, \mathsf{Enc}, \mathsf{Dec})$ is an IND-CCA-secure cryptosystem. Then, we mount a wide-strong adversary who creates a legitimate tag, corrupts it, then simulate it to the reader, except that the encryption of $(\mathsf{ID}, K_{\mathsf{ID}}, N) = m_1 \cdots m_n$ is modified as follows: after computing $E^1(m_i)$ to encrypt each bit of the plaintext, he multiplies them by z. Finally,

$$e = E^0_{\mathsf{pk}_0}(z \cdot E^1_{\mathsf{pk}_1}(m_1)\| \cdots \|z \cdot E^1_{\mathsf{pk}_1}(m_n))$$

Clearly, the decryption of e by the reader is unchanged if and only if $\xi = 0$. Otherwise, all bits are flipped and lead to an incorrect nonce, so the protocol fails. As the adversary gets $\mathsf{Result}(\pi)$ from the reader, this bit is thus equal to $1 - \xi$. Although the blinder knows how the ciphertext was forged, he cannot compute ξ when (G^1, E^1, D^1) is secure. So, no blinder can simulate the $\mathsf{Result}(\pi)$ oracle and we do not have wide-strong privacy.

Public-key cryptography is necessary. We can similarly show that a wide-strong private RFID system can define a public-key cryptosystem. So, it is unlikely that we could construct one based on symmetric cryptography only. More concretely, if we create two tags ID_0 and ID_1 then corrupt both of them, their state is equivalent to a public key. Alice could send a bit b to Bob by simulating ID_b using the public key while Bob would simulate the reader with the secret key. We can show that if the scheme is wide-strong private, then we have a public cryptographic scheme in the sense of [37]. Hence, public-key cryptography is necessary.

3   The HPVP11 Model

In [23], Hermans *et al.* proposed a quite simpler privacy model (the HPVP11 model herein).

To define the HPVP11 model, we revisit the oracle calls of the adversary. All oracles work the same except CreateTag, DrawTag, and Corrupt. Namely,

$$\mathsf{CreateTag(ID)}$$

always create a legitimate tag.

$$\mathsf{DrawTag(ID_0, ID_1) \to vtag}$$

draws either the tag $\mathsf{ID_0}$ (in the left world) or the tag $\mathsf{ID_1}$ (in the right world), and returns a fresh identifier vtag. It is not allowed to use as input an $\mathsf{ID_b}$ which was input of a previous $\mathsf{DrawTag} \to \mathsf{vtag}$ such that vtag was not freed. In addition to this,

$$\mathsf{Corrupt(ID) \to S}$$

now works on the true identity ID of the tag instead of the one of an anonymous tag, and it is not allowed if the corresponding tag was input of a previous $\mathsf{DrawTag}$ and was not freed since then.[2]

The main difference is that the game first flips a coin b and uses the left world for $b = 0$ and the right world for $b = 1$. The goal of the adversary is to guess b. We have P-privacy if for any adversary in the class P, the probability to correctly guess b is lower than $\frac{1}{2}$ plus some negligible advantage.

Surprisingly, they even proved that based on IND-CCA security, the PKC RFID system is wide-strong private in their model. Hence, our proof that IND-CCA security is not sufficient shows that the PKC protocol can be wide-strong private in the HPVP11 sense but not in the OV12 sense. So, HPVP11 privacy does not imply OV12 privacy. However, looking closer at what it means in practice, we can wonder to what extend the proof that IND-CCA security is not enough for OV12 privacy implies any privacy threat. Indeed, the inability to simulate the Result oracle in our counterexample does not seem to imply any leakage in identifying information. So, HPVP11 privacy may be enough in practice.

4 Strong Privacy in Distance Bounding

In distance bounding (DB) protocols, the tag wants to prove its proximity to the reader. There are several threat models. With honest tags, we have to face to *man-in-the-middle* attacks (MiM) trying to make the reader accept a proof of proximity although no tag is actually close. MiM-security is also called HP-security (as for *Honest Prover*) in [41,43]. With malicious tags, we consider *distance fraud* (DF), where no tag is close to the reader, *distance hijacking* (DH), where a honest tag is close to the reader but the malicious one far away tries to pass the protocol, and *collusion fraud* (CF), where the malicious tag can be helped by a close-by malicious adversary. CF-resistance is formalized in [41,43] in terms of *soundness* of the proximity proof: essentially, we show that if the protocol succeeds, then we can extract the secret of the identified tag from the

---

[2] Some variants allow this but do not disclose states depending on possible ongoing sessions (typically: the volatile memory). So, extra care must be taken with stateful protocols.

view of participants which are close to the reader. So, there is no better CF than the trivial one consisting of giving the secret of the tag to the close-by adversary. In symmetric DB, the tag and the reader are assumed to share a secret. In public-key DB, the tag holds a key pair but shares no secret with the reader. In this paper, we concentrate on strong privacy. Since this requires public-key cryptography (as already mentioned), there is no need for limiting ourselves to symmetric DB. So, we only consider public-key DB.

Privacy in public-key DB. The first public-key DB protocol to offer privacy is the HPO protocol [24]. However, it does not offer strong privacy [44]. In [13], it was suggested to transform a symmetric DB protocol into a public-key DB protocol using a key agreement protocol. We can wonder how privacy can be preserved. The first concrete example is the privDB protocol [42]. It is depicted on Fig. 2 (taken from [42]). There, symDB denotes a one-time symmetric DB protocol (such as OTDB on Fig. 3). We use a signature scheme Sign/Verify and a cryptosystem Enc/Dec. The function Validate(pk) is used to "validate" a public key, i.e. either to check that it belongs to a database, or to check a certificate (which could be pk itself).

In public-key DB, the tag has a key pair $(\mathsf{sk}, \mathsf{pk})$ and the public key K_P of the system. We modify the PKC protocol as follows: instead of encrypting $\mathsf{ID}\|K_{\mathsf{ID}}\|N$, we now encrypt $s\|\mathsf{pk}\|\mathsf{Sign}_{\mathsf{sk}}(N)$ where s is a random key. Then, the

$$
\begin{array}{ll}
\textbf{Reader} & \textbf{Tag} \\
\text{secret key: } \mathsf{sk}_R & \text{secret key: } \mathsf{sk}_T \\
\text{public key: } \mathsf{pk}_R & \text{public key: } \mathsf{pk}_T
\end{array}
$$

$$\text{pick } N \xrightarrow{\quad N \quad} \text{pick } s,\ \sigma = \mathsf{Sign}_{\mathsf{sk}_T}(N)$$

$$s\|\mathsf{pk}\|\sigma = \mathsf{Dec}_{\mathsf{sk}_R}(e) \xleftarrow{\quad e \quad} e = \mathsf{Enc}_{\mathsf{pk}_R}(s\|\mathsf{pk}_T\|\sigma)$$

$$\mathsf{Verify}_{\mathsf{pk}}(\sigma, N) \text{ and } \mathsf{Validate}(\mathsf{pk}) \xleftrightarrow{\ \mathsf{symDB}(s)\ }$$

$$\text{output: } \mathsf{pk}$$

Fig. 2. privDB: Private public-key DB [42].

$$
\begin{array}{ll}
\textbf{Reader} & \textbf{Tag} \\
\text{secret key: } s & \text{secret key: } s
\end{array}
$$

initialization phase

$$\text{pick } m \in \{0,1\}^{2n} \xrightarrow{\quad m \quad} a = s \oplus m$$

challenge phase
for $i = 1$ to n

$$\text{pick } c_i \in \{0,1\}, \text{ start timer}_i \xRightarrow{\quad c_i \quad}$$

$$\text{stop timer}_i \xLeftarrow{\quad r_i \quad} r_i = a_{2i+c_i-1}$$

verification phase

$$a = s \oplus m$$

$$\text{check timer}_i \leq 2B, \ r_i = a_{2i+c_i-1}$$

Fig. 3. OTDB: One-time symmetric DB [42].

reader no longer needs the secret of the tag. The identity is obtained by pk and it is enough to authenticate the tag using the signature on N. The value s can further be used as the result of a key agreement. Hence, the tag and the reader can now use s to run a symmetric DB protocol. This is the principle of the privDB protocol [42] which is wide-strong private (in the HPVP11 sense) and secure DB[3].

Strengthening ProProx. We recall on Fig. 4 [43] a (simplified) version of ProProx. There, we use a homomorphic bit commitment scheme Com such that

$$\mathsf{Com}(b; \rho) = \theta^b \rho^2$$

in a group such that $\theta^2 = 1$ and θ has no square root, and a deterministic vector commitment scheme

$$\mathsf{Com}_H(\mathsf{sk}) = (\mathsf{Com}(\mathsf{sk}_1; H(\mathsf{sk}, 1)), \ldots, \mathsf{Com}(\mathsf{sk}_s; H(\mathsf{sk}, s)))$$

There is no required assumption on the hash function H except that Com_H must be one-way. This is the case when H is a random oracle (and sk is not too small), but H does not necessarily need to be a random oracle in this construction. We also use a zero-knowledge proof $\mathsf{ZKP}_\kappa(z_{i,j}; \zeta_{i,j})$ that there exists some $\zeta_{i,j}$ such that $z_{i,j} = \zeta_{i,j}^2$ for all i, j. We can use parallel instances of the protocol from Fig. 5 [43] with enough challenges to that the soundness probability is κ. There, we use a trapdoor commitment scheme (Gen, Commit, Equiv).

Reader		**Tag**
public: pk	pk = $\mathsf{Com}_H(\mathsf{sk})$	secret: sk

initialization phase
for $i = 1$ to n and $j = 1$ to s
                                                pick $a_{i,j} \in \mathbf{Z}_2$, $\rho_{i,j}$
                    $\xleftarrow{\quad A_{i,j} \quad}$ $A_{i,j} = \mathsf{Com}(a_{i,j}; \rho_{i,j})$

challenge phase
for $i = 1$ to n and $j = 1$ to s
pick $c_{i,j} \in \mathbf{Z}_2$
start timer$_{i,j}$ $\xRightarrow{\quad c_{i,j} \quad}$ receive $c'_{i,j}$
receive $r_{i,j}$, stop timer$_{i,j}$ $\xleftarrow{\quad r'_{i,j} \quad}$ $r'_{i,j} = a_{i,j} + c'_{i,j} b_{i,j} + c'_{i,j} \mathsf{sk}_j$

verification phase
check timer$_{i,j} \leq 2B$ for all i, j
$z_{i,j} = A_{i,j} \left(\theta^{b_{i,j}} \mathsf{pk}_j\right)^{c_{i,j}} \theta^{-r_{i,j}}$ $\xleftarrow{\quad ZKP_\kappa(z_{i,j}; \zeta_{i,j}; i, j) \quad}$ $\zeta_{i,j} = \rho_{i,j} H(\mathsf{sk}, j)^{c'_{i,j}}$

Fig. 4. ProProx: Sound public-key DB [43].

---

[3] More precisely, it defeats distance fraud, man-in-the-middle attacks, and distance hijacking, but not collusion fraud, as shown on Table 1.

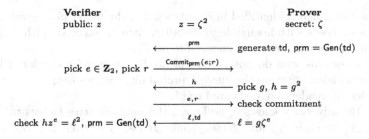

Fig. 5. ZKP($z : \zeta$): a zero-knowledge proof of existence of ζ such that $z = \zeta^2$ [43].

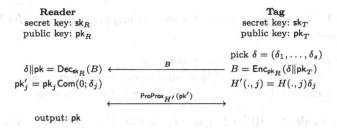

Fig. 6. eProProx: a privacy extension for ProProx.

As shown on Table 1, ProProx is the only public-key DB protocol with full security. However, it does not protect privacy. We can extend ProProx into a protocol eProProx as shown on Fig. 6 to add privacy protection. If $\mathsf{ProProx}_H(\mathsf{pk})$ denotes the protocol from Fig. 4, we just change the function H (as used by the tag) into a function H' and the public key pk (as used by the reader) into pk$'$. Essentially, we blind the public key of the tag so that it does not leak from ZKP. Interestingly, the encryption step in this extension is similar to the PKC protocol from Fig. 1. We can indeed use this encrypted channel to identify by transmitting pk: now, pk is given as an output of the reader instead as an input.

We state the security results for eProProx as they are stated for ProProx in [43]. We however simplified it (in more details, we took $p_{\mathsf{noise}} = 0$ and $\tau = n$).

Theorem 1. *The eProProx protocol is a sound, MiM-secure, DF-resistant, and DH-resistant proof of proximity under the assumption that*

- Com *is a perfectly binding, computationally hiding, and homomorphic bit commitment;*
- Com$_H$ *is one-way;*
- ZKP$_\kappa$ *is a complete and κ-sound computationally zero-knowledge proof of membership for $\kappa = $ negl.*

Proof. Since the cryptosystem plays no role in the security, we assume without loss of generality that $\delta\|\mathsf{pk}_T$ is sent in clear in B. We let Γ_0 be a security game. We make a new game Γ_1 which first picks one tag pk at random and succeeds in this is the tag which is identified in the attack. So, the target pk is given first. If this game succeeds with negligible probability, then Γ_0 succeeds with negligible probability as well. So, we can concentrate on Γ_1.

Reader sessions who do not receive pk in B can just be simulated by the adversary without affecting the success probability. So, we obtain a new game Γ_2 in which all readers are dedicated to pk.

Since the adversary knows δ, he knows the multiplicative factors to change pk_j into pk'_j in each $z_{i,j}$ and $H(sk, j)$ into $H'(sk, j)$ in each $\zeta_{i,j}$. So, we can construct an adversary against $\mathsf{ProProx}_H(pk)$. Then, we apply the security results from [41,43].   □

Theorem 2. *The* eProProx *protocol is wide-strong private in the HPVP11 sense under the assumption that*

– Enc/Dec *is an IND-CCA-secure cryptosystem;*
– Com *is a computationally hiding homomorphic bit commitment;*
– ZKP_κ *is a computationally zero-knowledge proof of membership.*

Proof. We consider the HPVP11 game Γ_0. Without loss of generality, we assume that drawn tags run a single session of the protocol (indeed, they can be freed and drawn again to run more sessions).

We first reduce to a game in which no different tag sessions pick the same δ vector. So, they never produce the same B, due to the correctness of the cryptosystem. We obtain a game Γ_1 producing the same output as Γ_0, except with negligible probability.

We observe that in the privacy game, the output pk on the reader side plays no role and that the reader only needs pk' to run $\mathsf{ProProx}_{H'}(pk')$. Namely, δ and H' are of no use to the reader. So, we can change the protocol by having the reader saying to the adversary whether pk is a valid key, returning pk', and stopping. Then, the reader messages as in Γ_1 can be fully simulated by the adversary. We obtain a game Γ_2 in which the reader is only decrypting B, checking pk, computing pk', and releasing it.

Next, we change the game by making sure that if a session π receives B which was previously issued by one vtag after encrypting some $\delta \| pk_T$, then π does not use the decryption algorithm but rather continues directly with δ and $pk = pk_T$. Clearly, the simulation is perfect. We let Γ_3 denote the new game.

Then, by using hybrids, we replace in Γ_3 every B issued by vtag by the encryption of some random junk string. Thanks to the IND-CCA security, we obtain a new game Γ_4 which produces the same output, except with negligible probability. So, in Γ_4, it is as if we had a protocol in which vtag has some perfectly secure channel to transmit δ and pk_T to π but the adversary can plug or unplug this channel.

Then, we change again the protocol by having the tag to release pk'. It is already known that pk_T is valid. So, the adversary need not ask for it to the reader. Hence, we can now suppress the private channel to the reader, then even give sk_R to the adversary and completely get rid of the reader. We obtain a privacy game Γ_5 against a protocol in which there are only tags who first pick δ, compute pk', release pk', and run $\mathsf{ProProx}_{H'}(pk')$.

We now construct hybrid games of Γ_5. The ith hybrid is using the right world for the first $i - 1$ DrawTag queries and the left world for all queries starting from the $(i + 1)$th one. Let vtag be the ith drawn tag. Note that vtag runs a single session of the protocol. By giving the secret of all tags to the adversary, we can get rid of all tags except vtag. We can then apply the zero-knowledge property of $\mathsf{ProProx}_{H'}(pk')$ [41,43] to simulate the view of the adversary and produce the same output in the left or right world of the hybrid, except with negligible probability, by only getting pk' from vtag. Clearly, pk' is just a random commitment of sk. So, we can use the hiding property of Com to deduce that the left and right worlds of the hybrid produce the same output except with negligible probability.

So, the left and the right worlds of Γ_5 are producing the same output except with negligible probability. □

5 Conclusion

As we have seen, we now have pretty mature privacy models for RFID and protocols reaching their stronger flavors. So far, these models fully cover *unilateral authenticated identification* protocols, in which a tag identifies to a reader. These models could be enriched to cover other protocols: we could consider DB protocols in which the tag is already identified, we could consider *bilateral identification* protocols, we could consider protocols with *mutual authentication* (such as in [1,36]). In general, even if we do have a general model for elementary protocol, it is not clear that we could compose private elementary protocols for free. More research must be done for *composable privacy*.

For completeness, we mention that we only discussed privacy related to identifying information. Some other forms of privacy are discussed in the literature, such as the *location privacy* [27–29].

Acknowledgements. This work was partly sponsored by the ICT COST Action IC1403 Cryptacus in the EU Framework Horizon 2020.

References

1. Armknecht, F., Sadeghi, A.-R., Visconti, I., Wachsmann, C.: On RFID privacy with mutual authentication and tag corruption. In: Zhou, J., Yung, M. (eds.) ACNS 2010. LNCS, vol. 6123, pp. 493–510. Springer, Heidelberg (2010)

2. Avoine, G.: Cryptography in Radio Frequency Identification and Fair Exchange Protocols. PhD thesis no. 3407, EPFL (2005). http://library.epfl.ch/theses/?nr=3407

3. Avoine, G., Dysli, E., Oechslin, P.: Reducing time complexity in RFID systems. In: Preneel, B., Tavares, S. (eds.) SAC 2005. LNCS, vol. 3897, pp. 291–306. Springer, Heidelberg (2006)

4. Bay, A., Boureanu, I., Mitrokotsa, A., Spulber, I., Vaudenay, S.: The Bussard-Bagga and other distance-bounding protocols under attacks. In: Kutyłowski, M., Yung, M. (eds.) Inscrypt 2012. LNCS, vol. 7763, pp. 371–391. Springer, Heidelberg (2013)

5. Bellare, M., Palacio, A.: Towards plaintext-aware public-key encryption without random oracles. In: Lee, P.J. (ed.) ASIACRYPT 2004. LNCS, vol. 3329, pp. 48–62. Springer, Heidelberg (2004)

6. Bocchetti, S.: Security and Privacy in RFID Protocols. Master Thesis (2006)

7. Boureanu, I., Vaudenay, S.: Optimal proximity proofs. In: Lin, D., Yung, M., Zhou, J. (eds.) Inscrypt 2014. LNCS, vol. 8957, pp. 170–190. Springer, Heidelberg (2015)

8. Boureanu, I., Mitrokotsa, A., Vaudenay, S.: Towards secure distance bounding. In: Moriai, S. (ed.) FSE 2013. LNCS, vol. 8424, pp. 55–68. Springer, Heidelberg (2014). http://eprint.iacr.org/2015/208.pdf

9. Boureanu, I., Mitrokotsa, A., Vaudenay, S.: Secure & lightweight distance-bounding. In: Avoine, G., Kara, O. (eds.) Lightweight Cryptography for Security and Privacy. LNCS, vol. 8162, pp. 97–113. Springer, Heidelberg (2013)

10. Boureanu, I., Mitrokotsa, A., Vaudenay, S.: Practical & Provably Secure Distance-Bounding. To appear in the proceedings of ISC'13. Also [12,11]

11. Boureanu, I., Mitrokotsa, A., Vaudenay, S.: Practical & Provably Secure Distance-Bounding. IACR Eprint 2013/465 report (2013). http://eprint.iacr.org/2013/465.pdf. Also [12,10]

12. Boureanu, I., Mitrokotsa, A., Vaudenay, S.: Practical and provably secure distance-bounding. J. Comput. Secur. (JCS) **23**(2), 229–257 (2015). Also [10,11]

13. Boureanu, I., Vaudenay, S.: Challenges in distance bounding. Security & Privacy **13**(1), 41–47 (2015)

14. Brands, S., Chaum, D.: Distance bounding protocols. In: Helleseth, T. (ed.) EUROCRYPT 1993. LNCS, vol. 765, pp. 344–359. Springer, Heidelberg (1994)

15. Bussard, L., Bagga, W.: Distance-bounding proof of knowledge to avoid real-time attacks. In: Sasaki, R., Qing, S., Okamoto, E., Yoshiura, H. (eds.) Security and Privacy in the Age of Ubiquitous Computing. IFIP Advances in Information and Communication Technology, vol. 181, pp. 223–238. Springer, Heidelberg (2005)

16. Dent, A.: The cramer-shoup encryption scheme is plaintext-aware in the standard model. In: Vaudenay, S. (ed.) Advances in Cryptology - EUROCRYPT 2006. LNCS, vol. 4004, pp. 289–307. Springer, Heidelberg (2006)

17. Dimitriou, T.: A lightweight RFID protocol to protect against traceability and cloning attacks. In: Conference on Security and Privacy for Emerging Areas in Communication Networks (SecureComm'05), Athens, Greece. IEEE (2005). http://ieeexplore.ieee.org/iel5/10695/33755/01607559.pdf?arnumber=1607559

18. Dürholz, U., Fischlin, M., Kasper, M., Onete, C.: A formal approach to distance-bounding RFID protocols. In: Lai, X., Zhou, J., Li, H. (eds.) ISC 2011. LNCS, vol. 7001, pp. 47–62. Springer, Heidelberg (2011)

19. Feldhofer, M., Dominikus, S., Wolkerstorfer, J.: Strong authentication for RFID systems using the AES algorithm. In: Joye, M., Quisquater, J.-J. (eds.) CHES 2004. LNCS, vol. 3156, pp. 357–370. Springer, Heidelberg (2004)

20. Fischlin, M., Onete, C.: Terrorism in distance bounding: modeling terrorist-fraud resistance. In: Jacobson, M., Locasto, M., Mohassel, P., Safavi-Naini, R. (eds.) ACNS 2013. LNCS, vol. 7954, pp. 414–431. Springer, Heidelberg (2013)

21. Gambs, S., Onete, C., Robert, J.-M.: Prover anonymous and deniable distance-bounding authentication. In: ACM Symposium on Information, Computer and Communications Security (ASIACCS'14), Kyoto, Japan, pp. 501–506. ACM Press (2014)

22. Goldwasser, S., Micali, S.: Probabilistic encryption. J. Comput. Syst. Sci. **28**(2), 270–299 (1984)
23. Hermans, J., Pashalidis, A., Vercauteren, F., Preneel, B.: A new RFID privacy model. In: Atluri, V., Diaz, C. (eds.) ESORICS 2011. LNCS, vol. 6879, pp. 568–587. Springer, Heidelberg (2011)
24. Hermans, J., Peeters, R., Onete, C.: Efficient, secure, private distance bounding without key updates. In: ACM Conference on Security and Privacy in Wireless and Mobile Networks WISEC'13, Budapest, Hungary, pp. 195–206. ACM (2013)
25. Juels, A., Weis, S.: Defining Strong Privacy for RFID. Technical report 2006/137, IACR (2006). http://eprint.iacr.org/2006/137
26. Kılınç, H., Vaudenay, S.: Optimal Proximity Proofs Revisited. To appear in ACNS'15
27. Mitrokotsa, A., Onete, C., Vaudenay, S.: Mafia fraud attack against the RC distance-bounding protocol. In: Proceedings of the RFID-TA'12, Nice, France, pp. 74–79. IEEE (2012)
28. Mitrokotsa, A., Onete, C., Vaudenay, S.: Location Leakage in Distance Bounding: Why Location Privacy does not Work. IACR Eprint 2013/776 report (2013). http://eprint.iacr.org/2013/776.pdf
29. Mitrokotsa, A., Onete, C., Vaudenay, S.: Location leakage in distance bounding: why location privacy does not work. Comput. Secur. **45**, 199–209 (2014)
30. Molnar, D., Wagner, D.: Privacy and security in library RFID: issues, practices, and architectures. In: 11th ACM Conference on Computer and Communications Security, pp. 210–219. ACM Press, Washington DC, USA (2004)
31. Ng, C.Y., Susilo, W., Mu, Y., Safavi-Naini, R.: RFID privacy models revisited. In: Jajodia, S., Lopez, J. (eds.) ESORICS 2008. LNCS, vol. 5283, pp. 251–266. Springer, Heidelberg (2008)
32. Ohkubo, M., Suzuki, K., Kinoshita, S.: Cryptographic approach to a privacy friendly tag. Presented at the RFID Privacy Workshop, MIT, USA (2003)
33. Ohkubo, M., Suzuki, K., Kinoshita, S.: Efficient hash-chain based RFID privacy protection scheme. Presented at the International Conference on Ubiquitous Computing (Ubicomp'04), Workshop Privacy: Current Status and Future Directions, Nottingham, UK (2004)
34. Ohkubo, M., Suzuki, K.: RFID privacy issues and technical challenges. Commun. ACM **48**, 66–71 (2005)
35. Ouafi, K., Vaudenay, S.: Strong privacy for RFID systems from plaintext-aware encryption. In: Pieprzyk, J., Sadeghi, A.-R., Manulis, M. (eds.) CANS 2012. LNCS, vol. 7712, pp. 247–262. Springer, Heidelberg (2012)
36. Paise, R.-I., Vaudenay., S.: Mutual authentication in RFID. In: ACM Symposium on Information, Computer and Communications Security (ASIACCS'08), Tokyo, Japan, pp. 292–299. ACM Press (2008)
37. Rudich, S.: The use of interaction in public cryptosystems. In: Feigenbaum, J. (ed.) CRYPTO 1991. LNCS, vol. 576, pp. 242–251. Springer, Heidelberg (1992)
38. Vaudenay, S.: RFID privacy based on public-key cryptography. In: Rhee, M.S., Lee, B. (eds.) ICISC 2006. LNCS, vol. 4296, pp. 1–6. Springer, Heidelberg (2006)
39. Vaudenay, S.: On privacy models for RFID. In: Kurosawa, K. (ed.) Advances in Cryptology - ASIACRYPT 2007. LNCS, vol. 4833, pp. 68–87. Springer, Heidelberg (2007)
40. Ouafi, K., Vaudenay, S.: Strong privacy for RFID systems from plaintext-aware encryption. In: Pieprzyk, J., Sadeghi, A.-R., Manulis, M. (eds.) CANS 2012. LNCS, vol. 7712, pp. 247–262. Springer, Heidelberg (2012)

41. Vaudenay, S.: Proof of Proximity of Knowledge. IACR Eprint 2014/695 report (2014). http://eprint.iacr.org/2014/695.pdf. Also [43]
42. Vaudenay, S.: Private and secure public-key distance bounding. In: Böhme, R., Okamoto, T. (eds.) FC 2015. LNCS, vol. 8975, pp. 207–216. Springer, Heidelberg (2015)
43. Vaudenay, S.: Sound proof of proximity of knowledge. In these proceedings. Also [41]
44. Vaudenay, S.: Privacy failure in public-Key distance-bounding protocols. IET Inf. Secur. J
45. Weis, S.A., Sarma, S.E., Rivest, R.L., Engels, D.W.: Security and privacy aspects of low-cost radio frequency identification systems. In: Hutter, D., Müller, G., Stephan, W., Ullmann, M. (eds.) Security in Pervasive Computing. LNCS, vol. 2802, pp. 201–212. Springer, Heidelberg (2004)

Fundamental

From Stateful Hardware to Resettable Hardware Using Symmetric Assumptions

Nico Döttling[1]([⊠]), Daniel Kraschewski[2],
Jörn Müller-Quade[3], and Tobias Nilges[3]

[1] Aarhus University, Aarhus, Denmark
nico.doettling@cs.au.dk
[2] TNG Technology Consulting GmbH, Munich, Germany
[3] Karlsruhe Institute of Technology, Karlsruhe, Germany

Abstract. Universally composable multi-party computation is impossible without setup assumptions. Motivated by the ubiquitous use of secure hardware in many real world security applications, Katz (EUROCRYPT 2007) proposed a model of tamper-proof hardware as a UC-setup assumption. An important aspect of this model is whether the hardware token is allowed to hold a state or not. Real world examples of tamper-proof hardware that can hold a state are expensive hardware security modules commonly used in mainframes. Stateless, or resettable hardware tokens model cheaper devices such as smartcards, where an adversarial user can cut off the power supply, thus resetting the card's internal state.

A natural question is how the stateful and the resettable hardware model compare in their cryptographic power, given that either the receiver or the sender of the token (and thus the token itself) might be malicious. In this work we show that any UC-functionality that can be implemented by a protocol using a single untrusted stateful hardware token can likewise be implemented using a single untrusted resettable hardware token, assuming only the existence of one-way functions.

We present two compilers that transform UC-secure protocols in the stateful hardware model into UC-secure protocols in the resettable hardware model. The first compiler can be proven secure assuming merely the existence of one-way functions. However, it (necessarily) makes use of computationally rather expensive non-black-box techniques. We provide an alternative second compiler that replaces the expensive non-black-box component of the first compiler by few additional seed OTs. While this

N. Döttling—The authors acknowledge support from the Danish National Research Foundation and The National Science Foundation of China (under the grant 61061130540) for the Sino-Danish Center for the Theory of Interactive Computation, within which part of this work was performed; and also from the CFEM research center (supported by the Danish Strategic Research Council) within which part of this work was performed. Supported by European Research Commission Starting Grant no. 279447.

D. Kraschewski—Part of work done while at Technion, Israel. Supported by the European Union's Tenth Framework Programme (FP10/2010-2016) under grant agreement no. 259426 – ERC Cryptography and Complexity.

M.-H. Au and A. Miyaji (Eds.): ProvSec 2015, LNCS 9451, pp. 23–42, 2015.
DOI: 10.1007/978-3-319-26059-4_2

second compiler introduces the seed OTs as additional setup assumptions, it is computationally very efficient.

Keywords: Tamper-proof hardware · Universal composability · Protocol compilers

1 Introduction

Tamper-proof hardware has gained a lot of interest in the design of UC-secure [5] protocols. Many cryptographic tasks that are impossible in the plain model can be realized using tamper-proof hardware, e.g. *Program Obfuscation* [2]. It turns out that several flavors of tamper-proof hardware have different cryptographic strengths. On the one hand there are *stateful* tokens, which allow for very efficient and UC-secure oblivious transfer (OT) protocols even without computational assumptions [14,15,19]. On the other hand, *resettable*, or equivalently *stateless*, tokens are strictly weaker: it was shown that unconditional OT cannot be achieved with stateless tokens [18]. Nevertheless the distinction between both models is very relevant, because in real-world applications it is considered to be much more difficult to manufacture stateful tamper-proof tokens than stateless or resettable tokens. Removing the dependency on stateful hardware by an improved protocol design can greatly simplify the manufacturing process and also reduce the costs. This leads to the following question:

Is it possible to implement any UC-functionality using a single resettable tamper-proof hardware and assuming only one-way functions?

We answer this question affirmatively. We shall first motivate the setting. There are protocol compilers by Kilian [25] and Ishai et al. [23] basing general (UC-)secure multi-party computation (MPC) on OT without additional computational assumptions. Recent results in the area of efficient information-theoretically secure OT protocols include [14,15]. Their results, however, are based on stateful tamper-proof hardware. Considering the above-mentioned impossibility result of Goyal et al. [18], who show that unconditionally secure OT with *any* number of resettable tokens is impossible, it becomes obvious that converting a protocol like [15] such that only resettable tokens are necessary cannot be achieved without further assumptions.

One of the weakest common assumptions in cryptography is the existence of one-way functions and it turns out that these suffice for our goal. It was previously known that one-way functions suffice for UC-secure OT with stateless tokens [19], but they need many tokens to obtain this result. For our solution, instead of adapting an OT protocol such that it uses a resettable token, we present two compilers that transform any protocol based on stateful tokens into a protocol based on resettable tokens. This allows for many improvements in previous protocols, because any statistically secure protocol using a single untrusted stateful token can be transformed into a computationally secure protocol using a single untrusted resettable token and one-way functions.

1.1   Our Contribution

We present two compilers that basically use the same technique to achieve resettability of the token: The sender has to authenticate the query that the receiver wants to input into the token. For the first compiler, we generalize and improve upon a technique that is implicit in [17], where resettability is obtained by having the sender sign every query the receiver will provide to the token. The second compiler is stated in the OT-hybrid model and makes no further assumptions.

In more detail, given a protocol where a stateful token is sent from the sender to the receiver, we extend the protocol as follows. For the first compiler, a key pair for a signature scheme is created by the sender. For each token invocation, the receiver commits to its input and sends the commitment to the sender. The sender signs the commitment and sends it back to the receiver. At this point, care must be taken not to introduce a channel between the sender and the token. Otherwise, the token and/or the sender party could gather complete information about the messages sent and received by the receiver party. This would make aborts possible that are correlated with the receivers secret input and thus cannot be simulated in the UC framework. Therefore, the receiver does not show any signature to the token, but instead provides a resettably-sound zero-knowledge argument of knowledge (rsZKAoK) of the commitment and the signature. Recent results by Chung et al. [9] and Bitansky and Paneth [3] show that such resettably-sound zero-knowledge arguments of knowledge can be based on the existence of one-way functions. This technique guarantees that any information generated by the sender during a protocol run remains oblivious to the token.

Additionally, we present a compiler that works in the OT-hybrid model (without any computational assumptions) and can, e.g., be used to implement many OT instances from few "seed OTs" and a resettable token. The raw version of this compiler uses one OT per bit sent from the receiver to the token, but by using Merkle trees (or sig-com trees [9] respectively; see Sect. 2.5), we can compress the number of bits to be authenticated. The main idea is that the sender only has to authenticate a single message of small size, namely the root of such a tree. To stay true to the goal of using only one-way functions, however, we cannot directly use a Merkle tree. Instead, we show how the sig-com scheme proposed by [9] can be applied to our scenario. The same compression technique applies to both our compilers, which also allows us to keep the amount of proofs for the rsZKAoK-based compiler at a minimum. For protocols that use more than one token, our compilers can be invoked successively, replacing all the stateful tokens by resettable tokens.

Our rsZKAoK-based compiler can be used to obtain several improvements on existing protocols concerning resettable hardware. We highlight the following contribution: The combination of the OT protocol by Döttling et al. [15] with our compiler yields a round-efficient OT protocol based on one-way functions and a single untrusted resettable token. This yields the first OT-protocol using a single resettable token and only symmetric computational assumptions. Prior to our result, the best known approach to obtain UC-secure OT with a single resettable token was to use the token to generate a common reference string [17] and use an efficient OT-protocol in the CRS-model, e.g. the protocol of Peikert et al. [30]. Implementing OT in the common reference string model, however, requires much stronger computational assumptions (e.g., doubly enhanced trapdoor permutations, number-theoretic or lattice assumptions). Alternatively, [19] presented a protocol for OT based on resettable hardware and one-way functions, but their construction needs polynomially many tokens. Thus the question of obtaining OT from a single resettable hardware token using only one-way functions was left open by prior works.

Döttling et al. [17] and Choi et al. [8] showed that, if only a single resettable token is issued, then even simple functionalities cannot be implemented only with black-box techniques. We circumvent this impossibility result by using resettably-sound zero-knowledge argument of knowledge, which are inherently non-black-box. Moreover, Goyal et al. [18] showed there exists no unconditionally secure protocol implementing OT using any number of resettable tokens. Thus, computational assumptions are necessary to implement OT using a single resettable token. Considering the computational assumptions and number of resettable tokens used, our compiler yields an optimal UC-secure OT-protocol.

1.2 Efficiency

The compilers require one round of interaction between the token issuer and the receiver per token message. With a few exceptions in the area of non-interactive computation [15,17,19], protocols based on tamper-proof hardware already require interaction between the sender and the receiver. Moreover, in the scenario of a single token, Döttling et al. [17] show that interaction is necessary to UC-realize any functionality based on resettable hardware. Thus the induced overhead is minimal with respect to communication, even more so since typically token-based protocols are constant round.

The main efficiency drawback is incurred by the use of non-black-box zero-knowledge. However, in current protocols [3,9] the honest prover is not required to execute a universal argument, so that the efficiency is comparable to a general zero-knowledge protocol. With a zero-knowledge protocol tailored to the statements in our protocol the efficiency can be further improved.

1.3 Further Related Work

The model of tamper-proof hardware considered in this paper was introduced by Katz [24]. Further formalizations of different tamper-proof hardware tokens can be found in [17,19]. Physically uncloneable functions (PUFs) [4,28,29] only allow for MPC if the PUFs are not malicious [10,33], but this is out of the scope of our work.

Resettability was first considered in the context of zero-knowledge protocols. The case of a resettable prover was analyzed by Canetti et al. [6] while the case of resettable verifiers was treated by Barak et al. [1] with several follow up works, e.g. [3,9,13]. Later, simultaneously resettable zero-knowledge protocols were presented [3,12,13]. These works made it possible to transform stateful into stateless protocols. Goyal and Sahai [21] present a compiler that transforms any semi-honest secure protocol into a resettably secure protocol using similar techniques to ours. They also show that general resettable MPC with honest majority is possible where all parties are resettable. Another compiler due to Goyal and Maji [20] allows to compile almost any semi-honest secure protocol into a fully resettable protocol. However, neither [21] nor [20] achieve UC-security.

While all of the above-mentioned works do not make use of tamper-proof hardware, Chandran et al. [7] present a protocol for general UC-secure MPC with resettable tokens, but they need to exchange several tokens and rely on strong cryptographic assumptions, namely enhanced trapdoor permutations. Goyal et al. [19] construct a protocol for UC-secure MPC assuming only one-way functions, but they also need polynomially many resettable tokens.

In the context of statistically UC-secure OT, Goyal et al. [19] present a protocol using several stateful tokens. The protocols of Döttling et al. [14,15] improve upon this result by achieving UC-secure OT using only a single stateful token. In [18] it was shown that statistically secure OT is impossible with stateless tokens (unless parties can encapsulate tokens into each other), but statistical commitments are possible. Their commitment construction was improved by [11] to achieve UC-security. Given an upper bound on the number of resets, Döttling et al. [16] show that resettable tamper-proof hardware allows for unconditionally UC-secure OT. Another recent result by [8] implements UC-secure OT from CRHFs and two bidirectionally exchanged stateless tokens. Leaky tokens, which reveal additional information to malicious receivers, were considered in [2,31], but this is again out of the scope of our work.

2 Preliminaries

In the following we denote by k a security parameter. We abbreviate probabilistic polynomial time by PPT. We use the standard notions of negligible functions, statistical indistinguishability and computational indistinguishability.

2.1 The UC-Framework

The *Universal Composability* (UC) framework was introduced by Canetti [5]. It differentiates between an *ideal model* and a *real model*. In the real model an adversary $\mathcal{A}$ coordinates the behavior of all corrupted parties while the uncorrupted parties follow the protocol. An environment $\mathcal{Z}$ representing an outside observer can read all messages and outputs of the protocol parties. The same setup also holds for the ideal model, but the adversary is replaced by a simulator $\mathcal{S}$ that simulates the behavior of $\mathcal{A}$, and all participating parties are replaced by dummy parties that only pass on any message that they receive. Security is proven by comparing a protocol Π in the real model with an ideal functionality $\mathcal{F}$ in the ideal model. An ideal functionality is secure per definition and represents a trusted third party that provides a functionality. All communication between a protocol party and the ideal functionality is assumed to be authenticated. Tamper-proof hardware is also modeled as an ideal functionality, further details can be found in Sect. 3.

By $\mathsf{Real}_{\Pi}^{\mathcal{A}}(\mathcal{Z})$ we denote the output of the environment $\mathcal{Z}$ when interacting with the real model, by $\mathsf{Ideal}_{\mathcal{F}}^{S}(\mathcal{Z})$ we denote the output of $\mathcal{Z}$ when interacting with the ideal model. A protocol is said to compose securely if for any environment $\mathcal{Z}$, which is plugged to either the ideal model or the real model, the view is (computationally, statistically or perfectly) indistinguishable.

We assume static corruption (i.e. the adversary does not adaptively change corruption) and prove our results in this framework.

2.2 Signature Schemes

A signature scheme SIG consists of three PPT algorithms KeyGen, Sign and Verify.

- KeyGen(1^k) generates a key pair consisting of a verification key vk and a signature key sgk.
- Sign$_{\mathsf{sgk}}(m)$ takes a message m and outputs a signature σ on this message.
- Verify$_{\mathsf{vk}}(m, \sigma)$ takes as input a verification key vk, a message m and a presumed signature σ on this message. It outputs 1 if the signature is correct and 0 otherwise.

We will use existentially unforgeable (EUF-CMA secure) signatures and will briefly recall the security definition. The experiment creates a key pair (sgk, vk). An adversary $\mathcal{A}$ has access to a verification key vk and a signing oracle $\mathcal{O}^{\mathsf{Sign}_{\mathsf{sgk}}(\cdot)}$. The adversary can now query the oracle with messages and obtains signatures to these messages. If $\mathcal{A}$ manages to create a signature σ^* for an arbitrary message m without querying $\mathcal{O}^{\mathsf{Sign}_{\mathsf{sgk}}(\cdot)}$ with m such that Verify$_{\mathsf{vk}}(m, \sigma^*) = 1$ it wins the experiment.

A signature scheme SIG is called EUF-CMA-secure if the probability that a PPT adversary wins the above specified experiment is negligible. EUF-CMA secure signature schemes can be constructed from one-way functions [27,32].

2.3 Commitment Schemes

We will use 2-move commitment schemes in our compiler. In such a commitment-scheme, the receiver first chooses a key k, sends k to the sender of the commitment, who computes a commitment $c = \mathsf{com}_k(m; r)$ for a message m using randomness r and sends c to the receiver. The sender can unveil the commitment by sending (m, r) to the receiver, who checks if $c = \mathsf{com}_k(m; r)$ holds.

We will require such a commitment scheme to be statistically binding, which means that for a given commitment $c = \mathsf{com}_k(m; r)$, the unveil (m, r) is unique, except with negligible probability over the choice of k. Naor [26] constructs 2-move statistically binding commitment schemes using only pseudorandom generators, if one considers their first message from the receiver as the key. As the latter can be constructed from one-way functions [22], this yields a 2-move statistically binding commitment scheme based on one-way functions.

2.4 Resettably-Sound Zero-Knowledge Arguments of Knowledge

Due to the fact that our protocol runs in the resettable token model, we use resettably-sound zero-knowledge arguments of knowledge for our proofs. We give a definition for resettably-sound zero-knowledge arguments of knowledge.

Definition 1. *A resettably-sound zero-knowledge argument of knowledge system for a language* $L \in \mathcal{NP}$ *(with witness-relation* $\mathcal{R}_L$ *and witness-set* $w_L(x) = \{w : (x, w) \in \mathcal{R}_L\}$*) consists of a pair of PPT-machines* (P, V)*, where the verifier* V *is resettable, such that there exist two PPT-machines* Sim *and* Ext *and the following conditions hold.*

- *Completeness. For every* $(x, w) \in \mathcal{R}_L$ *it holds that* $\Pr[\langle P(w), V \rangle(x) = 1] = 1$.
- *Computational Soundness. For every* $x \notin L$ *and every PPT-machine* P* *it holds that* $\Pr[\langle P^*, V \rangle(x) = 1] < \mathsf{negl}(|x|)$.
- *Computational Zero-Knowledge. For every* $(x, w) \in \mathcal{R}_L$ *and every stateful or resettable PPT* V* *it holds that the distributions* Real $= \{\langle P(w), V^* \rangle(x)\}$ *and* Ideal $= \{\mathsf{Sim}(x, V^*)\}$ *are computationally indistinguishable.*
- *Proof of Knowledge. For every* $x \in L$ *and every PPT-machine* P* *there exists a negligible* ν *such that* $\Pr[\mathsf{Ext}(x, P^*) \in w_L(x)] > \Pr[\langle P^*, V \rangle(x) = 1] - \nu$.

It will be convenient to rephrase the computational zero-knowledge property as follows. Given that a simulator Sim exists with $\{\langle P(w), V^* \rangle(x)\} \approx_c \{\mathsf{Sim}(x, V^*)\}$, we can always construct a *prover-simulator* $\mathsf{P}_{\mathsf{Sim}}$ such that it holds that $\{\langle P(w), V^* \rangle(x)\} \approx_c \{\langle \mathsf{P}_{\mathsf{Sim}}(V^*), V^* \rangle(x)\}$. Such a prover-simulator can be constructed as follows. $\mathsf{P}_{\mathsf{Sim}}$ first runs $\mathsf{Sim}(x, V^*)$ to obtain a simulated view of V*. From this view it takes the prover-messages and uses these prover-messages in its own interaction with V*. Thus it holds $\{\langle \mathsf{P}_{\mathsf{Sim}}(V^*), V^* \rangle(x)\} \approx_c \{\mathsf{Sim}(x, V^*)\}$ and we are done.

Recent constructions of rsZK arguments of knowledge are based on one-way functions [3,9].

2.5 Sig-Com Schemes

As an alternative to collision resistant hash functions, Chung et al. [9] propose sig-com schemes. They show that such a scheme is compressing and has a collision resistance property similar to collision resistant hash functions, but requires only one-way functions. In comparison to hash functions, however, sig-com schemes require interaction between two parties: one party creates the signature and verification keys, and sends the verification key to the other party. The other party sends a commitment to its input and obtains a signature on the commitment, i.e. the party with the signature key acts as a signature oracle. This separation is due to the fact that if the party that holds the input for the sig-com tree also possesses the secret key to the signature scheme, the security of the signature scheme (and hence the collision resistance property) does no longer hold. The commitments to the input are necessary, because otherwise the sender could abort depending on the received message. The commit-then-sign step can be applied to create a tree analogous to Merkle trees.

Definition 2 ([9]). *Let* SIG = (Gen, Sign, Verify) *be a strong length-n signature scheme and let* com *be a non-interactive commitment scheme. Define* SIG' = (Gen', Sign', Verify') *to be a triple of PPT machines defined as follows:*

- Gen' = Gen.
- $\text{Sign}'_{\text{sgk}}(m)$: *compute a commitment* $c = \text{com}(m; r)$ *using a uniformly selected* r, *and let* $\sigma = \text{Sign}_{\text{sgk}}(c)$; *output* (σ, r).
- $\text{Verify}'_{\text{vk}}(m, \sigma, r)$: *output 1 iff* $\text{Verify}_{\text{vk}}(\text{com}(m; r), \sigma) = 1$.

Definition 3 ([9]). *Let* SIG = (Gen, Sign, Verify) *be a strong length-n signature scheme, let* com *be a non-interactive commitment scheme, and let* SIG' = (Gen', Sign', Verify') *be the sig-com scheme corresponding to* SIG *and* com. *Let* (sgk, vk) *be a key pair of* SIG', *and* s *be a string of length* 2^d. *A sig-com tree for* s *w. r. t.* (sgk, vk) *is a complete binary tree of depth* d, *defined as follows.*

- *A leaf* l_γ *indexed by* $\gamma \in \{0, 1\}^d$ *is set as the bit at position* γ *in* s.
- *An internal node* l_γ *indexed by* $\gamma \in \bigcup_{i=0}^{d-1} \{0, 1\}^i$ *satisfies that there exists some* r_γ *such that* $\text{Verify}'_{\text{vk}}((l_{\gamma 0}, l_{\gamma 1}), l_\gamma, r_\gamma) = 1$. *(By* $l_{\gamma 0}, l_{\gamma 1}$ *we denote the left and right child of an inner node* l_γ.)

Note that sig-com trees have a collision resistance property in the following sense: no adversary with oracle access to a signature oracle SIG can output a root and a sequence of signatures for both 0 and 1 for any leaf γ. This property stems from the binding property of the commitment and the unforgeability of the signature scheme.

3   Ideal Functionalities

In this section we define the ideal functionalities we will use later. Here we only consider the two-party case with a sender S and a receiver R. The following definition for a stateful wrapper functionality is based on [19,24].

Functionality $\mathcal{F}_{\text{wrap}}^{\text{stateful}}$ (parametrized by a security parameter k and a polynomial runtime bound $p(\cdot)$).

- **Create** Upon receiving (create, $\mathcal{P}, p(\cdot)$) from S, where $\mathcal{P}$ is a Turing machine, send create to R and store $\mathcal{P}$.
- **Execute** Upon receiving (run, w) from R, check if a create-message has already been sent by S, if not output $\bot$. Run $\mathcal{P}(w)$ for at most $p(k)$ steps, and let m be the output. Save the current state of $\mathcal{P}$. Output m to R

We use the wrapper functionality for resettable functionalities as defined in [17].

Functionality $\mathcal{F}_{\text{wrap}}^{\text{resettable}}$ (parametrized by a security parameter k and a polynomial runtime bound $p(\cdot)$).

- Create Upon receiving $(\texttt{create}, \mathcal{P}, p(\cdot))$ from S, where $\mathcal{P}$ is a Turing machine, send create to R and store $\mathcal{P}$.
- Execute Upon receiving $(\texttt{run}, w)$ from R, check if a create-message has already been sent by S, if not output $\bot$. Run $\mathcal{P}(w)$ for at most $p(k)$ steps, and let m be the output. Save the current state of $\mathcal{P}$. Output m to R
- Reset (Adversarial Receiver only) Upon receiving reset from R, reset the Turing machine $\mathcal{P}$ to its initial state.

In the sequel, we will use the notation $\mathcal{P}$ for programs (given as code, Turing-machine etc.) and $\mathcal{T}$ for the instance of the wrapper-functionality $\mathcal{F}_{\text{wrap}}^{\text{resettable}}$, resp. $\mathcal{F}_{\text{wrap}}^{\text{stateful}}$, in which $\mathcal{P}$ runs.

4 Compiler

In the following we present two compilers that allow to convert a protocol that makes a single call to a *stateful* token into a protocol that uses a *resettable* token.

We need to make some assumptions on the structure of the underlying stateful protocol Π_s. W.l.o.g the protocol can be divided into the following phases.

- A setup phase in which the sender sends a token program T to $\mathcal{F}_{\text{wrap}}^{\text{stateful}}$.
- Communication between the sender and the receiver.
- An invocation of the token by the receiver.

The token program from the setup phase will be used in the resettable protocol as well, albeit the setup phase will be extended by additional steps. Any interaction between the two parties of the protocol (not the communication with the token) will be left untouched.

The basic idea underlying our compilers is to let the sender *authenticate* the message for the token, while being oblivious of what the actual message to the token is. Instead of invoking the stateful token in the underlying protocol directly, we will additionally insert a communication step with the sender. Though the receiver can still perform reset-attacks, it will not be able to change its input after a reset.

We will assume that the input protocol Π_s has dummy-messages query and ack, where an honest receiver sends the message query to the sender before querying the token, and waits until the sender replies with ack before proceeding. We do not require a corrupted receiver to send the query message before querying the token. Therefore any protocol Π_s can be converted into this form, while preserving its security guarantees.

4.1   Protocol Using Resettably-Sound Zero-Knowledge

Outline. The compiler $\mathcal{C}_{ZK}$ (cf. Fig. 1) alters the underlying protocol as follows. Before the execution of Π_s a signature key-pair (sgk, vk) and a key k for a commitment scheme (cf. Sect. 2.3) are created by the sender and sent to the receiver. Then Π_s is carried out. When the token code of the underlying protocol is sent to the wrapper functionality, the sender chooses a seed s for a pseudorandom function and constructs a new token.

During token invocation of the original protocol, we enhance the communication of the token and the receiver as follows. Instead of just sending an input inp to the token, the receiver first commits to its input inp and sends the commitment to the sender. The sender then computes a signature σ on the commitment c and sends the signature to the receiver. Now the receiver checks if the signature is valid and queries the token with its input. Additionally, the receiver starts a resettably-sound zero-knowledge argument of knowledge to prove that it knows a signature on a commitment to the input. If the verifier accepts, the token outputs the output out of the underlying functionality on input inp.

We stress that it is essential that the token cannot learn the signature σ on the commitment c, otherwise both token and sender have a covert channel by which they can communicate, which cannot be simulated. To eliminate this channel, we use a zero-knowledge proof which hides the signature from the token.

Proof of Security. *Corrupted Receiver.* Let $\mathcal{A}_R$ be the dummy-adversary for a corrupted receiver for the protocol Π_r. We will construct an adversary $\mathcal{A}'_R$ (cf. Fig. 2) against the protocol Π_s. $\mathcal{A}'_R$ needs to simulate a resettable token to $\mathcal{A}_R$, while it has itself access to a non-resettable stateful token.

Lemma 1. *For every PPT-environment $\mathcal{Z}$, it holds that the random variables* $\mathsf{Real}^{\mathcal{A}_R}_{\Pi_r}(\mathcal{Z})$ *and* $\mathsf{Real}^{\mathcal{A}'_R}_{\Pi_s}(\mathcal{Z})$ *are computationally indistinguishable.*

As Π_s is UC-secure, there exists a simulator $\mathcal{S}_R$ such that $\mathsf{Real}^{\mathcal{A}'_R}_{\Pi_s}(\mathcal{Z}) \approx \mathsf{Ideal}^{\mathcal{S}_R}_{\mathcal{F}}(\mathcal{Z})$. This yields the desired $\mathsf{Real}^{\mathcal{A}_R}_{\Pi_r}(\mathcal{Z}) \approx \mathsf{Ideal}^{\mathcal{S}_R}_{\mathcal{F}}(\mathcal{Z})$.

Proof. Let $\mathcal{Z}$ be a PPT environment. We will prove the indistinguishability of $\mathsf{Real}^{\mathcal{A}_R}_{\Pi_r}(\mathcal{Z})$ and $\mathsf{Real}^{\mathcal{A}'_R}_{\Pi_s}(\mathcal{Z})$ by a series of indistinguishable hybrid experiments.

Hybrid $\mathcal{H}_0$. Simulator $\mathcal{S}_0$ simulates $\mathsf{Real}^{\mathcal{A}_R}_{\Pi_r}$.

Hybrid $\mathcal{H}_1$. Identical to $\mathcal{H}_0$, except that simulator $\mathcal{S}_1$ replaces the pseudo"-random-function $\mathsf{F}_s(\cdot)$ by a random-oracle H.

Hybrid $\mathcal{H}_2$. Identical to $\mathcal{H}_1$, except for the following. $\mathcal{S}_2$ checks – after V accepts – if a tuple (inp', out') has already been stored. If so and inp' $\neq$ inp, it aborts. Moreover, if no such tuple exists it will store (inp, out), where out is the output of the token. From the view of $\mathcal{Z}$, this is identical to $\mathsf{Real}^{\mathcal{A}_R}_{\Pi_s}$.

Compiler $\mathcal{C}_{ZK}$

Let $\mathcal{F}$ be a two-party UC-functionality. Let com_k denote a 2-move commitment scheme and $\mathsf{SIG} = (\mathsf{KeyGen}, \mathsf{Sign}, \mathsf{Verify})$ an EUF-CMA secure signature-scheme. Let (P, V) be a resettably-sound zero-knowledge argument-of-knowledge system for the NP-language $L = \{(\mathsf{vk}, \mathsf{inp}) | \exists \sigma, c, r : \mathsf{Verify}_{\mathsf{vk}}(c, \sigma) = 1 \wedge c = \mathsf{com}(\mathsf{inp}; r)\}$. Further let F be a pseudorandom function.

Input: Protocol Π_s UC-implementing $\mathcal{F}$ in the $\mathcal{F}_{\mathsf{wrap}}^{\mathsf{stateful}}$-hybrid model.

Output: Protocol Π_r UC-implementing $\mathcal{F}$ in the $\mathcal{F}_{\mathsf{wrap}}^{\mathsf{resettable}}$-hybrid model.

Setup (Before execution of Π_s):

- **(Sender)** Generate a key pair $(\mathsf{sgk}, \mathsf{vk}) \leftarrow \mathsf{KeyGen}(1^\lambda)$ and choose a key $k \in \{0,1\}^\lambda$ for the commitment scheme uniformly at random. Send $(\mathsf{setup}, \mathsf{vk}, k)$ to R.
- **(Receiver)** Upon receiving a message $(\mathsf{setup}, \mathsf{vk}, k)$ from S, store vk and k.

Rewriting the token-code:

(Sender) Once S inputs a token code T into $\mathcal{F}_{\mathsf{wrap}}^{\mathsf{stateful}}$ do the following.

- Choose a seed $s \in \{0,1\}^\lambda$ for the pseudorandom function F uniformly at random.
- Construct a token-code T′ which upon receiving a message $(\mathsf{input}, \mathsf{inp})$ from R sets up a verifier V with input $(\mathsf{vk}, \mathsf{inp})$, random-tape $\mathsf{F}_s(\mathsf{inp})$ and runs V. It forwards the messages sent by V to R and vice versa. If V rejects, it aborts. If V accepts, it continues the execution of T with input inp and forwards T's output to R.
- Input T′ into $\mathcal{F}_{\mathsf{wrap}}^{\mathsf{resettable}}$.

Token-invocation:

- **(Receiver)** Let inp be R's input to the token. Compute $c = \mathsf{com}_k(\mathsf{inp}; r)$ and send (query, c) to S.
- **(Sender)** Upon receiving a message (query, c) from R, compute $\sigma = \mathsf{Sign}_{\mathsf{sgk}}(c)$. Send (ack, σ) to R.
- **(Receiver)** Upon receiving a message (ack, σ) from S, check if $\mathsf{Verify}_{\mathsf{vk}}(c, \sigma) = 1$ holds, if not abort. Otherwise send $(\mathsf{input}, \mathsf{inp})$ to the token. Setup a prover P with input $(\mathsf{vk}, \mathsf{inp})$, witness-input (σ, c, r) and run P. Forward the messages sent by P to the token and vice versa. Continue R's computation once the token outputs out.

Fig. 1. Stateless compiler using resettably-sound zero-knowledge.

Computational indistinguishability of $\mathcal{H}_0$ and $\mathcal{H}_1$ follows straightforwardly by the pseudorandomness of the pseudorandom-function F_s. The interesting part is the computational indistinguishability of $\mathcal{H}_1$ and $\mathcal{H}_2$.

Adversary-Simulator $\mathcal{A}'_R$

- **Setup:** Generate a key pair $(\mathsf{sgk}, \mathsf{vk}) \leftarrow \mathsf{KeyGen}(1^k)$ and choose $k \in \{0,1\}^n$ uniformly at random. Send $(\mathsf{setup}, \mathsf{vk}, k)$ to $\mathcal{A}_R$. Setup a simulated-random oracle H.
- **Token-Invocation:**
  - Once $\mathcal{A}_R$ wants to send a message (query, c) to S, compute $\sigma = \mathsf{Sign}_{\mathsf{sgk}}(c)$. Send query to S. Once S responds with ack, send (ack, σ) to $\mathcal{A}_R$.
  - Once $\mathcal{A}_R$ wants to input a message $(\mathsf{input}, \mathsf{inp})$ to $\mathcal{F}_{\mathsf{wrap}}^{\mathsf{resettable}}$, setup a verifier V with input $(\mathsf{vk}, \mathsf{inp})$, random-tape $\mathsf{H}(\mathsf{inp})$ and run V. Forward the messages sent by V to $\mathcal{A}_R$ and vice versa. If V rejects, abort. If V accepts, check if a tuple $(\mathsf{inp}', \mathsf{out}')$ has been stored. If yes and it holds $\mathsf{inp}' \neq \mathsf{inp}$, abort. If yes and it holds $\mathsf{inp}' = \mathsf{inp}$, send out' to $\mathcal{A}_R$. If no, send inp to $\mathcal{F}_{\mathsf{wrap}}^{\mathsf{stateful}}$, let out be the corresponding output, send out to $\mathcal{A}_R$ and store the tuple $(\mathsf{inp}, \mathsf{out})$.

Fig. 2. Adversary-simulator $\mathcal{A}'_R$ for $\mathcal{C}_{\mathsf{ZK}}$.

We claim that $\mathcal{H}_1$ and $\mathcal{H}_2$ are computationally indistinguishable, provided that the argument system (P, V) fulfills the computational resettable soundness property, the commitment scheme com is statistically binding and the signature scheme SIG is EUF-CMA secure.

Clearly, if $\mathcal{S}_2$ does not abort after V accepts, the views of $\mathcal{Z}$ are identical in $\mathcal{H}_1$ and $\mathcal{H}_2$. We will thus show that this event happens at most with negligible probability, establishing indistinguishability of $\mathcal{H}_1$ and $\mathcal{H}_2$.

Since the commitment-scheme com is statistically binding, the event that there exist distinct (inp_1, r_1) and (inp_2, r_2) with $\mathsf{com}_k(\mathsf{inp}_1; r_1) = \mathsf{com}_k(\mathsf{inp}_2; r_2)$ has only negligible probability (over the choice of k). We can thus assume that each commitment c has a unique unveil (inp, r).

Assume now that the probability that $\mathcal{S}_2$ aborts after V accepts is non-negligible. We distinguish two cases:

1. The probability ϵ that $\mathcal{A}_R$ successfully proves a false statement in one of the invocations of (P, V) is non-negligible.
2. The probability ϵ that $\mathcal{A}_R$ successfully proves a false statement in one of the invocations of (P, V) is negligible.

In the first case, we can construct a corrupted prover P^* that breaks the soundness property of the argument-system P, V. P^* simulates $\mathcal{S}_1$ faithfully until the argument-system (P, V) is started. Then, P^* announces the statement $(\mathsf{vk}, \mathsf{inp})$ and forwards all messages sent by $\mathcal{A}_R$ to his own verifier V and vice versa. Clearly, from $\mathcal{A}_R$'s (and thus $\mathcal{Z}$'s) view, $\mathcal{S}_1$ and P^*'s simulation are identically distributed. Thus, P^*'s chance of successfully proving a false statement is at least ϵ, contradicting the soundness property of (P, V).

In the second case, we will argue that $\mathcal{A}_R$ must be able to successfully forge a signature σ for a message c, contradicting the EUF-CMA security of SIG. We will therefore construct an adversary $\mathcal{B}$ that breaks the EUF-CMA security of SIG with non-negligible probability, leading to the desired contradiction. Let Ext be a knowledge-extractor for the argument-of-knowledge system (P, V). $\mathcal{B}$ simulates $\mathcal{S}_2$ faithfully except for the following. Instead of generating $(\mathsf{sgk}, \mathsf{vk})$ itself, it will use vk provided by the EUF-CMA experiment. $\mathcal{B}$ uses $\mathcal{A}_\mathsf{R}$ and $\mathcal{Z}$ to construct a malicious prover P^*, which simply consists in continuing the computation of $\mathcal{A}_\mathsf{R}$ and $\mathcal{Z}$ until the argument-system terminates. $\mathcal{B}$ now runs the extractor Ext on P^* and obtains a witness (σ^*, c^*, r^*) for a statement $(\mathsf{vk}, \mathsf{inp}^*)$. If it holds $\mathsf{Verify}_{\mathsf{vk}}(c^*, \sigma^*) = 1$, then $\mathcal{B}$ outputs the forge (c^*, σ^*). Otherwise it outputs $\perp$.

Clearly, from the view of $\mathcal{Z}$, both $\mathcal{S}_2$ and $\mathcal{B}$'s simulation are identically distributed. Since we assume that $\mathcal{S}_2$ aborts with non-negligible probability and P^* proves a true statement, except with negligible probability, the extractor Ext returns a witness (σ^*, c^*, r^*) with non-negligible probability. As we conditioned on the event that $\mathcal{S}_2$ aborts and the commitment c^* has a unique unveil, it must hold that (c^*, σ^*) is, with non-negligible probability, a valid forge. This however contradicts the EUF-CMA security of SIG, which concludes the proof. $\qquad\square$

Corrupted Sender. We move on to prove the security against a corrupted sender by stating a simulator (cf. Fig. 3).

Adversary-Simulator $\mathcal{A}_\mathsf{S}'$

- **Setup:** Once $\mathcal{A}_\mathsf{S}$ sends a message $(\mathsf{setup}, \mathsf{vk}, k)$ store vk and k.
- **Rewriting the Token-code:** Once S inputs a token code T^* into $\mathcal{F}_{\mathrm{wrap}}^{\mathrm{resettable}}$ construct a token-code $\mathsf{T}^\dagger$ with the following functionality.
  Upon receiving a message $(\mathsf{input}, \mathsf{inp})$ from R, run T^* with input $(\mathsf{input}, \mathsf{inp})$. Halt the computation of T^* and construct a corrupted verifier V^* from T^*. Setup a prover-simulator $\mathsf{P}_{\mathsf{Sim}}$ with input $(\mathsf{vk}, \mathsf{inp})$ and witness-input V^* and run $\mathsf{P}_{\mathsf{Sim}}$. Forward the messages between $\mathsf{P}_{\mathsf{Sim}}$ and T^* and vice versa. Once T^* outputs out, send out to R.
  Input $\mathsf{T}^\dagger$ into $\mathcal{F}_{\mathrm{wrap}}^{\mathrm{stateful}}$.
- **Token-Invocation:** Upon receiving a message query from R, compute $c = \mathsf{com}_k(0; r)$. Send (query, c) to $\mathcal{A}_\mathsf{S}$. Let (ack, σ) be the output of $\mathcal{A}_\mathsf{S}$. Check if it holds $\mathsf{Verify}_{\mathsf{vk}}(c, \sigma) = 1$, if not abort. Otherwise send ack to R.

Fig. 3. Adversary-simulator $\mathcal{A}_\mathsf{S}'$ for $\mathcal{C}_{\mathrm{ZK}}$.

Lemma 2. *For every PPT-environment $\mathcal{Z}$, it holds that the random variables* $\mathsf{Real}_{\Pi_r}^{\mathcal{A}_\mathsf{S}}(\mathcal{Z})$ *and* $\mathsf{Real}_{\Pi_s}^{\mathcal{A}_\mathsf{S}'}(\mathcal{Z})$ *are computationally indistinguishable.*

Again, as Π_s is UC-secure, there exists a simulator $\mathcal{S}_\mathsf{S}$ such that $\mathsf{Real}_{\Pi_s}^{\mathcal{A}_\mathsf{S}'}(\mathcal{Z}) \approx \mathsf{Ideal}_{\mathcal{F}}^{\mathcal{S}_\mathsf{S}}(\mathcal{Z})$, which yields the desired $\mathsf{Real}_{\Pi_r}^{\mathcal{A}_\mathsf{S}}(\mathcal{Z}) \approx \mathsf{Ideal}_{\mathcal{F}}^{\mathcal{S}_\mathsf{S}}(\mathcal{Z})$

Proof. Let $\mathcal{Z}$ be a PPT environment. We will prove the indistinguishability of $\mathsf{Real}_{\Pi_r}^{\mathcal{A}_\mathsf{S}}(\mathcal{Z})$ and $\mathsf{Real}_{\Pi_s}^{\mathcal{A}_\mathsf{S}'}(\mathcal{Z})$ by a series of indistinguishable hybrid experiments.

Hybrid $\mathcal{H}_0$. Simulator $\mathcal{S}_0$ simulates $\mathsf{Real}_{\Pi_r}^{\mathcal{A}_\mathsf{S}}$.

Hybrid $\mathcal{H}_1$. Identical to $\mathcal{H}_0$, except that during invocation of the token, R does not setup and run a prover P with input (vk, inp) and witness-input (σ, c, r), but instead runs the prover-simulator P_{Sim} with input (vk, inp) and witness-input V^*, where V^* is a corrupted verifier that is constructed from T^*.

Hybrid $\mathcal{H}_2$. Identical to $\mathcal{H}_1$, except that the commitment c sent to $\mathcal{A}_S$ is computed by $c = com_k(0; r)$ instead of $c = com_k(inp; r)$. From the view of $\mathcal{Z}$, this is identical to $\mathsf{Real}_{\Pi_s}^{\mathcal{A}_S'}$.

Indistinguishability of the hybrids $\mathcal{H}_0$ and $\mathcal{H}_1$ follows directly from the computational zero-knowledge property of the system (P, V). Since the commitment scheme com is computationally binding, the hybrids $\mathcal{H}_1$ and $\mathcal{H}_2$ are computationally indistinguishable from the view of $\mathcal{Z}$ as well. This can be established by a simple hybrid-argument, where a $\mathcal{Z}$ distinguishing the two experiments can be used to break the hiding-property of com.   □

Remark 1. The above compiler can easily be extended to allow for multiple messages. Then, in each step of the token invocation the token receiver has to query the sender on a commitment and provide a proof to the token, that this commitment was signed by the sender. For each message, a counter is added such that the receiver cannot query the token "out-of-sync". If the token is reset, its counter will not match the counter of the sender and thus the token will abort.

4.2 Protocol Using UC-Secure Seed-OTs

Outline. The compiler $\mathcal{C}_{OT}$ depicted in Fig. 4 adds a step to the underlying protocol Π_s, which authenticates the token input. This time, the authentication is done by using UC-secure OTs. Before the execution of Π_s, the token sender creates two random strings (s_0^i, s_1^i) for every bit of the message inp that the receiver will input into the token. Let $inp(i)$ denote the i-th bit of inp. During the setup, the receiver obtains one of these random strings, namely $s_{inp(i)}^i$, for each of his input bits. Since the receiver does not learn any $s_{1-inp(i)}^i$, he is bitwise committed to his input, while the sender does not learn anything about it.

All random values $((s_0^1, s_1^1), \ldots, (s_0^k, s_1^k))$ that the sender created are stored in the token functionality. When the token is invoked on input $(inp, (s_{j_1}^1, \ldots, s_{j_k}^k))$, the tokens checks that these values are consistent with the random values of the OTs. If that is the case, the token will evaluate the underlying token functionality on inp and forward the output out.

Proof of Security. Please note that the security reduction is information-theoretic, but depending on the realization of $\mathcal{F}$, the protocol might still only be computationally secure.

Corrupted Receiver. Let $\mathcal{A}_R$ be the dummy-adversary for a corrupted sender for the protocol Π_r. We will construct an adversary $\mathcal{A}_R'$ against the protocol Π_s (cf. Fig. 5).

Compiler $\mathcal{C}_{\text{OT}}$

Let $\mathcal{F}$ be a two-party UC-functionality. Let $k = |\text{inp}|$ be the input length of the token receiver's message inp to the token in Π_s. S and R have access to k $\mathcal{F}_{\text{OT}}$-functionalities.

Input: Protocol Π_s UC-implementing $\mathcal{F}$ in the $\mathcal{F}_{\text{wrap}}^{\text{stateful}}$-hybrid model.

Output: Protocol Π_r UC-implementing $\mathcal{F}$ in the $\mathcal{F}_{\text{wrap}}^{\text{resettable}}$-hybrid model.

Setup (Before execution of Π_s):

- **(Sender)** S creates $2k$ random strings $S = ((s_0^1, s_1^1), \ldots, (s_0^k, s_1^k))$, $s_j^i \in \{0,1\}^\lambda$ and inputs them into the k $\mathcal{F}_{\text{OT}}$-functionalities.
- **(Receiver)** R inputs $\text{inp}(1), \ldots, \text{inp}(k)$ into the corresponding $\mathcal{F}_{\text{OT}}$ and obtains $(s_{\text{inp}(1)}^1, \ldots, s_{\text{inp}(k)}^k)$.

Rewriting the token-code:

(Sender) Once S inputs a token code T into $\mathcal{F}_{\text{wrap}}^{\text{stateful}}$ do the following. Construct a token-code T' which upon receiving a message $(\text{input}, \text{inp}, (s_{j_1}^1, \ldots, s_{j_k}^k))$, $j \in \{0,1\}$ from R checks that $s_j^i \in S$ for all $i \in \{1, \ldots, k\}$. If this is the case, it continues the execution of T with input inp and forwards whatever T outputs. Then input T' into $\mathcal{F}_{\text{wrap}}^{\text{resettable}}$.

Token-invocation:

1. R sends a message query to S, who replies with a message ack.
2. R sends the previously obtained random strings with the message $(\text{input}, \text{inp}, (s_{j_1}^1, \ldots, s_{j_k}^k))$ to the token and continues the normal computation once the token outputs out.

Fig. 4. Stateless compiler using k seed-OTs.

Lemma 3. *For every (PPT-)environment $\mathcal{Z}$, it holds that the random variables* $\text{Real}_{\Pi_r}^{\mathcal{A}_R}(\mathcal{Z})$ *and* $\text{Real}_{\Pi_s}^{\mathcal{A}_R'}(\mathcal{Z})$ *are indistinguishable.*

Proof. The only difference between $\text{Real}_{\Pi_r}^{\mathcal{A}_R}(\mathcal{Z})$ and $\text{Real}_{\Pi_s}^{\mathcal{A}_R'}(\mathcal{Z})$ is the abort of $\mathcal{A}_R'$ in case $\text{inp}' \neq \text{inp}$. For this event to happen, $\mathcal{A}_R$ has to guess a string $s_j^i \in S$ of length λ for any $i \in \{1, \ldots, k\}, j \in \{0,1\}$. The probability for this event is obviously negligible in the security parameter λ. $\square$

Since the protocol Π_s is UC-secure, there exists a simulator S_R such that $\text{Real}_{\Pi_s}^{\mathcal{A}_R'}(\mathcal{Z}) \approx \text{Ideal}_{\mathcal{F}}^{S_R}(\mathcal{Z})$. Thus, $\text{Real}_{\Pi_r}^{\mathcal{A}_R}(\mathcal{Z}) \approx \text{Ideal}_{\mathcal{F}}^{S_R}(\mathcal{Z})$ follows from the above lemma.

Corrupted Sender. Let $\mathcal{A}_S$ be the dummy-adversary for a corrupted sender for the protocol Π_r. We will construct an adversary $\mathcal{A}_S'$ against the protocol Π_s (cf. Fig. 6).

Adversary-Simulator $\mathcal{A}'_{\mathsf{R}}$

- **Setup:** Create $2k$ random strings $S = ((s_0^1, s_1^1), \ldots, (s_0^k, s_1^k))$ and simulate k $\mathcal{F}_{\mathsf{OT}}$ instances. Obtain the choice-bits $c_i, i \in \{1, \ldots, k\}$ and thereby learn inp.
- **Token-Invocation:**
  - Once $\mathcal{A}_{\mathsf{R}}$ sends query, forward query to S. Once S responds with ack, send ack to $\mathcal{A}_{\mathsf{R}}$.
  - Once $\mathcal{A}_{\mathsf{R}}$ wants to input a message $(\text{input}, \text{inp}', (s_{j_1}^1, \ldots, s_{j_k}^k))$ to $\mathcal{F}_{\mathsf{wrap}}^{\text{resettable}}$, check if inp = inp' and $s_j^i \in S \forall i$, if not abort. Query $\mathcal{F}_{\mathsf{wrap}}^{\text{stateful}}$ on inp and let out be the result. Send out to $\mathcal{A}_{\mathsf{R}}$.

Fig. 5. Adversary-simulator $\mathcal{A}'_{\mathsf{R}}$ for $\mathcal{C}_{\mathsf{OT}}$.

Adversary-Simulator $\mathcal{A}'_{\mathsf{S}}$

- **Setup:** Simulate the $\mathcal{F}_{\mathsf{OT}}$-functionalities and obtain all values $((s_0^1, s_1^1), \ldots, (s_0^k, s_1^k))$.
- **Rewriting the Token-code:** Once S inputs a token code T^* into $\mathcal{F}_{\mathsf{wrap}}^{\text{resettable}}$, create a token code $\mathsf{T}^\dagger$ as follows:
  - On input a message $(\text{input}, \text{inp})$, select $(s_{\mathsf{Inp}(1)}^1, \ldots, s_{\mathsf{Inp}(k)}^k)$.
  - Run T^* with input $(\text{input}, \text{inp}, (s_{\mathsf{Inp}(1)}^1, \ldots, s_{\mathsf{Inp}(k)}^k))$ and let out be the result. Send out to R.
  Input $\mathsf{T}^\dagger$ into $\mathcal{F}_{\mathsf{wrap}}^{\text{stateful}}$.

Fig. 6. Adversary-simulator $\mathcal{A}'_{\mathsf{S}}$ for $\mathcal{C}_{\mathsf{OT}}$.

Lemma 4. *For every (PPT-)environment $\mathcal{Z}$, it holds that the random variables* $\mathsf{Real}_{\Pi_r}^{\mathcal{A}_{\mathsf{S}}}(\mathcal{Z})$ *and* $\mathsf{Real}_{\Pi_s}^{\mathcal{A}'_{\mathsf{S}}}(\mathcal{Z})$ *are indistinguishable.*

Proof. $\mathsf{Real}_{\Pi_r}^{\mathcal{A}_{\mathsf{S}}}(\mathcal{Z})$ and $\mathsf{Real}_{\Pi_s}^{\mathcal{A}_{\mathsf{S}}'}(\mathcal{Z})$ are identically distributed, because after obtaining all labels $((s_0^1, s_1^1), \ldots, (s_0^k, s_1^k))$, a normal protocol run is simulated. □

5 Optimizations

Recall that the compiler $\mathcal{C}_{\mathsf{ZK}}$ can straightforwardly be extended to allow for multiple messages between token and receiver. However, this would lead to an inefficient zero-knowledge proof for each message. Also, it seems difficult to change the compiler $\mathcal{C}_{\mathsf{OT}}$ such that it allows for more than a single message due to the fixed amount of seed-OTs.

In case that the receiver has non-adaptive queries for the token, these problems can be overcome. By non-adaptive queries, we mean that the i-th token query does not depend on the $(i-1)$-th query. A very simple solution is to just concatenate all messages into a single message and have the sender authenticate this message. However, this needs quite a lot of seed-OTs and also the amount of data that has to be sent to the sender is very large.

A more refined solution to the problem is the following. Instead of using the normal token input as the message that shall be authenticated by the sender, the receiver computes a Merkle tree with all non-adative messages in the leaves. Then, the sender authenticates the root of the Merkle tree, and the receiver only has to use the compiler for the root message. From there on, for each of the initial non-adaptive messages he sends the path through the tree and the corresponding message to the token, which can verify that the path is consistent with the root.

This improvement leads to a single message of small size during the authentication step of $\mathcal{C}_{\text{ZK}}$ and $\mathcal{C}_{\text{OT}}$ respectively. This construction has one drawback: the Merkle tree relies on collision resistant hash functions. Considering our initial goal to achieve a compiler using only one-way functions, we replace the Merkle tree with the recent construction of *sig-com trees* [9].

We will briefly sketch how sig-com trees can be used in our scenario. Additionally to the normal setup, the token sender creates a key pair $(\text{vk}_h, \text{sk}_h)$ and extends the token functionality as follows. Upon receiving (sign, x) the token returns $\text{Sign}_{\text{sk}_h}(x)$, basically implementing a signature oracle. Further, upon receiving $(\text{check}, \text{path})$, the token checks that path constitutes a valid path given the root of a sig-com tree. The verification key vk_h is given to the token receiver. The rest of the compiler is carried out as described above. During the protocol run, instead of directly giving the non-adaptive messages to the sender, the receiver first uses the resettable token to create a signature tree and verifies each obtained signature with vk_h. Since all inputs are committed to in advance of the oracle calls, the token does not learn the inputs. Then the rest of the protocol proceeds normally: The sender authenticates the root of the sig-com tree, and the receiver has to present a path through the sig-com tree for each of the non-adaptive messages.

Simulation of this enhancement against a corrupted sender is quite simple. Since the commitments on the receiver inputs are never opened (but only used in zero-knowledge arguments of knowledge), the simulator can still just pick all-zero inputs, then use the token to create a corresponding sig-com tree, and proceed as before. Our indistinguishability proofs for the original compilers just carry over; otherwise the commitments on the receiver inputs would not be hiding. If the receiver is corrupted, the binding property of the commitments on his inputs and the collision resistance of the sig-com tree guarantee that the token can still be queried only with messages that were authenticated by the sender. It follows again that our indistinguishability proofs for the original compilers just carry over.

6 Implications

In this section we will briefly discuss the implications of applying our compiler to existing protocols. We want to focus on UC-secure oblivious transfer protocols. Previous constructions based on resettable tokens were either dependent on the fact that several hardware tokens had to be exchanged [8] or made use of stronger computational assumptions [7]. In fact, it was shown that, using only black-box techniques, OT can only be achieved by exchanging two tokens [8] or by sending a large amount of tokens in one direction [7,19].

The only known solution using a single resettable hardware token can be constructed by using the recent work of [17] (which makes inherent use of non-black-box techniques). They create a CRS with a single resettable token and by plugging in an efficient OT protocol in the CRS model, e.g. [30], an OT protocol using a single resettable token can be obtained. OT protocols in the CRS model, however, cannot be based on one-way functions and thus stronger cryptographic assumptions are needed. In the context of stateful tokens, very efficient constructions are known, e.g. [15]. By plugging the protocol of Döttling et al. [14,15] into one of our compilers, we obtain the most efficient OT-protocol based on resettable hardware to date (the protocol of [14,15] only gives an a priori fixed amount of OTs). The compiler $\mathcal{C}_{ZK}$ uses non-black-box techniques, so the above-mentioned impossibility result does not hold. We can further improve the efficiency of this protocol by performing random OTs with non-adaptive token inputs. This allows us to use the optimization from Sect. 5, thereby making only a single call to the sender. Additionally, the compiler $\mathcal{C}_{OT}$ allows to extend a fixed amount of UC-OTs (the seed-OTs of the compiler) to a (fixed but independent) number of UC-OTs by using the protocol of [14,15].

References

1. Barak, B., Goldreich, O., Goldwasser, S., Lindell, Y.: Resettably-sound zero-knowledge and its applications. In: FOCS, pp. 116–125 (2001)
2. Bitansky, N., Canetti, R., Goldwasser, S., Halevi, S., Kalai, Y.T., Rothblum, G.N.: Program obfuscation with leaky hardware. In: Lee, D.H., Wang, X. (eds.) ASIACRYPT 2011. LNCS, vol. 7073, pp. 722–739. Springer, Heidelberg (2011)
3. Bitansky, N., Paneth, O.: On the impossibility of approximate obfuscation and applications to resettable cryptography. In: STOC (2013)
4. Brzuska, C., Fischlin, M., Schröder, H., Katzenbeisser, S.: Physically uncloneable functions in the universal composition framework. In: Rogaway, P. (ed.) CRYPTO 2011. LNCS, vol. 6841, pp. 51–70. Springer, Heidelberg (2011)
5. Canetti, R.: Universally composable security: a new paradigm for cryptographic protocols. In: FOCS, pp. 136–145 (2001)
6. Canetti, R., Goldreich, O., Goldwasser, S., Micali, S.: Resettable zero-knowledge (extended abstract). In: STOC, pp. 235–244 (2000)
7. Chandran, N., Goyal, V., Sahai, A.: New constructions for UC secure computation using tamper-proof hardware. In: Smart, N.P. (ed.) EUROCRYPT 2008. LNCS, vol. 4965, pp. 545–562. Springer, Heidelberg (2008)
8. Choi, S.G., Katz, J., Schröder, D., Yerukhimovich, A., Zhou, H.-S.: (Efficient) Universally composable oblivious transfer using a minimal number of stateless tokens. In: Lindell, Y. (ed.) TCC 2014. LNCS, vol. 8349, pp. 638–662. Springer, Heidelberg (2014)
9. Chung, K.M., Pass, R., Seth, K.: Non-black-box simulation from one-way functions and applications to resettable security. In: STOC (2013)

10. Dachman-Soled, D., Fleischhacker, N., Katz, J., Lysyanskaya, A., Schröder, D.: Feasibility and infeasibility of secure computation with malicious PUFs. In: Garay, J.A., Gennaro, R. (eds.) CRYPTO 2014, Part II. LNCS, vol. 8617, pp. 405–420. Springer, Heidelberg (2014)

11. Damgård, I., Scafuro, A.: Unconditionally secure and universally composable commitments from physical assumptions. In: Sako, K., Sarkar, P. (eds.) ASIACRYPT 2013, Part II. LNCS, vol. 8270, pp. 100–119. Springer, Heidelberg (2013)

12. Deng, Y., Feng, D., Goyal, V., Lin, D., Sahai, A., Yung, M.: Resettable cryptography in constant rounds – the case of zero knowledge. In: Lee, D.H., Wang, X. (eds.) ASIACRYPT 2011. LNCS, vol. 7073, pp. 390–406. Springer, Heidelberg (2011)

13. Deng, Y., Goyal, V., Sahai, A.: Resolving the simultaneous resettability conjecture and a new non-black-box simulation strategy. In: FOCS, pp. 251–260 (2009)

14. Döttling, N., Kraschewski, D., Müller-Quade, J.: Unconditional and composable security using a single stateful tamper-proof hardware token. In: Ishai, Y. (ed.) TCC 2011. LNCS, vol. 6597, pp. 164–181. Springer, Heidelberg (2011)

15. Döttling, N., Kraschewski, D., Müller-Quade, J.: David & goliath oblivious affine function evaluation - asymptotically optimal building blocks for universally composable two-party computation from a single untrusted stateful tamper-proof hardware token. IACR Cryptology ePrint Archive 2012, p. 135 (2012)

16. Döttling, N., Kraschewski, D., Müller-Quade, J., Nilges, T.: General statistically secure computation with bounded-resettable hardware tokens. In: Dodis, Y., Nielsen, J.B. (eds.) TCC 2015, Part I. LNCS, vol. 9014, pp. 319–344. Springer, Heidelberg (2015)

17. Döttling, N., Mie, T., Müller-Quade, J., Nilges, T.: Implementing resettable UC-functionalities with untrusted tamper-proof hardware-tokens. In: Sahai, A. (ed.) TCC 2013. LNCS, vol. 7785, pp. 642–661. Springer, Heidelberg (2013)

18. Goyal, V., Ishai, Y., Mahmoody, M., Sahai, A.: Interactive locking, zero-knowledge PCPs, and unconditional cryptography. In: Rabin, T. (ed.) CRYPTO 2010. LNCS, vol. 6223, pp. 173–190. Springer, Heidelberg (2010)

19. Goyal, V., Ishai, Y., Sahai, A., Venkatesan, R., Wadia, A.: Founding cryptography on tamper-proof hardware tokens. In: Micciancio, D. (ed.) TCC 2010. LNCS, vol. 5978, pp. 308–326. Springer, Heidelberg (2010)

20. Goyal, V., Maji, H.K.: Stateless cryptographic protocols. In: FOCS, pp. 678–687 (2011)

21. Goyal, V., Sahai, A.: Resettably secure computation. In: Joux, A. (ed.) EUROCRYPT 2009. LNCS, vol. 5479, pp. 54–71. Springer, Heidelberg (2009)

22. Håstad, J., Impagliazzo, R., Levin, L.A., Luby, M.: A pseudorandom generator from any one-way function. SIAM J. Comput. **28**(4), 1364–1396 (1999)

23. Ishai, Y., Prabhakaran, M., Sahai, A.: Founding cryptography on oblivious transfer – efficiently. In: Wagner, D. (ed.) CRYPTO 2008. LNCS, vol. 5157, pp. 572–591. Springer, Heidelberg (2008)

24. Katz, J.: Universally composable multi-party computation using tamper-proof hardware. In: Naor, M. (ed.) EUROCRYPT 2007. LNCS, vol. 4515, pp. 115–128. Springer, Heidelberg (2007)

25. Kilian, J.: Founding cryptography on oblivious transfer. In: STOC, pp. 20–31 (1988)

26. Naor, M.: Bit commitment using pseudorandomness. J. Cryptology **4**(2), 151–158 (1991)

27. Naor, M., Yung, M.: Universal one-way hash functions and their cryptographic applications. In: STOC, pp. 33–43 (1989)

28. Ostrovsky, R., Scafuro, A., Visconti, I., Wadia, A.: Universally composable secure computation with (malicious) physically uncloneable functions. In: Johansson, T., Nguyen, P.Q. (eds.) EUROCRYPT 2013. LNCS, vol. 7881, pp. 702–718. Springer, Heidelberg (2013)
29. Pappu, R.S.: Physical One-Way Functions. Ph.D. thesis, MIT (2001)
30. Peikert, C., Vaikuntanathan, V., Waters, B.: A framework for efficient and composable oblivious transfer. In: Wagner, D. (ed.) CRYPTO 2008. LNCS, vol. 5157, pp. 554–571. Springer, Heidelberg (2008)
31. Prabhakaran, M., Sahai, A., Wadia, A.: Secure computation using leaky tokens. In: Esparza, J., Fraigniaud, P., Husfeldt, T., Koutsoupias, E. (eds.) ICALP 2014. LNCS, vol. 8572, pp. 907–918. Springer, Heidelberg (2014)
32. Rompel, J.: One-way functions are necessary and sufficient for secure signatures. In: STOC, pp. 387–394 (1990)
33. Rührmair, U.: Oblivious transfer based on physical unclonable functions. In: Acquisti, A., Smith, S.W., Sadeghi, A.-R. (eds.) TRUST 2010. LNCS, vol. 6101, pp. 430–440. Springer, Heidelberg (2010)

Constrained Verifiable Random Functions from Indistinguishability Obfuscation

Bei Liang[1,2,3]([✉]), Hongda Li[1,2,3], and Jinyong Chang[1,3]

[1] State Key Laboratory of Information Security, Institute of Information Engineering
of Chinese Academy of Sciences, Beijing, China
{liangbei,lihongda,changjinyong}@iie.ac.cn
[2] Data Assurance and Communication Security Research Center of Chinese Academy
of Sciences, Beijing, China
[3] University of Chinese Academy of Sciences, Beijing, China

Abstract. Constrained verifiable random functions (VRFs) were first explicitly introduced by Fuchsbauer (SCN'14) as an extension of the standard concept of VRFs. In a standard VRF, there is a secret key sk that enables one to evaluate the function at any point of its domain, and enables generation of a proof that the function value is computed correctly. While, in a constrained VRF, it is allowed to derive constrained key sk_S for subset S (of the domain) from sk, which enables evaluation of function and generation of proofs *only* at points in S and nowhere else. In fact, there are many open questions in the study of VRFs, especially constructing them from a wide variety of cryptographic assumptions.

In this work, we show how to construct constrained VRFs with respect to a set system, which can be described by a polynomial-size circuit C, from one-way functions together with indistinguishability obfuscation (iO). Our construction may be interesting for at least two reasons:

- Given the results of Brakerski et al. (TCC09) and Fiore et al. (TCC12), in which they proved that VRFs cannot be constructed from one-way permutations and trapdoor permutations in a black-box manner, it is interesting to study their construction from other stronger cryptographic primitives. Our construction shows that one-way functions plus iO are sufficient.
- Compared to the multilinear-map-based construction of constrained VRFs (SCN'14), our iO-based one has its particular advantage:
  - In current multilinear-based constrained VRFs, since the level of their group is $n + d_C$ where n is the bit-length of input and d_C is the depth of circuit C, public key is dependent on the depth of circuit. However, our iO-based construction does not have this limitation since our public key is an obfuscated program which is independent on the circuit.

Keywords: Constrained VRFs · Puncturable PRFs · Commitment schemes · Indistinguishability obfuscation

This research is supported by the Strategy Pilot Project of Chinese Academy of Sciences (Grant No. Y2W0012203).

M.-H. Au and A. Miyaji (Eds.): ProvSec 2015, LNCS 9451, pp. 43–60, 2015.
DOI: 10.1007/978-3-319-26059-4_3

1   Introduction

Verifiable Random Functions (VRFs) were proposed by Micali, Rabin and Vadhan [17]. Informally, a VRF behaves similar to a pseudorandom function (see Goldreich, Goldwasser and Micali [10]) and also enables a verifier to verify, given an input x, an output y and a proof π, that the function has been correctly computed on x. More precisely, a VRF is associated with a secret key sk and a corresponding public verification key pk. As usual, sk allows the evaluation of function $y = F_{sk}(x)$ on any input x and the generation of a proof $\pi = P_{sk}(x)$. This proof can be used in conjunction with pk to convince a verifier that y is the correct output on input x. For security, VRFs must satisfy the provability (or correctness), uniqueness and pseudorandomness properties. *Uniqueness* guarantees that the verifier cannot accept two different values for an input x, even if pk is generated dishonestly; *Pseudorandomness* states that having only pk and oracle access to $F_{sk}(\cdot)$ and $P_{sk}(\cdot)$, the value $y = F_{sk}(x)$ looks random to any polynomially bounded adversary who did not query $F_{sk}(x)$ explicitly.

Due to their strong properties, VRFs are a fascinating primitive that have several theoretical and practical applications. Abdalla et al. [1] provided a nice summary of applications, including resettable zero-knowledge proofs [16] and verifiable transaction escrow schemes [14], to name a few.

However, most existing constructions of VRFs either allow only a small input space of polynomially-bounded size, or do not achieve full adaptive security under a static complexity assumption. To our knowledge, the few known constructions [1,13] of fully-secure VRFs with exponential-size input space are based on non-interactive, so-called "q-type" assumptions [12]. Hence, constructing VRFs with large input space and full adaptive security from a static complexity assumption seems to be a challenging task. Still, there are many open questions in the study of VRFs, especially their relations to more widely studied cryptographic primitives and constructions from a wide variety of cryptographic assumptions. Brakerski et al. [3] showed that VRFs cannot be constructed from one-way permutations in a black-box way. And Fiore et al. [7] also proved VRFs cannot be based on the existence of trapdoor permutations in a black-box manner. In this work we attempt to ask an ambitious question: *Is it possible to construct VRFs from one-way functions, combing with other assumption (such as the existence of indistinguishability obfuscation (iO))?*

Constrained VRFs. As the notion of constrained PRFs explicitly introduced by Boneh and Waters [6], recently Fuchsbauer [8] has defined a extended notion of VRFs which he called constrained VRFs. Informally, a constrained VRF is a special kind of VRF that allows one to derive a constrained key sk_S with respect to some set $S \subseteq \mathcal{X}$ from the master secret key sk. The constrained key sk_S allows the computation of $F(sk, x)$ and $P(sk, x)$ only for $x \in S$. *Pseudorandomness* should also hold for constrained VRFs against adversaries that obtain constrained keys of their choice (in addition to public key, function values and proofs for input points of their choice). Moreover, an additional *constraint-hiding* property is also needed for constrained VRFs, which states that the proof does not reveal which key (secret key or constrained key) was used to compute it.

By adding a level in the group hierarchy based on the constructions of constrained PRFs given by Boneh and Waters [6], Fuchsbauer [8] also provides two instantiation of constrained VRFs for "bit-fixing" sets and sets that can be decided by a polynomial-size circuit under the DDH assumption adapted to the multilinear-map environment.

Our Contribution. In this paper, assuming the existence of iO and one-way functions, we also propose a construction of constrained VRFs with respect to a set system which can be described by a polynomial-size circuit C. More precisely, based on iO, we provide a generic construction of constrained VRFs from puncturable PRFs and commitment scheme, which both can in turn be built from one-way functions. We remark that, although constrained VRFs were already constructed by Fuchsbauer from multilinear maps [8], our iO-based one has its particular feature.

- In current multilinear-based constrained VRFs with respect to a set system, which can be described by a polynomial-size circuit C, since the level of their group is $n + d_C$ where n is the bit-length of input and d_C is the depth of circuit C, public key is dependent on the depth of circuit. However, our iO-based construction does not have this limitation since our public key is an obfuscated program which is independent on the circuit.

Now, we would like to briefly introduce our construction and underlying ideas. In [17], Micali et al. showed that, for the purpose of constructing a VRF, it is sufficient to construct a verifiable unpredictable function (unique signature [11]). Lysyanskaya [15] provided a specific construction of unique signature and adopted the security proof slightly to show that such unique signature is also a verifiable unpredictable function which implies verifiable random function. In the light of these results, we consider using a specific construction of unique signature to build a VRF. In fact, our constrained VRF shares some of the spirit of the unique signature scheme of Bitansky and Paneth [5], which is further inspired by Sahai-Waters's signature scheme [19]. In Sahai-Waters's and Bitansky-Paneth's signature schemes, the secret signing key is key K for a PRF PRF_K, and signature σ on message x is simply $\sigma = \mathsf{PRF}(K, x)$. Therefore, we define the evaluation of function on input x as the first bit of $\sigma = b\|r$, which means $y = F(sk, x) = b$, and the proof π for $F(sk, x) = b$ is the string r. To verify a tuple (x, y, π) is simply done by computing $f(y\|\pi)$ and comparing it to the value $f(\mathsf{PRF}(K, x))$, where f is an injective one-way function.

Unfortunately, the one-wayness of f is not enough to derive the pseudorandomness of b. Hence, we additionally employ a non-interactive perfectly-binding commitment scheme. Now, the verification algorithm is simply to compare $\mathsf{Com}(y; \pi)$ with the value $\mathsf{Com}(\mathsf{PRF}(K, x))$. While the public key pk is an obfuscation of the program outputting the value $\mathsf{Com}(\mathsf{PRF}(K, x))$ for input x with the hardwired PRF key. The constrained key for a set S is an obfuscation of the program $\mathsf{ConstrainedKey}_{K,S}$ which with hardwired secret key K and set S, takes as inputs x, and if $x \in S$ computes $\mathsf{PRF}(K, x) = b\|r$ and outputs $(y = b, \pi = r)$; else if $x \notin S$, outputs $(\bot, \bot)$.

Indeed, the properties of provability, uniqueness and constraint-hiding can be directly verified according to the perfectly binding and computational hiding properties of the commitment scheme. To prove the selective pseudorandomness is a more challenging task and we will apply the "puncturing technique" of Sahai and Waters [19], where we surgically remove a key element of a program, but in a way that does not alter input/output functionality, coupled with the computationally hiding property of the commitment Com.

Concretely, our selective pseudorandomness security proof is formed by a sequence of games, in which the latter is obtained by making some proper modifications of the former. In game 1, we replace the obfuscation of the program Verify_K with an obfuscation of an equivalent program $\text{Verify}_{K(x^*),c^*}$. This program operates the same as the original except on input x^*, where x^* is the point the attacker selectively chose to attack (before seeing the public key). At this point, instead of computing $\text{PRF}(K, x^*) = t^* = b^* \| r^*$ and $c^* = \text{Com}(b^*; r^*)$, the program is simply hardwired a constant c^* to output. Therefore, the program $\text{Verify}_{K(x^*),c^*}$ computes the same function as Verify_K. In addition, the program is not given the full PRF key K, but instead is given a punctured PRF key $K(x^*)$. By the security of iO, the advantage of any poly-time attacker must be negligibly close between these two hybrids. In game 2 on attacker's Prove-query, the challenger responds by punctured key $K(x^*)$, which is identical to that responds by full PRF key K, except that on input x^*, it outputs $(\perp, \perp)$. In game 3 on attacker's Constrainedkey-query, the challenger also responds by punctured key $K(x^*)$. Since, for constrained key query, the attacker only allows to ask for set $S \in \mathcal{S}$ satisfying $x^* \notin S$, the punctured key $K(x^*)$ can also compute evaluations and proofs on every input $x \in S$, which is the same as responding by PRF key K. Having punctured out x^*, in game 4, we replace t^* with a totally random value chosen from the range of the PRFs. The advantage between these games must also be close due to the indistinguishability at punctured points property of PRFs. In game 5, we replace the bit y^* with a random independent bit. By the computational hiding property of Com, the advantage of any poly-time attacker must be negligibly close between these two games.

Organization. The rest of this paper is organized as follows. In Sect. 2 we introduce the basic tools underlying our construction. In Sect. 3 we introduce the notions of constrained VRFs that are considered in this work. In Sect. 4 we present our generic construction of constrained VRFs and prove its security. Conclusion is presented in Sect. 5.

2 Preliminaries

2.1 Indistinguishability Obfuscation

Here we recall the notion of indistinguishability obfuscation which was originally proposed by Barak et al. [2]. The formal definition we present below is from [9].

Definition 1 (Indistinguishability obfuscation [9]). *A probabilistic polynomial time (PPT) algorithm iO is said to be an indistinguishability obfuscator for a circuits class $\{\mathcal{C}_\lambda\}$, if the following conditions are satisfied:*

- *For all security parameters $\lambda \in \mathbb{N}$, for all $C \in C_\lambda$, for all inputs x, we have that*

$$\Pr[C'(x) = C(x) : C' \leftarrow i\mathcal{O}(\lambda, C)] = 1.$$

- *For any (not necessarily uniform) PPT adversaries (Samp, D), there exists a negligible function $\mathrm{negl}(\cdot)$ such that the following holds: if $\Pr[\forall x, C_0(x) = C_1(x) : (C_0, C_1, \sigma) \leftarrow \mathsf{Samp}(1^\lambda)] > 1 - \mathrm{negl}(\lambda)$, then we have:*

$$\left| \Pr[D(\sigma, i\mathcal{O}(\lambda, C_0)) = 1 : (C_0, C_1, \sigma) \leftarrow \mathsf{Samp}(1^\lambda)] \right.$$
$$\left. - \Pr[D(\sigma, i\mathcal{O}(\lambda, C_1)) = 1 : (C_0, C_1, \sigma) \leftarrow \mathsf{Samp}(1^\lambda)] \right| \leq \mathrm{negl}(\lambda).$$

In a recent work, Garg et al. [9] gave the first candidate construction of indistinguishability obfuscator $i\mathcal{O}$ for all polynomial size circuits under novel algebraic hardness assumptions. In this paper, we will take advantage of such indistinguishability obfuscators for all polynomial size circuits.

2.2 Puncturable PRFs

Puncturable PRF introduced by Sahai and Waters [19] is considered as a simple type of constrained PRF [6], where a PRF is only defined on a subset of the input space. Informally speaking, puncturable PRFs are PRFs for which a punctured key can be derived that allows evaluation of the PRF on all inputs, except for any polynomial-size set of inputs. The definition is formulated as in [19].

Definition 2. *A puncturable family of PRFs F mapping is given by a triple of Turing Machines $(\mathsf{Key}_F, \mathsf{Puncture}_F, \text{ and } \mathsf{Eval}_F)$, and a pair of computable functions $\tau_1(\cdot)$ and $\tau_2(\cdot)$, satisfying the following conditions:*

- *[**Functionality preserved under puncturing**] For every PPT adversary $\mathcal{A}$ such that $\mathcal{A}(1^\lambda)$ outputs a set $S \subseteq \{0,1\}^{\tau_1(\lambda)}$, then for all $x \in \{0,1\}^{\tau_1(\lambda)}$ where $x \notin S$, we have that:*

$$\Pr[\mathsf{Eval}_F(K, x) = \mathsf{Eval}_F(K_S, x) : K \leftarrow \mathsf{Key}_F(1^\lambda), K_S = \mathsf{Puncture}_F(K, S)] = 1.$$

- *[**Pseudorandom at punctured points**] For every PPT adversary $(\mathcal{A}_1, \mathcal{A}_2)$ such that $\mathcal{A}_1(1^\lambda)$ outputs a set $S \subseteq \{0,1\}^{\tau_1(\lambda)}$ and state σ, consider an experiment where $K \leftarrow \mathsf{Key}_F(1^\lambda)$ and $K_S = \mathsf{Puncture}_F(K, S)$. Then we have*

$$\left| \Pr[\mathcal{A}_2(\sigma, K_S, S, \mathsf{Eval}_F(K, S)) = 1] - \Pr[\mathcal{A}_2(\sigma, K_S, S, U_{\tau_2(\lambda) \cdot |S|}) = 1] \right| = \mathrm{negl}(\lambda),$$

where $\mathsf{Eval}_F(K, S)$ denotes the concatenation of $\mathsf{Eval}_F(K, x_1), \ldots, \mathsf{Eval}_F(K, x_k)$ where $S = \{x_1, \ldots, x_k\}$ is the enumeration of the elements of S in lexicographic order, $\mathrm{negl}(\cdot)$ is a negligible function, and $U_{\tau_2(\lambda) \cdot |S|}$ denotes the uniform distribution over $\tau_2(\lambda) \cdot |S|$ bits.

Theorem 1. *[19] If one-way functions exist, then for all efficiently computable functions $\tau_1(\lambda)$ and $\tau_2(\lambda)$, there exists a puncturable PRFs family that maps $\tau_1(\lambda)$ bits to $\tau_2(\lambda)$ bits.*

Definition 3. *[19] A statistically injective (puncturable) PRFs family with fail-ure probability $\epsilon(\cdot)$ is a family of (puncturable) PRFs F such that with probability $1 - \epsilon(\cdot)$ over the random choice of key $K \leftarrow \mathsf{Key}_F(1^\lambda)$, we have that $F(K, \cdot)$ is injective.*

Theorem 2. *[19] If one-way functions exist, then for all efficiently computable functions $\tau_1(\lambda)$, $\tau_2(\lambda)$, and $e(\lambda)$ such that $\tau_2(\lambda) \geq 2\tau_1(\lambda) + e(\lambda)$, there exists a puncturable statistically injective PRFs family with failure probability $2^{-e(\lambda)}$ that maps $\tau_1(\lambda)$ bits to $\tau_2(\lambda)$ bits.*

2.3 Commitment Schemes [18]

A non-interactive commitment scheme $\mathsf{Com} : \{0,1\}^{\ell(\lambda)} \times \{0,1\}^{\ell_1(\lambda)} \to \{0,1\}^{\ell_2(\lambda)}$ is a PPT algorithm that takes as input a string x and outputs $c \leftarrow \mathsf{Com}(x; r)$. A non-interactive perfectly binding commitment scheme must satisfy the *perfectly binding* and *computationally hiding* properties:

- **Perfectly Binding:** This property states that two different strings cannot have the same commitment. More formally, $\forall x_1 \neq x_2$ and r_1, r_2,

$$\mathsf{Com}(x_1; r_1) \neq \mathsf{Com}(x_2; r_2).$$

- **Computationally Hiding:** For all strings x_0 and x_1 (of the same length), for all PPT adversaries $\mathcal{A}$, we have that:

$$\left| \Pr[\mathcal{A}(\mathsf{Com}(x_0)) = 1] - \Pr[\mathcal{A}(\mathsf{Com}(x_1)) = 1] \right| \leq negl(\lambda).$$

We note that a non-interactive perfectly binding and computationally hiding commitment scheme which will be used in our construction in Sect. 4 can be constructed based on any one-way permutation [4].

3   Constrained Verifiable Random Functions

In this section, we define the syntax and security properties of a constrained ver-ifiable random function (VRF) family. The syntax for constrained VRFs roughly follows in the line of Fuchsbauer [8].

Recall that a verifiable random function [17] is defined over a secret key space $\mathcal{K}$, a domain $\mathcal{X}$, a range $\mathcal{Y}$ and a proof space $\mathcal{P}$ (and these sets may be parameterized by the security parameter λ). The VRF is a function $F : \mathcal{K} \times \mathcal{X} \to \mathcal{Y}$ that can be computed by a deterministic polynomial time algorithm and associated with another deterministic polynomial time algorithm $P : \mathcal{K} \times \mathcal{X} \to \mathcal{P}$ that outputs proof.

Definition 4. *A function $F : \mathcal{K} \times \mathcal{X} \to \mathcal{Y}$ is said to be a constrained verifiable random function with respect to a set system $\mathcal{S} \subseteq 2^{\mathcal{X}}$ if there exists a constrained-key space $\mathcal{K}'$ and a tuple of polynomial time algorithms (Setup, Constrain, Prove and Verify) as follows:*

- $Setup(1^\lambda)$ is a probabilistic polynomial-time algorithm that on inputs the security parameter λ, outputs a pair of keys (PK, SK), and the description of VRF $F(SK, \cdot)$ and $P(SK, \cdot)$.
- $Constrain(SK, S)$ is a randomized polynomial-time algorithm that takes as input a VRF key $SK \in \mathcal{K}$ and the description of a set $S \in \mathcal{S}$, and outputs a constrained key $SK_S \in \mathcal{K}'$.
- $Prove(SK_S, x)$ is a deterministic polynomial-time algorithm that takes as input a constrained key $SK_S \in \mathcal{K}'$ and $x \in \mathcal{X}$, and outputs a pair $(y, \pi) \in (\mathcal{Y} \times \mathcal{P}) \cup \{(\bot, \bot)\}$ of a function value and a proof.
- $Verify(PK, x, y, \pi)$ takes as input public key pk, $x \in \mathcal{X}$, $y \in \mathcal{Y}$, and proof $\pi \in \mathcal{P}$, and outputs a bit.

We require the tuple (Setup, Constrain, Prove and Verify) satisfying the following properties:

Provability. For all $\lambda \in \mathbb{N}$, all $(PK, SK) \leftarrow Setup(1^\lambda)$, all $S \in \mathcal{S}$, all $SK_S \leftarrow Constrain(SK, S)$, all $x \in \mathcal{X}$ and $(y, \pi) \leftarrow Prove(SK_S, x)$ it holds that:

- If $x \notin S$ then $(y, \pi) = (\bot, \bot)$;
- If $x \in S$ then $y = F(SK, x)$ and $Verify(PK, x, y, \pi) = 1$.

Uniqueness. For all $\lambda \in \mathbb{N}$, all PK, all $x \in \mathcal{X}$, $y_0, y_1 \in \mathcal{Y}$ and $\pi_0, \pi_1 \in \mathcal{P}$ such that $y_0 \neq y_1$, the following holds for either $i = 0$ or $i = 1$:

$$Verify(PK, x, y_i, \pi_i) = 0.$$

Constraint-Hiding. This notion ensures that the proof computed with a constrained key should be distributed like the proof computed with the actual secret key. Formally, we require that there exist a PPT algorithm $P : \mathcal{K} \times \mathcal{X} \rightarrow \mathcal{P}$, such that for all $\lambda \in \mathbb{N}$, all $(PK, SK) \leftarrow Setup(1^\lambda)$, all $S \in \mathcal{S}$, all $SK_S \leftarrow Constrain(SK, S)$, all $x \in S$ the following holds: the second output, π, of $Prove(SK_S, x)$ and the output of $P(SK, x)$ is identical.

Pseudorandomness. Intuitively, we require that even after obtaining several constrained keys as well as several function values and corresponding proofs at points of the attacker's choosing, the function looks random at all points that the attacker cannot compute himself. This intuition can be formalized by the following security game $\mathbf{Exp}_{\mathcal{A}}^{Pse}(\lambda)$ for $\lambda \in \mathbb{N}$ between a challenger and an adversary $\mathcal{A} = (\mathcal{A}_1, \mathcal{A}_2)$.

<u>**Experiment $\mathbf{Exp}_{\mathcal{A}}^{Pse}(\lambda)$**</u>

1. $(PK, SK) \leftarrow Setup(1^\lambda)$;
2. $(x^*, state) \leftarrow \mathcal{A}_1^{Func(SK, \cdot), Constrain(SK, \cdot)}(PK)$; //$Func(SK, \cdot) = (F(SK, \cdot), P(SK, \cdot))$.
3. $b \xleftarrow{\$} \{0, 1\}$;
4. $y_0 \leftarrow F(SK, x^*)$; $y_1 \xleftarrow{\$} \mathcal{Y}$;
5. $b' \leftarrow \mathcal{A}_2^{Func(SK, \cdot), Constrain(SK, \cdot)}(state, y_b)$;

6. *output 1 iff $b' = b$, x^* was not asked to the Func$(SK, \cdot)$ oracle and x^* was also not in any set which has been asked to the Constrain$(SK, \cdot)$ oracle.*

We define the advantage of $\mathcal{A}$ succeeding in the experiment $\mathbf{Exp}_{\mathcal{A}}^{Pse}(\lambda)$ as

$$Adv_{\mathcal{A}}^{Pse}(\lambda) = 2 \cdot \Pr[\mathbf{Exp}_{\mathcal{A}}^{Pse}(\lambda) = 1] - 1.$$

A constrained VRF with respect to S is pseudorandom if for all PPT adversaries $\mathcal{A} = (\mathcal{A}_1, \mathcal{A}_2)$ the advantage $Adv_{\mathcal{A}}^{Pse}(\lambda) \le negl(\lambda)$, where $negl(\lambda)$ is a negligible function.

Selectively-Secure Constrained VRFs. We also consider the selective security of constrained VRF that we call selectively-secure constrained VRF. Informally speaking, a selectively secure constrained VRF is a constrained VRF with a relaxed pseudorandomness property in which the adversary is required to choose the challenge input value x^* before seeing the public key PK.

More formally, a constrained VRF is selectively-secure if it satisfies the constrained VRF definition given above except that the pseudorandomness property is replaced by the following selective variant:

Selective Pseudorandomness. For all PPT adversaries $\mathcal{A} = (\mathcal{A}_1, \mathcal{A}_2)$, we require that the advantage $\mathcal{A}$ succeeds in the experiment $\mathbf{Exp}_{\mathcal{A}}^{\mathsf{Sel\text{-}Pse}}(\lambda)$ is negligible, that is

$$Adv_{\mathcal{A}}^{\mathsf{Sel\text{-}Pse}}(\lambda) = 2 \cdot \Pr[\mathbf{Exp}_{\mathcal{A}}^{\mathsf{Sel\text{-}Pse}}(\lambda) = 1] - 1 \le negl(\lambda),$$

where $negl(\lambda)$ is a negligible function.

Experiment $\mathbf{Exp}_{\mathcal{A}}^{\mathsf{Sel\text{-}Pse}}(\lambda)$

1. $(x^*, \mathsf{state}) \leftarrow \mathcal{A}_1(1^\lambda)$;
2. $(PK, SK) \leftarrow \mathsf{Setup}(1^\lambda)$;
3. $b \xleftarrow{\$} \{0,1\}$;
4. $y_0 \leftarrow F(SK, x^*)$; $y_1 \xleftarrow{\$} \mathcal{Y}$;
5. $b' \leftarrow \mathcal{A}_2^{\mathsf{Func}(SK,\cdot),\mathsf{Constrain}(SK,\cdot)}(\mathsf{state}, y_b)$; //Func$(SK, \cdot) = (F(SK, \cdot), P(SK, \cdot))$.
6. output 1 iff $b' = b$, x^* was not asked to the Func$(SK, \cdot)$ oracle and x^* also was not in any set which has been asked to the Constrain$(SK, \cdot)$ oracle.

Note that in our definition of pseudorandomness we only allow the adversary to issue a single challenge query (but multiple queries to the other two oracles). This restricted notion defined above however implies the multi-challenge notion via a standard hybrid argument.

4   Generic Construction of Constrained VRFs

In this section, we describe our construction of constrained VRFs in details. The construction is parameterized over a security parameter λ and has input space $\mathcal{M} = \mathcal{M}(\lambda) = \{0,1\}^{n(\lambda)}$ for some polynomial function $n(\cdot)$ and range space $\mathcal{Y} = \{0, 1\}$. It will rely on the following primitives:

- A statistically injective puncturable PRF ($\mathsf{Key_{PRF}}$, $\mathsf{Puncture_{PRF}}$, $\mathsf{Eval_{PRF}}$), that accepts inputs of length $n(\lambda)$ and outputs strings of length $\ell(\lambda)+1$. If one-way functions exist, then such a statistically injective puncturable PRF exists.
- A perfectly binding commitment scheme Com which takes as input a bit b and randomness $r \in \{0,1\}^{\ell(\lambda)}$ and outputs $\mathsf{Com}(b;r) \in \{0,1\}^{\ell'(\lambda)}$.

VRF.Setup(1^λ): On input 1^λ, the VRF.Setup algorithm firstly samples a PRF key $K \leftarrow \mathsf{Key_{PRF}}(1^\lambda)$ and sets the secret key $SK = K$. Next, it creates the program Verify_K defined below as Fig. 1, the size of which is padded to be the maximum of itself and program $\mathsf{Verify}_{K(x^*),c^*}$ of Fig. 3. Set $PK = i\mathcal{O}([\mathsf{Verify}_K])$.

On input $x \in \{0,1\}^n$, compute $t = \mathsf{PRF}(K,x)$ and parse $t = b\|r \in \{0,1\} \times \{0,1\}^{\ell(\lambda)}$. The function value and the proof for input $x \in \{0,1\}^n$ are defined as

$$F(SK = K, x) = y = b, \quad P(SK, x) = \pi = r.$$

VRF.Constrain$(SK = K, S)$: On input a secret key $SK = K$ and a set $S \in \mathcal{S}$, VRF.Constrain algorithm builds the program $\mathsf{ConstrainedKey}_{SK,S}$ defined below as Fig. 2, the size of which is padded to be the maximum of itself and program $\mathsf{ConstrainedKey}_{K(x^*),S_j}$ of Fig. 4. It outputs $SK_S = i\mathcal{O}([\mathsf{ConstrainedKey}_{SK,S}])$.

VRF.Prove(SK_S, x): Given a constrained key SK_S for a set S and input $x \in \{0,1\}^n$, the VRF.Prove(SK_S, x) algorithm runs $SK_S(x)$, namely $i\mathcal{O}([\mathsf{ConstrainedKey}_{SK,S}])(x)$, and outputs the responds.

VRF.Verify(PK, x, y, π): Since PK consists of the obfuscated program $i\mathcal{O}([\mathsf{Verify}_K])$, where the Verify_K program is defined as Fig. 1, the VRF.Verify algorithm evaluates the obfuscated program $i\mathcal{O}([\mathsf{Verify}_K])$ with inputs x and obtains $c \leftarrow i\mathcal{O}([\mathsf{Verify}_K])(x)$. Then it checks if $c = \mathsf{Com}(y;\pi)$. Output 1 if true; else output 0.

Verify_K

Hardwired into the circuit: Key of the PRF K.
Input to the circuit: $x \in \{0,1\}^n$.
Algorithm:
    1. Compute $t = \mathsf{PRF}(K,x)$ and parse $t = b\|r \in \{0,1\} \times \{0,1\}^{\ell(\lambda)}$.
    2. Output $c = \mathsf{Com}(b;r)$.

Fig. 1. Program Verify_K

Theorem 3. *If $i\mathcal{O}$ is a secure indistinguishability obfuscator, $PRF(K,\cdot)$ is a secure puncturable PRF, Com is a perfectly binding commitment scheme, then our constrained VRFs given above is a selectively secure constrained VRF as defined in Sect. 3.*

ConstrainedKey$_{SK,S}$

Hardwired into the circuit: Key of the PRF K and the set $S \in \mathcal{S}$.
Input to the circuit: $x \in \{0,1\}^n$.
Algorithm:
   1. If $x \in S$, do as the followings:
      – Compute $t = \mathsf{PRF}(K,x)$ and parse $t = b\|r \in \{0,1\} \times \{0,1\}^{\ell(\lambda)}$.
      – Outputs $F(SK = K, x) = y = b$ and $P(SK, x) = \pi = r$.
   2. Otherwise, return $(\bot, \bot)$.

Fig. 2. Program ConstrainedKey_SK, S

Proof. The *provability* property can be verified in a straightforward manner from our above construction.

Moreover, given a punctured key SK_S derived from SK for a set S and $x \in \{0,1\}^n$ with $x \in S$, we see that when running the $\mathsf{VRF.Prove}(SK_S = i\mathcal{O}([\mathsf{ConstrainedKey}_{SK,S}]), x)$ algorithm, the value computed from $i\mathcal{O}([\mathsf{ConstrainedKey}_{SK,S}])(x)$ is equal to $(y = b, \pi = r)$ where $b\|r = \mathsf{PRF}(K, x)$. Therefore, the outputs $(y = b, \pi = r)$ satisfy verification equation $c = \mathsf{Com}(y; \pi)$.

The *uniqueness* property follows from the perfectly binding property of the commitment scheme. More precisely, assume that there exist a public key PK, a value $x \in \{0,1\}^n$ and values $(y_0, \pi_0), (y_1, \pi_1) \in \{0,1\} \times \{0,1\}^\ell$ satisfying that

$$y_0 \neq y_1 \wedge \mathsf{VRF.Verify}(PK, x, y_0, \pi_0) = 1 \wedge \mathsf{VRF.Verify}(PK, x, y_1, \pi_1) = 1.$$

That is $y_0 \neq y_1$ but $\mathsf{Com}(y_0; \pi_0) = \mathsf{Com}(y_1; \pi_1)$. This contradicts with the perfectly binding property of Com.

The *constraint-hiding* property is also obvious, since for $x \in \{0,1\}^n$, the proof $P(SK = K, x) = r$ where $b\|r = \mathsf{PRF}(K, x)$, is precisely the value that $\mathsf{VRF.Prove}(SK_S = K_S, x)$ outputs for any set S with $x \in S$.

Finally we show *selective pseudorandomness*, which will require more works. We prove it via a sequence of games (depicted in Table 1), where Game$_0$ denotes the original selective pseudorandomness security game in Sect. 3 with the challenge bit b fixed to 0 and the Game$_9$ corresponds to security game with the challenge bit b fixed to 1. We first present the games and subsequently show (based on the security of different primitives) that any poly-time attacker's advantage in each game must be negligibly close to that of the previous one. Suppose that $\mathcal{A}$ makes $Q_{\mathsf{Prove}} = Q_{\mathsf{Prove}}(\lambda)$ Prove queries and $Q_{\mathsf{Con}} = Q_{\mathsf{Con}}(\lambda)$ ConstrainedKey queries.

Sequence of Games
Game$_0$. This game is the original security game $\mathbf{Exp}_{\mathcal{A}}^{\mathsf{Sel-Pse}}(\lambda)$ in Sect. 3 instantiated by our construction of constrained VRF with the challenge bit b fixed to 0, which means challenger returns $y = F(SK, x^*)$ to attacker.

1. $\mathcal{A}$ first chooses a challenge $x^* \in \{0,1\}^n$.

Table 1. The games used in the proof of Theorem. We highlight the changes between the games with a red backgound. The arrows above the games indicate the security reduction to get from Game i to Game $i + 1$. $\mathsf{Po}(K, \cdot)$ stands for the Prove oracle and $\mathsf{C}(K, \cdot)$ stands for the ConstrainedKey oracle.

G0:Game 0G0r	G1:Game 1G1r	G2:Game 2G2r	G3:Game 3G3r
$x^* \leftarrow A_1(1^\lambda)$	$x^* \leftarrow A_1(1^\lambda)$	$x^* \leftarrow A_1(1^\lambda)$	$x^* \leftarrow A_1(1^\lambda)$
$K \leftarrow \mathsf{Key}_{\mathsf{PRF}}(1^\lambda)$	$K \leftarrow \mathsf{Key}_{\mathsf{PRF}}(1^\lambda)$	$K \leftarrow \mathsf{Key}_{\mathsf{PRF}}(1^\lambda)$	$K \leftarrow \mathsf{Key}_{\mathsf{PRF}}(1^\lambda)$
	$K(x^*) \leftarrow \mathsf{Punctured}(K, x^*)$	$K(x^*) \leftarrow \mathsf{Punctured}(K, x^*)$	$K(x^*) \leftarrow \mathsf{Punctured}(K, x^*)$
$b^*\|r^* = \mathsf{PRF}(K, x^*)$	$b^*\|r^* = \mathsf{PRF}(K, x^*)$	$b^*\|r^* = \mathsf{PRF}(K, x^*)$	$b^*\|r^* = \mathsf{PRF}(K, x^*)$
	$c^* = \mathsf{Com}(b^*; r^*)$	$c^* = \mathsf{Com}(b^*; r^*)$	$c^* = \mathsf{Com}(b^*; r^*)$
$PK = i\mathcal{O}([\mathsf{Verify}_K])$	$PK = i\mathcal{O}([\mathsf{Verify}_{K(x^*),c^*}])$	$PK = i\mathcal{O}([\mathsf{Verify}_{K(x^*),c^*}])$	$PK = i\mathcal{O}([\mathsf{Verify}_{K(x^*),c^*}])$
$y^* = b^*$	$y^* = b^*$	$y^* = b^*$	$y^* = b^*$
$b' \leftarrow A_2^{\mathsf{Po}(K,\cdot),\mathsf{C}(K,\cdot)}(y^*)$	$b' \leftarrow A_2^{\mathsf{Po}(K,\cdot),\mathsf{C}(K,\cdot)}(y^*)$	$b' \leftarrow A_2^{\mathsf{Po}(K(x^*),\cdot),\mathsf{C}(K,\cdot)}(y^*)$	$b' \leftarrow A_2^{\mathsf{Po}(K(x^*),\cdot),\mathsf{C}(K(x^*),\cdot)}(y^*)$
output 1 iff $b' = 0$	output 1 iff $b' = 0$	output 1 iff $b' = 0$	output 1 iff $b' = 0$

G7:Game 7G7r	G6:Game 6G6r	G5:Game 5G5r	G4:Game 4G4r
$x^* \leftarrow A_1(1^\lambda)$	$x^* \leftarrow A_1(1^\lambda)$	$x^* \leftarrow A_1(1^\lambda)$	$x^* \leftarrow A_1(1^\lambda)$
$K \leftarrow \mathsf{Key}_{\mathsf{PRF}}(1^\lambda)$	$K \leftarrow \mathsf{Key}_{\mathsf{PRF}}(1^\lambda)$	$K \leftarrow \mathsf{Key}_{\mathsf{PRF}}(1^\lambda)$	$K \leftarrow \mathsf{Key}_{\mathsf{PRF}}(1^\lambda)$
$K(x^*) \leftarrow \mathsf{Punctured}(K, x^*)$	$K(x^*) \leftarrow \mathsf{Punctured}(K, x^*)$	$K(x^*) \leftarrow \mathsf{Punctured}(K, x^*)$	$K(x^*) \leftarrow \mathsf{Punctured}(K, x^*)$
$b^*\|r^* = \mathsf{PRF}(K, x^*)$	$b^*\|r^* = \mathsf{PRF}(K, x^*)$	$t^* \leftarrow \{0,1\}^{\ell+1}, t^* = b^*\|r^*$	$t^* \leftarrow \{0,1\}^{\ell+1}, t^* = b^*\|r^*$
$c^* = \mathsf{Com}(b^*; r^*)$	$c^* = \mathsf{Com}(b^*; r^*)$	$c^* = \mathsf{Com}(b^*; r^*)$	$c^* = \mathsf{Com}(b^*; r^*)$
$PK = i\mathcal{O}([\mathsf{Verify}_{K(x^*),c^*}])$	$PK = i\mathcal{O}([\mathsf{Verify}_{K(x^*),c^*}])$	$PK = i\mathcal{O}([\mathsf{Verify}_{K(x^*),c^*}])$	$PK = i\mathcal{O}([\mathsf{Verify}_{K(x^*),c^*}])$
$b \leftarrow \{0,1\}, y^* = b$	$b \leftarrow \{0,1\}, y^* = b$	$b \leftarrow \{0,1\}, y^* = b$	$y^* = b^*$
$b' \leftarrow A_2^{\mathsf{Po}(K(x^*),\cdot),\mathsf{C}(K(x^*),\cdot)}(y^*)$	$b' \leftarrow A_2^{\mathsf{Po}(K(x^*),\cdot),\mathsf{C}(K(x^*),\cdot)}(y^*)$	$b' \leftarrow A_2^{\mathsf{Po}(K(x^*),\cdot),\mathsf{C}(K(x^*),\cdot)}(y^*)$	$b' \leftarrow A_2^{\mathsf{Po}(K(x^*),\cdot),\mathsf{C}(K(x^*),\cdot)}(y^*)$
output 1 iff $b' = 0$	output 1 iff $b' = 0$	output 1 iff $b' = 0$	output 1 iff $b' = 0$

G8:Game 8G8r	G9:Game 9G9r
$x^* \leftarrow A_1(1^\lambda)$	$x^* \leftarrow A_1(1^\lambda)$
$K \leftarrow \mathsf{Key}_{\mathsf{PRF}}(1^\lambda)$	$K \leftarrow \mathsf{Key}_{\mathsf{PRF}}(1^\lambda)$
$K(x^*) \leftarrow \mathsf{Punctured}(K, x^*)$	
$b^*\|r^* = \mathsf{PRF}(K, x^*)$	
$c^* = \mathsf{Com}(b^*; r^*)$	
$PK = i\mathcal{O}([\mathsf{Verify}_{K(x^*),c^*}])$	$PK = i\mathcal{O}([\mathsf{Verify}_K])$
$b \leftarrow \{0,1\}, y^* = b$	$b \leftarrow \{0,1\}, y^* = b$
$b' \leftarrow A_2^{\mathsf{Po}(K,\cdot),\mathsf{C}(K,\cdot)}(y^*)$	$b' \leftarrow A_2^{\mathsf{Po}(K,\cdot),\mathsf{C}(K,\cdot)}(y^*)$
output 1 iff $b' = 0$	output 1 iff $b' = 0$

2. The challenger randomly samples a PRFs key $K \leftarrow \mathsf{Key}_{\mathsf{PRF}}(1^\lambda)$ and sets $SK = K$ and $b = 0$. Next, it creates the obfuscated program $i\mathcal{O}([\mathsf{Verify}_K])$ where the program Verify_K is defined as Fig. 1 and padded to be of appropriate size. The challenger sets $PK = i\mathcal{O}([\mathsf{Verify}_K])$ and passes it to attacker.

3. On attacker's constrained key queries and prove queries, the challenger responds as follows:
   - On any Prove query for $x_i \in \{0,1\}^n$ where $i \in [1, Q_{\mathsf{Prove}}]$, the challenger compute $\mathsf{PRF}(K, x_i) = t_i$; then parse $t_i = b_i\|r_i \in \{0,1\} \times \{0,1\}^\ell$. If $x_i \neq x^*$ for $i \in [1, Q_{\mathsf{Prove}}]$, returns $(y_i = b_i, \pi_i = r_i)$; else return $(\bot, \bot)$.
   - On any ConstrainedKey query for set $S_j \in \mathcal{S}$, where $j \in [1, Q_{\mathsf{Con}}]$, if $x^* \notin S_j$, the challenger returns $SK_{S_j} \leftarrow i\mathcal{O}([\mathsf{ConstrainedKey}_{SK,S_j}])$, where the program $\mathsf{ConstrainedKey}_{SK,S_j}$ is defined as Fig. 2; else returns $\bot$.

4. Challenger sends a VRF evaluation $y^* = b^*$ at the challenged input, where

$$\mathsf{PRF}(K, x^*) = b^*\|r^* \in \{0,1\} \times \{0,1\}^\ell.$$

5. $\mathcal{A}$ outputs b' and wins if $b = b'$.

Game$_1$. This game is identical to the Game$_0$, except that the public key PK is created as an obfuscation of the program Verify$_{K(x^*),c^*}$ of Fig. 3, that is $PK = i\mathcal{O}([\text{Verify}_{K(x^*),c^*}])$. Precisely speaking, the challenger randomly samples a PRFs key $K \leftarrow \text{Key}_{\text{PRF}}(1^\lambda)$ and compute $K(x^*) \leftarrow \text{Punctured}_{\text{PRF}}(K, x^*)$. Let $t^* = b^*\|r^* = \text{PRF}(K, x^*)$ and $c^* = \text{Com}(b^*; r^*)$. The challenger modifies the Verify$_K$ program as follows: firstly it hardwires $c^* \in \{0,1\}^{\ell'}$ in the program. Then it adds an "if" statement at the start that output c^* if the input $x = x^*$. Because this "if" statement is in place, we can safely puncture key K at this position. Thus, we replace the secret key K of the program Verify$_K$ with puncturable key $K(x^*)$.

Verify$_{K(x^*),c^*}$

Hardwired into the circuit: Punctured key $K(x^*)$ and $c^* \in \{0,1\}^{\ell'}$.
Input to the circuit: $x \in \{0,1\}^n$.
Algorithm:
    1. If $x = x^*$, outputs c^*.
    2. If $x \neq x^*$, do as follows:
       – Compute $t = \text{PRF}(K(x^*), x)$ and parse $t = b\|r \in \{0,1\} \times \{0,1\}^\ell$.
       – Outputs $c = \text{Com}(b; r)$.

Fig. 3. Program Verify_$K(x^*)$, c^*

Game$_2$. This game is identical to the Game$_1$, except that the challenger responds by puncturable key $K(x^*)$ on attacker's Prove queries. More precisely, on attacker's Prove query for $x_i \in \{0,1\}^n$ where $i \in [1, Q_{\text{Prove}}]$, the challenger compute $\text{PRF}(K(x^*), x_i) = t_i$; then parse

$$t_i = b_i\|r_i \in \{0,1\} \times \{0,1\}^\ell.$$

If $x_i \neq x^*$ for $i \in [1, Q_{\text{Prove}}]$, returns $(y_i = b_i, \pi_i = r_i)$; else return $(\perp, \perp)$.

Game$_3$. This game is identical to the Game$_2$, except that the challenger responds by puncturable key $K(x^*)$ on attacker's constrained key queries. More precisely, on attacker's ConstrainedKey query for set $S_j \in \mathcal{S}$ where $j \in [1, Q_{\text{Con}}]$, if $x^* \notin S_j$, the challenger returns

$$SK_{S_j} \leftarrow i\mathcal{O}([\text{ConstrainedKey}_{K(x^*),S_j}]),$$

where the program ConstrainedKey$_{K(x^*),S_j}$ is defined as Fig. 4; else returns $\perp$.

Game$_4$. This game is identical to the Game$_3$, except that the challenger randomly chooses $t^* \in \{0,1\}^{\ell+1}$ instead of computing by $\text{PRF}(K, x^*)$.

Game$_5$. This game is identical to the Game$_4$, except that the challenger replaces the evaluation y^* of VRF on challenged point x^* with a random independent bit.

ConstrainedKey$_{K(x^*),S_j}$

Hardwired into the circuit: Punctured key $K(x^*)$ and the set $S_j \in S$.
Input to the circuit: $x \in \{0,1\}^n$.
Algorithm:
   1. If $x \in S_j$, do as the followings:
      – Compute $t = \mathsf{PRF}(K(x^*), x)$ and parse $t = b\|r \in \{0,1\} \times \{0,1\}^\ell$;
      – Outputs $F(SK = K, x) = y = b$ and $P(SK, x) = \pi = r$.
   2. Otherwise, return $(\bot, \bot)$.

Fig. 4. Program ConstrainedKey_K(x*), S_j

Game$_6$. This game is identical to the Game$_5$, except that the challenger obtains $t^* \leftarrow \mathsf{PRF}(K, x^*)$ instead of randomly choosing from $\{0,1\}^{\ell+1}$.

Game$_7$. This game is identical to the Game$_6$, except that the challenger responds by secret key K on attacker's Prove queries instead of by puncturable key $K(x^*)$.

Game$_8$. This game is identical to the Game$_7$, except that the challenger responds by secret key K on attacker's Constrained key queries instead of by puncturable key $K(x^*)$.

Game$_9$. This game is identical to the Game$_8$, except that the public key PK is created as an obfuscation of the program Verify$_K$ of Fig. 1 instead of Verify$_{K(x^*),c^*}$.

We observe that in this final game the attacker receives a random value y^* on the challenged point x^*, which is exactly the original security game $\mathbf{Exp}_{\mathcal{A}}^{\mathsf{Sel\text{-}Pse}}(\lambda)$ in Sect. 3 with the challenge bit b fixed to 1.

Indistinguishability Proofs Between Games
Let $\mathsf{Adv}_{\mathcal{A},i}$ denote the advantage of adversary $\mathcal{A}$ in Game$_i$ of guessing the bit b. We now establish via a sequence of lemmas that the difference of the attacker's advantage between each adjacent game is negligible.

Lemma 1. *If $i\mathcal{O}$ is a secure indistinguishability obfuscator, then for all PPT $\mathcal{A}$ we have that*

$$\mathsf{Adv}_{\mathcal{A},0} - \mathsf{Adv}_{\mathcal{A},1} = \mathsf{negl}_{01}(\lambda)$$

for some negligible function $\mathsf{negl}_{01}(\lambda)$.

Proof. We prove this lemma by giving a reduction to the indistinguishability security of the obfuscation. We describe and analyze a PPT reduction algorithm $\mathcal{B}$ that plays the indistinguishability obfuscation security game with $\mathcal{A}$. First, $\mathcal{B}$ receives a challenged input $x^* \in \{0,1\}^n$ from adversary $\mathcal{A}$. $\mathcal{B}$ then randomly samples a PRFs key $K \leftarrow \mathsf{Key}_{\mathsf{PRF}}(1^\lambda)$ and computes $K(x^*) \leftarrow \mathsf{Punctured}_{\mathsf{PRF}}(K, x^*)$. Let $t^* = b^*\|r^* = \mathsf{PRF}(K, x^*)$ and $c^* = \mathsf{Com}(b^*; r^*)$. Next it creates two circuits as $C_0 = \mathsf{Verify}_K$ of Fig. 1 and $C_1 = \mathsf{Verify}_{K(x^*),c^*}$ of Fig. 3. It submits both of these to the $i\mathcal{O}$ challenger and receives back a program C which it passes to the attacker in step 2. It executes steps 3–5 as in Game_0. If the attacker wins (i.e. $b' = b$), then $\mathcal{B}$ guesses '0' to indicated that C was and obfuscation of C_0; otherwise, it guesses '1' to indicate it was an obfuscation of C_1.

We observe that when C is generated as an obfuscation of C_0, then $\mathcal{B}$ gives exactly the view of Game_0 to $\mathcal{A}$. Otherwise if C is chosen as an obfuscation of C_1 the view is of Game_1. In addition, the programs are functionally equivalent. The only difference in the programs is that the response is hardwired in for the challenge point x^*. Therefore if $\text{Adv}_{\mathcal{A},0} - \text{Adv}_{\mathcal{A},1}$ is non-negligble, $\mathcal{B}$ must also have non-negligible advantage against the indistinguishability obfuscation game.

Lemma 2. *If puncturable PRF $\text{PRF}(K, \cdot)$ preserves functionality under puncturing, then for all PPT $\mathcal{A}$ we have that*

$$\text{Adv}_{\mathcal{A},1} - \text{Adv}_{\mathcal{A},2} = negl_{12}(\lambda)$$

for some negligible function $negl_{12}(\lambda)$.

Proof. To prove this lemma we will consider a hybrid argument. Let Q_{Prove} be the number of Prove queries issued by some attacker $\mathcal{A}$. For $i \in [0, Q_{\text{Prove}}]$ we define $\text{Game}_{1,i}$ to be the same as Game_1 except that the first i private key queries of step 3 are handled as in Game_2 and the last $Q_{\text{Prove}} - i$ are handled as in Game_1. We observe that $\text{Game}_{1,0}$ is the same as Game_1 and that $\text{Game}_{1,Q_{\text{Prove}}}$ is the same as Game_2. Thus to prove security we need to establish that no attacker can distinguish between $\text{Game}_{1,i}$ and $\text{Game}_{1,i+1}$ for $i \in [0, Q_{\text{Prove}} - 1]$ with non-negligible advantage.

The difference between $\text{Game}_{1,i}$ and $\text{Game}_{1,i+1}$ is the response on the $(i+1)$-th Prove queries, which is computed by $\text{PRF}(K, x_{i+1}) = t_{i+1}$ in $\text{Game}_{1,i}$ and by $\text{PRF}(K(x^*), x_{i+1}) = t_{i+1}$ in $\text{Game}_{1,i+1}$. Since it is required that the Prove queries on inputs $x_i \in \{0,1\}^n$ satisfy $x_i \neq x^*$ for $i \in [1, Q_{\text{Prove}}]$, for $x_{i+1} \neq x^*$ we have $\text{PRF}(K, x_{i+1}) = \text{PRF}(K(x^*), x_{i+1})$ due to the *functionality preserving property under puncturing* of puncturable PRF. Therefore the response on the $(i + 1)$-th Prove queries in $\text{Game}_{1,i}$ and $\text{Game}_{1,i+1}$ is identical. Then for all PPT $\mathcal{A}$ we have that $\text{Adv}_{\mathcal{A},(1,i)} - \text{Adv}_{\mathcal{A},(1,i+1)} = negl(\lambda)$ for some negligible function negl.

Lemma 3. *If $i\mathcal{O}$ is a secure indistinguishability obfuscator, then for all PPT $\mathcal{A}$ we have that*

$$\text{Adv}_{\mathcal{A},2} - \text{Adv}_{\mathcal{A},3} = negl_{23}(\lambda)$$

for some negligible function $negl_{23}(\lambda)$.

Proof. To prove this lemma we will consider a hybrid argument. Let Q_{Con} be the number of constrained key queries issued by some attacker $\mathcal{A}$. For $i \in [0, Q_{\text{Con}}]$ we define $\text{Game}_{2,i}$ to be the same as Game_2 except that the first i private key queries of step 3 are handled as in Game_3 and the last $Q_{\text{Con}} - i$ are handled as in Game_2. We observe that $\text{Game}_{2,0}$ is the same as Game_2 and that $\text{Game}_{2,Q_{\text{Con}}}$ is the same as Game_3. Thus to prove security we need to establish that no attacker can distinguish between $\text{Game}_{2,i}$ and $\text{Game}_{2,i+1}$ for $i \in [0, Q_{\text{Con}} - 1]$ with non negligible advantage. The difference between $\text{Game}_{2,i}$ and $\text{Game}_{2,i+1}$ is the response on the $(i+1)$-th Constrained key queries, which is $i\mathcal{O}([\text{ConstrainedKey}_{SK,S_{i+1}}])$ in $\text{Game}_{2,i}$ and $i\mathcal{O}([\text{ConstrainedKey}_{K(x^*),S_{i+1}}])$ in $\text{Game}_{2,i+1}$.

We describe and analyze a PPT reduction algorithm $\mathcal{B}$ that plays the indistinguishability obfuscation security game with $\mathcal{A}$. First, $\mathcal{B}$ receives a challenged input $x^* \in \{0,1\}^n$ from adversary $\mathcal{A}$. $\mathcal{B}$ then randomly samples a PRFs key $K \leftarrow \text{Key}_{\text{PRF}}(1^\lambda)$ and compute $K(x^*) \leftarrow \text{Punctured}_{\text{PRF}}(K, x^*)$. Let $t^* = b^*\|r^* = \text{PRF}(K, x^*)$ and $c^* = \text{Com}(b^*; r^*)$. Next, $\mathcal{B}$ creates the obfuscated program $i\mathcal{O}([\text{Verify}_{K(x^*),c^*}])$ where program $\text{Verify}_{K(x^*),c^*}$ is defined as Fig. 3 and padded to be of appropriate size, and passes it to attacker. On attacker's Prove query for $x_i \in \{0,1\}^n$ where $i \in [1, Q_{\text{Prove}}]$, $\mathcal{B}$ compute $\text{PRF}(K(x^*), x_i) = t_i$; then parse $t_i = b_i\|r_i \in \{0,1\} \times \{0,1\}^\ell$. If $x_i \neq x^*$ for $i \in [1, Q_{\text{Prove}}]$, returns $(y_i = b_i, \pi_i = r_i)$; else return $(\bot, \bot)$. For the first i constrained key queries $\mathcal{B}$ answers as in Game_3. For query $i+1$ it creates two circuits as $C_0 = \text{ConstrainedKey}_{SK,S_{i+1}}$ of Fig. 2 and $C_1 = \text{ConstrainedKey}_{K(x^*),S_{i+1}}$ of Fig. 4 where $S_{i+1} \in \mathcal{S}$ is the set queried for. It submits both of them to the $i\mathcal{O}$ challenger and receives back a program C which it passes to the attacker as $SK_{S_{i+1}}$. $\mathcal{B}$ answers the rest of the constrained key queries as in Game_2. Finally $\mathcal{B}$ sends a VRF evaluation $y^* = b^*$ at the challenged input. And $\mathcal{A}$ outputs b'. If $\mathcal{A}$ wins (i.e. $b' = b$), then $\mathcal{B}$ guesses '0' to indicated that C was and obfuscation of C_0; otherwise, it guesses '1' to indicate it was an obfuscation of C_1.

We observe that when C is generated as an obfuscation of C_0, then $\mathcal{B}$ gives exactly the view of $\text{Game}_{2,i}$ to $\mathcal{A}$. Otherwise if C is chosen as an obfuscation of C_1 the view is of $\text{Game}_{2,i+1}$. In addition, the program C_0 and C_1 behaves identically on every input. The reason is that for set S_{i+1} s.t. $x^* \notin S_{i+1}$, if $x \in S_{i+1}$ the output of two circuits are $C_0(x) = (y_{i+1} = b_{i+1}, \pi_{i+1} = r_{i+1}) = C_1(x)$ where $b_{i+1}\|r_{i+1} = \text{PRF}(K(x^*), x_{i+1}) = \text{PRF}(K, x_{i+1})$; if $x \notin S_{i+1}$ the output both are $(\bot, \bot)$. Therefore if $\text{Adv}_{\mathcal{A},(2,i)} - \text{Adv}_{\mathcal{A},(2,i+1)}$ is non-negligible, $\mathcal{B}$ must also have non-negligible advantage against the indistinguishability obfuscation game.

Lemma 4. *If $\text{PRF}(K, \cdot)$ is a secure puncturable PRF, then for all PPT $\mathcal{A}$ we have that*

$$\text{Adv}_{\mathcal{A},3} - \text{Adv}_{\mathcal{A},4} = \text{negl}_{34}(\lambda)$$

for some negligible function $\text{negl}_{34}(\lambda)$.

Proof. We prove this lemma by giving a reduction to the pseudorandomness property at punctured points for punctured PRFs. We describe and analyze a PPT reduction algorithm $\mathcal{B}$ that plays the puncturable PRF security game. $\mathcal{B}$ receives a challenged input $x^* \in \{0,1\}^n$ from adversary $\mathcal{A}$ and submits it back to the punctured PRF challenger. It receives back a punctured key $K(x^*)$ and a challenge value $t^* \in \{0,1\}^{\ell+1}$. $\mathcal{B}$ parses $t^* = b^*\|r^* \in \{0,1\} \times \{0,1\}^\ell$ and compute $c^* = \text{Com}(b^*; r^*)$. Next, it creates the obfuscated program $i\mathcal{O}([\text{Verify}_{K(x^*),c^*}])$ where the program $\text{Verify}_{K(x^*),c^*}$ is created as Fig. 3 and passes it to $\mathcal{A}$. On attacker's Prove query since $\mathcal{B}$ has punctured key $K(x^*)$, it responds as in Game_2. On attacker's ConstrainedKey query $\mathcal{B}$ responds by punctured key $K(x^*)$ as in

Game₃. Finally $\mathcal{B}$ sends a VRF evaluation $y^* = b^*$ at the challenged input and $\mathcal{A}$ outputs b'. If $\mathcal{A}$ wins (i.e. $b' = b$), then $\mathcal{B}$ guesses '1' to indicate that $t^* = \text{PRF}(K, x^*)$; otherwise, it outputs '0' to indicate that t^* was chosen randomly.

We observe that when t^* is generated as $\text{PRF}(K, x^*)$, then $\mathcal{B}$ gives exactly the view of Game₃ to $\mathcal{A}$. Otherwise if t^* is chosen randomly, the view is of Game₄. Therefore if $\text{Adv}_{\mathcal{A},3} - \text{Adv}_{\mathcal{A},4}$ is non-negligible, $\mathcal{B}$ must also have non-negligible advantage against the security of the puncturable PRF.

Lemma 5. *If Com is a computationally hiding commitment scheme, then for all PPT $\mathcal{A}$ we have that*

$$\text{Adv}_{\mathcal{A},4} - \text{Adv}_{\mathcal{A},5} = negl_{45}(\lambda)$$

for some negligible function $negl_{45}(\lambda)$.

Proof. We prove this lemma by giving a reduction to the computational hiding property of the commitment scheme. We describe and analyze a PPT reduction algorithm $\mathcal{B}$ that plays the computational hiding security game with $\mathcal{A}$. $\mathcal{B}$ firstly receives a challenged input $x^* \in \{0,1\}^n$ from $\mathcal{A}$. Then it randomly samples a PRFs key $K \leftarrow \text{Key}_{\text{PRF}}(1^\lambda)$ and compute $K(x^*) \leftarrow \text{Punctured}_{\text{PRF}}(K, x^*)$. $\mathcal{B}$ randomly samples random $t^* \in \{0,1\}^{\ell+1}$ and parse $t^* = b^* \| r^* \in \{0,1\} \times \{0,1\}^\ell$. It submits $b_0 = b^*, b_1 = 1 - b^*$ to the commitment scheme challenger, and receives back a challenge value $c^* = \text{Com}(b_\alpha)$. Next, $\mathcal{B}$ randomly chooses $\beta \leftarrow \{0,1\}$, and creates the obfuscated program $i\mathcal{O}([\text{Verify}_{K(x^*),c^*}])$ as in Fig. 3 and passes it to $\mathcal{A}$. On attacker's Prove query since $\mathcal{B}$ has punctured key $K(x^*)$, it responds as in Game₂. On attacker's ConstrainedKey query $\mathcal{B}$ responds by punctured key $K(x^*)$ as in Game₃. Finally $\mathcal{B}$ sends a VRF evaluation $y^* = b_\beta$ to $\mathcal{A}$. Since if $\alpha = \beta$ then $\mathcal{B}$ gives exactly the view of Game₄ to A; if $\alpha = 1 - \beta$ then the view is of Game₅. Therefore, if the attacker wins (i.e. $\beta = \alpha$), then $\mathcal{B}$ outputs β to indicate that $c^* = \text{Com}(b_\beta)$; otherwise, it outputs $1 - \beta$ to indicate that $c^* = \text{Com}(b_{1-\beta})$.

Lemma 6. *If $\text{PRF}(K, \cdot)$ is a secure puncturable PRF, then for all PPT $\mathcal{A}$ we have that*

$$\text{Adv}_{\mathcal{A},5} - \text{Adv}_{\mathcal{A},6} = negl_{56}(\lambda)$$

for some negligible function $negl_{56}(\lambda)$.

The proof of this lemma is analogous to that of Lemma 4.

Lemma 7. *If $\text{PRF}(K, \cdot)$ is a secure puncturable PRF, then for all PPT $\mathcal{A}$ we have that*

$$\text{Adv}_{\mathcal{A},6} - \text{Adv}_{\mathcal{A},7} = negl_{67}(\lambda)$$

for some negligible function $negl_{67}(\lambda)$.

The proof of this lemma is analogous to that of Lemma 3.

Lemma 8. *If $i\mathcal{O}$ is a secure indistinguishability obfuscator, then for all PPT $\mathcal{A}$ we have that*

$$Adv_{\mathcal{A},7} - Adv_{\mathcal{A},8} = negl_{78}(\lambda)$$

for some negligible function $negl_{78}(\lambda)$.

The proof of this lemma is analogous to that of Lemma 2.

Lemma 9. *If $i\mathcal{O}$ is a secure indistinguishability obfuscator, then for all PPT $\mathcal{A}$ we have that*

$$Adv_{\mathcal{A},8} - Adv_{\mathcal{A},9} = negl_{89}(\lambda)$$

for some negligible function $negl_{89}(\lambda)$.

The proof of this lemma is analogous to that of Lemma 1.

Putting all the facts above together, our main theorem follows.

5   Conclusion

In this paper, we propose a generic construction of constrained VRFs w.r.t. a set system, which can be described by a polynomial-size circuit C, from one-way functions together with indistinguishability obfuscation (iO). In our construction, the public key is independent of the depth of circuit.

References

1. Abdalla, M., Catalano, D., Fiore, D.: Verifiable random functions from identity-based key encapsulation. In: Joux, A. (ed.) EUROCRYPT 2009. LNCS, vol. 5479, pp. 554–571. Springer, Heidelberg (2009)
2. Barak, B., Goldreich, O., Impagliazzo, R., Rudich, S., Sahai, A., Vadhan, S.P., Yang, K.: On the (im)possibility of obfuscating programs. In: Kilian, J. (ed.) CRYPTO 2001. LNCS, vol. 2139, pp. 1–18. Springer, Heidelberg (2001)
3. Brakerski, Z., Goldwasser, S., Rothblum, G.N., Vaikuntanathan, V.: Weak verifiable random functions. In: Reingold, O. (ed.) TCC 2009. LNCS, vol. 5444, pp. 558–576. Springer, Heidelberg (2009)
4. Blum, M.: Coin flipping by telephone-a protocol for solving impossible problems. In: COMPCON, pp. 133–137. IEEE Computer Society (1982)
5. Bitansky, N., Paneth, O.: ZAPs and non-interactive witness indistinguishability from indistinguishability obfuscation. In: Dodis, Y., Nielsen, J.B. (eds.) TCC 2015, Part II. LNCS, vol. 9015, pp. 401–427. Springer, Heidelberg (2015)
6. Boneh, D., Waters, B.: Constrained pseudorandom functions and their applications. In: Sako, K., Sarkar, P. (eds.) ASIACRYPT 2013, Part II. LNCS, vol. 8270, pp. 280–300. Springer, Heidelberg (2013)
7. Fiore, D., Schröder, D.: Uniqueness is a different story: impossibility of verifiable random functions from trapdoor permutations. In: Cramer, R. (ed.) TCC 2012. LNCS, vol. 7194, pp. 636–653. Springer, Heidelberg (2012)

8. Fuchsbauer, G.: Constrained verifiable random functions. In: Abdalla, M., De Prisco, R. (eds.) SCN 2014. LNCS, vol. 8642, pp. 95–114. Springer, Heidelberg (2014)

9. Garg, S., Gentry, C., Halevi, S., Raykova, M., Sahai, A., Waters, B.: Candidate indistinguishability obfuscation and functional encryption for all circuits. In: FOCS (2013)

10. Goldreich, O., Goldwasser, S., Micali, S.: How to construct random functions. J. ACM **33**(4), 792–807 (1986)

11. Goldwasser, S., Ostrovsky, R.: Invariant signatures and non-interactive zero-knowledge proofs are equivalent. In: Brickell, E.F. (ed.) CRYPTO 1992. LNCS, vol. 740, pp. 228–245. Springer, Heidelberg (1993)

12. Hohenberger, S., Waters, B.: Constructing verifiable random functions with large input spaces. In: Gilbert, H. (ed.) EUROCRYPT 2010. LNCS, vol. 6110, pp. 656–672. Springer, Heidelberg (2010)

13. Jager, T.: Verifiable random functions from weaker assumptions. Cryptology ePrint Archive, Report 2014/799 (2014)

14. Jarecki, S.: Handcuffing big brother: an abuse-resilient transaction escrow scheme. In: Cachin, C., Camenisch, J.L. (eds.) EUROCRYPT 2004. LNCS, vol. 3027, pp. 590–608. Springer, Heidelberg (2004)

15. Lysyanskaya, A.: Unique signatures and verifiable random functions from the DH-DDH separation. In: Yung, M. (ed.) CRYPTO 2002. LNCS, vol. 2442, pp. 597–612. Springer, Heidelberg (2002)

16. Micali, S., Reyzin, L.: Soundness in the public-key model. In: Kilian, J. (ed.) CRYPTO 2001. LNCS, vol. 2139, pp. 542–565. Springer, Heidelberg (2001)

17. Micali, S., Rabin, M., Vadhan, S.: Verifiable random functions. In: Proceedings of 40th IEEE Symposium on Foundations of Computer Science (FOCS), pp. 120–130. IEEE Computer Society Press (1999)

18. Naor, M.: Bit commitment using pseudorandomness. J. Cryptology **4**(2), 151–158 (1991)

19. Sahai, A., Waters, B.: How to use indistinguishability obfuscation: deniable encryption, and more. In: STOC, pp. 475–484 (2014)

An Improved Attack for Recovering Noisy RSA Secret Keys and Its Countermeasure

Noboru Kunihiro$^{(\boxtimes)}$

The University of Tokyo, Tokyo, Japan
kunihiro@k.u-tokyo.ac.jp

Abstract. This paper discusses how to recover RSA secret keys from their noisy version observed by side-channel attacks. At CRYPTO2009, Heninger and Shacham proposed a polynomial time algorithm which recovers an original secret key from some fraction of secret key bits. Then, at CRYPTO2010, Henecka et al. proposed a polynomial time algorithm recovering a correct secret key from the noisy secret key bits with some errors. Then they gave the bound such that the secret key can be recovered in polynomial time. At PKC2013, Kunihiro et al. presented a key-recovery algorithm from the erroneous version of secret key bits with erasures and errors. They also gave a condition for recovering the secret key and its theoretical bound. They pointed out that there is a small gap between their derived condition and the theoretical bound and closing the gap is an open problem. In this paper, we first improve the bound and reduce the computational cost by introducing tighter inequalities than the Hoeffding bound and choosing aggressive parameter settings. Our obtained bound is asymptotically optimal. Further, we show a practical countermeasure against the secret key extraction attack based on our analysis. In the countermeasure, some of the bits in the secret key are intentionally flipped and then the secret key with errors is stored in the memory. With the help of the intentionally added errors, the security is enhanced. For example, it results to be secure against the attacker extracting the secret key with an error rate 0.13 by intentionally adding a 0.15 fraction of errors. Finally, we revisit asymmetric error cases and give a provable bound for crossover probabilities.

Keywords: RSA cryptosystem · Key-recovery · Physical cryptanalysis · Error correction

1 Introduction

1.1 Background

In security analysis of the RSA cryptosystem [13], physical cryptanalysis is also important in addition to number-theoretic attacks. For example, some fraction of secret key bits may be leaked, or some of the secret key bits with error may be observed by physical attacks such as side-channel attacks and cold boot

© Springer International Publishing Switzerland 2015
M.-H. Au and A. Miyaji (Eds.): ProvSec 2015, LNCS 9451, pp. 61–81, 2015.
DOI: 10.1007/978-3-319-26059-4_4

attack [2]. If the amount of leaked information is small enough, there does not occur any problem since the attacker cannot recover the secret key from the extracted key bits. It is an important issue to evaluate the amount of information leakage that enable the key recover.

In the RSA [13], a modulus $N = pq$ is a product of two distinct primes and integers e and d satisfy $ed \equiv 1 \pmod{(p-1)(q-1)}$. The public (or encryption) key is (N, e) and the secret (or decryption) key is (N, d). It is recommended in PKCS#1 standard [12] to use $(p, q, d, d_p, d_q, q^{-1} \bmod p)$ for secret key, where $d_p = d \bmod p - 1$ and $d_q = d \bmod q - 1$. The above tuples is composed of the additional components $p, q, d_p, d_q, q^{-1} \bmod p$ in addition to d, which allows a fast decryption by using Chinese Remainder Theorem. Several studies about the physical cryptanalysis against PKCS#1 standard have been proposed from the proposal of cold boot attack [2].

At CRYPTO2009, Heninger and Shacham (HS) [5] proposed a polynomial time attack on RSA, which recovers the secret key from some fraction of the key bits. We denote the probability that each bit is erased by δ, which implies that $(1 - \delta)$-fraction is given. Their algorithm recovers the secret key in polynomial time when $\delta < 0.73$. At CRYPTO2010, Henecka, May and Meurer (HMM) [4] considered the symmetric error case where each key bits are flipped with the same crossover probability. Then, they presented the expected polynomial time attack which recovers the secret key from the noisy one. We denote the probability that each bit is flipped by ϵ. Their algorithm recovers the secret key in polynomial time when $\epsilon < 0.237$.

At Asiacrypt2012, Paterson, Polychroniadou and Sibborn (PPS) [11] presented an efficient algorithm which works when each bit is *asymmetrically flipped*. It means that two possible bit flips $0 \to 1$ and $1 \to 0$ have different probability. Their algorithm takes a maximum likelihood based approach while the HMM algorithm takes a threshold based approach. Further, they showed that the condition will be improved to $\epsilon < 0.243$ for the symmetric error cases.

At PKC2013, Kunihiro, Shinohara and Izu (KSI) [9] considered the unified case; the both of error and erasure occur, and they presented the polynomial time attack which recovers the secret key from the noisy one. Letting δ be the erasure probability and ϵ be the error probability, they showed that the secret key can be recovered in polynomial time when $\epsilon + \delta/2 \leq 1/2 - 0.263\sqrt{1 - \delta}$. If $\delta = 0$ (erasure-free case), then the above condition is simplified into $\epsilon < 0.237$ and then it is completely equivalent to the HMM result. They show the theoretical bound for key-recovering in polynomial; we cannot recover the secret key in polynomial time if $(1 - \delta)(1 - H(\frac{\epsilon}{1-\delta})) < \frac{1}{5}$, where $H(\cdot)$ is the so-called binary entropy function. They pointed out that there is a small gap between the derived condition and the theoretical bound. At CHES2014, Kunihiro and Honda gave an analysis for analog leakage [8]. Their analysis is also valid for discrete leakage and includes the results of PPS [11]. However, they gave no consideration of erasures in secret key bits.

In 2014, the Heartbleed Bug was found in Open SSL cryptographic software library [6]. The bug allows stealing the secret information under the normal conditions. The attackers can access at most 64 KByte for a single heartbeat without abnormal happening to the logs. Attackers can keep requesting arbitrary number of 64 KByte chunks of memory content. Then, using the bug the attacker can obtain the some fraction of the secret key.

1.2 Our Contributions

In this paper, we mainly discuss the case that the symmetric bit-flip and erasure occurs in RSA secret keys bits, which we call *Secret-Key Extraction Attack*.

Our first contribution is to improve the bound for the erasure rate δ and the error rate ϵ from the bound derived in [9]. We give a tighter analysis by aggressive parameters setting. We show that we can recover the correct secret key in polynomial time provided

$$(1 - \delta) \left(1 - H \left(\frac{\epsilon}{1 - \delta} \right) \right) > \frac{1}{5}.$$

Our result shows that the achievable bound is improved from $1 - \delta - 2\epsilon \geq \sqrt{\frac{2(1-\delta)\ln 2}{5}}$. Consider the case of 2048-bit RSA and $\delta = 0.5$ case. The KSI algorithm recovers the original secret key from the noisy key bits with up to $328(= 0.064 \times 1024 \times 5)$ errors. On the other hand, our algorithm recovers one from the noisy key bits with up to $374(= 0.073 \times 1024 \times 5)$ errors.

Our second contribution is to give a practical countermeasure against the secret-key extraction attack. At the countermeasure, a legitimate decryptor (or signer) first adds small random errors to the original secret key (that is, each bit is flipped with a small probability, denoted by ϵ'), and then stores the secret key with errors into the memory (side-channel attack scenario)/server (The Heartbleed Bug scenario). The decryptor then throws out the original secret key sequence. In each decryption process, he first reconstructs the correct secret key from stored noisy erroneous version of the secret key and then executes a usual decryption process. Suppose that the attacker can extract the secret key with error rate ϵ and erasure rate δ by a side-channel attack from the decryptor's storage. Typical examples of this kind of attacks are given as follows: (i) the whole secret key bits can be obtained but some fraction of bits are bit-flipped ($\epsilon > 0, \delta = 0$), (ii) some fraction of secret key bits can be obtained without any error ($\delta > 0, \epsilon = 0$).

We show that our countermeasure prevents the type (i) secret-key extracting attack with error rate ϵ if we set ϵ' as

$$\frac{0.243 - \epsilon}{1 - 2\epsilon} \leq \epsilon' \leq 0.243.$$

For example, our countermeasure is valid if we set ϵ' as $0.15 \leq \epsilon' \leq 0.243$ for $\epsilon = 0.13$.

Then, we show that our countermeasure prevents the type (ii) secret-key extracting attack with erasure rate δ if we set ϵ' as

$$(1 - \delta)(1 - H(\epsilon')) < \frac{1}{5}.$$

For example, if we set $\epsilon' = 0.15$, the attacker needs to extract the secret key bits with the erasure rate $\delta < 0.49$ for recovering the secret key in polynomial time. If we set $\epsilon' = 0.24$, the attacker needs to extracts the secret key bits with the erasure rate $\delta < 0.024$. In this case, the attacker needs to obtain almost all the noisy secret key for recovering the original secret key; a 0.976 fraction of the secret key is necessary.

Our third contribution is about asymmetric error cases. We give a *provable* bound for asymmetric error cases. Concretely, provided $\beta < 0.653$, we can recover the secret key efficiently. This part comes from theoretical interests.

2   Preliminaries

This section presents an overview of methods using binary trees to recover the secret key of the RSA cryptosystem [13]. We first explain a binary tree-based approach introduced by Heninger and Shacham [5] and then describe the methods of Henecka et al. [4] and Kunihiro et al. [9].

2.1   Notation

We use the same notation as [9]. We give a detailed in explanation in Appendix A for self-contained. Throughout the paper, we denote by $\log x$ the binary logarithm to base 2, and we denote by $\ln x$ the natural logarithm to base e ≈ 2.71828. We denote the bit-length of N by n. For a t-bit sequence $\boldsymbol{x} = (x_{t-1}, \ldots, x_0) \in \{0,1\}^t$, we denote the i-th bit of $\boldsymbol{x}$ by $x[i] = x_i$, where $x[0]$ is the least significant bit of $\boldsymbol{x}$. Let $\tau(M)$ denote the largest exponent such that $2^{\tau(M)} | M$.

2.2   HS Algorithm [5] – Recovering RSA Secret Keys by Using Binary Trees–

We review the work of [5]. First, we discuss the key setting of the RSA cryptosystem [13], especially of the PKCS #1 standard [12]. The public key is (N, e) and the secret key is $\mathbf{sk} = (p, q, d, d_p, d_q, q^{-1} \bmod p)$. As in the previous works, we also ignore the last component $q^{-1} \bmod p$ in the secret key.

The public and secret keys have the following relations: $N = pq, ed \equiv 1 \pmod{(p-1)(q-1)}, ed_p \equiv 1 \pmod{p-1}, ed_q \equiv 1 \pmod{q-1}$. From the key setting, there exist some integers k, k_p, k_q such that

$$N = pq, ed = 1 + k(p-1)(q-1), ed_p = 1 + k_p(p-1), ed_q = 1 + k_q(q-1). \quad (1)$$

Suppose that we know the exact values of k, k_p, and k_q. There exist five unknowns (p, q, d, d_p, d_q) in Eq. (1).

The small public exponent e is usually used in practical applications [14], so we suppose that e is small enough such that $e \leq 2^{16} + 1$ in the same manner as [4,5,9,11].

Heninger and Shacham introduced a binary-tree-based technique for recovering the secret key $\mathbf{sk}$. We denote the correct secret key by $\mathbf{sk}$, and the noisy secret key corresponding to **sk** by $\overline{\mathbf{sk}}$. We also denote by m the number of involved secret keys. For example, $m = 5$ if $\mathbf{sk} = (p, q, d, d_p, d_q)$ is involved; $m = 2$ if $\mathbf{sk} = (p, q)$ is involved.

Here we explain how to recover secret keys, taking $\mathbf{sk} = (p, q, d, d_p, d_q)$ as an example. We first explain how to generate the tree. Since p and q are $n/2$ bit prime numbers and half of the most significant bit (MSB) of d is efficiently computable, there exist at most $2^{n/2}$ candidates for each secret key in (p, q, d, d_p, d_q).

Heninger and Shacham [5] define the i-th bit slice for each bit index i and we denote it by

$$\mathbf{slice}(i) := (p[i], q[i], d[i + \tau(k)], d_p[i + \tau(k_p)], d_q[i + \tau(k_q)]).$$

Assume that we have computed a partial solution $\mathbf{sk'} = (p', q', d', d'_p, d'_q)$ up to $\mathbf{slice}(i - 1)$. Heninger and Shacham [5] applied Hensel's lemma to Eq. (1) and presented the following equations

$$p[i] + q[i] = (N - p'q')[i] \bmod 2, \tag{2}$$

$$d[i + \tau(k)] + p[i] + q[i] = (k(N + 1) + 1 - k(p' + q') - ed')[i + \tau(k)] \bmod 2, \tag{3}$$

$$d_p[i + \tau(k_p)] + p[i] = (k_p(p' - 1) + 1 - ed'_p)[i + \tau(k_p)] \bmod 2, \tag{4}$$

$$d_q[i + \tau(k_q)] + q[i] = (k_q(q' - 1) + 1 - ed'_q)[i + \tau(k_q)] \bmod 2. \tag{5}$$

We can easily see that $p[i], q[i], d[i + \tau(k)], d_p[i + \tau(k_p)]$, and $d_q[i + \tau(k_q)]$ are not independent. Each Hensel lift yields exactly two candidate solutions. Then, the number of all candidates is given by $2^{n/2}$.

Next we explain a pruning step. Since a random fraction of bits is assumed to be known with certainty, the tree can be pruned that are not consistent with known bits. The analysis in [5] shows that the size of trees remains in polynomial in n if $\delta < 0.73$.

2.3 HMM Algorithm [4] and KSI Algorithm [9]

First, we briefly explain the HMM algorithm [4]. It performs t Hensel lifts for some parameter t. Then, the binary tree is separated into partial trees whose depth is t, and then the pruning step is performed for each partial tree. Actually, mt bits of the node sequence from the root node of the partial tree to the leaf node of the partial tree are compared with the corresponding bit of $\overline{\mathbf{sk}}$. If the Hamming distance between the partial sequence of $\overline{\mathbf{sk}}$ and the candidate is larger than $C \in [0, mt]$, the leaf node is discarded. How to set C is crucial in the HMM algorithm. Henecka et al. considered the two following restrictions, which help to decide how to choose parameters (t, C). Note that $\mathbb{E}[X]$ is the mean of a random variable X.

Restriction 1. Let $Z_{b,i}$ be the number of bad candidates generated from one bad partial solution at the i-th pruning step. Then, we choose parameters (t, C) so that $\mathbb{E}[Z_{b,i}] \leq 1/2$ holds.

Restriction 2. For each pruning step, we choose parameters (t, C) so that the probability with that the correct node is discarded is less than $1/n$.

By properly choosing parameters C and t, Henecka et al. showed the following results. The HMM algorithm recovers the secret keys (p, q, d, d_p, d_q) in computation time $O(n^{2+\frac{\ln 2}{5\zeta^2}})$ if the error rate ϵ is not larger than $0.237 - \zeta$ for any positive ζ. For general m of the involved secret information, the secret key can be recovered in computation time $O(n^{2+\frac{\ln 2}{m\zeta^2}})$ provided that $\epsilon \leq 1/2 - \sqrt{\ln 2/2m} - \zeta$.

The following heuristic assumption is made in the analysis in [4] and we also use the same assumption in our analysis.

Heuristic Assumption 1. Every solution generated by applying the expansion phase to an incorrect partial solution is an ensemble of t randomly chosen bit slices.

Remark 1. Paterson et al. introduced the weaker randomness assumption and evaluated the success condition under the assumption [11]. In the analysis of Sect. 3, we employ the stronger (not weaker) randomness assumption for precisely evaluating the computational complexity.

KSI algorithm [9] is a unified variant of the HS algorithm [5] and HMM algorithm [4]. It is based on HMM algorithm, but, skips the erasure symbols and employs the Hamming distance in the pruning phase. The threshold for the Hamming distance is variable according to the number of skipped erasure symbols in their method; while it is fixed in the HMM algorithm. In Sect. 3, we present an improved algorithm from [9]. The algorithm itself is entirely the same as the KSI algorithm [9]. The difference from the analysis in [9] is how to set the parameter in the pruning phase.

We revisit how to choose the thresholds in the pruning phase, which is important in our analysis. First, we review the facts about probability theory and information theory and then introduce the so-called Chernoff–Hoeffding bound. We note that the analysis in [4] uses the Hoeffding bound.

2.4 Reviews for Probability Theory and Information Theory

We recall some basic definitions and theorems on a probability theory and information theory, which are necessary for our analysis. We concentrate on the case of binary sources.

Definition 1 (Binomial distribution). Let X be a random variable following the binomial distribution with parameters n and p. We write $X \sim \text{Bin}(n, p)$. The probability that $X = k$ for $k = 0, 1, \ldots, n$ is given by

$$\Pr[X = k] = \binom{n}{k} p^k (1-p)^{n-k}.$$

Definition 2 (Binary Entropy [1]). The binary entropy function $H(x)$ is defined by $H(x) := -x \log x - (1-x) \log(1-x)$.

Definition 3 (Kullback–Leibler Divergence [1]**).** Consider two distributions P and Q on $\{0, 1\}$. Let $P(0) = 1 - p, P(1) = p, Q(0) = 1 - q, Q(1) = q$. The Kullback–Leibler divergence between P and Q is defined by

$$D(P\|Q) := p \log \frac{p}{q} + (1-p) \log \frac{1-p}{1-q}.$$

For simplicity, we use a notation $D(p, q)$ instead of $D(P\|Q)$.

It follows Definition 3 that the Kullback–Leibler divergence is always non-negative and $D(p, q) = 0$ if and only if $p = q$.

We denote a uniform distribution on $\{0, 1\}$ by U, which implies $U(0) = U(1) = 1/2$. It directly follows Definition 3 that we have

$$D(P\|U) = D(p, 1/2) = p \log(2p) + (1-p) \log 2(1-p) = 1 - H(p).$$

The following is known about the binary entropy function $H(x)$.

Proposition 1. The binary entropy function $H(x)$ can be represented by the following sum of infinite series

$$H(x) = 1 - \frac{1}{\ln 2} \sum_{u=1}^{\infty} \frac{(1-2x)^{2u}}{2u(2u-1)}.$$

For the binomial distribution, the following is well-known.

Proposition 2 (The Hoeffding Bound [7]**).** Suppose that $X \sim \text{Bin}(n, p)$. Then, for all every $0 < \gamma < 1$, we have

$$\Pr[X \leq n(p - \gamma)] \leq \exp(-2n\gamma^2) \text{ and } \Pr[X \geq n(p + \gamma)] \leq \exp(-2n\gamma^2).$$

Our Main Tools for Analysis. The Hoeffding bound for the binomial distribution is a crucial tool in the analysis of [4,9]. It is a well-known and easy-to-use bound, whereas a tighter bound is also known. The tighter bound can make us evaluate the success condition and the computational cost of recovering the secret key more precisely. We introduce the bound for the binomial distribution in terms of the Kullback–Leibler divergence.

Proposition 3 (Chernoff–Hoeffding Bound). Suppose that $X \sim \text{Bin}(n, p)$. Then, for every $0 < \gamma < 1$, we have

$$\Pr[X \leq n(p - \gamma)] \leq \exp(-nD(p - \gamma, p) \ln 2) \text{ and}$$
$$\Pr[X \geq n(p + \gamma)] \leq \exp(-nD(p + \gamma, p) \ln 2).$$

For a proof of Proposition 3, see [10]. See Appendix B for the relation between two bounds. From Proposition 3, we directly have the following corollary.

Corollary 1. Suppose that $X \sim \text{Bin}(n, 1/2)$. For all every $0 < \gamma < 1$, we have

$$\Pr[X \leq n(1/2 - \gamma)] \leq \exp(-n(1 - H(1/2 - \gamma)) \ln 2) = 2^{-n(1 - H(1/2 - \gamma))}$$

3 Improving the KSI Bound by Chernoff–Hoeffding Bound

3.1 The KSI Algorithm

For self-contained, we first review the KSI algorithm [9] in more details, which recovers the original secret key from the noisy secret key bits with erasures and errors. In the algorithm, we divide the sequence into a T-bit subsequence skipping erasure bits in $\overline{\mathbf{sk}}$ for some fixed positive integer T. Here we denote by t_i the length of a node sequence that is newly generated for the i-th pruning step, and denote by Δ_i the number of E in $\overline{\mathbf{sk}}$ at the i-th pruning step. Since the condition $T \geq m$ practically holds, we have that $t_i = \lceil (T + \Delta_i)/m \rceil$ or $\lceil (T + \Delta_i)/m \rceil - 1$. In contrast, we use threshold values $C_1, \ldots, C_\ell$ when $\overline{\mathbf{sk}}$ is separated into ℓ subsequences. Theorem 1 in Sect. 3.2 provides how to set each C_i. Note that unknown values of k, k_p and k_q are efficiently computable from $\overline{\mathbf{sk}}$.

The KSI Algorithm[9]
Input: Public key (N, e), noisy secret key bits $\overline{\mathbf{sk}}$ with an error rate ϵ and an erasure probability δ and a parameter T.
Output: Correct secret key $\mathbf{sk}$
Initialization phase. Calculate (k, k_p, k_q) and $\mathbf{slice}(0)$ and compute the depth t_i of subtree and $(C_1, \ldots, C_\ell)$ used in the pruning phase
    From $i = 1$ to ℓ, perform the following Expansion and Pruning Phases:
Expansion phase (at i-th round). Generate a candidate set from the public key (N, e) and the partial solution $\mathbf{sk'}$ by using Eqs. (2)–(5). Compute t_i slices: $\mathbf{slice}(\sum_{j=1}^{i-1} t_j + 1), \mathbf{slice}(\sum_{j=1}^{i-1} t_j + 2), \ldots, \mathbf{slice}(\sum_{j=1}^{i} t_j)$ and generate a partial tree whose depth is $t_i + 1$.
Pruning phase (at i-th round). For every new candidate $\mathbf{sk'}$, calculate the Hamming distance between the expanded slices: $\mathbf{slice}(\sum_{j=1}^{i-1} t_j + 1), \ldots,$ $\mathbf{slice}(\sum_{j=1}^{i} t_j)$ and the corresponding bits of $\overline{\mathbf{sk}}$. If the Hamming distance is larger than C_i, discard the partial solution.
Finalization phase. Test whether each candidate solution is indeed $\mathbf{sk}$ with the help of public information.

3.2 Improved Bounds for Erasure and Error Case

We show how to improve the achievable bound from [9]. The main difference between KSI and our algorithms is how to set the threshold C_i. Then, we concentrate a discussion on the choice of C_i.

Theorem 1. Suppose that Assumption 1 holds. Let (N, e) be an RSA public key with n-bit N and fixed e. We choose

$$T = \left\lceil \frac{\log n}{D(\epsilon + \zeta, \epsilon)} \right\rceil \text{ and } C_i = T\left(\frac{1}{2} + \gamma_i\right), \tag{6}$$

where γ_i is positive real number satisfying

$$T\left(1 - H\left(\frac{1}{2} - \gamma_i\right)\right) = t_i + 1 \tag{7}$$

and t_i and Δ_i are defined in Sect. 3.1. Furthermore, let $\overline{\mathbf{sk}} = (\overline{\mathbf{sk}}_1, \ldots, \overline{\mathbf{sk}}_m)$ be an RSA secret key with noise rate ϵ such that

$$\frac{1}{2} + \gamma_i \leq 1 - \frac{(T + \Delta_i)\epsilon}{T} - \zeta \tag{8}$$

for every i. Then, Restrictions 1 and 2 hold for every fixed $\zeta > 0$. Our method corrects $\overline{\mathbf{sk}}$ in expected time $\mathcal{O}(n^{2+2(\frac{\ln 2}{mD(\epsilon+\zeta,\epsilon)} + \frac{\Delta}{m}\frac{\ln 2}{\ln n})})$ with success probability at least $1 - \left(\frac{(1-\delta)mD(\epsilon+\zeta,\epsilon)}{2\ln n} + \frac{1}{n}\right)$, where $\Delta = \max\{\Delta_i\}$ and $\delta mn/2 = \sum \Delta_i$.

We omit the proof since we take the same strategy as in [9]. The main difference between the proof in [9] and our proof comes from using the different setting of C_i, which is based on Proposition 3. See the full version for the proof of the theorem.

From Theorem 1, we have the following theorem.

Theorem 2. Suppose that Assumption 1 holds and that the number of erasure bits is Δ for each block. We choose

$$T = \left\lceil \frac{\log n}{D(\epsilon + \zeta, \epsilon)} \right\rceil, \quad t = \frac{T + \Delta}{m}, \quad \text{and } C = T\left(\frac{1}{2} + \gamma'\right),$$

where γ' is the solution of the equation $(1 - \delta)(1 - H(\frac{1}{2} - x)) = (1 + \frac{1}{t})\frac{1}{m}$. Further, let $\overline{\mathbf{sk}}$ be an RSA secret key with error rate

$$(1 - \delta)\left(1 - H\left(\frac{\epsilon}{1 - \delta} + \zeta\right)\right) \geq \left(1 + \frac{1}{t}\right)\frac{1}{m}.$$

Then, our algorithm recovers the correct secret key in average time $O\left(n^{2 + \frac{2}{mD(\epsilon+\zeta,\epsilon)} + \delta t\frac{\ln 2}{\ln n}}\right)$ with success probability at least $1 - \left(\frac{mD(\epsilon+\zeta,\epsilon)}{\log n} + \frac{1}{n}\right)$. Then our method satisfies Restrictions 1 and 2 for every fixed $\zeta > 0$. It also corrects $\overline{\mathbf{sk}}$ in expected time $\mathcal{O}(n^{2+2(\frac{\ln 2}{mD(\epsilon+\zeta,\epsilon)} + \delta t\frac{\ln 2}{\ln n})})$ with success probability at least $1 - \left(\frac{(1-\delta)mD(\epsilon+\zeta,\epsilon)}{2\log n} + \frac{1}{n}\right)$.

Proof. We begin with the discussion of Eq. (8) in the analysis of our method. For simplicity, we consider only the case where all Δ_i's are the same[1]. Suppose that $\overline{\mathbf{sk}}$ is separated into ℓ subsequences. Then, each part consists of $mn/2\ell$ bits. By letting $t = n/2\ell$, we have $\Delta = \delta tm$ and $T = tm - \Delta = (1 - \delta)tm$, so we can say

---

[1] For a large enough T, it holds with high probability. More precisely, all of Δ_i takes the value close to $\delta T/(1 - \delta)$ with overwhelming probability, which can be proved by the similar analysis of [5].

that γ' in Theorem 1 satisfies that $1 - H\left(\dfrac{1}{2} - \gamma'\right) = \left(1 + \dfrac{1}{t}\right)\dfrac{1}{m}\dfrac{1}{1-\delta}$. Hence, in this case, the upper bound (8) implies that

$$\frac{1}{2} + \gamma' \leq 1 - \epsilon - \frac{\delta\epsilon}{1-\delta} - \zeta.$$

We can transform the condition as follows:

$$\Longrightarrow \frac{\epsilon}{1-\delta} + \zeta \leq \frac{1}{2} - \gamma' \Longrightarrow H\left(\frac{\epsilon}{1-\delta} + \zeta\right) \leq H\left(\frac{1}{2} - \gamma'\right)$$

$$\Longrightarrow 1 - H\left(\frac{\epsilon}{1-\delta} + \zeta\right) \geq 1 - H\left(\frac{1}{2} - \gamma'\right) = \left(1 + \frac{1}{t}\right)\frac{1}{m}\frac{1}{1-\delta}$$

$$\Longrightarrow (1-\delta)\left(1 - H\left(\frac{\epsilon}{1-\delta} + \zeta\right)\right) \geq \left(1 + \frac{1}{t}\right)\frac{1}{m}.$$

Then, we have the condition.

Remark 2. For sufficiently large n, t goes to the infinity, and the success probability is close to 1. Hereafter, we ignore the term "ζ" for simplicity, and we just write the success condition as

$$(1-\delta)\left(1 - H\left(\frac{\epsilon}{1-\delta}\right)\right) \geq \frac{1}{m}. \qquad (9)$$

Figure 1 illustrates a region in which the attack succeed for ϵ and δ.

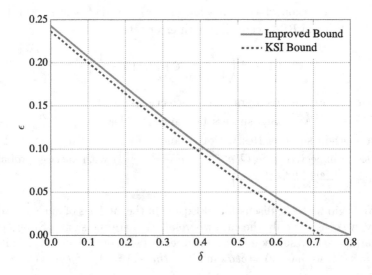

Fig. 1. Success region for ϵ and ϵ'

Remark 3. We show no implementation results here since the numerical experimental results will be exactly the same as [9]. See [9] for concrete experimental results if needed.

We give different settings of parameters C_i in Appendix C. The first one enables us to calculate C_i in analytic way and the last one interpolates KSI and our algorithms.

4 Practical Countermeasure Against Secret-Key Extraction Attack

4.1 Attack Model

In this section, we focus on the case $m = 5$. Suppose that an attacker can extract the secret key with a small enough error rate, say, $\epsilon = 0.1$. Since $\epsilon = 0.1 < 0.243$, the attacker can easily recover the correct secret key from the extracted secret key by HMM algorithm or PPS algorithm. Can we protect this kind of attacks? In this section, we propose a simple countermeasure against the secret key extraction attack by applying our results.

We consider the following two types of adversaries. The first type of adversary obtains the whole secret key with some errors. The second type of adversary obtains some fraction of the secret key without any error. We further divide the latter type of adversary into two classes. The first one obtains multiple bits at random positions; the second one obtains a single bit at a random position on the whole memory in each trial and repeats the trial for multiple times. The Heartbleed Bug is categorized into the latter class of attacks[2].

If an attacker can obtain the whole secret key without any error, his ability is completely equivalent to that of the legitimate decryptor. Hence, in this setting, there is no hope to prevent the attacker recovering the secret key. However, if there is a gap between their abilities, we have a chance to prevent it by amplifying the gap. Consider the following attacker model.

Definition 4 ((ϵ, δ)-Adversary). We denote by (ϵ, δ)–adversary an attacker that extracts the secret key with error rate ϵ and erasure rate δ from the storage.

4.2 Simple (but Ineffective) Countermeasures

The easiest countermeasure against this kind of attacker will be to encrypt RSA secret key bits under another encryption key, and then discard original RSA secret key and store encrypted secret key. In decryption phase, the decryptor first recovers the original RSA secret key from the encrypted one and then decrypt a ciphertext by using RSA secret key. With the help of the countermeasure, the original RSA secret key will be kept secret against the secret-key extraction attack. However, the countermeasure has the following disadvantages:

---

[2] Harrison and Xu discussed attacks that expose the private key of an OpenSSH serve and an Apache HTTP server and gave several countermeasures at different layers [3].

- The decryptor needs to recover the original secret key in each decryption phase, which requires additional computational costs.
- The decryptor needs to store additional secret information.

Especially, the latter disadvantage is critical. This countermeasure causes a new challenging problem of key management for the additional secret information.

The general strategy for preventing the key recovery is to add randomness in storing secret keys and to remove (or canceling) the randomness. The most common method in side-channel attack scenario is to add $r(p-1)(q-1), r_p(p-1), r_q(q-1)$ to d, d_p, d_q for random small r, r_p, r_q and then store $d + r(p-1)(q-1), d_p + r_p(p-1), d_q + r_q(q-1)$ instead of d, d_p, d_q. In decryption phase, added randomness r, r_p, r_q are cancelled automatically since $C^{d+r(p-1)(q-1)} = C^d C^{r(p-1)(q-1)} = C^d$. This countermeasure works well for protecting d, d_p and d_q. However, this kind of countermeasure cannot be applied to hiding p and q. Then, we need another type of countermeasure.

4.3   Our Countermeasure

We propose a new practical countermeasure, which does not rely on another encryption key. Our countermeasure against the (ϵ, δ)-Adversary is given as follows. A legitimate decryptor's work is composed of the following two phases: Setup phase and Decryption phase. He executes Setup phase only once but executes Decryption phase for each actual decryption.

- (Setup Phase)
  1. Estimate a non-negative real numbers ϵ and δ, which corresponds to the ability of attackers.
  2. Choose ϵ' (how to choose ϵ' is discussed later).
  3. Store the degraded secret key; each bit in the original secret key is intentionally bit-flipped with probability ϵ'.
  4. Discard the original secret key.
- (Decryption Phase)
  1. Reconstruct the original secret key from the stored secret key.
  2. Decrypt the ciphertext by using reconstructed secret key.

If we use a larger ϵ', we can protect against stronger adversaries; while we need more computational time for the decryption process. Then, it is important to properly set ϵ'.

The compounded erasure and error rates are given by δ and $\epsilon + \epsilon' - 2\epsilon\epsilon' - \epsilon'\delta$, respectively through the intentional bit-flip by the legitimate decryptor and the extraction of secret keys by attackers. They are verified by calculating $\Pr(0 \to E) = \epsilon'\delta + (1-\epsilon')\delta = \delta$ and $\Pr(0 \to 1) = \epsilon'(1-\epsilon-\delta) + (1-\epsilon')\epsilon = \epsilon + \epsilon' - 2\epsilon\epsilon' - \epsilon'\delta$, where E is an erasure symbol. Then, from Eq. (9) the success condition of (ϵ, δ)-adversary for recovering the correct secret key in polynomial time is given by

$$(1-\delta)\left(1 - H\left(\frac{\epsilon + \epsilon' - 2\epsilon\epsilon' - \epsilon'\delta}{1-\delta}\right)\right) > \frac{1}{m}. \tag{10}$$

Our countermeasure needs to recover the original RSA secret key. However, it does not need additional secret information for it, which is an advantage of our countermeasure.

There are two (possible) obstacles for our countermeasure. The first one is a time delay due to the key-recovery step. The other is a low success probability for the key-recovery. We show that the above obstacles can be removed if we properly set ϵ'.

The experimental results given in [4, 11] show that, the original secret key can be reconstructed rather fast (less than one second) with high probability (over than 0.8) if $\epsilon' \leq 0.15$. These results imply that it is practical to set $\epsilon' = 0.15$ for real situations. Hereafter, we mention the case $\epsilon' = 0.15$.

The problem of our countermeasure is that the success probability of recovering the secret key is not 1, which implies that the legitimate decryptor also may not recover the original secret key. However, we can easily solve the problem by choosing a *good* noise in advance which enables a decryptor to recover the secret key. Concretely, Step 3 in Setup Phase will be changed as follows. Prior to storing the degraded secret key, the decryptor checks whether the secret key can be really recovered from the degraded key. If the key-recovery fails, discard the degraded key and generate a new (degraded) key with a random seed. If the key-recovery succeeds, go to Step 4 and store the parameters used in key-recovery algorithm (they are not secret information). Since our key-recovery algorithm is deterministic, our countermeasure always works.

Summarizing the above discussion, if we carefully choose degraded version of the secret key under the setting $\epsilon' = 0.15$, we can recover the original secret key in practical time. Note that no addition secret information is required in our countermeasure.

4.4   Analyses Against Two Types of Adversaries

The Whole Secret Key Can Be Obtained with Errors: $\delta = 0, \epsilon > 0$
Plugging $\delta = 0$ into Eq. (10), the success condition for the attack can be transformed into

$$H(\epsilon + \epsilon' - 2\epsilon\epsilon') < 1 - \frac{1}{m}.$$

Then, if ϵ and ϵ' satisfy an inequity: $\epsilon + \epsilon' - 2\epsilon\epsilon' < 0.243$ for $m = 5$, the adversary can recover the secret key. The value ϵ' should be $\epsilon' < 0.243$ so that the legitimate decryptor can execute the decryption procedure. So as to guarantee that an attacker can never recover the correct secret key in polynomial time, $\epsilon + \epsilon' - 2\epsilon\epsilon'$ should be larger than 0.243.

Summing up, when (ϵ, ϵ') satisfy the both of $\epsilon' < 0.243$ and $\epsilon + \epsilon' - 2\epsilon\epsilon' > 0.243$, the proposed countermeasure is effective against $(\epsilon, 0)$-adversary. The condition for ϵ' is explicitly given by

$$\frac{0.243 - \epsilon}{1 - 2\epsilon} < \epsilon' < 0.243. \tag{11}$$

Figure 2 illustrates a region for ϵ and ϵ' to make the countermeasure be secure.

We give two typical examples. Suppose that the attacker's power for extracting secret keys is weak or key bits are robustly protected. Consider $(\epsilon, 0)$-adversary with $\epsilon > 0.243$. In this case, the attack never succeeds even if ϵ' is set as $\epsilon' = 0$. Then, in this case, the decryptor does not need to implement any countermeasures. Conversely, suppose that the attacker's power is rather high. From the above discussion, the countermeasure is effective by adequately choosing ϵ'. For example, setting ϵ' as $0.15 < \epsilon' < 0.243$ makes the storage system to be secure when $\epsilon = 0.13$. This implies that under the setting $\epsilon' = 0.15$, the legitimate decryptor can efficiently recover the original secret key and our countermeasure prevents the key-recover attack for $(\epsilon, 0)$-adversary with $\epsilon > 0.13$.

A Random Fraction Is Obtained Without Any Error: Implications to the Heartbleed Bug: Plugging $\epsilon = 0$ into Eq. (10), the success condition for the attack can be transformed into

$$(1 - \delta)(1 - H(\epsilon'))) > \frac{1}{m}. \tag{12}$$

Figure 3 illustrates a region for δ and ϵ' to make the countermeasure be secure.

The $(0, \delta)$-adversary with $\delta > 0.49$ cannot recover the secret key if we set $\epsilon' = 0.15$. In this case, the adversary must collect a half of the secret key in this case.

If we adopt more aggressive setting, say, $\epsilon' = 0.24$, the attacker needs to obtain almost all of the secret keys. Concretely, more than a $0.976(= 1 - 0.024)$ fraction is necessary for recovering the secret key.

Suppose that the attacker steals only one bit at a random position in a storage. We denote by M the number of bits in the storage and by L the bit length of the secret key. We first evaluate the average number of trials for obtaining αL-bit for some positive α less than 1. It is estimated by

$$\frac{M}{L} + \frac{M}{L - 1} + \cdots + \frac{M}{L(1 - \alpha)}. \tag{13}$$

By the simple analysis, it is upper bounded by

$$M\left(\frac{1}{L} + \frac{1}{L - 1} + \cdots + \frac{1}{L(1 - \alpha)}\right) < M\frac{\alpha}{1 - \alpha}. \tag{14}$$

Note that it does not depend on L. If $\alpha = 0.2$, (that is, the erasure rate $\delta = 0.8$), it is upper bounded by $0.25M$.

Equation (14) is not a so tighter bound if α is close to 1. From the so-called coupon collectors argument [10], the upper bound is given by

$$M\left(\frac{1}{L} + \frac{1}{L - 1} + \cdots + \frac{1}{1}\right) < M(\ln L + 0.5772). \tag{15}$$

For typical 2048-bit RSA case, the value is evaluated by $9.12M$ since $L = 2048/2 \times 5 = 5120$.

This result implies that the attacker needs about 36 times harder tasks if our countermeasure is applied; $0.25M$ trials without our countermeasure and $9.12M$ trials with our countermeasure ($\epsilon' = 0.24$).

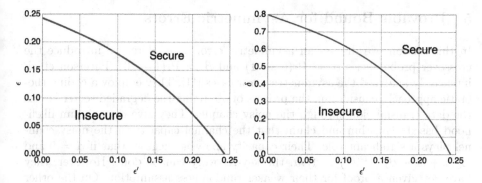

Fig. 2. Secure/Insecure region for (ϵ, ϵ') **Fig. 3.** Secure/Insecure region for (δ, ϵ')

4.5 Information-Theoretic View of our Countermeasure

For simplicity, we focus on the erasure-free case. We show a connection between our countermeasure and a key exchange scheme via eavesdropper channel [1]. First, we give a quick review of a key exchange scheme via eavesdropper channel. Suppose that Initiator and Responder want to share common secret key bits via binary symmetric channel with crossover probability ϵ'. Its channel capacity is given by $1 - H(\epsilon')$. Shannon's noisy channel coding theorem states that Initiator and Responder can share the secret key bits with error probability 0 asymptotically if an information rate R is less than the channel capacity $1 - H(\epsilon')$.

Suppose that Eavesdropper can receive the information with crossover probability ϵ in addition to ϵ', which is one between Initiator and Eavesdropper. As a result, we can say that the crossover probability of the channel between Initiator and Eavesdropper is $\epsilon + \epsilon' - 2\epsilon\epsilon'$. Its channel capacity is given by $1 - H(\epsilon + \epsilon' - 2\epsilon\epsilon')$.

The converse of channel coding theorem states that if $1 - H(\epsilon + \epsilon' - 2\epsilon\epsilon') < R$, Initiator and Eavesdropper cannot share the common key bits with probability 0 asymptotically. Summing up, if ϵ, ϵ' and R satisfy an inequality $1 - H(\epsilon + \epsilon' - 2\epsilon\epsilon') < R < 1 - H(\epsilon')$, Responder can share the key bits, and Eavesdropper cannot share one.

We explain that our countermeasure is similar to the key exchange scheme via eavesdropping channel. Suppose that Initiator chooses p, which is one component of the original secret key as the common key bits and wants to send p. And suppose that by some encoding procedure, p is encoded to $\mathbf{sk} = (p, q, d_L, d_p, d_q)$, where d_L is the least half of d. An information rate is given by $1/5$. In our countermeasure, Responder has the noisy secret key with crossover probability ϵ', and $(\epsilon, 0)$-adversary obtains a more noisy secret key with crossover probability $\epsilon + \epsilon' - 2\epsilon\epsilon'$, respectively. Then, if ϵ and ϵ' satisfy the following inequality $1 - H(\epsilon + \epsilon' - 2\epsilon\epsilon') < \frac{1}{5} < 1 - H(\epsilon')$, the legitimate decryptor can recover the secret keys, and the adversary cannot recover it. This condition is completely equivalent to Eq. (11) since the solution of the equation $H(x) = 4/5$ is $x = 0.243$.

5   Provable Bound for Asymmetric Errors

In this section, we discuss an asymmetric error case. Here, we introduce the crossover probabilities $\alpha := \Pr(0 \to 1)$ and $\beta := \Pr(1 \to 0)$. Paterson et al. intensively analyzed the asymmetric error cases [11]. They employ a coding theoretic approach; considering the process of obtaining the degraded secret key as the data transmission through the noisy channel. They give a maximum likelihood based algorithm and claim that the channel capacity of the noisy channel plays a significant role. Their capacity analysis suggests that if $\alpha = 0$ and $\log(1 + (1 - \beta)^{\beta/(1-\beta)}) > 1/m$, the key-recovery can be done. However, they have not given a proof for their weaker randomness assumption. On the other hand, Kunihiro et al. proved that if the symmetric capacity is larger than $1/m$, we can recover the correct secret key under the same assumption in [8]. Since the symmetric capacity is generally smaller than the channel capacity for asymmetry cases, the achievable bound is less than expected. We give a bound for asymmetric error cases according to [8].

First, we define (so-called a mutual information) $I(\alpha, \beta; P)$ as follows:

$$I(\alpha, \beta; P) = H((1 - \alpha)P + (1 - P)\beta) - P(H(\alpha)) - (1 - P)H(\beta).$$

Putting $P = 1/2$, we obtain the symmetric capacity[3]:

$$I(\alpha, \beta; 1/2) = H\left(\frac{1}{2} + \frac{\beta - \alpha}{2}\right) - \frac{H(\alpha)}{2} - \frac{H(\beta)}{2}.$$

From Theorem 2 in [8], the success condition for recovering keys is given by

$$H\left(\frac{1}{2} + \frac{\beta - \alpha}{2}\right) - \frac{H(\alpha)}{2} - \frac{H(\beta)}{2} > \frac{1}{m}. \tag{16}$$

Remark 4. Putting $\alpha = \beta = \epsilon$, we have the condition: $H(\frac{1}{2}) - H(\epsilon) = 1 - H(\epsilon) > \frac{1}{m}$, which is equal to that for the symmetric error. This equality comes from the fact that the symmetric capacity and the channel capacity are equivalent if the error is symmetric.

First, we discuss the idealized cold boot case: $\alpha = 0$. Plugging $\alpha = 0$ into Eq. (16), we obtain the condition. In this case, the key-recovery succeeds if

$$H\left(\frac{1 + \beta}{2}\right) - \frac{H(\beta)}{2} > \frac{1}{m}. \tag{17}$$

We compare the bounds derived by Paterson et al. and our bounds based on Eq. (17). Table 1 shows the maximal values of β for $m = 2, 3, 5$. As predicted, the bounds in [11] are slightly larger than ours. It shows that the analysis in [11] overestimated the achievable bounds. According to the numerical experiments

---

[3] The channel capacity is obtained by maximizing $I(\alpha, \beta; P)$ by optimizing P for fixed α and β.

Table 1. Comparison of maximal values of β between [11] and Ours

	Paterson et al. [11]	Ours
$m = 2$	0.304	0.294
$m = 3$	0.486	0.473
$m = 5$	0.666	0.653

Table 2. Maximal values of β for various α

	$\alpha = 0$	$\alpha = 0.001$	$\alpha = 0.01$	$\alpha = 0.1$
$m = 2$	0.294	0.289	0.261	0.120
$m = 3$	0.473	0.467	0.432	0.260
$m = 5$	0.653	0.646	0.609	0.419

presented in [11], we can recover keys up to $\beta = 0.63$ with a non-zero success rate for $m = 5$, which validates our analysis.

We return to the general case: $0 \neq \alpha < \beta$. In this case, the success condition is given by Eq. (16). Table 2 shows the maximal values of β for various values α. We can see that even if $\alpha \neq 0$ (say, $\alpha = 0.001$), we can succeed to recover the secret key for some β (say, $\beta < 0.646$).

Acknowledgement. This research was supported by CREST, JST and supported by JSPS KAKENHI Grant Number 25280001. We would like to thank Yuji Suga for telling us the connection between the Heartbleed Bug and our theoretical analysis.

A   Hamming Distance Between Two Sequences with Erasures

We use the same notation in [9]. For a t-bit binary sequence $\boldsymbol{a} = (a_{t-1}, \ldots, a_0)$, the Hamming weight of $\boldsymbol{a}$ is defined by $\mathrm{Hw}(\boldsymbol{a}) := \sum_{i=0}^{t-1} a_i$. For two t-bit binary sequences $\boldsymbol{a}, \boldsymbol{b} \in \{0,1\}^t$, the Hamming distance between $\boldsymbol{a}$ and $\boldsymbol{b}$ is defined by $\mathrm{Hw}(\boldsymbol{a} \oplus \boldsymbol{b})$, where $\oplus$ is a bit-wise XOR. The Hamming distance between $\boldsymbol{a}$ and $\boldsymbol{b}$ is equal to the number of positions at which the corresponding symbols in $\boldsymbol{a}$ and $\boldsymbol{b}$ are different.

Then, we define the Hamming distance between two t-bit sequences as follows. The symbol of one sequence (Sequence 1) is $\{0,1\}$ and that of the other sequence (Sequence 2) is $\{0, 1, \mathrm{E}\}$, where E is an erasure symbol. We denote the number of positions at which the corresponding symbols are different by h. We also denote the number of symbols E in Sequence 2 by a. We define the Hamming distance b between two sequences by $b := h - a$.

B   Relation Between the Hoeffding Bound and the Chernoff–Hoeffding Bound

In the analysis in [4,9], the Hoeffding bound plays an important role; whereas in our analysis, the Chernoff–Hoeffding bound is important. We review the relation among two bounds and verify that the Chernoff–Hoeffding bound is tighter than the Hoeffding bound.

Let X be a random variable on an alphabet $\mathcal{X}$. For two probability distributions P_1 and P_2 on $\mathcal{X}$, define a statistical distance $||P_1 - P_2|| = \sum_{a \in \mathcal{X}} |P_1(a) - P_2(a)|$. We focus on a binary alphabet case. Letting $P_1(0) = 1 - p_1, P_1(1) = p_1, P_2(0) = 1 - p_2, P_2(1) = p_2$, we have $||P_1 - P_2|| = |p_1 - p_2| + |p_2 - p_1| = 2|p_1 - p_2|$.

It is well known that Kullback–Leibler Divergence and the statistical distance have the following relation [1]: $D(P_1||P_2) \geq \frac{1}{2\ln 2}||P_1 - P_2||^2$. Then, we have for a binary alphabet case,

$$D(P_1||P_2) = D(p_1, p_2) \geq \frac{(2|p_1 - p_2|)^2}{2\ln 2} = \frac{2(p_1 - p_2)^2}{\ln 2}, \tag{B.1}$$

which implies that the Chernoff–Hoeffding bound (Proposition 3) is tighter than the Hoeffding bound (Proposition 2).

By plugging $p_1 = 1/2 - x$ and $p_2 = 1/2$ into Eq. (B.1), we have

$$D\left(\frac{1}{2} - x, \frac{1}{2}\right) \geq \frac{2x^2}{\ln 2}.$$

C   Another Parameter Choices

For simplicity, we only consider the erasure free case: $\delta = 0$. We can easily extend to the case for $\delta > 0$.

C.1   How to Choose γ Analytically

In Theorem 1, γ' is set as the solution of the equation: $1 - H\left(\frac{1}{2} - x\right) = \left(1 + \frac{1}{t}\right)/m$. It is impossible to find the solution in the analytical way. We introduce a semi-optimal setting of γ, which enables us to find γ analytically.

As similar as Proposition 2, we have the following.

Proposition 4 (Generalized Hoeffding Bound with Degree 2). Suppose that $X \sim \text{Bin}(n, 1/2)$. Then, for all every $0 < \gamma < 1$, we have

$$\Pr[X \leq n(1/2 - \gamma)] \leq \exp\left(-n\left(2\gamma^2 + \frac{4}{3}\gamma^4\right)\right).$$

If we use Proposition 4 instead of Proposition 2, we have the following theorem.

Theorem 3. Suppose that Heuristic Assumption 1 holds. Let $\zeta > 0$ be an arbitrary positive real number. Let (N, e) be an RSA public key with n-bit N and fixed e. We choose

$$t = \left\lceil \frac{\log n}{mD(\epsilon + \zeta, \epsilon)} \right\rceil \quad \text{and} \quad C = mt\left(\frac{1}{2} + \gamma_2\right),$$

where γ_2 is the solution of the equation $2x^2 + \frac{4}{3}x^4 = (1 + \frac{1}{t})\frac{1}{m}$. Further, let $\overline{\mathbf{sk}}$ be an RSA secret key with error rate $\epsilon \le \frac{1}{2} - \gamma_2 - \zeta$. Then, our algorithm recovers a correct secret key in average time $O\left(n^{2 + \frac{2}{mD(\epsilon+\zeta,\epsilon)}}\right)$ with success probability at least $1 - \left(\frac{mD(\epsilon+\zeta,\epsilon)}{\log n} + \frac{1}{n}\right)$.

We show that we can analytically find γ_2. Since the value γ_2 is a solution of the equation: $2x^2 + \frac{4}{3}x^4 = (1 + \frac{1}{t})\frac{\ln 2}{m}$, we have γ_2 is analytically given by

$$\gamma_2 = \frac{\sqrt{\sqrt{9 + \frac{12(1+\frac{1}{t})\ln 2}{m}} - 3}}{2}.$$

For sufficiently large n,

$$\gamma_2 \approx 0.257638.$$

for $m = 5$. Then, we can recover the secret key for sufficiently large n when $\epsilon < 0.5 - 0.257638 - \zeta = 0.242 - \zeta$, which is very close to the condition in Theorem 2.

C.2 More Extension

The discussion of this section just includes theoretical interests rather than practical meanings.

Proposition 4 can be extended to the following.

Proposition 5 (Generalized Hoeffding Bound with Higher Degree). For a fixed positive integer k, we define a polynomial $G_k(x)$ with degree $2k$ by

$$G_k(x) := \sum_{u=1}^{k} \frac{(2x)^{2u}}{2u(2u-1)}.$$

Suppose that $X \sim \mathrm{Bin}(n, 1/2)$. Then, for all every $0 < \gamma < 1$, we have

$$\Pr[X \le n(1/2 - \gamma)] \le \exp(-n(G_k(\gamma))).$$

Proposition 5 includes Propositions 2 and 4, which means that if $k = 1$ then $G_1(x) = 2x^2$, which corresponds to Proposition 2; if $k = 2$ then $G_2(x) = 2x^2 + \frac{4}{3}x^4$, which corresponds to Proposition 4. It follows from Proposition 3 that $k = \infty$ case corresponds to Theorem 2 since

$$G_\infty(x) = \left(1 - H\left(\frac{1}{2} - x\right)\right)\ln 2.$$

If we use Proposition 5 instead of using Propositions 2 or 4, we have the following theorem.

Theorem 4. Suppose that Heuristic Assumption 1 holds. Let $\zeta > 0$ be an arbitrary positive real number. Let (N, e) be an RSA public key with n-bit N and fixed e. We choose

$$t = \left\lceil \frac{\log n}{mD(\epsilon + \zeta, \epsilon)} \right\rceil \text{ and } C = mt\left(\frac{1}{2} + \gamma_k\right),$$

where γ_k is the solution of the equation $G_k(x) = (1 + \frac{1}{t})\frac{1}{m}$. Further, let $\overline{sk}$ be an RSA secret key with error rate $\epsilon \leq \frac{1}{2} - \gamma_k - \zeta$. Then, our algorithm recovers correct secret key in an average time $O\left(n^{2 + \frac{2}{mD(\epsilon + \zeta, \epsilon)}}\right)$ with success probability at least $1 - \left(\frac{mD(\epsilon + \zeta, \epsilon)}{\log n} + \frac{1}{n}\right)$.

If we set $k = 1$, we have the slightly improved version of the HMM result, which reduces in complexity. If we set $k = \infty$, we have the equivalent theorem to Theorem 2. We believe that the analysis in this section helps better understanding of the HMM algorithm [4].

References

1. Cover, C.M., Thomas, J.A.: Elements of Information Theory, 2nd edn. Wiley-Interscience, Hoboken (2006)
2. Halderman, J.A., Schoen, S.D., Heninger, N., Clarkson, W., Paul, W., Calandrino, J.A., Feldman, A.J., Appelbaum, J., Felten, E.W.: Lest we remember: cold boot attacks on encryption keys. In: Proceedings of USENIX Security Symposium, pp. 45–60 (2008)
3. Harrison, K., Xu, S.: Protecting cryptographic keys from memory disclosure attacks. In: Proceedings of IEEE/IFIP DSN, pp. 137–143 (2007)
4. Henecka, W., May, A., Meurer, A.: Correcting errors in RSA private keys. In: Rabin, T. (ed.) CRYPTO 2010. LNCS, vol. 6223, pp. 351–369. Springer, Heidelberg (2010)
5. Heninger, N., Shacham, H.: Reconstructing RSA private keys from random key bits. In: Halevi, S. (ed.) CRYPTO 2009. LNCS, vol. 5677, pp. 1–17. Springer, Heidelberg (2009)
6. The Heartbleed Bug. http://heartbleed.com/
7. Hoeffding, W.: Probability inequalities for sums of bounded random variables. J. Am. Stat. Assoc. 58(301), 13–30 (1963)
8. Kunihiro, N., Honda, J.: RSA meets DPA: recovering RSA secret keys from noisy analog data. In: Batina, L., Robshaw, M. (eds.) CHES 2014. LNCS, vol. 8731, pp. 261–278. Springer, Heidelberg (2014)
9. Kunihiro, N., Shinohara, N., Izu, T.: Recovering RSA secret keys from noisy key bits with erasures and errors. In: Kurosawa, K., Hanaoka, G. (eds.) PKC 2013. LNCS, vol. 7778, pp. 180–197. Springer, Heidelberg (2013)
10. Mitzenmacher, M., Upfal, E.: Probability and Computing: Randomized Algorithms and Probabilistic Analysis. Cambridge University Press, New York (2005)
11. Paterson, K.G., Polychroniadou, A., Sibborn, D.L.: A coding-theoretic approach to recovering noisy RSA keys. In: Wang, X., Sako, K. (eds.) ASIACRYPT 2012. LNCS, vol. 7658, pp. 386–403. Springer, Heidelberg (2012)

12. PKCS #1 Standard for RSA. http://www.rsa.com/rsalabs/node.asp?id=2125
13. Rivest, R., Shamir, A., Adleman, L.: A method for obtaining digital signatures and public-key cryptosystems. Commun. ACM **21**(2), 120–126 (1978)
14. Yilek, S., Rescorla, E., Shacham, H., Enright, B., Savage, S.: When private keys are public: results from the 2008 debian OpenSSL vulnerability, IMC 2009, pp. 15–27. ACM Press (2009)

Protocol

Augmented Secure Channels and the Goal of the TLS 1.3 Record Layer

Christian Badertscher[1]([✉]), Christian Matt[1], Ueli Maurer[1], Phillip Rogaway[2], and Björn Tackmann[3]

[1] Department of Computer Science, ETH Zurich, Zürich, Switzerland
{badertsc,mattc,maurer}@inf.ethz.ch
[2] Department of Computer Science, University of California, Davis, USA
rogaway@cs.ucdavis.edu
[3] Department of Computer Science & Engineering,
University of California, San Diego, USA
btackmann@eng.ucsd.edu

Abstract. Motivated by the wide adoption of authenticated encryption and TLS, we suggest a basic channel abstraction, an *augmented secure channel* (ASC), that allows a sender to send a receiver messages consisting of two parts, where one is privacy-protected and both are authenticity-protected. Working in the tradition of constructive cryptography, we formalize this idea and provide a construction of this kind of channel using the lower-level tool authenticated-encryption.

We look at recent proposals on TLS 1.3 and suggest that the criterion by which their security can be judged is quite simple: do they construct an ASC? Due to this precisely defined goal, we are able to give a natural construction that comes with a rigorous security proof and directly leads to a proposal on TLS 1.3 that is provably secure.

1 Introduction

This paper defines and investigates a new abstraction of a secure channel. We call it an *augmented secure channel*, or ASC. Like most types of channels, an ASC lets a sender Alice send messages to a receiver Bob. But unlike more conventional types of channels, each message has designated private and non-private parts. An active adversary Eve occupies the system, but is limited to seeing the length of the private portion and the contents of the non-private portion of each message—and to entirely shutting down the channel. In particular, the adversary cannot inject messages or induce out-of-order message delivery. Additionally, the non-private portion can contain an implicit part, already known to the receiver, that is not transmitted but still authenticated, e.g., to bind the message to a given context.

The service an ASC provides is motivated by the ascendancy of both TLS and authenticated encryption. We take the rise of these tools, and what they deliver, as an indication that customary conceptualizations of secure channels may not have been rich enough to deliver the service that protocol designers routinely need.

© Springer International Publishing Switzerland 2015
M.-H. Au and A. Miyaji (Eds.): ProvSec 2015, LNCS 9451, pp. 85–104, 2015.
DOI: 10.1007/978-3-319-26059-4_5

Authenticated Encryption. While ASCs are closely related to schemes for authenticated encryption (AE) and authenticated encryption with associated data (AEAD), an ASC and an AE/AEAD-scheme are very different things. An ASC is a reasonably high-level object: an abstract *resource* that parties can employ, getting compositional guarantees when they do. Our formulation of ASCs will be in the tradition of *constructive cryptography* [16,17]. In contrast, an AEAD-scheme is a comparatively low-level primitive: it is a tuple of algorithms that is "good" in some particular, complexity-theoretic sense.

The AEAD notion emerged over a sequence of works [2,3,12,13,22–24] having two distinct purposes: to minimize the misuse of symmetric encryption primitives and to gain efficiency advantages over generic composition schemes (i.e., traditional ways to meld privacy-only encryption schemes and message-authentication codes). But in moving from conventional encryption to AEAD, the basic conception of what symmetric encryption *is* was thoroughly revamped: authenticity became an intrinsic part of the goal; so too did the allowance of (non-private) associated data A; while probabilism, formerly seen as indispensable, was surfaced and subsumed by a nonce N. Roughly said, an AEAD-scheme would nowadays be defined as a triple of algorithms $\Pi = (\mathcal{K}, \mathcal{E}, \mathcal{D})$ where a computationally-reasonable adversary $\mathcal{A}$ has poor advantage at distinguishing encryption and decryption oracles $(\mathcal{E}_K(N, A, M), \mathcal{D}_K(N, A, C))$ from a pair of oracles $(\$(N, A, M), \bot(N, A, C))$, where K is generated by $\mathcal{K}$, the $\$(N, A, M)$ oracle returns an appropriate number of random bits, the $\bot(N, A, C)$ oracle always returns $\bot$, the adversary repeats no nonce N in queries to its first oracle, and queries that would result in trivial wins are disallowed.

The new conceptualization for symmetric encryption gained surprisingly rapid acceptance. The IEEE, IETF, ISO, and NIST all stepped in to standardize AEAD-schemes (e.g., in NIST SP 800-38C and SP 800-38D, IEEE 802.11i, ISO 19772, and IETF RFC 3610, 5116, 5288, 5297, and 7253). Methods that had been previously embedded in widely-deployed systems and standards, (e.g., SSH, and SSL) were recognized as attempts—sometimes rather clumsy ones—to achieve AE/AEAD. Revisions to widely-used protocols started to deploy the ready-built solutions to AEAD rather than the *ad hoc* and error-prone mechanisms that had provided no real abstraction boundaries other that of block ciphers, hash functions, or MACs.

Understanding the Goal of TLS. A long line of work analyzes the security of TLS (mainly versions prior to 1.3) [8,9,11,14,15,19,20,25]. Several recent papers [11,15] use a security notion called Authenticated and Confidential Channel Establishment (ACCE), a game-based definition that models both the handshake and the record layer, as TLS versions prior to 1.3 could formally not be proved as the composition of the two sub-protocols. Motivated by the adoption of AEAD as well as the better separation of the two sub-protocols in TLS 1.3, we give a novel interpretation for the goal of the TLS record layer: constructing a specific instantiation of an ASC, from insecure communication and a shared secret key constructed by the handshake sub-protocol. Indeed, messages in the TLS record protocol consist of private and non-private parts, which are both authenticated.

We show how a generic ASC construction directly leads to this specific instantiation of an ASC. We thereby obtain a provably secure TLS record protocol. Our proposal differs from the current draft for TLS 1.3 by slightly reducing the size of transmitted records and the number of elements in the authenticated data, as well as a different choice of the nonces.

The Gap between a Scheme's Security Properties and its Use. Classical cryptographic definitions, including the AEAD definition reviewed above, do not capture in which contexts a scheme satisfying them can securely be used. They consider a specific attack model and give certain capabilities to an adversary that tries to win some game, but it is not *a priori* clear which capabilities an adversary has in a particular application, or even what her final goal is. To illustrate our point, consider the standard notions for encryption schemes, IND-CPA and IND-CCA. While IND-CCA is stronger, it is not obvious in which applications an IND-CCA encryption scheme is needed and where IND-CPA would suffice. These considerations are highly security-relevant. For complex protocols like TLS or IPSec, one has to make sure that any overall attack can be translated to an attack against the CPA or CCA game or another hardness assumption; only then the protocol is sound. But such analyses are complex and cannot be reused for the analysis of other protocols or attack models.

To solve this problem, we divide a complex protocol into several less complex *construction steps*. Each step specifies precisely what is assumed and what is achieved. Following the tradition of constructive cryptography[1] (CC) [16,17], we model guarantees and expectations as *resources* that provide a specified service to each party. Every party possesses an *interface* to the resources via which it can request that service. We consider resources with three interfaces, labeled A (for Alice), B (for Bob) and E (for Eve). The construction notion of CC provides the following compositional guarantee: a constructed resource can be used in any other construction as an assumed resource. We obtain modularity in the sense that the overall security follows automatically from individual security proofs.

The approach has already been applied successfully in many other contexts. For example, the results in [5,6] shed new light on the definitions of public-key encryption schemes and even led to a new security definition.

2 Preliminaries

Notation. We describe our systems with pseudocode using the following conventions: We write $x \leftarrow y$ for assigning the value y to the variable x. For a distribution $\mathcal{D}$ over some set, $x \leftarrow \mathcal{D}$ denotes sampling x according to $\mathcal{D}$. For a finite set X, $x \leftarrow X$ denotes assigning to x a uniformly random value in X. Typically queries to systems consist of a suggestive keyword and a list of arguments (e.g., (send, M) to send the message M). We ignore keywords in writing the domains of arguments, e.g., (send, M) $\in \mathcal{M}$ indicates that $M \in \mathcal{M}$.

---

[1] We suspect that alternative definitional frameworks, like treating ASCs in the UC framework [4] or RSIM [1,21], would yield closely related findings.

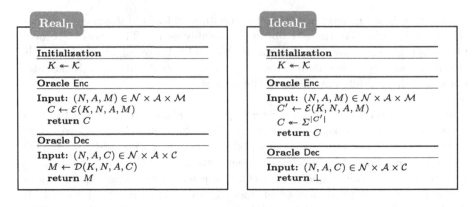

Fig. 1. Real and ideal security game for AEAD-schemes.

AEAD. Let Σ be an alphabet (a finite nonempty set). Typically an element of Σ is a bit ($\Sigma = \{0,1\}$) or a byte ($\Sigma = \{0,1\}^8$). For a string $x \in \Sigma^*$, $|x|$ denotes its length. We define the syntax of a scheme for authenticated encryption with associated data (AEAD) following [22].

Definition 1. *An AEAD-scheme Π is a triple of algorithms $\Pi = (\mathcal{K}, \mathcal{E}, \mathcal{D})$, where $\mathcal{K}$ is a randomized algorithm that samples a key $K \in \Sigma^*$, $\mathcal{E}$ is a deterministic algorithm that maps a key $K \in \Sigma^*$, a nonce $N \in \mathcal{N}$, additional data $A \in \mathcal{A}$, and a message $M \in \mathcal{M}$ to a ciphertext $C \in \mathcal{C}$, and $\mathcal{D}$ is a deterministic algorithm that maps $(K, N, A, C) \in \Sigma^* \times \mathcal{N} \times \mathcal{A} \times \mathcal{C}$ to $\mathcal{M} \cup \{\bot\}$. We assume the domains $\mathcal{N}$, $\mathcal{A}$, $\mathcal{M}$, and $\mathcal{C}$ are equal to Σ^* and require for all $K, N, A, M \in \Sigma^*$ that $\mathcal{D}(K, N, A, \mathcal{E}(K, N, A, M)) = M$. We further require the length of a ciphertext $|\mathcal{E}(K, N, A, M)|$ only depend on the length of the corresponding message $|M|$.*

We define the security game for AEAD-schemes using the all-in-one formulation from [10]. A scheme is considered secure if all valid and efficient adversaries $\mathcal{A}$ have poor advantage according to the following definition.

Definition 2. *We define the advantage of an adversary $\mathcal{A}$ as the difference in the probability that it outputs 1 in the real and ideal games defined in Fig. 1:*

$$\mathbf{Adv}_{\Pi}^{\mathrm{ae}}(\mathcal{A}) := \Pr\left[\mathcal{A}^{\mathbf{Real}_{\Pi}} = 1\right] - \Pr\left[\mathcal{A}^{\mathbf{Ideal}_{\Pi}} = 1\right].$$

An adversary is valid *if it does not repeat Enc or Dec queries, does not ask queries Enc(N, A, M) and Enc(N, A', M') (i.e., does not repeat nonces), and does not ask a query Dec(N, A, C) where C was returned by a preceding query Enc(N, A, M).*

3   Revisiting the Functionality and Modeling of Communication Channels

In constructive cryptography, communication channels are modeled as resources with three interfaces: Interface A for sender Alice, interface B for receiver Bob, and interface E for adversary Eve. Different types of such channels have been studied that differ in the capabilities of the adversary Eve [6,16,18].

In the following paragraphs, we present a formalization of secure and insecure channels and argue why in many applications users might need more services than provided by either. To resolve this mismatch, we introduce a new type of channel, which we call *augmented secure channel (ASC)*, that provides those missing functionalities.

3.1 Existing Formalizations

Insecure Channel. The insecure channel **IC** allows messages to be input repeatedly at interface A. Each message is subsequently leaked at the E-interface. At interface E, arbitrary messages (including those that were previously input at interface A) can be injected such that they are delivered to B. This channel does not give any security guarantees to Alice and Bob. A formal description is provided in Fig. 2.

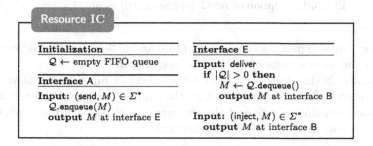

Fig. 2. The insecure channel resource.

Secure Channel. The typical formalization of a secure channel follows the same basic structure as an insecure channel but where the ability of the adversary is limited to seeing the length of the transmitted messages and to deliver messages input at interface A. In particular, the adversary cannot inject new messages or induce out-of-order message delivery. A description of the secure channel can be derived from Fig. 2 by omitting the inject-query and by restricting the leakage at interface E to $|M|$ on inputs (send, M) at interface A.

3.2 What Service Should a Secure Channel Provide?

In many relevant security protocols, like TLS, transmitted data packets are usually divided into a header part and a payload part. While both are required to be authentic, only the payload has to remain confidential.

We further observe that the header often contains context information since binding a message to a given context is good security-engineering practice. Moreover, parts of the context are already known to the receiver. This part does not have to be transmitted but should still be authenticated. This suggests splitting

---

Resource ASC

Initialization

    $S \leftarrow$ empty FIFO queue
    $\mathcal{R} \leftarrow$ empty FIFO queue
    halt $\leftarrow 0$

Interface A

Input: $(\text{send}, E, I, M) \in \mathcal{H}_\mathrm{E} \times \mathcal{H}_\mathrm{I} \times \mathcal{M}$
    $S.\text{enqueue}((E, I, M))$
    output $(E, |M|)$ at interface E

Interface B

Input: $(\text{fetch}, I) \in \mathcal{H}_\mathrm{I}$
    if $|\mathcal{R}| > 0$ **and** halt $= 0$ **then**
        $(E', I', M') \leftarrow \mathcal{R}.\text{dequeue}()$
        if $I' = I \neq \bot$ **then**
            output M' at interface B
        else
            halt $\leftarrow 1$
            output $\bot$ at interface B

Interface E

Input: deliver
    if $|S| > 0$ **and** halt $= 0$ **then**
        $(E, I, M) \leftarrow S.\text{dequeue}()$
        $\mathcal{R}.\text{enqueue}((E, I, M))$
        output (newMsg, E) at interface B

Input: $(\text{injectStop}, E) \in \mathcal{H}_\mathrm{E}$
    if halt $= 0$ **then**
        $\mathcal{R}.\text{enqueue}((\bot, \bot, \bot))$
        output (newMsg, E) at interface B

Fig. 3. Description of **ASC**, an augmented secure channel.

the header into two parts: an explicit part and an implicit part that describe the unknown and known parts of the header, respectively.

We conclude that there is a need for an abstract functionality that allows one to transmit a message together with the explicit part of a header such that the message remains private and the message as well as both the explicit and the implicit part of the header are authenticated.

Augmented Secure Channel. We now present the channel abstraction that formalizes the desired service. The augmented secure channel **ASC** is described in Fig. 3: The sender can provide a triple consisting of the explicit part of a header $E \in \mathcal{H}_\mathrm{E}$, the implicit part of the header $I \in \mathcal{H}_\mathrm{I}$, and a message $M \in \mathcal{M}$. The message remains confidential and the explicit part of the header is leaked at the adversarial interface. If the receiver knows the implicit part of the header, he can recover the message using the query (fetch, I) and verify the authenticity of the message and both parts of the header. If the verification fails, the system stops delivering messages and signals an error by outputting $\bot$. The adversary has the ability to deliver messages and to inject a special element that will terminate the channel at the receiver's side once fetched. Delivering a message notifies the receiver of the new message and provides him with the explicit part of the header.

4 Constructing an Augmented Secure Channel via Authenticated Encryption

After motivating the need for the new channel **ASC**, we now show how to construct it using an AEAD-scheme. We first introduce the assumed resources from which we construct **ASC** and describe the protocol that achieves this construction. We finally prove the security of our construction.

4.1 Assumed Resources

We construct the augmented secure channel from an insecure channel **IC** and a shared secret key. We introduce a shared key resource $\mathbf{SK}_\mathcal{K}$ for some key distribution $\mathcal{K}$ that initially chooses a key according to $\mathcal{K}$ and on input getKey at interface A or B, outputs this key at the corresponding interface; interface E remains inactive. See Fig. 4 for pseudocode. We denote by $[\mathbf{SK}_\mathcal{K}, \mathbf{IC}]$ the resource that provides at each interface access to the corresponding interface of both the key and the channel. The resource $\mathbf{SK}_\mathcal{K}$ can be constructed by some key exchange protocol, e.g., during the TLS handshake.

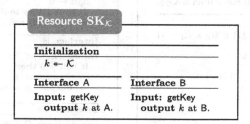

Fig. 4. The shared secret key resource.

4.2 Protocol

A protocol is modeled in constructive cryptography as a pair of *converters* that specify the actions of both honest parties Alice and Bob. A converter is a system with two interfaces: the *inner interface* in is connected to an interface of a resource and the *outer interface* out becomes the new connection point of that resource towards the environment. Attaching a converter to an interface changes the local behavior at that interface and hence yields a new resource.[2]

For an AEAD-scheme $\Pi = (\mathcal{K}, \mathcal{E}, \mathcal{D})$, we present the protocol $(\mathsf{enc}_\Pi, \mathsf{dec}_\Pi)$ as pseudocode in Fig. 5. The converter for the sender, enc_Π, accepts inputs of the form (send, E, I, M) at its outer interface and encrypts the message M using $\mathcal{E}$. The nonce is implemented as a counter, the additional data[3] is $H = (E, I)$ and the key is provided by the key-resource $\mathbf{SK}_\mathcal{K}$. An encoding of the resulting ciphertext and the explicit part of the header is output to the insecure channel **IC**.

---

[2] For example, the resource $\mathsf{enc}_\Pi{}^A\mathsf{dec}_\Pi{}^B\,[\mathbf{SK}_\mathcal{K}, \mathbf{IC}]$ is obtained by attaching Alice's converter enc_Π at interface A and Bob's converter dec_Π at interface B of $[\mathbf{SK}_\mathcal{K}, \mathbf{IC}]$, where the interfaces are indicated by superscripts.

[3] Here, $(E, I) \in \mathcal{H}_E \times \mathcal{H}_I$ denotes an encoding of that pair as an element in $\mathcal{A}$. Abusing notation, we generally do not distinguish between a tuple and its encoding as an element in Σ^*.

The receiver converter dec_Π receives inputs from **IC** and queues the header-ciphertext pairs internally in a queue $\mathcal{Q}$. For each newly arrived message a notification is output at the outer interface. The next ciphertext C in the queue is decrypted if dec_Π is invoked with the implicit part of the corresponding header. The parameters for decryption are again the header as the additional data, the counter as the nonce and the shared key. On success, the corresponding plaintext is output at the outer interface. If decryption fails, the converter stops and signals an error by outputting $\perp$.

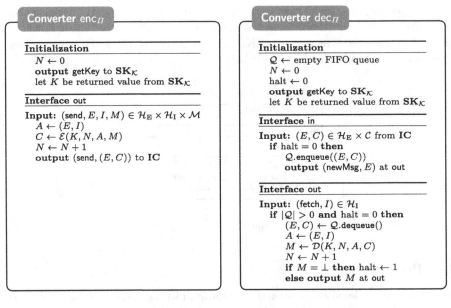

Fig. 5. The protocol converters for the sender (left) and the receiver (right) that construct **ASC** via an AEAD-scheme $\Pi = (\mathcal{K}, \mathcal{E}, \mathcal{D})$.

4.3   The Construction Notion

In order to show that the protocol $(\mathsf{enc}_\Pi, \mathsf{dec}_\Pi)$ constructs **ASC** from $[\mathbf{SK}_\mathcal{K}, \mathbf{IC}]$ in the sense of constructive cryptography, we have to prove the *availability condition* and the *security condition* that are derived from the general construction notion in [16].

Random Experiments. Both conditions make statements about random experiments **DR** in which a distinguisher **D** plays the role of an interactive environment for some resource **R**. The distinguisher **D** is a system that provides inputs to the connected resource and receives the outputs generated by the resource. For example, $\mathbf{D}(\mathsf{enc}_\Pi{}^\mathsf{A}\mathsf{dec}_\Pi{}^\mathsf{B}\,[\mathbf{SK}_\mathcal{K}, \mathbf{IC}])$ is the experiment that captures "the protocol in action" in the environment provided by **D**. More concretely, in each step of these experiments, the distinguisher provides an input to one of the interfaces A, B, or E and observes the output that is generated in reaction to that input. This process continues iteratively by having $\mathbf{D}$ providing adaptively the next input and receiving the next output. The experiment ends by $\mathbf{D}$ outputting a bit 0 or 1 that indicates its guess to which system it is connected. The *distinguishing advantage* of $\mathbf{D}$ for two resources $\mathbf{R}$ and $\mathbf{S}$ is defined as

$$\Delta^{\mathbf{D}}\left(\mathbf{R},\mathbf{S}\right) \;=\; \Pr\left[\mathbf{D}\mathbf{R}=1\right] - \Pr\left[\mathbf{D}\mathbf{S}=1\right].$$

Availability Condition. The first condition captures the situation when no attacker interferes with the protocol execution. We require that in this case, the intended functionality is available to the honest parties. This condition can be seen as a correctness condition for the protocol.

No attacker being present is formalized by a special converter dlv that is attached at interface E and always ensures the *delivery* of messages. Concretely, on any input at its inner interface, dlv outputs deliver to the channel connected to its inner interface and does not provide any service at its outer interface. Formally, the availability condition places a bound on the advantage in distinguishing the systems $\mathrm{enc}_\Pi{}^A\mathrm{dec}_\Pi{}^B\mathrm{dlv}^E\,[\mathbf{SK}_{\mathcal{K}},\mathbf{IC}]$ and $\mathrm{dlv}^E\,\mathbf{ASC}$, i.e., a bound on

$$\Delta^{\mathbf{D}}\left(\mathrm{enc}_\Pi{}^A\mathrm{dec}_\Pi{}^B\mathrm{dlv}^E\,[\mathbf{SK}_{\mathcal{K}},\mathbf{IC}],\mathrm{dlv}^E\,\mathbf{ASC}\right)$$
$$= \Pr\left[\mathbf{D}\left(\mathrm{enc}_\Pi{}^A\mathrm{dec}_\Pi{}^B\mathrm{dlv}^E\,[\mathbf{SK}_{\mathcal{K}},\mathbf{IC}]\right)=1\right] - \Pr\left[\mathbf{D}\left(\mathrm{dlv}^E\,\mathbf{ASC}\right)=1\right]$$

for any distinguisher $\mathbf{D}$.

Security Condition. The second condition captures the situation where an adversary attacks the protocol execution using its capabilities at interface E. The effects of such an attack have to be indistinguishable from the effects in the system corresponding to the constructed resource with some simulator attached at the adversarial interface. This captures that all attacks on the protocol can be translated by a simulator to an attack on the constructed resource. Turned around, if the constructed resource is secure by definition, there is no successful attack on the protocol. More concretely, the security condition places a bound on the advantage in distinguishing the systems $\mathrm{enc}_\Pi{}^A\mathrm{dec}_\Pi{}^B\,[\mathbf{SK}_{\mathcal{K}},\mathbf{IC}]$ and $\mathrm{sim}_{\mathrm{ASC}}^E\,\mathbf{ASC}$ for some simulator $\mathrm{sim}_{\mathrm{ASC}}$, i.e., a bound on

$$\Delta^{\mathbf{D}}\left(\mathrm{enc}_\Pi{}^A\mathrm{dec}_\Pi{}^B\,[\mathbf{SK}_{\mathcal{K}},\mathbf{IC}],\mathrm{sim}_{\mathrm{ASC}}^E\,\mathbf{ASC}\right)$$
$$= \Pr\left[\mathbf{D}\left(\mathrm{enc}_\Pi{}^A\mathrm{dec}_\Pi{}^B\,[\mathbf{SK}_{\mathcal{K}},\mathbf{IC}]\right)=1\right] - \Pr\left[\mathbf{D}\left(\mathrm{sim}_{\mathrm{ASC}}^E\,\mathbf{ASC}\right)=1\right]$$

for any distinguisher $\mathbf{D}$.

4.4   Proof of the Construction

The following two lemmata relate the AEAD-security game to the distinguishing advantage in the availability and security condition, respectively. Note that the availability condition does not follow directly from the correctness of the AEAD-scheme. This is because it is not excluded that a ciphertext gets decrypted to some message $M \neq \bot$ if the wrong additional data is supplied, while the system $\mathsf{dlv}^E \mathbf{ASC}$ always returns $\bot$ if the wrong value for I is input at interface B. We need the security of the AEAD-scheme to conclude that such invalid decryptions can only occur with small probability.

Lemma 1. *There is an (efficient) transformation ρ described in the proof that maps distinguishers $\mathbf{D}$ for two resources to valid adversaries $\mathcal{A} = \rho(\mathbf{D})$ for the AEAD-security game such that*

$$\Delta^{\mathbf{D}}\left(\mathsf{enc}_\Pi{}^A\mathsf{dec}_\Pi{}^B\mathsf{dlv}^E\,[\mathbf{SK}_\mathcal{K}, \mathbf{IC}], \mathsf{dlv}^E\,\mathbf{ASC}\right) \leq \mathbf{Adv}_\Pi^{ae}(\rho(\mathbf{D})).$$

Proof. In $\mathsf{enc}_\Pi{}^A\mathsf{dec}_\Pi{}^B\mathsf{dlv}^E\,[\mathbf{SK}_\mathcal{K}, \mathbf{IC}]$, the converter dlv is attached at interface E and answers any output produced by $\mathbf{IC}$ with the input deliver. This essentially converts $\mathbf{IC}$ into a reliable transmission channel: whatever pair (E, C) is input by converter enc_Π, it is immediately delivered to dec_Π that outputs a notification (newMsg, E) at its outer interface. Furthermore, if the ith input at interface A is $(\mathsf{send}, E_i, I_i, M_i)$, and the ith input at interface B is (fetch, I_i), then the output at interface B is M_i. The same holds for system $\mathsf{dlv}^E\mathbf{ASC}$. Only if the ith input at interface B is (fetch, I_i') for $I_i' \neq I_i$, then the behavior of the two systems can differ: While $\mathsf{dlv}^E\mathbf{ASC}$ always returns $\bot$ in this case, for $\mathsf{enc}_\Pi{}^A\mathsf{dec}_\Pi{}^B\mathsf{dlv}^E\,[\mathbf{SK}_\mathcal{K}, \mathbf{IC}]$ it is possible that a message $M \neq \bot$ is returned. Since this is the only difference between the two systems, we can upper bound the distinguishing advantage by the probability that $\mathbf{D}$ can provoke such an output at interface B when interacting with $\mathsf{enc}_\Pi{}^A\mathsf{dec}_\Pi{}^B\mathsf{dlv}^E\,[\mathbf{SK}_\mathcal{K}, \mathbf{IC}]$. It remains to bound the probability of this event, subsequently denoted by $\mathcal{F}$.

Note that $\mathcal{F}$ occurs exactly if the decryption algorithm of the AEAD-scheme returns a message $M \neq \bot$ on input a different additional data than used for encryption. Based on this observation, we build an adversary $\mathcal{A}$ that emulates a view towards distinguisher $\mathbf{D}$ that is identical to an interaction of $\mathbf{D}$ with $\mathsf{enc}_\Pi{}^A\mathsf{dec}_\Pi{}^B\mathsf{dlv}^E\,[\mathbf{SK}_\mathcal{K}, \mathbf{IC}]$ if $\mathcal{A}$ gets access to its real oracles. The probability of provoking event $\mathcal{F}$ is preserved in this case. In contrast, if $\mathcal{A}$ gets access to the ideal oracles, the condition for event $\mathcal{F}$ cannot be satisfied as we argue below. This is a suitable distinguishing criterion.

More formally, the reduction ρ is defined as follows: The adversary $\mathcal{A} = \rho(\mathbf{D})$ initially sets $N_A, N_B \leftarrow 0$, initializes an empty FIFO queue $\mathcal{Q}$, and then emulates an execution to $\mathbf{D}$ as follows. When $\mathbf{D}$ inputs (send, E, I, M) at interface A, $\mathcal{A}$ ask the query $(N_A, (I, E), M)$ to the oracle Enc to receive the answer C. It then executes $N_A \leftarrow N_A + 1$ and $\mathcal{Q}.\mathsf{enqueue}((E, I, M, C))$, and emulates the output (newMsg, E) at interface B for $\mathbf{D}$. Inputs (fetch, I') at interface B are ignored if $\mathcal{Q}$ is empty. Otherwise, $\mathcal{A}$ executes $(E, I, M, C) \leftarrow \mathcal{Q}.\mathsf{dequeue}()$. If $I' = I$, it sets $M' = M$; if $I' \neq I$, it asks the query $(N_B, (I', E), C)$ to the oracle Dec to receive the answer M'. It then sets $N_B \leftarrow N_B + 1$ and emulates the output M' at interface B for $\mathbf{D}$.

If $M' \neq \bot$ and $I' \neq I$ (i.e., the event $\mathcal{F}$ occurs), $\mathcal{A}$ stops and returns 1. If $M' = \bot$, $\mathcal{A}$ ignores subsequent inputs at interface B. When $\mathbf{D}$ outputs a bit and $\mathcal{F}$ has not occurred, $\mathcal{A}$ returns 0. Observe that if $\mathcal{A}$ gets access to the ideal oracles, the conditions of event $\mathcal{F}$ cannot be met. We conclude the proof by noting that $\mathcal{A}$ is a valid adversary and $\mathbf{Adv}_{\Pi}^{\mathrm{ae}}(\rho(\mathbf{D}))$ equals the probability of the event $\mathcal{F}$.   □

The next lemma implies the security condition of the construction:

Lemma 2. *For the simulator* $\mathrm{sim}_{\mathrm{ASC}}$ *defined in Fig. 6, there is an (efficient) transformation* ρ' *described in the proof that maps distinguishers* $\mathbf{D}$ *for two resources to valid adversaries* $\mathcal{A} = \rho'(\mathbf{D})$ *for the AEAD-security game such that*

$$\Delta^{\mathbf{D}}\left(\mathrm{enc}_{\Pi}{}^{\mathsf{A}}\mathrm{dec}_{\Pi}{}^{\mathsf{B}}[\mathbf{SK}_{\mathcal{K}},\mathbf{IC}],\mathrm{sim}_{\mathrm{ASC}}^{\mathsf{E}}\,\mathbf{ASC}\right) \leq \mathbf{Adv}_{\Pi}^{\mathrm{ae}}(\rho'(\mathbf{D})).$$

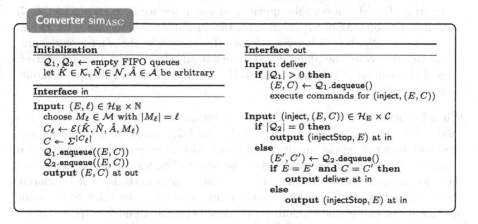

Fig. 6. The simulator for the security condition of the construction of $\mathbf{ASC}$.

Proof. Let $\mathbf{D}$ be a distinguisher for $\mathrm{enc}_{\Pi}{}^{\mathsf{A}}\mathrm{dec}_{\Pi}{}^{\mathsf{B}}[\mathbf{SK}_{\mathcal{K}},\mathbf{IC}]$ and $\mathrm{sim}_{\mathrm{ASC}}^{\mathsf{E}}\mathbf{ASC}$. We define an adversary $\mathcal{A} = \rho'(\mathbf{D})$ for the AEAD-security game as follows. The adversary $\mathcal{A}$ initially sets $N_A, N_B, \mathtt{flag} \leftarrow 0$, initializes an empty FIFO queue $\mathcal{S}$ and two empty lists[4] $\mathcal{L}$ and $\mathcal{R}$, and then emulates an execution of $\mathbf{D}$ by translating inputs of the distinguisher to oracle queries as well as answers from the oracles to outputs of the resource for $\mathbf{D}$. There are four types of inputs $\mathbf{D}$ can make:

(send, E, I, M) **at interface A:** If $\mathcal{R}$ contains strictly less than $N_A + 1$ elements, $\mathcal{A}$ asks the query $(N_A, (E, I), M)$ to the oracle Enc and receives the answer C. It then stores (N_A, E, I, M, C) in the list $\mathcal{L}$, emulates the output (E, C) at interface E for $\mathbf{D}$, sets $N_A \leftarrow N_A + 1$, and executes $\mathcal{S}.\mathrm{enqueue}((E, C))$.
If $\mathcal{R}$ contains at least $N_A + 1$ elements, there is a pair $\mathcal{R}[N_A] = (E, C)$. $\mathcal{A}$ asks the query $(N_A, (E, I), C)$ to the oracle Dec to receive the plaintext M. If

---

[4] For a list L, we denote by $L \parallel x$ the list L with x appended. Furthermore, the ith element of a list L with n elements is denoted by $L[i]$ for $i \in \{0, \ldots, n-1\}$.

$M \neq \perp$, $\mathcal{A}$ sets flag $\leftarrow 1$, returns 1 as its decision and halts. If $M = \perp$, the tuple $(N_A, E, I, \perp, C)$ is stored in $\mathcal{L}$ and $\mathcal{A}$ asks the query $(N_A, (E, I), M)$ to the oracle Enc, receives the answer C and stores (N_A, E, I, M, C) in the list $\mathcal{L}$. Finally, $\mathcal{A}$ emulates the output (E, C) at interface E for **D**, sets $N_A \leftarrow N_A + 1$, and executes $\mathcal{S}$.enqueue$((E, C))$.

deliver **at interface E:** If $|\mathcal{S}| > 0$, $\mathcal{A}$ executes $(E, C) \leftarrow \mathcal{S}$.dequeue() followed by $\mathcal{R} \leftarrow \mathcal{R} \parallel (E, C)$. If $\perp$ has not been output at interface B, $\mathcal{A}$ emulates the output (newMsg, E) at interface B.

(inject, (E, C)) **at interface E:** The adversary $\mathcal{A}$ executes $\mathcal{R} \leftarrow \mathcal{R} \parallel (E, C)$. If $\perp$ has not been output at interface B, $\mathcal{A}$ emulates the output (newMsg, E) at interface B.

(fetch, I) **at interface B:** If $\mathcal{R}$ is empty, the input is ignored. Otherwise, $\mathcal{A}$ executes $(E, C) \leftarrow \mathcal{R}[N_B]$. If $(N_B, E, I, \perp, C)$ is in $\mathcal{L}$, $\mathcal{A}$ emulates the output $\perp$ at interface B and ignores subsequent inputs at interface B. If (N_B, E, I, M, C) is in $\mathcal{L}$ for some $M \in \mathcal{M}$, $\mathcal{A}$ emulates the output M at interface B for **D** and sets $N_B \leftarrow N_B + 1$. Otherwise, $\mathcal{A}$ asks the query $(N_B, (E, I), C)$ to the oracle Dec to receive the plaintext M. The output M is emulated at interface B and the counter N_B is incremented. If $M = \perp$, $\mathcal{A}$ ignores subsequent inputs at interface B.

When **D** outputs a bit b and if flag $= 0$, $\mathcal{A}$ returns b and halts. Note that $\mathcal{A}$ is a valid adversary since it asks at most one Enc and Dec query for each nonce (and therefore does not repeat queries) and never asks a query to the oracle Dec for a ciphertext that has been returned by a query to Enc for the same parameters (because for such ciphertext, the corresponding tuple is in the list $\mathcal{L}$). To analyze the success probability of $\mathcal{A}$, let F be the random variable that takes on the value of flag at the end of the random experiment between $\mathcal{A}$ and $\mathbf{Real}_\Pi$.

We claim that the view of **D** when connected to $\mathrm{sim}_{\mathrm{ASC}}^{\mathsf{E}} \mathbf{ASC}$ is identical to the view emulated by $\mathcal{A}$ with access to the ideal oracles. Additionally, the view of **D** when connected to $\mathrm{enc}_\Pi{}^{\mathsf{A}}\mathrm{dec}_\Pi{}^{\mathsf{B}} [\mathbf{SK}_\mathcal{K}, \mathbf{IC}]$ is identical to the view emulated by $\mathcal{A}$ with access to the real oracles as long as flag $= 0$. This implies the statement of the lemma:

$$\mathbf{Adv}_\Pi^{\mathrm{ae}}(\mathcal{A}) = \Pr[\mathcal{A}^{\mathbf{Real}_\Pi} = 1] - \Pr[\mathcal{A}^{\mathbf{Ideal}_\Pi} = 1]$$

$$= \Pr[F = 1] + \Pr[F = 0] \cdot \underbrace{\Pr[\mathcal{A}^{\mathbf{Real}_\Pi} = 1 \mid F = 0]}_{= \Pr[\mathbf{D}(\mathrm{enc}_\Pi{}^{\mathsf{A}}\mathrm{dec}_\Pi{}^{\mathsf{B}}[\mathbf{SK}_\mathcal{K}, \mathbf{IC}]) = 1]} - \Pr[\mathcal{A}^{\mathbf{Ideal}_\Pi} = 1]$$

$$\geq \Pr\left[\mathbf{D}\left(\mathrm{enc}_\Pi{}^{\mathsf{A}}\mathrm{dec}_\Pi{}^{\mathsf{B}}[\mathbf{SK}_\mathcal{K}, \mathbf{IC}]\right) = 1\right] - \Pr\left[\mathbf{D}\left(\mathrm{sim}_{\mathrm{ASC}}^{\mathsf{E}} \mathbf{ASC}\right) = 1\right]$$

$$= \Delta^{\mathbf{D}}\left(\mathrm{enc}_\Pi{}^{\mathsf{A}}\mathrm{dec}_\Pi{}^{\mathsf{B}}[\mathbf{SK}_\mathcal{K}, \mathbf{IC}], \mathrm{sim}_{\mathrm{ASC}}^{\mathsf{E}} \mathbf{ASC}\right).$$

To prove this claim, we distinguish the possible inputs by **D** and compare the resulting outputs:

(send, E, I, M) **at interface A:** In system $\mathrm{enc}_\Pi{}^{\mathsf{A}}\mathrm{dec}_\Pi{}^{\mathsf{B}} [\mathbf{SK}_\mathcal{K}, \mathbf{IC}]$, the converter enc_Π evaluates $C \leftarrow \mathcal{E}(K, N, (E, I), M)$, where N is the number of sent messages before this input. The explicit part E of the header is sent together with C over **IC**, which outputs the pair (E, C) at interface E. The same output is emulated by $\mathcal{A}$ in the real game since the oracle Enc in this case also evaluates the algorithm $\mathcal{E}$.

In the system $\text{sim}^{\mathsf{E}}_{\text{ASC}}$ **ASC**, the triple (E, I, M) is inserted into the senders queue of **ASC** and the pair $(E, |M|)$ is output to the simulator sim_{ASC}, which in turn generates a uniformly random ciphertext C of the same length as ciphertexts for M. Note that by Definition 1, the length of ciphertexts only depend on the length of the message, so the values of $\hat{K}$, $\hat{N}$, and $\hat{A}$ used by sim_{ASC} to determine this length are irrelevant. The simulator then stores (E, C) in its own queue for later reference and outputs this pair at interface E. Note that Enc in **Ideal**$_\Pi$ generates ciphertexts with the same distribution, so the view emulated by $\mathcal{A}$ is identical.

deliver **at interface** E: If the sender's queue it non-empty, the next element (E, C) is dequeued from it and **D** receives the output (newMsg, E) from interface B if there has not been an output $\perp$ in both systems and in the emulated view.

$(\mathsf{inject}, (E, C))$ **at interface** E: In $\text{enc}_\Pi{}^{\mathsf{A}}\text{dec}_\Pi{}^{\mathsf{B}}\,[\mathbf{SK}_\mathcal{K}, \mathbf{IC}]$, the injected pair is inserted into the receiver's queue of the converter dec_Π and the notification (newMsg, E) is output at interface B.

In $\text{sim}^{\mathsf{E}}_{\text{ASC}}$ **ASC**, the simulator checks whether the injected pair is equal to the top-element (E', C') of its queue $\mathcal{Q}_2$. If this is the case, the simulator outputs deliver with the effect that the notification (newMsg, E) is output at interface B. If $(E, C) \neq (E', C')$, sim_{ASC} injects a stop element by $(\mathsf{injectStop}, E)$, which also yields the output (newMsg, E) at interface B. Note that by definition of **ASC**, this element is guaranteed to yield $\perp$ when fetched at interface B.

We see that in the emulation by $\mathcal{A}$, **D** receives (newMsg, E) from interface B if there has not been an output $\perp$ before at interface B. The same holds for both systems $\text{enc}_\Pi{}^{\mathsf{A}}\text{dec}_\Pi{}^{\mathsf{B}}\,[\mathbf{SK}_\mathcal{K}, \mathbf{IC}]$ and $\text{sim}^{\mathsf{E}}_{\text{ASC}}$ **ASC** in an interaction with **D**.

(fetch, I) **at interface** B: Assume this is the ith input at interface B, there have been at least i inputs deliver or inject at interface E, and there has not been an output $\perp$ so far (otherwise the input is always ignored). In the system $\text{enc}_\Pi{}^{\mathsf{A}}\text{dec}_\Pi{}^{\mathsf{B}}\,[\mathbf{SK}_\mathcal{K}, \mathbf{IC}]$, the converter dec_Π retrieves the top element of its queue. This value is equal to the ith delivered or injected pair (E, C) at interface E. The converter dec_Π then computes $M \leftarrow \mathcal{D}(K, i - 1, (E, I), C)$ and outputs M.

In the view emulated by $\mathcal{A}$ in the real game, (E, C) also corresponds to the ith delivered or injected pair. If the tuple $(i - 1, E, I, M, C)$ is found in $\mathcal{L}$ for some $M \in \mathcal{M}$, M is output at interface B. By the correctness of the AEAD-scheme, M is then equal to the output of the algorithm $\mathcal{D}$ for the corresponding parameters. If no such tuple is in $\mathcal{L}$, $\mathcal{A}$ decrypts C with the corresponding parameters using the oracle Dec and also outputs the resulting message at interface B. Since the real oracle Dec evaluates $\mathcal{D}$, we conclude that the views are identical in this case.

In $\text{sim}^{\text{E}}_{\text{ASC}} \textbf{ASC}$, the resource checks whether $I = I'$, where (E', I', M') is the next element in the queue $\mathcal{R}$. If this is the case, it outputs M' at interface B, otherwise it outputs $\perp$. Furthermore, only those elements can be successfully fetched that do not correspond to stop-elements $(\perp, \perp, \perp)$. By construction of the simulator, the ith element of the sender's queue is only delivered if the ith injected pair (E, C) at interface E matches the simulated pair output at interface E in reaction to the ith input $(\text{send}, E', I', M')$ at interface A. In any other case, a stop-element is injected into the receiver's queue.

To determine whether the values of the ith injection match the simulated values for the ith input at interface A, sim_{ASC} maintains the queue $\mathcal{Q}_2$ such that its top element, after i injections, stores exactly these values. Note that the queue $\mathcal{Q}_1$ on the other hand is only needed to simulate the queue of the insecure channel $\textbf{IC}$ in the real world and to figure out the next message in the simulation of a deliver-request.

In the view emulated by $\mathcal{A}$ in the ideal game, the list $\mathcal{L}$ ensures that the same message M' is output at interface B if all the values match as above. Furthermore, if there is not a match, the output is $\perp$ because the ideal oracle Dec always returns $\perp$. In particular, the condition that the ith simulated pair correspond to the ith injected pair is equivalent to requiring that the tuple $(i - 1, E, I, M, C)$, for some message M, is an element of $\mathcal{L}$. Hence, the views for $\textbf{D}$ are also identical in this case.

This concludes the proof of the claim and thus of the lemma.   □

The following theorem summarizes the results from Lemmas 1 and 2.

Theorem 1. *The protocol* $(\text{enc}_\Pi, \text{dec}_\Pi)$ *constructs* $\textbf{ASC}$ *from* $[\textbf{SK}_\mathcal{K}, \textbf{IC}]$. *More specifically, we have for the simulator* sim_{ASC} *in Fig. 6 and for all distinguishers* $\textbf{D}$

$$\Delta^{\textbf{D}} \left(\text{enc}_\Pi{}^{\text{A}} \text{dec}_\Pi{}^{\text{B}} \text{dlv}^{\text{E}} [\textbf{SK}_\mathcal{K}, \textbf{IC}], \text{dlv}^{\text{E}} \textbf{ASC} \right) \leq \textbf{Adv}^{\text{ae}}_\Pi(\rho(\textbf{D}))$$

$$\text{and} \quad \Delta^{\textbf{D}} \left(\text{enc}_\Pi{}^{\text{A}} \text{dec}_\Pi{}^{\text{B}} [\textbf{SK}_\mathcal{K}, \textbf{IC}], \text{sim}^{\text{E}}_{\text{ASC}} \textbf{ASC} \right) \leq \textbf{Adv}^{\text{ae}}_\Pi(\rho'(\textbf{D})),$$

where ρ *and* ρ' *are the reductions defined in the proofs of Lemmas 1 and 2, respectively.*

5   The Goal of the TLS 1.3 Record Layer

Version 1.3 of TLS is currently in draft state at the IETF.[5] Unlike TLS 1.2, the new version of the record payload protection protocol mandates AEAD ciphers[6] and the format of the authenticated data has changed. More specifically, in the

---

[5] We refer to the most recent draft (retrieved on August 28, 2015) that is available for download at https://tools.ietf.org/html/draft-ietf-tls-tls13-08.

[6] Previous versions of TLS supported MAC-then-Encrypt modes.

current draft, the authenticated data in TLS 1.3 consists of the sequence number of the current fragment, the protocol version, and the message type, e.g., whether it is an "alert," a "handshake," or an "application" message. The nonce of the AEAD cipher is chosen in a specific way based on the sequence number.[7] This section treats the record protocol and assumes that a shared key has been derived in the TLS handshake.

5.1 Formalizing the Goal of TLS Record Payload Protection

What does it mean for the TLS record layer to be secure? We propose a simple answer to this question in the form of a new channel abstraction. Each packet in the TLS record layer contains a payload and specifies its associated type. While the entire packet is authenticated, only the content of the packet has to be private and hidden from the attacker. This resembles a specific type of channel: a secure channel where messages are tagged with a non-private type-flag from the set of types $\mathcal{T} := \{0, \ldots, 255\}$. The TLS record payload protection can be considered secure if it provably constructs this secure channel. We formalize this channel as the resource $\mathbf{SEC}_{\mathrm{TLS}}$ and provide a formal description thereof in Fig. 7.[8]

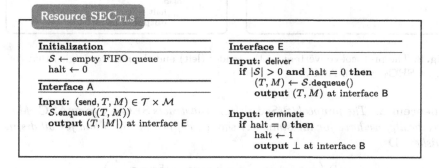

Fig. 7. Description of the channel $\mathbf{SEC}_{\mathrm{TLS}}$.

Note that in contrast to **ASC**, the channel $\mathbf{SEC}_{\mathrm{TLS}}$ does not contain an implicit part of the header and messages are directly delivered to Bob without the need to fetch them. Therefore, $\mathbf{SEC}_{\mathrm{TLS}}$ does not allow the authentication of data without sending it. One can thus view $\mathbf{SEC}_{\mathrm{TLS}}$ as an augmented secure channel that is more restricted than **ASC** but also simpler to use.

---

[7] Until draft 5, the choice of the nonce was not specified, and it was transmitted together with the ciphertext.

[8] While applications usually provide data to TLS as a sequence of multi-byte strings, TLS only guarantees that the same stream of bytes, as the concatenation of the individual strings, is delivered. TLS does not guarantee that the boundaries between the multi-byte strings are preserved as chosen by the application, cf. [7]. The message M in Fig. 7 is to be understood as the multi-byte string used within the TLS protocol, which is not necessarily the same as chosen by the higher-level application.

5.2 Achieving the Goal

In this section, we present a construction of the channel $\mathbf{SEC}_{\mathrm{TLS}}$ from $\mathbf{ASC}$. To this end, we introduce the protocol (tlsSnd, tlsRcv), which is described in Fig. 8 and manages the usage of the resource $\mathbf{ASC}$. We adhere closely to the current TLS specification in setting the corresponding values. The implicit part I of the header consists of the protocol version V (which corresponds to $\{3,4\}$ and consists of two bytes[9]) and the explicit part E consists of the message type T (one byte).

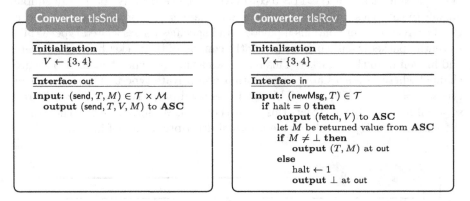

Fig. 8. The protocol converters for the sender (left) and the receiver (right) that construct $\mathbf{SEC}_{\mathrm{TLS}}$ from $\mathbf{ASC}$.

Theorem 2. *The protocol* (tlsSnd, tlsRcv) *constructs* $\mathbf{SEC}_{\mathrm{TLS}}$ *from* $\mathbf{ASC}$. *More specifically, we have for the simulator* $\mathrm{sim}_{\mathrm{TLS}}$ *defined in Fig. 9 and for all distinguishers* $\mathbf{D}$

$$\Delta^{\mathbf{D}}\left(\mathrm{tlsSnd}^{\mathsf{A}}\mathrm{tlsRcv}^{\mathsf{B}}\mathrm{dlv}^{\mathsf{E}}\mathbf{ASC}, \mathrm{dlv}^{\mathsf{E}}\mathbf{SEC}_{\mathrm{TLS}}\right) = 0 \qquad (1)$$

$$and \quad \Delta^{\mathbf{D}}\left(\mathrm{tlsSnd}^{\mathsf{A}}\mathrm{tlsRcv}^{\mathsf{B}}\mathbf{ASC}, \mathrm{sim}_{\mathrm{TLS}}^{\mathsf{E}}\mathbf{SEC}_{\mathrm{TLS}}\right) = 0. \qquad (2)$$

Proof. The availability condition (1) is easy to verify: On input (send, T, M) at interface A, the system $\mathrm{dlv}^{\mathsf{E}}\mathbf{SEC}_{\mathrm{TLS}}$ directly outputs (T, M) at interface B. The same holds for system $\mathrm{tlsSnd}^{\mathsf{A}}\mathrm{tlsRcv}^{\mathsf{B}}\mathrm{dlv}^{\mathsf{E}}\mathbf{ASC}$: On input (send, T, M), the converter tlsSnd inputs (send, T, V, M) to $\mathbf{ASC}$. The converter tlsRcv then obtains the notification (newMsg, T) and queries (fetch, V) to $\mathbf{ASC}$, which results in the output M from $\mathbf{ASC}$, which in turn triggers tlsRcv to output (T, M). Since the two systems behave identically, every distinguisher has advantage 0 in distinguishing them, i.e., (1) follows.

To verify the security condition (2), we distinguish the possible inputs to the system:

Input (send, T, M) **at interface** A: In the system $\text{tlsSnd}^A\text{tlsRcv}^B\textbf{ASC}$, this input results in the converter tlsSnd inputting (send, T, V, M) to **ASC**, which yields the output $(T, |M|)$ at interface E of **ASC**. In $\text{sim}^E_{\text{TLS}}\textbf{SEC}_{\text{TLS}}$, the values $(T, |M|)$ are given to the simulator, which then outputs $(T, |M|)$ at its outer interface.

Input deliver **at interface** E: In $\text{tlsSnd}^A\text{tlsRcv}^B\textbf{ASC}$, if the queue S in **ASC** is empty, nothing happens. Otherwise, the converter tlsRcv receives the notification (newMsg, T). Then, tlsRcv inputs (fetch, V) to **ASC** if it has not already halted. In this case, there have been only inputs deliver at interface E and therefore the verification within **ASC** succeeds. Thus, tlsRcv obtains the message M and outputs (T, M).

In $\text{sim}^E_{\text{TLS}}\textbf{SEC}_{\text{TLS}}$, the simulator inputs deliver to $\textbf{SEC}_{\text{TLS}}$. If S in $\textbf{SEC}_{\text{TLS}}$ is empty, nothing happens. Otherwise, the next tuple (T, M) in S is output at interface B if the channel has not halted before.

Input (injectStop, T) **at interface** E: In the system $\text{tlsSnd}^A\text{tlsRcv}^B\textbf{ASC}$, the notification (newMsg, T) is output to tlsRcv. The converter tlsRcv then outputs (fetch, V) to **ASC** and since the element is an inserted empty element, the verification within **ASC** fails and tlsRcv outputs $\bot$ and stops by setting halt $\leftarrow 1$.

In $\text{sim}^E_{\text{TLS}}\textbf{SEC}_{\text{TLS}}$, sim_{TLS} terminates the session, which causes the output $\bot$ at interface B and results in no further messages being processed by Bob.

To see that the two described systems behave identically, we only have to observe that they both terminate the session if an empty message is injected into the channel and that all inputs are delivered in order until termination. We again conclude that every distinguisher has advantage 0 in distinguishing these systems, i.e., we obtain (2). This completes the proof.   □

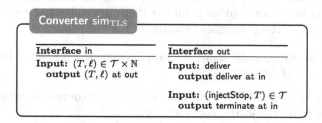

Fig. 9. The simulator for the security condition of the construction of $\textbf{SEC}_{\text{TLS}}$.

5.3   Using the Protocol in TLS 1.3

We have shown that (tlsSnd, tlsRcv) constructs $\textbf{SEC}_{\text{TLS}}$ from **ASC**. Since by Theorem 1, the protocol $(\text{enc}_\Pi, \text{dec}_\Pi)$ constructs the channel **ASC** from a shared secret key and an insecure channel, we can invoke the composition theorem of constructive cryptography to conclude that the composition of both protocols

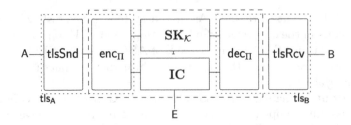

Fig. 10. Illustration of the composed protocol $(\text{tls}_A, \text{tls}_B)$. For a secure AEAD-scheme, the resource $\text{enc}_\Pi{}^A\text{dec}_\Pi{}^B[\mathbf{SK}_\mathcal{K}, \mathbf{IC}]$ inside the dashed box in the center is indistinguishable from $\text{sim}_{\text{ASC}}^E\mathbf{ASC}$.

constructs $\mathbf{SEC}_{\text{TLS}}$ from a shared key $\mathbf{SK}_\mathcal{K}$ and an insecure channel $\mathbf{IC}$. See Fig. 10 for a graphical illustration of the composed protocol $(\text{tls}_A, \text{tls}_B)$.

The protocol for the sender tls_A works as follows: On input (send, T, M), the message M is encrypted with a call to the AEAD-scheme as $C \leftarrow \mathcal{E}(K, N, A, M)$, where K is the shared key retrieved from $\mathbf{SK}_\mathcal{K}$, N is the internal counter and $A = (T, V)$ is the additional data. Finally, the pair (T, C) is sent over the insecure channel.

The protocol for the receiver tls_B works analogously: On input a new pair (T, C) from $\mathbf{IC}$, the ciphertext is decrypted to $M \leftarrow \mathcal{D}(K, N, A, C)$, where N is the internal counter, A is the additional data, and K is the shared key as above. Note that the implicit part of the header is fixed and provided by tlsRcv immediately after receiving the notification (newMsg, T) from dec_Π.

In summary, the protocol $(\text{tls}_A, \text{tls}_B)$ provably achieves the goal of the TLS record layer. Note that the key resource $\mathbf{SK}_\mathcal{K}$ is constructed by the handshake protocol if both parties are authenticated. In [14], the authors consider the more general case where only one party is authenticated, which yields a weaker key resource. We have chosen the setting where both sides are authenticated to simplify the presentation, but we point out that our result can be generalized to the more general setting straightforwardly.

Our Proposal. Our results shown in this paper suggest minor modifications to the current draft of TLS 1.3:

1. The nonce of the AEAD scheme can be set to the counter value left-padded with zeros to be of the appropriate length.
2. The sequence number can be removed from the additional data part.
3. After the handshake, the version number does not need to be transmitted explicitly as part of the TLS record. However, it should still be part of the additional data.

Our proposal comes with a rigorous security proof, which guarantees that our choice of parameters is adequate. For example, this clarifies that the nonce need not be unpredictable or derived from other values, which is a priori unclear.

We are aware that item 3 would require a new structure of TLS fragments and hence there might be objections against this change. However, we stress that only respecting item 1 and item 2 of our proposal is also secure (i.e., constructs SEC_{TLS}). The proof for the case where the version number is moved to the explicit part of the header is essentially identical to the one presented in Sect. 5.2.

Acknowledgments. Ueli Maurer was supported by the Swiss National Science Foundation (SNF), project no. 200020-132794. Björn Tackmann was supported by the Swiss National Science Foundation (SNF) via Fellowship no. P2EZP2_155566 and the NSF grants CNS-1116800 and CNS-1228890. Much of the work on this paper was done while Phil Rogaway was visiting Ueli Maurer's group at ETH Zurich. Many thanks to Ueli for hosting that sabbatical. Rogaway was also supported by NSF grants CNS-1228828 and CNS-1314885.

References

1. Backes, M., Pfitzmann, B., Waidner, M.: The reactive simulatability (RSIM) framework for asynchronous systems. Inf. Comput. **205**(12), 1685–1720 (2007)
2. Bellare, M., Namprempre, C.: Authenticated encryption: relations among notions and analysis of the generic composition paradigm. In: Okamoto, T. (ed.) ASIACRYPT 2000. LNCS, vol. 1976, pp. 531–545. Springer, Heidelberg (2000)
3. Bellare, M., Rogaway, P.: Encode-then-encipher encryption: how to exploit nonces or redundancy in plaintexts for efficient cryptography. In: Okamoto, T. (ed.) ASIACRYPT 2000. LNCS, vol. 1976, pp. 317–330. Springer, Heidelberg (2000)
4. Canetti, R.: Universally composable security: a new paradigm for cryptographic protocols. In: 42nd IEEE Symposium on Foundations of Computer Science, pp. 136–145. IEEE (2001)
5. Canetti, R., Krawczyk, H., Nielsen, J.B.: Relaxing chosen-ciphertext security. In: Boneh, D. (ed.) CRYPTO 2003. LNCS, vol. 2729, pp. 565–582. Springer, Heidelberg (2003)
6. Coretti, S., Maurer, U., Tackmann, B.: Constructing confidential channels from authenticated channels—public-key encryption revisited. In: Sako, K., Sarkar, P. (eds.) ASIACRYPT 2013, Part I. LNCS, vol. 8269, pp. 134–153. Springer, Heidelberg (2013)
7. Fischlin, M., Günther, F., Marson, G.A., Paterson, K.G.: Data is a stream: security of stream-based channels. In: Gennaro, R., Robshaw, M. (eds.) CRYPTO 2015. LNCS, vol. 9216, pp. 545–564. Springer, Heidelberg (2015)
8. Gajek, S., Manulis, M., Pereira, O., Sadeghi, A.-R., Schwenk, J.: Universally composable security analysis of TLS. In: Baek, J., Bao, F., Chen, K., Lai, X. (eds.) ProvSec 2008. LNCS, vol. 5324, pp. 313–327. Springer, Heidelberg (2008)
9. He, C., Sundararajan, M., Datta, A., Derek, A., Mitchell, J.: A modular correctness proof of IEEE 802.11i and TLS. In: Proceedings of the ACM Conference on Computer and Communications Security (ACM CCS 2005), pp. 2–15 (2005)
10. Hoang, V.T., Krovetz, T., Rogaway, P.: Robust authenticated-encryption AEZ and the problem that it solves. In: Oswald, E., Fischlin, M. (eds.) EUROCRYPT 2015. LNCS, vol. 9056, pp. 15–44. Springer, Heidelberg (2015)
11. Jager, T., Kohlar, F., Schäge, S., Schwenk, J.: On the security of TLS-DHE in the standard model. In: Safavi-Naini, R., Canetti, R. (eds.) CRYPTO 2012. LNCS, vol. 7417, pp. 273–293. Springer, Heidelberg (2012)

12. Jutla, C.S.: Encryption modes with almost free message integrity. In: Pfitzmann, B. (ed.) EUROCRYPT 2001. LNCS, vol. 2045, pp. 529–544. Springer, Heidelberg (2001)

13. Katz, J., Yung, M.: Unforgeable encryption and chosen ciphertext secure modes of operation. In: Schneier, B. (ed.) FSE 2000. LNCS, vol. 1978, pp. 284–299. Springer, Heidelberg (2001)

14. Kohlweiss, M., Maurer, U., Onete, C., Tackmann, B., Venturi, D.: (De-)Constructing TLS. Cryptology ePrint Archive, Report 2014/020 (2014)

15. Krawczyk, H., Paterson, K.G., Wee, H.: On the security of the TLS protocol: a systematic analysis. In: Canetti, R., Garay, J.A. (eds.) CRYPTO 2013, Part I. LNCS, vol. 8042, pp. 429–448. Springer, Heidelberg (2013)

16. Maurer, U.: Constructive cryptography – a new paradigm for security definitions and proofs. In: Mödersheim, S., Palamidessi, C. (eds.) TOSCA 2011. LNCS, vol. 6993, pp. 33–56. Springer, Heidelberg (2012)

17. Maurer, U., Renner, R.: Abstract cryptography. In: Chazelle, B. (ed.) The Second Symposium on Innovations in Computer Science, ICS 2011, pp. 1–21. Tsinghua University Press (2011)

18. Maurer, U., Rüedlinger, A., Tackmann, B.: Confidentiality and integrity: a constructive perspective. In: Cramer, R. (ed.) TCC 2012. LNCS, vol. 7194, pp. 209–229. Springer, Heidelberg (2012)

19. Morrissey, P., Smart, N.P., Warinschi, B.: A modular security analysis of the TLS handshake protocol. In: Pieprzyk, J. (ed.) ASIACRYPT 2008. LNCS, vol. 5350, pp. 55–73. Springer, Heidelberg (2008)

20. Paterson, K.G., Ristenpart, T., Shrimpton, T.: Tag size *Does* matter: attacks and proofs for the TLS record protocol. In: Lee, D.H., Wang, X. (eds.) ASIACRYPT 2011. LNCS, vol. 7073, pp. 372–389. Springer, Heidelberg (2011)

21. Pfitzmann, B., Waidner, M.: A model for asynchronous reactive systems and its application to secure message transmission. In: Proceedings of the 2001 IEEE Symposium on Security and Privacy, pp. 184–200. IEEE Computer Society (2001)

22. Rogaway, P.: Authenticated-encryption with associated-data. In: Proceedings of the 9th ACM Conference on Computer and Communications Security, pp. 98–107. ACM (2002)

23. Rogaway, P., Bellare, M., Black, J.: OCB: a block-cipher mode of operation for efficient authenticated encryption. ACM Trans. Inf. Syst. Secur. (TISSEC) **6**(3), 365–403 (2003)

24. Rogaway, P., Shrimpton, T.: A provable-security treatment of the key-wrap problem. In: Vaudenay, S. (ed.) EUROCRYPT 2006. LNCS, vol. 4004, pp. 373–390. Springer, Heidelberg (2006)

25. Wagner D., Schneier, B.: Analysis of the SSL 3.0 protocol. In: USENIX - Workshop on Electronic Commerce, pp. 29–40 (1996)

Sound Proof of Proximity of Knowledge

Serge Vaudenay[(✉)]

EPFL, 1015 Lausanne, Switzerland
serge.vaudenay@epfl.ch
http://lasec.epfl.ch

Abstract. Public-key distance bounding schemes are needed to defeat relay attacks in payment systems. So far, only five such schemes exist, but fail to fully protect against malicious provers. In this paper, we solve this problem. We provide a full formalism to define the proof of proximity of knowledge (PoPoK). Protocols should succeed if and only if a prover holding a secret is within the proximity of the verifier. Like proofs of knowledge, these protocols must satisfy completeness, soundness (protection for the honest verifier), and security (protection for the honest prover). We construct ProProx, the very first sound PoPoK.

1 Introduction

Relay attacks can be a serious threat against applications such as NFC-based payment: for small payments, there is typically no action required on the creditcard or smartphone (beyond approaching to the terminal) such as typing a PIN code. So, a man-in-the-middle adversary could just relay communications between the payment device of the victim and the terminal to make payments on the behalf of the holder. The limit of the speed of communication was proposed to solve this problem [4]. Brands and Chaum [11] introduced the notion of *distance-bounding protocol* to prove that a *prover* is close enough to a *verifier*. This relies on information being local and unable to travel faster than the speed of light. So, an RFID reader can identify when participants are close enough because the round-trip communication time in challenge/response rounds have been small enough.

The literature considers several threat models.

- *Relay attack*: an adversary relay messages between a far-away honest prover and a verifier, trying to make the verifier accept. This is extended by *Mafia fraud* [15] where the adversary can also modify messages. This is further extended by *Man-in-the-Middle attack* [6,8,9] where the attack follows a learning phase where the prover could be close-by. In *Impersonation fraud* [2], the prover is absent and the adversary tries to impersonate the prover to the verifier. These threat models have in common that the prover is honest.
- *Distance fraud* [11]: a far-away malicious prover tries to pass the protocol.
- *Terrorist fraud* [15]: a far-away malicious prover, with the help of an adversary, tries to make the verifier accept, but without giving the adversary any advantage to later pass the protocol alone. This extends to *Collusion fraud* [6,8,9]

© Springer International Publishing Switzerland 2015
M.-H. Au and A. Miyaji (Eds.): ProvSec 2015, LNCS 9451, pp. 105–126, 2015.
DOI: 10.1007/978-3-319-26059-4_6

where the goal of the adversary is to run a man-in-the-middle attack. Terrorist fraud is also related to the notion of *soundness* [25]: whenever the verifier accepts, there must be an extractor who can reconstruct the secret of the prover based on the view of all close-by participants, possibly after several iterations. An hybrid model between distance fraud and terrorist fraud is the one of *Distance hijacking* [14]: A far-away prover takes advantage of some honest, active provers to make the verifier accept.

One of the first models to capture these notions was proposed by Avoine *et al.* [1]. However, it was not formal enough. Then, two parallel models were developed: the BMV model [6,8,9] and the DFKO model [16]. There exist many symmetric distance-bounding protocols but so far only the SKI protocol [5–7,9] (based on the BMV model), the Fischlin-Onete (FO) protocol [18] (based on the DFKO model), and DB1, DB2, and their extensions [10,24] (combining both SKI and FO in the BMV model) provide an all-encompassing proven security.

Public-Key Distance Bounding. In interactive proofs, the prover does not share a secret key with the verifier. The verifier only knows a public key. However, so far, only the following distance-bounding protocols are in the public key model: the Brands-Chaum protocol [11], the Bussard-Bagga protocol [12], the Hermans-Peeters-Onete (HPO) protocol [22][1], and PrivDB [26]. The Bussard-Bagga protocol was broken by Bay et al. [3] and none of the others protect against terrorist fraud. Additionally, the protocol VSSDB was presented at the BalkanCryptSec'14 conference by Gambs *et al.* It is based on the random oracle model, but the instanciability is questionable, as it requires a NIZK proof on statements of form $\{x : c = f(x, H(x))\}$ where H is a random oracle. As far as we know, this does not exist. So, the problem of making a fully secure public-key distance-bounding protocol is still open.

In Table 1 we update the list from [26] with all known public-key distance bounding protocols and the proven status of their security with respect to Man-in-the-Middle (MiM), Distance Fraud (DF), Distance Hijacking (DH), Collusion Fraud (CF), Privacy, and Strong privacy.

Contribution. In clear, our contributions in this paper are as follows.

- We adapt the framework of [10] in the BMV model to provide a full formalization of public-key distance-bounding. We specify our new primitive: the *proof of proximity of knowledge (PoPoK)*.
- We change the definition of soundness from [10,25] to make it closer to the one of interactive proofs. So, our model is pretty natural and nicely connects recent work on distance bounding (such as the BMV model [6,8,9]) and interactive proofs.
- We construct ProProx, the very first sound PoPoK. It is based on the quadratic residuosity problem, using the Goldwasser-Micali encryption [20,21] as a homomorphic perfectly binding commitment $\mathsf{Com}(b; \rho)$ and the Fiat-Shamir protocol [17]. We also use a function H which is assumed to be such that $x \mapsto$

---

[1] A variant of the HPO protocol offers anonymous authentication [19].

Table 1. Existing public-key distance bounding protocols

Protocol	MiM	DF	DH	CF	Privacy	Strong privacy
Brands-Chaum [11]	secure	secure	insecure	insecure	insecure	insecure
DBPK-Log [12]		insecure		insecure	insecure	insecure
HPO [22]	secure	secure		insecure	secure	insecure
GOR [19]	secure	secure	insecure	insecure	insecure	insecure
privDB [26]	secure	secure	secure	insecure	secure	secure
ProProx (this paper)	secure	secure	secure	secure	insecure	insecure
eProProx [27]	secure	secure	secure	secure	secure	secure

$(\mathsf{Com}(b_1; H(x,1)), \ldots, \mathsf{Com}(b_n; H(x,n)))$ is a one-way function, where $x = (b_1, \ldots, b_n)$. (An easy instance is when H is a random oracle.)

- We provide a technique to prove security and soundness. Essentially, we construct a straightline extractor based on the "Fundamental Lemma" and prove that the protocol is zero-knowledge.

2 Model and Definitions

We refine the security definitions and other tools from the BMV model [6,8,9,25]. Constructions depend on some security parameter λ which is omitted for more readability. A *constant* does not depend on λ, while parameters defining cryptographic constructions do. Algorithms run in probabilistic polynomial-time (PPT) in terms of λ. A real function $f(\lambda)$ is negligible if for any d, we have $f(\lambda) = \mathcal{O}(\lambda^{-d})$, as $\lambda \to +\infty$. We denote $f(\lambda) = \mathsf{negl}(\lambda)$. We also define

$$\mathsf{Tail}(n, \tau, \rho) = \sum_{i=\tau}^{n} \binom{n}{i} \rho^i (1 - \rho)^{n-i}$$

2.1 Computational, Communication, and Adversarial Models

In our settings, participants are interactive Turing machines running PPT algorithms. We follow the BMV model [6,8,9]: we assume that participants have a *location* which is an element of a metric space $\mathcal{S}$, with a distance function d. If a participant π_1 at a location loc_1 executes a special command $\mathsf{send}(\pi_2, m)$ at time t to send a message m to a participant π_2 at location loc_2, the message m is received by π_2 at time $t + d(\mathsf{loc}_1, \mathsf{loc}_2)$. Furthermore, any malicious participant π_3 at some location loc_3 could see this message m at time $t + d(\mathsf{loc}_1, \mathsf{loc}_3)$. We assume no authentication: π_2 does not know if the message really comes from π_1. There is however an exception preventing m from being delivered to π_2: if π_2 is honest and some (malicious) participant π_3 at some location loc_3 has sent a special signal $\mathsf{corrupt}(\pi_1, \pi_2)$ at time t', m is not delivered to π_2 if

$t+d(\mathsf{loc}_1, \mathsf{loc}_2) \geq t'+d(\mathsf{loc}_3, \mathsf{loc}_2)$. This condition is a consequence of the information traveling with a speed limit: whenever a malicious participant π_3 corrupts a $\pi_1 \to \pi_2$ channel, π_2 will only receive the messages from π_1 until his corruption signal emitted from π_3 reaches π_2.

Note that once the $\pi_1 \to \pi_2$ channel is corrupted, π_3 can still see the message m sent by π_1 and decide to send any m' to π_2, either depending on m if he waits to receive m, or not. The crux is that either m' is independent of m, or it is delivered at a later time, when $d(\mathsf{loc}_1, \mathsf{loc}_2) < d(\mathsf{loc}_1, \mathsf{loc}_3) + d(\mathsf{loc}_3, \mathsf{loc}_2)$.

The communication model is only used to prove the "Fundamental Lemma". We take here a version of it inspired from [24].

Lemma 1 (Fundamental Lemma). *Assume a multiparty protocol execution with a distinguished participant $\mathcal{V}$, the set* Far *of all participants within a distance to $\mathcal{V}$ larger than B, and the set* Close *of all other participants. At some time t in the execution, $\mathcal{V}$ broadcasts a random challenge c based on some fresh coins and waits for a response r for up to $2B$ time. (If no answer is received, we set $r = \bot$.) We let $\exp_c$ be the experiment in which the challenge is equal to c. For each instance U, we denote by View_U his initial view. For $U \neq \mathcal{V}$, this is common to all $\exp_c$. We further denote by $\mathsf{Incoming}_U^c(E)$ the list of all incoming messages seen by U until time $t+2B-d(\mathcal{V}, U)$ in $\exp_c$ and coming from an instance in a set E. Finally, $\mathsf{Outgoing}_{\mathcal{V}}$ denotes all messages sent by $\mathcal{V}$ before time t. This is common to all $\exp_c$. There exists an algorithm Algo such that for all c and c_0, we have in $\exp_c$ that*

$$r = \mathsf{Algo}\left(c, (\mathsf{View}_U)_{U \in \mathsf{Close}}, (\mathsf{Incoming}_U^{c_0}(\mathsf{Far}))_{U \in \mathsf{Close} \cup \{\mathcal{V}\}}, \mathsf{Outgoing}_{\mathcal{V}}\right)$$

If Close *is empty, we can further write $r = \mathsf{Algo}(\mathsf{Incoming}_{\mathcal{V}}^{c_0}(\mathsf{Far}))$.*

To make the lemma short: r cannot depend on any message which was sent from a far away U after receiving c. So, if we simulate $\exp_{c_0}$ in a straightline way, we can compute for each c what would have been r if c was sent instead of c_0.

We provide below a detailed proof of this lemma in the BMV model.

Proof. We first show that there exists an algorithm such that for all c,

$$r = \mathsf{Algo}\left(c, (\mathsf{View}_U)_{U \in \mathsf{Close}}, (\mathsf{Incoming}_U^c(\mathsf{Far}))_{U \in \mathsf{Close} \cup \{\mathcal{V}\}}, \mathsf{Outgoing}_{\mathcal{V}}\right)$$

Indeed, we show below that for each $U \in \mathsf{Close}$ we can compute the view of U at time $t+2B-d(\mathcal{V}, U)$. Then, we can see if U sends a message r to $\mathcal{V}$. We can also see in $\mathsf{Incoming}_{\mathcal{V}}^c(\mathsf{Far})$ if there is a message r coming from far away. We can then compute the first of these messages which arrives to $\mathcal{V}$. We note that if r comes from some $U \in \mathsf{Close}$, then it must have been sent no later than $t+2B-d(\mathcal{V}, U)$. So, it must be among the computed messages.

Then, we show that for all $U \in \mathsf{Close} \cup \{\mathcal{V}\}$, $\mathsf{Incoming}_U^c(\mathsf{Far})$ is independent from c, so we can replace c by c_0. Indeed, every message w in $\mathsf{Incoming}_U^c(\mathsf{Far})$ is seen by some $U \in \mathsf{Close} \cup \{\mathcal{V}\}$ at time $t' \leq t+2B-d(\mathcal{V}, U)$ and comes from some

$U' \in$ Far. So, it must have been sent at time $t' - d(U, U') \leq t + 2B - d(\mathcal{V}, U) - d(U, U') \leq t + 2B - d(\mathcal{V}, U') \leq t + B$. We define exp' like in exp_c, except that each participant U'' is stopped at time $t + B - d(U', U'')$. In exp', $\mathcal{V}$ is stopped before time t, so c is not used. We show by induction that for each U'', the view of U'' at the stopping time of U'' is the same in exp_c and exp'. We deduce that w is independent from c_0.

What remains to be shown is that for each $U \in$ Close we can compute the view of U at time $t + 2B - d(\mathcal{V}, U)$. This is shown by induction on the time. Indeed, this view is composed of the initial view View_U of U and of the incoming messages. These messages either come from $\mathcal{V}$, so are either c or something in $\mathsf{Outgoing}_\mathcal{V}$, or come from $U' \in$ Close, so can have been computed in the view of U', by induction, or come from $U' \in$ Far, so is in $\mathsf{Incoming}_U$. $\qquad\square$

Participants can move, but not faster than communication. For simplicity, we assume that far-away participants (as defined in Definition 3) remain far away during the entire execution. Honest participants move as instructed by the adversary.

We sometimes consider that when an honest participant receives a message from another honest participant, it may be subject to noise. As for malicious participants, we could assume that they use a better equipment which eliminates noise. Also: whenever the honest-to-honest communication is not time-sensitive, we may also assume that they use error correction means so that the communication is noiseless.

2.2   PoPoK: Proofs of Proximity of Knowledge

Definition 2 (Proof of proximity of knowledge). *A proof of proximity of knowledge (PoPoK) is a tuple* $(\mathcal{K}, \mathsf{Kgen}, P, V, B)$, *consisting of: a key space* $\mathcal{K}$ *depending on a security parameter* λ, *with elements of polynomially-bounded size in terms of* λ; *a PPT algorithm* Kgen; *a two-party PPT protocol* $(P(\mathsf{sk}), V(\mathsf{pk}))$, *where* $P(\mathsf{sk})$ *is the* <u>proving algorithm</u> *and* $V(\mathsf{pk})$ *is the* <u>verifying algorithm</u>; *a distance bound* B. *The algorithm* Kgen *maps the secret* $\mathsf{sk} \in \mathcal{K}$ *to a public key* pk. pk *is given as input to all participants. At the end of the protocol,* $V(\mathsf{pk})$ *sends a final message* Out_V. *He accepts* $(\mathsf{Out}_V = 1)$ *or rejects* $(\mathsf{Out}_V = 0)$.

The protocol must be such that when running $P(\mathsf{sk})$ *and* $V(\mathsf{pk})$ *at locations within a distance up to* B, *in a noiseless environment, the verifier always accepts. This property is called* <u>completeness</u>.

If the protocol specifies a list of time-critical challenge/response exchanges, we say that it is complete with <u>noise</u> *probability* p_{noise} *if, in an environment in which all challenge/response rounds are independently corrupted with probability* p_{noise} *and other exchanges are not subject to noise, the probability that the verifier accepts is* $1 - \mathsf{negl}(\lambda)$.

In practice, if we want to have $B = 10\,\mathrm{m}$, assuming that an adversary can do computation in negligible time, the timer for receiving a response r to a challenge c in Lemma 1 should be limited to 67 ns. So, an honest prover at a zero distance must respond within less than 67 ns. This clearly excludes any cryptographic computation. To be realistic, a PoPoK can only consider boolean (or very small) challenges and responses when it comes to use Lemma 1.

We adopt the multiparty setting from [10] and only adapt it to accommodate public-key distance bounding. We consider a setting with participants which are called either *provers, verifiers,* or *other actors.* In public-key settings, we assume only one verifier $\mathcal{V}$ (other verifiers can be taken as *other actors*). Similarly, we often assume that provers correspond to the same identity so share the same secret sk (provers with other secrets are considered as *other actors*). Other actors are malicious by default. The difference between malicious provers and malicious actors is in the input: they receive sk or only pk.

We assume that participants run their algorithm only once. Multiple executions are modeled by multiple instances which can be at different location or time. We only assume that instances of honest provers never run concurrently. A malicious prover may however clone himself at different locations and run many algorithms concurrently.

Definition 3 (Experiment). *Given a PoPoK ($\mathcal{K}$, Kgen, P, V, B), we define an* experiment *exp by several* participants *who are a* verifier $\mathcal{V}$, provers, *and other* actors, *and each* instance *of the participants. Instances who are within a distance of at most B to $\mathcal{V}$ are said* close-by. *Instances who are within a distance larger than B to $\mathcal{V}$ are called* far-away. *We say that the prover is* always far-away *if all its instances are far away. We adopt a static adversarial model: either the prover is honest, in which case all its instances run the P(sk) algorithm, or the prover is malicious, in which case its instances can run any PPT algorithm.*

If the prover is honest, its instances are assumed to be non-concurrent: *at each time, it must be defined which is the current instance. An instance of a honest participant can only be active if it is the current one and if it has received a special* Activate *message from a malicious participant. The first current instance must be defined in the experiment. Instances store an address of the next current instance. This address can be updated by a special* Destination *message from a malicious participant. It can also receive a special* Halt *message making the algorithm terminate, and a special* Move *message. After receiving this message and as soon as the algorithm terminated, the instance sends a special* Moving *message to the instance specified in his destination address. Only current instances can send this message to an instance of the same participant.[2]*

At the beginning of the experiment, for malicious provers, (sk, pk) is set arbitrarily. If the provers are honest, sk $\in \mathcal{K}$ is randomly selected and pk = Kgen(sk) is computed. Then, sk is given as input to all prover instances, while pk is given as input to all participants. $\mathcal{V}$ runs V(pk). All participants are then activated and run concurrently. (If the prover is honest, only one is activated.) The experiment terminates when $\mathcal{V}$ produces its final output Out_V.

We formalize security following [10].

---

[2] All these special messages are defined in order to avoid participants moving faster than messages and to allow arbitrary movements influenced by the adversary.

Definition 4 (Honest Prover Security of PoPoK). *We say that a PoPoK* $(\mathcal{K}, \mathsf{Kgen}, P, V, B)$ *is* <u>HP-secure</u> *if* $\Pr[\mathsf{Out}_V = 1] = \mathsf{negl}(\lambda)$ *for any experiment with a single prover, where the prover is honest and always far-away from* V.

This definition clearly captures relay attacks, Mafia fraud [15], man-in-the-middle attacks in general, and even models (like in [6,8,9]) which distinguish a learning phase (with provers which could be close-by) and an attack phase (with far-away provers).

We now formalize the protection for the honest verifier. Intuitively, we want that if the proof is accepted, it must be because the information about the secret sk is in the close-by neighborhood.

Definition 5 (Soundness of PoPoK). *Given a function* $p(\lambda)$, *we say that a PoPoK* $(\mathcal{K}, \mathsf{Kgen}, P, V, B)$ *is* $p(\lambda)$*-sound if for any experiment* exp *in which* $\Pr[\mathsf{Out}_V = 1] > p(\lambda)$, *there exists an algorithm* $\mathcal{E}$ *called* <u>extractor</u>, *with the following property.* exp *defines an oracle which simulates an execution of* exp *and returns the views of all participants which are close-by (excluding* V*) and the transcript of the protocol seen by* V. $\mathcal{E}$ *can invoke the oracle many times. Then,* $\mathcal{E}$ *finally outputs* sk' *such that* $\mathsf{Kgen}(\mathsf{sk}') = \mathsf{pk}$, *using an expected time complexity of* $\frac{\mathsf{Poly}(\lambda)}{\Pr[\mathsf{Out}_V = 1] - p(\lambda)}$.

This is trivial for experiments with a close-by prover as sk is in the view of the prover. For experiments with no close-by participant at all, the transcript as seen by V would leak. Otherwise, close-by actors would extract the prover's credential. So, a far away malicious prover is bound to leak.

Compared to the soundness of interactive proofs, our notion uses a straight-line extractor: we extract the secret from close-by participants without rewinding them and after several independent executions. This makes the treatment of multiparty settings much easier. As we will see, our extractor essentially uses Lemma 1. Interestingly, the extractor is also used to prove HP-security: if the protocol is zero-knowledge, the oracle extractor can be transformed into a stand-alone extractor which contradicts the one-wayness of Kgen.

Clearly, our definition nicely connects the infamous terrorist-fraud resistance to the soundness of interactive proofs. To compare with the literature, we could see that terrorist frauds in our model make the secret leak instead of only making man-in-the-middle attack feasible as in the notion of collusion fraud proposed in [6,8,9], and on which the SKI protocol is based, or only making impersonation attack feasible as in [10]. Our soundness is thus stronger.

Our notion and the one of [10] are close to soundness as defined in [25], except that we no longer require $1/\Pr[\mathsf{Out}_V = 1]$ to be polynomial. Also, compared to [10], we no longer need the condition on the success of the experiment to extract and we call an oracle $\mathcal{O}$ many times instead of using m views.

Just like other notions of TF-resistance, soundness is incomparable with SimTF-security [16] or GameTF-security [18] in the DFKO model.

Definition 6 (Distance-fraud security). *A PoPoK* $(\mathcal{K}, \mathsf{Kgen}, P, V, B)$ *resists to* <u>distance fraud</u> *if for any experiment* exp *where all participants are far away from* V, *we have that* $\Pr[\mathsf{Out}_V = 1] = \mathsf{negl}(\lambda)$.

We adapt the definition of distance-hijacking security from [26].

Definition 7 (Resistance to Distance Hijacking [26]). *We say that the PoPoK ($\mathcal{K}$, Kgen, P, V, B) is DH-secure if for all PPT algorithms K and $\mathcal{A}$, the following game makes $\mathcal{V}$ accept with negligible probability:*

1: pick sk′ $\in \mathcal{K}$, pk′ = Kgen(sk), K(pk′) → (sk, pk); if pk = pk′, the game aborts
2: let $\mathcal{A}$ run $\mathcal{A}$(sk, pk, pk′), let $\mathcal{V}$ runs V(pk), let P′, P_1', P_2', . . . run P(sk′)
3: let $\mathcal{A}$ interact with P′, P_1', P_2' . . . and $\mathcal{V}$ concurrently until the initialization phase ends for $\mathcal{V}$
4: let P′ and $\mathcal{V}$ continue interacting with each other until the challenge phase ends for $\mathcal{V}$; $\mathcal{A}$ receives the exchanged messages but remains passive
5: let $\mathcal{A}$ continue interacting with P′, P_1', P_2' . . . and $\mathcal{V}$ concurrently during the verification phase

3   ProProx: A PoPoK Scheme

3.1   Building Blocks

Perfectly Binding Bit Commitment. Depending on the security parameter λ, we use a (multiplicative) group structure with two Abelian groups L and G and an element θ such that G is generated by L and θ, $\theta \notin L$, and L is the set of all squares of G. We further assume that it is easy to do group operations and comparisons in G and to sample elements in G uniformly.[3] Finally, we assume it is computationally hard to distinguish elements from L and from G.

We define $\mathsf{Com}(b; \rho) = \theta^b \rho^2$ for a bit b and a random $\rho \in G$, like in the Goldwasser-Micali cryptosystem [20,21]. So, Com is computationally hiding as defined by Definition 8. We will not require any secret key to extract b, although there *exists* a function Com^{-1} such that $\mathsf{Com}^{-1}(\mathsf{Com}(b; \rho)) = b$ for all $b \in \{0, 1\}$ and $\rho \in G$. We will rather use the homomorphic properties of the commitment and prove the correct commitment in a zero-knowledge way.

Definition 8 (Bit commitment). *A bit commitment consists of a PPT algorithm Com taking as input λ, a bit $b \in \mathbf{Z}_2$, and some random $\rho \in G$. It computes $\mathsf{Com}(b; \rho) \in G$. We define the following properties: (1). homomorphic: for all $b, b' \in \mathbf{Z}_2$ and $\rho, \rho' \in G$, $\mathsf{Com}(b; \rho)\mathsf{Com}(b'; \rho') = \mathsf{Com}(b + b'; \rho\rho')$; (2). perfectly binding: for all $b, b' \in \mathbf{Z}_2$ and $\rho, \rho' \in G$, $\mathsf{Com}(b; \rho) = \mathsf{Com}(b'; \rho')$ implies $b = b'$; (3). computationally hiding: for ρ random, the distributions of $\mathsf{Com}(0; \rho)$ and $\mathsf{Com}(1; \rho)$ are computationally indistinguishable.*

For instance, we can take a Blum integer N, i.e., $N = PQ$ for two distinct primes P and Q which are congruent to 3 modulo 4. We set L to the set of quadratic residues modulo N and $\theta = -1$: a residue modulo N such that $\left(\frac{\theta}{P}\right) = \left(\frac{\theta}{Q}\right) = -1$. The algorithm Com is given N and θ. We sample $r \in G$ by $r = \theta^b \rho^2 \bmod N$, for $b \in \mathbf{Z}_2$ and $\rho \in \mathbf{Z}_N^*$. Distinguishing G from L is the (supposedly hard) quadratic residuosity problem. In this case, N is assumed to come from a Common Reference String (CRS).

---

[3] So, we can sample an element of L uniformly by taking r^2 with r uniform in G.

A Zero-Knowledge Proof for z Being a Square. We use the Fiat-Shamir protocol [17]. Namely, we show that z is a commitment to zero with a witness ζ (i.e., $z = \zeta^2$) with the protocol from Fig. 1, based on a perfectly hiding trapdoor commitment. Concretely, we use Definitions 9 and 10 with the $\mathcal{NP}$ language L of all squares. If $z = \zeta^2$, we say that z is a member of L with witness ζ.

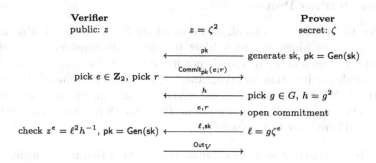

Fig. 1. ZKP($z : \zeta$): a sound and zero-knowledge proof for z being a square.

Definition 9 (Sound proof of membership). *An interactive proof for a language L is a pair $(P(\zeta), V(z))$ of PPT algorithms such that 1. completeness: for any $z \in L$ with witness ζ, $\Pr[\mathrm{Out}_V = 1 : P(\zeta) \leftrightarrow V(z)] = 1$; 2. κ-soundness: for any $z \notin L$ and any algorithm P^* then $\Pr[\mathrm{Out}_V = 1 : P^* \leftrightarrow V(z)] \leq \kappa$.*

Definition 10 (Zero-knowledge protocol). *A protocol $(P(\zeta), V(z))$ for a language L is computationally zero-knowledge for $P(\zeta)$ if for any PPT interactive machine $V^*(z, \mathsf{aux})$ there exists a PPT algorithm $S(z, \mathsf{aux})$ and a negligible ε such that for any PPT distinguisher, any $(z : \zeta) \in L$, and any aux, the advantage for distinguishing the final view of $V^*(z, \mathsf{aux})$ in $P(\zeta) \leftrightarrow V^*(z, \mathsf{aux})$ and the output of $S(z, \mathsf{aux})$ is bounded by ε.*

The protocol of Fig. 1 is $\frac{1}{2}$-sound and zero-knowledge. It must be run k times in parallel to achieve a soundness level $\kappa = 2^{-k}$. We denote it by $\mathsf{ZKP}_\kappa(z : \zeta)$.

By using parallel composition, we extend the protocol to prove that $z_1, \ldots, z_k$ are some commitments to zero with witness $\zeta_1, \ldots, \zeta_k$ respectively, and denote it by $\mathsf{ZKP}_\kappa(z_1, \ldots, z_k : \zeta_1, \ldots, \zeta_k)$. I.e., it succeeds with probability up to κ if there exists i such that $z_i \notin L$.

(Perfectly Binding) Deterministic Commitment. Given a hash function H making coins for Com, we define a deterministic commitment by

$$\mathsf{Com}_H(\mathsf{sk}) = (\mathsf{Com}(\mathsf{sk}_1; H(\mathsf{sk}, 1)), \ldots, \mathsf{Com}(\mathsf{sk}_s; H(\mathsf{sk}, s)))$$

for $\mathsf{sk} \in \mathbf{Z}_2^s$. We assume that Com_H is a one-way function (as defined by Definition 11). We assume the existence of Com and H such that Com_H is one-way as independent primitives. This is the case in particular when H is a random oracle, but H is not necessarily assumed to be a random oracle. Constructions without using a random oracle are left to future work.

Definition 11 (One-way function). *We consider a function* Com *taking as input* λ *and a message* sk $\in \mathbf{Z}_2^s$ *which is computable in deterministic polynomial time. The function is one-way if for any algorithm receiving* Com(sk), *for* sk $\in \mathbf{Z}_2^s$ *random, the probability that it outputs* sk *is negligible.*

3.2   The ProProx Protocol

We define the ProProx protocol, as depicted on Fig. 2 (there, double arrows indicate messages which can be subject to noise). We consider s (the size of the secret), n (the number of rounds per iteration), τ (the minimal number of correct rounds per iteration for acceptance) as functions in terms of the security parameter λ. We assume s and n are asymptotically linear. We use a matrix $b \in \mathbf{Z}_2^{sn}$. The use of b will only appear in Theorem 18 to treat distance fraud. There, we will consider two variants.

Variant I: b is constant and the columns must have a Hamming weight of $\lfloor \frac{n}{2} \rfloor$
   to make sure that $b_{i,j} + x_j \neq 0$ in half of the rounds. This requires $n \geq 2$.
Variant II: b is randomly selected by V and sent to P during the initialization
   phase. This requires $n \geq 1$.

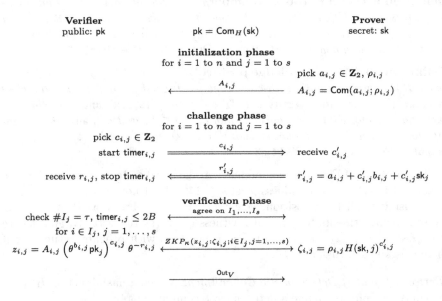

Fig. 2. ProProx: a sound and secure PoPoK.

The prover holds a secret sk $\in \mathbf{Z}_2^s$ and the public key is pk $=$ Com$_H$(sk). We iterate s times and in parallel a protocol which we call an iteration and which corresponds to an index j. First, the prover selects n bits $a_{1,j}, \ldots, a_{n,j} \in \mathbf{Z}_2$ and commits to them using some fresh coins $\rho_{1,j}, \ldots, \rho_{n,j}$, respectively. So, $A_{i,j} =$ Com$(a_{i,j}; \rho_{i,j})$, $i = 1, \ldots, n$. The $A_{i,j}$'s are sent to the verifier.

In the challenge phase, we have n time-critical rounds (in each iteration). These rounds may be subject to noise. The verifier picks a challenge $c_{i,j} \in \mathbf{Z}_2$ at random and sends it to the prover. The prover receives $c'_{i,j}$ (which may be different, due to noise). He computes his response $r'_{i,j} = a_{i,j} + c'_{i,j}b_{i,j} + c'_{i,j}\mathsf{sk}_j$ and sends it back to the verifier at once. The verifier receives $r_{i,j}$. The verifier measures the elapsed time $\mathsf{timer}_{i,j}$ taken to receive $r_{i,j}$ after $c_{i,j}$ was sent. Below, p_{noise} is the probability that some noise corrupts a challenge/response round. We assume that the noise corrupts each round independently.

Thus, the $c'_{i,j} \mapsto r'_{i,j}$ function maps one bit to one bit.

In the verification phase, the prover and the verifier determine a set I_j of τ round indices which they believe are correct. The way this agreement is done is not important (as long as the prover does not leak). Then, the verifier checks whether I_j has cardinality τ and the corresponding timers are small enough. If this fails, the verifier rejects. As a concrete instance for I_j agreement, we suggest that the prover sends (through the lazy noiseless channel) the $c'_{i,j}$ and $r'_{i,j}$ to the verifier. The verifier then takes the first τ rounds for which $c_{i,j} = c'_{i,j}$, $r_{i,j} = r'_{i,j}$, and $\mathsf{timer}_{i,j} \leq 2B$ to define I_j and sends I_j to the prover. If there are not enough correct rounds, the protocol aborts.

Next, the prover and the verifier run the interactive proof ZKP_κ to show that the responses $r_{i,j}$'s are consistent with the $A_{i,j}$'s and pk_j's. Namely, for all j and $i \in I_j$, they compute

$$z_{i,j} = A_{i,j}\left(\theta^{b_{i,j}}\mathsf{pk}_j\right)^{c_{i,j}}\theta^{-r_{i,j}}, \quad \zeta_{i,j} = \rho_{i,j}H(\mathsf{sk},j)^{c'_{i,j}}$$

Since $A_{i,j} = \theta^{a_{i,j}}\rho_{i,j}^2$ and $\mathsf{pk}_j = \theta^{\mathsf{sk}_j}H(\mathsf{sk},j)^2$, it is easy to verify that $r_{i,j} = a_{i,j} + c_{i,j}b_{i,j} + c_{i,j}\mathsf{sk}_j$ is equivalent to the existence of $\zeta_{i,j}$ such that $z_{i,j} = \zeta_{i,j}^2$. That is, $z_{i,j} \in L$. If this fails, the protocol aborts. When the protocol aborts, the verifier sends $\mathsf{Out}_V = 0$. Otherwise, he sends $\mathsf{Out}_V = 1$.

3.3   Analysis

Theorem 12 (Completeness). *Let $\varepsilon > 0$ be a constant. We assume either that $n = \Omega(\lambda)$ and $\frac{\tau}{n} < 1 - p_{\mathsf{noise}} - \varepsilon$ or that $p_{\mathsf{noise}} = 0$. We assume that* Com *is a homomorphic bit commitment [Definition 8] and that* ZKP_κ *is complete [Definition 9]. The ProProx protocol is a PoPoK which fails with probability bounded by*

$$p_{\mathsf{Comp}} = 1 - \mathsf{Tail}\left(n, \tau, 1 - p_{\mathsf{noise}}\right)^s \tag{1}$$

when the challenge/response rounds are subject to a noise level of p_{noise} [Definition 2].

Proof. Completeness for $p_{\mathsf{noise}} = 0$ is trivial. Proving completeness when $\frac{\tau}{n} < 1 - p_{\mathsf{noise}} - \varepsilon$ is straightforward: in an iteration, we have less than τ noiseless rounds with probability $1 - \mathsf{Tail}(n, \tau, 1 - p_{\mathsf{noise}}) < e^{-2\varepsilon^2 n}$ due to the Chernoff-Hoeffding bound (Lemma 13), which is negligible since $n = \Omega(\lambda)$. Then, the completeness failure is bounded by p_{Comp} which is also negligible.   □

We recall here some useful bound on the tail of the binomial distribution.

Lemma 13 (Chernoff-Hoeffding bound [13,23]). *For any ε, n, τ, q we have $\frac{\tau}{n} < q - \varepsilon \implies \mathsf{Tail}(n, \tau, q) > 1 - e^{-2\varepsilon^2 n}$ and $\frac{\tau}{n} > q + \varepsilon \implies \mathsf{Tail}(n, \tau, q) < e^{-2\varepsilon^2 n}$.*

We construct an extractor giving an output which is close to the secret.

Lemma 14 (Straightline extractor). *Under the assumption that Com is a perfectly binding homomorphic bit commitment, and that ZKP_κ is a κ-sound proof of membership, for any experiment, there is a PPT algorithm $\mathsf{Extract}$ which takes the views of all close-by participants and the transcript of the protocol seen by $\mathcal{V}$ and which aborts if $\mathcal{V}$ rejects, otherwise produces a vector $\mathsf{sk}' \in \{0,1\}^s$. For any w, the probability that $\mathcal{V}$ accepts and the Hamming distance between sk and sk' is at least $w + 1$ is lower than*

$$p_{\mathsf{Sound}} = \mathsf{Tail}\left(\left\lceil\frac{n}{2}\right\rceil, \tau - \left\lfloor\frac{n}{2}\right\rfloor, \frac{1}{2}\right)^{w+1} + \kappa \qquad (2)$$

We will often define $p_B = \mathsf{Tail}(\lceil\frac{n}{2}\rceil, \tau - \lfloor\frac{n}{2}\rfloor, \frac{1}{2})$. We note that if we assume that $s = \Omega(\lambda)$ and $\tau \geq n - (\frac{1}{2} - 2\varepsilon)\lceil\frac{n}{2}\rceil$ with a constant ε, we have $\frac{\tau - n + \lceil\frac{n}{2}\rceil}{\lceil\frac{n}{2}\rceil} \geq \frac{1}{2} + 2\varepsilon$. So, $p_B \leq e^{-8\varepsilon^2 n}$ due to the Chernoff-Hoeffding bound (Lemmma 13), which is negligible. This case will be use subsequently.

Proof. We assume that we have an experiment making $\mathcal{V}$ accept with probability p. We define $p_B = \mathsf{Tail}(\lceil\frac{n}{2}\rceil, \tau - \lfloor\frac{n}{2}\rfloor, \frac{1}{2})$.

We take the viewpoint of $\mathcal{V}$. Since we have a perfectly binding commitment, the value pk_j uniquely defines $\mathsf{sk}_j = \mathsf{Com}^{-1}(\mathsf{pk}_j)$, and the value of $A_{i,j}$ uniquely defines $a_{i,j} = \mathsf{Com}^{-1}(A_{i,j})$. (We stress that we need not compute these values, we just mathematically define them given the view of the verifier.) The purpose of the proof is to show that we can extract a good approximation of sk (i.e., at a distance lower than w), except with some negligible probability p_{Sound}.

Let $p = \Pr[\mathsf{Out}_V = 1]$. Let S be the event that for all j and for at least τ values of i (for each j), we have $r_{i,j} = a_{i,j} + c_{i,j}(b_{i,j} + \mathsf{sk}_j)$ (where the values are those seen by $\mathcal{V}$). In the case where the statement proven by ZKP_κ is true, for all j and $i \in I_j$, $z_{i,j}$ is clearly a commitment to zero. Due to the homomorphic property of Com, we know that $z_{i,j}$ is the commitment to $a_{i,j} + c_{i,j}(b_{i,j} + \mathsf{sk}_j) - r_{i,j}$. So, we deduce that S occurs. By using the κ-soundness of ZKP_κ (Definition 9), we deduce $\Pr[\mathsf{Out}_V = 1 | \neg S] \leq \kappa$. So, $\Pr[\neg S, \mathsf{Out}_V = 1] \leq \kappa$.

Since the $c_{i,j}$ challenges are sent in sequence, in what follows we denote by $c_q = c_{i_q, j_q}$ the qth challenge sent. We further denote by ρ all random coins of the experiment except those defining the challenges. So, we compute probabilities over the independent distributions of ρ and all $c_{i,j}$.

Thanks to Lemma 1, we can write $r_{i,j} = \mathsf{Algo}_{i,j}(c_{i,j}, \mathsf{Data}_{i,j})$ with $\mathsf{Data}_{i,j} = (\mathsf{Views}, \mathsf{Incoming}_{i,j}, \mathsf{Outgoing}_{i,j})$, where Views lists the initial view of close-by participants, $\mathsf{Incoming}_{i,j}$ gives the list of incoming messages from far away that they can see until the sender can see $c_{i,j}$, and $\mathsf{Outgoing}_{i,j}$ includes the list of outgoing messages from $\mathcal{V}$ before $c_{i,j}$. Note that $\mathsf{Data}_{i,j}$ can be computed from the final views of the close-by participants but depends on the selected challenges before $c_{i,j}$. So, thanks to Lemma 1, we can compute in this case both $\mathsf{resp}_{i,j}(0) = \mathsf{Algo}_{i,j}(0, \mathsf{Data}_{i,j})$ and $\mathsf{resp}_{i,j}(1) = \mathsf{Algo}_{i,j}(1, \mathsf{Data}_{i,j})$ without rewinding (i.e., from the final view only). Since $r_{i,j}$ is supposed to be $a_{i,j} + c_{i,j}(b_{i,j} + \mathsf{sk}_j)$, we can compute the guess $\xi_{i,j} = \mathsf{resp}_{i,j}(1) - \mathsf{resp}_{i,j}(0) - b_{i,j}$ for sk_j. (Note that if the answer $r_{i,j}$ comes to $\mathcal{V}$ from far-away, we can still apply Lemma 1 and deduce that the answer is the same for $c_{i,j} = 0$ and $c_{i,j} = 1$, so $\xi_{i,j} = -b_{i,j}$.) In all cases, we can always compute the vectors $\xi_j = (\xi_{1,j}, \ldots, \xi_{n,j})$ of guesses for sk_j. The extractor is taking all $\mathsf{Algo}_{i,j}(., \mathsf{Data}_{i,j})$ to compute ξ_j then $\mathsf{sk}'_j = \mathsf{majority}(\xi_j)$ for all j.

Given c, if $a_{i,j} + c(b_{i,j} + \mathsf{sk}_j) = \mathsf{resp}_{i,j}(c)$, we say that the answer to $c_{i,j} = c$ is correct relative to the previous challenges (we recall that $\mathsf{Data}_{i,j}$ depends on all challenges which are sent before $c_{i,j}$). Based on ρ, we construct a binary tree T of depth ns in which a node at depth q corresponds to the selection of c_q. We denote by $G(c|c_1, \ldots, c_{q-1})$ the predicate that c is correct relative to $c_1, \ldots, c_{q-1}$. Let $S_T^{c_1, \ldots, c_q}$ be an s-tuple of integers such that $(S_T^{c_1, \ldots, c_q})_j = \#\{q' \leq q; j_{q'} = j, G(c_{q'}|c_1, \ldots, c_{q'-1})\}$. This counts how many good answers we had until step q for the $c_{.,j}$ challenges which are based on sk_j. We let S_ρ denote the event that $(S_T^{C_1, \ldots, C_{ns}})_j \geq \tau$ for all j where $C_1, \ldots, C_{ns}$ are the random challenges from the experiment. $\mathcal{V}$ only accepts when S_ρ holds. Let $R_T^{c_1, \ldots, c_q}$ be an s-tuple of integers such that $(R_T^{c_1, \ldots, c_q})_j = \#\{q' \leq q; j_{q'} = j, G(0|c_1, \ldots, c_{q'-1}), G(1|c_1, \ldots, c_{q'-1})\}$. This counts how many times both values lead to good answers for the $c_{.,j}$ challenges. If $G(0|c_1, \ldots, c_{q'-1})$ and $G(1|c_1, \ldots, c_{q'-1})$ hold, then $\xi_{i_q, j_q} = \mathsf{sk}_j$. So, if $(R_T^{c_1, \ldots, c_{ns-1}})_j \geq \lfloor \frac{n}{2} \rfloor + 1$, we have $\mathsf{sk}'_j = \mathsf{sk}_j$. We let W_ρ be the number of j such that $(R_T^{C_1, \ldots, C_{ns}})_j \leq \lfloor \frac{n}{2} \rfloor$. We show below that for all ρ, $\Pr[S_\rho, W_\rho > w] \leq p_{\mathsf{Sound}} - \kappa$ over the distribution of the $c_{i,j}$. By averaging over ρ, we have $\Pr[S, W > w] \leq p_{\mathsf{Sound}} - \kappa$. Thus, by splitting with the S and $\neg S$ events,

$$\Pr[W > w, \mathsf{Out}_V = 1] \leq \Pr[\neg S, \mathsf{Out}_V = 1] + \Pr[S, W > w] \leq p_{\mathsf{Sound}}$$

So, having that $\mathcal{V}$ accepts and the extractor gives at least $w + 1$ errors occurs with probability bounded by p_{Sound}, which is what we wanted to prove.

To show that $\Pr[S_\rho, W_\rho > w] \leq p_{\mathsf{Sound}} - \kappa$ in the fixed tree T, we first modify the tree in a way which only make this probability increase. Namely, we add more $G(c_q|c_1, \ldots, c_{q-1})$ so that for all j, $(R_T^{c_1, \ldots, c_{ns}})_j$ is either n or $\lfloor \frac{n}{2} \rfloor$. Then, we show a more general property. We consider a balanced binary tree of depth q with some indexing $q \leftrightarrow (i_q, j_q)$. We denote q_j the number of $k \in \{1, \ldots, q\}$ such that $j_k = j$. So, $q = q_1 + \cdots + q_s$. We let $W_T(J, w)$ be the event that for at least $w + 1$ values of $j \in J$ we have $(R_T^{c_1, \ldots, c_q})_j \leq q_j - \lceil \frac{n}{2} \rceil$, for other values of j we have $(R_T^{c_1, \ldots, c_q})_j = q_j$, and for all $j \in J$ we have $(S_T^{C_1, \ldots, C_q})_j \geq \tau - (n - q_j)$. We show that for all J, τ_j's, and μ_j's, we have

$$\Pr\left[W_T(J, w), \bigwedge_{j \notin J} (S_T^{C_1, \ldots, C_q})_j \geq \tau_j, (R_T^{C_1, \ldots, C_q})_j \leq \mu_j\right]$$

$$\leq p_B^{w+1} \times \prod_{j \notin J} \mathsf{tail}\left(q_j - \mu_j, \tau_j - \mu_j, \frac{1}{2}\right) \tag{3}$$

Then, we apply it with $J = \{1, \ldots, s\}$. We obtain $\Pr[S_\rho, W_\rho > w] \le p_B^{w+1} = p_{\mathsf{Sound}} - \kappa$.

The (3) property is proven by induction on q. It is trivial for $q = 0$. Assuming it holds for $q - 1$, we prove it for q by looking at the two subtrees T_0 and T_1 of T. We have

$$(S_T^{c_1,\ldots,c_q})_j = (S_{T_{c_1}}^{c_2,\ldots,c_q})_j \qquad (R_T^{c_1,\ldots,c_q})_j = (R_{T_{c_1}}^{c_2,\ldots,c_q})_j \qquad \text{if } j \ne j_1$$
$$(S_T^{c_1,\ldots,c_q})_j = (S_{T_{c_1}}^{c_2,\ldots,c_q})_j + 1_{G(c_1)} \quad (R_T^{c_1,\ldots,c_q})_j = (R_{T_{c_1}}^{c_2,\ldots,c_q})_j + 1_{G(0),G(1)} \quad \text{if } j = j_1$$

If $j_1 \notin J$ or $G(0) \wedge G(1)$ holds, $W_T(J, w)$ is equivalent to $W_{T_{c_1}}(J', w')$ for $J' = J$ and $w' = w$. If now $j_1 \in J$ and $\neg G(0) \vee \neg G(1)$ holds, we define $\tau_{j_1} = \tau - (n - q_{j_1})$, $\mu_{j_1} = q_{j_1} - \lceil \frac{n}{2} \rceil$, $J' = J - \{j_1\}$, and $w' = w - 1$. Then, $W_T(J, w)$ is equivalent to, $(S_T^{C_1,\ldots,C_q})_{j_1} \ge \tau_{j_1}$, $(R_T^{c_1,\ldots,c_q})_{j_1} = \mu_{j_1}$, and $W_{T_{C_1}}(J', w')$. So,

$$\Pr\left[W_T(J, w), \bigwedge_{j \notin J} (S_T^{C_1,\ldots,C_q})_j \ge \tau_j, (R_T^{C_1,\ldots,C_q})_j \le \mu_j \right]$$

$$= \sum_{c_1=0}^{1} \Pr\left[W_T(J, w), \bigwedge_{j \notin J} (S_T^{c_1,C_2,\ldots,C_q})_j \ge \tau_j, (R_T^{c_1,C_2,\ldots,C_q})_j \le \mu_j, C_1 = c_1 \right]$$

$$\le \sum_{c_1=0}^{1} \Pr\left[W_{T_{c_1}}(J', w'), \bigwedge_{j \notin J'} (S_T^{c_1,C_2,\ldots,C_q})_j \ge \tau_j, (R_T^{c_1,C_2,\ldots,C_q})_j \le \mu_j, C_1 = c_1 \right]$$

$$= \sum_{c_1=0}^{1} \frac{1}{2} \Pr\left[W_{T_{c_1}}(J', w'), \bigwedge_{j \notin J'} (S_{T_{c_1}}^{C_2,\ldots,C_q})_j \ge \tau_j - 1_{j=j_1,G(c_1)}, (R_{T_{c_1}}^{C_2,\ldots,C_q})_j \le \mu_j - 1_{j=j_1,G(0),G(1)} \right]$$

$$\le \sum_{c_1=0}^{1} \frac{1}{2} p_B^{w'+1} \prod_{j \notin J'} \mathsf{tail}\left(q_j - 1_{j=j_1} - \mu_j + 1_{j=j_1,G(0),G(1)}, \tau_j - 1_{j=j_1,G(c_1)} - \mu_j + 1_{j=j_1,G(0),G(1)}, \frac{1}{2} \right)$$

When $j_1 \in J'$, this proves (3). For $j_1 \notin J'$, we obtain

$$p_B^{w'+1} \left(\sum_{c_1=0}^{1} \frac{1}{2} \mathsf{tail}\left(q_{j_1} - 1 - \mu_{j_1} + 1_{G(0),G(1)}, \tau_{j_1} - 1_{G(c_1)} - \mu_{j_1} + 1_{G(0),G(1)}, \frac{1}{2} \right) \right)$$

$$\times \prod_{\substack{j \notin J' \\ j \ne j_1}} \mathsf{tail}\left(q_j - \mu_j, \tau_j - \mu_j, \frac{1}{2} \right)$$

If both $G(0)$ and $G(1)$ are true the sum in parentheses is clearly equal to $\mathsf{tail}(q_{j_1} - \mu_{j_1}, \tau_{j_1} - \mu_{j_1}, \frac{1}{2})$. If either $G(0)$ or $G(1)$ is true but not both, the sum is

$$\frac{1}{2} \mathsf{tail}\left(q_{j_1} - 1 - \mu_{j_1}, \tau_{j_1} - \mu_{j_1}, \frac{1}{2} \right) + \frac{1}{2} \mathsf{tail}\left(q_{j_1} - 1 - \mu_{j_1}, \tau_{j_1} - 1 - \mu_{j_1}, \frac{1}{2} \right)$$

which is also equal to $\mathsf{tail}(q_{j_1} - \mu_{j_1}, \tau_{j_1} - \mu_{j_1}, \frac{1}{2})$. Finally, if neither $G(0)$ nor $G(1)$ hold, the sum is $\mathsf{tail}(q_{j_1} - 1 - \mu_{j_1}, \tau_{j_1} - \mu_{j_1}, \frac{1}{2})$ which is bounded by $\mathsf{tail}(q_{j_1} - \mu_{j_1}, \tau_{j_1} - \mu_{j_1}, \frac{1}{2})$. So, in all cases this proves (3). $\qquad \square$

Theorem 15 (Soundness). *We assume that* Com *is a perfectly binding homomorphic bit commitment, and that* ZKP_κ *is a κ-sound proof of membership.* *ProProx is a p_{Sound}-sound proof of proximity, where p_{Sound} is defined by (2).*

More precisely, for all constant w, if the experiment succeeds with probability $p > p_{\mathsf{Sound}}$ there exists an extractor following Definition 5 with complexity

$$T_{\mathsf{exp}}.\mathcal{O}\left(\frac{1}{p - p_{\mathsf{Sound}}}\right) + T_{\mathsf{Com}_H}.\mathcal{O}\left(B_w^s\right)$$

where T_{exp} is the complexity of the experiment, T_{Com_H} is the complexity to compute Com_H, and $B_w^s = \sum_{i=0}^{w}\binom{s}{i}$. The second term is actually the complexity of an exhaustive search with B_w^s iterations on sk until pk $= \mathsf{Com}_H(\mathsf{sk})$.

To use (2) with concrete parameters, w is chosen as the maximal value such that an adversary could afford an exhaustive search of B_w^s trials.

Proof. We can use the extractor of Lemma 14 on views taken from an experiment run. If $\mathcal{V}$ rejects, the extraction produces nothing. We iterate this extraction $\mathcal{O}(\frac{1}{p})$ times until one experiment succeeds. So, we obtain for sure a guess sk' for sk (with possible errors). The probability that at least w errors occurs in the extracted pairs is bounded by $\frac{p_{\mathsf{Sound}}}{p}$. When there are less errors, we can correct them by exhaustive search in time $T_{\mathsf{Com}_H}.\mathcal{O}(B_w^s)$ (which is polynomial). If this fails (i.e., if it gives no preimage of pk by Com_H) as some extracted pairs may have too many errors, we can just iterate. With a number of iterations of $\mathcal{O}\left(\left(1 - \frac{p_{\mathsf{Sound}}}{p}\right)^{-1}\right)$, we finally extract sk. The overall expected complexity is thus $\mathsf{Poly}(\lambda)/(p - p_{\mathsf{Sound}})$. More precisely, it is $T_{\mathsf{exp}}.\mathcal{O}\left(\frac{1}{p-p_{\mathsf{Sound}}}\right) + T_{\mathsf{Com}_H}.\mathcal{O}\left(B_w^s\right)$. $\square$

Our technique to prove HP-security relies on Lemma 14 and zero-knowledge.

Lemma 16 (Zero-knowledge). *Under the assumption that* Com *is a computationally hiding bit commitment and that* ZKP_κ *is a computationally zero-knowledge proof of membership, The ProProx protocol is zero-knowledge following Definition 10. More precisely, for any malicious verifier, given a simulator for ZKP_κ of complexity T_{Sim} producing views which are p_{ZKP}-indistinguishable to the real ones, we construct a simulator for ProProx of complexity $T_{\mathsf{Sim}} + ns.T_{\mathsf{Com}}$ and producing views which are p_{ZK}-indistinguishable to the real ones, where*

$$p_{\mathsf{ZK}} = p_{\mathsf{ZKP}} + ns.p_{\mathsf{Com}} \qquad (4)$$

where p_{Com} is the bound on the hiding property of Com.

Proof. We have to prove that, given two participants $P(\mathsf{sk})$ and $V^*(\mathsf{pk}, \mathsf{aux})$, there exists a simulator $S(\mathsf{pk}, \mathsf{aux})$ such that $V^*(\mathsf{pk}, \mathsf{aux}) \leftrightarrow P(\mathsf{sk})$ produces a view of $V^*(\mathsf{pk}, \mathsf{aux})$ which is computationally indistinguishable from the output of $S(\mathsf{pk}, \mathsf{aux})$. We actually construct a sequence of simulations. We define an interactive $V'(\mathsf{pk}, \mathsf{aux})$ to replace $V^*(\mathsf{pk}, \mathsf{aux})$, and some interactive $P'(\mathsf{sk})$ and P'' to replace $P(\mathsf{sk})$.

We denote $\bar{z}$ the vector of all $z_{i,j}$ for $j = 1, \ldots, s$ and $i \in I_j$, and $\bar{\zeta}$ the vector of all $\zeta_{i,j}$. We split $V^*(\mathsf{pk}, \mathsf{aux})$ into two protocols $V_1(\mathsf{pk}, \mathsf{aux})$ and $V_2(\bar{z}, \mathsf{aux}')$, where V_1 mimics V^* until the $\mathsf{ZKP}_\kappa(\bar{z} : \bar{\zeta})$ protocol must start. V_2 executes only $\mathsf{ZKP}_\kappa(\bar{z} : \bar{\zeta})$ where aux' is the final view of $V_1(\mathsf{pk}, \mathsf{aux})$. The final view of $V_2(\bar{z}, \mathsf{aux}')$ is of form $v = (\bar{z}, \mathsf{aux}', t)$. We write $g(v) = (\mathsf{aux}', t)$, which is the final view of $V^*(\mathsf{pk}, \mathsf{aux})$. Similarly, we split $P(\mathsf{sk})$ into $P_1(\mathsf{sk})$ and $P_2(\mathsf{sk}, u)$ where (sk, u) is the view of $P_1(\mathsf{sk})$. Running either $V^*(\mathsf{pk}, \mathsf{aux}) \leftrightarrow P(\mathsf{sk})$ and taking the final view of V^*, or $V_1(\mathsf{pk}, \mathsf{aux}) \leftrightarrow P_1(\mathsf{sk})$, $V_2(\bar{z}, \mathsf{aux}') \leftrightarrow P_2(\mathsf{sk}, u)$, then taking $g(v)$ is the same. This simulation is illustrated on the left-hand side of Fig. 3.

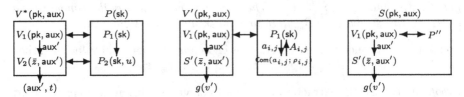

Fig. 3. Applying a ZK reduction.

First, $V'(\mathsf{pk}, \mathsf{aux})$ runs a simulation of $V_1(\mathsf{pk}, \mathsf{aux})$ interacting with $P_1(\mathsf{sk})$. Then, $V'(\mathsf{pk}, \mathsf{aux})$ runs the simulator $S'(\bar{z}, \mathsf{aux}')$ of the $\mathsf{ZKP}_\kappa(\bar{z} : \bar{\zeta})$ protocol associated to the verifier $V_2(\bar{z}, \mathsf{aux}')$ with complexity T_{Sim}. Let v' be the output of $S'(\bar{z}, \mathsf{aux}')$. Finally, $V'(\mathsf{pk}, \mathsf{aux})$ produces $g(v')$ as an output. This simulation is illustrated on the middle of Fig. 3. Due to the zero-knowledge property of $\mathsf{ZKP}_\kappa(\bar{z} : \bar{\zeta})$, v' is p_{ZKP}-indistinguishable from the final view of $V_2(\bar{z}, \mathsf{aux}')$. So, the final view of $V'(\mathsf{pk}, \mathsf{aux})$ in $V'(\mathsf{pk}, \mathsf{aux}) \leftrightarrow P_1(\mathsf{sk})$ and the final view of $V^*(\mathsf{pk}, \mathsf{aux})$ in $V^*(\mathsf{pk}, \mathsf{aux}) \leftrightarrow P(\mathsf{sk})$ are p_{ZKP}-indistinguishable.

Note that $P_1(\mathsf{sk})$ makes no longer extra use of the coins ρ_i's (as $P_2(\mathsf{sk}, u)$ does in ZKP_κ). So, the commitment can be outsourced to a challenger playing the real-or-random hiding game for Com. We modify $P_1(\mathsf{sk})$ into an algorithm $P'(\mathsf{sk})$ who sets $A_{i,j}$ to the commitment to some random bit instead of $a_{i,j}$. Thanks to the hiding property of Com applied ns times, the output of $V'(\mathsf{pk}, \mathsf{aux}) \leftrightarrow P_1(\mathsf{sk})$ and of $V'(\mathsf{pk}, \mathsf{aux}) \leftrightarrow P'(\mathsf{sk})$ are $ns.p_{\mathsf{Com}}$-indistinguishable.

Finally, r_i' in $P'(\mathsf{sk})$ is now uniformly distributed and independent from all the rest, so we change $P'(\mathsf{sk})$ into an algorithm P'' which sends a random r_i' instead. Note that P'' no longer needs sk. So, the view of V^* in $V^*(\mathsf{pk}, \mathsf{aux}) \leftrightarrow P(\mathsf{sk})$ and the output of $V'(\mathsf{pk}, \mathsf{aux}) \leftrightarrow P''$ are indistinguishable. This defines a simulator $S(\mathsf{pk}, \mathsf{aux})$, as illustrated on the right-hand-side of Fig. 3.   □

Theorem 17 (HP-Security). *We assume that Com is a perfectly binding, and computationally hiding homomorphic bit commitment, that Com_H is one-way, and that ZKP_κ is a κ-sound computationally zero-knowledge proof of membership for $\kappa = \mathsf{negl}(\lambda)$. For all w, we take an experiment with r instances of the honest prover and we split it into r successive experiments, with one honest prover per splitted experiment. Each of them is associated to a simulator Sim_i for the ZKP_κ protocol and we denote by T_{Sim_i} the complexity of the simulator. Assuming that the experiment succeeds with probability at least*

$$p_{\mathsf{Sec}} = p_{\mathsf{Sound}} + r.p_{\mathsf{ZK}} + p_{\mathsf{Com}} \tag{5}$$

(where p_{Sound} is defined by (2)) we construct an inversion algorithm for Com_H with complexity

$$\sum_{i=1}^{r} T_{\mathsf{Sim}_i} + T_{\mathsf{Com}_H}.\mathcal{O}\left(B_w^s\right) + rns.T_{\mathsf{Com}}$$

where p_{ZK}, p_{Com}, and T_{Com} are defined as in Lemma 16, T_{Com_H} is the complexity of Com_H, and B_w^s is defined in Theorem 15. For $s = \Omega(\lambda)$ and that $\tau \geq n - (\frac{1}{2} - 2\varepsilon)\lceil\frac{n}{2}\rceil$ with a constant ε, p_{Sec} is negligible. So, ProProx is HP-secure.

Proof. We consider an experiment exp with an honest always far-away prover. Let p be the probability that $\mathcal{V}$ accepts. We want to show that $p = \mathsf{negl}(\lambda)$.

We define $p_B = \mathsf{Tail}(\lceil\frac{n}{2}\rceil, \tau - \lfloor\frac{n}{2}\rfloor, \frac{1}{2})$. We use Lemma 14 to extract the vector sk' when $\mathcal{V}$ accepts, with at least w errors to sk with probability bounded by p_{Sound}. Then, by a $T_{\mathsf{Com}_H}.\mathcal{O}(B_w^s)$-time exhaustive search on the errors, we correct sk' and check if we obtain a preimage of Com_H like in Theorem 15. This gives sk in polynomial time and a probability of success of at least $p - p_{\mathsf{Sound}}$, by playing with some non-concurrent instances of $P(\mathsf{sk})$. For each of the non-concurrent instances of $P(\mathsf{sk})$, we then use the ZK property of $P(\mathsf{sk})$ to construct an algorithm inverting Com_H with probability of success of at least $p - p_{\mathsf{Sound}} - r.p_{\mathsf{ZK}}$, where r is the number of $P(\mathsf{sk})$ instances in one experiment. By assumption on Com_H, this must be bounded by some negligible p_{Com}. So, we have $p \leq p_{\mathsf{Sec}}$ with p_{Sec} defined by Eq. (5). The values κ, p_{ZK}, and p_{Com} are negligible, while r is polynomial and w is constant. So, p_{Sound} and p_{Sec} are negligible. □

Note that a malicious prover can run a distance fraud in each round such that $b_{i,j} = \mathsf{sk}_j$, as $r_{i,j}$ no longer depends on $c_{i,j}$. For $\mathsf{sk} = 0$ (as allowed in the malicious prover model) and $b = 0$, this can be done in all rounds, so we can have a distance fraud. There is no contradiction with soundness: an observer seeing that the verifier accepts can deduce that sk_j is likely to be zero, for all j. So, the malicious prover leaks.

To have distance fraud resistance, we adopt a trick from DB2 [10]: we select a vector b_j with Hamming weight $\lfloor\frac{n}{2}\rfloor$ so that half of the rounds will really use $c_{i,j}$. Actually, b_j has a maximal distance to the repetition code.

Theorem 18 (DF-Resistance). *We assume that Com is a perfectly binding bit commitment and that ZKP_κ is a κ-sound proof of membership for $\kappa = \mathsf{negl}(\lambda)$. Every distance fraud in ProProx succeeds with a probability bounded by*

$$p_{\mathsf{DF}} = \begin{cases} \kappa + \mathsf{Tail}\left(\lfloor\frac{n}{2}\rfloor, \tau - \lceil\frac{n}{2}\rceil, \frac{1}{2}\right)^s & in\ variant\ I \\ \kappa + \left(\frac{3}{4}\right)^{ns} & in\ variant\ II \end{cases} \tag{6}$$

For $n = \Omega(\lambda)$ and $\tau \geq n - (\frac{1}{2} - 2\varepsilon)\lfloor\frac{n}{2}\rfloor$ with a constant ε, p_{DF} is negligible. So, ProProx is DF-resistant.

Proof. We concentrate on the jth iteration. Let w_j be the weight of the vector $b_j \oplus (\mathsf{sk}_j, \ldots, \mathsf{sk}_j)$. Due to the perfectly binding property, the view of $\mathcal{V}$ uniquely defines sk_j and $a_{i,j}$. Thanks to Lemma 1, $r_{i,j}$ is obtained from $\mathsf{Incoming}_\mathcal{V}(\mathsf{Far})$, so independent from $c_{i,j}$. So, for $b_{i,j} \neq \mathsf{sk}_j$ (which happens for w_j rounds), we have that $\Pr[r_{i,j} = a_{i,j} + c_{i,j}b_{i,j} + c_{i,j}\mathsf{sk}_j] = \frac{1}{2}$. So, the probability that the statement in ZKP_κ holds is bounded by $\prod_{j=1}^{s} \mathsf{Tail}(w_j, \tau - n + w_j, \frac{1}{2})$ which is negligible for $\frac{\tau - n + w_j}{w_j} \geq \frac{1}{2} + 2\varepsilon$, due to the Chernoff-Hoeffding bound (Lemma 13) for $n = \Omega(\lambda)$. Due to the fact that ZKP_κ is sound, the verifier accepts with probability bounded by $\kappa + \mathsf{Tail}(\lfloor \frac{n}{2} \rfloor, \tau - \lceil \frac{n}{2} \rceil, \frac{1}{2})^s$ in the first variant of the protocol. In the second variant, we first note that $E(\mathsf{Tail}(w_j, \tau - n + w_j, \frac{1}{2})) = E(2^{-w_j}) = \left(\frac{3}{4}\right)^n$ since $n = \tau$. So, the verifier accepts with probability bounded by $\kappa + \left(\frac{3}{4}\right)^{ns}$. $\square$

We also treat distance hijacking [14] specifically.

Theorem 19 (DH-Resistance). *We assume that* Com *is a perfectly binding bit commitment, that* Com_H *is one-way, and that* ZKP_κ *is a κ-sound proof of membership for* $\kappa = \mathsf{negl}(\lambda)$. *For any constant w, given a DH attack succeeding with probability at least*

$$p_{\mathsf{DH}} = \begin{cases} \kappa + \mathsf{Tail}\left(n, \tau, \frac{1}{2}\right)^w & \text{in variant } I \\ \kappa + \left(\frac{1}{2}\right)^{w\lceil \frac{n}{2} \rceil} & \text{in variant } II \end{cases} \tag{7}$$

we can construct an inversion algorithm for Com_H *with complexity* $T_{\mathsf{Com}_H}.\mathcal{O}\left(s^w\right)$ *where* T_{Com_H} *is the complexity of* Com_H. *For* $n = \Omega(\lambda)$ *and* $\tau \geq n - (\frac{1}{2} - 2\varepsilon)\lceil \frac{n}{2} \rceil$ *with a constant ε, p_{DH} is negligible. So, ProProx is DH-resistant.*

Proof. We consider a DH attack with a malicious prover $P^* = P(\mathsf{sk})$ with a public key pk and an honest prover $P' = P(\mathsf{sk}')$ with a public key pk'. During the initialization, P' chooses some $a'_{i,j}$ bits which are committed in some $A'_{i,j}$. He also receives some $b'_{i,j}$ bits while V has some $b_{i,j}$ bits. The malicious prover P^* sends some $A_{i,j}$ to V and we denote $a_{i,j} = \mathsf{Com}^{-1}(A_{i,j})$. During the challenge phase, V and P' interact in a noisy channel. We write $r'_{i,j} = e_{i,j} + a'_{i,j} + c_{i,j}(b'_{i,j} + \mathsf{sk}'_i)$ the response by P', where $\Pr[e_{i,j} = 1] = p_{\mathsf{noise}}$ and all $e_{i,j}$ are independent. As the verifier expects $r_{i,j} = a_{i,j} + c_{i,j}(b_{i,j} + \mathsf{sk}_j)$, this holds if and only if $a_{i,j} + a'_{i,j} + e_{i,j} = c_{i,j}(b_{i,j} + b'_{i,j} + \mathsf{sk}_j + \mathsf{sk}'_j)$. This can only hold with probability $\frac{1}{2}$ when the content of the parenthesis is equal to 1.

Let w_j be the number of i such that $b_{i,j} + b'_{i,j} \neq \mathsf{sk}_j + \mathsf{sk}'_j$. Clearly, the jth iteration has τ correct responses with probability bounded by $\mathsf{Tail}(w_j, \tau - n + w_j, \frac{1}{2})$. If $w_j \geq \lceil \frac{n}{2} \rceil$, this is bounded by $\mathsf{Tail}(\lceil \frac{n}{2} \rceil, \tau - \lfloor \frac{n}{2} \rfloor, \frac{1}{2})$. Otherwise, the probability is bounded by 1, but the majority of $b_{i,j} + b'_{i,j}$ matches $\mathsf{sk}_j + \mathsf{sk}'_j$ so the adversary deduces sk'_j. Let w be the number of j such that $w_j \geq \lceil \frac{n}{2} \rceil$. Clearly, the responses are overall acceptable with a probability bounded by $\mathsf{Tail}(\lceil \frac{n}{2} \rceil, \tau - \lfloor \frac{n}{2} \rfloor, \frac{1}{2})^w$. Due to the soundness of ZKP_κ, the probability of success is bounded by $\kappa + \mathsf{Tail}(\lceil \frac{n}{2} \rceil, \tau - \lfloor \frac{n}{2} \rfloor, \frac{1}{2})^w$. Furthermore, by the majority decoding, we have an inversion algorithm for Com_H with complexity $\mathcal{O}\left(s^w.T_{\mathsf{Com}_H}\right)$.

We note that when b is fixed in the protocol, w_j is equal to either 0 or n. So, in the first variant of the protocol, the same analysis as above concludes to a probability of success bounded by $\kappa + \mathsf{Tail}(n, \tau, \frac{1}{2})^w$. In the second variant, we have $n = \tau$ and the probability simplifies to $2^{-w\lceil \frac{n}{2}\rceil}$.   □

3.4   Simplification in the Noiseless Communications Case

The protocol could be simplified in noiseless environment. For this, we would take $n = \tau$. There is clearly no need to agree on I_j which is always the full set $I_j = \{1, \ldots, n\}$. The protocol is much simpler. Variant I and Variant II use in (6) the bounds $\left(\frac{1}{2}\right)^{\lfloor \frac{n}{2}\rfloor s}$ and $\left(\frac{3}{4}\right)^{ns}$, respectively. For n even, the Variant I is better, but if we want to lower n down to $n = 1$, we must use Variant II.

3.5   Concrete Parameters

To see if the proven bounds Eqs. (2), (5), (6), and (7) are tight or not, we look at the best known attacks. They correspond to the following probabilities of success:

$$p_{\mathsf{DF}}^{\mathsf{I}} = \mathsf{Tail}\left(\left\lfloor \frac{n}{2}\right\rfloor, \tau - \left\lceil \frac{n}{2}\right\rceil, \frac{1}{2}\right)^s \qquad p_{\mathsf{DF}}^{\mathsf{II}} = \left(\frac{3}{4}\right)^{ns}$$

$$p_{\mathsf{Sec}} = p_{\mathsf{DH}} = \mathsf{Tail}\left(n, \tau, \frac{1}{2}\right)^s \qquad p_{\mathsf{Sound}} = \mathsf{Tail}\left(\left\lceil \frac{n}{2}\right\rceil, \tau - \left\lfloor \frac{n}{2}\right\rfloor, \frac{1}{2}\right)^s$$

where p_{DF} depends on Variant I or Variant II. The DF attack with success probability p_{DF} consists of guessing c_i in half of the rounds for which $b_{i,j} \neq \mathsf{sk}_j$. So, the proven bound Eq. (6) is pretty tight.

The MF attack with success probability p_{Sec} follows the post-ask strategy: the adversary first guesses the answers to all challenges then plays with the prover with the same challenges. Clearly, there is a gap between p_{Sec} and the proven bound of Eq. (5). The DH case is similar: the malicious prover commits to some random $a_{i,j}$ which will make the correspondence between $c_{i,j}$ and $r_{i,j}$ between P' correct for P with probability $\frac{1}{2}$.

The TF attack with success probability p_{Sound} consists of giving a table of all $c'_{i,j} \mapsto r'_{i,j}$ which is corrupted in half of the rounds (selected at random) in each iteration, so that it gives no information about sk_j. Having the table $c'_{i,j} \mapsto r'_{i,j}$ corrupted means that one of the two entries (selected at random) is flipped. There is also a gap with the proven bound Eq. (2).

So, it may be the case that either the bounds Eqs. (2), (5), and (7) can be improved, or that there exist better attacks. To select the parameters, we could either use the *proven* bounds or the above equations based on the best known attacks that we call the *empirical* bounds.

As concrete parameters, we could suggest $\lambda = 80$ bits as the security parameter and a modulus N of $1\,024$ bits. Then, we look for n and τ which minimize the total number of rounds n while keeping $p_{\mathsf{Comp}} \approx 1 - 2^{-7}$ and different objectives:

we propose several vectors of parameters to reach the online security of either $\sigma = 2^{-20}$ (*high*) or $\sigma = 2^{-10}$ (*low*), with *proven* bounds or *empirical* bound, and with either $p_{\text{noise}} = 1\%$ or the noiseless variant ($p_{\text{noise}} = 0$) from Sect. 3.4. In the computation of Eqs. (2) and (5), we took $\kappa = \frac{\sigma}{4}$ and w such that the exhaustive search is not more for a random s-bit string, i.e., $B_w^s \leq 2^\lambda$. For that, we took $s = \lambda + 1$ and $w = \lceil \frac{s}{2} \rceil$.

The total number of rounds is ns.

Security	Bounds	p_{noise}	ns	s	n	w	τ	Variant	p_{Comp}	p_{DF}	p_{Sec}	p_{Sound}	p_{DH}
high	proven	1%	648	81	8	41	6	I	$1 - 2^{-8}$	2^{-22}	2^{-21}	2^{-21}	2^{-22}
high	empirical	1%	640	80	8	–	6	I	$1 - 2^{-8}$	2^{-43}	2^{-223}	2^{-43}	2^{-223}
low	proven	1%	567	81	7	41	5	I	$1 - 2^{-9}$	2^{-12}	2^{-12}	2^{-12}	2^{-12}
low	empirical	1%	560	80	7	–	5	I	$1 - 2^{-9}$	2^{-15}	2^{-171}	2^{-43}	2^{-171}
high	proven	0	162	81	2	41	2	I	1	2^{-22}	2^{-22}	2^{-22}	2^{-22}
high	empirical	0	160	80	2	–	2	I	1	2^{-80}	2^{-160}	2^{-80}	2^{-160}
low	proven	0	162	81	2	41	2	I	1	2^{-12}	2^{-12}	2^{-12}	2^{-12}
low	empirical	0	160	80	2	–	2	I	1	2^{-80}	2^{-160}	2^{-80}	2^{-160}
high	proven	0	81	81	1	41	1	II	1	2^{-22}	2^{-22}	2^{-22}	2^{-22}
high	empirical	0	80	80	1	–	1	II	1	2^{-33}	2^{-80}	2^{-80}	2^{-80}

Clearly, there is a big gap between proven and empirical parameters in the high security values. We can observe that the noise has a huge impact on the complexity. Sometimes, the obtained parameters with low and high security are the same. This comes from p_{Sec} and p_{Sound} being basically equal to κ. As we can see, the noiseless case with $n = 1$ and $s = 80$ offers pretty efficient parameters.

For other parameters, ns may look high. However, we shall keep in mind that distance bounding rounds are exchanging bits very quickly. A challenge/response round shall take much less than 100 ns. So, even by "wasting" 10 μs in between rounds, $ns = 648$ takes less than 7 ms. So, the round-complexity is not so important. What matters more is the impact on other cryptographic operations. Indeed, the prover needs to compute ns commitments, so $\frac{3}{2}ns$ multiplications, and $-\tau s \log_2 \kappa$ parallel rounds of ZKP, so $-\frac{3}{2}\tau s \log_2 \kappa$ multiplications. So, $\frac{3}{2}(n - \tau \log_2 \kappa)s$ multiplications in total. Hence, we shall consider the regular tricks to perform batch ZKP proofs to reduce the complexity.

4   Conclusion

We proposed ProProx, the very first PoPoK addressing soundness. It is provably secure. A remaining challenge is to construct a more efficient PoPoK. Another open question would be to have a tight security proof for ProProx.

Acknowledgements. This work was partly sponsored by the ICT COST Action IC1403 Cryptacus in the EU Framework Horizon 2020.

References

1. Avoine, G., Bingöl, M., Kardas, S., Lauradoux, C., Martin, B.: A framework for analyzing RFID distance bounding protocols. J. Comput. Secur. **19**(2), 289–317 (2011)
2. Avoine, G., Tchamkerten, A.: An efficient distance bounding RFID authentication protocol: balancing false-acceptance rate and memory requirement. In: Samarati, P., Yung, M., Martinelli, F., Ardagna, C.A. (eds.) ISC 2009. LNCS, vol. 5735, pp. 250–261. Springer, Heidelberg (2009)
3. Bay, A., Boureanu, I., Mitrokotsa, A., Spulber, I., Vaudenay, S.: The bussard-bagga and other distance-bounding protocols under attacks. In: Kutyłowski, M., Yung, M. (eds.) Inscrypt 2012. LNCS, vol. 7763, pp. 371–391. Springer, Heidelberg (2013)
4. Beth, T., Desmedt, Y.G.: Identification tokens – or: solving the chess grandmaster problem. In: Menezes, A., Vanstone, S.A. (eds.) CRYPTO 1990. LNCS, vol. 537, pp. 169–176. Springer, Heidelberg (1991)
5. Boureanu, I., Mitrokotsa, A., Vaudenay, S.: Secure and lightweight distance-bounding. In: Avoine, G., Kara, O. (eds.) LightSec 2013. LNCS, vol. 8162, pp. 97–113. Springer, Heidelberg (2013)
6. Boureanu, I., Mitrokotsa, A., Vaudenay, S.: Practical & Provably Secure Distance-Bounding. IACR Eprint 2013/465 report (2013)
7. Boureanu, I., Mitrokotsa, A., Vaudenay, S.: Towards secure distance bounding. In: Moriai, S. (ed.) FSE 2013. LNCS, vol. 8424, pp. 55–68. Springer, Heidelberg (2014)
8. Boureanu, I., Mitrokotsa, A., Vaudenay, S.: Practical & Provably Secure Distance-Bounding. To appear in the Proceedings of ISC 2013 (2013)
9. Boureanu, I., Mitrokotsa, K., Vaudenay, S.: Practical and provably secure distance-bounding. J. Comput. Secur. (JCS) **23**(2), 229–257 (2015)
10. Boureanu, I., Vaudenay, S.: Optimal proximity proofs. In: Lin, D., Yung, M., Zhou, J. (eds.) Inscrypt 2014. LNCS, vol. 8957, pp. 170–190. Springer, Heidelberg (2015)
11. Brands, S., Chaum, D.: Distance bounding protocols. In: Helleseth, T. (ed.) EUROCRYPT 1993. LNCS, vol. 765, pp. 344–359. Springer, Heidelberg (1994)
12. Bussard, L., Bagga, W.: Distance-bounding proof of knowledge to avoid real-time attacks. In: Sasaki, R., Qing, S., Okamoto, E., Yoshiura, H. (eds.) Security and Privacy in the Age of Ubiquitous Computing. IFIP AICT, vol. 181, pp. 223–238. Springer, Heidelberg (2005)
13. Chernoff, H.: A measure of asymptotic efficiency for tests of a hypothesis based on the sum of observations. Ann. Math. Stat. **23**(4), 493–507 (1952)
14. Cremers, C.J.F., Rasmussen, C.J.F., Schmidt, B., Čapkun, S.: Distance hijacking attacks on distance bounding protocols. In: IEEE Symposium on Security and Privacy S&P'12, San Francisco, California, USA, pp. 113–127. IEEE Computer Society (2012)
15. Desmedt, Y.: Major security problems with the "Unforgeable" (Feige-)Fiat-shamir proofs of identity and how to overcome them. In: Congress on Computer and Communication Security and Protection Securicom 1988, Paris, France, pp. 147–159. SEDEP Paris France (1988)
16. Dürholz, U., Fischlin, M., Kasper, M., Onete, C.: A formal approach to distance-bounding RFID protocols. In: Lai, X., Zhou, J., Li, H. (eds.) ISC 2011. LNCS, vol. 7001, pp. 47–62. Springer, Heidelberg (2011)
17. Fiat, A., Shamir, A.: How to prove yourself: practical solutions to identification and signature problems. In: Odlyzko, A.M. (ed.) CRYPTO 1986. LNCS, vol. 263, pp. 186–194. Springer, Heidelberg (1987)

18. Fischlin, M., Onete, C.: Terrorism in distance bounding: modeling terrorist-fraud resistance. In: Jacobson, M., Locasto, M., Mohassel, P., Safavi-Naini, R. (eds.) ACNS 2013. LNCS, vol. 7954, pp. 414–431. Springer, Heidelberg (2013)

19. Gambs, S., Onete, C., Robert, J.-M.: Prover anonymous and deniable distance-bounding authentication. In: ACM Symposium on Information, Computer and Communications Security (ASIACCS 2014), Kyoto, Japan, pp. 501–506. ACM Press (2014)

20. Goldwasser, S., Micali, S.: Probabilistic encryption and how to play mental poker keeping secret all partial information. In: Proceedings of the 14th ACM Symposium on Theory of Computing, San Fransisco, California, USA, pp. 365–377. ACM Press (1982)

21. Goldwasser, S., Micali, S.: Probabilistic encryption. J. Comput. Syst. Sci. **28**, 270–299 (1984)

22. Hermans, J., Peeters, R., Onete, C.: Efficient, secure, private distance bounding without key updates. In: ACM Conference on Security and Privacy in Wireless and Mobile Networks WISEC 2013, Budapest, Hungary, pp. 195–206. ACM (2013)

23. Hoeffding, W.: Probability inequalities for sums of bounded random variables. J. Am. Stat. Assoc. **58**, 13–30 (1963)

24. Kılınç, H., Vaudenay, S.: Optimal Proximity Proof Revisited. To appear in ACNS 2015 (2015)

25. Vaudenay, S.: On modeling terrorist frauds. In: Susilo, W., Reyhanitabar, R. (eds.) ProvSec 2013. LNCS, vol. 8209, pp. 1–20. Springer, Heidelberg (2013)

26. Vaudenay, S.: Private and secure public-key distance bounding. In: Böhme, R., Okamoto, T. (eds.) FC 2015. LNCS, vol. 8975, pp. 207–216. Springer, Heidelberg (2015)

27. Vaudenay, S.: On Privacy for RFID. In: Au, M.-H., Miyaji, A. (eds.) ProvSec 2015. LNCS, vol. 9451, pp. 3–20. Springer, Heidelberg (2015)

Multi-party Computation with Small Shuffle Complexity Using Regular Polygon Cards

Kazumasa Shinagawa[1,2]($\boxtimes$), Takaaki Mizuki[3], Jacob C.N. Schuldt[2],
Koji Nuida[2], Naoki Kanayama[1], Takashi Nishide[1], Goichiro Hanaoka[2],
and Eiji Okamoto[1]

[1] University of Tsukuba, Tsukuba, Japan
shinagawa@cipher.risk.tsukuba.ac.jp
[2] National Institute of Advanced Industrial Science and Technology,
Tsukuba, Japan
[3] Tohoku University, Sendai, Japan

Abstract. It is well-known that a protocol for any function can be constructed using only cards and various shuffling techniques (this is referred to as a *card-based protocol*). In this paper, we propose a new type of cards called regular polygon cards. These cards enable a new encoding for multi-valued inputs while the previous works can only handle binary inputs. We furthermore propose a new technique for constructing a card-based protocol for any n-ary function with small shuffle complexity. This is the first general construction in which the shuffle complexity is independent of the complexity (size/depth) of the desired functionality, although being directly proportional to the number of inputs. The construction furthermore supports a wide range of cards and encodings, including previously proposed types of cards. Our techniques provide a method for reducing the number of shuffles in card-based protocols.

Keywords: Multi-party computation · Card-based protocol · Polygon cards · Shuffle complexity

1 Introduction

1.1 Background

Since the seminal work of den Boer [2], many card-based protocols have been proposed, which can securely compute a function by applying shuffles to sequences of cards [1–13]. Compared to computer-based protocols, a card-based protocol can be performed without the use of computers and electricity. Thus, this type of protocol is suitable when computers are not available or the parties do not trust the security of computers-based protocols (although card-based protocols require a different set of trust assumptions). Moreover, it is easy to understand the correctness and the security of card-based protocols since they do not rely on complicated reductions to mathematical problems which may be hard to verify and understand for non-experts.

© Springer International Publishing Switzerland 2015
M.-H. Au and A. Miyaji (Eds.): ProvSec 2015, LNCS 9451, pp. 127–146, 2015.
DOI: 10.1007/978-3-319-26059-4_7

The *Five-Card Trick* [2] is the first card-based protocol, in which two parties can securely compute the AND function of their secret inputs, using five cards that have two types of front sides ([♣], [♡]) and identical backs ([×]). In the subsequent works [1,3–13], many card-based protocols are proposed which focus on feasibility results and reducing the number of cards required in the protocols. In 2009, Mizuki and Sone [8] proposed composable AND, XOR, and COPY protocols using six, four, and six cards, respectively. (It is possible to compute any functions by composing these protocols.) These results [8] are the most efficient construction for the elementary boolean functions with respect to a commonly used encoding scheme in which each input bit is encoded using two cards (a *two-cards-per-bit encoding scheme*). For any n-ary boolean function, Nishida et al. [10] showed that it is possible to construct a $(2n+6)$-card protocol using a two-cards-per-bit encoding scheme. In 2014, Mizuki and Shizuya [7] showed that under a *one-card-per-bit encoding scheme*[1] it is possible to construct composable AND, XOR, and COPY protocols using three, two, and three cards with rotationally symmetric backs. (A protocol for any n-ary function using only $n + 3$ cards can easily be obtained by combining the result from [10] with the encoding scheme in [7].)

While previous results show that it is feasible to construct a protocol for an arbitrary function using a small number of cards, it is unknown how to construct a protocol with small shuffle complexity. Since shuffles are the most costly operations, a large number of shuffles immediately imply a large computational overhead. Let f be a function and let $|f|$ be the smallest number of gates (AND/XOR/COPY) in circuits implementing f. In this case, we can obtain a protocol for f using the previous AND/XOR/COPY protocols to evaluate the circuit for f, which yields a shuffle complexity of exactly $|f|$. We stress that even if a protocol has an asymptotic small number of shuffles (e.g. polynomial in $|f|$), it is not always considered to be efficient. For card-based protocols, it is desirable that the shuffle complexity is as low as possible (with small coefficients), and ideally, that it is independent of the complexity of the desired functionality.

1.2   Our Contribution

Our main contributions are as follows: (1) We first propose a new type of cards, regular polygon cards, that can deal with multi-valued inputs directly. As a result, we can construct a protocol for an arbitrary linear function with small shuffle complexity. (2) We define a new notion, which we call oblivious conversion. This enables the construction of a protocol for any functions with small shuffle complexity. (3) We show that the regular polygon cards enable the construction of an efficient voting protocol for multiple candidates. Our protocols

---

[1] We stress that the two-card-per-bit encoding schemes are important since the one-card-per-bit encoding scheme [7] needs unnatural shuffle for computing the AND function. Thus, it is still meaningful to improve protocols under the two-cards-per-bit encoding schemes.

Table 1. Comparison between our protocols and previous protocols

	Type of cards	Shuffle Complexity	Number of cards
o Addition and Subtraction over $\mathbb{Z}/m\mathbb{Z}$			
[3,8] based	standard	$O(\log m)$	$O(\log m)$
Ours	m-sided	1	2
o Multiplication by $a \in \mathbb{Z}/m\mathbb{Z}$			
[3,8] based	standard	$O(\log a \cdot \log m)$	$O(\log a \cdot \log m)$
Ours	m-sided	$\lceil \log_2 a \rceil + 1$	$\lceil \log_2 a \rceil + 2$
o Protocol for an arbitrary $f : (\mathbb{Z}/m\mathbb{Z})^n \to \mathbb{Z}/m\mathbb{Z}$			
[10] based	standard	$O(m^n \cdot \log m)$	$2((n+1)\lceil \log_2 m \rceil + 2)$
Ours	m-sided	n	$mn + m^n$
o Protocol for an arbitrary $f : (\mathbb{Z}/2\mathbb{Z})^n \to \mathbb{Z}/2\mathbb{Z}$			
[10]	standard	$O(2^n)$	$2(n+3)$
Ours	standard	n	$2(n + 2^n)$

Table 2. Comparison between our voting protocol and previous voting protocol

	# of voters	# of candi.	Input timing	# of shuffles	# of cards
[3] (standard)	any n	2	restricted	$O(n \log n)$	$2\lceil \log_2 n \rceil + 6$
Ours (Sect. 4)	n ($n < m$)	any ℓ	no restriction	n	$\ell^n + \ell n$
Ours (Sect. 5)	n ($n < m$)	any ℓ	no restriction	$n + 1$	$(n + 2)\ell$

using regular m-sided polygon cards have smaller shuffle complexity than protocols using the previously proposed cards ♣, ♡ (the cards are referred to as *standard* in Table 1).

Regular Polygon Cards. The regular m-sided polygon cards (Fig. 1) have $(360/m)°$ rotational symmetry, and have a value corresponding to an element of $\mathbb{Z}/m\mathbb{Z}$. The card with rotationally symmetric backs proposed by Mizuki and Shizuya [7] (in the context of one-card-per-bit encoding schemes) can be regarded as a regular 2-sided polygon card. Our work introduces the first card-based protocols for multi-valued inputs while all previous works [1–13] only consider binary inputs. Using the m-sided polygon cards, it is possible to construct addition, subtraction, and copy protocols over $\mathbb{Z}/m\mathbb{Z}$ using only a single shuffle while protocols based on [8,10] use $O(\log m)$ shuffles (see Table 1, Addition and Subtraction). We also construct a protocol for multiplication by a constant $a \in \mathbb{Z}/m\mathbb{Z}$ using only $\lceil \log_2 a \rceil + 1$ shuffles while protocols based on [8,10] use $O(\log a \cdot \log m)$ shuffles (see Table 1, Multiplication). Composing our protocols, we can securely compute an arbitrary linear function while maintaining a small shuffle complexity.

Oblivious Conversion. We define a new notion, oblivious conversion, which is a generalization of oblivious transfer. This is a protocol that takes as inputs an encoding of $x \in \mathbb{Z}/m_0\mathbb{Z}$ and a function $f : \mathbb{Z}/m_0\mathbb{Z} \to \mathbb{Z}/m_1\mathbb{Z}$, and outputs an encoding of $f(x) \in \mathbb{Z}/m_1\mathbb{Z}$. By applying an oblivious conversion n times, it is possible to construct protocols for arbitrary n-ary functions (see Table 1, Protocol for an arbitrary f). This approach can be applied to various cards (and encodings) including the regular polygon cards and the previously proposed cards ($\clubsuit$, $\heartsuit$). Here, a protocol for $f : \bigotimes_{i=0}^{n-1} \mathbb{Z}/m_i\mathbb{Z} \to \mathbb{Z}/m_n\mathbb{Z}$ (i.e., the domain of f is n tuples in which each element belongs to $\mathbb{Z}/m_i\mathbb{Z}$) is regarded as an MPC protocol for f with n parties $P_0, P_1, \cdots, P_{n-1}$ where P_i holds the secret input $x_i \in \mathbb{Z}/m_i\mathbb{Z}$. Thus, an MPC protocol for any n-ary function can be obtained by applying oblivious conversion by n times. The shuffle complexity of the obtained protocol is small, and it does not depend on the complexity (size/depth) of the function to be evaluated.

Voting Protocol. While oblivious conversion allows the generic construction of protocols with a small shuffle complexity, it might still be possible to construct even more efficient protocols for specific functionalities. We specifically construct an efficient voting protocol for multiple candidates. For n voters and ℓ candidates, using the regular m-sided polygon cards ($m > n$), our protocol uses $n+1$ shuffles and $(n+2)\ell$ cards, while a protocol based on oblivious conversion uses n shuffles and $\ell^n + \ell n$ cards.

1.3 Related Works

In 1993, Crépeau and Kilian [1] achieved protocols implementing any functionality by constructing composable elementary protocols (COPY/XOR/AND). In 2009, Mizuki and Sone [8] constructed composable elementary protocols using fewer cards, by applying a new shuffle called a *random bisection cut*. To evaluate a function that has $|f|$ gates (COPY/XOR/AND), the shuffle complexity of the obtained protocol is exactly $|f|$. On the other hand, our construction (Sect. 4) requires only n shuffles where n is the number of inputs to the function.

Mizuki, Asiedu, and Sone [3] constructed a voting protocol with n voters and 2 candidates, using $2\lceil \log_2 n \rceil + 6$ cards. However, this protocol restricts the timing of the voter inputs in order to reduce the number of required cards; an unrestricted protocol requires $O(n)$ cards to encode the voter inputs. Our protocol is unrestricted, requires n cards, and makes use of $n + 1$ shuffles. In contrast, the protocol from [3] requires $O(n \log n)$ shuffles (see Table 2).

2 Our New Cards and Model of Protocols

In this section, we propose *regular polygon cards*, and define protocols and the security based on regular polygon cards as well as the standard notion of security.

2.1 Regular Polygon Cards

We first propose new cards called *regular polygon cards*, which are conceptually different from previous cards ($\clubsuit$, $\heartsuit$). A regular m-sided polygon card encodes an element of $\mathbb{Z}/m\mathbb{Z}$, while previous works use two cards to encode an element of $\mathbb{Z}/2\mathbb{Z}$. From now on, we use $\mathbb{Z}_m$ to denote $\mathbb{Z}/m\mathbb{Z}$.

Definition 1 (Regular Polygon Card). *A card is called a* regular *m-sided* polygon card *if the front side of the card has no rotational symmetry and the back side of the card has* $(360/m)°$ *rotational symmetry.*

Note that m, in a regular m-sided polygon card, does not refer to the shape of the cards, but the symmetry of the back side of the card. Indeed, for all $m = m_0 m_1$, a regular m-sided polygon card is both a regular m_0-sided polygon card and a regular m_1-sided polygon card. In the case of $m = 2$, a regular 2-sided polygon card refer to a card with a 180° rotationally symmetric pattern [7].

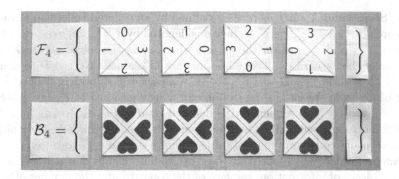

Fig. 1. An example of regular 4-sided polygon cards

Set of Cards. The cards (Fig. 1) are an example of regular m-sided polygon cards ($m = 4$). Letting the front side of a card correspond to a value of $\mathbb{Z}_m$ decided by the card's rotation, a set of front side cards $\mathcal{F}_m$ is obtained as $\mathcal{F}_m = \{0, 1, \cdots, m-1\}$. (See the upper four cards in Fig. 1; the value of a card corresponds to the number shown in the top of the card.) Using $[\![x]\!]$ to denote a card put face-down[2] whose value is x, a set of back side cards $\mathcal{B}_m$ is obtained as $\mathcal{B}_m = \{[\![0]\!], [\![1]\!], \cdots, [\![m-1]\!]\}$ (see the lower four cards in Fig. 1). A set of cards $\mathcal{C}_m$ is defined by $\mathcal{C}_m = \mathcal{F}_m \cup \mathcal{B}_m$. Let rot_m and flip_m be a rotation function and a flip function, s.t., $\mathsf{rot}_m, \mathsf{flip}_m : \mathcal{C}_m \to \mathcal{C}_m$. The rotation function rot_m takes $x \in \mathcal{F}_m$ or $[\![x]\!] \in \mathcal{B}_m$ as input, and outputs $x - 1 \in \mathcal{F}_m$ or $[\![x+1]\!] \in \mathcal{B}_m$, respectively. (Note that both of $x \to x - 1$ and $[\![x]\!] \to [\![x+1]\!]$ correspond to the same rotation operation.) The flip function flip_m takes $x \in \mathcal{F}_m$ or $[\![x]\!] \in \mathcal{B}_m$ as input, and outputs $[\![x]\!] \in \mathcal{B}_m$ or $x \in \mathcal{F}_m$, respectively. From now on, we often omit m and denote $\mathcal{C}_m, \mathcal{F}_m, \mathcal{B}_m, \mathsf{rot}_m, \mathsf{flip}_m$ as $\mathcal{C}, \mathcal{F}, \mathcal{B}, \mathsf{rot}, \mathsf{flip}$. Using rot and flip, any card $[\![x]\!] \in \mathcal{B}$ or $x \in \mathcal{F}$ can be expressed by operations on $[\![0]\!]$, i.e., $[\![x]\!] = \mathsf{rot}^x([\![0]\!])$ and $x = \mathsf{flip}(\mathsf{rot}^x([\![0]\!]))$. We define a *face function* face which expresses the face of cards. For $[\![x]\!] \in \mathcal{B}$, $\mathsf{face}([\![x]\!]) = \times$, and for $x \in \mathcal{F}$, $\mathsf{face}(x) = \text{``}x\text{''}$, where $\times$ and "$x$" are symbols. Thus, the face function is a function that takes an element of $\mathcal{C}$ as input, and outputs an element of a set of symbols $\{\text{``0''}, \text{``1''}, \cdots, \text{``}m-1\text{''}, \times\}$.

---

[2] We assume that the direction of flipping is predetermined.

Fig. 2. An example of a sequence whose face is ("1", $\times^3$, "0"^{3}, "2")

Stack/Sequence. A *stack of cards* is defined by an ordered collection of cards. For t cards $c_0, c_1, \cdots, c_{t-1} \in \mathcal{C}$, a stack d is denoted by $d = c_0 \circ c_1 \circ \cdots \circ c_{t-1} \in \mathcal{C}^t$ (the top is c_0 and c_{t-1} is on the table), where $\mathcal{C}^t$ is the set of all stacks of t cards. Note that a card $c \in \mathcal{C}$ is a special case of a stack. We use $\mathcal{D}$ to denote a set of all stacks, i.e., $\mathcal{D} = \bigcup_{i=1}^{\infty} \mathcal{C}^i$. A *sequence (of stacks)* is defined by a vector of multiple stacks (see an example of a sequence in Fig. 2). For k stacks $d_0, d_1, \cdots, d_{k-1} \in \mathcal{D}$, a sequence $\boldsymbol{d}$ is denoted by $\boldsymbol{d} = (d_0, d_1, \cdots, d_{k-1}) \in \mathcal{D}^k$. The difference between a stack and a sequence is that a stack is a single object while a sequence consists of multiple objects. For a stack $d = c_0 \circ c_1 \circ \cdots \circ c_{t-1}$, the *face function* is defined by $\mathsf{face}(d) = (\mathsf{face}(c_0), t)$. This means that a face of stacks have two pieces of information; the face of the top card and the number of cards in the stack[3]. From now on, we use $(\mathsf{face}(c))^t$ to denote $(\mathsf{face}(c), t)$. For example, for an encoding $[\![x]\!] \in \mathcal{B}$ and a card $c \in \mathcal{C}$, $\mathsf{face}([\![x]\!] \circ c) = (\mathsf{face}([\![x]\!]))^2 = \times^2$. For a sequence $\boldsymbol{d} = (d_0, d_1, \cdots, d_{k-1}) \in \mathcal{D}^k$, the *face function* is defined by $\mathsf{face}(\boldsymbol{d}) = (\mathsf{face}(d_0), \mathsf{face}(d_1), \cdots, \mathsf{face}(d_{k-1}))$ (see Fig. 2).

Encoding. For a finite set X, an *encoding* is defined as an injective function E which maps $x \in X$ to a tuple of back side cards $\mathcal{B}^k$, where k is the length of the encoding. This is also called a *commitment* in previous card-based protocols. For an encoding E over $\mathbb{Z}_m$, we often omit "mod m", e.g., we use $\mathsf{E}(x - 1)$ to denote $\mathsf{E}(x - 1 \bmod m)$. The most natural encoding is the one that maps $x \in \mathbb{Z}_m$ to $\mathsf{E}(x) = [\![x]\!]$. Unless otherwise noted, this is the encoding we use. (In Sects. 4 and 5, we use other encodings to achieve a small shuffle complexity.)

2.2   Operations

We now define operations for sequences; permutation, rotation, flip, shuffle, composition/decomposition, and insert/delete.

Permutation. Let S_k be the symmetric group of degree k. For a permutation of k objects $\sigma \in S_k$, we define a *permutation operation* σ that takes as input a sequence $\boldsymbol{d} = (d_0, d_1, \ldots, d_{k-1}) \in \mathcal{D}^k$ and outputs $\sigma(\boldsymbol{d})$. We define a useful permutation $\mathsf{cyc}_k \in S_k$ that takes $(d_0, d_1, \ldots, d_{k-1})$, and outputs $(d_1, \ldots, d_{k-1}, d_0)$.

---

[3] The number of cards in a stack would be revealed by the thickness of the stack.

We often omit the degree k and denote cyc_k as cyc.

$$(d_0, d_1, \ldots, d_{k-1}) \xrightarrow{\text{Perm } \sigma} (d_{\sigma^{-1}(0)}, d_{\sigma^{-1}(1)}, \ldots, d_{\sigma^{-1}(k-1)}).$$

$$(d_0, d_1, \ldots, d_{k-1}) \xrightarrow{\text{Perm cyc}} (d_1, \ldots, d_{k-1}, d_0).$$

Rotation. We define a *rotation operation* that takes as input a stack $d \in \mathcal{D}$ and outputs $\mathsf{rot}(d)$. Here, the rotated stack, $\mathsf{rot}(d)$, corresponds to subtracting 1 (modulo m) to the value of all front side cards $c \in \mathcal{F}$, and adding 1 from the value of all back side cards $c \in \mathcal{B}$ in the stack d. By $\mathsf{rot}^i(d)$ we denote the rotation operation applied i times. For $[\![x]\!]$ and a public number a, we can obtain $[\![x + a]\!]$ by applying $\mathsf{rot}^a([\![x]\!])$. We use the following notation.

$$d \xrightarrow{\text{Rot}} \mathsf{rot}(d). \qquad\qquad d \xrightarrow{\text{Rot}^i} \mathsf{rot}^i(d).$$

Flip. We define a *flip operation* that takes as input a card $c \in \mathcal{C}$ and outputs $\mathsf{flip}(c)$ which corresponds to the card c flipped around. For example, given the back side card $[\![x]\!]$, $\mathsf{flip}(x)$ corresponds to the front side x. When the input is a single back side card, we sometimes refer to the flip operation as open. We use the following notation.

$$c \xrightarrow{\text{Flip}} \mathsf{flip}(c).$$

Shuffle. In this paper, we use two shuffles, called a cyclic shuffle and a rotation shuffle. Let a sequence $d = (d_0, d_1, \cdots, d_{k-1}) \in \mathcal{D}^k$ satisfy $\mathsf{face}(d_0) = \mathsf{face}(d_1) = \cdots = \mathsf{face}(d_{k-1})$. We define a *cyclic shuffle* that takes as input a sequence d as above and outputs $\mathsf{cyc}^r(d)$ where r is uniformly chosen from $\mathbb{Z}_k$. (We assume that nobody knows the value r except when all parties are corrupted by an adversary.) Let a stack $d \in \mathcal{D}$ satisfy $\mathsf{face}(d) = \mathsf{face}(\mathsf{rot}(d)) = \cdots = \mathsf{face}(\mathsf{rot}^{m-1}(d))$. (Thus, the top of stack d is a back side card.) We define a *rotation shuffle* that takes as input a stack d as above and outputs $\mathsf{rot}^r(d)$ where r is uniformly chosen from $\mathbb{Z}_m$. (Similarly, we assume that nobody knows the value r.) As far as we know, all shuffles used in previous works can be expressed by the combination of the operations defined here[4]. As in previous works, we can securely operate a cyclic shuffle and a rotation shuffle[5].

$$(d_0, d_1, \cdots, d_{k-1}) \xrightarrow{\text{CycShffl}} \mathsf{cyc}_k^r(d_0, d_1, \cdots, d_{k-1}).$$

$$d \xrightarrow{\text{RotShffl}} \mathsf{rot}^r(d).$$

---

[4] The "cyclic shuffle" used in [2] and the random bisection cut proposed in [8] corresponds to one of our cyclic shuffles. Similarly, the shuffle used in [7] and the "rotation shuffle" used in [12] corresponds to one of the our rotation shuffles.

[5] We demonstrate how to securely obtain a cyclic shuffle. Let $P_0, \cdots, P_{n-1}$ be the parties participating in the protocol. P_0 chooses a uniformly random value $r_0 \in \mathbb{Z}_k$ and applies cyc^{r_0} to d, and sends $\mathsf{cyc}^{r_0}(d)$ to P_1. Similarly, P_i receives d', chooses $r_i \in \mathbb{Z}_k$, and sends $\mathsf{cyc}^{r_i}(d')$ to P_{i+1}. Finally, P_{n-1} outputs $\mathsf{cyc}^r(d)$ where $r = r_0 + \cdots + r_{n-1}$. Nobody knows the uniform random value r except when all parties are corrupted by an adversary assuming parties are *honest-but-curious*.

Composition/Decomposition. We define a *composition operation* that takes as input a pair of cards (c_0, c_1) where $c_0, c_1 \in \mathcal{C}$ and outputs a stack $c_0 \circ c_1 \in \mathcal{C}^2$. We define a *decomposition operation* as the inverse operation of a composition, i.e., it takes $c_0 \circ c_1 \in \mathcal{C}^2$ and outputs (c_0, c_1). Similarly, we define a *flip composition operation* that takes (c_0, c_1) where $c_0, c_1 \in \mathcal{C}$ and outputs $c_0 \circ \mathsf{flip}(c_1) \in \mathcal{C}^2$, and *flip decomposition operation* that is the inverse operation of a flip composition. We use the following notation.

$$(c_0, c_1) \xrightarrow{\mathsf{Comp}} c_0 \circ c_1. \qquad\qquad c_0 \circ c_1 \xrightarrow{\mathsf{Decomp}} (c_0, c_1).$$

$$(c_0, c_1) \xrightarrow{\mathsf{FComp}} c_0 \circ \mathsf{flip}(c_1). \qquad c_0 \circ c_1 \xrightarrow{\mathsf{FDecomp}} (c_0, \mathsf{flip}(c_1)).$$

Insert/Delete. We define an *insert operation* that takes as input a sequence $(d_0, d_1, \cdots, d_{k-1}) \in \mathcal{D}^k$ and outputs $(0, d_0, d_1, \cdots, d_{k-1}) \in \mathcal{D}^{k+1}$. Oppositely, we define a *delete operation* that takes a sequence $(d_0, d_1, \cdots, d_{k-1}) \in \mathcal{D}^k$ and outputs $(d_1, \cdots, d_{k-1}) \in \mathcal{D}^{k-1}$. Note that using permutation and rotation operations we can easily insert/delete any card at any position. We use the following notation.

$$(d_0, d_1, \cdots, d_{k-1}) \xrightarrow{\mathsf{Insert}} (0, d_0, d_1, \cdots, d_{k-1}).$$

$$(d_0, d_1, \cdots, d_{k-1}) \xrightarrow{\mathsf{Del}} (d_1, \cdots, d_{k-1}).$$

We have now defined all operations used in our protocols. However, we would like to apply these operations to a subsequence of the sequence. (For example, we want to apply a shuffle to a half of sequence.) For this reason, we use (naturally) extended operations that apply to a subsequence as follows.

$$(d_0, d_1, d_2, \cdots, d_{k-1}) \xrightarrow{\mathsf{RotShffl}\ \{0,1\}} (\mathsf{rot}^r(d_0), \mathsf{rot}^r(d_1), d_2, \cdots, d_{k-1}).$$

$$(c_0, c_1, d_2, \cdots, d_{k-1}) \xrightarrow{\mathsf{Flip}\ \{0,1\}} (\mathsf{flip}(c_0), \mathsf{flip}(c_1), d_2, \cdots, d_{k-1}).$$

$$(d_0, d_1, d_2, \cdots, d_{k-1}) \xrightarrow{\mathsf{Comp}\ \{1,2\}} (d_0, d_1 \circ d_2, d_3, \cdots, d_{k-1}).$$

$$(d_0, d_1, \cdots, d_{k-1}) \xrightarrow{\mathsf{Del}\ \{1,k-1\}} (d_0, d_2, d_3, \cdots, d_{k-2}).$$

We use $\mathcal{O}$ to denote the set of extended operations as above. Here, we stress that the shuffles are special operations[6]. We use $\mathcal{O}_S$ to denote the set of shuffles. The set of shuffles is a proper subset of the set of extended operations ($\mathcal{O}_S \subset \mathcal{O}$).

2.3   Model

Protocol. We define a protocol using regular m-sided polygon cards as follows.

Definition 2 (Protocol). *A protocol Π taking input $(x_0, x_1, \cdots, x_{n-1})$ is specified by $\langle (P_0, P_1, \cdots, P_{n-1}), (\mathsf{E}, \mathsf{E}'), \pi \rangle$, where P_i is a party who holds the secret*

---

[6] All operations except shuffles output a sequence in a deterministic way. However, shuffles output a sequence in a probabilistic way under a uniformly random value r.

value x_i, E and E' are the input and output encodings, and π is a transition function that takes as input a vector of faces of sequences, and outputs an element of $\mathcal{O} \cup \{\perp\}$. The protocol Π proceeds as follows.

1. *P_i submits $\mathsf{E}(x_i)$ in public. Let $c_0 := (\mathsf{E}(x_0), \mathsf{E}(x_1), \cdots, \mathsf{E}(x_{n-1}))$ be the initial sequence, and let $C_0 := (c_0)$ be the initial vector of sequences.*
2. *Iteratively proceed as follows: For a vector $C_i = (c_0, c_1, \cdots, c_i)$, apply the operation $\tau_i := \pi(\mathsf{face}(c_0), \cdots, \mathsf{face}(c_i))$ to the sequence c_i, and obtain the sequence $c_i + 1$.*
   - *When $\tau_i \notin \mathcal{O}_S$ (τ_i is not a shuffle operation), all parties publicly obtain $c_i + 1$ by applying τ_i to c_i, i.e., $c_i \xrightarrow{\tau_i} c_i + 1$. Note that all of these operations proceed in public.*
   - *When $\tau_i \in \mathcal{O}_S$ (τ_i is a shuffle operation), all parties invoke a shuffle protocol for c_i, and obtain $c_i + 1$. In the shuffle protocol, each party P_i generates a uniformly random value r_i privately, and apply cyc^{r_i} or rot^{r_i} to the sequence. As a result, all parties obtain the sequence obtained from applying cyc^r or rot^r where $r := r_0 + r_1 + \cdots + r_{n-1}$. We use $c_i \xrightarrow{\tau_i(r)} c_i + 1$ to denote a shuffle under the random value r.*
   - *When $\tau_i = \perp$, all of the parties output $c_{\mathrm{our}} := c_i$ as an output sequence.*

For a protocol Π with input $x = (x_0, x_1, \cdots, x_{n-1})$ we use $\mathsf{Trans}(\Pi, x)$ to denote the transcript of an execution of $\Pi(x)$, including the random values generated by the parties as part of the protocol:

$$\mathsf{Trans}(\Pi, x) \to ((\mathsf{face}(c_0), \mathsf{face}(c_1), \cdots, \mathsf{face}(c_\ell)), \mathsf{face}(c_{\mathrm{out}}), r_0, r_1, \cdots, r_n - 1)$$

where ℓ is the number of generated sequences, c_{out} is the output sequence c_{out}, and r_i is a vector of random values[7] used by P_i.

Security. As in standard multi-party computation, we define security via a simulation-based security experiment. Intuitively, our notion of security captures that any set of corrupt users cannot learn anything about the secret input of honest users, expect for the output of the protocol. More specifically, for a protocol to be secure, we require that there exist an efficient simulator which can simulate the corrupt user's view of the protocol execution, without access to the honest user's input. We define a perfect security for a protocol Π as follows.

Definition 3 (Perfect Security). *Let Π be a protocol. We say that Π is perfectly secure if for any $\mathfrak{C} \subsetneq \mathbb{Z}_n$ there exists an efficient algorithm $\mathcal{S}$ such that for any $x = (x_0, x_1, \cdots, x_{n-1})$ the outputs of the experiments $\mathsf{Exp}^0_{\Pi, \mathfrak{C}}(x)$ and $\mathsf{Exp}^1_{\Pi, \mathfrak{C}, \mathcal{S}}(x)$ are distributed identically.*

$\mathsf{Exp}^0_{\Pi, \mathfrak{C}}(x)$	$\mathsf{Exp}^1_{\Pi, \mathfrak{C}, \mathcal{S}}(x)$
$\mathsf{Trans}(\Pi, x)$	$\mathsf{Trans}(\Pi, x)$
$\to (\mathsf{face}(C), \mathsf{face}(c_{\mathrm{out}}), \{r_i\}_{i \in \mathbb{Z}_n});$	$\to (\mathsf{face}(C), \mathsf{face}(c_{\mathrm{out}}), \{r_i\}_{i \in \mathbb{Z}_n});$
$\mathsf{view} := (\mathsf{face}(C), \{(x_i, r_i)\}_{i \in \mathfrak{C}});$	$\mathcal{S}(\{x_i\}_{i \in \mathfrak{C}}, \mathsf{face}(c_{\mathrm{out}})) \to \mathsf{view}';$
output $\mathsf{view};$	*output* $\mathsf{view}';$

---

[7] When there are no shuffles in a transcript, the vector r_i should be an empty vector.

Efficiency. For a protocol Π, the *card complexity* and the *shuffle complexity* are defined as the worst-case number of cards and shuffles required in Π, respectively. We evaluate the efficiency of protocols with respect to the card complexity and shuffle complexity. Note that these complexities are not necessarily related, and cannot be compared directly. Furthermore, since the shuffle operation is the only randomized operation, the shuffle complexity can also be seen as a measure for demanding a protocol is with respect to random number generation.

3 Efficient Protocols Using Regular Polygon Cards

In this section, using properties of regular m-sided polygon cards, we construct protocols for linear functions over $\mathbb{Z}_m$. Linear functions are all functions that can be expressed as a composition of multiplications by a constant and additions. In particular, we construct four protocols as follows.

– Addition Protocol : $(\llbracket x_0 \rrbracket, \llbracket x_1 \rrbracket) \xrightarrow{\mathsf{Add}} \llbracket x_0 + x_1 \rrbracket$.
– Subtraction Protocol : $(\llbracket x_0 \rrbracket, \llbracket x_1 \rrbracket) \xrightarrow{\mathsf{Sub}} \llbracket x_1 - x_0 \rrbracket$.
– Copy Protocol : $\llbracket x \rrbracket \xrightarrow{\mathsf{Copy}\ k} (\underbrace{\llbracket x \rrbracket, \llbracket x \rrbracket, \cdots, \llbracket x \rrbracket}_{k})$.
– Multiplication by Constant Protocol : $\llbracket x \rrbracket \xrightarrow{\mathsf{Mult}\ a} \llbracket ax \rrbracket$.

Composing them, we can securely compute an arbitrary linear function over $\mathbb{Z}_m$.

3.1 Addition, Subtraction, and Copy Protocols

We construct an *addition protocol* over $\mathbb{Z}_m$ using regular m-sided polygon cards. It takes as inputs two encodings $\llbracket x_0 \rrbracket$ and $\llbracket x_1 \rrbracket$, and outputs an encoding of the sum $\llbracket x_0 + x_1 \rrbracket$. Our idea is simple. Firstly, using a rotation shuffle, we obtain two encodings $\llbracket x_0 + r \rrbracket$ and $\llbracket x_1 - r \rrbracket$, and open the former to learn the value $\epsilon := x_0 + r$. Since ϵ is masked by the random value r, ϵ reveals no information about x_0. Once ϵ is opened in public, we can easily obtain $\llbracket x_0 + x_1 \rrbracket$ from $\llbracket x_1 - r \rrbracket$ by applying an ϵ-times rotation. The most important part in our addition protocol is generating the rotation and the inverse rotation $\llbracket x_0 + r \rrbracket$ and $\llbracket x_1 - r \rrbracket$. You can see the demonstration movie (https://youtu.be/9Tid6X-9r-c).

Addition Protocol (Add)

Secret Information : $(x_0, x_1) \in (\mathbb{Z}_m, \mathbb{Z}_m)$.
Input : $(\llbracket x_0 \rrbracket, \llbracket x_1 \rrbracket)$.
Output $\llbracket x_0 + x_1 \bmod m \rrbracket$. (We omit "mod m" in the description.)

1. Apply a flip composition to $(\llbracket x_0 \rrbracket, \llbracket x_1 \rrbracket)$.

$$(\llbracket x_0 \rrbracket, \llbracket x_1 \rrbracket) \xrightarrow{\mathsf{FComp}} \llbracket x_0 \rrbracket \circ \mathsf{flip}(\llbracket x_1 \rrbracket).$$

---

2. Apply a rotation shuffle to $[\![x_0]\!] \circ \mathsf{flip}([\![x_1]\!])$.

$$([\![x_0]\!] \circ \mathsf{flip}([\![x_1]\!])) \xrightarrow{\mathsf{RotShffl}} \mathsf{rot}^r([\![x_0]\!]) \circ \mathsf{rot}^r(\mathsf{flip}([\![x_1]\!]))$$
$$= [\![x_0 + r]\!] \circ \mathsf{flip}([\![x_1 - r]\!]).$$

3. Apply a flip decomposition to $[\![x_0 + r]\!] \circ \mathsf{flip}([\![x_1 - r]\!])$. Open the 1st card $[\![x_0 + r]\!]$, and learn a value $\epsilon := x_0 + r \bmod m$ publicly.

$$[\![x_0 + r]\!] \circ \mathsf{flip}([\![x_1 - r]\!]) \xrightarrow{\mathsf{FDecomp}} ([\![x_0 + r]\!], [\![x_1 - r]\!]) \xrightarrow{\mathsf{Open}\ \{0\}} (\epsilon, [\![x_1 - r]\!]).$$

4. Delete the front card ϵ. Apply ϵ-times rotation to $[\![x_1 - r]\!]$.

$$(\epsilon, [\![x_1 - r]\!]) \xrightarrow{\mathsf{Del}\ \{0\}} [\![x_1 - r]\!] \xrightarrow{\mathsf{Rot}\ \epsilon} [\![x_0 + x_1]\!].$$

Theorem 1. *The above addition protocol is perfectly secure.*

Proof. The faces of the sequence in the above addition protocol are the following.

$$(\times, \times) \xrightarrow{\mathsf{FComp}} (\times^2) \xrightarrow{\mathsf{RotShffl}} (\times^2) \xrightarrow{\mathsf{FDecomp}} (\times, \times) \xrightarrow{\mathsf{Open}} (\text{``}\epsilon\text{''}, \times) \xrightarrow{\mathsf{Del}} (\times) \xrightarrow{\mathsf{Rot}} (\times).$$

In the sequences, $\epsilon = x_0 + r$ is a uniformly random value in $\mathbb{Z}_m$ since r is a uniformly random value in $\mathbb{Z}_m$. For any subset $\mathfrak{C} \subsetneq \mathbb{Z}_n$, the simulator $\mathcal{S}$ is constructed as follows. $\mathcal{S}$ takes $\{x_i\}_{i \in \mathfrak{C}}$ and a face of the output sequence $(\times)$ as inputs, chooses uniformly random r_i' and $\epsilon' \in \mathbb{Z}_m$, and outputs the following.

$$(((\times, \times), (\times^2), (\times^2), (\times, \times), (\text{``}\epsilon'\text{''}, \times), (\times), (\times)), \{x_i, r_i'\}_{i \in \mathfrak{C}}).$$

This is the same as the real distribution. Therefore, our addition protocol Add is perfectly secure. □

In the addition protocol, if we use $[\![x_0]\!] \circ \mathsf{flip}([\![x_1]\!]) \circ \mathsf{flip}([\![x_2]\!]) \cdots \circ \mathsf{flip}([\![x_{k-1}]\!])$ instead of $[\![x_0]\!] \circ \mathsf{flip}([\![x_1]\!])$, then it is possible to apply an x_0-addition operation to $k-1$ encodings by using a rotation shuffle (Single Instruction Multiple Data, SIMD operation).

$$([\![x_0]\!], [\![x_1]\!], \cdots, [\![x_{k-1}]\!]) \xrightarrow{\mathsf{Add}} ([\![x_0 + x_1]\!], \cdots, [\![x_0 + x_{k-1}]\!]).$$

Using this property, we immediately obtain a copy protocol by applying our addition protocol to $[\![x]\!]$ and $[\![0]\!]$s, i.e., $([\![x]\!], [\![0]\!], \cdots, [\![0]\!]) \xrightarrow{\mathsf{Add}} ([\![x]\!], \cdots, [\![x]\!])$. We use the following notation for our k-copy protocol.

$$[\![x]\!] \xrightarrow{\mathsf{Copy}\ k} \underbrace{([\![x]\!], [\![x]\!], \cdots, [\![x]\!])}_{k}.$$

In the addition protocol, if we use $[\![x_0]\!] \circ [\![x_1]\!]$ instead of $[\![x_0]\!] \circ \mathsf{flip}([\![x_1]\!])$, then we obtain a subtraction protocol. Similarly, it is possible to operate a SIMD operation in our subtraction as follows.

$$([\![x_0]\!], [\![x_1]\!], \cdots, [\![x_{k-1}]\!]) \xrightarrow{\mathsf{Sub}} ([\![x_1 - x_0]\!], \cdots, [\![x_{k-1} - x_0]\!]).$$

Clearly, it is possible to apply a SIMD operation for $[\![x_0]\!]$-addition, $[\![x_0]\!]$-subtraction, and copy for $[\![x_0]\!]$. For example, the following operation can be obtained from a rotation shuffle.

$$([\![x_0]\!], [\![x_1]\!], [\![x_2]\!], [\![x_3]\!]) \rightarrow ([\![x_1 + x_0]\!], [\![x_2 - x_0]\!], [\![x_3 - x_0]\!], [\![x_0]\!], [\![x_0]\!]).$$

3.2 Protocol for Multiplication by a Constant

A protocol for multiplication by a constant, that takes an encoding $[\![x]\!]$ and a constant $a \in \mathbb{Z}_m$ as inputs and outputs $[\![ax]\!]$, can be constructed by just applying our addition protocol a times. Using a binary representation $a = a_0 + 2a_1 + \cdots + 2^{\ell-1}a_{\ell-1}$, it is widely known how to reduce the complexity for a multiplication. (We refer to this as the *binary method.*) In our model, we can apply the binary method and obtain a protocol using only $O(\log a)$-times rotation shuffles as follows.

1. Let $a \in \mathbb{Z}_m$ denote a constant represented by $a = a_0 + 2a_1 + \cdots + 2^{\ell-1}a_{\ell-1}$ where $a_i \in \{0, 1\}$.
2. Repeat the following from $i = 0$ to $\ell - 1$.
   (a) If $a_i = 0$, then apply our 2-copy protocol to $[\![2^i x]\!]$, otherwise apply our 3-copy protocol to $[\![2^i x]\!]$.
   (b) For two encodings of $[\![2^i x]\!]$, apply our addition protocol and obtain an encoding of $[\![2^{i+1} x]\!]$.
3. For all encodings generated as above, apply our addition protocol and obtain an encoding of $[\![ax]\!]$.

Let ℓ_a be the number of a_i that satisfies $a_i = 1$. The shuffle complexity of the above protocol is $(2\lceil \log_2 a \rceil + \ell_a - 1)$ rotation shuffles.

In the rest of this section, we show that it is possible to construct a multiplication by constant protocol whose shuffle complexity is only $(\lceil \log_2 a \rceil + 1)$ rotation shuffles. The basic idea is to use a SIMD operation of our addition protocol. Our multiplication by constant protocol is denoted by $[\![x]\!] \xrightarrow{\text{Mult } a} [\![ax]\!]$.

Multiplication by Constant Protocol (Mult)

Secret Information : $x \in \mathbb{Z}_m$.
Input : $[\![x]\!]$.
Output $[\![ax]\!]$.
Let $\ell = \lceil \log_2 a \rceil$ and $a - 1 = \sum_{j=0}^{\ell-1} 2^j \cdot b_j$ where $b_j \in \{0, 1\}$. Note that we use a binary representation of $a - 1$, while the standard binary method using that of a.

1. Invoke our $(\ell + 1)$-copy protocol to $[\![x]\!]$.

$$[\![x]\!] \xrightarrow{\text{Copy } \ell+1} (\underbrace{[\![x]\!], \cdots, [\![x]\!]}_{\ell+1}).$$

2. Repeat the following operation for $i = 0, 1, \cdots, \ell - 1$ the following operation. For clarity, we first demonstrate the 0th step and then the i-th step. In the 0th step, invoke our addition protocol Add as follows: if $b_0 = 1$, then add the leftmost $[\![x]\!]$ to all others $[\![x]\!]$, otherwise add the leftmost $[\![x]\!]$ to all others $[\![x]\!]$ except from the rightmost $[\![x]\!]$.

$$(\underbrace{[\![x]\!], \cdots, [\![x]\!]}_{\ell}, [\![x]\!]) \xrightarrow{\text{Add}} \begin{cases} (\underbrace{[\![2x]\!], \cdots, [\![2x]\!]}_{\ell-1}, [\![x]\!]) & \text{if } b_0 = 0. \\ (\underbrace{[\![2x]\!], \cdots, [\![2x]\!]}_{\ell-1}, [\![2x]\!]) & \text{if } b_0 = 1. \end{cases}$$

In i-th step $(i > 0)$, the current sequence is $s = (\overbrace{[\![w]\!], \cdots, [\![w]\!]}^{\ell-i}, [\![w_i]\!])$ where $w = 2^i x$, and $w_i = (\sum_{j=0}^{i-1} 2^j b_j + 1)x$. If $b_i = 1$, then add $[\![w]\!]$ to all others. If $b_i = 0$, then add $[\![w]\!]$ to all others except from $[\![w_i]\!]$.

$$(\underbrace{[\![w]\!], \cdots, [\![w]\!]}_{\ell-i}, [\![w_i]\!]) \xrightarrow{\text{Add}} \begin{cases} (\underbrace{[\![2w]\!], \cdots, [\![2w]\!]}_{\ell-i-1}, [\![w_i]\!]) & \text{if } b_i = 0. \\ (\underbrace{[\![2w]\!], \cdots, [\![2w]\!]}_{\ell-i-1}, [\![w_i + w]\!]) & \text{if } b_i = 1. \end{cases}$$

3. Finally, the current sequence is a card $[\![w_\ell]\!]$, where $w_\ell = (\sum_{j=0}^{\ell-1} 2^j b_j + 1)x = ax$. The output is the card $[\![w_\ell]\!]$.

Theorem 2. *The above multiplication protocol is perfectly secure.*

Proof. The faces of the sequence in the above multiplication protocol are the following.

$$(\times) \xrightarrow{\text{Copy}} (\underbrace{\times, \times, \cdots, \times}_{\ell+1}) \xrightarrow{\text{Add}} (\underbrace{\times, \times, \cdots, \times}_{\ell}) \xrightarrow{\text{Add}} \cdots \xrightarrow{\text{Add}} (\times, \times) \xrightarrow{\text{Add}} (\times).$$

For any subset $\mathfrak{C} \subsetneq \mathbb{Z}_n$, the simulator $\mathcal{S}$ is constructed as follows. $\mathcal{S}$ takes $\{x_i\}_{i \in \mathfrak{C}}$ and the face of the output sequence $(\times)$ as inputs, chooses uniformly random $r'_{i,j}$ and $\epsilon'_j \in \mathbb{Z}_m$ (for $i \in \mathfrak{C}$ and $j \in \{0, 1, \cdots, \ell\}$), and outputs $(\mathsf{face}(C'), \{x_i, r'_{i,0}, r'_{i,1}, \cdots, r'_{i,\ell}\}_{i \in \mathfrak{C}})$. (Note that $\mathsf{face}(C')$ can be easily generated from ϵ'_j and the transition function π.) This is the same as the real distribution. Therefore, our multiplication protocol Mult_a is perfectly secure. $\square$

4 Efficient Protocols Using Oblivious Conversion

In this section, we construct protocols for any function $f : \bigotimes_{i=0}^{n-1} \mathbb{Z}_{m_i} \to \mathbb{Z}_{m_n}$ with small shuffle complexity using a new protocol, an *oblivious conversion*. A protocol based on oblivious conversion has a small shuffle complexity, but use a large number of cards. In general, there is a trade-off between a specific construction and a generic (oblivious conversion based) construction, in terms of the shuffle complexity and the number of cards. (For example, the specific multiplication by $a \in \mathbb{Z}_m$ (Sect. 3.2) uses $\lceil \log_2 a \rceil + 1$ rotation shuffles and $\lceil \log_2 a \rceil + 2$ cards while a multiplication protocol based on oblivious conversion uses 1 cyclic shuffle and $2m$ cards (Example 1).) Our oblivious conversion can be applied to general encodings (see Corollary 1). Thus, for general encodings we can construct protocols for any functions with small shuffle complexity (see Corollary 2).

For two finite cyclic groups $\mathbb{Z}_{m_0}, \mathbb{Z}_{m_1}$, let f be a function s.t. $f : \mathbb{Z}_{m_0} \to \mathbb{Z}_{m_1}$, and let $\mathsf{E}_0, \mathsf{E}_1$ be encodings on $\mathbb{Z}_{m_0}, \mathbb{Z}_{m_1}$, respectively. An *oblivious conversion* is defined by a protocol, that takes $\mathsf{E}_0(x), \mathsf{E}_1(f(0)), \mathsf{E}_1(f(1)), \cdots, \mathsf{E}_1(f(m_0 - 1))$ as inputs, and outputs $\mathsf{E}_1(f(x))$. In our definition, an oblivious transfer can be seen as an oblivious conversion. Indeed, if two parties P_0 and P_1 plays a receiver and a sender, i.e., P_0 chooses x, and P_1 chooses f, then the oblivious conversion is equal to an oblivious transfer.

Firstly, we construct an oblivious conversion for $f : \mathbb{Z}_m \to \mathbb{Z}_m$, where the input and output encodings are the standard encoding $[\![\cdot]\!]$. You can see the demonstration movie (https://youtu.be/hlAetm66iRU).

Oblivious Conversion

Secret Information : $x \in \mathbb{Z}_m$.
Input : $([\![x]\!], \boldsymbol{f})$ where $\boldsymbol{f} = ([\![f(0)]\!], [\![f(1)]\!], \cdots, [\![f(m-1)]\!])$.
Output : $[\![f(x)]\!]$.

1. Invoke our m-copy protocol for $[\![x]\!]$, apply a $(i-1)$-times rotation to i-th card from the left $(i = 1, 2, \cdots, m)$, and obtain $\boldsymbol{x} = ([\![x]\!], [\![x-1]\!], [\![x-2]\!], \cdots, [\![x-(m-1)]\!])$.

$$([\![x]\!], \boldsymbol{f}) \xrightarrow{\text{Copy } m} (\underbrace{[\![x]\!], \cdots, [\![x]\!]}_{m}, \boldsymbol{f}) \xrightarrow{\text{Rot}} (\boldsymbol{x}, \boldsymbol{f}).$$

   We see the sequence as a matrix as follows.

$$\begin{pmatrix} \boldsymbol{x} \\ \boldsymbol{f} \end{pmatrix} = \begin{pmatrix} [\![x]\!] & [\![x-1]\!] & \cdots & [\![0]\!] & \cdots & [\![x-(m-1)]\!] \\ [\![f(0)]\!] & [\![f(1)]\!] & \cdots & [\![f(x)]\!] & \cdots & [\![f(m-1)]\!] \end{pmatrix}.$$

2. Apply a composition operation to each column and make a sequence $\boldsymbol{w} := (w_0, w_1, \cdots, w_{m-1})$ where $w_i = [\![x-i]\!] \circ [\![f(i)]\!]$. Apply a cyclic shuffle to the sequence, and then decompose it.

$$\begin{pmatrix} \boldsymbol{x} \\ \boldsymbol{f} \end{pmatrix} \xrightarrow{\text{Comp}} \boldsymbol{w} \xrightarrow{\text{CycShffl}} \mathsf{cyc}^r(\boldsymbol{w}) \xrightarrow{\text{Decomp}} \begin{pmatrix} \mathsf{cyc}^r(\boldsymbol{x}) \\ \mathsf{cyc}^r(\boldsymbol{f}) \end{pmatrix}.$$

3. Open the first card of $\mathsf{cyc}^r(\boldsymbol{x})$, and learn the value $\epsilon := x - r \bmod m$. Delete the top column in the matrix.

4. Apply an ϵ-times cyclic permutation to the sequence.

$$\mathsf{cyc}^r(\boldsymbol{f}) \xrightarrow{\text{Perm cyc}^\epsilon} \mathsf{cyc}^x(\boldsymbol{f}).$$

5. The 1st card of $\mathsf{cyc}^x(\boldsymbol{f})$ is $[\![f(x)]\!]$, this is the output.

$$([\![f(x)]\!], [\![f(x+1)]\!], \cdots, [\![f(x+m-1)]\!]) \xrightarrow{\text{Del}} [\![f(x)]\!].$$

Theorem 3. *The above oblivious conversion is perfectly secure.*

Proof. In the case of $m = 4$, the faces of the sequence in the above protocol are the following.

$$(\times, \times, \times, \times, \times) \xrightarrow{\text{Copy}} (\times, \times, \times, \times, \times, \times, \times, \times) \xrightarrow{\text{Rot}} (\times, \times, \times, \times, \times, \times, \times, \times) \longrightarrow$$

$$\begin{pmatrix} \times & \times & \times & \times \\ \times & \times & \times & \times \end{pmatrix} \xrightarrow{\text{Comp}} (\times^2, \times^2, \times^2, \times^2) \xrightarrow{\text{CycShffl}} (\times^2, \times^2, \times^2, \times^2) \xrightarrow{\text{Decomp}} \begin{pmatrix} \times & \times & \times & \times \\ \times & \times & \times & \times \end{pmatrix}$$

$$\xrightarrow{\text{Open}} \begin{pmatrix} \text{``}\epsilon\text{''} & \times & \times & \times \\ \times & \times & \times & \times \end{pmatrix} \xrightarrow{\text{Del}} (\times, \times, \times, \times) \xrightarrow{\text{cyc}^\epsilon} (\times, \times, \times, \times) \xrightarrow{\text{Del}} (\times).$$

For any subset $\mathfrak{C} \subsetneq \mathbb{Z}_n$, $\mathcal{S}$ takes $\{x_i\}_{i \in \mathfrak{C}}$ and the face of the output sequence $(\times)$ as inputs, chooses uniformly random $r_i' \in \mathbb{Z}_m$ (for $i \in \mathfrak{C}$) and $\epsilon' \in \mathbb{Z}_m$, and outputs $(\mathsf{face}(\boldsymbol{C}'), \{x_i, r_i'\}_{i \in \mathfrak{C}})$. (Note that $\mathsf{face}(\boldsymbol{C}')$ can be easily generated from ϵ' and the transition function π.) This is the same as the real distribution. Therefore, our oblivious conversion is perfectly secure. $\qquad\square$

In above protocol, using an encoding E_1 instead of $[\![\cdot]\!]$, we can obtain an oblivious conversion protocol that takes $\boldsymbol{f} = (\mathsf{E}_1(f(0)), \cdots, \mathsf{E}_1(f(m-1)))$ as inputs. Similarly, if an encoding E_0 can execute Step 1 in the protocol, then we can use $\mathsf{E}_0(x)$ instead of $[\![x]\!]$ as input. This is formally stated in the following.

Corollary 1. *For cyclic groups $\mathbb{Z}_{m_0}, \mathbb{Z}_{m_1}$, let $f : \mathbb{Z}_{m_0} \to \mathbb{Z}_{m_1}$ be a function and $\mathsf{E}_0, \mathsf{E}_1$ be encodings on X, Y such that there exists integers k_0, k_1 that satisfies for all $x \in \mathbb{Z}_{m_0}$ $\mathsf{face}(\mathsf{E}_0(x)) = \times^{k_0}$ and $\mathsf{face}(\mathsf{E}_1(f(x))) = \times^{k_1}$. If the encoding E_0 supports the computation of $(\mathsf{E}_0(x), \mathsf{E}_0(x-1), \cdots, \mathsf{E}_0(x-(m_0-1)))$ from $\mathsf{E}_0(x)$ by applying ℓ shuffles, then there exists an oblivious conversion for f with only $\ell + 1$ shuffles.*

This can be easily proven from the construction of our oblivious conversion.

Example 1 (Multiplication by a Constant Protocol). *For a function $f : \mathbb{Z}_m \to \mathbb{Z}_m$ defined as $f(x) = ax$, and encodings $\mathsf{E}_0(\cdot) = \mathsf{E}_1(\cdot) = [\![\cdot]\!]$, the oblivious conversion for f is a protocol of multiplication by a constant a.*

Example 2 (Square Protocol). *For a function $f : \mathbb{Z}_m \to \mathbb{Z}_m$ defined as $f(x) = x^2$, and encodings $\mathsf{E}_0(\cdot) = \mathsf{E}_1(\cdot) = [\![\cdot]\!]$, the oblivious conversion for f is a square protocol.*

Example 3 (Modulus Switch). *For a function* $f : \mathbb{Z}_{m_0} \to \mathbb{Z}_{m_1}$ *defined as* $f(x) = (x \bmod m_1)$, *and encodings* $\mathsf{E}_0(x) = [\![x]\!]$ *(the natural encoding of regular* m_0*-sided polygon cards)* $\mathsf{E}_1(y) = [\![y]\!]$ *(the natural encoding of regular* m_1*-sided polygon cards), the oblivious conversion for* f *is a modulus switch protocol.*

For all $x \in \mathbb{Z}_{m_0}$, if an encoding E_0 satisfies $\mathsf{cyc}(\mathsf{E}_0(x)) = \mathsf{E}_0(x - 1 \bmod m_0)$, then we can obtain an oblivious conversion which has a lower shuffle complexity. For such an encoding, there exists a constant k which satisfies $\mathsf{E}(x) \in \mathcal{B}^{km}$, since $\mathsf{cyc}^m(\mathsf{E}(x)) = \mathsf{E}(x - m) = \mathsf{E}(x)$. Thus, we can use $\mathsf{E}(x)$ instead of x in Step 2. As a result, we obtain an oblivious conversion using only a cyclic shuffle.

Example 4 (Encodings for Small Shuffle Complexity). *For* $\mathbb{Z}_m$, *let* $\mathsf{E}_A(x) = ([\![x]\!], [\![x - 1]\!], \cdots, [\![x - (m - 1)]\!]) \in \mathcal{B}^m$, *and* $\mathsf{E}_B(x) = ([\![y_0]\!], [\![y_1]\!], \cdots, [\![y_{m-1}]\!]) \in \mathcal{B}^m$ *where* $y_j = 0$ *for* $(j \neq x)$ *and* $y_x = 1$. *And then* E_A *and* E_B *satisfy* $\forall x [\mathsf{cyc}_k(\mathsf{E}(x)) = \mathsf{E}(x - 1)]$. *Furthermore, let* E_C *be an encoding which have redundancy, s.t.* $\mathsf{E}_C(x) = (\mathsf{E}_A(x), \mathsf{E}_A(x)) \in \mathcal{B}^{2m}$. *Then* E_C *satisfies* $\forall x [\mathsf{cyc}_{2k}(\mathsf{E}_C(x)) = \mathsf{E}_C(x - 1)]$.

MPC for Small Shuffle Complexity. It is possible to construct a secure MPC for any function using only our oblivious conversion. We use $(\alpha_i)_{i=0}^{m-1}$ to denote the sequence $(\alpha_0, \alpha_1, \cdots, \alpha_{m-1})$. For a function $f : \bigotimes_{i=0}^{n-1} \mathbb{Z}_{m_i} \to \mathbb{Z}_{m_n}$ and an output encoding E_n, we first define a sequence $\boldsymbol{f}$ as follows.

$$\boldsymbol{f}^{(x_0, \cdots, x_{n-3}, x_{n-2})} := (\mathsf{E}_n(f(x_0, \cdots, x_{n-2}, i)))_{i=0}^{m_{n-1}-1}$$

$$\boldsymbol{f}^{(x_0, \cdots, x_{n-3})} := (\boldsymbol{f}^{(x_0, \cdots, x_{n-3}, i)})_{i=0}^{m_{n-2}-1}$$

$$\vdots$$

$$\boldsymbol{f}^{(x_0)} := (\boldsymbol{f}^{(x_0, i)})_{i=0}^{m_1-1}$$

$$\boldsymbol{f} := (\boldsymbol{f}^{(i)})_{i=0}^{m_0-1}$$

Let $\mathsf{E}_0, \mathsf{E}_1, \cdots, \mathsf{E}_{n-1}$ be encodings over $\mathbb{Z}_{m_0}, \mathbb{Z}_{m_1}, \cdots, \mathbb{Z}_{m_{n-1}}$, respectively. Given encodings of inputs $\{\mathsf{E}_i(x_i)\}_{i \in \mathbb{Z}_n}$ and $\boldsymbol{f}$, we can obtain the output sequence $\mathsf{E}_n(f(x_0, \cdots, x_{n-1}))$ as follows.

$$(\mathsf{E}_0(x_0), \boldsymbol{f}) \xrightarrow{\mathsf{OC}} \boldsymbol{f}^{(x_0)}$$

$$(\mathsf{E}_1(x_1), \boldsymbol{f}^{(x_0)}) \xrightarrow{\mathsf{OC}} \boldsymbol{f}^{(x_0, x_1)}$$

$$\vdots$$

$$(\mathsf{E}_{n-2}(x_{n-2}), \boldsymbol{f}^{(x_0, \cdots, x_{n-3})}) \xrightarrow{\mathsf{OC}} \boldsymbol{f}^{(x_0, \cdots, x_{n-3}, x_{n-2})}$$

$$(\mathsf{E}_{n-1}(x_{n-1}), \boldsymbol{f}^{(x_0, \cdots, x_{n-3}, x_{n-2})}) \xrightarrow{\mathsf{OC}} \mathsf{E}_n(f(x_0, \cdots, x_{n-1}))$$

where $\xrightarrow{\mathsf{OC}}$ denotes applying the oblivious conversion.

Corollary 2. *For cyclic groups* $\mathbb{Z}_{m_0}, \mathbb{Z}_{m_1}, \cdots, \mathbb{Z}_{m_n}$, *let* $f : \bigotimes_{i=0}^{n-1} \mathbb{Z}_{m_i} \to \mathbb{Z}_{m_n}$ *be a function and let* E_i ($i \in \{0, 1, \cdots, n - 1\}$) *and* E_n *be encodings on* $\mathbb{Z}_{m_i}$ *and*

$\mathbb{Z}_{m_n}$ such that there exists integers $k_0, k_1, \cdots, k_n$ that satisfies for all $x_i \in \mathbb{Z}_{m_i}$ $\mathsf{face}(\mathsf{E}_i(x_i)) = \times^{k_i}$ $(i \in \{0, 1, \cdots, n-1\})$ and $\mathsf{face}(\mathsf{E}_n(f(x_0, x_1, \cdots, x_{n-1}))) = \times^{k_n}$. If for all $\mathbb{Z}_{m_i}$ $(i \in \{0, 1, \cdots, n-1\})$ the encoding E_i supports the computation of $(\mathsf{E}_i(x), \mathsf{E}_i(x-1), \cdots, \mathsf{E}_i(x-(m_i-1)))$ from $\mathsf{E}(x)$ by applying ℓ_i shuffles, then there exists a card-based protocol for f with only $\sum_{i=0}^{n-1}(\ell_i + 1)$ shuffles. In particular, if each E_i satisfies $\forall x \in \mathbb{Z}_{m_i}[\mathsf{cyc}^r(\mathsf{E}_i(x)) = \mathsf{E}_i(x-r)]$ $(i \in \{0, 1, \cdots, n-1\})$, then there exists a card-based protocol for f with only n cyclic shuffles.

This corollary can be easily proven from the above discussion.

5   Efficient Voting Protocol for Multiple Candidates

Using our oblivious conversion (Sect. 4), it is possible to construct a protocol for any n-ary function with n cyclic shuffles. Since protocols based on oblivious conversion are generic constructions, they require a large number of cards. Therefore, it might be possible to construct a more efficient protocol in terms of both the shuffle complexity and the number of cards by considering a protocol tailored to a specific functionality. In this section, we construct an efficient voting protocol for ℓ candidates and n voters. Assume each voter P_i holds $x_i \in \mathbb{Z}_\ell$, i.e., P_i supports the x_i-th candidate. For $x \in \mathbb{Z}_\ell$, let $\mathsf{E}_v(x)$ be an encoding for voting as follows[8]

$$\mathsf{E}_v(x) := \mathsf{cyc}_\ell^{-x}(\underbrace{[\![1]\!], [\![0]\!], [\![0]\!], \cdots, [\![0]\!]}_{\ell}).$$

Clearly, this encoding satisfies $\forall x [\mathsf{cyc}_\ell(\mathsf{E}_v(x)) = \mathsf{E}_v(x - 1 \bmod \ell)]$. Our voting protocol takes n encodings $\mathsf{E}_v(x_0), \mathsf{E}_v(x_1), \cdots, \mathsf{E}_v(x_{n-1})$ as inputs, and outputs $\boldsymbol{y} = ([\![y_0]\!], \cdots, [\![y_{\ell-1}]\!])$ where y_j is the number of votes for the j-th candidate. (Note that our voting protocol outputs encodings of the number of votes, thus we can apply an arbitrary functionality to the outputs.) The shuffle complexity of our voting protocol is $n+1$ cyclic shuffles while a protocol using our oblivious conversion has only n cyclic shuffles. However, the number of cards is only $(n+2)\ell$ while the protocol using our oblivious conversion needs $O(\ell^n)$.

For the simplicity, we show a voting protocol with 2 voters. It is easy to extend this to a voting protocol with n voters for an arbitrary n.

Voting Protocol with 2 Voters and ℓ Candidates

Secret Information : $(x_0, x_1) \in \mathbb{Z}_\ell^2$.
Input : $\mathsf{E}_v(x_0), \mathsf{E}_v(x_1)$.
Output : $([\![y_0]\!], \cdots, [\![y_{\ell-1}]\!])$ where $y_i = |\{j | x_j = i\}|$.

---

[8] The encoding E_v is just equal to E_B (Sect. 4, Example 4).

1. We deal with the input sequence $(E_v(x_0), E_v(x_1))$ as a matrix as bellow. Insert $E_v(0) = (\llbracket 1 \rrbracket, \llbracket 0 \rrbracket, \cdots, \llbracket 0 \rrbracket)$ and all-zero sequence $\mathbf{0} = (\llbracket 0 \rrbracket, \cdots, \llbracket 0 \rrbracket)$.

$$\begin{pmatrix} E_v(x_0) \\ \hline E_v(x_1) \end{pmatrix} \xrightarrow{\text{Insert}} \begin{pmatrix} E_v(x_0) \\ \hline E_v(x_1) \\ \hline \llbracket 1 \rrbracket \ \llbracket 0 \rrbracket \ \cdots \ \llbracket 0 \rrbracket \ \llbracket 0 \rrbracket \\ \llbracket 0 \rrbracket \ \llbracket 0 \rrbracket \ \cdots \ \llbracket 0 \rrbracket \ \llbracket 0 \rrbracket \end{pmatrix} = \begin{pmatrix} E_v(x_0) \\ \hline E_v(x_1) \\ \hline E_v(0) \\ \hline \mathbf{0} \end{pmatrix}.$$

2. Apply a composition to each column and make a sequence $\boldsymbol{w_0} = (w_{0,0}, w_{0,1}, \cdots, w_{0,\ell-1})$. (Note that each $w_{0,i}$ contains 4 cards.) Apply a cyclic shuffle to $\boldsymbol{w_0}$, and decompose it.

$$\begin{pmatrix} E_v(x_0) \\ \hline E_v(x_1) \\ \hline E_v(0) \\ \hline \mathbf{0} \end{pmatrix} \xrightarrow{\text{Comp}} \boldsymbol{w_0} \xrightarrow{\text{CycShffl}} \mathsf{cyc}^{r_0}(\boldsymbol{w_0}) \xrightarrow{\text{Decomp}} \begin{pmatrix} E_v(x_0 - r_0) \\ \hline E_v(x_1 - r_0) \\ \hline E_v(-r_0) \\ \hline \mathsf{cyc}^{r_0}(\mathbf{0}) \end{pmatrix}.$$

3. Open the first row and learn the value $\epsilon_0 := x_0 - r_0$, and delete the first row. For the bottom sequence $\mathsf{cyc}^{r_0}(\mathbf{0})$, apply a rotation rot to ϵ_0-th card from the right, i.e., x_0-th card of $\mathbf{0}$. (Note that we refer to the rightmost card as the "0th" card.) Let $\mathsf{cyc}^{r_0}(\boldsymbol{z_0})$ be the bottom sequence.

4. Apply a composition to each column and make a sequence $\boldsymbol{w_1} = (w_{1,0}, w_{1,1}, \cdots, w_{1,\ell-1})$. (Note that each $w_{1,i}$ contains 3 cards.) Apply a cyclic shuffle to $\boldsymbol{w_1}$, and decompose it.

$$\begin{pmatrix} E_v(x_1 - r_0) \\ \hline E_v(-r_0) \\ \hline \mathsf{cyc}^{r_0}(\boldsymbol{z_0}) \end{pmatrix} \xrightarrow{\text{Comp}} \boldsymbol{w_1} \xrightarrow{\text{CycShffl}} \mathsf{cyc}^{r_1}(\boldsymbol{w_1}) \xrightarrow{\text{Decomp}} \begin{pmatrix} E_v(x_1 - r) \\ \hline E_v(-r) \\ \hline \mathsf{cyc}^{r}(\boldsymbol{z_0}) \end{pmatrix}.$$

where $r = r_0 + r_1$.

5. Open the first row and learn the value $\epsilon_1 := x_1 - r$, and delete the first row. For the bottom sequence $\mathsf{cyc}^{r}(\boldsymbol{z_0})$, apply a rotation rot to ϵ_1-th card from the right, i.e., x_1-th card of $\boldsymbol{z_0}$. Let $\mathsf{cyc}^{r}(\boldsymbol{z_1})$ be the bottom sequence.

6. Apply a composition to each column and make a sequence $\boldsymbol{w_2} = (w_{2,0}, w_{2,1}, \cdots, w_{2,\ell-1})$. (Note that each $w_{2,i}$ contains 2 cards.)

$$\begin{pmatrix} E_v(-r) \\ \hline \mathsf{cyc}^{r}(\boldsymbol{z_1}) \end{pmatrix} \xrightarrow{\text{Comp}} \boldsymbol{w_2} \xrightarrow{\text{CycShffl}} \mathsf{cyc}^{r_2}(\boldsymbol{w_2}).$$

7. Open the 1st row, and learn the value $\epsilon_2 := -(r + r_2)$. Delete the 1st row, and apply $\mathsf{cyc}^{\epsilon_2}$ to $\mathsf{cyc}^{r+r_2}(\boldsymbol{z_1})$. Output the sequence $\boldsymbol{z_1}$.

$$\begin{pmatrix} E_v(-(r + r_2)) \\ \hline \mathsf{cyc}^{r+r_2}(\boldsymbol{z_1}) \end{pmatrix} \xrightarrow{\text{Del}} \mathsf{cyc}^{r+r_2}(\boldsymbol{z_1}) \xrightarrow{\mathsf{cyc}^{\epsilon_2}} \boldsymbol{z_1}.$$

Theorem 4. *The above voting protocol is perfectly secure.*

Proof. In the case of $\ell = 3$, the faces of the sequence in the above voting protocol are the following.

$$\begin{pmatrix} \times \times \times \\ \times \times \times \\ \times \times \times \end{pmatrix} \xrightarrow{\text{Insert}} \begin{pmatrix} \times \times \times \\ \times \times \times \\ \times \times \times \\ \times \times \times \end{pmatrix} \xrightarrow[\text{CycShffl}]{\text{Comp}} (\times^4, \times^4, \times^4) \xrightarrow{\text{Decomp}} \begin{pmatrix} \times \times \times \\ \times \times \times \\ \times \times \times \end{pmatrix} \xrightarrow{\text{Open}}$$

$$\begin{pmatrix} \epsilon_0 \\ \hline \times \times \times \\ \times \times \times \\ \times \times \times \end{pmatrix} \xrightarrow[\text{Rot}]{\text{Del}} \begin{pmatrix} \times \times \times \\ \times \times \times \\ \times \times \times \end{pmatrix} \xrightarrow[\text{CycShffl}]{\text{Comp}} (\times^3, \times^3, \times^3) \xrightarrow{\text{Decomp}} \begin{pmatrix} \times \times \times \\ \times \times \times \\ \times \times \times \end{pmatrix} \xrightarrow{\text{Open}}$$

$$\begin{pmatrix} \epsilon_1 \\ \hline \times \times \times \\ \times \times \times \end{pmatrix} \xrightarrow[\text{Rot}]{\text{Del}} \begin{pmatrix} \times \times \times \\ \times \times \times \end{pmatrix} \xrightarrow[\text{CycShffl}]{\text{Comp}} (\times^2, \times^2, \times^2) \xrightarrow{\text{Decomp}} \begin{pmatrix} \times \times \times \\ \times \times \times \end{pmatrix} \xrightarrow{\text{Open}}$$

$$\begin{pmatrix} \epsilon_2 \\ \hline \times \times \times \end{pmatrix} \xrightarrow{\text{Del}} (\times, \times, \times) \xrightarrow{\text{cyc}^{\epsilon_2}} (\times, \times, \times).$$

where ϵ_i is the face of the opening i.e., $\epsilon_i = (\text{``}\epsilon_{i,0}\text{''}, \text{``}\epsilon_{i,1}\text{''}, \text{``}\epsilon_{i,2}\text{''})$ where $E_v(\epsilon_i) = (\epsilon_{i,0}, \epsilon_{i,1}, \epsilon_{i,2})$. For any subset $\mathfrak{C} \subsetneq \mathbb{Z}_n$, $\mathcal{S}$ takes $\{x_i\}_{i \in \mathfrak{C}}$ and the face of the output sequence ($\times$) as inputs, chooses uniformly random $r'_{i,j} \in \mathbb{Z}_m$ and $\epsilon'_{j,k} \in \mathbb{Z}_m$ (for $i \in \mathfrak{C}$, $j \in \{0, 1, \cdots, n\}$, and $k \in \{0, 1, \cdots, \ell - 1\}$), and outputs $(\text{face}(C'), \{x_i, r'_{i,0}, r'_{i,1}, \cdots, r'_{i,n}\}_{i \in \mathfrak{C}})$. (Note that $\text{face}(C')$ can be easily generated from $\epsilon'_{j,k}$ and the transition function π.) This is the same as the real distribution. In general, for an arbitrary ℓ, we can construct the simulator $\mathcal{S}$ similarly. Therefore, our voting protocol is perfectly secure. $\square$

Acknowledgment. The authors would like to thank members of the study group "Shin-Akarui-Angou-Benkyou-Kai" for the valuable discussions and helpful comments, and thank the anonymous reviewers for their comments. This work was partially supported by JSPS KAKENHI Grant Numbers 26330001 and 26330151, Kurata Grant from The Kurata Memorial Hitachi Science and Technology Foundation, and JSPS A3 Foresight Program.

References

1. Crépeau, C., Kilian, J.: Discreet solitary games. In: Stinson, D.R. (ed.) CRYPTO 1993. LNCS, vol. 773, pp. 319–330. Springer, Heidelberg (1994)
2. den Boer, B.: More efficient match-making and satisfiability. In: Quisquater, J.-J., Vandewalle, J. (eds.) EUROCRYPT 1989. LNCS, vol. 434, pp. 208–217. Springer, Heidelberg (1990)
3. Mizuki, T., Asiedu, I.K., Sone, H.: Voting with a logarithmic number of cards. In: Mauri, G., Dennunzio, A., Manzoni, L., Porreca, A.E. (eds.) UCNC 2013. LNCS, vol. 7956, pp. 162–173. Springer, Heidelberg (2013)
4. Mizuki, T., Fumishige, U., Sone, H.: Securely computing XOR with 10 cards. Australas. J. Comb. **36**, 279–293 (2006)

5. Mizuki, T., Kumamoto, M., Sone, H.: The five-card trick can be done with four cards. In: Wang, X., Sako, K. (eds.) ASIACRYPT 2012. LNCS, vol. 7658, pp. 598–606. Springer, Heidelberg (2012)

6. Mizuki, T., Shizuya, H.: A formalization of card-based cryptographic protocols via abstract machine. Int. J. Inf. Sec. **13**, 15–23 (2014)

7. Mizuki, T., Shizuya, H.: Practical card-based cryptography. In: Ferro, A., Luccio, F., Widmayer, P. (eds.) FUN 2014. LNCS, vol. 8496, pp. 313–324. Springer, Heidelberg (2014)

8. Mizuki, T., Sone, H.: Six-card secure AND and four-card secure XOR. In: Deng, X., Hopcroft, J.E., Xue, J. (eds.) FAW 2009. LNCS, vol. 5598, pp. 358–369. Springer, Heidelberg (2009)

9. Niemi, V., Renvall, A.: Secure multiparty computations without computers. Theor. Comput. Sci. **191**(1–2), 173–183 (1998)

10. Nishida, T., Hayashi, Y., Mizuki, T., Sone, H.: Card-based protocols for any boolean function. In: Jain, R., Jain, S., Stephan, F. (eds.) TAMC 2015. LNCS, vol. 9076, pp. 110–121. Springer, Heidelberg (2015)

11. Nishida, T., Mizuki, T., Sone, H.: Securely computing the three-input majority function with eight cards. In: Dediu, A.-H., Martín-Vide, C., Truthe, B., Vega-Rodríguez, M.A. (eds.) TPNC 2013. LNCS, vol. 8273, pp. 193–204. Springer, Heidelberg (2013)

12. Shinagawa, K., Mizuki, T., Schuldt, J., Nuida, K., Kanayama, N., Nishide, T., Hanaoka, G., Okamoto, E.: Secure multi-party computation using polarizing cards. In: Tanaka, K., Suga, Y. (eds.) IWSEC 2015. LNCS, vol. 9241, pp. 281–297. Springer, Heidelberg (2015)

13. Stiglic, A.: Computations with a deck of cards. Theor. Comput. Sci. **259**(1–2), 671–678 (2001)

Authenticated Encryption and Key Exchange

Forward-Secure Authenticated Symmetric Key Exchange Protocol: New Security Model and Secure Construction

Suvradip Chakraborty[1], Goutam Paul[2]([⊠]), and C. Pandu Rangan[1]

[1] Department of Computer Science and Engineering,
Indian Institute of Technology Madras, Chennai, India
{suvradip1111,prangan55}@gmail.com
[2] Cryptology and Security Research Unit (CSRU),
R. C. Bose Centre for Cryptology and Security,
Indian Statistical Institute, Kolkata, India
goutam.paul@isical.ac.in

Abstract. While a lot of work has been done on the design and security analysis of PKI-based authenticated key exchange (AKE) protocols, very few exist in the symmetric key setting. The first provably secure symmetric AKE was proposed by Bellare and Rogaway (BR) in CRYPTO 1994 and so far this stands out as the most prominent one for symmetric key setting. In line with the significant progress done for PKI based system, we propose a stronger model than the BR model for symmetric key based system. We assume that the adversary can launch active attacks. In addition, the adversary can also obtain long term secret keys of the parties and the internal states of parties by getting access to their ephemeral secrets (or internal randomness) by means of appropriate oracle queries. The salient feature of our model is the way we handle active adversaries even in the test session.

We also design a symmetric key AKE construction that is provably secure against active adversaries in our new model using weak primitives. Dodis et al. (EUROCRYPT 2012) used weak Pseudo Random Functions (wPRF) and weak Almost-XOR Universal hash function family (wAXU) to design a three-pass one-sided authentication protocol in the symmetric key paradigm. A direct application of their techniques yields a four-pass (two-round) symmetric key AKE protocol with mutual authentication. Our construction uses particular instances of these weak primitives and introduces a novel technique called input-swapping to achieve a three-pass symmetric key AKE protocol with mutual authentication resisting active attacks (even in the test session). Our construction is proven secure in the Random oracle Model under the DDH assumption.

Keywords: Authenticated key exchange · Input swapping · Random oracle · Key evolving · Perfect forward secrecy · Weak pseudo random functions · Weak almost universal hash functions

© Springer International Publishing Switzerland 2015
M.-H. Au and A. Miyaji (Eds.): ProvSec 2015, LNCS 9451, pp. 149–166, 2015.
DOI: 10.1007/978-3-319-26059-4_8

1   Introduction

Key exchange protocols allow two parties to establish secure communication over an untrusted network by setting up shared keys. Authenticated Key Exchange protocol (AKE) allows two parties not only to share a session secret key but also to mutually authenticate each other. After the key is securely established between the two parties, the key is used for encrypting messages among the two parties.

Most symmetric key encryption systems assume that the two parties share a common secret. Thus, before exchanging the actual data, the two parties first need to establish such a shared secret. For this, they usually first run a *key agreement* protocol over the public channel to agree on a symmetric key. We refer the established key by key agreement protocol as Long Term key (LTK) between a pair of parties.

In symmetric key set up, key exchange protocols broadly fall under two categories: *i. Server-based* key exchange protocols where the presence of a trusted server is assumed and all the parties have a LTK shared with the server; all the communication between the two parties take place via the server [NS78, OR87, GNY90] and *ii. Server-less* key exchange protocols where the presence of a trusted server is not required but it is assumed that the communicating parties share a LTK between themselves [Sat90, BR94, CJ97]. In this paper we focus on Server-less two party symmetric key exchange protocol.

While the communicating parties may use their LTKs to securely exchange messages for confidentiality or authenticity, it is generally considered a bad practice. This is because even if the pre-shared keys or LTKs have good entropy, the key tends to weaken with use; this is the reason why session keys are used instead and changed frequently. Hence, there is a need for key derivation based on pre-shared keys.Generally, for each session, the parties generate a session randomness, called *ephemeral secret key* and use that to generate the session key. This session key can be applied to subsequent network systems including live conference, online video games, collaborative work spaces and much more.

The Diffie-Hellman protocol [DH76] was the first key-exchange protocol not requiring a pre-shared static secret between the parties. It does not however enforce authentication between the parties, and is therefore vulnerable to man-in-the-middle attacks. After that, many *authenticated key-exchange* (AKE) protocols were proposed [JKL04, BLL07, CL08, CY08, LCZ07]; either they are insecure or their security is proved in an ad-hoc manner and later on some attacks would be presented.The attacked systems were either modified in a minor way to just overcome the proposed attack or abandoned altogether. This prompted the need for formal models for AKE problem and robust protocols for AKE whose security is proved formally in these models. Starting from the seminal work of Bellare and Rogaway [BR94], progressive stronger models were proposed by several authors such as [LMQ+03, Ust08, Kra05, SEVB10, MU08, CK01, LLM07, Sho99]. However all these are defined for the PKI based systems.

Surprisingly, after the first formal model for AKE was proposed by Bellare and Rogaway [BR94] for symmetric key system, no further progress has happened in refining the system for symmetric key settings considering stronger classes of adversaries. Several authors have presented protocols for AKE in the symmetric key set up such as [NS78,OR87] etc. However, none of them were proved and they were shown to be susceptible to various classes of attacks [Boy90,CJ97,BGH+92]. In fact many of the ISO-9798 family of protocols were shown to vulnerable to various classes of attacks [BCM13].

Our first contribution is that we propose a new model for a symmetric key AKE that allows the adversary to have far more power than the BR model [BR94]. More specifically, the adversary can obtain session randomness of party, long term keys of a parties. In particular we allow the adversary to obtain all information other than those which allow him to trivially compute the session key for a particular session (as defined by the freshness condition in Sect. 3.3). Moreover we allow the adversary to be fully active even in the test session. We define what it means for a symmetric key AKE to be secure in our new model.

We then give a construction of a three-pass symmetric key exchange protocol from *weak Pseudo Random Functions* (wPRF) and *weak Almost-XOR Universal hash function family* (wAXU). Dodis et al. [DKPW12] showed how to construct a three-pass authentication protocol from wPRF secure against *active* attacks. If we use the techniques of [DKPW12] to obtain mutual authentication, it will result in a four-pass (two-round) symmetric key AKE. We improve upon this direct application of their scheme by showing how to obtain a three-pass actively secure symmetric key AKE using secure instances of the same primitives which provides mutual authentication. For this, we introduce a new technique, called *input swapping*. Ours is the *first* construction that achieves security against fully active adversaries and at the same time provide mutual authentication of both parties in only *three-pass* using weaker primitives than MAC or PRF. Our proposed construction is also efficient and is secure under the *Decisional Diffie Hellman* (DDH) assumption in the Random Oracle (RO) model.

Our construction is also *forward secure*. So even if an adversary can get the long term secret key (LTK) between two parties, he cannot infer the previously established session keys between them. The concept of *perfect forward secrecy* was first defined by Gunther [Gün90] and used in protocols like Station-to-Station (STS) [DVOW92], SASI [Chi07]. These protocols update the LTKs at regular interval of time and irreversibly, i.e., if an adversary gets hold of a LTK K_t at time interval t say, he cannot infer the previous LTKs before time period t, since it will require the adversary to break the one-wayness of some function. These schemes are called *Key-Evolving Schemes* (KES). The time interval after which the LTKs should be updated depends from application to application depending on the level of security they want to achieve. They can be updated after each session, or they may be updated after every ϱ interval of time. The first approach is generally not followed due to the concurrent nature of AKE protocols. It may happen that multiple instances of the same protocol is running between different parties. If the LTKs are updated after each session, it may cause some other sessions to abort. So generally the second approach is followed which is far more suitable for distributed setting like the Internet. However on the downside, if we use the second approach for key evolution we do not achieve perfect forward secrecy in its entirely, whereas if we update the LTKs after each session we achieve perfect forward secrecy. The faster the LTKs are evolved more forward secrecy is achieved. We also evolve the LTKs at regular time intervals or *epoch*. The duration of each epoch after which the LTK needs to be updated or evolved depends on the application. If the level of security needs to be high, then the key refreshment needs to be done frequently. However it should not be the case that the key refreshment rate gets greater than the rate at which the session key is actually established between the parties. In some sense our constructions are also *key-evolving*. So we can achieve perfect forward secrecy due to the key evolving nature of our protocol and also due to the fact that in each session the parties choose independent randomness.

1.1 Our Contributions

To summarize what we have said earlier in the previous section our main contributions are as follows:

1. We propose a new model for a symmetric forward-secure AKE that is more powerful than the BR model [BR94]. In addition, our model has the capability to handle active adversaries even in the test session.
2. We propose a concrete three-pass symmetric key AKE protocol secure in our new model withstanding active adversaries. The security of this protocol is proved under the *Decisional Diffie Hellman* (DDH) assumption in the random oracle model.
3. Our construction uses much weaker primitives like *weak Pseudo Random Functions* (wPRF) and *weak Almost-XOR Universal hash function family* (wAXU) as in [DKPW12]. However, with the introduction of a new technique which we call *input swapping*, combined with these primitives, we can complete our protocol in three-passes.
4. Our protocol also achieves *perfect forward security*. We achieve this by a key evolving strategy and also sampling independent randomness for each party in each session.

2   Preliminaries

In this section, we define all the notations we would be using throughout the paper. We also provide some standard definitions and state the complexity assumptions required for our constructions.

2.1 Notations

The set of integers modulo an integer p is denoted by $\mathbb{Z}_p$. Let $[n]$ denote the set of integers $\{1, 2, \ldots, n\}$ where $n \in \mathbb{N}$, the set of all natural numbers. For a set X, $x \in_R X$ denotes that x is randomly sampled from the set X. We denote by

λ the security parameter and it will be given in unary to the algorithms. All the algorithms will run in time polynomial in the size of the security parameter. Let $\{0,1\}^*$ denote the set of all binary strings and $\{0,1\}^n$ denote the set of all binary strings of length n. The length of a string $x \in \{0,1\}^*$ is denoted by $|x|$. Let p be a large prime of order λ where $p = 2q + 1$ and q is a prime number. Let $\mathbb{G}$ be a multiplicative subgroup of $\mathbb{Z}_p^*$ with prime order q and let g be a generator for $\mathbb{G}$. A function $f : \mathbb{N} \to \mathbb{R}$ is called *negligible* if it vanishes faster than the inverse of any polynomial, i.e., for a constant $c > 0$ and sufficiently large n, $f(n) < n^{-c}$. We define $\mathsf{DLOG}(x)$ to denote the discrete logarithm of x with base g.

2.2   Some Standard Definitions

Definition 1. Weak Pseudo-Random Functions(wPRF). *A function family* $\mathcal{F} = \{f_K\}_{K \in \mathcal{K}} : \mathbb{D} \to \mathbb{F}$ *where* $\mathcal{K}$ *is the key space, is said to be a weak PRF family if for any polynomial-sized* k, *randomly chosen* $f \in_R \mathcal{F}$, *and* $r_1, r_2, \ldots r_k \in_R \mathbb{D}$, *the distribution of* $(r_1, f(r_1)), (r_2, f(r_2)), \ldots, (r_k, f(r_k))$ *is computationally indistinguishable from the uniform distribution over* $(\mathbb{D}, \mathbb{F})^k$, *i.e., an adversary for a weak-PRF aims to distinguish a random member of the family from a truly random function after observing a polynomially-bounded number of samples. A wPRF is called* (t, Q, ϵ)-*wPRF if for a* t-*time adversary* $\mathcal{A}$ *making at most* Q *queries to the function, the advantage in distinguishing the above two distributions is at most* ϵ.

Definition 2. Almost Universal Hash Family. *A family of keyed hash functions* $\{\mathcal{H}_k : \mathbb{D} \to \mathbb{F}\}_{k \in \mathcal{K}}$ *is* ρ-*almost universal if* $\forall x_1 \neq x_2 \in \mathbb{D}$, $Pr_{k \in_R \mathcal{K}}[h_k(x_1) = h_k(x_2)] \leq \rho$ *holds.*

Definition 3. Pairwise Independent Hash Family. *A hash family* $H : \mathbb{D} \to \mathbb{F}$ *is called pairwise independent if* $\forall x_1, x_2 \in \mathbb{D}$ *and* $x_1 \neq x_2$, *and* $y_1, y_2 \in \mathbb{F}$, $Pr_{h \in_R H}[h(x_1) = y_1 \wedge h(x_2) = y_2] = \frac{1}{|\mathbb{F}|^2}$.

Definition 4. Weak-Almost XOR-Universal (wAXU) hash family. *A family of keyed hash functions* $\{\mathcal{H}_k : \mathbb{D} \to \mathbb{F}\}_{k \in \mathcal{K}}$ *is* δ-*wAXU if for* $x_1, x_2 \in_R \mathbb{D}$ *with* $x_1 \neq x_2$, *and a* $y \in \mathbb{F}$, *we have* $Pr_{k \in_R \mathcal{K}}[h_k(x_1) \oplus h_k(x_2) = y] \leq \delta$.

If $\forall x_1 \neq x_2$ *and for any* $y \in \mathbb{F}$, $Pr_{k \in_R \mathcal{K}}[h_k(x_1) \oplus h_k(x_2) = y] \leq \delta$ *holds, then it is called* δ-*AXU. If* $\delta = \frac{1}{|\mathbb{F}|}$, *it is called (perfectly) XOR-universal.*

Without loss of generality we can assume that the output of all the functions can be embedded into a finite field. Example if the output size of a wPRF is n bits, one can embed the output of the wPRF into a finite field of size 2^n. The simplest way this can be done is considering the function output $t \in \{0,1\}^n$ as a polynomial in a finite field $\mathbb{F} = (\mathbb{Z}_2^n, +, \times)$ for suitable defined addition and multiplication operations.

2.3   Complexity Assumption

In this section, we present a brief overview of the hard problem assumption.

Definition 5. *Decisional Diffie-Hellman Problem (DDH) - Given* $(g, g^\alpha,$
$g^\beta, h) \in \mathbb{G}^4$ *for unknown* $\alpha, \beta \in \mathbb{Z}_q^*$, *where* $\mathbb{G}$ *is a cyclic prime order multiplicative group with* g *as a generator and* q *the order of the group, the DDH problem in* $\mathbb{G}$ *is to check whether* $h \stackrel{?}{=} g^{\alpha\beta}$.

The advantage of any probabilistic polynomial time algorithm $\mathcal{A}$ in solving the DDH problem in $\mathbb{G}$ is defined as

$$Adv_{\mathcal{A}}^{DDH} = |Pr\left[\mathcal{A}(g, g^\alpha, g^\beta, g^{\alpha\beta}) = 1\right] - Pr\left[\mathcal{A}(g, g^\alpha, g^\beta, h) = 1\right] \mid \alpha, \beta \in \mathbb{Z}_q^*|$$

The DDH Assumption is that, for any probabilistic polynomial time algorithm $\mathcal{A}$, the advantage $Adv_{\mathcal{A}}^{DDH}$ is negligibly small.

3   Our Security Model

In order to define what is meant by the security of an authenticated symmetric key exchange protocol, we need to formally define the security model and to define the powers of an adversary in this model. We assume there are n parties $P_1, \ldots, P_n$ each modeled by a probabilistic polynomial time Turing machine (PPTM). We assume the parties $P_1, \ldots, P_n$ are connected over point-to-point links over which the messages can be exchanged between them. Since our AKE is *key evolving*, the LTKs between the parties are fixed for a particular epoch only and they are refreshed at the expiration of each epoch. In particular, the lth epoch is denoted by T_l and it represents the time interval $[a_{l-1}, a_l]$ $\forall l \geq 1$. In each epoch T_l, the parties P_i and P_j will have a LTK shared among them denoted by $LTK_{ij}^{(l)}$ $\forall l \geq 1$. We denote the current epoch as T_t throughout the paper. We assume that at the beginning of each epoch, the LTKs of all the parties are updated simultaneously. Without loss of generality, we assume throughout the paper that when two parties communicate with each other, they do so in the same epoch. We now define the concept of a session and define the powers of an adversary in our model. Next, we define the concept of partner session in this setting and what it means for a session to be fresh. Finally, we define the security of an symmetric AKE protocol in this model.

3.1   Session

A typical AKE protocol between two parties consists of several passes between the parties wishing to establish a common session key. Let us denote the two parties executing an instance of the protocol by A and B. Let us further assume that A is the initiator and B is the responder for this execution of the protocol. The set of all actions carried out by A during the execution of the protocol is called *session* of A. Similarly we define the session corresponding to B.

Every session is uniquely identified by a label called *session identifier*. A session corresponding to the party A consists of a (small) finite number of passes executed by A. In a typical pass executed by A:

1. A may perform some local computations that may depend on the values received from B or locally generated by A and
2. A may communicate certain values to B or *aborts*.

The state of a typical pass, say the ith pass is described by the 5-tuple $\hat{P}_i = (sid_{AB}, A, B, in_i, out_i)$ where A is the *owner* of the session, sid_{AB} is the session identifier, B is the *peer*, in_i denotes the values A had received from B prior to the execution of this pass and out_i is the set of values that A sends to B in this pass.

If A is the initiator of the protocol then the state of the first pass is denoted as $(sid_{AB}, A, B, \_\_\_, out_1)$ because this being the first pass of the session A would not have received any value from B. Since a session comprises of several passes, we define the state of a session corresponding to A as $(sid_{AB}, A, B, IN, OUT, role)$ where A is the owner of the session and B is the peer for the session, $role = \mathcal{I}$ if A is the initiator of the protocol and $role = \mathcal{R}$ if A is the responder of the protocol, $IN = \bigcup\limits_{i=1}^{n} in_i$, where n is the number of passes and in_i is the values received from B in the ith pass and $OUT = \bigcup\limits_{i=1}^{n} out_i$ where out_i denotes the values that A sends to B.

Several sessions may run concurrently at each party. Since a party can have multiple concurrent sessions running within it, it has to maintain the states of all these sessions. However these session states are independent of each other as all the sessions use independent randomness and hence their states are to be stored separately. The shared secret key obtained at the end of this session is called the *session key*. On successful completion of a session, each entity outputs the *session key* and deletes the *session state*. A session may not get completed, and may enter into *abort* state, and in this case no *session key* is generated.

3.2 Adversary

The adversary $\mathcal{A}$ is also modeled as a PPTM which has the capability to launch active attacks in all the session including the test session apart from his eavesdropping capability on the protocol messages. In order to model real life attacks we allow the adversary to obtain more information such as the long term secret key of parties. Since our protocol is key evolving (i.e. the long term secret keys of users changes after a certain lifetime) we allow the adversary to obtain the LTKs at a certain time period. Similarly the adversary can also obtain ephemeral secret key of users during a particular session. In our security model since we allow the adversary to launch active attacks even in the test session, we disallow the adversary to make corrupt queries in the test session for the current epoch. This restriction is quite natural and is an obvious one. In fact, if we allow the adversary to obtain the LTK of the parties in the test session, ephemeral keys of the parties and also allow the adversary to launch active in the test session, it would be impossible to design any protocol as discussed in Sect. 4.3. Thus we need to impose some restriction on the allowed queries when we make the adversary active in all sessions, including the test session. The information that the adversary gets is modeled by the following oracle queries:

- $Send(P_i, P_j, m, t)$: This query models the capabilities of an adversary to perform the *active man-in-the-middle* attacks. Here t represents the index of the current epoch T_t. The following sequence of actions are assumed to take place:
  1. Case (i) $m \neq 0$
     - Party P_i sends m in this pass to party P_j.
     - If P_j does not abort, it sends a response say r_j to P_i.
     - The value r_j is given to the adversary.
  2. Case (ii) $m = 0$
     - Party P_i initiates a new session with party P_j.
     - If P_j does not abort, it sends a response say r_j to P_i.
     - The value r_j is given to the adversary.
- $LTK\_Reveal(i, j, t)$: This query will return $LTK_{ij}^{(l)}$ $\forall 1 \leq l < t$ where t denotes the index of the current epoch T_t, i.e., it allows the adversary to obtain the LTKs of user P_i and P_j in all the previous epochs excluding the current epoch T_t.
- $Ephemeral\_Reveal(sid_{ij}^{(t)})$: This query reveals the ephemeral secret key of the session $sid_{ij}^{(t)}$, i.e., the value $rand_i$ of the current epoch T_t.
- $SK\_Reveal(sid_{ij}^{(t)})$: The queries reveals the session key of a completed session $sid_{ij}^{(t)}$ for the current epoch T_t.

After some polynomial amount of interactions, A may choose a specific session as *Test* session provided the session is completed and fresh as per Definition 9. We denote the chosen session as $Test(sid_{ij}^{(t)})$. Only one query of this form is allowed.

- $Test(sid_{ij}^{(t)})$: In response to the test query, a bit $b \in \{0, 1\}$ is randomly generated. If $b = 0$, the session key is given to the adversary $\mathcal{A}$. If $b = 1$, a uniformly chosen random value from the set of valid session keys is returned to $\mathcal{A}$.

  After the Test query has been issued, the adversary can continue querying provided that the test session remains fresh. Note that while $\mathcal{A}$ can issue polynomial number of queries like *Send*, *LTK_Reveal*, *Ephemeral_Reveal* queries he can issue only one *Test* query.

3.3 Few Important Definitions

Before defining the Sym-AKE security notion, we need to define what is meant by *session partnership* or a *matching* session.

Definition 6. Session Partnership. *Two sessions* $sid_{ij}^{(t)} = (P_i, P_j, OUT, IN, role)$ *and* $sid_{ji}^{\prime(t)} = (P_j, P_i, OUT', IN', role')$ *are said to be partnered session or matching sessions iff:*

1. $OUT = IN'$ and $IN = OUT'$.
2. $role \neq role'$.

We now define the condition for the freshness of a session.

Definition 7. Local Exposure of Session. *Let Π be a protocol, and P_i and P_j be two honest parties, $sid_{ij}^{(t)}$ the identifier of a completed session at P_i with peer P_j, and $sid_{ji}^{'(t)}$ the matching session's identifier. The session $sid_{ij}^{(t)}$ is said to be locally exposed to an adversary $\mathcal{A}$ if only $\mathcal{A}$ issued a $SK\_Reveal(sid_{ij}^{(t)})$.*

Definition 8. Exposure of Session. *A session $sid_{ij}^{(t)}$ is said to be exposed if (a) it is locally exposed, or (b) its matching session $sid_{ji}^{'(t)}$ exists and is locally exposed.*

Definition 9 (Session Freshness). *A session that is not exposed is called a fresh session.*

Remark 1. Note that the adversary can ask the following combinations of queries:

1. $LTK\_Reveal\,(i,j,t)$ where $1 \leq l < t$ and $Ephemeral\_Reveal(sid_{ij}^{(t)})$.
2. $LTK\_Reveal\,(i,j,t)$ where $1 \leq l < t$ and $Ephemeral\_Reveal(sid_{ji}^{'(t)})$.

The goal of the adversary is to guess whether the challenge is a true session key or a randomly selected key. We say the adversary is successful if he manages to distinguish the session key from a random value with a noticeable probability bounded away from $\frac{1}{2}$ in any non-obvious way. More formally let us define the security of a symmetric key AKE protocol as in Definition 10.

Definition 10 (Sym-AKE security). *The protocol Π is said to be Sym-AKE-secure, if no polynomially bounded adversary can distinguish a fresh session key from a random value, chosen from the distribution of session keys, with probability significantly greater than 1/2. An adversary $\mathcal{A}$ outputs his guess b' in the test session. The adversary wins the game if he guesses the challenge b correctly, i.e., $b' = b$. The advantage of $\mathcal{A}$ against Π in the Sym-AKE model is defined as*

$$Adv_{\mathcal{A}}^{\Pi, Sym\text{-}AKE} = \Pr[b' = b] - \tfrac{1}{2}.$$

The protocol Π is defined to be Sym-AKE secure iff the following two conditions hold:

1. *If two honest parties complete matching sessions, then, except with negligible probability, they both compute the same session key. (Correctness)*
2. *For any probabilistic polynomial-time adversary $\mathcal{A}$, $Adv_{\mathcal{A}}^{\Pi, Sym\text{-}AKE}$ is negligible.*

4   Symmetric Key Exchange Protocol Resilient to Fully Active (FA) Adversaries

In this section, we give our construction of a symmetric key exchange protocol that can handle fully active adversaries. We give the adversary the power to additionally launch active attacks on the test session. Note that it is trivial to achieve security against FA adversaries in *one-round* by simply MAC-ing or applying a secure pseudo-random function (PRF) on the values sent across by the parties. More precisely party P_i can simply perform a MAC on the value χ_i by using the LTKs shared between P_i and P_j (keyed MAC), i.e., let $y = MAC_K(\chi_i, P_i, P_j)$. Now party P_i sends $\langle P_i, \chi_i, y \rangle$ to party P_j who can verify the authenticity of the MAC. After this party P_j can simply perform a MAC on the value χ_j by using the LTKs shared between P_j and P_i, i.e., let $y' = MAC_K(\chi_j, P_j, P_i)$. Party P_j then sends $\langle P_j, \chi_j, y' \rangle$ to party P_i. Party P_i can verify the authenticity of the MAC sent from P_j and engage in session key exchange. Another way of achieving security against FA adversaries is by using a PRF with the seed of the PRF being the LTK shared between P_i and P_j.

But instead of using MAC or PRF we use weaker primitives like Weak Pseudo Random Functions (wPRF) and weak Almost XOR Universal (wAXU) hash functions to achieve resilience against FA adversaries. We propose a three-pass symmetric key AKE resilient to FA adversaries using concrete instances of these weaker primitives.

4.1   Intuition Behind our Construction

NAXOS trick [LLM07] is one of the standard tool that is used to construct secure key exchange protocols in public key paradigm. We, for the first time, introduce the NAXOS trick in symmetric key setting. We generate a pseudo-ephemeral key $\tilde{K}$ by hashing the long term shared secret key between the parties (LTK) and the ephemeral randomness chosen by the parties in each session $(rand_k$ where $k \in i, j)$, i.e., $\tilde{K} \leftarrow H_1(LTK, rand_k)$. The value $\tilde{K}$ is never stored, and so the adversary must learn both LTK and $rand_k$ to compute $\tilde{K}$. So the adversary needs to query LTK_Reveal on one of the two parties and also $Ephemeral\_Reveal$ on any one of the two parties in the current epoch, but this type of query is not allowed in our model. So in our protocol, the initiator of the session must compute $\tilde{K} = H(LTK, rand)$ twice: once during sending $g^{\tilde{K}}$ and once during computing the secret session key from the received values. This is done to avoid to storing this pseudo ephemeral value, which when compromised can allow the adversary to compute the shared secret session key. But in addition to safeguard against active attacks in the test session we use wPRF and wAXU hash functions to achieve authentication of parties. However to achieve a three-pass symmetric key AKE using these primitives in *three-pass* is challenging. The main idea we employ is a trick what we call the *input swapping* technique. Using this trick we get a three-pass symmetric key exchange protocol with mutual authentication of parties in the presence of FA adversaries. The idea is to swap the inputs of the wPRF and the wAXU hash functions during the computation of values at the two parties as shown in Algorithm 1. More precisely, a party computes the function sampled randomly from the wPRF family on it's local input and evaluates the hash function sampled randomly from the wAXU on the input received from the other party. Now the adversary receives the values sent by one party (owner) and also the tag value computed by its peer (responder) in the second pass. Now he has to forge the tag value of the owner. The tag values computed by the owner and responder have their inputs swapped in the wPRF and the wAXU functions. So the security intuition is that even receiving the tag value from the receiver in the second pass and the values sent by the owner in the first pass will not help the adversary to forge the tag value sent from the owner in the third pass. Also if the adversary tries to tamper with the values sent by the owner or the receiver or both he will be caught during verification since the adversary does not possess the long term secret keys of the current epoch held by the parties.

4.2 Protocol Π: A Three-Pass Protocol Secure Against FA Adversaries

In this section we present the concrete construction of a protocol that is secure against fully active adversaries in our new security model. Let P_i and P_j be the two parties participating in the protocol. Our construction provides mutual authentication of both the parties involved in the session key establishment and in addition are *forward-secure*.

Setup: Choose a group $\mathbb{G}$ of prime order q and let g be a generator of $\mathbb{G}$. We assume the DDH problem is hard in $\mathbb{G}$. Let the keyspace $\mathcal{K}_1 = \mathcal{K}_2 = \mathbb{Z}_q^*$. Let $\mathcal{F} = \{f_{K_1} : \mathbb{G} \to \mathbb{G}\}_{K_1 \in \mathcal{K}_1}$ be a weak pseudo random function(wPRF) family and $\mathcal{H} = \{h_{K_2} : \mathbb{G} \to \mathbb{G}\}_{K_2 \in \mathcal{K}_2}$ be a weak Almost XOR-Universal (wAXU) hash function family. We may define $f_{K_1}(x) = x^{K_1}$ and $h_{K_2}(y) = y^{K_2}$ so that f is a wPRF under the DDH assumption and h is a also a wAXU hash function by DDH as well [DKPW12]. Choose a collision resistant hash function $H_1 : \mathbb{Z}_p^* \times \mathbb{Z}_q^* \to \mathbb{Z}_q^*$ and a non-invertible collision resistant *key derivation function* KDF $: \mathbb{Z}_q^* \times \{0,1\}^* \times \{0,1\}^* \to \mathbb{Z}_q^*$.

Long Term KeyGen: For every pair of users, say P_i and P_j the Long Term KeyGen algorithm produces a long term key LTK $= K = \langle K_1, K_2 \rangle \in \mathcal{K}_1 \times \mathcal{K}_2$ and we assume that this common key is securely available with both the parties P_i and P_j.

Session Key Establishment: The two users P_i and P_j choose secret ephemeral exponents $rand_i$ and $rand_j$ respectively and compute the values χ_i and χ_j respectively. They now engage in an interactive three-pass key establishment protocol as shown in Algorithm 1. Party P_j computes a tag v_j using the keyed function f chosen uniformly at random from the wPRF family and a keyed hash function h uniformly at random from the wAXU family. The party P_j applies the function f on its local input (χ_j) and the function h on the input received from

160   S. Chakraborty et al.

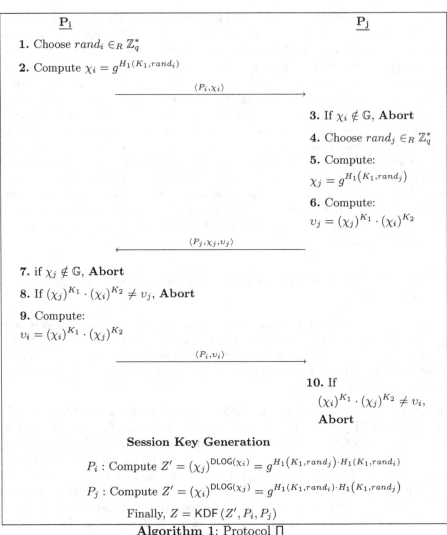

Algorithm 1: Protocol Π

P_i (i.e., χ_i). Party P_j then send the values χ_j and the computed tag value v_j to P_i. Party P_i then verifies the tag using the secret key $K = \langle K_1, K_2 \rangle$ and the received value χ_j. If the verification goes through, P_i computes the tag value v_i and sends it over to P_j and proceed with the session key generation phase. Notice that here we are also using our technique of *input swapping*, i.e., the inputs to the functions f_{K_1} and h_{K_2} are swapped in the computation of v_j and v_i). P_j then verifies the received tag value from P_i using the LTK $K = \langle K_1, K_2 \rangle$. If the verification goes through, it proceeds with the session key generation phase. Finally at the end of the protocol both the users P_i and P_j compute the same session key Z' as shown and compute the final session key using the secure KDF.

Remark 2. The protocol consists of two sends by the owner of the session and only one send by the responder (peer) per session. Here each party needs to perform four exponentiations, two calls to the wPRF function f and two calls to the wAXU hash function h.

Remark 3. The values χ_k where $k \in \{i, j\}$ are freshly generated for every session. In a preprocessing or a setup stage, the two users generate large number of ephemeral secret values and stores them in the table T_k. For each session, user P_k extracts a fresh value from the table T_k and uses them to generate the session keys for that session.

Remark 4. The value of the LTK $K = \langle K_1, K_2 \rangle$ is updated or *evolved* in each epoch. So the protocol Π is a key-evolving scheme (KES) and also since the values of the ephemeral keys generated in each session are random and independent of each other, it also achieves forward secrecy.

4.3   Need for Disallowing *LTK_Reveal* Query in the Test Session for the Current Epoch

In this section we show that by incorporating active attacks in the test session, it is impossible to achieve any kind of security for the AKE protocol if the long term keys of the parties of the current epoch are given to the adversary. In particular this is not a requirement specific to symmetric key settings only. In public key AKE also the same restriction holds. In particular if we allow *LTK_Reveal* (i, j, l) oracle service to the adversary for the current epoch T in the test session, then the adversary must be given the LTK K (or private keys in public key settings) shared between parties P_i and P_j for the current epoch. If the adversary $\mathcal{B}$ gets hold of the LTK shared between the two parties and he is allowed to perform active attacks he can successfully launch an *impersonation* attack as shown in Algorithm 2 when he is allowed to query the LTK of P_i and P_j in the current epoch . He can simply chose any session randomness on behalf of any one of the parties and can impersonate that party. Since the adversary also knows the LTK, the authentication at the other end (peer) will go through. This shows an *impossibility* result for allowing the LTK for the current epoch to be revealed to a FA adversary in the test session. The adversary can fool the party P_j into believing that he shares a key with party P_i and he can compute the same session key as party P_i. This represents a successful impersonation attack. In particular we show an impersonation attack on our protocol Π if we allow LTK of current epoch to be given to $\mathcal{B}$. In order to tackle this attack we allow only *LTK_Reveal* (i, j, l) where $1 \leq l \leq k - 1$ and do not reveal the LTK for the current epoch T_k between the users involved in the test session query in our new model. But note that he can even get the LTKs of the users involved in the test session for previous epochs. Hence from the above discussion we get the following proposition:

Proposition 1. *For any key-evolving two-party symmetric key AKE protocol, if we allow the Long Term Key (LTK) of the parties of the current epoch to get revealed to a Fully Active adversary, we cannot hope for any sort of security.*

P_i	Adversary	P_j

$$\xrightarrow{\chi_i} \qquad\qquad \xrightarrow{\chi_i}$$

1. Compute : $\tilde{\chi}_j = g^{H_1(K_1, \overline{rand_j})}$ $\xleftarrow{\chi_j, v_j}$

$\xleftarrow{\tilde{\chi}_j, \tilde{v}_j}$ 2. Compute $\tilde{v}_j = (\tilde{\chi}_j)^{K_1} \cdot (\chi_i)^{K_2}$:

$\xrightarrow{v_i = (\chi_i)^{K_1} \cdot (\tilde{\chi}_j)^{K_2}}$ 3. Compute : $\tilde{v}_i = (\chi_i)^{K_1} \cdot (\chi_j)^{K_2}$ $\xrightarrow{\tilde{v}_i}$

Session Key Computation:

P_i : Compute $Z_1 = (\tilde{\chi}_j)^{\mathsf{DLOG}(\chi_i)} = g^{H_1(K_1, \overline{rand_j}) \cdot H_1(K_1, rand_i)}$

P_j : Compute $Z_2 = (\chi_i)^{\mathsf{DLOG}(\chi_j)} = g^{H_1(K_1, rand_i) \cdot H_1(K_1, rand_j)}$

$\mathcal{B}$: Compute $Z_1 = (\chi_i)^{\mathsf{DLOG}(\tilde{\chi}_j)} = g^{H_1(K_1, rand_i) \cdot H_1(K_1, \overline{rand_j})}$

Algorithm 2: Impersonation Attack on Π in Presence of $LTK\_Reveal(i, j, t)$ where $1 \le l \le t$

4.4 Security Proof of Π

In this section we give the security proof of our protocol Π discussed in Sect. 4.2.

Theorem 1. *For any fully active AKE adversary $\mathcal{A}$ against our protocol Π, running in time $\tilde{t}$ and having advantage $\mathsf{Adv}_{\mathcal{A}}^{\Pi, Sym\text{-}AKE}$, that activates at most m sessions, we construct a DDH solver $\mathcal{S}$ with advantage $\mathsf{Adv}_{\mathcal{S}}^{DDH}$, a discrete logarithm solver τ with advantage $\mathsf{Adv}_{\tau}^{\mathsf{DLOG}}$ such that:*

$$\mathsf{Adv}_{\mathcal{A}}^{\Pi, Sym\text{-}AKE} \le \frac{m^2}{2} \cdot \mathsf{Adv}_{\mathcal{S}}^{DDH} - \mathsf{Adv}_{\tau}^{\mathsf{DLOG}} - \frac{1}{2}\left(1 - \frac{1}{|G|}\right).$$

where $\mathcal{S}$ runs in time $O(\tilde{t} \cdot m)$ and τ runs in time $O(\tilde{t})$ and $|G|$ denotes the size of the underlying group.

Proof. Let $\mathcal{A}$ be an adversary against our protocol Π. In accordance with our security model, the adversary $\mathcal{A}$ is allowed to make session activation queries. A query of the form $Send(P_i, P_j)$ makes user P_i perform **Step 1-2** of our protocol, and create a session with identifier $(P_i, P_j, \langle P_i, \chi_i, \eta_i \rangle, \star, \mathcal{I})$. On a query $(P_i, P_j, \langle P_i, \chi_i, \eta_i \rangle)$, P_j creates a session with identifier $(P_j, P_i, \langle P_j, \chi_j, \eta_j \rangle, \langle P_i, \chi_i, \eta_i \rangle, \mathcal{R})$. The query $(P_i, P_j, \langle P_i, \chi_i, \eta_i \rangle, \langle P_j, \chi_j, \eta_j \rangle, \mathcal{R})$ makes P_i update the session identifier $(P_i, P_j, \langle P_i, \chi_i, \eta_i \rangle, \star, \mathcal{I})$ (if any) to $(P_i, P_j, \langle P_i, \chi_i, \eta_i \rangle, \langle P_j, \chi_j, \eta_j \rangle, \mathcal{I})$ and perform **Step 4-6** of our protocol. The adversary is also allowed to make the following queries: $Ephemeral\_Reveal$, LTK_Reveal, SK_Reveal. Since the session key is computed as $H_2(\sigma)$ where $\sigma = (Z', P_i, P_j)$, the adversary can distinguish a fresh session key from a random session key in two ways:

- **Guessing Attack:** $\mathcal{A}$ guesses the test session key correctly.
- **Key Replication Attack:** $\mathcal{A}$ succeeds in making two non-matching sessions compute the same session key and then $\mathcal{A}$ simply issues a session key reveal query on one of the sessions and uses that key in the other session.

- **Forging Attack:** $\mathcal{A}$ computes the value σ and issues the H_2 digest query to get the session key.

Under the Random Oracle (RO) model, the first two attacks cannot succeed, except with negligible probability. Key Replication attack will not succeed, because if $\chi_i \neq \chi_i'$, or $\chi_j \neq \chi_j'$, or $\eta_i \neq \eta_i'$ or $\eta_j \neq \eta_j'$ or $P_i \neq P_i'$ or $P_j \neq P_j'$, and no substring of P_i matches P_j, then the probability that $H_2(\sigma_i, P_i, P_j) = H_2(\sigma_i', P_i', P_j')$ is negligible and vice versa. Thus it is enough to analyze the event E where E is defined as the event "$\mathcal{A}$ succeeds in forging the session key of a fresh session denoted by $sid_0 = (P_i, P_j, \langle \chi_{i_0}, \eta_{i_0}, P_i \rangle, \langle \chi_{j_0}, \eta_{j_0}, P_j \rangle, \varsigma)$". We will show that if $\mathcal{A}$ mounts a successful forgery, then we will be able to construct a DDH solver $\mathcal{S}$ which uses $\mathcal{A}$ as a subroutine.

Analysis of E. If event E occurs with non-negligible probability, using $\mathcal{A}$ we can build a DDH solver that succeeds with non-negligible probability.

$\mathcal{S}$ simulates $\mathcal{A}$'s environment, with n parties $P_1, \ldots, P_n$. Since $\mathcal{A}$ is polynomial (in $|q|$), we suppose that each party is activated at most m times ($m, n \leq \mathcal{L}(|q|$ for some polynomial $\mathcal{L}$). $\mathcal{S}$ chooses P_i, P_j randomly such that $i, j \in [n]$, and $t \in_R [m]$ (with these choices, $\mathcal{S}$ is guessing the test session). The challenger is given the DDH problem instance $\langle \mathbb{G}, g, q, p, C = g^\alpha, D = g^\beta, T \rangle$ where $T = g^{\alpha\beta}$ or T is random.

If the adversary queries on a value σ to the key derivation oracle KDF, the solver $\mathcal{S}$ looks up its corresponding list L_{KDF} to see if the value corresponding to the query is already listed in the list If the KDF *Oracle* was already queried with σ as input, the challenger extracts the value Z from the list L_{KDF} and returns the value. Otherwise it chooses a random value from the distribution of session keys and returns it to the adversary.

The solver $\mathcal{S}$ sets $\chi_{i_0} \leftarrow C$ and $\chi_{j_0} \leftarrow D$. Note that $\mathcal{S}$ does not know the values of $H_1(K, rand_{i0})$ and $H_1(K, rand_{j0})$ and the values of $H_1(K, rand_{i0})$ and $H_1(K, rand_{j0})$ is implicitly set to a and b respectively. We claim that if the adversary wins in the forging attack, $\mathcal{S}$ can solve the DDH challenge. Indeed the session key for the selected test session is of the form $KDF(\sigma)$ where σ includes the value $CDH(\chi_{i_0}, \chi_{j_0})$, i.e., $CDH(C, D)$. The adversary $\mathcal{A}$ cannot detect whether it is in the simulated session or the actual session unless it queried σ to the KDF function. Hence to win $\mathcal{A}$ must have queried on the KDF at the point σ. So if the adversary guesses the session key correctly, the solver $\mathcal{S}$ outputs 1 indicating it is a DDH tuple, else it outputs 0 indicating it is a random tuple.

Now $\mathcal{A}$ is allowed to make $EphemeralReveal(sid_{ij_0}^t)$, $EphemeralReveal$ $(sid_{ji_0}^t)$, but he is not allowed to ask both:

i. $(LTK\_Reveal(i, j, l), EphemeralReveal(sid_{ij_0}^t)$ where $l = t$ or
ii. $(LTK\_Reveal(i, j, l), EphemeralReveal(sid_{ji_0}^t)$ where $l = t$.

If sid_0 is indeed the test session, the only way $\mathcal{A}$ can distinguish the simulated session from the true session is it makes queries on $(K, rand_{i0})$ or $(K, rand_{j0})$ (by which $\mathcal{A}$ can find out $H_1(K, rand_{i0})$ or $H_1(K, rand_{j0})$). However $\mathcal{A}$ is not allowed to make these queries to reveal both $(K, rand_{i0})$ or $(K, rand_{j0})$. Hence for this $\mathcal{A}$ needs to find out the discrete logarithms of either $g^{H_1(K,rand_{i0})}$ or $g^{H_1(K,rand_{j0})}$. This corresponds to the hypothetical discrete logarithm solver τ in Theorem 1. Moreover since, $\mathcal{A}$ can activate at most m sessions and make at most $\tilde{t}$ KDF oracle queries, its total running time is $O(\tilde{t} \cdot m)$.

Probability Analysis: The solver $\mathcal{S}$ picks up two parties P_i and P_j and picks a session and its matching session randomly. So the probability that $\mathcal{A}$ picks one of the selected sessions as test session and another as its matching session is $\frac{1}{\binom{m}{2}} = \frac{2}{m(m-1)}$. The advantage of the DDH solver is related to the sum of the advantages of our AKE adversary $\mathcal{A}$ and the discrete logarithm solver τ. Let us define the event E: probability that the adversary $\mathcal{A}$ queries the KDF at the point σ as defined before. Now the advantage of the DDH solver $\mathcal{S}$ is equal to the probability that the adversary $\mathcal{A}$ outputs $b' = b$ (the challenge bit).

$$\Pr[b' = b] = \Pr[b' = b|E] \cdot \Pr[E] + \Pr[b' = b|\neg E] \cdot \Pr[\neg E]$$

Now let us analyze the probability of the event E.

$$\Pr[E] \geq \frac{2}{m(m-1)} \left(\mathrm{Adv}_{\mathcal{A}}^{\Pi,\mathbf{Sym\text{-}AKE}} + \mathrm{Adv}_{\tau}^{\mathrm{DLOG}} \right) \geq$$
$$\frac{2}{m^2} \left(\mathrm{Adv}_{\mathcal{A}}^{\Pi,\mathbf{Sym\text{-}AKE}} + \mathrm{Adv}_{\tau}^{\mathrm{DLOG}} \right)$$

So, we have:

$$\Pr[b' = b] \geq 1. \frac{2}{m(m-1)} \left(\mathrm{Adv}_{\mathcal{A}}^{\Pi,\mathbf{Sym\text{-}AKE}} + \mathrm{Adv}_{\tau}^{\mathrm{DLOG}} \right) + \frac{1}{2} \cdot \left(1 - \frac{1}{|G|} \right)$$

$$\text{or } \mathrm{Adv}_{\mathcal{S}}^{DDH} \geq 1. \frac{2}{m(m-1)} \left(\mathrm{Adv}_{\mathcal{A}}^{\Pi,\mathbf{Sym\text{-}AKE}} + \mathrm{Adv}_{\tau}^{\mathrm{DLOG}} \right) + \frac{1}{2} \cdot \left(1 - \frac{1}{|G|} \right)$$

$$\text{or } \mathrm{Adv}_{\mathcal{A}}^{\Pi,\mathbf{Sym\text{-}AKE}} \leq \frac{m^2}{2} \cdot \mathrm{Adv}_{\mathcal{S}}^{DDH} - \mathrm{Adv}_{\tau}^{\mathrm{DLOG}} - \frac{1}{2} \left(1 - \frac{1}{|G|} \right).$$

By our assumption, both $\mathrm{Adv}_{\mathcal{S}}^{DDH}$ and $\mathrm{Adv}_{\tau}^{\mathrm{DLOG}}$ are negligible. Hence $\mathrm{Adv}_{\mathcal{A}}^{\Pi,\mathbf{Sym\text{-}AKE}}$ is also negligible.   □

Thus, Theorem 1 ensures the security of our authenticated symmetric key AKE protocol.

5   Conclusion and Future Work

We propose a new security model for symmetric key AKE. Our model gives much more power to the adversary and also captures security against fully active adversaries, i.e., adversaries who are active in all the sessions including the test session. We also present a concrete construction providing security in our new security model for symmetric key AKE.

We show how to achieve a three-pass symmetric key AKE secure against fully active adversaries without using MACs or pseudorandom functions. Specifically, we use secure instances of weaker primitives like weak PRF and wAXU hash functions. However, achieving a three-pass AKE using wPRFs and wAXU functions is non-trivial and for this we introduce a novel technique which we call input swapping technique. Our construction is proven secure in the random oracle model under the DDH assumption. We leave open the problem of construction of a symmetric key AKE protocol in our new security model using weaker primitives, resisting fully active adversaries in the standard model.

Acknowledgments. The first two authors sincerely thank Rishiraj Bhattacharyya for a few technical discussions during the early stage of this work, that clarified some doubts on this topic. Part of this work was done while the first author was visiting R. C. Bose Centre for Cryptology and Security, Indian Statistical Institute, Kolkata during the Summer of 2015, and the third author was visiting the Simons Institute for the Theory of Computing, supported by the Simons Foundation and by the DIMACS/Simons Collaboration in Cryptography through NSF grant #CNS-1523467. The second author is also grateful to the Project CoEC (Centre of Excellence in Cryptology), Indian Statistical Institute, Kolkata, funded by the Government of India, for partial support towards this project.

References

[BCM13] Basin, D., Cremers, C., Meier, S.: Provably repairing the iso/iec 9798 standard for entity authentication. J. Comput. Secur. **21**(6), 817–846 (2013)

[BGH+92] Bird, R.S., Gopal, I., Herzberg, A., Janson, P., Kutten, S., Molva, R., Yung, M.: Systematic design of two-party authentication protocols. In: Feigenbaum, J. (ed.) CRYPTO 1991. LNCS, vol. 576, pp. 44–61. Springer, Heidelberg (1992)

[BLL07] Byun, J.K., Lee, D.H., Lim, J.I.: Ec2c-paka: An efficient client-to-client password-authenticated key agreement. Inf. Sci. **177**(19), 3995–4013 (2007)

[Boy90] Boyd, C.: Hidden assumptions in cryptographic protocols. IEE Proc. E (Comput. Digital Tech.) **137**(6), 433–436 (1990)

[BR94] Bellare, M., Rogaway, P.: Entity authentication and key distribution. In: Stinson, D.R. (ed.) CRYPTO 1993. LNCS, vol. 773, pp. 232–249. Springer, Heidelberg (1994)

[Chi07] Chien, H.-Y.: Sasi: A new ultralightweight rfid authentication protocol providing strong authentication and strong integrity. IEEE Trans. Dependable Secure Comput. **4**(4), 337–340 (2007)

[CJ97] Clark, J.A., Jacob, J.L.: A survey of authentication protocol literature: Version 1.0. (1997)

[CK01] Canetti, R., Krawczyk, H.: Analysis of key-exchange protocols and their use for building secure channels. In: Pfitzmann, B. (ed.) EUROCRYPT 2001. LNCS, vol. 2045, pp. 453–474. Springer, Heidelberg (2001)

[CL08] Cao, T., Lei, H.: Privacy-enhancing authenticated key agreement protocols based on elliptic curve cryptosystem. Acta Electronica Sinica **36**(2), 397 (2008)

[CY08] Cheng, H., Yang, G.: Ekaes: An efficient key agreement and encryption scheme for wireless sensor networks. J. Electron. (China) **25**(4), 495–502 (2008)

[DH76] Diffie, W., Hellman, M.E.: New directions in cryptography. IEEE Trans. Inf. Theory **22**(6), 644–654 (1976)

[DKPW12] Dodis, Y., Kiltz, E., Pietrzak, K., Wichs, D.: Message authentication, revisited. In: Pointcheval, D., Johansson, T. (eds.) EUROCRYPT 2012. LNCS, vol. 7237, pp. 355–374. Springer, Heidelberg (2012)

[DVOW92] Diffie, W., Van Oorschot, P.C., Wiener, M.J.: Authentication and authenticated key exchanges. Des. Codes Crypt. 2(2), 107–125 (1992)

[GNY90] Gong, L., Needham, R., Yahalom, R.: Reasoning about belief in cryptographic protocols. In: Proceedings of the 1990 IEEE Computer Society Symposium on Research in Security and Privacy, pp. 234–248. IEEE (1990)

[Gün90] Günther, C.G.: An identity-based key-exchange protocol. In: Quisquater, J.-J., Vandewalle, J. (eds.) EUROCRYPT 1989. LNCS, vol. 434, pp. 29–37. Springer, Heidelberg (1990)

[JKL04] Jeong, I.R., Katz, J., Lee, D.-H.: One-round protocols for two-party authenticated key exchange. In: Jakobsson, M., Yung, M., Zhou, J. (eds.) ACNS 2004. LNCS, vol. 3089, pp. 220–232. Springer, Heidelberg (2004)

[Kra05] Krawczyk, H.: HMQV: a high-performance secure Diffie-Hellman protocol. In: Shoup, V. (ed.) CRYPTO 2005. LNCS, vol. 3621, pp. 546–566. Springer, Heidelberg (2005)

[LCZ07] Rongxing, L., Cao, Z., Zhu, H.: An enhanced authenticated key agreement protocol for wireless mobile communication. Comput. Stand. Interfaces 29(6), 647–652 (2007)

[LLM07] LaMacchia, B.A., Lauter, K., Mityagin, A.: Stronger security of authenticated key exchange. In: Susilo, W., Liu, J.K., Mu, Y. (eds.) ProvSec 2007. LNCS, vol. 4784, pp. 1–16. Springer, Heidelberg (2007)

[LMQ+03] Law, L., Menezes, A., Minghua, Q., Solinas, J., Vanstone, S.: An efficient protocol for authenticated key agreement. Des. Codes Crypt. 28(2), 119–134 (2003)

[MU08] Menezes, A., Ustaoglu, B.: Comparing the pre- and post-specified peer models for key agreement. In: Mu, Y., Susilo, W., Seberry, J. (eds.) ACISP 2008. LNCS, vol. 5107, pp. 53–68. Springer, Heidelberg (2008)

[NS78] Needham, R.M., Schroeder, M.D.: Using encryption for authentication in large networks of computers. Commun. ACM 21(12), 993–999 (1978)

[OR87] Otway, D., Rees, O.: Efficient and timely mutual authentication. ACM SIGOPS Operating Syst. Rev. 21(1), 8–10 (1987)

[Sat90] Satyanarayanan, M.: Scalable, secure, and highly available distributed file access. Computer 23(5), 9–18 (1990)

[SEVB10] Sarr, A.P., Elbaz-Vincent, P., Bajard, J.-C.: A new security model for authenticated key agreement. In: Garay, J.A., De Prisco, R. (eds.) SCN 2010. LNCS, vol. 6280, pp. 219–234. Springer, Heidelberg (2010)

[Sho99] Shoup, V.: On formal models for secure key exchange. Citeseer (1999)

[Ust08] Ustaoglu, B.: Obtaining a secure and efficient key agreement protocol from (h) mqv and naxos. Des. Codes Crypt. 46(3), 329–342 (2008)

Full PRF-Secure Message Authentication Code Based on Tweakable Block Cipher

Yusuke Naito[✉]

Mitsubishi Electric Corporation,
Kanagawa, Japan
Naito.Yusuke@ce.MitsubishiElectric.co.jp

Abstract. We propose a new message authentication code (MAC) based on a tweakable block cipher (TBC). We prove that the new MAC is a pseudo-random function (PRF) up to $O(2^n)$ queries, that is, full PRF-security, where the output length of the TBC is n bits. We note that although Yasuda proposed a full PRF-secure MAC based on a compression function (CF), that does not offer a full PRF-secure TBC-based MAC due to the PRF/PRF switch. Hence our MAC is the first full PRF-secure one based on a TBC.

Keywords: Message authentication code · Full PRF-security · Tweakable block cipher

1 Introduction

Message Authentication Codes (MACs) are often realized by MAC constructions using block ciphers (BCs), compression functions (CFs) and tweakable block ciphers (TBCs). The security goal of MACs is commonly a pseudo-random function or PRF-security where BCs, CFs and TBCs are assumed to be pseudo-random permutations (PRPs), PRFs, and tweakable pseudo-random permutations (TPRPs), respectively.

Many MACs have been designed so that the internal state lengths are equal to the output ones of the underlying primitives. These MACs are vulnerable to the birthday attack on the internal states. In this case, the PRF-advantage is generally bounded by the birthday bound, that is, $O(\ell^2 q^2/2^n)$, where n is the output length of the underlying function, q is the total number of queries to the MAC oracle, and ℓ is the maximum length of each query.[1] Hence these MACs are PRF-secure up to $O(2^{n/2}/\ell)$ queries. We call PRF-secure MACs up to Q queries "Q PRF-secure MACs".

These MACs are endangered by the birthday attack when n is small and ℓ is large. Hence designing a MAC such that the number of queries is improved

---

[1] Several works such as [4,17] use the total query complexity σ instead of q and ℓ. Then the birthday bound is written as $O(\sigma^2/2^n)$. Note that we use q and ℓ in order to focus on removing the ℓ factor and improving the q factor.

© Springer International Publishing Switzerland 2015
M.-H. Au and A. Miyaji (Eds.): ProvSec 2015, LNCS 9451, pp. 167–182, 2015.
DOI: 10.1007/978-3-319-26059-4_9

and the influence of ℓ is removed is one of important research topics. Especially, designing a MAC that achieves $O(2^n)$ PRF-security is an ultimate goal. We call such MAC "a full PRF-secure MAC".

So far several papers attempt to design such MACs.

Counter-Based and Parallelizable MACs. Bellare et al. [1] proposed XOR MAC and Bernstein [3] proposed PCS. These MACs are based on CFs and achieve $O(2^{n/2})$ PRF-security, that is, the influence of ℓ is removed. These MACs employ counter-based parallelizable constructions where for message blocks $m_1, \ldots, m_l$ and a PRF $f_K(\cdot, \cdot)$ with a key K, the output of the MAC is defined by $c_i \leftarrow f_K(i, m_i)$ $(i = 1, \ldots, l)$; $tag \leftarrow f_K(0, c_1 \oplus \cdots \oplus c_l)$. This MAC is PRF-secure as long as no collision occurs in the xored values of $c_1 \oplus \cdots \oplus c_l$. Therefore, the counter-based parallelizable MAC is a PRF up to $O(2^{n/2})$ queries.

Later, Yasuda [20] and Zhang [22] proposed BC-based MACs that are variants of PMAC [4,17] and achieve $O(2^{n/2})$ PRF-security.

MACs with Double-Length Internal States. Yasuda [19] proposed a BC-based MAC called PMAC_Plus that is a variant of PMAC. PMAC_Plus has $2n$-bit internal states and thus resists the birthday attack. To obtain $2n$-bit internal states, the first n bits are updated by using xor operations and the remaining n bits are updated by using xor operations and multiplications by 2 over the multiplication subgroup of $GF(2^n)$. He proved that PMAC_Plus achieves $O(2^{2n/3}/\ell)$ PRF-security.

Yasuda [21] proposed a CF-based MAC. To remove the influence of ℓ, the idea of the counter-based parallelizable construction is used, and to resist the birthday attack, the idea of PMAC_Plus is used. He proved that this MAC achieves full PRF-security.

Motivation. Although these studies showed that when using BCs or CFs, parallelizable, counter-based, and double-length internal state MACs have an aptitude for achieving full PRF-security, we wondered if it can be achieved from another primitive, that is, a TBC whose concept was introduced by Liskov et al. [13]. A TBC offers distinct permutations by distinct tweaks and retweaking is less costly than changing its secret key. Recently, thanks to the CAESAR competition [2], highly efficient TBCs have been proposed (e.g., [7,9–12]). Hence it is interesting to study the design of full PRF-secure TBC-based MACs.

We note that we cannot obtain a full secure TBC-based MAC from Yasuda's MAC [21], since we need the PRF/PRP switch.

Our Result: Full PRF-Secure TBC-Based MAC. We propose a full PRF-secure TBC-based MAC PMAC_TBC1k that uses the idea of parallelizable, counter-based, and double-length internal state MACs. We denote a TBC using a key K and a tweak tw by $\widetilde{E}_K^{tw}$.

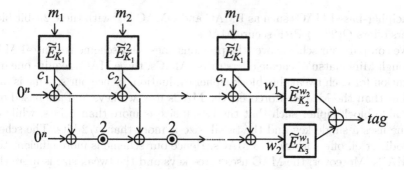

Fig. 1. 3-key TBC-based MAC for l message blocks $m_1, m_2, \ldots, m_l$

First we consider a simple example that is a 3-key TBC-based MAC. This construction is given in the Fig. 1 where the tweak size is n bits, K_1, K_2 and K_3 are secret keys and "$\odot 2$" represents a multiplication by 2 over the multiplication subgroup of $GF(2^n)$. This MAC employs the idea of the PMAC_Plus construction to resist the birthday attack, which offers $2n$-bit internal states, and employs the idea of the counter-based parallelizable construction in order to remove the influence of ℓ, where counters are inputted as tweaks. In the finalization phase, $\widetilde{E}_{K_2}$ and $\widetilde{E}_{K_3}$ are used. Intuitively, thanks to the counter-based parallelizable construction, we have only to consider a collision of inputs to the finalization phase which are corresponding with (w_1, w_2). Thanks to the $2n$-bit internal state, no collision occurs up to $O(2^n)$ queries. If no collision occurs then one of tweaks in the finalization phase is a fresh value, thereby the MAC returns a random value. Hence this MAC achieves full PRF-security. In the Sect. 3, we prove the PRF-security of the 3-key MAC.

The main scheme PMAC_TBC1k is a single key MAC whose finalization phase is slightly different from PMAC_TBC3k. Though the PMAC_TBC1k structure is analogous to the PMAC_TBC3k one, we elaborate the finalization phase in order to reduce the number of keys and support TBCs whose tweak lengths are $n/2$ bits or more. Then we prove that PMAC_TBC1k attains full PRF-security. The detail is given in the Sect. 4.

We note that our MAC construction is different from Yasuda's CF-based one. The internal state size of our MAC is $2n$ bits, while that of Yasuda's MAC is $4n$ bits. And our MAC calls a TBC two times in the finalization phase, while Yasuda's MAC calls a CF three times.

Related Works. Minematsu [15] proposed a $2n$-bit block cipher based on a tweakable block cipher with n-bit tweaks, which uses two keys and requires two multiplications over the multiplication subgroup of $GF(2^n)$ and two tweakable block cipher evaluations. And later Dodis et al. [5] proposed a different construction from Minematsu's one, which does not use the multiplications, uses three keys, and requires three tweakable block cipher evaluations. Combining blockcipher-based MACs such as PMAC and OMAC [8][2] with these $2n$-bit block ciphers offers $O(2^n/\ell)$ PRF-secure MACs.

We compare our scheme over the previous ones. Our scheme is a rate-1 MAC. Although Minematsu's scheme offers rate-1 MACs, these MACs require one multiplication for each tweakable block cipher evaluation. Hence our scheme is more efficient than the MACs. Moreover, the MACs use two keys and are based on a tweakable block cipher such that the tweak size is more than n bits, while our scheme uses a single key and the tweak size is more than $n/2$ bits. The scheme by Dodis et el. offers a rate-2/3 MACs. Hence our scheme is more efficient than the MACs. Moreover, the MAC uses three keys and the tweak size is more than n bits.

Several studies such as [6,16] succeeded in removing the influence of ℓ by employing probabilistic constructions. Such MACs require pseudo-random generators and must attach each generated random salt to each tag, which results in a larger tag size. On the other hand, our MAC is deterministic and thus does not require pseudo-random generators.

2   Notations and Security Definitions

Notations. ε is an empty string. 0^x is the bit string that consists of x zeros if $x > 0$ and $0^x = \varepsilon$ if $x \leq 0$. For some finite set X, $x \xleftarrow{\$} X$ means that an element is sampled uniformly at random from X and is set to x. For a bit string x and positive integers i, j such that $1 \leq i \leq j \leq |x|$, $x[i,j]$ is the substring of x from the left most i-th bit to the left most j-th bit. For example, for $x = 1000111$, $x[2,5] = 0001$. For a positive integer n, $\mathsf{Perm}(\{0,1\}^n)$ is the set of all permutations with n-bit blocks. For positive integers t, n, $\mathsf{Perm}(\{0,1\}^t, \{0,1\}^n)$ is the set of all tweakable permutations with t-bit tweaks and n-bit blocks. For $\widetilde{P} \in \mathsf{Perm}(\{0,1\}^t, \{0,1\}^n)$ and $tw \in \{0,1\}^t$, $\widetilde{P}(tw, \cdot)$ is a permutation with n-bit blocks. We denote $\widetilde{P}(tw, \cdot)$ by $\widetilde{P}^{tw}(\cdot)$. For positive integers k, t, n, $\mathsf{BC}(\{0,1\}^k, \{0,1\}^t, \{0,1\}^n)$ is the set of all tweakable block cipher with k-bit keys, t-bit tweaks and n-bit blocks. For $\widetilde{E} \in \mathsf{BC}(\{0,1\}^k, \{0,1\}^t, \{0,1\}^n)$, $tw \in \{0,1\}^t$ and $K \in \{0,1\}^k$, $\widetilde{E}(K, tw, \cdot)$ is a permutation with n-bit blocks. We denote $\widetilde{E}(K, tw, \cdot)$ by $\widetilde{E}_K^{tw}(\cdot)$. $\mathbf{D}^{\mathcal{O}} \Rightarrow 1$ is the event that $\mathbf{D}$ outputs 1 when interacting with one or more oracles $\mathcal{O}$.

Let $\mathrm{GF}(2^n)$ denote the field with 2^n points and let $\mathrm{GF}(2^n)^*$ denote the multiplication subgroup of this field which contains $2^n - 1$ points. We interchangeably think of a point a in $\mathrm{GF}(2^n)$ in any of the following ways: as an n-bit string $a_{n-1} \cdots a_1 a_0 \in \{0,1\}^n$ and as a formal polynomial $a_{n-1}\mathrm{x}^{n-1} + \cdots + a_1\mathrm{x} + a_0 \in \mathrm{GF}(2^n)$. Hence we need to fix an irreducible polynomial $a(\mathrm{x}) = \mathrm{x}^n + a_{n-1}\mathrm{x}^{n-1} + \cdots + a_1\mathrm{x} + a_0$. This paper uses the irreducible polynomial with the property that the element $2 = \mathrm{x}$ generates the entire multiplication

---

[2] These MACs achieve $O(2^n/\ell^{1/2})$ PRF-security when using a block cipher with $2n$-bit blocks.

group $GF(2^n)^*$ of order $2^n - 1$. Examples are $a(\mathbf{x}) = \mathbf{x}^{64} + \mathbf{x}^4 + \mathbf{x}^3 + \mathbf{x} + 1$ for $n = 64$ and $a(\mathbf{x}) = \mathbf{x}^{128} + \mathbf{x}^7 + \mathbf{x}^2 + \mathbf{x} + 1$ for $n = 128$.

PRF-Security. Let $\mathcal{F}_K$ be a keyed function using a secret key $K \xleftarrow{\$} \{0,1\}^k$ and $\mathcal{R}$ be a random function which is chosen uniformly at random from all functions with the same domain and range as $\mathcal{F}_K$. In the PRF-security game for $\mathcal{F}_K$, a distinguisher **D** interacts with either $\mathcal{F}_K$ or a random function $\mathcal{R}$, and tries to distinguish $\mathcal{F}_K$ from $\mathcal{R}$. The advantage of the PRF-security of $\mathcal{F}_K$ is defined as follows.

$$\mathbf{Adv}_{\mathcal{F}}^{\mathsf{prf}}(\mathbf{D}) := \Pr[\mathbf{D}^{\mathcal{F}_K} \Rightarrow 1] - \Pr[\mathbf{D}^{\mathcal{R}} \Rightarrow 1]$$

We call the world with $\mathcal{F}_K$ "a real world" and the world with $\mathcal{R}$ "an ideal world". We say $\mathcal{F}_K$ is a PRF if for any **D**, the above advantage is small.

TPRP-Security. Our security proof assumes that a tweakable block cipher is a tweakable pseudo-random permutation (TPRP). Let $\widetilde{E} \in \mathsf{BC}(\{0,1\}^k, \{0,1\}^t, \{0,1\}^n)$ be a tweakable block cipher. Let $K \xleftarrow{\$} \{0,1\}^k$ be a secret key of the tweakable block cipher. Let $\widetilde{P} \xleftarrow{\$} \mathsf{Perm}(\{0,1\}^t, \{0,1\}^n)$ be a tweakable random permutation. In the TPRP-security game for $\widetilde{E}_K$, a distinguisher **D** interacts with either $\widetilde{E}_K$ or $\widetilde{P}$, and tries to distinguish $\widetilde{E}_K$ from $\widetilde{P}$. The advantage of the TPRP-security of $\widetilde{E}_K$ is defined as follows.

$$\mathbf{Adv}_{\widetilde{E}}^{\mathsf{tprp}}(\mathbf{D}) := \Pr[\mathbf{D}^{\widetilde{E}_K} \Rightarrow 1] - \Pr[\mathbf{D}^{\widetilde{P}} \Rightarrow 1]$$

We say $\widetilde{E}_K$ is a TPRP if for any **D**, the above advantage is small. Note that **D** is given query access to *only* the forward oracle $\widetilde{E}_K/\widetilde{P}$ (not given query access to its inverse).

3   Simple Construction: 3-Key MAC from Tweakable Block Cipher

In this section, we consider a 3-key MAC construction PMAC_TBC3k.

3.1   Specification of PMAC_TBC3k

Let $\widetilde{E} \in \mathsf{BC}(\{0,1\}^k, \{0,1\}^t, \{0,1\}^n)$ be a tweakable blockcipher with k-bit keys, t-bit tweaks, and n-bit blocks such that $t \geq n$. Let $K_1, K_2, K_3 \xleftarrow{\$} \{0,1\}^k$ be secret keys. We denote PMAC_TBC3k using $\widetilde{E}_{K_1}, \widetilde{E}_{K_2}, \widetilde{E}_{K_3}$ by PMAC_TBC3k[$\widetilde{E}_{K_1}, \widetilde{E}_{K_2}, \widetilde{E}_{K_3}$]. Upon a message m, PMAC_TBC3k[$\widetilde{E}_{K_1}, \widetilde{E}_{K_2}, \widetilde{E}_{K_3}$]$(m)$ is defined as follows.

1. $(w_1, w_2) \leftarrow Int[\widetilde{E}_{K_1}](m)$

2. $tag \leftarrow \widetilde{E}_{K_2}^{w_1 \| 0^{t-n}}(w_2) \oplus \widetilde{E}_{K_3}^{w_2 \| 0^{t-n}}(w_1)$
3. Return tag

$Int[\widetilde{E}_{K_1}](m)$ is defined as follows.

1. $m^* \leftarrow m \| 10^*$
2. Partition m^* into n-bit blocks $m_1 \| \cdots \| m_l$
3. For $i = 1$ to l do $c_i \leftarrow \widetilde{E}_{K_1}^i(m_i)$
4. $w_1 \leftarrow c_1 \oplus \cdots \oplus c_l$; $w_2 \leftarrow 2^{l-1} \cdot c_1 \oplus 2^{l-2} \cdot c_2 \oplus \cdots \oplus c_l$
5. Return (w_1, w_2)

$m^* \leftarrow m \| 10^*$ means that first padding m with appending $1 \| 0 \cdots 0$ with the minimum number of zeros so that the length becomes a multiple of n, and then the padded value $m \| 10^*$ is assigned to m^*. Note that $\texttt{PMAC\_TBC3k}[\widetilde{E}_{K_1}, \widetilde{E}_{K_2}, \widetilde{E}_{K_3}]$ does not accept messages such that $l \geq 2^n$. For $i = 2^{l-1}, \ldots, 0$, $2^i \cdot c_1$ means the multiplication by 2^i and c_1 over $GF(2^n)^*$. Note that $2^{l-1} \cdot c_1 \oplus 2^{l-2} \cdot c_2 \oplus \cdots \oplus c_l$ can be calculated by $l - 1$ multiplications by 2 and $l - 1$ xor operations.

3.2   PRF-Security

The following theorem shows that $\texttt{PMAC\_TBC3k}[\widetilde{E}_{K_1}, \widetilde{E}_{K_2}, \widetilde{E}_{K_3}]$ is full PRF-secure if $\widetilde{E}_{K_1}, \widetilde{E}_{K_2}$, and $\widetilde{E}_{K_3}$ are TPRPs.

Theorem 1. *Let $\mathbf{D}$ be a distinguisher making at most q queries and running time in T such that each query has at most ℓ message blocks, that is, $l \leq \ell$. Then there exists a distinguisher $\mathbf{D}^*$ such that*

$$\mathbf{Adv}_{\texttt{PMAC\_TBC3k}}^{\mathsf{prf}}(\mathbf{D}) \leq \frac{0.5q^2}{(2^n - q)^2} + 3 \cdot \mathbf{Adv}_{\widetilde{E}}^{\mathsf{tprp}}(\mathbf{D}^*).$$

$\mathbf{D}^*$ *makes at most $(\ell + 2)q$ queries and runs in time $\mathcal{O}(T + \ell q)$.*

3.3   Proof of Theorem 1

To simplify the proof, we fix the tweak size $t = n$. We note that this proof can be carried over into that of the case with $t > n$.

Firstly, we replace the underlying primitive from $(\widetilde{E}_{K_1}, \widetilde{E}_{K_2}, \widetilde{E}_{K_3})$ to three tweakable random permutations $\widetilde{P}_1, \widetilde{P}_2, \widetilde{P}_3 \xleftarrow{\$} \mathsf{Perm}(\{0,1\}^n, \{0,1\}^n)$. This replacement yields the term $3 \cdot \mathbf{Adv}_{\widetilde{E}}^{\mathsf{tprp}}(\mathbf{D}^*)$ in the bound of Theorem 1.

Hence the remaining work is to bound the following difference that is the PRF-advantage of $\texttt{PMAC\_TBC3k}[\widetilde{P}_1, \widetilde{P}_2, \widetilde{P}_3]$.

$$\Pr[\mathbf{D}^{\texttt{PMAC\_TBC3k}[\widetilde{P}_1, \widetilde{P}_2, \widetilde{P}_3]} \Rightarrow 1] - \Pr[\mathbf{D}^{\mathcal{R}} \Rightarrow 1]$$

We consider the case where $\mathbf{D}$ interacts with L where $L = \texttt{PMAC\_TBC3k}[\widetilde{P}_1, \widetilde{P}_2, \widetilde{P}_3]$ in the real world and $L = \mathcal{R}$ in the ideal. Without loss of generality, we assume that $\mathbf{D}$ makes no repeated query.

We prove the PRF-security by using three games which start at the real world and end at the ideal world. We denote these games by Game 1, Game 2, and Game 3. By G_i, we denote an event that $\mathbf{D}$ outputs 1 in Game i. Hereafter we denote L in Game i by L_i. Then we have

$$\Pr[\mathbf{D}^{\mathtt{PMAC\_TBC3k}[\widetilde{P}_1, \widetilde{P}_2, \widetilde{P}_3]} \Rightarrow 1] - \Pr[\mathbf{D}^{\mathcal{R}} \Rightarrow 1]$$
$$= \Pr[G_1] - \Pr[G_3] = (\Pr[G_1] - \Pr[G_2]) + (\Pr[G_2] - \Pr[G_3]).$$

Hereafter we bound the differences $\Pr[G_i] - \Pr[G_{i+1}]$ ($i = 1, 2$). Note that we define L_2 before bounding $\Pr[G_1] - \Pr[G_2]$.

Bound of $\Pr[G_1] - \Pr[G_2]$. First we define an oracle $\mathcal{F}_{1,2}$. Upon a query m, $\mathcal{F}_{1,2}(m)$ is defined as follows, where T_{Int} is a (initially empty) table and bad is a flag that is initially false.

1. $(w_1, w_2) \leftarrow Int[\widetilde{P}_1](m)$

2. If $\exists (w_1, w_2) \in T_{Int}$ then bad $\leftarrow$ true; $\boxed{tag \xleftarrow{\$} \{0,1\}^n; \text{Return } tag}$

3. $T_{Int} \xleftarrow{\cup} \{(w_1, w_2)\}$; $tag \leftarrow \widetilde{P}_2^{w_1}(w_2) \oplus \widetilde{P}_3^{w_2}(w_1)$
4. Return tag

We define L_2 as $\mathcal{F}_{1,2}$ with the boxed statement. We note that $\mathcal{F}_{1,2}$ without the boxed statement is equal to L_1. Since L_1 and L_2 are equivalent until $\mathbf{D}$ sets bad, the fundamental lemma of game playing [2] ensures that

$$\Pr[G_1] - \Pr[G_2] \leq \Pr[\mathbf{D}^{L_2} \text{ sets bad}].$$

We bound $\Pr[\mathbf{D}^{L_2} \text{ sets bad}]$. First fix $i \in [1, q]$. We evaluate the probability that $\mathbf{D}^{L_2}$ sets bad at the i-th query. Fix $j \in [1, i-1]$. Let $w_1^{(i)}$ and $w_2^{(i)}$ be w_1 and w_2 defined at the i-th query. $w_1^{(i)}$, $w_2^{(i)}$, $w_1^{(j)}$ and $w_2^{(j)}$ have the following forms.

$$w_1^{(i)} = c_1^{(i)} \oplus c_2^{(i)} \oplus \cdots \oplus c_{l_i}^{(i)} \qquad w_2^{(i)} = 2^{l_i - 1} \cdot c_1^{(i)} \oplus 2^{l_i - 2} \cdot c_2^{(i)} \oplus \cdots \oplus c_{l_i}^{(i)}$$
$$w_1^{(j)} = c_1^{(j)} \oplus c_2^{(j)} \oplus \cdots \oplus c_{l_j}^{(j)} \qquad w_2^{(j)} = 2^{l_j - 1} \cdot c_1^{(j)} \oplus 2^{l_j - 2} \cdot c_2^{(j)} \oplus \cdots \oplus c_{l_j}^{(j)}$$

$w_1^{(i)} = w_1^{(j)}$ and $w_2^{(i)} = w_2^{(j)}$ imply that

$$c_1^{(i)} \oplus c_2^{(i)} \oplus \cdots \oplus c_{l_i}^{(i)} = c_1^{(j)} \oplus c_2^{(j)} \oplus \cdots \oplus c_{l_j}^{(j)}$$
$$2^{l_i - 1} \cdot c_1^{(i)} \oplus 2^{l_i - 2} \cdot c_2^{(i)} \oplus \cdots \oplus c_{l_i}^{(i)} = 2^{l_j - 1} \cdot c_1^{(j)} \oplus 2^{l_j - 2} \cdot c_2^{(j)} \oplus \cdots \oplus c_{l_j}^{(j)}$$

We analyze the probability that the above equations hold. We consider the following cases.

- $l_i \neq l_j$:
  The equations provide a unique solution set for two random variables, so the probability that the equations hold is bounded by $1/(2^n - (i-1))^2$.

- $\left(l_i = l_j\right) \wedge \left(\exists t \in [1, l_i] \text{ s.t. } c_t^{(i)} \neq c_t^{(j)}\right) \wedge \left(\forall s \in [1, l_i] \text{ with } s \neq t : c_s^{(i)} = c_s^{(j)}\right)$:
  The above equations never hold.
- $\left(l_i = l_j\right) \wedge \left(\exists t, s \in [1, l_i] \text{ with } t \neq s \text{ s.t. } c_t^{(i)} \neq c_t^{(j)} \text{ and } c_s^{(i)} \neq c_s^{(j)}\right)$:
  The equations provide a unique solution set for two random variables, so the probability that the equations hold is bounded by $1/(2^n - (i-1))^2$.

We thus have

$$\Pr[G_1] - \Pr[G_2] \leq \sum_{i=1}^{q} \frac{i-1}{(2^n - (i-1))^2} \leq \frac{0.5q^2}{(2^n - q)^2} \ .$$

Bound of $\Pr[G_2] - \Pr[G_3]$. We show that L_2 and L_3 are indistinguishable. Note that $L_3 = \mathcal{R}$.

Lemma 1. L_2 and L_3 are indistinguishable.

Proof. We show that for a query m, $L_2(m)$ is chosen uniformly at random from $\{0,1\}^n$.

Upon a query m, if $(w_1, w_2) \in T_{Int}$ holds then tag is chosen uniformly at random from $\{0,1\}^n$. If $(w_1, w_2) \notin T_{Int}$ then $(w_1, w_2) \notin T_{Int}$ holds, thereby w_1 or w_2 is a new tweak. Hence, $\widetilde{P}^{w_2}(w_1)$ or $\widetilde{P}^{w_1}(w_2)$ is chosen uniformly at random from $\{0,1\}^n$, and tag is chosen uniformly at random from $\{0,1\}^n$.

Thus L_2 behaves like a random function.   □

Hence we have $\Pr[G_2] - \Pr[G_3] = 0$.

Bound of Advantage. Hence we have

$$\mathbf{Adv}_{\mathsf{PMAC\_TBC3k}}^{\mathrm{prf}}(\mathbf{D}) \leq \frac{0.5q^2}{(2^n - q)^2}.$$

3.4   Remark

By using a tweakable block cipher with $t \geq n + 2$, one can obtain a single-key and full PRF-secure MAC. To obtain a single-key MAC, we separate tweaks by using two bits of tweaks. For example, the first two bits of tweaks of $\widetilde{E}_{K_1}$, $\widetilde{E}_{K_2}$, and $\widetilde{E}_{K_3}$ are defined as 00, 10, and 11, respectively. Then K_2 and K_3 are replaced with K_1. Consequently, one can see that $\widetilde{E}_{K_1}^{00\|*}$, $\widetilde{E}_{K_1}^{10\|*}$, and $\widetilde{E}_{K_1}^{11\|*}$ are distinct tweakable block ciphers. Note that Theorem 1 can be carried over into the PRF-security of the single-key MAC if the tweak length satisfies the relation that $t \geq n + 2$.

In the next section, we propose a single-key MAC based on a TBC with $t \geq 3$.

4 Full PRF-Secure, Single-Key MAC from Tweakable Block Cipher

We propose a single-key MAC construction PMAC_TBC1k. PMAC_TBC1k uses the tweak separation that is discussed in the Subsect. 3.4. We note that PMAC_TBC1k supports TBCs with $t \geq 3$, while PMAC_TBC3k does not support TBCs with $t < n$. Hence the PRF-security proof of PMAC_TBC3k cannot be carried over into that of PMAC_TBC1k.

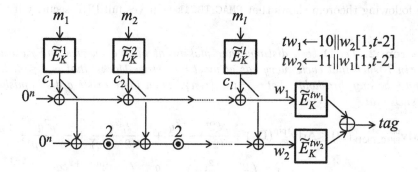

Fig. 2. PMAC_TBC1k for l message blocks $m_1, \ldots, m_l$

4.1 Specification of PMAC_TBC1k

Let $\widetilde{E} \in \mathsf{BC}(\{0,1\}^k, \{0,1\}^t, \{0,1\}^n)$ be a tweakable block cipher with k-bit keys, t-bit tweaks, and n-bit blocks such that $t \geq 3$. Let $K \xleftarrow{\$} \{0,1\}^k$ be a secret key. We denote PMAC_TBC1k using $\widetilde{E}_K$ by PMAC_TBC1k$[\widetilde{E}_K]$. Upon an input m PMAC_TBC1k$[\widetilde{E}_K](m)$ is defined as follows.

1. $(w_1, w_2) \leftarrow Int[\widetilde{E}_K](m)$
2. $(tw_1, tw_2) \leftarrow (10\|w_2[1, \min\{t, n\} - 2], 11\|w_1[1, \min\{t, n\} - 2])$
3. $tag \leftarrow \widetilde{E}_K^{tw_1 \| 0^{t-n}}(w_1) \oplus \widetilde{E}_K^{tw_2 \| 0^{t-n}}(w_2)$
4. Return tag

$Int[\widetilde{E}_K](m)$ is defined as follows.

1. $m^* \leftarrow m \| 10^*$
2. Partition m^* into n-bit blocks $m_1 \| \cdots \| m_l$
3. For $i = 1$ to l do $c_i \leftarrow \widetilde{E}_K^i(m_i)$
4. $w_1 \leftarrow c_1 \oplus \cdots \oplus c_l$; $w_2 \leftarrow 2^{l-1} \cdot c_1 \oplus 2^{l-2} \cdot c_2 \oplus \cdots \oplus c_l$
5. Return (w_1, w_2)

$m^* \leftarrow m\|10^*$ means that first padding m with appending $1\|0\cdots 0$ with the minimum number of zeros so that the length becomes a multiple of n, and then the padded value $m\|10^*$ is assigned to m^*. Note that PMAC_TBC1k$[\widetilde{E}_K]$ does not accept messages such that $l \geq 2^{t-1}$ bits. Hence the left most bit of a tweak in Int is 0. The Fig. 2 shows the PMAC_TBC1k construction using a tweakable block cipher with $t \leq n$.

4.2   PRF-Security

The following theorem shows that PMAC_TBC1k achieves full PRF-security if $t \geq n/2$.

Theorem 2. *Let* **D** *be a distinguisher making at most q queries and running time in T such that each query has at most ℓ message blocks, that is, $l \leq \ell$. Let ρ and ξ be any thresholds. Let $\gamma = \min\{t, n\}$. Then there exists a distinguisher* **D*** *such that*

$$\mathbf{Adv}^{\mathrm{prf}}_{\mathrm{PMAC\_TBC1k}}(\mathbf{D}) \leq \mathbf{Adv}^{\mathrm{tprp}}_{\widetilde{E}}(\mathbf{D}^*) + \frac{\rho\xi 2^{n-\gamma+2}q}{(2^n-q)^2} + \frac{2\rho^2 q}{2^n(2^n-q)} + \frac{\rho^2 q}{(2^n-\rho)^2}$$

$$+ 2^{\gamma-1} \times \left(\frac{2^{n-\gamma+2}eq}{\rho(2^n-q)}\right)^\rho + \frac{q}{\xi} \times \left(\frac{2^{n-\gamma+2}eq}{(\xi-1)(2^n-q)^2}\right)^{\xi-1}.$$

D* *makes at most $(\ell+2)q$ queries and runs in time $\mathcal{O}(T + \ell q)$.*

Now we analyze the above bound. We assume that $\mathbf{Adv}^{\mathrm{tprp}}_{\widetilde{E}}(\mathbf{D}^*)$ is negligible compared with other terms.

Firstly we consider the case where $t = n$. Then $\gamma = n$. Tweakable block ciphers such as [7,10,11] cover this case. We define $\rho := n$ and $\xi := 2n$. Then we have

$$\mathbf{Adv}^{\mathrm{prf}}_{\mathrm{PMAC\_TBC1k}}(\mathbf{D}) \leq \mathbf{Adv}^{\mathrm{tprp}}_{\widetilde{E}}(\mathbf{D}^*) + \frac{8n^2 q}{(2^n-q)^2} + \frac{2n^2 q}{2^n(2^n-q)} + \frac{n^2 q}{(2^n-n)^2}$$

$$+ \left(\frac{8eq}{n(2^n-q)}\right)^n + \left(\frac{8eq}{(2n-1)(2^n-q)^2}\right)^{2n-1},$$

assuming $q \leq 2^n$. In this case, PMAC_TBC1k is a PRF up to $O(2^n)$ queries, that is, full PRF-security is achieved. We note that this bound also holds on the cases where $t \geq n$.

Secondly we consider the case where $t = n/2$. Then $\gamma = n/2$. Tweakable block ciphers such as [11,12] cover this case. We define $\rho := 2^{n/2}$ and $\xi := 3$.

Then we have

$$\mathbf{Adv}^{\mathrm{prf}}_{\mathtt{PMAC\_TBC1k}}(\mathbf{D}) \leq \mathbf{Adv}^{\mathrm{tprp}}_{\widetilde{E}}(\mathbf{D}^*) + \frac{12 \times 2^n q}{(2^n - q)^2} + \frac{2q}{2^n - q} + \frac{2^n q}{(2^n - 2^{n/2})^2}$$

$$+ 2^{n/2-1} \times \left(\frac{4eq}{2^n - q}\right)^{2^{n/2}} + \frac{q}{3} \times \left(\frac{4 \cdot 2^{n/2} eq}{2(2^n - q)^2}\right)^2$$

$$\leq \mathbf{Adv}^{\mathrm{tprp}}_{\widetilde{E}}(\mathbf{D}^*) + \frac{12 \times 2^n q}{(2^n - q)^2} + \frac{2q}{2^n - q} + \frac{q}{2^n - 2^{n/2+1}}$$

$$+ \left(\frac{8eq}{2^n - q}\right)^{2^{n/2}} + \left(\frac{2 \cdot 2^n eq}{(2^n - q)^2}\right)^2,$$

assuming $q \leq 2^n$. In this case, $\mathtt{PMAC\_TBC1k}$ is also a PRF up to $O(2^n)$ queries. We note that this bound also holds on the cases where $t \geq n/2$.

4.3   Proof of Theorem 2

To simplify this proof, we assume that $t \leq n$. Note that this proof can be carried over into the case where $t > n$.

Firstly, we replace the underlying function of $\mathtt{PMAC\_TBC1k}$ from $\widetilde{E}_K$ to a tweakable random permutation $\widetilde{P} \xleftarrow{\$} \mathsf{Perm}(\{0,1\}^t, \{0,1\}^n)$. This replacement yields the term $\mathbf{Adv}^{\mathrm{tprp}}_{\widetilde{E}}(\mathbf{D}^*)$ in the bound of Theorem 2.

Hence the remaining work is to bound the following difference that is the PRF-advantage of $\mathtt{PMAC\_TBC1k}[\widetilde{P}]$.

$$\Pr[\mathbf{D}^{\mathtt{PMAC\_TBC1k}[\widetilde{P}]} \Rightarrow 1] - \Pr[\mathbf{D}^{\mathcal{R}} \Rightarrow 1]$$

We consider the case where $\mathbf{D}$ interacts with L where $L = \mathtt{PMAC\_TBC1k}[\widetilde{P}]$ in the real world and $L = \mathcal{R}$ in the ideal. Without loss of generality, we assume that $\mathbf{D}$ makes no repeated query.

We bound the PRF-advantage by using three games which start at the real world and end at the ideal world. We denote these games by Game 1, Game 2, and Game 3. By G_i, we denote an event that $\mathbf{D}$ outputs 1 in Game i. Hereafter we denote L in Game i by L_i. Then we have

$$\Pr[\mathbf{D}^{\mathtt{PMAC\_TBC1k}[\widetilde{P}]} \Rightarrow 1] - \Pr[\mathbf{D}^{\mathcal{R}} \Rightarrow 1] = \Pr[G_1] - \Pr[G_3]$$

$$= \sum_{i=1}^{2} (\Pr[G_i] - \Pr[G_{i+1}]).$$

Hereafter we bound the differences $\Pr[G_i] - \Pr[G_{i+1}]$ $(i = 1, 2)$. Note that we define L_2 before bounding $\Pr[G_1] - \Pr[G_2]$.

Bound of $\Pr[G_1] - \Pr[G_2]$. First we define an oracle $\mathcal{G}$. Upon a query m, $\mathcal{G}(m)$ is defined as follows, where $\mathsf{Tweak}_1(\widetilde{P})$, $\mathsf{Tweak}_2(\widetilde{P})$, and $\mathcal{T}$ are (initially empty) tables.

1. $(w_1, w_2) \leftarrow Int[\widetilde{P}](m); (tw_1, tw_2) \leftarrow (10\|w_2[1, t-2], 11\|w_1[1, t-2])$
2. If $\exists tw_1 \in \mathsf{Tweak}_1(\widetilde{P}), tw_2 \in \mathsf{Tweak}_2(\widetilde{P})$ then $\boxed{tag \xleftarrow{\$} \{0,1\}^n; \text{goto Step 4}}$
3. $tag \leftarrow \widetilde{P}^{tw_1}(w_1) \oplus \widetilde{P}^{tw_2}(w_2)$
4. $\mathsf{Tweak}_1(\widetilde{P}) \xleftarrow{\cup} \{tw_1\}; \mathsf{Tweak}_2(\widetilde{P}) \xleftarrow{\cup} \{tw_2\}; \mathcal{T} \xleftarrow{\cup} \{w_1\|w_2[1, t-2]\}$
5. Return tag

We define L_2 as $\mathcal{G}$ with the boxed statement. We note that L_1 is equal to $\mathcal{G}$ without the boxed statement. Although $\mathcal{T}$ does not effect the above procedure, we use $\mathcal{T}$ in the following analysis.

Let Gdiff be an monotone event in Game 2 where firstly Gdiff = false, and if the behavior of L_2 is distinct from that of L_1 then true is set in Gdiff. Hence $\Pr[G_1] = \Pr[G_2|\neg\mathsf{Gdiff}]$. Then,

$$\Pr[G_1] - \Pr[G_2] \leq |\Pr[G_1] - (\Pr[G_2 \wedge \mathsf{Gdiff}] + \Pr[G_2 \wedge \neg\mathsf{Gdiff}])|$$
$$\leq |\Pr[G_1] - (\Pr[G_2|\neg\mathsf{Gdiff}] \cdot \Pr[\neg\mathsf{Gdiff}] + \Pr[G_2 \wedge \mathsf{Gdiff}])|$$
$$\leq |\Pr[G_1] \cdot (1 - \Pr[\neg\mathsf{Gdiff}]) - \Pr[G_2 \wedge \mathsf{Gdiff}]|$$
$$\leq \max\{1 - \Pr[\neg\mathsf{Gdiff}], \Pr[\mathsf{Gdiff}]\} = \Pr[\mathsf{Gdiff}].$$

Hence we bound $\Pr[\mathsf{Gdiff}]$ that is the probability that **D** sets true into Gdiff when interacting with L_2.

We define two multi-collision events mcoll_1 and mcoll_2, where

$$\mathsf{mcoll}_1 \Leftrightarrow \exists i \in \{1, 2\} \text{ s.t. } \exists tw^{(1)}, \ldots, tw^{(\rho)} \in \mathsf{Tweak}_i(\widetilde{P}) \text{ s.t. } tw^{(1)} = \cdots = tw^{(\rho)}$$
$$\mathsf{mcoll}_2 \Leftrightarrow \exists u^{(1)}, \ldots, u^{(\xi)} \in \mathcal{T} \text{ s.t. } u^{(1)} = \cdots = u^{(\xi)}$$

where ρ and ξ are any thresholds. Then we have

$$\Pr[\mathsf{Gdiff}] = \Pr[\mathsf{Gdiff} \wedge (\mathsf{mcoll}_1 \vee \mathsf{mcoll}_2)] + \Pr[\mathsf{Gdiff} \wedge \neg(\mathsf{mcoll}_1 \vee \mathsf{mcoll}_2)]$$
$$\leq \Pr[\mathsf{mcoll}_1] + \Pr[\mathsf{mcoll}_2] + \Pr[\mathsf{Gdiff}|\neg(\mathsf{mcoll}_1 \vee \mathsf{mcoll}_2)].$$

▶ **Bound of $\Pr[\mathsf{mcoll}_1]$:** Fix $i \in \{1, 2\}$ and $tw^{(1)}, \ldots, tw^{(\rho)} \in \mathsf{Tweak}_i(\widetilde{P})$, and $tw \in \{0, 1\}^{t-2}$. Then the probability that $tw^{(1)} = \cdots = tw^{(\rho)} = 1\|b\|tw$ is at most $\left(\frac{2^{n-t+2}}{2^n - q}\right)^\rho$ where $b = 0$ if $i = 1$ and $b = 1$ if $i = 2$. We thus have

$$\Pr[\mathsf{mcoll}_1] \leq 2 \times 2^{t-2} \times \binom{q}{\rho} \times \left(\frac{2^{n-t+2}}{2^n - q}\right)^\rho \leq 2^{t-1} \times \left(\frac{2^{n-t+2}eq}{\rho(2^n - q)}\right)^\rho,$$

using Stirling's approximation ($x! \geq (x/e)^x$ for any x).

▶ **Bound of $\Pr[\mathsf{mcoll}_2]$:** Fix $u^{(1)}, \ldots, u^{(\xi)} \in \mathcal{T}$. Then the probability that $u^{(1)} = \cdots = u^{(\xi)}$ is at most $\left(\frac{2^{n-t+2}}{2^n - q} \times \frac{1}{2^n - q}\right)^{\xi-1}$, since for $i, j \in \{1, \ldots, \xi\}$ with $i \neq j$, $u^{(i)} = u^{(j)}$ provides a unique solution set for two random variables (this fact was discussed in the proof of Theorem 1). We thus have

$$\Pr[\mathsf{mcoll}_2] \leq \binom{q}{\xi} \times \left(\frac{2^{n-t+2}}{(2^n - q)^2}\right)^{\xi-1} \leq \frac{q}{\xi} \times \left(\frac{2^{n-t+2}eq}{(\xi-1)(2^n - q)^2}\right)^{\xi-1},$$

using Stirling's approximation.

▶ **Bound of** $\Pr[\mathsf{Gdiff}|\neg(\mathsf{mcoll}_1 \vee \mathsf{mcoll}_2)]$: In this case, we have only to consider the difference between L_1 and L_2 when the conditions of the step 2: $tw_1 \in \mathsf{Tweak}_1(\widetilde{P})$ and $tw_2 \in \mathsf{Tweak}_2(\widetilde{P})$ hold.

Fix $i \in [1, q]$. We assume that $(\mathsf{mcoll}_1 \vee \mathsf{mcoll}_2) = \mathsf{false}$. We bound the probability that Gdiff becomes true at the i-th query. We consider the following four cases, where for $i = 1, 2$, $\mathsf{Dom}(\widetilde{P}^{tw_i})$ is the set of input blocks to $\widetilde{P}^{tw_i}$ which are already defined.

- **Case 1**: $\mathsf{Gdiff} = \mathsf{true} \wedge w_1 \in \mathsf{Dom}(\widetilde{P}^{tw_1}) \wedge w_2 \in \mathsf{Dom}(\widetilde{P}^{tw_2})$
- **Case 2**: $\mathsf{Gdiff} = \mathsf{true} \wedge w_1 \in \mathsf{Dom}(\widetilde{P}^{tw_1}) \wedge w_2 \notin \mathsf{Dom}(\widetilde{P}^{tw_2})$
- **Case 3**: $\mathsf{Gdiff} = \mathsf{true} \wedge w_1 \notin \mathsf{Dom}(\widetilde{P}^{tw_1}) \wedge w_2 \in \mathsf{Dom}(\widetilde{P}^{tw_2})$
- **Case 4**: $\mathsf{Gdiff} = \mathsf{true} \wedge w_1 \notin \mathsf{Dom}(\widetilde{P}^{tw_1}) \wedge w_2 \notin \mathsf{Dom}(\widetilde{P}^{tw_2})$

For Case 1, the probability that $w_1 \in \mathsf{Dom}(\widetilde{P}^{tw_1})$ holds is bounded by $\frac{\rho}{2^n - q}$ due to $\mathsf{mcoll}_1 = \mathsf{false}$. Then since $w_1 \in \mathsf{Dom}(\widetilde{P}^{tw_1})$ holds and $\mathsf{mcoll}_2 = \mathsf{false}$, the probability that $w_2 \in \mathsf{Dom}(\widetilde{P}^{tw_2})$ holds is bounded by $\frac{\xi \times 2^{n-t+2}}{2^n - q}$. Since the following inequation holds:

$$\Pr[\mathsf{Gdiff} = \mathsf{true} \wedge w_1 \in \mathsf{Dom}(\widetilde{P}^{tw_1}) \wedge w_2 \in \mathsf{Dom}(\widetilde{P}^{tw_2})]$$
$$\leq \Pr[w_1 \in \mathsf{Dom}(\widetilde{P}^{tw_1}) \wedge w_2 \in \mathsf{Dom}(\widetilde{P}^{tw_2})],$$

the probability that Case 1 holds at the i-th query is bounded by $\frac{\rho \xi 2^{n-t+2}}{(2^n - q)^2}$.

For Case 2, the probability that $w_1 \in \mathsf{Dom}(\widetilde{P}^{tw_1})$ is bounded by $\frac{\rho}{2^n - q}$. If $w_2 \notin \mathsf{Dom}(\widetilde{P}^{tw_2})$ then the output of L_1 at the i-th query is chosen uniformly at random from at least $2^n - \rho$ values of n bits, while L_2 is chosen uniformly at random from $\{0, 1\}^n$. Hence the probability that Gdiff becomes true at the i-th query is $\rho/2^n$. Since the following inequation holds:

$$\Pr[\mathsf{Gdiff} \wedge w_1 \in \mathsf{Dom}(\widetilde{P}^{tw_1}) \wedge w_2 \notin \mathsf{Dom}(\widetilde{P}^{tw_2})]$$
$$\leq \Pr[\mathsf{Gdiff} \wedge w_1 \in \mathsf{Dom}(\widetilde{P}^{tw_1})|w_2 \notin \mathsf{Dom}(\widetilde{P}^{tw_2})],$$

the probability that Case 2 holds at the i-th query is bounded by $\frac{\rho}{2^n - q} \times \frac{\rho}{2^n}$.

For Case 3, this analysis follows the analysis of Case 2, thereby the probability that Case 3 holds at the i-th query is bounded by $\frac{\rho}{2^n - q} \times \frac{\rho}{2^n}$.

For Case 4, we use the technique of fair sets developed by Lucks [14], which is the sampling technique of the xor of two random permutations. The probability that Case 4 holds at the i-th query is bounded by $\left(\frac{\rho}{2^n - \rho}\right)^2$. The detail analysis is given in Appendix A.

We thus have

$$\Pr[\mathsf{Gdiff}|\neg\mathsf{mcoll}] \leq \sum_{i=1}^{q} \left(\frac{\rho \xi 2^{n-t+2}}{(2^n - q)^2} + \frac{2\rho^2}{2^n(2^n - q)} + \frac{\rho^2}{(2^n - \rho)^2} \right)$$

$$\leq \frac{\rho \xi 2^{n-t+2} q}{(2^n - q)^2} + \frac{2\rho^2 q}{2^n(2^n - q)} + \frac{\rho^2 q}{(2^n - \rho)^2}.$$

▷ Bound of $\Pr[G_1] - \Pr[G_2]$: The sum of the above bounds yields the following bound.

$$\Pr[G_1] - \Pr[G_2] \le \frac{\rho\xi 2^{n-t+2}q}{(2^n - q)^2} + \frac{2\rho^2 q}{2^n(2^n - q)} + \frac{\rho^2 q}{(2^n - \rho)^2}$$
$$+ 2^{t-1} \times \left(\frac{2^{n-t+2}eq}{\rho(2^n - q)}\right)^{\rho} + \frac{q}{\xi} \times \left(\frac{2^{n-t+2}eq}{(\xi - 1)(2^n - q)^2}\right)^{\xi - 1}.$$

Bound of $\Pr[G_2] - \Pr[G_3]$. Note that $L_3 = \mathcal{R}$. We show that L_2 and L_3 are indistinguishable.

Lemma 2. L_2 and L_3 are indistinguishable.

Proof. We show that for a query m, $L_2(m)$ is chosen uniformly at random from $\{0,1\}^n$.

Upon a query m, if $tw_1 \in \mathsf{Tweak}_1(\widetilde{P})$ and $tw_2 \in \mathsf{Tweak}_2(\widetilde{P})$ hold then tag is chosen uniformly at random from $\{0,1\}^n$. Otherwise, since tw_1 or tw_2 is a new tweak, $\widetilde{P}^{w_2}(w_1)$ or $\widetilde{P}^{w_1}(w_2)$ is chosen uniformly at random from $\{0,1\}^n$. Hence tag is chosen uniformly at random from $\{0,1\}^n$.

Thus L_2 behaves like a random function.   □

Hence we have $\Pr[G_2] - \Pr[G_3] = 0$.

Bound of Advantage. The sum of the above bounds yields the following bound.

$$\Pr[\mathbf{D}^{\mathtt{PMAC\_TBC1k}[\widetilde{P}]} \Rightarrow 1] - \Pr[\mathbf{D}^{\mathcal{R}} \Rightarrow 1]$$
$$\le \frac{\rho\xi 2^{n-t+2}q}{(2^n - q)^2} + \frac{2\rho^2 q}{2^n(2^n - q)} + \frac{\rho^2 q}{(2^n - \rho)^2}$$
$$+ 2^{t-1} \times \left(\frac{2^{n-t+2}eq}{\rho(2^n - q)}\right)^{\rho} + \frac{q}{\xi} \times \left(\frac{2^{n-t+2}eq}{(\xi - 1)(2^n - q)^2}\right)^{\xi - 1}.$$

We note that when $t > n$, the second last term is $2^{n-1} \times \left(\frac{4eq}{\rho(2^n - q)}\right)^{\rho}$ and the last term is $\frac{q}{\xi} \times \left(\frac{4eq}{(\xi-1)(2^n - q)^2}\right)^{\xi - 1}$.

Acknowledgments. The author would like to thank reviewers for helpful comments.

A   Analysis of the XOR of Two Random Permutations $\widetilde{P}^{tw_1}$ and $\widetilde{P}^{tw_2}$

The following analysis is almost exactly the same as the one for Yasuda's analysis in [18,19] that follows the analysis for Lucks' SUM^2 construction [14].

In this case, we have only to analyze the case where the indistinguishability of the xor of two random permutations $\widetilde{P}^{tw_1}$ and $\widetilde{P}^{tw_2}$ from a random function under the following conditions.

- The input w_1 (resp., w_2) to $\widetilde{P}^{tw_1}$ (resp., $\widetilde{P}^{tw_2}$) is a fresh input
- The number of inputs to $\widetilde{P}^{tw_1}$ is at most $\rho - 1$ due to mcoll $=$ false and the same is true for $\widetilde{P}^{tw_2}$.

Then we simulate the xor of two random permutation and a random function by using the technique of fair sets developed by Lucks. In this case, a fair set R is chosen so that the number of pair $(tag_1, tag_2) \in R$ such that

$$tag = tag_1 \oplus tag_2$$

is the same for each $tag \in \{0,1\}^n$. For $(w_1, w_2) \in \{0,1\}^n \times \{0,1\}^n$, we unroll the outputs of $\widetilde{P}^{tw_1}$ into $Y_1 = \{tag_1^1, \ldots, tag_1^\alpha\}$, and the outputs of $\widetilde{P}^{tw_2}$ into $Y_2 = \{tag_2^1, \ldots, tag_2^\beta\}$. Let $Y_1^* \leftarrow \{0,1\}^n \backslash Y_1$ and $Y_2^* \leftarrow \{0,1\}^n \backslash Y_2$. Then we choose a fair set $R \subset Y_1^* \times Y_2^*$ as follows. For each $1 \le j_1 \le \alpha$ and $1 \le j_2 \le \beta$, we choose arbitrary representatives $(tag_1^{(j_1)}, tag_2^{(j_2)}) \in Y_1^* \times Y_2^*$ such that $tag_1^{(j_1)} \oplus tag_2^{(j_2)} = tag_1^{j_1} \oplus tag_2^{j_2}$. We then define $R \leftarrow Y_1^* \times Y_2^* \backslash \bigcup_{j_1, j_2} \{(tag_1^{(j_1)}, tag_2^{(j_2)})\}$. We see that, for each value $tag \in \{0,1\}^n$,

$$|\{(tag_1, tag_2) \in R \mid tag_1 \oplus tag_2 = tag\}| = 2^n - \alpha - \beta.$$

Hence R is a fair set. We note that $\alpha \le \rho - 1$ and $\beta \le \rho - 1$. Then for an input pair (w_1, w_2), tag is defined by the following procedure.

1. Choose a fair set $R \subset Y_1^* \times Y_2^*$
2. $(tag_1, tag_2) \overset{\$}{\leftarrow} Y_1^* \times Y_2^*$
3. If $(tag_1, tag_2) \notin R$ then $\boxed{(tag_1, tag_2) \overset{\$}{\leftarrow} R}$
4. $tag \leftarrow tag_1 \oplus tag_1$
5. Return tag

Since R is a fair set, the above procedure without the boxed statement simulates the xor of two random permutations where tag_1 is the output of $\widetilde{P}^{tw_1}$ for input w_1 and tag_2 is the output of $\widetilde{P}^{tw_2}$ for input w_2, and the above procedure with the boxed statement simulates a random function.

Then at one execution of the above procedure, the probability that the behavior of the xor function is different from that of a random function is bounded by

$$\frac{|Y_1^* \times Y_2^* \backslash R|}{|Y_1^* \times Y_2^*|} = \frac{\alpha\beta}{(2^n - \alpha)(2^n - \beta)} \le \frac{\rho^2}{(2^n - \rho)^2}.$$

Hence at the i-th query the probability that Case 4 holds is bounded by $\frac{\rho^2}{(2^n - \rho)^2}$.

References

1. Bellare, M., Guérin, R., Rogaway, P.: XOR MACs: new methods for message authentication using finite pseudorandom functions. In: Coppersmith, D. (ed.) CRYPTO 1995. LNCS, vol. 963, pp. 15–28. Springer, Heidelberg (1995)

2. Bernstein, D.J.: CAESAR: Competition for Authenticated Encryption: Security, Applicability, and Robustness
3. Bernstein, D.J.: How to stretch random functions: the security of protected counter sums. J. Cryptology **12**(3), 185–192 (1999)
4. Black, J.A., Rogaway, P.: A block-cipher mode of operation for parallelizable message authentication. In: Knudsen, L.R. (ed.) EUROCRYPT 2002. LNCS, vol. 2332, pp. 384–397. Springer, Heidelberg (2002)
5. Coron, J.-S., Dodis, Y., Mandal, A., Seurin, Y.: A domain extender for the ideal cipher. In: Micciancio, D. (ed.) TCC 2010. LNCS, vol. 5978, pp. 273–289. Springer, Heidelberg (2010)
6. Dodis, Y., Pietrzak, K.: Improving the security of MACs via randomized message preprocessing. In: Biryukov, A. (ed.) FSE 2007. LNCS, vol. 4593, pp. 414–433. Springer, Heidelberg (2007)
7. Grosso, V., Leurent, G., Standaert, F.-X., Varici, K., Durvaux, F., Gaspar, L., Kerckhof, S.: SCREAM & iSCREAM side-channel resistant authenticated encryption with masking. Submission to CAESAR (2014)
8. Iwata, T., Kurosawa, K.: OMAC: one-key CBC MAC. In: Johansson, T. (ed.) FSE 2003. LNCS, vol. 2887, pp. 129–153. Springer, Heidelberg (2003)
9. Jean, J., Nikolic, I., Peyrin, T.: Tweaks and keys for block ciphers: the TWEAKEY framework. In: Sarkar, P., Iwata, T. (eds.) Advances in Cryptology - ASIACRYPT 2014. Lecture Notes in Computer Science, vol. 8874, pp. 274–288. Springer, Heidelberg (2014)
10. Jean, J., Nikolić, I., Peyrin, T.: Deoxys v1. Submission to CAESAR (2014)
11. Jean, J., Nikolić, I., Peyrin, T.: Joltik v1. Submission to CAESAR (2014)
12. Jean, J., Nikolić, I., Peyrin, T.: KIASU v1. Submission to CAESAR (2014)
13. Liskov, M., Rivest, R.L., Wagner, D.: Tweakable block ciphers. In: Yung, M. (ed.) CRYPTO 2002. LNCS, vol. 2442, pp. 31–46. Springer, Heidelberg (2002)
14. Lucks, S.: The sum of PRPs is a secure PRF. In: Preneel, B. (ed.) EUROCRYPT 2000. LNCS, vol. 1807, pp. 470–484. Springer, Heidelberg (2000)
15. Minematsu, K.: Beyond-birthday-bound security based on tweakable block cipher. In: Dunkelman, O. (ed.) FSE 2009. LNCS, vol. 5665, pp. 308–326. Springer, Heidelberg (2009)
16. Minematsu, K.: How to thwart birthday attacks against MACs via small randomness. In: Hong, S., Iwata, T. (eds.) FSE 2010. LNCS, vol. 6147, pp. 230–249. Springer, Heidelberg (2010)
17. Rogaway, P.: Efficient instantiations of Tweakable blockciphers and refinements to modes OCB and PMAC. In: Lee, P.J. (ed.) ASIACRYPT 2004. LNCS, vol. 3329, pp. 16–31. Springer, Heidelberg (2004)
18. Yasuda, K.: The sum of CBC MACs is a secure PRF. In: Pieprzyk, J. (ed.) CT-RSA 2010. LNCS, vol. 5985, pp. 366–381. Springer, Heidelberg (2010)
19. Yasuda, K.: A new variant of PMAC: beyond the birthday bound. In: Rogaway, P. (ed.) CRYPTO 2011. LNCS, vol. 6841, pp. 596–609. Springer, Heidelberg (2011)
20. Yasuda, K.: PMAC with parity: minimizing the query-length influence. In: Dunkelman, O. (ed.) CT-RSA 2012. LNCS, vol. 7178, pp. 203–214. Springer, Heidelberg (2012)
21. Yasuda, K.: A parallelizable PRF-based MAC algorithm: well beyond the birthday bound. IEICE Trans. **96–A**(1), 237–241 (2013)
22. Zhang, Y.: Using an error-correction code for fast, beyond-birthday-bound authentication. In: Nyberg, K. (ed.) CT-RSA 2015. LNCS, vol. 9048, pp. 291–307. Springer, Heidelberg (2015)

Efficient Key Authentication Service for Secure End-to-End Communications

Mohammad Etemad$^{(\boxtimes)}$ and Alptekin Küpçü

Crypto Group, Koç University, İstanbul, Turkey
{metemad,akupcu}@ku.edu.tr

Abstract. After four decades of public key cryptography, both the industry and academia seek better solutions for the public key infrastructure. A recent proposal, the *certificate transparency* concept, tries to enable *untrusted* servers act as public key servers, such that any key owner can verify that her key is kept properly at those servers. Unfortunately, due to high computation and communication requirements, existing certificate transparency proposals fail to address the problem as a whole.

We propose a new efficient *key authentication service* (KAS). It uses server-side gossiping as the source of trust, and assumes servers are not all colluding. KAS stores all keys of each user in a separate hash chain, and always shares the last ring of the chain among the servers, ensuring the users that all servers provide the same view about them (i.e., no equivocation takes place). Storing users' keys separately reduces the server and client computation and communication dramatically, making our KAS a very efficient way of public key authentication. The KAS handles a key registration/change operation in $O(1)$ time using only $O(1)$ proof size; *independent of the number of users*. While the previous best proposal, CONIKS, requires the client to download 100 KB of proof per day, our proposal needs less than 1 KB of proof per key lifetime, while obtaining the same probabilistic guarantees as CONIKS.

Keywords: Certificate transparency · End-to-end encryption

1 Introduction

Many online services, ranging from financial services to health and social services, process sensitive data. Most of the sensitive information is transferred through the network, unencrypted or point-to-point encrypted [8]. The former reveals the data to everyone while the latter reveals the data only to those who perform decryption and re-encryption on the path to the destination. One of the breakthroughs to this regard was the invention of public key cryptography [2,10]. It is employed in end-to-end secure email and end-to-end encryption (E2EE). To provide security and prevent misuse, the data should be encrypted by the sender, transmitted encrypted, and decrypted by the receiver.

End-to-End Secure Email. Email is one of the oldest IT services for fast communication. Gmail initially launched with HTTPS support and uses an

© Springer International Publishing Switzerland 2015
M.-H. Au and A. Miyaji (Eds.): ProvSec 2015, LNCS 9451, pp. 183–197, 2015.
DOI: 10.1007/978-3-319-26059-4_10

encrypted connection for sending and receiving emails, but the encryption is not end-to-end, i.e., the Gmail server has access to the plaintext of all emails that are not encrypted explicitly by the sender.

End-to-End Encryption (E2EE) is required to solve the above-mentioned problem. Having easy access to the target's key, a party can encrypt a message directly with it. E2EE is being considered as an important building block in many recent schemes. Weber [12] used attribute-based encryption for secure end-to-end one-to-many mobile communication. Snake [1] is proposed as an end-to-end encrypted online social networking scheme, relying on establishment of shared keys between users at the start phase of friendship. E2EE is also used in several messaging service such as Apple iMessage and BlackBerry protected messenger [8]. The main problem with all these schemes is *key management*.

One caveat of public key cryptography is that it requires the communicating parties to obtain *genuine* keys of each other. If they had a secure physical channel (i.e., they could physically meet), they could have exchanged their public keys. Unfortunately, in the online world, a *trusted* party called *certificate authority* (CA) is required. A CA ensures the parties via issuing unforgeable cryptographic evidences (certificates) that the public key contained in the certificate does indeed belong to the party stated in the certificate. However,the CAs must be trusted, and sometimes this trust is broken [11]. Moreover, there are other applicability and usage problems such as storage, revocation, and distribution [9]. CAs are also valuable targets for adversaries through which they can attack the whole system. We need a new source of trust that cannot easily be compromised legally or under pressure, without being detected and revealed.

Certificate transparency is recently proposed to substitute the existing certificate authorities [7]. There is no single source of trust and all users and servers contribute to provide a web of trust among themselves. Following (efficient) schemes [8,11] added key revocation support, and used it as a general key management scheme for different applications such as end-to-end encrypted email. However, all these schemes impose a heavy computation and communication burden on both clients and servers, preventing its mass application. We propose an efficient key authentication service that performs key registration/change operations optimally (i.e., with $O(1)$ computation and communication).

Our contributions are as follows:

- We give the **first security definition** of a key authentication service, and prove our construction's security formally.
- Our KAS scheme performs key registration/change operations **optimally** with $O(1)$ server and client computation and $O(1)$ communication. Hence, we reduce the costs of the existing schemes [7,8,11] for each key registration/change operation by a factor of $\log n$, where n is the number of users.
- The total cost of the server in the previous schemes is $O(n \log n)$, since they compute the proof for all users on each key registration/change [7,11] or on each epoch [8]. A similar audit operation costs $O(n)$ in our KAS.
- Our scheme is **perfectly privacy-preserving**, i.e., proof of a key (of a user) does not depend on any other key (of another user), and hence, does not reveal any information about other users.

- For the first time, we consider **non-repudiation** for both client and server. In our scheme, a malicious client cannot frame an honest server.

1.1 Related Work

Laurie *et al.* [7] proposed **certificate transparency** for preventing certificate misuse by publishing the issued TLS certificates through publicly-auditable logs. The clients and some special entities (called *monitors* and *auditors*) will report any misbehavior through regularly verifying the logs. The logs are append-only Merkle hash trees. The tree has the property that any previous version is a subset of all following versions, through which the consistency of logs can be proven. On receipt of a new certificate, the log server appends it into the existing tree, commits to its new root, and returns both the new root and its commitment. The issuing user verifies the result and if it is correct, spreads it through *global gossiping*. All later verifications should be made against this new root.

Later, Laurie and Kasper [6] proposed **revocation transparency**, similar to certificate transparency, as a transparent mechanism for providing the list of revoked certificates and showing that all clients see the same list of revoked certificates. However, it is not efficient due to its space and time complexity that is *linear* in the number of revocations.

Ryan [11] proposed **enhanced certificate transparency** (ECT) that can also be used for secure end-to-end email or messaging without requiring a trusted certificate authority. ECT also solves the certificate revocation problem efficiently. There is an append-only Merkle tree as in [7] for handling certificate transparency, but in addition, there is another lexicographically ordered hash tree storing a constant number of revoked keys for each client, reducing the revocation complexity from $O(n)$ to $O(\log n)$, where n is the number of users.

Melara *et al.* [8] proposed **CONIKS** as an automated key management system. It consists of a number of key providers storing user-to-key bindings of users. The users can detect equivocations or unexpected key changes made by malicious providers. CONIKS provides the following security properties:*non-equivocation, binding consistency, and privacy-preserving bindings.*

Laurie *et al.* [7] and ECT [11] use **client-side gossiping**, which requires all clients to gossip with each other. This is very inefficient as it is required on each key change. Moreover, it requires a fully connected graph over all users during the gossiping. If the user are partitioned during gossiping, the server can *equivocate* since the others has no idea about the change that happened. CONIKS [8] uses **server-side gossiping**, which is much more efficient than the client-side gossiping, especially assuming a constant number of servers.

A problem with these schemes is the lack of **formal security definitions and proofs**. Moreover, organizing the keys in a tree data structure ties them altogether, which means that even if only one key changes, all users (except the one whose key has been changed) need to check the resulting new tree to make sure they are not affected. We store the user-to-key bindings separately, thus decreasing provider and client computation while increasing the privacy-preservation level. Another problem is that the **non-repudiation** property for all parties was not considered previously: one cannot show the origin of any potential inconsistency. A malicious client can try to frame an honest server, and neither party could provide evidence of honest behavior. We also address this issue. A comparison of these schemes is given in Table 1.

Table 1. A comparison of certificate transparency schemes. NR and PP stand for non-repudiation and privacy-preserving, respectively, and '×' means not fully supported.

Scheme	Update	Audit	Revocation	Gossiping	NR	PP
Laurie *et al.* [7]	$O(\log n)$	$O(n \log n)$	$O(n)$	Client-side	-	-
ECT [11]	$O(\log n)$	$O(n \log n)$	$O(\log n)$	Client-side	-	-
CONIKS [8]	$O(\log n)$	$O(n \log n)$	$O(\log n)$	Server-side	×	×
Our KAS	$O(1)$	$O(n)$	$O(1)$	Server-side	+	+

On a separate line of work, Wendlandt *et al.* [13] proposed Perspectives for authenticating a server's public key. It uses a number of (semi-)trusted hosts named *network notaries* that probe most of network services (e.g., SSH) and keep a history of their public keys over time. On receipt of an unauthenticated public key from a service, the client asks the notaries the history of keys used by that service to help her decide on whether to accept or reject it. Perspectives differs from the certificate transparency as it requires all notaries to be trusted.

1.2   Model

There are two parties in our model. The **providers** are the publicly available servers storing name-to-key bindings of the users. There are multiple providers each running in a different domain. Each provider manages a distinct set of clients, and shares information about them with other providers by gossiping, through a specific PKI. $\mathcal{P}$ represents the set of all providers. We use the terms *provider* and *server* interchangeably. For easier presentation, *home provider* is the provider a user registers her keys with.

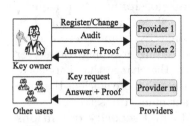

The **client** (or her device on her behalf) registers her (public) key in a provider and can access the keys of other clients through the (same or other) provider(s). We use the terms *client* and *user* interchangeably. We also differentiate between two kinds of users when they execute our protocols: The *key owner* registers, updates, and audits her own key, while the *other users* request the key of some key owner from the providers. In our scenarios, hereafter, we

Fig. 1. Our model.

assume that **Alice** is the **key owner**, and **Bob** is some **other user** who wants to communicate with Alice, hence, requests her key from the providers. Our model is depicted in Fig. 1.

Adversarial Model. We assume that the providers may be malicious, but not all providers collude (though some may). They may try to attack the integrity of the name-to-key bindings they store, or to equivocate and show different results for the same query coming from different users, while trying to be undetected. We assume honest behavior of the users *only* during the first key registration. But, they are *not* trusted for later key changes in the sense that they may later try to frame an honest provider. Our scheme provides non-repudiation for both the user and the provider, i.e., they cannot deny what they have already done, and helps find the origin of any inconsistency or misbehavior and provides cryptographic proofs to be used as evidence.

1.3 Overview

Public logs are proposed as an alternative to CAs that are not required to be trusted. Either client-side or server-side gossiping is used as the source of trust. The high level idea is that instead of trusting on only one entity, it is better to rely of a group of entities, hoping that not all of them misbehave simultaneously.

The existing solutions store keys of all users in an authenticated data structure, and hence, tie all keys together. This requires all users to check for their keys on any key registration/change. Instead, we store all keys of each user in a separate hash chain and remove the dependence between keys of different users. Each time a user registers a new key, the new key and the previous hash chain digest is hashed to obtain an new hash chain digest. Then, the home provider signs and shares this new digest with all other providers, i.e., we follow the server-side gossiping. This helps all providers keep the same view about the users.

To request a key, a user contacts a number of providers, and accepts the obtained key if they all provide the same view. She cannot rely on only one provider due to the possibility of equivocation.

2 Key Authentication Service

2.1 Preliminaries

Notation. We use $\|$ for concatenation, and $|X|$ to show the number of items in X. PPT means probabilistic polynomial time, and λ is the security parameter. A function $\nu(\lambda) : Z^+ \to [0, 1]$ is called *negligible* if $\forall$ positive polynomials p, $\exists$ a constant c such that $\forall \lambda > c$, $\nu(\lambda) < 1/p(\lambda)$. *Overwhelming* probability is greater than or equal to $1 - \nu(\lambda)$ for some negligible function $\nu(\lambda)$. By *efficient algorithms*, we mean those with expected running time polynomial in λ.

Interactive Protocols. We present our key authentication scheme as a set of interactive protocols between stateful clients and stateful servers, instead of separately-executed algorithms. Each protocol may receive inputs from both parties and may output some data at both parties. Hence, we represent a protocol as $\texttt{protocolName}(output_{client})(output_{server}) \leftarrow (input_{client})(input_{server})$.

Hash functions are functions that take arbitrary-length strings, and output strings of some fixed length. Let $h : \mathcal{K} * \mathcal{M} \to \mathcal{C}$ be a family of hash functions, whose members are identified by $k \in \mathcal{K}$. A hash function family is collision resistant if $\forall PPT$ adversaries $\mathcal{A}$, $\exists$ a negligible function $\nu(\lambda)$ such that: $Pr[k \leftarrow \mathcal{K}; (x, x') \leftarrow \mathcal{A}(h, k) : (x' \neq x) \wedge (h_k(x) = h_k(x'))] \leq \nu(\lambda)$ for security parameter λ (which is correlated to $|\mathcal{K}|$ and $|\mathcal{C}|$).

A **signature scheme** is a scheme for preserving message integrity, consisting of the following PPT algorithms [5]:

- $(sk, vk) \leftarrow$ Gen(1^λ): Generates a signing and verification key pair (sk, vk) using the security parameter λ.
- $\sigma \leftarrow$ Sign(sk, m): Generates a signature σ on a message m using the key sk.
- $\{$accept, reject$\} \leftarrow$ Verify (vk, m, σ): Checks whether σ is a correct signature on a message m, using the verification key vk, and outputs an acceptance or a rejection signal, accordingly.

2.2   Key Authentication Service Scheme

Definition 1 (KAS scheme). *A KAS scheme is composed of the following interactive protocols between a stateful user and a stateful provider:*

- $(vk_p)(sk_p, vk_p) \leftarrow$ Setup$(1^\lambda)(1^\lambda)$. The provider starts up this protocol to generate the signing and verification keys (sk_p, vk_p), given as input the security parameter λ, and shares the verification key with all users and providers. Essentially, we assume the providers' verification keys are part of some other well-established PKI.
- $(\sigma_i^u, $accept/reject$)(rvk_{i-1}^u, vk_i^u, \sigma_i^u) \leftarrow$ Register$(id_u, sk_{i-1}^u, sk_i^u, vk_i^u, vk_p)$ (sk_p, vk_p). The user registers/changes her key via a provider, given her ID id_u, her previous key sk_{i-1}^u (empty for the first time), and her new key pair (sk_i^u, vk_i^u) as input. For a key change, she should provide a revocation statement rvk_{i-1}^u signed with her previous signing key sk_{i-1}^u. The provider receives his key pair (sk_p, vk_p) as input, stores user's key, computes a signature σ_i^u on the result, and transfers it to the user. The user verifies it and outputs an acceptance or a rejection signal based on the result.
- $(vk_i^u, $accept/reject$)() \leftarrow$ Audit$(id_u, \{vk_p\}_{p \in \mathcal{P}})(info_u)$: A user initiates this protocol to retrieve the (latest) key of a user id_u. She specifies a subset of providers $P \subseteq \mathcal{P}$ at random and challenges them about the user id_u. The providers are given the user information $info_u$ as input and send back their latest view about the user id_u. If all challenged providers gave the *same* answer, she accepts and outputs the received key vk_i^u as the correct (latest) key of id_u, and **accept**. Otherwise, she outputs $\perp$ and **reject**.

Both users and providers keep their own local states during execution of the protocols. Each user stores her latest key and the respective provider's signature (and the previous ones if she has enough resources). The providers also store all keys received from the users along with the signatures they have computed. The key owner runs Audit to see if the providers keep a correct view about her. If Audit returns **accept** and the obtained key matches the locally-stored key, she outputs **accept**. Otherwise, she outputs **reject**.

2.3   Security Definitions of the Key Authentication Service

Definition 2 (Correctness). *considers the honest behavior of providers and users in a protocol execution. A key authentication scheme is correct if the following is satisfied with probability 1 over the randomness of the users and providers:*

Each execution of the Audit *protocol results in a key* vk_u, *which is the latest key registered by the key owner through the* Register *protocol. If such a user does not exist, it returns* ⊥.

Security Game. If the providers deviate from honest behavior by providing different answers to the same query for different users, the users should detect this with high probability. The security game $\text{AuthGame}_{\mathcal{A}}(\lambda)$ between a challenger $\mathcal{C}$ who plays the role of all users (key owners and others) and all non-adversarial providers[1], and the adversary $\mathcal{A}$ acting as the malicious providers, is defined as:

- **Initialization.** $\mathcal{C}$ runs the Setup protocol to initialize the environment on behalf of all non-adversarial providers, and shares their verification keys with $\mathcal{A}$. He stores the verification keys of malicious providers given by $\mathcal{A}$.
- **Adaptively Chosen Queries.** $\mathcal{A}$ asks the challenger to start a Register or an Audit protocol by providing the required information. For the Register protocol, he specifies a user and a provider that the user will register her key with. If the specified provider is a malicious one, $\mathcal{C}$ acts as the user in the corresponding registration protocol with $\mathcal{A}$. He also stores the signatures coming from $\mathcal{A}$. Otherwise, $\mathcal{C}$ registers the key locally (acting as both the user and a non-adversarial provider) and shares the resulting signature with $\mathcal{A}$. For the Audit protocol, $\mathcal{A}$ requests a user ID, and $\mathcal{C}$ performs the associated audit and verifies the answer, and notifies $\mathcal{A}$ about the result. The queries can be repeated polynomially-many times, in any order, adaptively.
- **Challenge.** $\mathcal{A}$ specifies a user and sends an audit request to $\mathcal{C}$, who initiates an Audit protocol, giving the specified user ID as input. He outputs the obtained key and accept if Audit accepts, and ⊥ and reject otherwise.

$\mathcal{A}$ wins the game if $\mathcal{C}$ accepts while the obtained key differs from the latest key $\mathcal{C}$ successfully registered on behalf of that user. The output of the game is defined to be 1 in this case.

Definition 3 (ϵ-Security). *A key authentication service scheme is ϵ-secure if $Pr[\text{AuthGame}_{\mathcal{A}}(\lambda) = 1] \leq \epsilon$ for any efficient adversary $\mathcal{A}$.*

3   Construction

Problems with Previous Proposals. Laurie *et al.* [7] builds an append-only Merkle hash tree and appends the new keys as they arrive. To be secure, after each new key registration/change, they distribute the root of the updated tree to the users who will gossip it among themselves to ensure that they all keep

---

[1] By our assumption that not all providers are colluding, there is at least one non-adversarial provider that the challenger will simulate.

the *same* latest view of the keys registered in the log. This requires all users to connect and contribute in gossiping. In case of any partitioning among the users, the server can easily equivocate. In addition, all users need to verify the new tree. The key owner wants to check that her key is correctly registered/changed, while the other users want to make sure that they are not affected by this key registration/change. This poses an unacceptably heavy burden on users.

To alleviate the problem, CONIKS [8] uses server-side gossiping. Although this relieves the users from gossiping, they still need heavy and frequent verifications. CONIKS goes further and divides the time into *epochs*, accumulates all key registration/change requests during each epoch, and applies them all at the beginning of the next epoch. If t key registration/change requests arrive in an epoch, instead of performing t consistency checks, a client performs only one consistency check. However, this comes at the cost of giving outdated keys for users whose keys are changed in an epoch, until the beginning of the next epoch.

Our Observations and Solution. A problem common to all existing solutions [6–8,11] is that they put all user-to-key bindings in a single data structure (i.e., a Merkle tree) on each provider. This ties all users together, and hence, forces all users to check whether or not any change in the data structure affects them, regardless of who initiated the change, which is a costly process. Instead, we store each user's data separately, preventing unwanted costly checks due to changes on other users. Even though on the surface it seems that we are gossiping more than just a root, the number of gossiping operations in our strategy is the same as in [6,7,11], since one value is gossiped on every key change (though we can also gossip per epoch as in CONIKS, leaving some vulnerability window). However, they need to update the Merkle tree with $O(\log n)$ cost, while we only add a new value into the corresponding hash chain with only $O(1)$ cost.

Storing users' data separately brings other important advantages: the resulting scheme is **perfectly privacy-preserving**, since the proof for the a user's key does not contain any information about other owners. Moreover, there is no need for consistency checks, which are very costly operations in [6,11]. Even though CONIKS reduces the cost of this operation using epochs, the consistency check problem is inherent in tree-based approaches: on each key registration/change (or a group of them in CONIKS), the provider updates the tree and distributes a new commitment. Then, *all* other owners should check the tree and ensure that their keys have not been changed.

Our KAS provides verifiable user-to-key binding service and consists of a number of providers each managing a subset of users. Each provider stores all registered keys of each user in its namespace in a separate hash chain. The provider, after adding the key into the respective chain, commits to (signs) the result, and sends it to the user for verification. Besides, he distributes (gossips) the last hash value in the chain and its signature to all other providers. To acknowledge the receipt, the other providers sign the received hash value, and return the signature to the initiating provider. Figure 2 shows our construction.

Let S=(Gen,Sign,Verify) be a secure signature scheme and $h : \{0,1\}^* \to \{0,1\}^l$ be a collision resistant hash function modeled as a random oracle. Construct a key authentication service scheme KAS=(Setup,Register,Audit) as:

- Setup$(1^\lambda)(1^\lambda)$:
  - Each provider runs $(sk_p, vk_p) = \text{S.Gen}(1^\lambda)$ and shares vk_p with his users and the other providers.
  - Each user stores vk_p of her home provider.
- Register$(id_u, sk^u_{i-1}, sk^u_i, vk^u_i, vk_p)(sk_p, vk_p)$:

  The key owner:
  - If $i > 1$, sets $rvk^u_{i-1} = \text{S.Sign}(sk^u_{i-1}, \text{'revocation statement'})$
  - Sends vk^u_i and rvk^u_{i-1} to her home provider.

  The home provider:
  - Finds the last registered key, vk^u_{i-1}, and the last computed hash, h^u_{i-1}, for user id_u.
  - If S.Verify$(vk^u_{i-1}, \text{'revocation statement'}, rvk^u_{i-1}) ==$ reject, outputs reject and exits.
  - Otherwise, computes $h^u_i = h(id_u||h^u_{i-1}||rvk^u_{i-1}||vk^u_i)$ and $\sigma^u_i = \text{S.Sign}(sk_p, h^u_i)$.
  - Sends $(id_u, h^u_i, \sigma^u_i)$ to the respective user and all other providers.

  Other providers:
  - Each other provider p_t first checks if S.Verify$(vk_p, h^u_i, \sigma^u_i) ==$ accept. If so, he computes $\sigma^{u,t}_i = \text{S.Sign}(sk_{p_t}, h^u_i)$, stores h^u_i and $\sigma^{u,t}_i$ locally, and sends $\sigma^{u,t}_i$ to the home provider.

  The home provider:
  - On receipt the acknowledgments $\sigma^{u,t}_i$, the home provider checks if S.Verify$(vk_{p_t}, h^u_i, \sigma^{u,t}_i) ==$ accept for all other providers p_t. He stores the correct ones, and reveals the incorrect ones.

  The key owner:
  - The key owner checks if $h^u_i == h(id_u||h^u_{i-1}||rvk^u_i||vk^u_i)$ and S.Verify$(vk_p, h^u_i, \sigma^u_i) ==$ accept. If so, she stores h^u_i and σ^u_i locally and outputs accept. Otherwise, she outputs reject and publishes misbehavior of the provider together with the corresponding h^u_i and σ^u_i as the proof, through public social networks.
- Audit$(id_u, \{vk_p\}_{p \in \mathcal{P}})(info_u)$:
  - The user selects a random subset of providers $P \subseteq \mathcal{P}$, and sends them the Audit(id_u) request.
  - The home provider replies with the latest information about the user being queried: $(h^u_{i-1}, rvk^u_{i-1}, vk^u_i, h^u_i)$.
  - The other providers reply with the latest hash value, h^{u,i_t}_i, received from the home provider about that user.
  - On receipt $(h^u_{i-1}, rvk^u_{i-1}, vk^u_i, h^u_i)$ from the home provider and h^{u,i_j}_i from other providers, the user checks if:
    * $h(id_u||h^u_{i-1}||rvk^u_{i-1}||vk^u_i) == h^u_i$. If not, misbehavior of the home provider is detected. She outputs $\perp$ and reject, publishes the misbehavior, and exits.
    * $h^u_i == h^{u,i_1}_i == h^{u,i_2}_i == \dots == h^{u,i_t}_i$, $\forall i_j \in P$. If so, she outputs vk^u_i and accept. Otherwise, she outputs $\perp$ and reject, publishes the misbehavior, and starts the misbehaving detection process.
  - (Owner Only) If the user audits for the key she owns, she also checks if the received key vk^u_i is the one she last registered. If so, outputs accept. Otherwise, she uses it with the signature she received during registration, publishes the misbehavior case, outputs reject, and exits.

Fig. 2. Construction of our key authentication service.

3.1 Description of the Operations

Register. When a user registers her key for the first time, she provides the home provider with her id, id_u, and her key, vk^u_1. (The user is assumed to be trusted for this operation.) The provider computes hash of this key as $h^u_1 = h(id_u||vk^u_1)$, signs it as $\sigma^u_1 = \text{Sign}(sk_p, h^u_1)$, and returns back both values. When the user is registering a key change (i.e., the previous key, the $(i-1)^{th}$ key, is revoked and she is providing a new one, the ith key), she should also prepare a revocation statement rvk^u_{i-1} signed with her previous key and give it to the provider along with id_u and vk^u_i. On receipt, the provider verifies rvk^u_{i-1}, and if it is accepted, computes $h^u_i = h(id_u||h^u_{i-1}||rvk^u_{i-1}||vk^u_i)$ and $\sigma^u_i = \text{Sign}(sk_p, h^u_i)$. In both cases, the provider returns h^u_i and σ^u_i to the user for verification. In addition, he distributes both values to all other providers, who will verify correctness of the signature and acknowledge by signing it if it is accepted. The home provider keeps the acknowledgments for detecting the source of later inconsistencies. The data structure for a key owner, Alice, on her home provider is a table as shown in Table 2. It contains all keys registered by Alice, all her key revocation statements, the home provider's signatures, and the other providers' acknowledgments.

Table 2. The data structure for a key owner, Alice, on her home provider.

Alice's keys	vk_1^{Alice}	vk_2^{Alice}, rvk_1	...	vk_i^{Alice}, rvk_{i-1}
Provider's signatures	$h_1^{Alice}, \sigma_1^{Alice}$	$h_2^{Alice}, \sigma_2^{Alice}$	...	$h_i^{Alice}, \sigma_i^{Alice}$
P_2's acknowledgments	$\sigma_1^{Alice,2}$	$\sigma_2^{Alice,2}$	...	$\sigma_i^{Alice,2}$
...	...	...	...	
P_m's acknowledgments	$\sigma_1^{Alice,m}$	$\sigma_2^{Alice,m}$	...	$\sigma_i^{Alice,m}$

Each provider stores the hash values and signatures he receives about users of the other providers in a similar table, as presented in Table 3. The information in these tables are used for answering the audit queries, which if passed, ensure the auditing user that all providers have the same view about the queried user, meaning that there is no equivocation, with high probability. In other words, the providers help to make a web of trust through ensuring the auditing user that they all confirm binding of the provided key (hash value) to the queried user.

Table 3. The information provider P_t keeps about Alice, a user of provider P_j.

P_j's signatures	$h_1^{Alice}, \sigma_1^{Alice}$	$h_2^{Alice}, \sigma_2^{Alice}$	...	$h_i^{Alice}, \sigma_i^{Alice}$
P_t's acknowledgments	$\sigma_1^{Alice,t}$	$\sigma_2^{Alice,t}$	...	$\sigma_i^{Alice,t}$

On receipt the answer, the key owner verifies the received signature to see if the home provider has correctly registered her key. She can compute either $h_1'^u = h(id_u || vk_1^u)$ or $h_i'^u = h(id_u || h_{i-1}^u || rvk_{i-1}^u || vk_i^u)$ (she knows all required information) and compare it with what received from the home provider: $h_1'^u == h_1^u$ for the first key registration or $h_i'^u == h_i^u$ for the subsequent key changes. If the test passed, she verifies the signature. If it is verified successfully too, she ensures that her key is correctly registered. Then, she can run an `Audit` protocol to see if the key registration is correctly reflected on the other providers.

`Audit`. From time to time, the key owner, Alice, checks if the providers keep storing her key and hash value intact. This is because other users cannot check authenticity of her keys. Hence, they rely on regular checks of Alice. If Alice detects equivocation or any other misbehavior, in addition to going to arbitration, she should somehow inform the other users about the misbehavior (e.g., via publishing in social networks [8]) and prevent them from using the fake or outdated keys registered in her name.

When another user, Bob, wants to communicate with Alice, he asks for Alice's key from the providers. If Bob requests Alice's key only from her home provider, the home provider may equivocate and give a fake or an outdated key to him. He needs to make sure, with high probability, that he retrieves a genuine key. Moreover, before obtaining the key, he should first check and ensure that there is no equivocation report by Alice.

Bob selects a random subset P of providers $\mathcal{P}$, and sends them the audit request. They return the last hash value they have received from the home provider. Bob also contacts Alice's home provider, who returns the last registered key, as well as information required to recompute the last hash in the chain. Bob then checks whether all received hash values are the same (otherwise an equivocation is detected). He also re-hashes the values provided by Alice's home provider. If everything verifies, he returns the obtained key and `accept`. Otherwise, he outputs $\perp$ and `reject`, and starts the misbehavior detection process.

The misbehavior detection probabilities are discussed in more detail in our full version [3]. Essentially, we obtain similar probabilities as in CONIKS [8].

Misbehavior Detection. When the key owner or another user discovers a misbehavior, she can trace and find its source. This is due to the non-repudiation property of our scheme. Since the key is distributed by the home provider only, and the other providers distribute the hash values, if the given key does not match the given hash value (all users can detect it), this can be used as the witness of home provider's misbehavior. If the given key matches the given hash value but it is not the genuine key (only the key owner can detect it), the home provider is misbehaving, and the key owner can use these values together with the home provider's signature received during the registration as the cryptographic proof of the misbehavior. However, she cannot claim that a given key is fake if she has already registered the key. The home provider can show this case using the signed revocation statement he received from the key owner.

Whenever the received hash values does not match each other (all users can detect it), a subset of providers are equivocating. The user (or any authority) asks the home provider acknowledgments of the other challenged providers, and asks the other challenged providers the signature they have received from the home provider. Verifying the signatures will reveal the misbehaving provider(s).

4 Analysis

4.1 KAS Security Proof

Correctness follows from the correctness of the hash function used by the providers. If the key owner has already been registered, the hash function guarantees that whenever her key is requested, the requesting party receives the correct key. If not, $\perp$ together with non-membership proof will be returned.

Theorem 1. *Our KAS scheme is secure according to Definition 3 provided that the underlying hash function is collision-resistant.*

Proof. We reduce the security of our KAS scheme to that of the underlying hash function. If a PPT adversary $\mathcal{A}$ wins the security game of our KAS scheme with non-negligible probability, we use it to construct another PPT algorithm $\mathcal{B}$ who breaks collision-resistance of the hash function, with non-negligible probability. $\mathcal{B}$ acts as the adversary in the hash function security game with the challenger $\mathcal{C}$. In parallel, $\mathcal{B}$ plays the role of the challenger in the KAS game with $\mathcal{A}$.

Initialization. $\mathcal{B}$ receives a hash function $h(.)$ from $\mathcal{C}$, and shares it with $\mathcal{A}$. The signature keys are generated and shared.

Adaptively Chosen Queries. $\mathcal{A}$ sends $\mathcal{B}$ a request to start a protocol, with the required information:

- For a `Register` protocol, a user ID, id_u, and a provider ID are given. $\mathcal{B}$ generates key pair (sk_i^u, vk_i^u) and the revocation statement rvk_{i-1} for the given user and stores them locally. If the given provider is non-adversarial, $\mathcal{B}$ computes $h_i^u = h(id_u \| h_{i-1}^u \| rvk_{i-1}^u \| vk_i^u)$, signs it as σ_i^u, stores h_i^u and σ_i^u locally, sends them to $\mathcal{A}$, and keeps the acknowledgments coming back. If the given provider is malicious, $\mathcal{B}$ asks $\mathcal{A}$ to register the key for the user, and stores and acknowledges the potential hashes and signatures coming back.
- For an `Audit` protocol about id_u, $\mathcal{B}$ selects a random subset of providers $P \subseteq \mathcal{P}$, as well as the user's home provider, and challenges them about id_u. For those challenged providers who are non-adversarial, $\mathcal{B}$ himself provides the answer, while the answer of the malicious ones are given by $\mathcal{A}$. On receipt all answers, $\mathcal{B}$ performs the audit verification as in the protocol. He also informs $\mathcal{A}$ about the result.

Challenge. The adversary specifies a user id_u and asks $\mathcal{B}$ to challenge him about this user. $\mathcal{B}$ runs the `Audit` protocol as described. If $\mathcal{B}$ accepts $\mathcal{A}$'s answer while the obtained key disagrees with his local knowledge, we consider two cases:

- The returned hash value(s) is the same as the locally-stored one. In this case, a collision is found. If $\mathcal{B}$ accepts $\mathcal{A}$'s answer with probability ϵ_1, we can use it to break security of the hash function with probability ϵ_1. Since the hash function is collision-resistant by assumption, ϵ_1 must be negligible, which means that $\mathcal{A}$ has negligible chance to pass $\mathcal{B}$'s verification successfully and win the game. Hence, our KAS scheme is secure in this regard assuming that the underlying hash function is collision-resistant.
- The returned hash values differ from the locally-stored one: that is an indication of an equivocation. The equivocation of providers is discussed in more detail in our full version [3]. It states that we can approximate the provider equivocation probability with $(1 - f)^k$ against the key owner and f^k against the other users, where f is the fraction of providers distributing fake hash values, and $k = |P|$ is the size of the challenged subset of providers. Moreover, they will mutually detect the equivocation with probability $1 - (f - f2)k$.

  Hence, our scheme is $(f - f^2)^k$-*equivocal*, which means that the equivocation detection probability increases very fast as we increase k. This is maximized when $f = 1/2$. Interestingly, increasing f (from $1/2$) decreases the detection probability (except if $f = 1$ where all providers are maliciously colluding).

  - When f is very small, the probability of misbehavior detection by Alice is not very high (e.g., when f=0.01, k=50 leads to detection probability $1 - (1 - 0.01)^{50}$=0.395). But, this means that the `Audit` protocol will select all honest providers for audit with high probability, and hence, the obtained key will be the correct key with high probability.
  - When f is close to 1, the key owner's probability of misbehavior detection is very high (e.g., when f=0.99, k=50 leads to detection probability $1 - (1 - 0.99)^{50}$, which is almost 1).

- These computations show only the results of one audit. But, the key owner audits regularly over the time. If the Audit protocol selects the providers uniformly, it is expected that after $|\mathcal{P}|/|P|$ audits, all providers will be challenged at least once. This means that the key owner will eventually detect the misbehavior.

To sum up, our KAS scheme is $\epsilon = (\epsilon_1, \epsilon_2)$-secure, i.e., the adversary can break it with probability ϵ_1, which is negligible in the security parameter if the underlying hash function is secure, and it is $(\epsilon_2 = (f - f^2)^k)$-equivocal meaning that the adversary can equivocate with a very small probability.

4.2   Asymptotic Comparison to Previous Work

Key Registration/Change. Since all users' data are tied together in the existing schemes, a key registration/change (or an epoch in CONIKS) forces the provider to generate proofs of size $O(\log n)$ for all users and send them to the respective users (consistency proofs). This requires total $O(n \log n)$ computation and communication cost at the provider, which are not taken into account in the previous work. This is an $O(1)$ operation in our KAS since the provider performs a constant number of operations and distributes constant-size proofs over the network on each update. However, the key owners of KAS audit the providers once in a time, roughly like an epoch in CONIKS. The providers reply only with the latest keys and hash values without any computation, which accounts for $O(n)$ server computation and communication, in total.

Gossiping. In CONIKS and our scheme, there is a gossiping at the provider side, whereas in the other two schemes gossiping is done at the client side. Note that in practice, we expect maybe only hundreds of providers whereas many millions of clients will take place in the system. Table 4 presents the comparison, showing an $O(\log n)$ decrease in all operations in our KAS.

Table 4. A comparison of key registration/change costs. n is the number of users.

Scheme	Provider		User		Gossiping
	Key Reg.	Proof Gen.	Comp.	Proof Size	
Laurie *et al.* [6]	$O(\log n)$	$O(n \log n)$	$O(\log n)$	$O(\log n)$	Client-side
ECT [11]	$O(\log n)$	$O(n \log n)$	$O(\log n)$	$O(\log n)$	Client-side
CONIKS [8]	$O(\log n)$	$O(n \log n)$	$O(\log n)$	$O(\log n)$	Server-side
Our KAS	$O(1)$	$O(1)$ $(O(n)$ audits$)$	$O(1)$	$O(1)$	Server-side

Key Revocation. The scheme given in [6] has no an efficient way for key revocation, hence, it needs to traverse the whole ADS with cost $O(n)$. But, the two others [8,11] can do it with $O(\log n)$ time and space complexity, i.e., the server should generate an $O(\log n)$ proof for each user (summing up to $O(n \log n)$ communication) in $O(n \log n)$ time. This is also an $O(1)$ operation in our scheme since there is no correlation between data of different users.

Audit. This operation is only needed in CONIKS and our scheme. Similarly, it requires $O(n \log n)$ and $O(n)$ server computation and communication in CONIKS and KAS, respectively. Moreover, the client computation and proof size are $O(\log n)$ and $O(1)$ in CONIKS and KAS, respectively.

4.3   Performance Analysis

Setup. To evaluate our KAS scheme, we implemented a prototype using the Cashlib library All experiments were performed on a 2.50 GHz machine with 24 cores (using a single core), with 16 GB RAM and Ubuntu 12.04 LTS operating system, hosting all our providers. Hence, the inter-provider communications were performed as loopback. The clients were deployed on a dualcore 2.5GHz laptop machine with 4 GB RAM, running Ubuntu 14.04 LTS, connected to the same LAN. We used settings similar to CONIKS: there are n=10M users registered at each provider, and each user changes her key once a year, which accounts for $\sim$ 27,400 changes per day. The security parameter $\lambda = 128$, and we use SHA-256 as the hash function and the DSA signature scheme with key pair size (2048,256) bits according to [4]. The numbers are averages of 50 runs.

Key Registration/Change. The client sends the home provider her new key (and revocation statement of the previous key), which has a fixed size. The provider computes hash of the key (32 B), signs the result (64 B), and shares the hash values and the signature with other providers, as well as the key owner. Therefore, the inter-provider communication is 96 KB in total when $|\mathcal{P}|$=1000, and the provider-user communication is only 96 B. *This happens for each client once per key lifetime, not per epoch as in CONIKS.*

The previous schemes require the provider to generate and send a consistency proof to each user on each key registration/change [6,11] (each epoch in CONIKS [8]). Considering that the proof is of size $O(\log n)$, where n is the number of users, and there are r key registrations/changes per day, each client receives and verifies $O(r \log n)$ proofs per day. This is $\sim$800 MB (for 10^9 users) in ECT and 100 KB (for 10^7 users) using the compressed proofs in CONIKS, per day.

The $O(n \log n)$ proof that the provider prepares and distributes over the network each time is more than 3.11 GB in total in CONIKS. Assuming 27,400 key changes and 288 epochs per day, the providers prepare and distribute more than 895 GB proof per day in CONIKS. The others [6,11] perform even worse. In our scheme, the providers perform a constant number of operations and distributes constant-size proofs, leading to a total of $\sim$2.5 MB of proof per day.

Computation Time. It takes ~ 0.5 ms for the provider in KAS to perform the key registration and send back the proof, while it takes ~ 2.6 s in CONIKS.

Audit. Assuming the key owners perform audit operations once in a time equal to a CONIKS epoch (i.e., 5 min), the providers return the already-computed hash values (and signatures in previous schemes), without any computation. During the normal operation, our providers respond with the latest hash values only. Assuming the challenge size k=50, each user receives a response of size $\sim$1.56

KB in our scheme, and ~4.68 KB in CONIKS, for each audit. These sum up to ~450 KB in our scheme, and ~1.31 MB in CONIKS, per day. For the providers, this is an $O(n)$ operation, which sums to ~305 MB of proof for one round of audit, and ~85 GB per day, in our scheme. While CONIKS will transfer ~915 MB of proof for one round of audit, and ~257.5 GB per day. Our KAS saves more than 67 % of the daily communication compared to CONIKS. The results are shown in Table 5.

Table 5. A comparison of audit proof sizes in KAS and CONIKS, k=50.

Scheme	Provider			User		
	Complexity	One epoch	Per day	Complexity	One Audit	Per day
CONIKS	$O(n \log n)$	915 MB	257.5 GB	$O(1)$	4.68 KB	1.31 MB
Our KAS	$O(n)$	305 MB	85 GB	$O(1)$	1.56 KB	450 KB

Acknowledgement. We would like to acknowledge the support of TÜBİTAK, the Scientific and Technological Research Council of Turkey, under project number 114E487.

References

1. Barenghi, A., Beretta, M., Federico, A.D., Pelosi, G.: Snake: An end-to-end encrypted online social network. In: HPCC, pp. 763–770. IEEE (2014)
2. Diffie, W., Hellman, M.E.: New directions in cryptography. IEEE Trans. Inf. Theory **22**(6), 644–654 (1976)
3. Etemad, M., Küpçü, A.: Efficient for secure end-to-end communications. Cryptology ePrint Archive, Report 2015/833 (2015)
4. Gallagher, P., Kerry, C.: Digital signature standard (dss). NIST, 2013. FIPS PUB 186-4
5. Goldwasser, S., Micali, S., Rivest, R.L.: A digital signature scheme secure against adaptive chosen-message attacks. SIAM **17**(2), 281–308 (1988)
6. Laurie, B., Kasper, E.: Revocation transparency. Google Research (2012). http://www.links.org/files/RevocationTransparency.pdf. Accessed on 20 April 2015
7. Laurie, B., Langley, A., Kasper, E.: Rfc 6962: Certificate transparency (2013)
8. Melara, M.S., Blankstein, A., Bonneau, J., Freedman, M.J., Felten, E.W.: Coniks: A privacy-preserving consistent key service for secure end-to-end communication (2014)
9. Naor, M., Nissim, K.: Certificate revocation and certificate update. IEEE J. Sel. Areas Commun. **18**(4), 561–570 (2000)
10. Rivest, R.L., Shamir, A., Adleman, L.: A method for obtaining digital signatures and public-key cryptosystems. Commun. ACM **21**(2), 120–126 (1978)
11. Ryan, M.D.: Enhanced certificate transparency and end-to-end encrypted mail. The Internet Society, Proceedings of NDSS (2014)
12. Weber, S.G.: Enabling end-to-end secure communication with anonymous and mobile receivers - an attribute-based messaging approach. Cryptology ePrint Archive, Report 2013/478 (2013)
13. Wendlandt, D., Andersen, D.G., Perrig, A.: Perspectives: improving ssh-style host authentication with multi-path probing. In: USENIX, pp. 321–334 (2008)

PPAE: Practical Parazoa Authenticated Encryption Family

Donghoon Chang[2](✉), Sumesh Manjunath R.[1],
and Somitra Kumar Sanadhya[2]

[1] TCS Innovation Labs, Pune, India
sumesh.manjunathr@tcs.com
[2] Indraprastha Institute of Information Technology, Delhi, India
{donghoon,somitra}@iiitd.ac.in

Abstract. The CAESAR competition for standardization of schemes for authenticated encryption has received 49 entries. Constructions such as Keyak, ICEPOLE, Artemia, NORX and Ascon use DuplexWrap and JHAE modes. DuplexWrap is based on the sponge construction and JHAE is based on the JH hash function. Andreeva et al. have recently defined a generalized sponge like construction called Parazoa hash family and provided indifferentiability security bound for the same. They had shown that the sponge as well as the JH hash function are instances of the parazoa construction with suitable choices of parameters. In our work, we define *PPAE* as an Authenticated Encryption family based on Parazoa construction. The proposed AE mode supports feed-forward operation which is lacking in sponge based AE constructions. We also provide security analysis of the *PPAE* family.

Keywords: Authenticated encryption family · Feed-forward · Provable security · Game-playing framework

1 Introduction

Authenticated Encryption (AE) was first introduced by Bellare et al. [4] in 2000. An AE scheme provides combined functionality of encryption as well as authentication. In recent times, there has been a lot of interest in the community towards efficient authenticated encryption schemes and their analysis. In January 2013, a competition was announced for Authenticated Ciphers [8], highlighting the importance and need of authenticated encryption schemes in the symmetric key setting. In the current phase of the competition, there are 49 candidate designs. Some of these are Keyak [7], ICEPOLE [14], Artemia [1], NORX [3] and Ascon [9]. Keyak and ICEPOLE are based on the duplex construction, NORX [3] and Ascon [9] are based on MonkeyDuplex [10] while Artemia is based on the JHAE [12] mode. The underlying design of MonkeyDuplex, DuplexWrap and JHAE are sponge-like hash functions. In [2], the authors have provided a generalized sponge-like hash construction called Parazoa Hash Family.

© Springer International Publishing Switzerland 2015
M.-H. Au and A. Miyaji (Eds.): ProvSec 2015, LNCS 9451, pp. 198–211, 2015.
DOI: 10.1007/978-3-319-26059-4_11

In this work, we define a sub family of Parazoa, called Practical Parazoa Hash (*PPH*) family. In *PPH*, we fix L_{in} as partial internal state XOR with message block and also L_{ex} outputs p Most Significant Bits (MSB) of internal state. Fixing L_{in} and L_{ex} still fulfills all the requirements of these functions as defined in [2]. Using this subfamily, we propose a nonce based *PPAE* family of Authenticated Encryption of Associated Data. *PPAE* supports feed-forward of message blocks as well as previous internal state strings. We provide a generalized privacy and authenticity security proof for *PPAE* hash family. Thus, we have proposed an Authenticated Encryption Mode based on sub-family of Parazoa which covers sponge construction also.

In [13], the security bound of sponge based authenticated encryptions is increased beyond $2^{\frac{c}{2}}$, where c is the capacity of sponge function. In this work, they have extensively proved for sponge based AE contructions. Sponge based construction doesn't support feed forward operation [11], therefore AE based on sponge also doesn't support feed forward operation. The parazoa family proposed by E. Andreeva et al. in [2] supports feed-forward of message block as well as internal state strings and thus our *PPAE*, which is based on parazoa also supports the feed-forward.

2   Preliminaries

We discuss the notation used in this paper and give a formal introduction to Authenticated Encryption and its security notions.

2.1   Notations

Let $\mathbb{Z}_2^*$ be set of bit strings of arbitrary length and $\mathbb{Z}_2^n$ be set of n-bit strings, where $n \in N$. Let $p\|q$ denote the concatenation of bit strings p and q. We use $\lceil V \rceil_n^x$ to denote "x" most significant bits of an n-bit string V, and $\lfloor V \rfloor_n^y$ to denote "y" least significant bits of the n-bit V. Further, $max(x,y)$ outputs the bigger of the two values x and y and $\perp$ is the invalid symbol.

2.2   Authenticated Encryption - *AE*

AE is a symmetric key encryption scheme which provides privacy as well as authenticity for a message. An AE scheme Π is defined as $\Pi = (\mathcal{K}, \mathcal{E}, \mathcal{D})$, where $\mathcal{K}$ is a key generation algorithm which chooses a secret key K uniformly random from a finite set, and $\mathcal{E}$ and $\mathcal{D}$ are encryption and decryption functions respectively. *AE* can use a nonce N. AE can also support an optional Associate Data (A). The encryption algorithm takes nonce N, Associated Data A, message M as input and output ciphertext C and Tag T. The decryption algorithm outputs the message M, if the tag T' produced from N, A, C matches the given tag T, else it returns $\perp$ (INVALID) and discards the message.

$$\text{Encryption algorithm} : \mathcal{E}_K(N, A, M) = (C, T),$$
$$\text{Decryption algorithm} : \mathcal{D}_K(N, A, C, T) = M \text{ or } \perp.$$

2.3 Security Notion for AE

We use the the security notion defined in [13] and we explain the same below.

2.3.1 Privacy. Consider a nonce-respecting adversary $\mathcal{A}$, interacting with either a real encryption oracle $\mathcal{E}_K(N, M)$ or an ideal function $\$(N, M)$. The goal of the adversary is to identify the unknown oracle. The adversary is given access to the ideal permutation π and its inverse π^{-1}. The advantage of the adversary is its ability to identify the oracle.

$$\mathbf{Adv}_{\Pi}^{priv}(\mathcal{A}) = \Pr[\mathcal{A}^{\mathcal{E}_K(\cdot,\cdot),\pi,\pi^{-1}} = 1] - \Pr[\mathcal{A}^{\$(\cdot,\cdot),\pi,\pi^{-1}} = 1]$$

2.3.2 Authenticity. The authenticity of an AE scheme is defined in terms of the ability of an adversary to produce a valid (N, C, T) pair without querying the encryption oracle (i.e. forge a valid tag).

The forging adversary $\mathcal{A}$ is given access to the encryption oracle $\mathcal{E}_K(\cdot, \cdot)$, decryption oracle $\mathcal{D}_K(\cdot, \cdot, \cdot)$, ideal permutation π and its inverse π^{-1}. Further, $\mathcal{A}$ is nonce respecting adversary (for encryption only) and queries these oracles for fixed number of times

The forging experiment $Exp_{\Pi}^{auth}(\mathcal{A})$, is defined as follows:

1. $\mathcal{A}$ can query π, π^{-1}, $\mathcal{E}_K(\cdot, \cdot)$ and $\mathcal{D}_K(\cdot, \cdot, \cdot)$ at most q_1, q_2, q_e and q_d times, respectively.
2. For every $\mathcal{E}_K(N, M)$ query, the encryption oracle output C, T and stores (N, C, T) in a set, say Z.
3. For every $\mathcal{D}_K(N, C, T)$ query, the decryption oracle decrypt C to get a valid message M. If M is valid and $(N, C, T) \notin Z$, then experiment outputs 1.
4. For every π and π^{-1} queries, corresponding permutations oracles are used.
5. After all queries are exhausted, the experiment outputs 0.

We say that $\mathcal{A}$ forges the scheme if $Exp_{\Pi}^{auth}(\mathcal{A}) = 1$.

The advantage of the Adversary $\mathcal{A}$ in forging the scheme Π is represented as

$$Adv_{\Pi}^{auth}(\mathcal{A}) = \Pr[Exp_{\Pi}^{auth}(\mathcal{A}) = 1].$$

3 Parazoa Family

Parazoa family of hash functions [2] is generalization of a Sponge based hash function. Parazoa uses s-bit IV and s-bit ideal permutation π. The padded message M is divided into k blocks of m-bit each. The Parazoa comprise of two main functions: the compression function f and the extraction function g. The compression function uses an s-bit state and one block of the message to update the state. $f : \mathbb{Z}_2^s \times \mathbb{Z}_2^m \to \mathbb{Z}_2^s$. The extraction function takes the previous state, processes it and outputs a p-bit P and the next state. $g : \mathbb{Z}_2^s \to \mathbb{Z}_2^s \times \mathbb{Z}_2^p$. Once the input blocks are processed by the f function, the extraction function g is called l times to produce n-bit hash digest where $lp \geq n$.

$$\mathcal{H}(M) = h, where : (M_1, \ldots \ldots, M_k) \leftarrow pad(M); V_0 \leftarrow IV$$
$$V_i \leftarrow f(V_{i-1}, M_i) \text{ for } i = 1, \ldots, k$$
$$(V_{k+i}, P_i) \leftarrow g(V_{k+i-1}) \text{ for } i = 1, \ldots, l$$
$$h \leftarrow fin(P_1, \ldots, P_l)$$

3.1 Compression Function f

Compression function f takes previous state and a message block M_i as input and processes it to produce a new state. It process in two steps. First, with the help of an injection function $L_{in} : \mathbb{Z}_2^s \times \mathbb{Z}_2^m \to \mathbb{Z}_2^s$, the message M is injected into the state V_{i-1}. This injected state is permuted using π to get an intermediate state y. This intermediate state is transformed and combined with previous state and M_i using $L_{out} : \mathbb{Z}_2^s \times Z_2^s \times \mathbb{Z}_2^m \to \mathbb{Z}_2^s$. Therefore, the compression function is defined as $f(V_{i-1}, M_i) = V_i$.

Let $C(x)$ be capacity set. Formally $C(x)$ is defined as follows. For any $x \in \mathbb{Z}_2^s$, $C(x) = \{V \in \mathbb{Z}_2^s \mid \exists M \in \mathbb{Z}_2^m \text{ s.t } L_{in}(V, M) = x\}$.

o The requirement for L_{in}:
  – For any given $x \in \mathbb{Z}_2^s$ and $V \in C(x)$, there exists exactly one $M \in \mathbb{Z}_2^m$ such that $L_{in}(V, M) = x$,
  – If $C(x) \cap C(x') \neq \emptyset$, then $C(x) = C(x')$.
o The requirement for L_{out}:
  – For any $(V, M) \in \mathbb{Z}_2^s \times \mathbb{Z}_2^m$, L_{out} must be bijection on the state.

3.2 Extraction Function g

Extraction function g takes s-bit state as input and produces p-bit output P_i along with an updated state, $L_{ex} : \mathbb{Z}_2^s \leftarrow \mathbb{Z}_2^p$. The only requirement of g-function is to be balanced. That is each $P \in \mathbb{Z}_2^p$ is equally likely to occur.

3.3 Finalization Function fin

The fin function combines l blocks of p-bits extracted from g-functions to produce an n-bit digest. In most of the cases, l blocks of p-bits are concatenated and then chopped to the required length of n bits. The fin function is required to be balanced. That is, each digest n is equally likely to occur from the given pl bits of string.

3.4 Padding Function pad

The pad function is an injective function which transforms arbitrary length message M into m-bit message blocks. The last block of the padded message, M_k, must satisfy the following condition: For any $x \in \mathbb{Z}_2^s$ and $(V', M') \in \mathbb{Z}_2^s \times \mathbb{Z}_2^m$:

$$L_{in}(x, M_k) \neq x \text{ and } L_{in}(L_{out}(x, V', M'), M_k) \neq x.$$

3.5   Indifferentiability of Parazoa Functions

The indifferentiablility of parazoa functions are proved based on the assumption that the underlying permutation π is ideal. We quote the relevant theorem from [2] for the secutity bound of Parazoa.

Theorem 1 (Indifferentiability). *Let π be a random s-bit permutation, and let RO be a random oracle. Let H be a Parazoa function parameterized by l, m, n, p, s, t. Let D be the distinguisher that makes at most q_1 left queries of maximal length $(U - 1)m$ bits, q_2 right queries and runs in time t, where $U \geq 1$. Then:*

$$Adv_{H,S}^{pro}(D) = O\left(\frac{((U+l)q_1 + q_2)^2}{2^{s-p-d}}\right),$$

where, simulator S, makes at most $q_s \leq q_2$ queries to RO and runs in the time $O(q_2^2)$.

The advantage of any adversary say $\mathcal{A}$, in differentiating a Parazoa function with a random oracle is $O\left(\frac{((U+l)q_1+q_2)^2}{2^{s-p-d}}\right)$ such that $\mathcal{A}$ can make at most q_1 queries to the hash function and q_2 queries to the underlying primitive used in the hash function. Each q_1 query can call the underlying primitive at most $U + l$ times.

Intuition on Capacity Loss d: In [2], $d \geq 0$ is the minimum value such that for any given x and fixed $P \in \mathbb{Z}_2^p$, there are at most 2^d couples (V, x) such that $V \in L_{ex}^{-1}(P)$. Thus, $|C(x)| \leq 2^{p+d}$ for any x. This is due to the fact that there is only one P which satisfies $L_{ex}(V) = P$ and the total number of P are 2^p.

In the indifferentiability proof, the simulator is required to choose V such that it doesn't belong to the set $C(x)$ to avoid collisions. Thus, the simulator can choose at most (2^{s-p-d}) values of V. Thus, $(s - p - d)$ bits of the state: *(a)* cannot be affected by the distinguisher by message injection, and *(b)* cannot be obtained by distinguisher through extraction. The parameter d can vary between 0 and $s - p$. When $d = 0$, then $(s-p)$ bits cannot be controlled by the adversary. Similarly when $d = s - p$, then the adversary has complete control over the state. In sponge construction $(s-p)$ is called the capacity C. If d increases, then $(S - p - d)$ decreases, thus it is termed the capacity loss.

4   Practical Parazoa Hash - *PPH*

For a secure AE scheme, the ciphertext should be influenced by message block. In order to ensure this with efficient implementation, we fix the L_{in} function as XOR. The addition modulo 2 function satisfies all the requirements for L_{in}. Our choice of the function is motivated by the fact that most of the practical designs such as Sponge, JH, FWP, FP modes have XOR as their L_{in} function. We denote this specific type of Parazoa hash family, as *"Practical Parazoa Hash"* function, *PPH*. The PPH construction is shown in Fig. 1. We use PPH as underlying construction for our Authenticated Encryption PPAE.

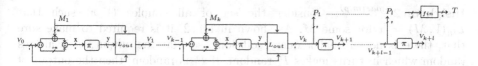

Fig. 1. Practical Parazoa Hash function. The message M, is padded using $pad()$ function, such that $pad(M) \rightarrow M_1 \| \ldots \| M_k$.

4.1 Compression Function f_p

The compression function f_p, is an instance of the Parazoa f-function. It satisfies all the requirement of L_{in}, L_{out} functions. Since XOR is used, for any given $x \in \mathbb{Z}_2^s$ and V, there will be only one $M \in \mathbb{Z}_2^s$, thus satisfying the requirement.

The $L_{in}(.,.)$ of f function is defined as XOR of m-bit M with m Most Significant Bit (MSB) of V_{i-1} and concatenating the XORed value with the $s - m$ least significant bits of V_{i-1}. More formally,

$$x = (\lceil V_{i-1} \rceil_s^m \oplus M_i) \| \lfloor V_{i-1} \rfloor_s^{s-m}.$$

4.2 Extraction Function g_p

Extraction function g_p is an instance of the g function of the Parazoa. The p-most significant bits of V_{i-1} are output as P. Thus L_{ex} function is defined as below:

$$L_{ex}(V_{i-1}) \rightarrow \lceil V_{i-1} \rceil^p = P_i.$$

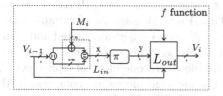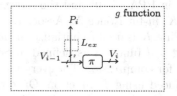

Fig. 2. f_p and g_p functions of PPH

4.3 Indifferentiability Bound of *PPH*

We define a lemma using the adversarial advantage as given in Theorem 1 with little modification to define the advantage of an adversary for the practical parazoa function.

Lemma 1. *The indifferentiability of PPH hash function is derived from Theorem [1].*

$$Adv_{H,S}^{pro}(D) = O\left(\frac{((U + l)q_1 + q_2)^2}{2^{s - max(m,p)}}\right),$$

where, m is the size of the message block.

Insight on $2^{s\text{-}max(m,p)}$: Consider the set of all couples (V, x) such that $L_{in}(V, M) = x$ for some M. As shown in Fig. 2, it is required to make sure that, there is no internal π query collisions, so that the output, y, is always random which in turns makes P_i random. If P_i is random, then the output of this hash function will be indifferentiable with random oracle. Therefore, the adversary has control over *(i)* Compression function through m-bit message M_i, *(ii)* Extraction function through p-bit output P_i.

For a fixed $P \in \mathbb{Z}_2^p$, there can be only one $\lceil V \rceil_m^p \in \mathbb{Z}_2^p$. Similarly, the message $M \in \mathbb{Z}_2^m$ can be controlled by the adversary. Therefore, for a given x and fixed M there is only one V. Therefore, out of the 2^s possible values for V, only $(2^{s-max(m-p)})$ values cannot be controlled by the adversary through M and P.

5   Practical Parazoa Authenticated Encryption Family (PPAE)

We propose a nonce based Associated Data supported Authenticated Encryption mode based on Practical Parazoa Hash family functions as described in Sect. 4. We describe PPAE, especially the modified f function to support the ciphertext. PPAE is shown in the Fig. 3.

5.1   Description

PPAE is a nonce based authenticated encryption mode which supports associated data A. It uses ideal permutation π as the underlying primitive. The IV used in PPAE is 0^s and the internal state is of size s bits. PPAE takes m-bit key K, m-bit Nonce N, Associated Data A and Message M of variable size.

First K is used to initialize the mode. N and A are concatenated and padded using *pad* function as defined in Sect. 3. For K and $pad(N\|A)$, f_p-function is used for compression. For every message block M_i, one block of ciphertext C_i is produced using f_a-function. Once all the message blocks are compressed, then g_p-function is used to produce the n-bit tag T. The PPAE construction is shown in Fig. 3.

$$\mathcal{PPH}_K(N, A, M) = (C, T); where$$
$$: (Z_1, \ldots, Z_a) \leftarrow pad(N\|A); (M_1, \ldots, M_k) \leftarrow pad(M)$$
$$V_i \leftarrow f_p(V_{i-1}, M_i) \text{ for } i = 1, \ldots, k; V_0 \leftarrow IV$$
$$(V_i, C_i) \leftarrow f_a(V_{i-1}, M_i) \text{ for } i = 1, \ldots, k; V_0 \leftarrow V_a$$
$$(V_{k+i}, P_i) \leftarrow g(V_{k+i-1}) \text{ for } i = 1, \ldots, l$$
$$C \leftarrow C_1\| \ldots \|C_k \text{ and } T \leftarrow fin(P_1, \ldots, P_l).$$

f_a-**function:** PPAE uses f_a-function as a modified version of f_p-function such that it produces ciphertext C_i for every M_i block. In this function, "m" most significant bits of the previous state $\lceil V_{i-1} \rceil_s^m$ are XOR'ed with the m-bit message M_i to form m-bit ciphertext C_i. The f_a-function is shown in Fig. 4.

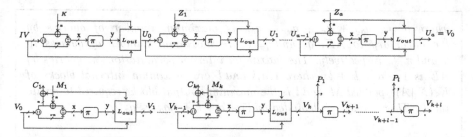

Fig. 3. The PPAE Construction. Nonce N, Associated Data A is concatenated and padded using $pad()$ function, such that $pad(N\|A) \to Z_1\|\ldots\|Z_a$. Similarly, the message M is also padded: $pad(M) \to M_1\|\ldots\|M_k$.

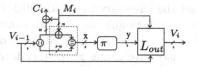

Fig. 4. f_a-function of PPAE

6 PPAE Security

6.1 PPAE: Privacy

Privacy of $PPAE$ is defined as the advantage of the nonce respecting adversary to distinguish ciphertext from random string. Game playing framework [5] is used to find the advantage of the adversary. We define 7 games where Game $G0$ is the $PPAE$ construction and Game $G7$ is a random oracle. The probability of the adversary to distinguish between each consecutive games are computed and union bound is applied to get the advantage of the adversary in distinguishing between a ciphertext and a random string.

The Theorem 2 provides the advantage of the adversary. Here AE means $PPAE$.

Theorem 2. (PPAE Privacy). *Let* **AE** *be the proposed Authenticated Encryption scheme which uses s-bit ideal permutation π and its inverse π^{-1} as its primitives. The internal input block is of size m bits and the output block after all the inputs are compressed in the s-bit states is of size p bits.*

The adversary $\mathcal{A}$ is given access to π, π^{-1} and the advantage of $\mathcal{A}$ to differentiate AE from RO is given by:

$$\boldsymbol{Adv}_{AE}^{priv}(\mathcal{A}) = Pr[\mathcal{A}_{\pi,\pi^{-1}}^{AE} = 1] - Pr[\mathcal{A}_{\pi,\pi^{-1}}^{RO} = 1]$$

$$\leq \frac{\sigma}{2^{s-1}} + \frac{q_{ae}}{2^m} + \frac{\sigma(\sigma-1)}{2^{s-max(m,p)+1}},$$

> where $\sigma = q_{ae} + q_\pi + q_{\pi^{-1}}$. q_{ae} is maximum number of queries by the adversary to AE, q_π and $q_{\pi^{-1}}$ are maximum number of queries to π and π^{-1}, respectively. The maximum internal permutation, π, queries by AE is $1 + a + k + l$, where $1, a, k$ and l are maximum internal blocks of $K, (N\|A)$, padded M and l is the maximum output blocks required to create tag T. Therefore, q_{ae} is bounded by $(1 + a + k + l)q_{ae} \le q_\pi$.

Proof. Game playing framework [5] is used to identify the adversary advantage for privacy of $PPAE$. Here, the initial game $G0$ represents $PPAE$ construction and $G7$ represents random oracle. These subsequent games from $G0$ is modified with *bad* events such that the adversary can distinguish the given two consecutive games. The advantage of distinguishing the two games is the probability of occurrence of these *bad* events. Thus summing all the probability of occurrence of *bad* events in all the consecutive games gives the advantage of the adversary in distinguishing $PPAE$ from random oracle.

In all the games K is chosen randomly from $\mathbb{Z}_2^m$ and $IV = 0^s$ to initialize the games. Each query takes Nonce, Associated Data and Message as input and returns corresponding Ciphertext and Tag. The adversary is nonce respecting.

Adversary can query π, π^{-1}, AE, at most $q_\pi, q_{\pi^{-1}}, q_{ae}$ times. Each q_{ae} queries π at most $(a + k + l + 1)$ times. Thus, q_{ae} is bounded by q_π such that $(a + k + l + 1)q_{ae} \le q_\pi$. We also define $\sigma = q_{ae} + q_\pi + q_{\pi^{-1}}$, overall internal permutation queries.

We define the term *state transition* where the input state is permuted to get a new output state. (i.e.) The input x is permuted using π to get y.

Game G0: $G0$ perfectly simulates $PPAE$. $G0$ takes (N, A, M) as input and simulates our construction and outputs ciphertext C and tag T. $PPAE$ queries uses π for state transition. π and π^{-1} outputs a random permutation that is for every new input, output is different and random.

$$\Pr[\mathcal{A}_{\pi,\pi^{-1}}^{AE} = 1] = \Pr[\mathcal{A}^{G0} = 1]. \tag{1}$$

Game G1: The π and π^{-1} queries simulates random function that is for every new input, output is random, need not be different. Thus, G1 and G0 are identical games until the outputs of π and π^{-1} queries collides with any of its previous outputs. This collision is denoted as *bad* event.

Set I_π stores all the (x, y) pairs of π and π^{-1} queries. Since π, π^{-1} is queried at most σ times by $PPAE$ as well as adversary, there should not be any collision within this σ pairs. The bad event occurs when any of the pairs collides.

$$\Pr[\mathcal{A}^{G1} = 1] - \Pr[\mathcal{A}^{G0} = 1] = \Pr[bad \leftarrow true]$$
$$\le \frac{\sigma}{2^s} \tag{2}$$

Game G2: In G2, $PPAE$ simulates random function and updates the set I_π. Since the set is synchronized, the adversary cannot distinguish between G1 and G2. Thus, G2 and G1 are identical from adversary point of view.

$$\Pr[\mathcal{A}^{G2} = 1] = \Pr[\mathcal{A}^{G1} = 1]. \tag{3}$$

Game G3: In this game we use PRP/PRF switching Lemma [5] to make sure that all the output of internal state are random. For any two distinct input string, random permutation always output distinct strings, whereas random function might output same string. Thus, the advantage of the adversary in distinguishing between random function and permutation is the probability of same string output for two different input strings.

For a secure Authenticated Encryption, the ciphertext must be random so that the adversary cannot distinguish with Random Oracle output. So, we must make sure that the output ciphertext in each internal state must be random.

Also, since the m-bit input message M_i is controlled by the adversary and the output, p-bit P_i is also known, our construction cannot rely on these bits for random string. The output string is from the output state bits of the internal state transition. To create a random output state bits, the input to the state transition must be different from all the previous inputs. Since $max(m, p)$-bit is controlled by the adversary, $s - max(m, p)$ bits needs to be different to make sure that input to the state transition is different.

Sets I_l and I_{lp} are used to store $s - m$ LSB of x and $s - p$ LSB of V_{k+i} (output of L_{out}) respectively. When $s - m$ LSB of input collides with I_l, it means that those bits have been already queried during the state transition. Even though the complete s-bit state may not be in I_π, but still we make sure that the input to state transition is different by choosing a random value from $\mathbb{Z}_2^{s-m}$ excluding the set I_l. Similarly I_{lp} is used in extraction phase of $PPAE$.

In function, $V_{i-1} \leftarrow L_{out}(y_{i-1}, V_{i-2}, M_{i-1})$, if V_{i-2}, M_{i-1} is fixed and y_{i-1} is random, then V_{i-1} is random. Since $V_{i-1} \oplus M_i = C_i$. Therefore, C_i is random.

Similarly, in extraction function which outputs p-bit P_i, we must make sure that $s - p$ bit is always different from the set I_p. Thus, for the complete construction, combining both the part, we must make sure that $s - max(m, p)$ bit is different which cannot be controlled by the adversary.

If the adversary guesses the key correctly, then with probability 1 it can differentiate between both the games. Since the key is random, the probability of guessing the m-bit key will also become *bad* event.

Games G2 and G3 are identical until there is collision in the $(s - m)$ LSB of x_i in the set I_l. The collision is denoted as *bad* event. If collision doesn't occur in x_i, then it is guaranteed that $\lceil V_{i-1} \rceil^m$ is random and $\lfloor V_{i-1} \rfloor^{s-m}$ is different.

$$\Pr[\mathcal{A}^{G3} = 1] - \Pr[\mathcal{A}^{G2} = 1] = \Pr[bad \leftarrow true] \tag{4}$$

Bad event occurs when the input x to π, collides with the elements in the set I_π. Let $Pr[\text{coll} = 1]$ be the probability of collisions which leads to occurrence of *bad* event. *Bad* event can also occur when the adversary guesses the key correctly. Thus,

$$\Pr[bad \leftarrow true] = \Pr[\text{coll} = 1] + \Pr[\text{key guess} \rightarrow correct] \tag{5}$$

Let $Pr[coll_i]$ means that there is no collision till $i - 1$ queries and collision occurs in the ith query. Therefore, $Pr[\text{coll} = 1]$ is given by:

$$\begin{aligned} \Pr[coll = 1] &= \Pr[coll_1 \vee coll_2 \vee \dots \vee coll_\sigma] \\ &\leq \Pr[coll_1] + \Pr[coll_2] + \dots + \Pr[coll_\sigma] \\ &\leq \frac{1}{2^{s-max(m,p)}} + \frac{2}{2^{s-max(m,p)}} + \dots + \frac{\sigma - 1}{2^{s-max(m,p)}} \\ &\leq \frac{\sigma(\sigma - 1)}{2^{s-max(m,p)+1}}. \end{aligned} \tag{6}$$

Since key is chosen randomly from $\mathbb{Z}_2^m$, the probability of guessing the key is given as below:

$$\Pr[\text{key guess} = 1] \leq \frac{q_{ae}}{2^m} \tag{7}$$

From Eqs. (5), (6) and (7) we can derive [3] as given below:

$$\Pr[\mathcal{A}^{G3} = 1] - \Pr[\mathcal{A}^{G2} = 1] \leq \frac{\sigma(\sigma - 1)}{2^{s-max(m,p)+1}} + \frac{q_{ae}}{2^m}. \tag{8}$$

Game G4: In this game, we assign the output of state transition such that there will be no collisions. While assigning the y value Fig. 3, it is made sure that $(s - max(m,p))$ MSB of V_i is random and remaining bits are different from the set I_l or I_{lp} as required. This makes ciphertext as well as all P_i random. Therefore, from adversary point of view, both the games are identical.

$$\Pr[\mathcal{A}^{G4} = 1] = \Pr[\mathcal{A}^{G3} = 1]. \tag{9}$$

Game G5: Till now, both $PPAE$ and π, π^{-1} queries are synchronized by using I_π queries. Where as, in G5, $PPAE$ queries doesn't depend on set I_π making $PPAE$ independent of π, π^{-1}. In G5, all the internal state transition x, y pairs are stored in the set I_{ae}, and similarly π, π^{-1} queries are stored in the set I_π. If any of the internal queries in $PPAE$ is present in I_π, then we denote it as bad event and vise versa. This makes AE and π, π^{-1} independent of each other.

$$\begin{aligned} \Pr[\mathcal{A}^{G5} = 1] - \Pr[\mathcal{A}^{G4} = 1] &= \Pr[bad \leftarrow true] \\ &\leq \frac{\sigma}{2^s}, \text{ where } \sigma = (a + k + 1)q_{ae} + q_\pi + q_{\pi^{-1}} \end{aligned} \tag{10}$$

Game G6: In G6, k-blocks of m-bit C_i and l-blocks of p-bit P_i is chosen randomly to create ciphertext C and tag T accordingly. In G5 also, C_i and P_i are random. Therefore, from adversarial point of view G5 and G6 are identical.

$$\Pr[\mathcal{A}^{G6} = 1] = \Pr[\mathcal{A}^{G5} = 1]. \tag{11}$$

Game G7: G7 perfectly simulates VIL Random Oracle. In G7, km bits of ciphertext as well as n bits of tag is chosen randomly. From adversary point of view both G7 and G6 are identical.

$$\Pr[\mathcal{A}^{G7} = 1] = \Pr[\mathcal{A}^{G6} = 1] = \Pr[\mathcal{A}^{RO}_{\pi, \pi^{-1}} = 1]. \tag{12}$$

Combining the probability difference between subsequent games, we will get the advantage of the adversary in differentiating $PPAE$ and Random Oracle.

Using the Eqs. (1), (2), (3), (8), (9), (10), (11) and (12), we give the advantage of adversary.

$$Adv_{AE}^{priv}(\mathcal{A}) = \Pr[\mathcal{A}_{\pi,\pi^{-1}}^{AE} = 1] + \Pr[\mathcal{A}_{\pi,\pi^{-1}}^{RO} = 1]$$

$$= (Pr[\mathcal{A}^{G0} = 1] - Pr[\mathcal{A}^{G1} = 1]) + (Pr[\mathcal{A}^{G1} = 1] - Pr[\mathcal{A}^{G2} = 1])$$

$$+ (Pr[\mathcal{A}^{G2} = 1] - Pr[\mathcal{A}^{G3} = 1]) + (Pr[\mathcal{A}^{G3} = 1] - Pr[\mathcal{A}^{G4} = 1])$$

$$+ (Pr[\mathcal{A}^{G4} = 1] - Pr[\mathcal{A}^{G5} = 1]) + (Pr[\mathcal{A}^{G5} = 1] - Pr[\mathcal{A}^{G6} = 1])$$

$$+ (Pr[\mathcal{A}^{G6} = 1] - Pr[\mathcal{A}^{G7} = 1])$$

$$Adv_{AE}^{priv}(\mathcal{A}) \leq \frac{\sigma}{2^{s-1}} + \frac{q_{ae}}{2^m} + \frac{\sigma(\sigma-1)}{2^{s-max(m,p)+1}}.$$

(13)

This completes the proof of Theorem 2.

6.2 PPAE: Authenticity

The authenticity of the $PPAE$ scheme is defined in terms of the ability of an adversary who can forge a valid (N, C, T) pair. The encryption and decryption functions in PPAE take key K and compress it and then answer queries from the adversary. Let us call these functions as encryption $\mathbf{E}^{\pi,\pi^{-1}}$ and decryption $\mathbf{D}^{\pi,\pi^{-1}}$ oracles respectively. For every (N, A, M) query to $\mathbf{E}^{\pi,\pi^{-1}}$, the output (C, T) is stored in a set I_{auth} along with the nonce N.

The adversary is given access to these oracles as well as to π and π^{-1}. Adversary $\mathcal{A}$ can query $\mathbf{E}^{\pi,\pi^{-1}}$, $\mathbf{D}^{\pi,\pi^{-1}}$, π and π^{-1} oracles at most $q_e, q_d, q_\pi, q_{\pi^{-1}}$ times, respectively. Each query q_e and q_d can query the permutations π and π^{-1} at most $a + k + l + 1$ times, where a, k, l are defined in Sect. 6.1. Finally, $\sigma_a = q_e + q_d + q_\pi + q_{\pi^{-1}}$ is the maximum number of queries allowed to $\mathcal{A}$.

The adversary $\mathcal{A}$ must be nonce-respecting for encryption queries only. After interacting with different oracles, $\mathcal{A}$ outputs (N, C, T). We say that $\mathcal{A}$ forged $PPAE$ scheme if the decryption oracle outputs M for the given $(N, C, T) \notin I_{auth}$. The experiment outputs 1 if the forgery was successful and 0 otherwise. Mathematically, we say that $\mathcal{A}$ forges the scheme if $Exp_{PPAE,\pi,\pi^{-1}}^{auth}(\mathcal{A}) = 1$. The advantage of the Adversary $\mathcal{A}$ in forging the scheme is denoted by:

$$Adv_{PPAE}^{auth}(\mathcal{A}) = \Pr[Exp_{PPAE,\pi,\pi^{-1}}^{auth}(\mathcal{A}) = 1].$$

(14)

Theorem 3 (Authenticity). *The authenticity of $PPAE$ is defined as the ability of any adversary to forge $PPAE$ after interacting with $PPAE, \pi, \pi^{-1}$ oracles. The ability is measured in terms of probability of an adversary to succeed in the forgery experiment.*

$$Pr[Exp_{PPAE,\pi,\pi^{-1}}^{auth}(\mathcal{A}) = 1] \leq O\left(\frac{((U+l+1)^2(\sigma_a)^2}{2^{s-max(m,p)}}\right) + \frac{\sigma_a}{2^n} + \frac{\sigma_a}{2^m}.$$

Proof (Authenticity). The proof of this theorem is not being provided here due to space restrictions. It will be provided in the extended version of this work.

7   Examples

In this section, Keyak is instantiated using $PPAE$ and derive the security bounds. Due to space constraint, more details will be provided in the extended version of this work.

7.1   Keyak

Keyak v1 [7] is one of the submissions to the CAESAR competition and is designed by the Keccak team. Keyak is based on the Duplex construction called DuplexWrap. This is similar to SpongeWrap [6] authenticated encryption mode.

Privacy of DuplexWrap. The privacy advantage of DuplexWrap is

$$\mathbf{Adv}^{\text{priv}}_{DuplexWrap[f,\rho]}(\mathcal{A}) \leq \frac{q_{ae}}{2^m} + \frac{\sigma(\sigma+1)}{2^{c+1}}. \tag{15}$$

According to DuplexWrap, the security parameter is capacity c, $c = s - max(m,p)$. Here, $q_{ae} \geq \sigma$. Therefore, the privacy advantage of DuplexWrap using $PPAE$ is

$$\mathbf{Adv}^{\text{priv}}_{DuplexWrap}(\mathcal{A}) \leq \frac{\sigma}{2^{s-1}} + \frac{\sigma}{2^m} + \frac{\sigma(\sigma-1)}{2^{c+1}}$$

Therefore, the privacy advantage of the adversary of DuplexWrap is within the $PPAE$ advantage given in Theorem 2.

Authenticity of DuplexWrap. The authenticity advantage of the adversary for DuplexWrap is shown in Eq. 16. Let the size of tag T be n bits and the number of invocations of random permutation including the decryption queries be σ_a.

$$\mathbf{Adv}^{\text{auth}}_{DuplexWrap[f,pad,r,p]}(\mathcal{A}) \leq \frac{q_{ae}}{2^m} + \frac{1}{2^n} + \frac{\sigma_a(\sigma_a+1)}{2^{c+1}}. \tag{16}$$

The authenticity advantage for DupplexWrap using PPAE is derived below.

$$\Pr[Exp^{auth}_{PPAE,\pi,\pi^{-1}}(\mathcal{A}) = 1] \leq \frac{\sigma_a}{2^m} + \frac{\sigma_a}{2^n} + O\left(\frac{((U+l+1)^2(\sigma_a)^2}{2^c}\right)$$

The higher bound compared to actual advantage is the extra cost for the general proof. Thus, the advantage of DuplexWrap is in accordance with advantage of $PPAE$.

8   Conclusion

In this work, we proposed $PPAE$, a new nonce based Authenticated Encryption with Associated Data family based on a variant of Parazoa hash family PPH. $PPAE$ supports feed-forward operations which was lacking in sponge based construction. We also provided its privacy and authenticity security based on the indifferentiability security bounds of Parazoa. We also showed that Keyak [7] belong to the $PPAE$ family and claim that Ascon [9] and NORX [3] also belong to the $PPAE$ family.

References

1. Alizadeh, J., Aref, M.R., Bagheri, N.: Artemia v1 (2014)
2. Andreeva, E., Mennink, B., Preneel, B.: The parazoa family: generalizing the sponge hash functions. Int. J. Inf. Sec. **11**(3), 149–165 (2012)
3. Aumasson, J.-P., Jovanovic, P., Neves, S.: NORX: parallel and scalable AEAD. In: Kutyłowski, M., Vaidya, J. (eds.) ICAIS 2014, Part II. LNCS, vol. 8713, pp. 19–36. Springer, Heidelberg (2014)
4. Bellare, M., Namprempre, C.: Authenticated encryption: relations among notions and analysis of the generic composition paradigm. In: Okamoto, T. (ed.) ASIACRYPT 2000. LNCS, vol. 1976, pp. 531–545. Springer, Heidelberg (2000)
5. Bellare, M., Rogaway, P.: The security of triple encryption and a framework for code-based game-playing proofs. In: Vaudenay, S. (ed.) EUROCRYPT 2006. LNCS, vol. 4004, pp. 409–426. Springer, Heidelberg (2006)
6. Bertoni, G., Daemen, J., Peeters, M., Van Assche, G.: Duplexing the sponge: single-pass authenticated encryption and other applications. In: Miri, A., Vaudenay, S. (eds.) SAC 2011. LNCS, vol. 7118, pp. 320–337. Springer, Heidelberg (2012)
7. Bertoni, G., Daemen, J., Peeters, M., Van Assche, G., Van Keer, R.: Keyak V1 (2014)
8. CAESAR. Competition for Authenticated Encryption: Security, Applicability, and Robustness (2013). http://competitions.cr.yp.to/caesar.html
9. Dobraunig, C., Eichlseder, M., Mendel, F., Martin, S.: Ascon V1 (2014)
10. Andreeva, E., Bilgin, B., Bogdanov, A., Luykx, A., Mennink, B., Mouha, N., Yasuda, K.: APE: Authenticated Permutation-Based Encryption for Lightweight Cryptography. Cryptology ePrint Archive, Report 2013/791 (2013). http://eprint. iacr.org/
11. Bertoni, G., Daemen, J., Peeters, M., Van Assche, G.: Sponge Functions. Ecrypt Hash Workshop 2007 (2007). http://sponge.noekeon.org/SpongeFunctions.pdf
12. Alizadeh, J., Aref, M.R., Bagheri, N.: JHAE: An Authenticated Encryption Mode Based on JH. Cryptology ePrint Archive, Report 2014/193 (2014). http://eprint. iacr.org/
13. Jovanovic, P., Luykx, A., Mennink, B.: Beyond $2^{c/2}$ security in sponge-based authenticated encryption modes. In: Sarkar, P., Iwata, T. (eds.) ASIACRYPT 2014. LNCS, vol. 8873, pp. 85–104. Springer, Heidelberg (2014)
14. Morawiecki, P., Gaj, K., Homsirikamol, E., Matusiewicz, K., Pieprzyk, J., Rogawski, M., Srebrny, M., Wojcik, M.: ICEPOLE: High-speed, Hardware-oriented Authenticated Encryption. Cryptology ePrint Archive, Report 2014/266 (2014). http://eprint.iacr.org/

Encryption and Identification

Lightweight Anonymous Authentication for Ad Hoc Group: A Ring Signature Approach

Xu Yang[1,2], Wei Wu[1,2]([✉]), Joseph K. Liu[3], and Xiaofeng Chen[4]

[1] Fujian Provincial Key Laboratory of Network Security and Cryptology,
School of Mathematics and Computer Science, Fujian Normal University,
Fuzhou 350117, Fujian, China
weiwu@fjnu.edu.cn
[2] State Key Laboratory of Cryptology, P. O. Box 5159, Beijing 100878, China
[3] Faculty of Information Technology, Monash University, Melbourne, VIC 3800,
Australia
joseph.liu@monash.edu
[4] State Key Laboratory of Integrated Service Networks (ISN),
Xidian University, Xi'an, China
xfchen@xidian.edu.cn

Abstract. Anonymous authentication protocol allows the system to authenticate a user anonymously. That is, the system knows that the requester is eligible to access, yet does not know his/her actual identity. Anonymous authentication is useful in many privacy-preserving applications such as wireless sensor networks and roaming. However, most of the anonymous authentication protocols are not lightweight. They all require a number of exponentiations or pairings which cannot be executed by lightweight devices such as sensors or RFID. In this paper, we propose a lightweight anonymous authentication protocol for *Ad Hoc* group. Our protocol contains only lightweight calculations such as hashing or modulus square but *not* exponentiation or pairing in both prover and verifier sides. The core primitive of our mechanism is a lightweight ring signature scheme. The security of our scheme can be reduced to the classic integer factorization assumption in the random oracle model.

1 Introduction

Privacy is an important factor in many areas. For example, no one wants his/her own daily behaviours, either location information in the physical world or web-browsing history in the cyber world, to be known by others. There exist various kinds of anonymization technologies that can help one become "anonymous" and protect user privacy. However, this will raise another security concern. There are many services that are designated for a particular group of users, for example, those who have paid and subscribed for the service. Being totally anonymous prevents the service provider telling whether a user belongs to the subscribed group or not. Thus we need a kind of *anonymous authentication* mechanism to ensure the authenticity of users while privacy is preserved simultaneously.

© Springer International Publishing Switzerland 2015
M.-H. Au and A. Miyaji (Eds.): ProvSec 2015, LNCS 9451, pp. 215–226, 2015.
DOI: 10.1007/978-3-319-26059-4_12

Ring signature is a good candidate to provide anonymous authentication, especially to ad hoc group. A ring signature scheme (for examples [1–6,8,9,13, 16,18,22,24,27–36,38,42–47]) allows members of a group to sign messages on behalf of the group without revealing their identities, i.e. signer anonymity. In addition, it is not possible to decide whether two signatures have been issued by the same group member. Different from a group signature scheme (for examples, [7,10,12]), the group formation is spontaneous and there is no group manager to revoke the identity of the signer. That is, under the assumption that each user is already associated with a public key of some standard signature scheme, a user can form a group by simply collecting the public keys of all the group members including his/her own. These diversion group members can be totally unaware of being conscripted into the group.

Ring signature schemes could be used for whistle blowing [38], anonymous membership authentication for ad hoc groups [9], anonymous data sharing [19], E-voting [14] and many other applications which do not want complicated group formation stage but require signer anonymity. For example, in the whistle blowing scenario, a whistleblower gives out a secret as well as a ring signature of the secret to the public. From the signature, the public can be sure that the secret is indeed given out by a group member while cannot figure out who the whistleblower is. At the same time, the whistleblower does not need any collaboration of other users who have been conscripted by him into the group of members associated with the ring signature. Hence the anonymity of the whistleblower is ensured and the public is also certain that the secret is indeed leaked by one of the group members associated with the ring signature.

Ring signature schemes can be used to derive other primitives as well. It had been utilized to construct non-interactive deniable ring authentication [40], perfect concurrent signature [41] and multi-designated verifiers signature [20].

Nevertheless, existing ring signature schemes need very heavy computations. *All* existing ring signature schemes require exponentiations, at least on the verification stage. (Some may require the execution of pairings, which is even computationally expensive) Usually the number of exponentiations required during the signing stage is proportional to the number of users included in the ring signature. Say, if the signature includes 10000 users, the signing stage requires at least 10000 exponentiations. This may not be a big problem for personal computers. However, the schemes will not be suitable in practice to be used in mobile devices as these computations will drain the battery quickly.

1.1   Our Contributions

In this paper, we address the problem specifically. Our solution does not require the signer or the verifier to execute any exponentiation or pairing. Both algorithms are considered heavy and not suitable for lightweight device (e.g. wireless sensor and RFID) to execute. Only hashing, modulus square and addition operations are needed in both stages. For a setting of n users, on average our new scheme requires $n + 4$ hashing, square and addition operations and one square-root operation for the signature generation. The verifier only requires n hashing, square and addition operations.

Note that our scheme is different from another primitive called online/offline ring signature [23]. Online/offline ring signature together with online/offline (identity-based) encryption [15,17,37], signcryption [25] and signature [26] belong to the paradigm of online/offline cryptogrpahy.

In an online/offline ring signature scheme, the signing part is splitted into two parts while some offline computations have to be completed before knowing the message and the set of public keys. While this will speed up the (online) signature generation, the verification cost of online/offline (ring) signature is not reduced. The scheme of [23] requires n exponentiations for verifying a ring signature containing n users. Nonetheless, despite the efficiency differences, both schemes are the same in terms of functionality. Thus we can regard our scheme is a further improvement of online/offline signature scheme in two ways: (1) We do not require any offline stage in the signing part; and (2) The verification is lightweight.

Paper Organisation. The remainder of this paper is organised as follows. Section 2 reviews the mathematical preliminaries and the syntax of ring signature. Our scheme is proposed in Sect. 3. Section 4 analyzes the performance of our scheme. We conclude the paper in Sect. 5.

2 Definitions

This section reviews the complexity assumption and definitions of ring signature.

2.1 Complexity Assumption

The security of our scheme relies on the factorization assumption with safe primes, which is defined as follows:

Definition 1 (Safe Prime). *p is a safe prime if it is of the form $2p' + 1$, where p' is also a prime.*

Definition 2 (Factorization Assumption with Safe Prime). *Let $N = pq$ where p and q are k-bit length safe primes. Given N as the input, the goal of an algorithm of $\mathcal{A}$ is to output an unordered pair (p, q). $\mathcal{A}$ has at least an advantage of ϵ if*

$$\Pr[\mathcal{A}(N) = p, q \mid N = pq] \geq \epsilon.$$

We say that the (ϵ, τ, k)-Factorization assumption holds if no algorithm running in time at most τ can solve the factorization problem with advantage at least ϵ, where the modulus is a product of two safe primes and each is with k-bit length.

Definition 3 (Quadratic Residues). *An integer $y \in Z_N^*$ is called a quadratic residue modulo N if there exists an integer $x \in Z_N^*$ such that: $x^2 = y \pmod{N}$. Let $QR(N)$ denote the set of quadratic residues modulo N.*

2.2 Security Model

Definition 4. *A ring signature scheme consists of three algorithms:*

- Key-Gen(k) → (sk, pk): Key-Gen is a probabilistic algorithm taking as input a security parameter k. It returns the user secret key sk and public key pk.
- Sign(L, sk, m) → σ: Sign is a probabilistic algorithm taking (L, m, sk) as input, where L is the list of n public keys to be included in the ring signature, sk is the secret key of the actual signer (such that the corresponding public key is included in L) and m is the message to be signed. It returns a signature σ.
- Verify(L, m, σ) → {Accept, Reject}. Verify is a deterministic algorithm taking (L, m, σ) as input, where L is the list of n public keys of the ring members and m, σ) is the message/ring-signature pair. It outputs either Accept or Reject.

The security of a ring signature scheme consists of two requirements, namely *Signer Ambiguity* and *Existential Unforgeability*. They are defined as follows.

Definition 5 (Signer Ambiguity). *Let $L = \{pk_1, \cdots, pk_n\}$ be the list of public keys and $L_{sk} = \{sk_1, \cdots, sk_n\}$ be the corresponding secret keys. Each key is generated by* Key-Gen. *A ring signature scheme is said to be unconditionally signer ambiguous if, for any L, any message m, and any signature $\sigma \leftarrow$ Sign(L, m, sk_π) where $sk_\pi \in L_{sk}$, any unbound adversary $\mathcal{A}$ accepts as inputs L, m and σ, outputs π with probability $1/n$.*

It means that even all the private keys are known, it remains uncertain that who, out of n possible signers, actually produced the ring signature. Note that we do not allow $\mathcal{A}$ to know the random coins used to generate the signature.

Definition 6 (Existential Unforgeability). *For a ring signature scheme with n public keys, the existential unforgeability is defined as the following game between a challenger and an adversary $\mathcal{A}$:*

1. The challenger runs algorithm Key-Gen. Let $L = \{pk_1, \cdots, pk_n\}$ be the set of n public keys and $L_{sk} = \{sk_1, \cdots, sk_n\}$ be the corresponding secret keys. $\mathcal{A}$ is given L.
2. $\mathcal{A}$ can adaptively queries the signing oracle q_S times: On input any message m and L' where $L' \subseteq L$ (the corresponding secret keys are denoted by L'_{sk}), the challenger returns a ring signature $\sigma \leftarrow$ Sign(L', m, sk_π), where $sk_\pi \in L'_{sk}$ and Verify(L', m, σ) = Accept.
3. Finally $\mathcal{A}$ outputs a tuple (L^*, m^*, σ^*).

$\mathcal{A}$ wins the game if:

1. $L^* \subseteq L$,
2. (L^*, m^*) has not been submitted to the signing oracle, and
3. Verify(L^*, m^*, σ^*) = Accept

We define $\mathcal{A}$'s advantage in this game to be $Adv(\mathcal{A}) = \Pr[\mathcal{A} \text{ wins}]$.

3   The Proposed Scheme

This section describes our proposal and its security analysis.

3.1   Construction

The details of our design are given as follows.

Key-Gen: Let κ be security parameters. Each user selects two safe primes p, q of length k-bit, such that $p = 2p' + 1, q = 2q' + 1$ where p', q' are also primes. The private key is (p, q) and public key is $N = pq$.

Sign: Let $L = \{N_1, \ldots, N_n\}$ be a list of n public keys to be included in the ring signature. Let $H_i : \{0,1\}^* \rightarrow \mathbb{Z}_{N_i}$ be some hash functions for $i = 1, \ldots, n$. H_i is a random oracle. W.l.o.g., we assume user n is the actual signer and thus the signer knows sk_n but not sk_i where $i = 1, \ldots, n - 1$. The actual signer executes the following steps:

1. Randomly generate $r_n \in_R \mathbb{Z}_{N_n}$, compute $c_1 = H_1(L, m, r_n)$.
2. (For $n > 1$ only) For $i = 1, \ldots, n - 1$, randomly generate $x_i \in_R \mathbb{Z}_{N_i}$ and compute $c_{i+1} = H_{i+1}(L, m, c_i + x_i^2 \mod N_i)$.
3. Compute $t_n = r_n - c_n \mod N_n$. If $t_n \notin QR(N)$, repeat the following steps until $t_n \in QR(N)$.
   - (For $n > 1$) choose another random $x_{n-1} \in_R \mathbb{Z}_{N_{n-1}}$ and compute $c_n = H_n(L, m, c_{n-1} + x_{n-1}^2 \mod N_{n-1})$.
   - (For $n = 1$) choose another random $r_1 \in_R \mathbb{Z}_{N_1}$ and compute $c_1 = H_1(L, m, r_1)$.
4. Compute $x_n = t_n^{1/2} \mod N_n$ using the knowledge of the factorization of N_n.

Output the signature $\sigma = (x_1, \ldots, x_n, c_1)$.

Verify: To verify a signature $\sigma = (x_1, \ldots, x_n, c_1)$ for message m and public keys $L = \{N_1, \ldots, N_n\}$, computes $r_i = c_i + x_i^2 \mod N_i$ for $i = 1, \ldots, n$ and $c_{i+1} = H_{i+1}(L, m, r_i)$ for $i \neq n$. The Verify algorithm accepts the signature if $c_1 = H_1(L, m, r_n)$. Otherwise, it rejects.

The correctness of our scheme is obvious and thus omitted.

3.2   Security Analysis

We will show that the proposed scheme is unconditionally signer ambiguous and existentially unforgeable.

Theorem 1. *Our ring signature scheme is unconditionally signer ambiguous.*

Proof. All x_i except x_n are taken randomly from $\mathbb{Z}_{N_i}$. At the closing point, $x_n \in \mathbb{Z}_{N_n}$ also distributes randomly as r_n is randomly chosen, c_n depends on previous x_{n-1} which is also a random number. Therefore, for fixed (L, m), $(x_1, \ldots, x_n)$ has $\prod_{i=1}^{n} N_i$ variation that are equally likely regardless of the closing point. The remaining c_1 is uniquely determined from L, m and x_i's and thus reveals no information of the actual signer.   □

Theorem 2. *Suppose the (ϵ', τ', k)-Factorization assumption holds, then our ring signature scheme with n users is $(\tau, q_s, q_h, \epsilon)$-secure against existential forgery under adaptive chosen message attacks in the random oracle model provided that:*

$$\epsilon' \leq \frac{\left(1 - \frac{q_h q_s}{N_{min}}\right)\left(1 - \frac{1}{N_{min}}\right)\epsilon}{q_h(q_h + 1)n}, \qquad \tau' = \tau$$

where N_{min} is the smallest modulus among n public keys, q_s is the maximum number of signing oracle queries allowed and q_h is the maximum number of H_i random oracle queries allowed.

Proof. The proof uses the approach described in [1]. (Readers may refer to [1] for some preliminary understanding.) Suppose the adversary $\mathcal{A}$ can forge the ring signature scheme with n users. We construct an algorithm $\mathcal{S}$ that uses $\mathcal{A}$ to solve the factorization problem.

<u>Setup:</u> $\mathcal{S}$ receives the problem instance N, which is the product of two safe prime numbers of length k-bit. $\mathcal{S}$ is asked to output a non-trivial factor of N.

$\mathcal{S}$ randomly chooses $\pi \in_R [1, n]$ and assigns the public key of user π to be N (the problem instance). For the other $n - 1$ users' public keys, $\mathcal{S}$ generates them according to the algorithm. $\mathcal{S}$ also chooses two integers u, v such that $1 \leq u \leq v \leq q_h$.

<u>Oracle Simulation:</u>

- H_i *Random Oracle:* For simplicity, the H_i random oracles are treated as single oracle that takes $Q_j = (i, L_j, m_j, r_j)$ as the j-th query and returns a random value that corresponds to $H_i(L_j, m_j, r_j)$ maintaining consistency against duplicated queries.
- *Signing Oracle:* Upon receiving the signing query for (L_j, m_j), $\mathcal{S}$ simulates the signing oracle in the following way.
    1. Randomly choose $c_1 \in_R \mathbb{Z}_{N_1}$.
    2. For $i = 1, \ldots, |L_j|$, randomly select integers $x_i \in_R \mathbb{Z}_{N_i}$, compute $r_i = x_i^2 + c_i \mod N_i$, and then compute $c_{i+1} = H_{i+1}(L_j, m_j, r_j)$ if $i \neq |L_j|$.
    3. Assign c_1 to the value of $H_1(L_j, m_j, r_{|L_j|})$.

<u>Output Calculation:</u> Since the queries form a ring, there exists at least one index, say κ, in $\{1, \ldots, n\}$ such that $Q_u = (\kappa + 1, L, m, r_\kappa)$ and $Q_v(\kappa, L, m, r_{\kappa-1})$ satisfy $u \leq v$. Namely, κ is in between the gap of query order. We call such (u, v) a gap

index. Note that $u = v$ happens only if $n = 1$, which means that the resulting L contains only one public-key. If there are two or more gap indices with regard to a signature, only the smallest one is considered.

At the beginning of the simulation, S has chosen a pair of index (u, v) randomly such that $1 \leq u \leq v \leq q_h$. If the guess is correct, S receives $Q_u = (\kappa + 1, L, m, r_\kappa)$ and $Q_v = (\kappa, L, m, r_{\kappa-1})$ so that (u, v) is a gap index. When query Q_v is made (u-th query has been already made by this moment), S returns $c_\kappa = r_\kappa - R \mod N_\kappa$ (where $R = r^2 \mod N_\kappa$ and $r \in_R N_\kappa$ is chosen by S) as the value of $H_\kappa(L, m, r_{\kappa-1})$. If A is successful in forgery, it outputs x_κ that satisfies $r_\kappa = c_\kappa + x_\kappa^2 \mod N_\kappa$. Since $r_\kappa = c_\kappa + R \mod N_\kappa$, we obtain x_κ as the square root of R with regard to N_κ. That is, $x_\kappa^2 = R \mod N_\kappa$ or $x_\kappa^2 = r^2 \mod N_\kappa$. With half probability, $x_\kappa \neq r$. That is, $x_\kappa - r$ and $x_\kappa + r$ are two non-trivial factors of N_κ.

Probability Analysis: S is successful if

1. A outputs a valid forged signature;
2. There is no abortion or failure in any oracle simulation; and
3. All guesses are correct.

Suppose A outputs a valid forged signature with probability at least ϵ.

S fails if Step 3 in the signing oracle simulation causes inconsistency in H_1. It happens with probability at most q_h/N_{min} where N_{min} is the smallest N_i in L. Hence, the simulation is successful q_s times with probability at least

$$\left(1 - \frac{q_h}{N_{min}}\right)^{q_s} \geq 1 - \frac{q_h q_s}{N_{min}}.$$

For H_i random oracle, with probability at least $1 - 1/N_{min}$, there exist queries $Q_j = (i + 1, L, m, r_i)$ for all $i = 1, \ldots, n$ due to the ideal randomness of hash function.

At the beginning of the simulation, B selects a pair of index (u, v). With probability $2/q_h(q_h + 1)$, the guess is correct. B needs to guess the index of the user corresponding to the (u, v) gap. B is correct if $\pi = \kappa$. This happens with probability $1/n$. Finally, with probability $1/2$, $x \neq r$ for the square root of R.

Combining all cases, the overall successful probability of B is at least

$$\frac{\left(1 - \frac{q_h q_s}{N_{min}}\right)\left(1 - \frac{1}{N_{min}}\right)\epsilon}{q_h(q_h + 1)n}$$

The running time of S is almost the same as τ as S runs A only once and the simulation cost for the signing oracle and the random oracles are assumed to be sufficiently smaller than τ. This contradicts the assumption that the (ϵ', τ', k)-Factorization assumption holds where

$$\epsilon' \leq \frac{\left(1 - \frac{q_h q_s}{N_{min}}\right)\left(1 - \frac{1}{N_{min}}\right)\epsilon}{q_h(q_h + 1)n}, \qquad \tau' = \tau$$

This completes our proof.   □

4   Efficiency Analysis

4.1   Comparison of Existing Ring Signatures

The following table (Table 1) summarizes the time complexities of existing ring signatures. We breakdown the time complexity of the protocol into the number of exponentiations (EXP) and pairings (PAIR) (the other operation such as hashing or multiplication is relatively small when compared to exponentiation and pairing)[1]. The running time of a pairing operation is about 2 to 3 times of an exponentiation. Let n be the size of the ring. We split the analysis into signing and verification. Note that no scheme in the comparison requires any pairing opeartions in the signing stage.

Table 1. Time complexities of existing ring signatures.

Scheme	# of EXP (sign)	# of EXP (verify)	# of PAIR (verify)
Rivest-Shamir-Tauman [38]	n	n	0
Abe-Ohkubo-Suzuki [1]	n	n	0
Dodis-Kiayias-Nicolosi-Shoup [18]	14	14	0
Chow-Wei-Liu-Yuen [13]	n	n	0
Shacham-Waters [39]	$4n + 3$	0	$2n + 3$
Chandran-Groth-Sahai [11]	$5 + 6\sqrt{n} + \frac{n+1}{3}$	3	$6 + 6\sqrt{n}$
Liu-Au-Susilo-Zhou [23]	2	n	0
Our Scheme	0	0	0

4.2   Running Time

We also implement our scheme to analyze the running time. Details are as follows:

- Equipment: Thinkpad x201s, Intel(R) Core™ I7 processor I7-640LM (2.13 GHz) with dual-core, 2.8 GB RAM running on 32 bits ubuntu 12.04
- Key length: 1024 bits

---

[1] Note that our scheme requires $n - 1$ square operations and 1 square root operation in the signing stage and n square operations in the verification stage. But since the running time of square and square root is far less than EXP and PAIR, we do not include these two operations in the comparison table.

- Number of running times: average by 80,000,000 times
- Library used: openSSL linux
- Running time: It takes 0.000568101266 ms for an additional operation over modulus (1024 bits), 0.003478101266 ms for a square operation over modulus (1024 bits), 12.877974683544 ms for an exponentiation operation over modulus (1024 bits). Suppose there are n users included in the signature. Our scheme takes around $(0.0040462 \times n)$ ms for signing and verification.

5   Conclusion

In this paper, we have proposed a lightweight anonymous authentication protocol, the essential of which is actually a lightweight ring signature scheme. It is lightweight in the sense that it does not contain any exponentiation or pairing in both prover and verifier sides. Instead, it only requires a few hashing and modulus square operations. We believe it is particular suitable for lightweight devices such as sensors and RFID and those applications that require authentication and privacy simultaneously. In the future, we may incorporate the technique from lattices [21] to further improve the efficiency while keeping all desired features.

Acknowledgement. The authors would like to thank anonymous reviewers for their helpful comments. This work is supported by National Natural Science Foundation of China (61472083, U1405255, 61402110), Fok Ying Tung Education Foundation (141065), Fujian Normal University Innovative Research Team (IRTL1207), the State Key Laboratory of Cryptology Research Fund (China), China 111 Project (No. B08038), Doctoral Fund of Ministry of Education of China (No. 20130203110004), Program for New Century Excellent Talents in University (No. NCET-13-0946), the Fundamental Research Funds for the Central Universities (Nos. BDY151402 and JB142001-14)

References

1. Abe, M., Ohkubo, M., Suzuki, K.: 1-out-of-n signatures from a variety of keys. In: Zheng, Y. (ed.) ASIACRYPT 2002. LNCS, vol. 2501, pp. 415–432. Springer, Heidelberg (2002)
2. Au, M.H., Liu, J.K., Susilo, W., Yuen, T.H.: Constant-size ID-based linkable and revocable-iff-linked ring signature. In: Barua, R., Lange, T. (eds.) INDOCRYPT 2006. LNCS, vol. 4329, pp. 364–378. Springer, Heidelberg (2006)
3. Au, M.H., Liu, J.K., Susilo, W., Yuen, T.H.: Certificate based (linkable) ring signature. In: Dawson, E., Wong, D.S. (eds.) ISPEC 2007. LNCS, vol. 4464, pp. 79–92. Springer, Heidelberg (2007)
4. Au, M.H., Liu, J.K., Susilo, W., Yuen, T.H.: Secure ID-based linkable and revocable-iff-linked ring signature with constant-size construction. Theor. Comput. Sci. **469**, 1–14 (2013)
5. Au, M.H., Liu, J.K., Susilo, W., Zhou, J.: Realizing fully secure unrestricted id-based ring signature in the standard model based on HIBE. IEEE Trans. Inf. Forensics Secur. **8**(12), 1909–1922 (2013)

6. Au, M.H., Liu, J.K., Yuen, T.H., Wong, D.S.: ID-based ring signature scheme secure in the standard model. In: Yoshiura, H., Sakurai, K., Rannenberg, K., Murayama, Y., Kawamura, S. (eds.) IWSEC 2006. LNCS, vol. 4266, pp. 1–16. Springer, Heidelberg (2006)

7. Bellare, M., Micciancio, D., Warinschi, B.: Foundations of group signatures: formal definitions, simplified requirements, and a construction based on general assumptions. In: Biham, E. (ed.) EUROCRYPT 2003. LNCS, vol. 2656, pp. 614–629. Springer, Heidelberg (2003)

8. Boneh, D., Gentry, C., Lynn, B., Shacham, H.: Aggregate and verifiably encrypted signatures from bilinear maps. In: Biham, E. (ed.) EUROCRYPT 2003. LNCS, vol. 2656, pp. 416–432. springer, heidelberg (2003)

9. Bresson, E., Stern, J., Szydlo, M.: Threshold ring signatures and applications to Ad-hoc groups. In: Yung, M. (ed.) CRYPTO 2002. LNCS, vol. 2442, pp. 465–480. Springer, Heidelberg (2002)

10. Camenisch, J.L., Stadler, M.A.: Efficient group signature schemes for large groups. In: Kaliski Jr., B.S. (ed.) CRYPTO 1997. LNCS, vol. 1294, pp. 410–424. Springer, Heidelberg (1997)

11. Chandran, N., Groth, J., Sahai, A.: Ring signatures of sub-linear size without random oracles. In: Arge, L., Cachin, C., Jurdziński, T., Tarlecki, A. (eds.) ICALP 2007. LNCS, vol. 4596, pp. 423–434. Springer, Heidelberg (2007)

12. Chaum, D., van Heyst, E.: Group signatures. In: Davies, D.W. (ed.) EUROCRYPT 1991. LNCS, vol. 547, pp. 257–265. Springer, Heidelberg (1991)

13. Chow, S.S., Liu, J.K., Wei, V.K., Yuen, T.H.: Ring signatures without random oracles. In: ASIACCS 2006, pp. 297–302. ACM Press (2006)

14. Chow, S.S.M., Liu, J.K., Wong, D.S.: Robust receipt-free election system with ballot secrecy and verifiability. In: Proceedings of the Network and Distributed System Security Symposium, NDSS 2008, San Diego, California, USA, 10th February - 13th February 2008. The Internet Society (2008)

15. Chow, S.S.M., Liu, J.K., Zhou, J.: Identity-based online/offline key encapsulation and encryption. In: Proceedings of the 6th ACM Symposium on Information, Computer and Communications Security, ASIACCS 2011, pp. 52–60. Hong Kong, China, 22–24 March 2011

16. Chow, S.S.M., Yiu, S.-M., Hui, L.C.K.: Efficient identity based ring signature. In: Ioannidis, J., Keromytis, A.D., Yung, M. (eds.) ACNS 2005. LNCS, vol. 3531, pp. 499–512. Springer, Heidelberg (2005)

17. Chu, C., Liu, J.K., Zhou, J., Bao, F., Deng, R.H.: Practical id-based encryption for wireless sensor network. In: Proceedings of the 5th ACM Symposium on Information, Computer and Communications Security, ASIACCS 2010, Beijing, China, April 13–16, 2010, pp. 337–340. ACM (2010)

18. Dodis, Y., Kiayias, A., Nicolosi, A., Shoup, V.: Anonymous identification in *Ad Hoc* groups. In: Cachin, C., Camenisch, J.L. (eds.) EUROCRYPT 2004. LNCS, vol. 3027, pp. 609–626. Springer, Heidelberg (2004)

19. Huang, X., Liu, J.K., Tang, S., Xiang, Y., Liang, K., Xu, L., Zhou, J.: Cost-effective authentic and anonymous data sharing with forward security. IEEE Trans. Comput. **64**(4), 971–983 (2015)

20. Laguillaumie, F., Vergnaud, D.: Multi-designated verifiers signatures. In: López, J., Qing, S., Okamoto, E. (eds.) ICICS 2004. LNCS, vol. 3269, pp. 495–507. Springer, Heidelberg (2004)

21. Ling, S., Nguyen, K., Wang, H.: Group signatures from lattices: simpler, tighter, shorter, ring-based. In: Katz, J. (ed.) PKC 2015. LNCS, vol. 9020, pp. 427–449. Springer, Heidelberg (2015)

22. Liu, D.Y.W., Liu, J.K., Mu, Y., Susilo, W., Wong, D.S.: Revocable ring signature. J. Comput. Sci. Technol. **22**(6), 785–794 (2007)
23. Liu, J.K., Au, M.H., Susilo, W., Zhou, J.: Online/offline ring signature scheme. In: Qing, S., Mitchell, C.J., Wang, G. (eds.) ICICS 2009. LNCS, vol. 5927, pp. 80–90. Springer, Heidelberg (2009)
24. Liu, J.K., Au, M.H., Susilo, W., Zhou, J.: Linkable ring signature with unconditional anonymity. IEEE Trans. Knowl. Data Eng. **26**(1), 157–165 (2014)
25. Liu, J.K., Baek, J., Zhou, J.: Online/offline identity-based signcryption revisited. In: Lai, X., Yung, M., Lin, D. (eds.) Inscrypt 2010. LNCS, vol. 6584, pp. 36–51. Springer, Heidelberg (2011)
26. Liu, J.K., Baek, J., Zhou, J., Yang, Y., Wong, J.W.: Efficient online/offline identity-based signature for wireless sensor network. Int. J. Inf. Sec. **9**(4), 287–296 (2010)
27. Liu, J.K., Susilo, W., Wong, D.S.: Ring signature with designated linkability. In: Yoshiura, H., Sakurai, K., Rannenberg, K., Murayama, Y., Kawamura, S. (eds.) IWSEC 2006. LNCS, vol. 4266, pp. 104–119. Springer, Heidelberg (2006)
28. Liu, J.K., Tsang, P.P., Wong, D.S.: Efficient verifiable ring encryption for Ad Hoc groups. In: Molva, R., Tsudik, G., Westhoff, D. (eds.) ESAS 2005. LNCS, vol. 3813, pp. 1–13. Springer, Heidelberg (2005)
29. Liu, J.K., Wei, V.K., Wong, D.S.: A separable threshold ring signature scheme. In: Lim, J.-I., Lee, D.-H. (eds.) ICISC 2003. LNCS, vol. 2971. Springer, Heidelberg (2004)
30. Liu, J.K., Wei, V.K., Wong, D.S.: Linkable spontaneous anonymous group signature for Ad Hoc groups. In: Wang, H., Pieprzyk, J., Varadharajan, V. (eds.) ACISP 2004. LNCS, vol. 3108, pp. 325–335. Springer, Heidelberg (2004)
31. Liu, J.K., Wong, D.S.: On the security models of (threshold) ring signature schemes. In: Park, C., Chee, S. (eds.) ICISC 2004. LNCS, vol. 3506, pp. 204–217. Springer, Heidelberg (2005)
32. Liu, J.K., Wong, D.S.: Linkable ring signatures: security models and new schemes. In: Gervasi, O., Gavrilova, M.L., Kumar, V., Laganá, A., Lee, H.P., Mun, Y., Taniar, D., Tan, C.J.K. (eds.) ICCSA 2005. LNCS, vol. 3481, pp. 614–623. Springer, Heidelberg (2005)
33. Liu, J.K., Wong, D.S.: Enhanced security models and a generic construction approach for linkable ring signature. Int. J. Found. Comput. Sci. **17**(6), 1403–1422 (2006)
34. Liu, J.K., Wong, D.S.: A more efficient instantiation of witness-indistinguishable signature. I. J. Network Secur. **5**(2), 199–204 (2007)
35. Liu, J.K., Wong, D.S.: Solutions to key exposure problem in ring signature. I. J. Network Secur. **6**(2), 170–180 (2008)
36. Liu, J.K., Yuen, T.H., Zhou, J.: Forward secure ring signature without random oracles. In: Qing, S., Susilo, W., Wang, G., Liu, D. (eds.) ICICS 2011. LNCS, vol. 7043, pp. 1–14. Springer, Heidelberg (2011)
37. Liu, J.K., Zhou, J.: An efficient identity-based online/offline encryption scheme. In: Abdalla, M., Pointcheval, D., Fouque, P.-A., Vergnaud, D. (eds.) ACNS 2009. LNCS, vol. 5536, pp. 156–167. Springer, Heidelberg (2009)
38. Rivest, R.L., Shamir, A., Tauman, Y.: How to leak a secret. In: Boyd, C. (ed.) ASIACRYPT 2001. LNCS, vol. 2248, pp. 552–565. Springer, Heidelberg (2001)
39. Shacham, H., Waters, B.: Efficient ring signatures without random oracles. In: Okamoto, T., Wang, X. (eds.) PKC 2007. LNCS, vol. 4450, pp. 166–180. Springer, Heidelberg (2007)
40. Susilo, W., Mu, Y.: Non-interactive deniable ring authentication. In: Lim, J.-I., Lee, D.-H. (eds.) ICISC 2003. LNCS, vol. 2971. Springer, Heidelberg (2004)

41. Susilo, W., Mu, Y., Zhang, F.: Perfect concurrent signature schemes. In: López, J., Qing, S., Okamoto, E. (eds.) ICICS 2004. LNCS, vol. 3269, pp. 14–26. Springer, Heidelberg (2004)
42. Tsang, P.P., Au, M.H., Liu, J.K., Susilo, W., Wong, D.S.: A suite of non-pairing ID-based threshold ring signature schemes with different levels of anonymity (extended abstract). In: Heng, S.-H., Kurosawa, K. (eds.) ProvSec 2010. LNCS, vol. 6402, pp. 166–183. Springer, Heidelberg (2010)
43. Tsang, P.P., Wei, V.K., Chan, T.K., Au, M.H., Liu, J.K., Wong, D.S.: Separable linkable threshold ring signatures. In: Canteaut, A., Viswanathan, K. (eds.) INDOCRYPT 2004. LNCS, vol. 3348, pp. 384–398. Springer, Heidelberg (2004)
44. Wong, D.S., Fung, K., Liu, J.K., Wei, V.K.: On the RS-code construction of ring signature schemes and a threshold setting of RST. In: Qing, S., Gollmann, D., Zhou, J. (eds.) ICICS 2003. LNCS, vol. 2836, pp. 34–46. Springer, Heidelberg (2003)
45. Yuen, T.H., Liu, J.K., Au, M.H., Susilo, W., Zhou, J.: Threshold ring signature without random oracles. In: Proceedings of the 6th ACM Symposium on Information, Computer and Communications Security, ASIACCS 2011, Hong Kong, China, March 22–24, 2011, pp. 261–267. ACM (2011)
46. Yuen, T.H., Liu, J.K., Au, M.H., Susilo, W., Zhou, J.: Efficient linkable and/or threshold ring signature without random oracles. Comput. J. 56(4), 407–421 (2013)
47. Zhang, F., Kim, K.: ID-based blind signature and ring signature from pairings. In: Zheng, Y. (ed.) ASIACRYPT 2002. LNCS, vol. 2501, pp. 533–547. Springer, Heidelberg (2002)

Reset-Secure Identity-Based Identification Schemes Without Pairings

Ji-Jian Chin[1]($\boxtimes$), Hiroaki Anada[2], and Syh-Yuan Tan[3]

[1] Faculty of Engineering, Multimedia University, 63000
Cyberjaya, Selangor, Malaysia
jjchin@mmu.edu.my

[2] Institute of System, Information Technologies and Nanotechnologies (ISIT),
Fukuoka SRP Center Building 7F, 2-1-22, Momochihama, Sawara-ku,
Fukuoka 814-0001, Japan

[3] Faculty of Information Science and Technology, Multimedia University, Jalan Ayer
Keroh Lama, 75450 Bukit Beruang, Melaka, Malaysia

Abstract. Identity-based identification (IBI) schemes are generally insecure against reset attacks since they are commonly constructed from
three-move Σ-protocols similar those of traditional public-key identification schemes. In 2009, Thorncharoensri et al. proposed the first IBI
scheme secure against impersonators who are able to perform concurrent-
reset attacks and is the only scheme that satisfies this notion of security in
literature to date. However, their scheme suffers from correctness issues
and is also constructed using pairings, which are known to be costly
operationally. In this paper, we utilize one of Bellare et al's methods
to reinforce the Schnorr-IBI scheme (and also its more-secure variant:
the Twin-Schnorr-IBI scheme) against reset attacks, therefore achieving
reset-secure IBI schemes without pairings.

Keywords: Identity-based · Identification · Reset-attack · Concurrent
attackers · Commitment schemes

1 Introduction

Identification schemes allow provers to authenticate themselves to a verifier without revealing anything about the secret being shared, other than the fact that
he/she knows the secret. The method lies in the three-move Σ-protocol that the
prover and verifier engage in to conduct this exchange, where the Σ-protocol
may be a zero-knowledge protocol, a witness-indistinguishability protocol, or
some other proof-of-knowledge protocol. In traditional public key identification
schemes, certificates were used to explicitly certify a user is the rightful owner
of his/her public key. As the number of users grow, so does the operational cost
of maintaining these certificates.

Shamir subsequently proposed the notion of identity-based cryptography,
where users can implicitly certify their private key using a public identity-
string [14]. Boneh and Franklin then proposed the first identity-based encryp-

© Springer International Publishing Switzerland 2015
M.-H. Au and A. Miyaji (Eds.): ProvSec 2015, LNCS 9451, pp. 227–246, 2015.
DOI: 10.1007/978-3-319-26059-4_13

tion scheme [3], whereas Kurosawa and Heng [9] and Bellare et al. [4] rigorously defined the first identity-based identification (IBI) schemes.

However, it is widely known that identification schemes that run three-move proof-of-knowledge protocols are generally insecure against reset attacks, where the attacker can reset a prover's state to any point in the protocol. Since IBI schemes share the same three-move proof-of-knowledge protocols as traditional public key identification schemes, this weakness is inherent in them as well.

1.1   Motivations

Reset attacks are the most powerful attack for IBI schemes and can be a very practical one as well. One scenario where reset attacks can happen, as mentioned by [2], is if the adversary captures a prover device, such as by stealing a smart card or smart phone. Even if the device was constructed securely, the adversary can still mount reset attacks by manipulating the power source of the device such as removing and restoring battery to reset it to an earlier state.

IBI schemes provide a solid authentication mechanism for facilitating access control, now even more so with the rise of usage of mobile devices with various communication technology such as QR codes, NFC and Bluetooth. There is great potential for IBI schemes to be implemented as a secure way to authenticate oneself using a smartphone. However, with IBI schemes known to be insecure against reset attacks, the inherent danger is if one loses that smartphone, the adversary will be able to recover the user secret key easily by resetting a run mid-protocol to recover the user secret key, even if the user secret key is password-encrypted. This is because the IBI scheme itself is not secure against reset attacks to begin with.

To further show how simple a reset attack can be conducted, we illustrate the reset attack with an example of the conventional Schnorr standard identification protocol. The protocol involves the exchange $\langle Y = g^y, c, z = y + cs \rangle$, where $y, c \xleftarrow{\$} \mathbb{Z}_p$, $g \in G$ is a generator for group G and s be the user secret key. In this protocol, Y is the prover's commitment, c is the verifier's challenge while z is the prover's response. A reset attacker can interact with a prover as a cheating verifier, obtaining $\langle Y = g^y, c_1, z_1 = y + c_1 s \rangle$ from the first run. It then resets the prover to the commitment step of the protocol where the prover had just sent Y and sends a new challenge c_2, to which it will receive a new response of $z_2 = y + c_2 s$. From here the adversary can easily extract the user secret key $s = \frac{(z_1 - z_2)}{c_1 - c_2}$. The same attack works for any Σ-protocol satisfying the soundness property and is applicable to identity-based identification schemes as well.

While work has been done to secure standard identification schemes against reset attacks by [2], little has been done to address the same issue for IBI schemes. Hence, the motivation of our research is to secure IBI schemes against such attacks. Additionally, since most IBI schemes in literature are already using Σ-protocols, our goal is to seek a suitable reinforcement method that can be applied to existing schemes to reinforce them against reset attacks, rather than to devise new schemes.

1.2   Related Work

In 2001, Bellare et al. proposed several methods to secure identification schemes against reset attacks [2]: constructions using stateless digital signatures, constructions using chosen-ciphertext secure encryption schemes, constructions using trapdoor commitment schemes and pseudorandom functions (PRFs), and lastly constructions using zero-knowledge proof of membership. It is worth mentioning that the techniques of deploying stateless digital signatures and secure encryption schemes reduce the number of steps of the identification protocol from three to two, while the zero-knowledge proof of membership technique (or resettable zero-knowledge technique) increases the number of rounds of the protocol, requires both prover and verifier to have public keys and does not work with witness indistinguishable protocols. Therefore only the trapdoor commitment scheme and PRF technique seems suitable to be applied generically to reinforce existing three-move IBI schemes in literature to be secure against reset-attack. We utilize this technique for our work as a concrete instantiation.

In 2009, Thorncharoensri et al. [15] proposed the first IBI scheme secure against reset attacks in the concurrent setting. Their proposed scheme did not follow any of Bellare et al's techniques and as far as we can tell, is an ad-hoc construction. Their scheme was constructed using bilinear pairings and security against concurrent reset attacks was proven under the 2-Strong Diffie-Hellman (SDH) assumption. However, their scheme suffers from several drawbacks. First of all, there are correctness issues with the verification equation, in that the LHS and RHS of the equation are not equivalent. Secondly, the 2-SDH assumption is not a well-studied one. It is unknown why the authors did not utilize the q-SDH assumption as Kurosawa and Heng's construction [10]. Lastly, the user secret keys consist of many components, and the size of the commitment message is also large in proportion. Adding the factor of keysize to the pairing operations that their scheme requires and the resulting scheme is considerably costly to operate.

1.3   Contributions

In this paper, we propose two pairing-free IBI schemes that are provable-secure against reset attacks as alternatives to Thorncharoensri et al.'s pairing-based one. For our concrete construction, we reinforce the Schnorr-IBI scheme [13] proposed by [8] to be secure against reset attacks. This is done by extending Bellare et al's trapdoor commitment scheme and PRF technique to the identity-based setting. We label our proposed scheme as Schnorr-RS-IBI.

Our reduction technique for providing provable security is first to imply that the Schnorr-IBI scheme is implicitly secure against active and concurrent attacks. The original author only provided the proof of security for Schnorr-IBI for security against passive attacks. We contribute by showing that if the reinforced Schnorr-RS-IBI is secure against reset attacks, the Schnorr-IBI is also secure against active and concurrent attacks, assuming the one-more discrete logarithm problem is intractable, using the same basic strategy in the reduction.

Both in construction and in proof of security, we offer some tweaks between efficiency and security, by allowing the option of selecting between hash function or pseudorandom function application. We provide the advantages and drawback of applying both tools in different scenarios and how their analysis affect the tightness of the security proof.

Lastly we show a second scheme which is obtained from reinforcing the Twin-Schnorr-IBI scheme from [7]. For this variant of Schnorr-IBI with two keys, its active and concurrent security is reduced directly from the discrete logarithm assumption. Therefore, in combining with the security bound from Pedersen's commitment which is also based on the discrete logarithm assumption, we obtain a tighter and more concrete bound for the proof of security. The strategy of this proof is also more straightforward. However, it comes at the cost of a slight increase in operational costs.

All proofs are done in the random oracle model [6].

We organize the rest of the paper as follows: In Sect. 2 we provide the notations and description of tools that we will use. In Sect. 3 we propose the pairing-free Schnorr IBI scheme secure against reset attacks and prove it secure in Sect. 4. In Sect. 5 we propose the stronger Twin-Schnorr IBI scheme secure against reset attacks and prove it secure in Sect. 6. We provide an efficiency analysis for both schemes in Sect. 7 and conclude with a brief description of how to extend to concurrent-reset-2 security in Sect. 8.

2   Preliminaries

Let $\{0,1\}^*$ denote the set of all bit strings while $\{0,1\}^n$ denotes the set of bit strings of length n. Let $x \xleftarrow{\$} S$ denote a randomly and uniformly chosen element x from a finite set S. If x_1 and x_2 are strings then let $x_1 \| x_2$ denote the concatenation of these strings. Let N denote the set of positive integers, and let $k \in N$ be the security parameter. Let $a = A(\cdot, \cdot \ldots; R)$ denote the randomized algorithm A outputting a upon arbitrary inputs and random coins R. At times $a = A(\cdot, \cdot \ldots)$ will be used as shorthand if the random coins were selected beforehand. Also, denote $\Pr[E] = \varepsilon$ denote the probability of event Z is ε, where $0 \leq \varepsilon \leq 1$.

2.1   Discrete Logarithm Assumption

The discrete logarithm problem (DLP) is given a group G of order p, where p is a large prime number, a generator g and a number $X = g^x$ where x is an integer, find x.

The discrete logarithm assumption states that no polynomial-time algorithm can solve the problem described above with advantage more than $\mathbf{Adv}_{G,q}^{DL}(k)$ where k is the security parameter.

2.2   One-More Discrete Logarithm Assumption

The one-more discrete logarithm problem (OMDLP) is described as an interactive game played by a challenger given two oracles $CHALL$ and $DLOG$.

The challenger obtains random numbers from $h \xleftarrow{\$} CHALL(1^k)$ and receives the discrete logarithm $x_h = DLOG(h)$ where $g^{x_h} = h$ when querying $DLOG$. To win the game, the challenger needs to query $CHALL$ significantly more than $DLOG$. In other words, the challenger needs to solve one instance of the discrete logarithm problem on its own.

The one-more discrete logarithm assumption states that no polynomial-time algorithm can win the game described above advantage more than $\mathbf{Adv}_{G,q,q_{DL}}^{OMDL}(k)$ where k is the security parameter.

2.3   (Reset-Secure) Identity-Based Identification Schemes

An IBI scheme consists of the following PPT algorithms: (**SETUP, EXTRACT, PROVE, VERIFY**).

1. **SETUP**: The Trusted Authority (TA) runs **SETUP** with the security parameter. It sets up and publishes the system parameters mpk but stores the master secret key msk in private.
2. **Extract**: When a user wishes to register on the system, it sends its identity-string ID to the TA, who will calculate and return a user secret key usk.
3. **Identification Protocol**: Since we are restricting our work to three-move IBI schemes, the identification protocol that is run between the Prover and Verifier consists of a three-move proof-of-knowledge Σ-protocol. However, for our reset-secure construction, we modify the above definition of the identification protocol to a four-move one. We define the challenge commit, commitment, challenge reveal and response moves of the extended Σ-protocol by $\Sigma_1, \Sigma_2, \Sigma_3$ and Σ_4 respectively. Lastly the verification check is denoted by Σ_{CHK}.
   (a) Σ_1:**CHA-COMMIT**: The verifier draws a random challenge CHA and commits to a challenge with a commitment $CHA - CMT$ using the trapdoor commitment scheme.
   (b) Σ_2:**COMMIT**: The prover follows with a identification commitment $ID - CMT$ to the verifier.
   (c) Σ_3:**CHA-REVEAL**: The verifier reveals $CHA - CMT$ by sending CHA to prover.
   (d) Σ_4:**RESPONSE**: The prover checks the committed value CHA and continues the protocol if true. The prover calculates the response to the verifier RSP based on the system parameters mpk, its user secret key usk, the commitment CMT, the verifier's challenge CHA and identity-string ID.
   The verifier accepts or rejects the prover's authentication attempt based on the result of the verification equation Σ_{CHK} that it calculates with the inputs of $\langle \text{mpk}, ID, CMT, CHA, RSP \rangle$.

The security of the IBI scheme is described by the following game played between impersonator I trying to impersonate a selected target identity of its choice and the challenger M. In the learning phase, M creates the system environment and generates and passes the public values mpk to I. I is then allowed to make the Extract Queries for specific identities, to which M will return the corresponding usk.

In addition, I is able to make the following Identification queries depending on its classification:

1. passive attacker: I is only allowed to receive fixed transcripts on conversations by ID.
2. active attacker: I interacts with M as the cheating verifier while M plays the prover to simulate a valid conversation session for I. If I is a concurrent attacker, it can run multiple sessions with multiple prover instances concurrently.
3. reset attacker: in addition to interacting with multiple sessions and multiple provers simulated by M, I can reset a particular run of the protocol to any state it wishes.

Once the learning phase ends, I begins the challenge phase. I outputs an identity on which it wishes to be challenged on. We follow the definition of concurrent-reset-1 (CR1) from [2], and disallow any further interaction with the oracles during the challenge phase. In contrast, concurrent-reset-2 (CR2) attackers allow I to continue oracle queries during the challenge phase. Securing against a CR2 adversary will require session identifiers as recommended by [2].

I runs the identification protocol now as the cheating prover with M as the verifier. I wins the game if it manages to convince M to accept with non-negligible probability.

The advantage of I attacking the reset-secure IBI scheme is bounded by $(\mathbf{Adv}^{CR1}_{RS-IBI,I}(k), q_e, q_I)$: where $\mathbf{Adv}^{CR1}_{RS-IBI,I}(k)$ is the advantage of I in the game above where q_e and q_I are the maximum number of Extract and Identification queries allowed respectively.

2.4   The Pedersen Trapdoor Commitment Scheme

A trapdoor commitment scheme consists of the following PPT algorithms: (**KEYGEN, COMMIT, REVEAL, EQUIVOCATION**).

1. **Keygen**: involves the setting up of the system parameters. This can be done with the help of a trusted third party or by the receiver.
2. **Commit**: the sender sends the commitment of a value to the receiver.
3. **Reveal**: the sender reveals the message that corresponds to the commitment that was sent earlier to the receiver.
4. **Equivocation**: with the trapdoor to the commitment scheme, the sender is able to change the message that was committed to another message that corresponds to the same commitment.

Trapdoor commitment schemes need to fulfill the following security properties:

1. hiding: any observing parties may not learn any information about the value being committed.

2. binding: a sender can only reveal the value that was committed to and not another value.
3. trapdoor: a sender can only break the binding property with the possession of the trapdoor.

We utilize the Pedersen Commitment (PC) Scheme [12] in our construction of reset-secure IBI schemes. The following definition utilizes the discrete logarithm group as defined previously.

1. **Keygen**: choose a generator $g \xleftarrow{\$} G$ and $a \xleftarrow{\$} \mathbb{Z}_q$ and publishes $h = g^a$.
2. **Commit**: to commit to a value m, the sender chooses $r \xleftarrow{\$} \mathbb{Z}_q$ and sends $c = g^m h^r$ to the receiver.
3. **Reveal**: the sender sends m, r to the receiver and the receiver accepts if $c = g^m h^r$.
4. **Equivocation**: if the sender possesses a it can change m to m' while retaining the commitment c by computing $r' = r + (m - m')a^{-1}$. Here (m', r') is also a valid opening to c.

The binding property of the Pedersen Commitment scheme is required to a provide security guarantee for the reset-secure IBI scheme. The advantage of an adversary A trying to break the binding property of the Pedersen commitment scheme, i.e. coming up with $(m, r), (m', r')$ that correspond to the same c, is bounded as $\mathbf{Adv}_{A,q_c}^{PC}(k)$, where A is allowed to make a maximum of q_c commitment/reveal queries.

2.5   Pseudorandom Functions

A pseudorandom function is an efficiently computable function that maps a domain to a range, but is indistinguishable from a truly random function. The security of a pseudorandom function is given by $\mathbf{Adv}_{D,q_{PRF}}^{PRF}(k)$, where a distinguisher D, given access to function drawn either from a family of PRF or from the set of truly random functions and is allowed to query q_{PRF} evaluations on it, cannot distinguish the function with probability more than $1/2$.

2.6   Collision-Resistant Hash Function

A collission-resistant hash function is a hash function where finding a, b where $H(a) = H(b)$ is difficult. Specifically, the probability of an attacker A finding such a collision is bounded by $\mathbf{Adv}_{A,q_H}^{Collision}(k)$ where q_H is the maximum number of evaluations possible before finding such a collision.

3   Construction of the Schnorr-RS-IBI Scheme

We construct the Schnorr-RS-IBI scheme as follows:

1. **Setup**: takes in the security parameter 1^k and generates the group G of order q. It picks a random generators $g \xleftarrow{\$} G$ and a random integer $x, a \xleftarrow{\$} \mathbb{Z}_q$. It sets $X = g^{-x}$ and $h = g^a$. It also chooses a hash function $H_1 : \{0,1\}^* \times G \times G \to \mathbb{Z}_q$. We provide two options for the second random function: either choose $H_2 : \{0,1\}^{pcl} \times G \to \mathbb{Z}_q$ for better efficiency, or $PRF : \{0,1\}^{pcl} \times G \to \mathbb{Z}_q$ for better security, where pcl denotes the length of the prover's random coins in bits. The master public key is $\mathsf{mpk} = \langle G, q, g, X, h, H_1, H_2/PRF \rangle$ while the master private key is $\mathsf{msk} = \langle x \rangle$.

2. **Extract**: takes in the user identity string ID, mpk and the msk. It picks a random integer $\tau \xleftarrow{\$} \mathbb{Z}_q$ and sets $V = g^\tau$. It then sets $s = \tau + x\alpha$ where $\alpha = H(\mathsf{ID}\|V\|X)$. The user private key is $\mathsf{usk} = (s, \alpha)$.

3. **Identification Protocol**: **Prover** takes in $\mathsf{mpk}, \mathsf{ID}$ and usk while **Verifier** takes in the mpk and ID. They run the identification protocol as follows:

    (a) Σ_1:The **Verifier** begins by picking a random integers $m, r \xleftarrow{\$} \mathbb{Z}_q$ and calculates $c = g^m h^r$.

    (b) Σ_2:The **Prover** sets $y = H_2(R_p\|c)$ or $y = PRF_{R_p}(c)$ depending on the choice of hash or pseudorandom function selected during **Setup** and sets $Y = g^y$. **Prover** also sets $V = g^s X^\alpha$ and sends Y, V to the **Verifier**.

    (c) Σ_3:The **Verifier** reveals m, r and sends the challenge to **Prover**.

    (d) Σ_4:The **Prover** calculates $c' = g^m h^r$ and checks if $c' = c$. If true it responds by setting $z = y + ms$ and sends z to the Verifier as its response. Otherwise it aborts.

    Σ_{CHK}: The verifier evaluates $\alpha' = H_1(\mathsf{ID}\|V\|X)$, checks if $g^z = Y(\frac{V}{X^{\alpha'}})^m$ and accepts if true.

To prove correctness:

$$Y(\frac{V}{X^\alpha})^m = (g^y)(\frac{g^s X^\alpha}{(X)^\alpha})^m = g^{y+ms} = g^z$$

4   Security Analysis for Schnorr-RS-IBI

Theorem 1. *The Schnorr-RS-IBI is* $(\mathbf{Adv}^{CR1}_{Schnorr-RS-IBI,I,q_e,q_I}(k))$- *secure against impersonation under concurrent-reset attacks if the OMDL problem is* $(\mathbf{Adv}^{OMDL}_{G,q,q_{DL}}(k))$- *hard, where*

$$\mathbf{Adv}^{CR1}_{S-RS-IBI,I,q_e,q_I}(k) \leq \sqrt{\frac{\mathbf{Adv}^{OMDL}_{M,G,q,q_{DL}}(k)e(1+q_e)}{(1 - \mathbf{Adv}^{PC}_{I,q_I}(k))}} + 1/q$$

and the Pedersen commitment scheme is $\mathbf{Adv}^{PC}_{I,q_I}(k)$-*secure, and* H_1 *and* H_2 *are modeled as random oracles.*

Proof. Assume that the Schnorr-RS-IBI scheme is not reset-secure, that is, a reset impersonator I exists that breaks the scheme with advantage $\mathbf{Adv}^{CR1}_{Schnorr-RS-IBI,I,q_e,q_I}(k)$. We then show an algorithm M that breaks the one-more discrete logarithm assumption with advantage $\mathbf{Adv}_{M,G,q,q_{DL}}^{OMDL}(k)$ by running I as a subroutine.

Learning Phase

M starts the simulation by querying $CHALL$ and obtains the initial challenge W_0. M then picks $x, a \overset{\$}{\leftarrow} \mathbb{Z}_q$ and keeps them as the master secret key msk. It calculates $X = g^{-x}$ and $h = g^a$ and sets up the two hash function $H_1 : \{0,1\}^* \times G \times G \to \mathbb{Z}_q$ and $H_2 : \{0,1\}^{pcl} \times G \to \mathbb{Z}_q$ as random oracles. It then passes mpk $= \langle G, q, g, X, h, H_1, H_2 \rangle$ to I.

HASH QUERY: M maintains a list of tuples $L_{H_1} = (\text{ID}, V, s, \alpha, coin_i)$ for H_1 queries. When a H_1 query is issued on an ID, M search in the list $L_{H_1} =< \text{ID}, V_i, s_i, \alpha, coin_i >$ and return α as the hash value. If no such record exists, M flips a $coin_i$ where $\Pr[coin_{=}0] = \sigma$.

1. If $coin_i = 0$, M creates a new record $< \text{ID}_i, V_i, s_i, \alpha_i, \perp, coin_i >$ where $s_i, \alpha_i \overset{\$}{\leftarrow} \mathbb{Z}_q$ and $V_i = g^{s_i} X^{\alpha_i}$.
2. If $coin_i = 1$, M creates a new record $< \text{ID}_i, V_i, \perp, \alpha_i, \beta_i, coin_i >$ where $\alpha_i, \beta_i \overset{\$}{\leftarrow} \mathbb{Z}_q$ and $V_i = W_0^{\beta_i}$.

For H_2 queries M keeps a record of $L_{H_2} = (\kappa, y_\kappa, ID_j, R_{ID_j}, c_\kappa, Y_\kappa)$. We elaborate H_2 queries in detail in the IDENTIFICATION query section.

EXTRACT QUERY: In phase 1, I is allowed to query the user secret keys for any user of its choice for up to q_e Extract queries. M runs the H_1 query on ID_i that is queried. With probability σ, M retrieves usk$_{\text{ID}_i} = \langle s_i, \alpha_i \rangle$ and returns it to I.

IDENTIFICATION QUERY: I is also allowed to make IDENTIFICATION queries, where I plays the cheating verifier while M has to simulate a prover instance on ID_j queried by I. I is limited to q_I such queries. For simplicity, we count a reset query as in the same category of IDENTIFICATION queries and increment the IDENTIFICATION query counter whenever I performs a reset action.

On receiving c_κ from I, M makes a H_2 query. M simulates $y_\kappa = H_2(R_{\text{ID}_j}||c_\kappa)$ by picking $y_\kappa \overset{\$}{\leftarrow} \mathbb{Z}_q$ and $R_{ID_j} \overset{\$}{\leftarrow} \{0,1\}^{pcl(k)}$, where $pcl(k)$ is the function length of the prover random coins. M then returns $Y_\kappa = g^{y_\kappa}$ to I for step Σ_2 and adds $< \kappa, y_\kappa, \text{ID}_j, R_{\text{ID}_j}, c_\kappa, Y_\kappa >$ to L_{H_2}. To distinguish between j which traces a particular identity's prover instance ID_j, we let κ denote the thread used for an instance of ID_j's protocol run, i.e. for ID_j, κ is used to track a particular conversation of $\langle c_\kappa, Y_\kappa, V, m_\kappa, r_\kappa, z_\kappa \rangle$ on the same R_{ID_j} random coins. Therefore $\kappa \le q_I$. Without loss of generality, we assume I will not send $c_\kappa, m_\kappa, r_\kappa$ to M such that $c_\kappa \ne g^{m_\kappa} h^{r_\kappa}$.

M checks ID_j on which it is queried on to see if $coin_j = 0$. If it is, M just retrieves $\langle s_j, \alpha_j \rangle$ and uses it to participate in the protocol with I.

Otherwise, if $coin_j = 1$, M retrieves ID_j's record from L_{H_1} and responds as follows:

1. Keep a counter ω for every $CHALL$ query.
2. Receive c_κ from I and changes state to Σ_2.

3. Query $CHALL$ for W_ω and set $Y_\kappa = W_\omega$. Enter $< \kappa, \perp, \mathsf{ID}_j, R_{\mathsf{ID}_j}, c_\kappa, Y_\kappa = W_\omega >$ to L_{H_2} and send Y_κ, V to I.
4. I reveals m_κ, r_κ in Σ_3.
5. M checks if $c_\kappa = g^{m_\kappa} h^{r_\kappa}$. If true, M queries $DLOG$ and sends $z_\kappa = DLOG(Y_\kappa(\frac{V_j}{X^{\alpha_j}})^{m_\kappa})$ to I.
6. M increases ω by 1. We stress that $(\omega + 1) \leq q_{DL} \leq \kappa \leq q_I = q_c = q_{H_2}$, where q_{DL} is the maximum number of queries to $DLOG$.

M will abort if it encounters a protocol run on prover instance ID_j in an ambiguous commitment case, i.e. I manages to send both $(m_\kappa, r_\kappa), (m'_\kappa, r'_\kappa)$ that correspond to the same c_κ. This means I has managed to break the binding property of the Pedersen commitment and is able to extract $\mathsf{usk}_{\mathsf{ID}_i}$ from the soundness of the original Schnorr-IBI protocol. The upper bound for this event happening is the advantage of breaking the binding property of the Pedersen Commitment scheme: $\mathbf{Adv}_{I,q_I}^{PC}(k)$.

Impersonation Phase

Once the learning phase ends and I begins the challenge phase, I outputs an identity ID^* which was not issued for $\mathsf{EXTRACT}$ queries and it wishes to be challenged on. M runs a H_1 query on ID^* if it has not yet done so, and checks the corresponding $coin$ for ID^*. If $coin = 0$, M aborts.

Since M holds a where $h = g^a$, it can use the equivocation property of the Pedersen commitment scheme to facilitate and ambiguous commitment case in order to retrieve 2 valid transcripts from I with the same commitment. M chooses $m_1, r_1 \overset{\$}{\leftarrow} \mathbb{Z}_q$ and generates $c^* = g^{m_1} h^{r_1}$ and sends c^* to I as Σ_1. I returns Y, V as Σ_2.

Continuing with the protocol, M now reveals m_1, r_1 to I in Σ_3. Since this is a valid reveal to c^*, I continues by sending z_1 as Σ_4. Once M ascertains the validity of z_1, M then resets the protocol to Σ_3 and reveals a separate m_2, r_2 that corresponds to c^*. This can be done by choosing $m_2 \overset{\$}{\leftarrow} \mathbb{Z}_q$ then setting $r_2 = r_1 + (m_1 - m_2)a^{-1}$. I can validate that this is a valid opening to c^* by checking:

$$c^* = g^{m_2} h^{r_2} = g^{m_2 + r_2 a} = g^{m_2 + (r_1 + (m_1 - m_2)a^{-1})a} = g^{m_2 + r_1 a + m_1 - m_2} = g^{m_1} h^{r_1} = c^*$$

Once I confirms that it is a valid opening, it sends z_2 as response for challenge m_2 instead. M can then extract the user secret key for ID^* as $s_{\mathsf{ID}^*} = \frac{z_2 - z_1}{m_2 - m_1}$.

M then finds the solution to the initial challenge $w_0 = [sID^* - x\alpha_{\mathsf{ID}^*}]\beta_{ID^*}^{-1}$ and proceeds to solve the remaining ω queries. This is done either by calculating $w_\omega = z_\omega - m_\omega(w_0\beta_{ID^*} - x\alpha\mathsf{ID}^*)$ for $\omega = \kappa$ threads where responses were generated for I. This way, M wins the OMDLP game by answering all discrete logarithm challenges using one less call to $DLOG$ oracle.

It remains to calculate the probability of M solving the OMDLP, given by the advantage of M: $\mathsf{Adv}_{M,G,q}^{OMDL}(k)$. This is given by Event A: I impersonates successfully and Event B: M does not abort. Event A is given by the reset lemma from [5]: $(\mathsf{Adv}_{TS-RS-IBI,I,q_e,q_I}^{CR1}(k) - 1/q)^2$.

$$\text{Adv}_{M,G,q}^{OMDL}(k) \geq \Pr[A \wedge B] \tag{1}$$

$$\geq \Pr[A|B]\Pr[B] \tag{2}$$

$$\geq (\text{Adv}_{S-RS-IBI,I,q_e,q_I}^{CR1}(k) - 1/q)^2 \Pr[B] \tag{3}$$

To calculate the probability of M does not abort we take into account the various scenarios where M may abort.

During the learning phase, M does not abort with probability σ for EXTRACT queries. For IDENTIFICATION queries, M may abort if it encounters an ambiguous commitment query by I, given by the upper bound $\text{Adv}_{I,q_I}^{PC}(k)$. Hence the probability of M does not abort during IDENTIFICATION is $1 - \text{Adv}_{I,q_I}^{PC}(k)$. During the impersonation phase, M does not abort with probability $1 - \sigma$.

Putting them together, M does not abort with probability $(\sigma)^{q_e}(1 - \text{Adv}_{I,q_I}^{PC}(k))(1 - \sigma)$. Taking the maximum value $\sigma_{max} = 1 - 1/(q_e + 1)$, we now have $\frac{1 - \text{Adv}_{I,q_I}^{PC}(k)}{e(q_e+1)}$ as the probability of M does not abort, where the value $[1 - 1/(q_e + 1)]^{q_e}$ approaches $1/e$ for large q_e.

Therefore the advantage of I in Theorem 1 is:

$$\text{Adv}_{M,G,q,q_{DL}}^{OMDL}(k) \geq (\text{Adv}_{S-RS-IBI,I,q_e,q_I}^{CR1}(k) - 1/q)^2 \frac{1 - \text{Adv}_{I,q_I}^{PC}(k)}{e(q_e+1)} \tag{4}$$

$$\text{Adv}_{S-RS-IBI,I,q_e,q_I}^{CR1}(k) \leq \sqrt{\frac{\text{Adv}_{M,G,q,q_{DL}}^{OMDL}(k)e(q_e+1)}{1 - \text{Adv}_{I,q_I}^{PC}(k)}} + 1/q \tag{5}$$

This ends the proof for the Schnorr-RS-IBI scheme. □

In the case where H_2 is instantiated using a collision-resistant hash function or replaced with a PRF, the Schnorr-RS-IBI remains secure under Theorems 2 and 3. The separation discussion for the proofs of these two theorems can also be found in the appendix.

Theorem 2. *The Schnorr-RS-IBI is* $(\mathbf{Adv}_{Schnorr-RS-IBI,I,q_e,q_I}^{CR1}(k))$*-secure against impersonation under concurrent-reset attacks if the OMDL problem is* $(\mathbf{Adv}_{G,q,q_{DL}}^{OMDL}(k))$*-hard, where*

$$\text{Adv}_{S-RS-IBI,I,q_e,q_I}^{CR1}(k) \leq \sqrt{\frac{\text{Adv}_{M,G,q,q_{DL}}^{OMDL}(k)e(1+q_e)}{(1 - \text{Adv}_{I,q_I}^{PC}(k))(1 - 2^{-k/2})}} + 1/q$$

and the Pedersen commitment scheme is $\mathbf{Adv}_{I,q_I}^{PC}(k)$*-secure,* H_1 *is modeled as a random oracle, and* H_2 *is a* $\mathbf{Adv}_{I,q_{H_2}}^{Collision}(k)$*-secure collision-resistant hash function.*

Theorem 3. *The Schnorr-RS-IBI is* $(\mathbf{Adv}_{Schnorr-RS-IBI,I,q_e,q_I}^{CR1}(k))$*-secure against impersonation under concurrent-reset attacks if the OMDL problem is* $(\mathbf{Adv}_{G,q,q_{DL}}^{OMDL}(k))$*-hard, where*

$$Adv_{S-RS-IBI,I,q_e,q_I}^{CR1}(k) \leq \sqrt{\frac{Adv_{M,G,q,q_{DL}}^{OMDL}(k)e(1+q_e)}{(1-Adv_{I,q_I}^{PC}(k))(1-2^{-k})}} + 1/q$$

and the Pedersen commitment scheme is $Adv_{I,q_I}^{PC}(k)$-secure, H_1 is modeled as a random oracle, and PRF is a $Adv_{I,q_I}^{PRF}(k)$-secure pseudorandom function.

5   Construction of the Twin-Schnorr-RS-IBI Scheme

For the second construction, we propose the Twin-Schnorr-RS-IBI scheme. The Twin-Schnorr-RS-IBI scheme is simpler to prove secure compared to the Schnorr-RS-IBI scheme because there are less cases that cause an abort for the simulation. The proving method utilized follows that of [11]. This translates to a tighter proof of security. Also, since it relies only on the DLP instead of OMDLP, it provides stronger security guarantees because a weaker assumption is used. All this comes at a slight increase in user secret key size as well as operational costs. We provide this scheme as a stronger but slower alternative to the Schnorr-RS-IBI scheme.

The details of the construction are as follows:

1. **Setup**: takes in the security parameter 1^k and generates the group G of order q. It picks two random generators $g_1, g_2 \xleftarrow{\$} G$ and two random integers $x_1, x_2, a \xleftarrow{\$} \mathbb{Z}_q$. It sets $X = g_1^{-x_1} g_2^{-x_2}$ and $h = g^a$. It also chooses three hash functions $H_1 : \{0,1\}^* \times G \times G \to \mathbb{Z}_q$, $PRF_1/H_2 : \{0,1\}^{pcl} \times G \to \mathbb{Z}_q$ and $PRF_2/H_3 : \{0,1\}^{pcl} \times G \to \mathbb{Z}_q$. The master public key is $\mathsf{mpk} = \langle G, q, g, X, h, H_1, H_2/PRF1, H_3/PRF2 \rangle$ while the master private key is $\mathsf{msk} = \langle x_1, x_2, a \rangle$.
2. **Extract**: takes in the user identity string ID, mpk and msk. It picks two random integers $\tau_1, \tau_2 \xleftarrow{\$} \mathbb{Z}_q$ and sets $V = g_1^{\tau_1} g_2^{\tau_2}$. It then sets $s_1 = \tau_1 + x_1\alpha$ and $s_2 = \tau_2 + x_2\alpha$ where $\alpha = H(\mathsf{ID}||X||V)$. The user private key is $\mathsf{usk} = (s_1, s_2, \alpha)$.
3. **Identification Protocol: Prover** takes in mpk, ID and usk while **Verifier** takes in the mpk and ID. They run the identification protocol as follows:
   (a) Σ_1: The **Verifier** begins by picking a random integers $m, r \xleftarrow{\$} \mathbb{Z}_q$ and calculates $c = g^m h^r$.
   (b) Σ_2: The **Prover** sets $y_1 = H_2(R_p||c), y_2 = H_3(R_p||c)$ or $y_1 = PRF1_{R_p}(c), y_1 = PRF2_{R_p}(c)$ depending on the choice of hash or pseudo-random function selected during **Setup** and sets $Y = g_1^{y_1} g_2^{y_2}$. **Prover** also sets $V = g_1^{s_1} g_2^{s_2} X^\alpha$ and sends Y, V to the **Verifier**.
   (c) Σ_3: The **Verifier** reveals m, r to **Prover**.
   (d) Σ_4: The **Prover** calculates $c' = g^m h^r$ and checks if $c' = c$. If true it responds by setting $z_1 = y_1 + cs_1, z_2 = y_2 + cs_2$ and sends z_1, z_2 to the Verifier as its response. Otherwise it aborts.
   Σ_{CHK}: The verifier evaluates $\alpha' = H_1(\mathsf{ID}||V||X)$, checks if $g_1^{z_1} g_2^{z_2} = Y(\frac{V}{X^\alpha})^m$ and accepts if true.

To prove correctness:

$$Y(\frac{V}{X^\alpha})^m = (g_1^{y_1} g_2^{y_2})(\frac{g_1^{s_1} g_2^{s_2} X^\alpha}{X^\alpha})^m = g_1^{y_1+ms_1} g_2^{y_2+ms_2} = g_1^{z_1} g_2^{z_2}$$

6 Security Analysis for Twin-Schnorr-RS-IBI

Theorem 4. *The Twin-Schnorr-RS-IBI is $Adv_{TS-RS-IBI,I,q_e,q_I}^{CR1}(k)$-secure against impersonation under concurrent-reset-1 attacks if the DL problem is $Adv_{M,G,q}^{DL}(k)$ hard, where*

$$Adv_{TS-RS-IBI,I,q_e,q_I}^{CR1}(k) \le \sqrt{\frac{Adv_{M,G,q}^{DL}(k)}{(1 - Adv_{I,q_I}^{PC}(k))}} + 1/q$$

and the Pedersen commitment scheme is $Adv_{I,q_I}^{PC}(k)$-secure, and H_1, H_2 and H_3 are modeled as random oracles.

Proof. Assume that the Twin-Schnorr-RS-IBI scheme is not reset-secure, that is, a reset impersonator I exists that breaks the scheme with advantage $Adv_{TS-RS-IBI,I,q_e,q_I}^{CR1}(k)$. We then show an algorithm M that breaks the discrete logarithm assumption with advantage $Adv_{M,G,q}^{DL}(k)$.

Learning Phase

M starts the simulation by taking in the discrete log instance $(g, g^z = Z)$. It sets $g_1 = g$ and $g_2 = Z$. Additionally it picks $x_1, x_2, a \xleftarrow{\$} \mathbb{Z}_q$ and keeps them as the master secret key msk. It calculates $X = g_1^{-x_1} g_2^{-x_2}$ and $h = g^a$ and picks $H_1 : \{0,1\}^* \times G \times G \to \mathbb{Z}_q$. M picks $H_2 : \{0,1\}^k \times G \to \mathbb{Z}_q$ and $H_3 : \{0,1\}^k \times G \to \mathbb{Z}_q$ and runs them as random oracles. It then passes mpk $= \langle G, q, g_1, g_2, X, h, H_1, H_2, H_3 \rangle$ to I.

EXTRACT QUERY: In phase 1, since M possesses the master secret keys x_1, x_2, it can answer any query from I. However, it limits I to q_e EXTRACT queries. M keeps two sets for users and their private keys: the set of honest users HU for which they have their usk created but not queried for to be used for IDEN-TIFICATION queries; the other set of corrupted users CU, contain the identities and private keys for users I has requested an EXTRACT query for. For each EXTRACT query on ID_i, M creates $usk_{ID_i} = \langle s_{1,ID_i}, s_{2,ID_i}, \alpha_{ID_i} \rangle$, sends it to I and transfers (ID_i, usk_{ID_i}) from HU to CU.

IDENTIFICATION QUERY: M allows I to make q_I IDENTIFICATION queries. For IDENTIFICATION queries requested on ID_j, if ID_j wasn't queried for EXTRACT before, M runs an EXTRACT query on it to generate usk_{ID_j} and uses it for the protocol and puts the (ID_j, usk_{ID_j}) entry in HU. Without loss of generality, we assume I will not send c_k, m_k, r_k to M such that $c_k \ne g^{m_k} h^{r_k}$.

Also, since H_2 and H_3 are modeled as random oracles, they provide no advantage to I at all with truly random outputs.

M will abort if it encounters a protocol run on prover instance ID_j in an ambiguous commitment case, i.e. I manages to send both $(m_\kappa, r_\kappa), (m'_\kappa, r'_\kappa)$ that correspond to the same c_κ. This means I has managed to break the binding property of the Pedersen commitment and is able to extract $\mathsf{usk}_{\mathsf{ID}_i}$ from the soundness of the original Schnorr-IBI protocol. The upper bound for this event happening is the advantage of breaking the binding property of the Pedersen Commitment scheme: $\mathbf{Adv}^{PC}_{I,q_I}(k)$.

Impersonation Phase

Once the learning phase ends and I begins the challenge phase, I outputs an identity one which it wishes to be challenged on ID^*. If $ID^* \notin \{\mathsf{ID}_1, \ldots, \mathsf{ID}_{q_e}\}$ was queried before as an EXTRACT query for its usk during the learning phase, M generates its usk now. M proceeds with the protocol with I this time as the verifier while I plays the cheating prover.

Since M holds a where $h = g^a$, it can use the equivocation property of the Pedersen commitment scheme to facilitate and ambiguous commitment case in order to retrieve 2 valid transcripts from I with the same commitment. In the same way, M obtains two valid conversations $< c^*, Y, V, m_1, r_1, z_{1,1}, z_{1,2} >, < c^*, Y, V, m_2, r_2, z_{2,1}, z_{2,2} >$.

M can then extract the user secret key for ID^* as $\tilde{s}_1 = \frac{z_{2,1} - z_{1,1}}{m_2 - m_1}$, $\tilde{s}_2 = \frac{z_{2,2} - z_{1,2}}{m_2 - m_1}$. Now, if $s_1 = \tilde{s}_1$ and $s_2 = \tilde{s}_2$, M aborts. Otherwise, M can solve the DLP by calculating:

$$g_1^{\tilde{s}_1} g_2^{\tilde{s}_2} = g_1^{s_1} g_2^{s_2} \tag{6}$$

$$g_1^{z(s_2 - \tilde{s}_2)} = g_1^{\tilde{s}_1 - s_1} \tag{7}$$

$$z(s_2 - \tilde{s}_2) = \tilde{s}_1 - s_1 \tag{8}$$

$$z = \frac{\tilde{s}_1 - s_1}{\tilde{s}_2 - s_2} \tag{9}$$

It remains to calculate the probability of M solving the DLP, given by the advantage of M: $\mathsf{Adv}^{DL}_{M,G,q}(k)$. This is given by Event A:M calculates z and Event B:M does not abort. Event A is given by the reset lemma from [5]: $\mathsf{Adv}^{CR1}_{TS-RS-IBI,I,q_e,q_I}(k) - 1/q)^2$.

$$\mathsf{Adv}^{DL}_{M,G,q}(k) \geq \Pr[A \wedge B] \tag{10}$$

$$\geq \Pr[A|B]\Pr[B] \tag{11}$$

$$\geq (\mathsf{Adv}^{CR1}_{TS-RS-IBI,I,q_e,q_I}(k) - 1/q)^2 \Pr[B] \tag{12}$$

To calculate the probability of M does not abort we take into account the various scenarios where M may abort.

In phase 1, M does not abort for Extract queries. However, M may abort if it encounters an ambiguous commitment query by I, given by the upper bound $\mathsf{Adv}^{PC}_{I,q_I}(k)$. Hence the probability M does not abort is $1 - \mathsf{Adv}^{PC}_{I,q_I}(k)$.

In phase 2, M will only abort if $\tilde{s}_1 = s_1$ and $\tilde{s}_2 = s_2$. This happens with probability $1/2^k$. Hence M will not abort with probability $1 - 1/2^k$.

Therefore for Theorem 4, the advantage of I is:

$$\mathsf{Adv}^{DL}_{M,G,q}(k) \geq (\mathsf{Adv}^{CR1}_{TS-RS-IBI,I,q_e,q_I}(k) - 1/q)^2 \qquad (13)$$
$$(1 - \mathsf{Adv}^{PC}_{I,q_I}(k))(1 - 1/2^k)$$

$$\mathsf{Adv}^{CR1}_{TS-RS-IBI,I,q_e,q_I}(k) \leq \sqrt{\frac{\mathsf{Adv}^{DL}_{M,G,q}(k)}{(1 - \mathsf{Adv}^{PC}_{I,q_I}(k))(1 - 1/2^k)}} + 1/q \qquad (14)$$

This completes the proof. □

In the case where H_2 is instantiated using a collision-resistant hash function or replaced with a PRF, the Twin-Schnorr-RS-IBI remains secure under Theorems 5 and 6. The separation discussion for the proofs of these two theorems can also be found in the appendix.

Theorem 5. *The Twin-Schnorr-RS-IBI is $\mathbf{Adv}^{CR1}_{TS-RS-IBI,I,q_e,q_I}(k)$-secure against impersonation under concurrent-reset-1 attacks if the DL problem is $\mathbf{Adv}^{DL}_{M,G,q}(k)$ hard, where*

$$\mathsf{Adv}^{CR1}_{TS-RS-IBI,I,q_e,q_I}(k) \leq \sqrt{\frac{\mathsf{Adv}^{DL}_{M,G,q}(k)}{(1 - \mathsf{Adv}^{PC}_{I,q_I}(k))(1 - 1/2^k)^2}} + 1/q$$

and the Pedersen commitment scheme is $\mathbf{Adv}^{PC}_{I,q_I}(k)$-secure, H_1 is modeled as a random oracle, and H_2 and H_2 are $\mathbf{Adv}^{Collision}_{I,q_{H_2}}(k)$-secure and $\mathbf{Adv}^{Collision}_{I,q_{H_3}}(k)$-secure collision-resistant hash functions respectively.

Theorem 6. *The Twin-Schnorr-RS-IBI is $\mathbf{Adv}^{CR1}_{TS-RS-IBI,I,q_e,q_I}(k)$-secure against impersonation under concurrent-reset-1 attacks if the DL problem is $\mathbf{Adv}^{DL}_{M,G,q}(k)$ hard, where*

$$\mathsf{Adv}^{CR1}_{TS-RS-IBI,I,q_e,q_I}(k) \leq \sqrt{\frac{\mathsf{Adv}^{DL}_{M,G,q}(k)}{(1 - \mathsf{Adv}^{PC}_{I,q_I}(k))(1 - 1/2^k)^2}} + 1/q$$

and the Pedersen commitment scheme is $\mathbf{Adv}^{PC}_{I,q_I}(k)$-secure, H_1 is modeled as a random oracle, and $PRF1, PRF2$ are $\mathbf{Adv}^{PRF}_{I,q_I}(k)$-secure pseudorandom functions.

7   Efficiency Analysis

In this section we provide a comparison of the operational costs for the schemes proposed, each with option to either use a hash function or PRF for the prover. It is also possible to pre-compute the value of V and storing it in the prover for both schemes to save cost. The operation costs are given in Table 1.

Table 1. Operational costs for Schnorr-RS-IBI and Twin-Schnorr-RS-IBI schemes.

Scheme	usk-size	Setup	Extract	Prover	Verifier
Schnorr-RS-IBI	2Zq	2E	1AZ 1MZ 1H 1E	1H/PRF 1AZ 1MZ 2G 5E	1H 4G 6E
Twin-Schnorr-RS-IBI	3Zq	1G 3E	2AZ 2MZ 1H 1G 2E	2H/PRF 2AZ 2MZ 4G 7E	1H 5G 7E
Schnorr-RS-IBI wP	3Zq	2E	1AZ 1MZ 1H 1E	1H 1AZ 1MZ 1G 2E	1H 4G 6E
Twin-Schnorr-RS-IBI wP	4Zq	1G 3E	2AZ 2MZ 1H 1G 2E	2H 2AZ 2MZ 2G 4E	1H 5G 7E

Legend: G-Group Element, Zq-Element in $\mathbb{Z}_q$, H-Hash Evaluations, P-PRF Evaluations, AZ-Addition in $\mathbb{Z}_q$, MZ-Multiplication in $\mathbb{Z}_q$, G-Group Multiplication, E-Exponentiations, wP-with Precomputation

8   Extension to Concurrent-Reset-2 Security

An adversary for concurrent-reset-2 security (CR2) differs from CR1 adversaries in that they can still conduct oracle queries during the challenge phase. In order to further strengthen the Schnorr-RS-IBI and Twin-Schnorr-RS-IBI schemes against CR2 adversaries, [2]'s technique of using session IDs and binding them with an identity-based Pedersen commitment can be deployed.

Briefly speaking, the identity-based Pedersen commitment scheme requries 3 generators $g_1, g_2, g_3 \xleftarrow{\$} G$. Given a message m, randomness r and an identity-string ID, generate a commitment $c = (g_1^{\text{ID}} g_2)^m g_3^r$.

To secure against CR2 attacks, an additional public key generator g_3 is required. For the protocol, the verifier selects a session identifier SID and commits it together with m, r using the identity-based Pedersen commitment. It sends both $c = (g^{SID} g_3)^m h^r$ and SID to the prover. Prover appends SID to its hash or PRF input string for evaluation for the exponent of y. The rest of the protocol proceeds as normal. At the end, both prover and verifier output SID to check if they are the same.

Acknowledgment. The authors are grateful to the Ministry of Education of the Government of Malaysia for their financial support for this research under The Fundamental Research Project Scheme (no. FRGS/2/2013/ICT07/MMU/03/5). The first and third author would also like to thank Prof. Kouichi Sakurai for hosting their visit to Institute of System, Information Technologies and Nanotechnologies (ISIT), Japan, during which much of the initial ideas for this paper was discussed. For the second author, this work is partially supported by Grants-in-Aid for Scientific Research of Japan Society for the Promotion of Science; Research Project Number: 15K00029.

A   Choices of H_2 (and H_3)

For the modeling of the randomness of $y = H_2(R_p||C)$ or $y = PRF_{R_P}(c)$ in the proof for the Schnorr-RS-IBI scheme, the three different treatments are provided on whether H_2 is modeled as a random oracle, as a collision-resistant hash function or as pseudorandom function. The previous proof viewed H_2 as random oracle. We now briefly discuss the changes needed on the proof to maintain the security of the Schnorr-RS-IBI if H_2 is either a collision-resistant hash function or a pseudorandom function. Similar arguments apply for the treatment of H_3 for the Twin-Schnorr-RS-IBI scheme.

A.1 Collision-Resistant Hash H_2 (and H_3)

Schnorr-RS-IBI

If H_2 is only collision-resistant, in the IDENTIFICATION QUERY, M queries $CHALL$ for W_ω and set $Y_\kappa = W_\omega^{H_2(R_p||c_\kappa)}$. M sends Y_κ, V to I for step Σ_2 and send $z_\kappa = DLOG(y_\kappa^{H_2(R_p||c_\kappa)}(\frac{V}{X^\alpha})^{m_\kappa})$ for step Σ_4.

I can win in the learning phase if it manages to find a collision for H_2 , i.e. finding a c_κ where $Y_\kappa = g^{H_2(R_{ID_i}||c_\kappa)} = g^{H_2(R_{ID_i}||c'_\kappa)}$ where $c_\kappa \neq c'_\kappa$. The event of this happening is given by $\mathbf{Adv}_{I,H_2,q_{H_2}}^{Collision}(k)$ where q_{H_2} is the maximum number of hash queries available. With probability σ, M just returns $Y_\kappa = g^{H_2(R_{ID_i}||c_\kappa)}$ as usual to I. With probability $1 - \sigma$, M queries $CHALL$ for W_κ and sets $Y_\kappa = W_\kappa^{H_2(R_{ID_j}||c_\kappa)}$. To I, this view is indistinguishable from $Y_\kappa = g^{H_2(R_{ID_j}||c_\kappa)}$.

During the learning phase, the probability of not aborting is if there are no collisions for H_2. This is given by $1 - \mathbf{Adv}_{I,q_{H_2}}^{Collision}(k)$. It is possible to substitute more concrete values for $\mathbf{Adv}_{I,H_2,q_{H_2}}^{Collision}(k)$. From [1], we know that hash functions offer security of up to $2^{k/2}$ for k-bit security. Therefore, we can replace this value to $(1 - 2^{-k/2})$ We add this event as an additional intersection for Event B to yield Theorem 2.

$$\mathbf{Adv}_{M,G,q,q_{DL}}^{OMDL}(k) \geq (\mathbf{Adv}_{S-RS-IBI,I,q_e,q_I}^{CR1}(k) - 1/q)^2) \quad (15)$$
$$\frac{(1 - \mathbf{Adv}_{I,q_I}^{PC}(k))(1 - 2^{-k/2})}{e(1 + q_e)}$$

$$\frac{\mathbf{Adv}_{M,G,q}^{OMDL}(k)}{(1 - \mathbf{Adv}_{I,q_I}^{PC}(k))(1 - 1/2^k)} \geq (\mathbf{Adv}_{TS-RS-IBI,I,q_e,q_I}^{CR1}(k) - 1/q)^2) \quad (16)$$

$$\mathbf{Adv}_{S-RS-IBI,I,q_e,q_I}^{CR1}(k) \leq \sqrt{\frac{\mathbf{Adv}_{M,G,q,q_{DL}}^{OMDL}(k)e(1 + q_e)}{(1 - \mathbf{Adv}_{I,q_I}^{PC}(k)))(1 - 2^{-k/2})}} + 1/q \quad (17)$$

Twin-Schnorr-RS-IBI

For the Twin-Schnorr-RS-IBI scheme, if H_2 and H_3 are treated as collision-resistant hash functions, M chooses $H_2 : \{0,1\}^k \times G \to \mathbb{Z}_q$ and $H_3 : \{0,1\}^k \times G \to \mathbb{Z}_q$ and passes them to I during setup.

During IDENTIFICATON queries, I wins if it manages to find a collision for H_2 and H_3. However, both collisions must happen simultaneously in order for I to win. This event is bounded by $\mathbf{Adv}_{I,H_2,q_{H_2}}^{Collision}(k) \times \mathbf{Adv}_{I,H_3,q_{H_3}}^{Collision}(k)$ where

q_{H_2} and q_{H_3} are the maximum number of hash queries available to H_2 and H_3 respectively. In this case, M sets $q_{H_2}, q_{H_3} \leq q_I$.

The probability of not aborting is if there are no collisions for both H_2 and H_3 simultaneously. This is given by $(1 - \mathbf{Adv}_{I,H_2,q_{H_2}}^{Collision}(k)\mathbf{Adv}_{I,H_3,q_{H_3}}^{Collision}(k))$. We can also substitute more concrete values for this bound as $(1 - \frac{1}{2^{k/2}}\frac{1}{2^{k/2}}) = 1 - \frac{1}{2^k}$. We add this event as an additional intersection for Event B to yield Theorem 5.

$$\mathbf{Adv}_{TS-RS-IBI,I,q_e,q_I}^{CR1}(k) \leq \sqrt{\frac{\mathbf{Adv}_{M,G,q}^{DL}(k)}{(1 - \mathbf{Adv}_{I,q_I}^{PC}(k))(1 - 1/2^k)^2}} + 1/q \quad (18)$$

A.2   Pseudorandom Functions (PRFs)

Schnorr-RS-IBI

If PRFs are used then our treatment to the proof changes slightly. During the setup phase, M will flip a coin $b \in \{0, 1\}$. If $b = 0$, f is sampled from a family of PRFs while $CHALL$ oracle is modified so that W_κ is sampled from a PRF function. If $b = 1$ then f is sampled from truly random functions and the regular $CHALL$ oracle is used, where W_κ is sampled truly randomly.

During IDENTIFICATION query, M queries $CHALL$ where W_ω was generated by a pseudorandom function with some arbitrary seed and send $Y_\kappa = W_\omega$ and V to I.

The advantage of I distinguishing PRF from random function is given by $\mathbf{Adv}_{I,q_I}^{PRF}(k)$. For M not aborting, we have $(1 - \mathbf{Adv}_{I,q_I}^{PRF}(k))$. Once again, obtaining concrete values from [1], since I does not know the inner workings of the PRF, the best evaluation it can have would be to check 2^k possibilities. Therefore we can replace $(1 - \mathbf{Adv}_{I,q_I}^{PRF}(k))$ with $1 - 1/2^k$. This yields the result of Theorem 3:

$$\mathbf{Adv}_{S-RS-IBI,I,q_e,q_I}^{CR1}(k) \leq \sqrt{\frac{\mathbf{Adv}_{M,G,q,q_{DL}}^{OMDL}(k)e(1 + q_e)}{(1 - \mathbf{Adv}_{I,q_I}^{PC}(k))(1 - 2^{-k})}} + 1/q \quad (19)$$

Twin-Schnorr-RS-IBI

For Twin-Schnorr-RS-IBI, if PRFs are used then during the setup phase, M will flip a coin $b \in \{0, 1\}$. If $b = 0$, $f_1, f_2 \leftarrow PRF$ are sampled from a family of PRFs whereas if $b = 1$, $f_1, f_2 \leftarrow RAND$ are sampled from the set of truly random functions to be used instead, where $f_1 : \{0, 1\}^{pcl} \times G \rightarrow \mathbb{Z}_q, f_2 : \{0, 1\}^{pcl} \times G \rightarrow \mathbb{Z}_q$. M passes these PRFs to I as part of the system parameters.

Whenever I requests for an IDENTIFICATION query on ID_j, M generates $Y_\kappa = g_1^{f_{1,R_{\mathsf{ID}_j}}(c_\kappa)} g_2^{f_{2,R_{\mathsf{ID}_j}}(c_\kappa)}$ and passes this value to I during Σ_2 when it receives c_κ from I in Σ_1.

Lastly if PRFs are used, then the advantage of I distinguishing a PRF from a random function is given by $\mathbf{Adv}_{I,q_I}^{PRF}(k)$. For M not aborting, we have

$(1 - \mathbf{Adv}_{I,q_I}^{PRF}(k))$. Once again, we can replace $(1 - \mathbf{Adv}_{I,q_I}^{PRF}(k))$ with $1 - 1/2^k$. This yields the same result as Theorem 5, but under different assumptions, so we label it as Theorem 6.

$$\mathbf{Adv}_{TS-RS-IBI,I,q_e,q_I}^{CR1}(k) \leq \sqrt{\frac{\mathbf{Adv}_{M,G,q}^{DL}(k)}{(1 - \mathbf{Adv}_{I,q_I}^{PC}(k))(1 - 1/2^k)^2}} + 1/q \qquad (20)$$

References

1. Bogdanov, A.: Lecture 6: Cryptographic hash functions. The Chinese University of Hong Kong (2012). Available on http://www.cse.cuhk.edu.hk/andrejb/csc5440/notes/12L6.pdf
2. Bellare, M., Fischlin, M., Goldwasser, S., Micali, S.: Identification protocols secure against reset attacks. In: Pfitzmann, B. (ed.) EUROCRYPT 2001. LNCS, vol. 2045, pp. 495–511. Springer, Heidelberg (2001)
3. Boneh, D., Franklin, M.: Identity-based encryption from the weil pairing. In: Kilian, J. (ed.) CRYPTO 2001. LNCS, vol. 2139, pp. 213–229. Springer, Heidelberg (2001)
4. Bellare, M., Namprempre, C., Neven, G.: Security proofs for identity-based identification and signature schemes. In: Cachin, C., Camenisch, J.L. (eds.) EUROCRYPT 2004. LNCS, vol. 3027, pp. 268–286. Springer, Heidelberg (2004)
5. Bellare, M., Palacio, A.: GQ and schnorr identification schemes: proofs of security against impersonation under active and concurrent attacks. In: Yung, M. (ed.) CRYPTO 2002. LNCS, vol. 2442, pp. 162–177. Springer, Heidelberg (2002)
6. Bellare, M., Rogaway, P.: Random oracles are practical: a paradigm for designing efficient protocols. In: ACM Conference on Computer and Communications Securitym, pp. 62–73. ACM (1993)
7. Chin, J.-J., Tan, S.-Y., Heng, S.-H., Phan, R.C.: Twin-Schnorr: a security upgrade for the schnorr identity-based identification scheme. Sci. World J. **2015**, 9 (2014). doi:10.1155/2015/237514. Article ID 237514
8. Heng, S.-H.: Design and analysis of some cryptographic primitives. Doctoral dissertation. Graduate School of Science and Engineering, Tokyo Institute of Technology (2004)
9. Kurosawa, K., Heng, S.-H.: From digital signature to ID-based identification/signature. In: Bao, F., Deng, R., Zhou, J. (eds.) PKC 2004. LNCS, vol. 2947, pp. 248–261. Springer, Heidelberg (2004)
10. Kurosawa, K., Heng, S.-H.: Identity-based identification without random oracles. In: Gervasi, O., Gavrilova, M.L., Kumar, V., Laganá, A., Lee, H.P., Mun, Y., Taniar, D., Tan, C.J.K. (eds.) ICCSA 2005. LNCS, vol. 3481, pp. 603–613. Springer, Heidelberg (2005)
11. Okamoto, T.: Provably secure and practical identification schemes and corresponding signature schemes. In: Brickell, E.F. (ed.) CRYPTO 1992. LNCS, vol. 740, pp. 31–53. Springer, Heidelberg (1993)
12. Pedersen, T.P.: Non-interactive and information-theoretic secure verifiable secret sharing. In: Feigenbaum, J. (ed.) CRYPTO 1991. LNCS, vol. 576, pp. 129–140. Springer, Heidelberg (1992)
13. Schnorr, C.-P.: Efficient identification and signatures for smart cards. In: Brassard, G. (ed.) CRYPTO 1989. LNCS, vol. 435, pp. 239–252. Springer, Heidelberg (1990)

14. Shamir, A.: Identity-based cryptosystems and signature schemes. In: Blakely, G.R., Chaum, D. (eds.) CRYPTO 1984. LNCS, vol. 196, pp. 47–53. Springer, Heidelberg (1985)
15. Thorncharoensri, P., Susilo, W., Mu, Y.: Identity-based identification scheme secure against concurrent-reset attacks without random oracles. In: Youm, H.Y., Yung, M. (eds.) WISA 2009. LNCS, vol. 5932, pp. 94–108. Springer, Heidelberg (2009)

Attribute-Based Encryption for Finite Automata from LWE

Xavier Boyen and Qinyi Li[✉]

Queensland University of Technology, Brisbane, Australia
qinyi.li@hdr.qut.edu.au

Abstract. We propose a construction of Attribute-Based Encryption for deterministic finite automata with bounded input length from lattices. The security of our construction can be reduced to the hardness of learning with errors (**LWE**) problem in the selective security model.

The main technique in our scheme is a novel way to securely encode the deterministic finite automata and the input string as a "matrix ribbon" that closely mimics the structure of the tape and supports simple operations that rely only on traditional preimage sampling on lattices.

Our result is the first direct construction of key-policy attribute-based encryption for deterministic finite automata. Comparing with the existing indirect constructions from lattices, our scheme is conceptually simpler and also more efficient.

1 Introduction

Attribute-Based Encryption (ABE) [15] is a promising cryptographic primitive that enables fine-grained access on encrypted data. In a Key-Policy ABE (KP-ABE) scheme, a decryption key is associated with a Boolean predicate $\phi(\cdot)$ and a message is encrypted along with a *public* string w of variables. The key decrypts the ciphertext if and only if $\phi(w)$ is true.

Significant effort in ABE systems is devoted to providing more flexible predicates ϕ and handling attributes w from a larger class of languages. Early ABE systems, such as the one proposed by Goyal et al. [15], were constructed from bilinear maps usually supporting (non)-monotone Boolean formulas as ϕ. Very recently, quantum leaps on ABE were made with the help of lattice-based cryptography in addition to a longer tradition of schemes based on bilinear maps. As a breakthrough, ABE schemes for Boolean circuits [7,11,13] were proposed either directly or indirectly based on the hardness of lattice problems.

A natural question on ABE is: can we make ϕ work for more powerful computational models? Waters [21] studied a KP-ABE system for *Deterministic Finite Automata* (DFAs) from bilinear maps that enables the key policy ϕ to be any deterministic finite automaton and supports an arbitrary length of input w. Briefly, a deterministic finite automaton or DFA machine $M = (Q, \Sigma, \delta, s_0, F)$

Q. Li—Research conducted with generous support from the Australian Research Council under Discovery Project grant ARC DP-140103885.

© Springer International Publishing Switzerland 2015
M.-H. Au and A. Miyaji (Eds.): ProvSec 2015, LNCS 9451, pp. 247–267, 2015.
DOI: 10.1007/978-3-319-26059-4_14

is a 5-tuple, where Q is a set of states, Σ is an alphabet with finite number of letters, $\delta : Q \times \Sigma \to Q$ is a transition function (which takes a current state, an input letter in Σ as input, and then "consumes" this letter to transit the machine into a new state), s_0 is a unique start state, and $F \subseteq Q$ is a set of accept states. In such a system, an authority generates public parameters and a master secret key. The key generation algorithm takes as input the master secret key, the description of a DFA machine M and outputs a decryption key Sk_M. To encrypt a message, a string w of letters from the alphabet Σ and a message are taken as inputs, and a ciphertext Ctx_w that is associated with w is output. Sk_M decrypts Ctx_w if the input string w is recognised by the DFA machine M, meaning that M starts from the state s_0, "consumes" the letters in w one-by-one and shifts to the new states by applying the transition function δ. After reading all the letters, M stops at a final accept state $s \in F$.

The key of realising such DFA-based KP-ABE is to ensure key holders apply transition function honestly, i.e., "consume" the letters in w sequentially rather than "jump over" intermediate letters, backtrack in time, or splice ciphertext fragments from different sources. At a high level, [21] overcomes this difficulty as follow. The component of decryption key of one transition function is designed to tie two neighbouring states. For each letter in w in the ciphertext, an ephemeral exponentiation is chosen and each ciphertext component is constructed by using the neighbouring ephemeral exponentiations to tie two sequential letters together. If the decryptor "jumps over" the ciphertext components, it could not cancel all the ephemeral exponentiation parameters and only gets a random garbage. Backtracking is made a non-issue by focusing on deterministic machines which have but a single execution path for each input string.

In terms of security, the KP-ABE scheme for DFAs in [21] has selective security where the adversary is required to target the challenge string before seeing the public parameters. With a new framework of dual system encryption [20], Attrapadung [5] showed the first adaptively secure DFA-based ABE scheme from bilinear maps.

1.1 Our Results

In this paper, we propose the first direct construction of ABE system for deterministic finite automata that supports polynomially bounded input length from lattices. (We refer to the construction as a "direct" construction in the sense that as in our case the DFAs are running in polynomial time, the existing ABE schemes for polynomial-size circuits are able to realise the same functionality by converting bounded DFAs into static circuits.) Our novel method for securely encoding bounded DFA machines is the major technical contribution.

An abstraction of the low-level lattice delegation techniques of Cash et al. and Agrawal et al. [1,10] and the Two-to-One recoding of Gorbunov et al. [13] figure in our construction. The key idea is deceptively simple; it attempts to preserve the natural structure of the DFA as much as possible.

- The input string is transcoded into a "matrix ribbon" that can be viewed as a literal (if large) input tape, to which a (noisy linear) transformation similar to Regev encryption is performed to produce an actual ciphertext.
- The evolving state of the machine is encoded as an appendage to the input tape using an additional stretch of "matrix ribbon".
- The transition rules operate on fragments of the "ribbon" (or the ciphertext derived from it) and are implemented as local matrix multiplications that map two ribbon fragments (one for the current state and one for the next input letter) into a single new ribbon fragment (that encodes the next state of the transition). Those transition rules are part of the private key (and each private key encodes an independent set of rules that define the particular DFA).
- Acceptance is reached when the entire ciphertext has been consumed and "digested" into one of the predictable accept states, for which a decryption key similar to the Regev scheme has been issued.

In order to simulate the scheme and provide a security reduction in the selective model, we partially "unroll" the DFA into an "execution graph" whose nodes are pairs $(state, time)$, where $state$ is the state of the automaton and $time$ is a negative integer that indicates how far away we are from having consumed all the provided input word (i.e. the ciphertext). Because with a deterministic machine each input word induces but a single path in the graph (though the paths can diverge then merge again), we are able to plant a lattice trapdoor in this graph, for each "matrix ribbon fragment" that departs from the challenge path induced by the challenge ciphertext. This allows us to answer all DFA private key queries, and exploit a successful decryption by the adversary in solving an LWE challenge.

Our construction is provably secure in the selective security model (or in the adaptive security model though standard complexity leveraging argument [6]) under the learning with errors (LWE) problem which is shown to be as hard as standard lattice problems [9,18,19]. We give efficiency comparisons of our direct construction with other indirect constructions from ABE schemes for circuits.

1.2   Related Work

Functional and Attribute-Based Encryption have a long research tradition in cryptography, starting with Identity-Based Encryption (IBE) the most basic form of functional encryption. A number of different IBE schemes were constructed by using bilinear maps [6] and lattices [1,10,12]. Both regular IBE and ABE fall into the category of public index functional encryption [8], because the encryption string w is public. Predicate encryption systems [2,14,16], another branch of functional encryption, are designed to provide privacy of w. Here we review some important ABE systems.

ABE for Circuits from Multi-linear Maps. Garg et al. [11] showed how to build KP-ABE schemes for Boolean circuits from DBDH-analogue assumptions in multilinear maps setting. While the difficulty of constructing ABE for general circuits, whose internal gates have multiple fan-out, comes from the backtracking attack, the irreversibility of multilinear maps provides a natural way to prevent such attack. One drawback of this approach is that there has been no accepted candidate for realising such an assumption, and known constructions of multilinear maps also require non-standard assumptions. Multi-linear maps also remain highly inefficient and impractical for the time being.

Two-to-One Recoding and ABE for Circuits. Gorbunov et al. [13] proposed a novel Two-to-One Recoding (TOR) framework and made use of it to construct an ABE scheme for Boolean circuits. An instantiation of the TOR framework is also given in [13] from the LWE assumption. In the LWE-based TOR instantiation, an encoding of a matrix $\mathbf{A}_0 \in \mathbb{Z}_q^{n \times m}$ with respect to secret $\mathbf{s} \in \mathbb{Z}_q^n$ and noise ν_0 is $\mathsf{encode}(\mathbf{A}_0, \mathbf{s}) = \mathbf{s}^\top \mathbf{A}_0 + \nu_0^\top$. Given a second encoding $\mathsf{encode}(\mathbf{A}_1, \mathbf{s}) = \mathbf{s}^\top \mathbf{A}_1 + \nu_1^\top$ and a target matrix $\mathbf{A}_{tgt} \in \mathbb{Z}_q^{n \times m}$, one can compute the encoding of $\mathbf{A}_{tgt}$ under the same $\mathbf{s}$ from a trapdoor basis of either $\mathbf{A}_0$ or $\mathbf{A}_1$: sample a low-norm Gaussian recoding matrix $\mathbf{R} \in \mathbb{Z}^{2m \times m}$ such that $[\mathbf{A}_0 \mid \mathbf{A}_1] \cdot \mathbf{R} = \mathbf{A}_{tgt} \pmod{q}$ and compute the encoding $\mathsf{encode}(\mathbf{A}_{tgt}, \mathbf{s}) = [\mathsf{encode}(\mathbf{A}_0, \mathbf{s}) \mid \mathsf{encode}(\mathbf{A}_1, \mathbf{s})] \cdot \mathbf{R}$. In order to evaluate the gates of circuits in the TOR-based ABE scheme, two values of input wires are targeted by $\mathbf{A}_0$, $\mathbf{A}_1$ and the value of the outgoing wire is associated with $\mathbf{A}_{tgt}$. A legitimate user uses the recoding matrix $\mathbf{R}$, which serves as a component of decryption key, to compute the encoding of $\mathbf{A}_{tgt}$.

A weak version of the TOR framework was also presented in [13] with instantiations from a broader class of assumptions, including the LWE and DBDH assumptions. In the LWE-based weak TOR scheme, the recoding matrix $\mathbf{R} \in \mathbb{Z}^{m \times m}$ connects two original matrices $\mathbf{A}_0$, $\mathbf{A}_1$ and the target matrix $\mathbf{A}_{tgt}$ through $\mathbf{A}_0 + \mathbf{A}_1 \cdot \mathbf{R} = \mathbf{A}_{tgt} \pmod{q}$ and only the trapdoor from $\mathbf{A}_1$ is needed to sample $\mathbf{R}$. According to [13], the LWE-based weak TOR scheme leads to an LWE-based ABE scheme for branching programs.

We note however, that while a deterministic finite automaton can in theory be represented as a branching program, a special kind of execution tree, such representation is undesirable because it is exponential in the input word length. One of the ways in which we avoid such exponential blow-up in the present paper, is by only partially unrolling the DFA execution, omitting the part of the execution history that no longer has any relevance to the remainder of the execution. Hence the corresponding structure in our case is not a tree but a directed acyclic graph with *undirected cycles* of a highly constrained type. Such special graph representation of a DFA machines also prevents us from directly using the GVW's weak TOR whose backtrackable property leads to directed cycles. We resolve this problem in a different way.

Key-Homomorphic Encryption and ABE for Circuits. Boneh et al. [7] recently introduced the notion of Fully Key-Homomorphic Public-Key Encryption (FKHE) with an instantiation from the LWE assumption. Two important applications of the LWE-based FKHE scheme proposed in [7] are compression of garbled circuits and a KP-ABE scheme for arithmetic (Boolean) circuits. The basic idea of the KP-ABE scheme in [7] is the follow. A ciphertext associated with an attribute string $\mathbf{x} = x_1 x_2 \ldots x_\ell \in \{0, 1\}^\ell$ has the LWE form

$\mathbf{s}^\top \cdot [\mathbf{A}|\mathbf{A}_1 + x_1\mathbf{G}| \ldots |\mathbf{A}_\ell + x_\ell\mathbf{G}] + \nu^\top$ where $\mathbf{A}, \mathbf{G}$, and $\mathbf{A}_i$ are public matrices in $\mathbb{Z}_q^{n \times m}$, and $\mathbf{A}_i$ is associated with the attribute x_i. A decryption key for a ℓ-input Boolean circuit C is a "short" basis of lattice $\Lambda_q^\perp([\mathbf{A}|\mathbf{A}_C])$ where the matrix $\mathbf{A}_C$ is uniquely and publicly defined by the circuit C and matrices $\mathbf{A}_1, \ldots, \mathbf{A}_\ell$. The surprising feature of the scheme is that there is a *publicly known* trapdoor for the lattice $\Lambda_q^\perp(\mathbf{G})$ which allows the decryptor to transfer above ciphertext into a new ciphertext $\mathbf{s}^\top \cdot [\mathbf{A}|\mathbf{A}_C + C(\mathbf{x})\mathbf{G}] + \tilde{\nu}^\top$. If $C(\mathbf{x}) = 0$, then the short basis of $\Lambda_q^\perp([\mathbf{A}|\mathbf{A}_C])$ enables decryption. A major selling point of this approach is to achieve KP-ABE for circuits where the size of the private key depends only on the circuit depth.

2   Preliminaries

Notations: For a positive integer n, $[n]$ denotes the set of positive integers no greater than n, i.e. $\{1, 2, \ldots, n\}$. Let $|n|$ be the absolute value of integer n. We use bold capital letters to denote matrices (e.g. $\mathbf{A}$), bold lowercase letters to denote vectors (e.g. $\mathbf{d}$) and regular lowercase letters to denote scalars (e.g. c). For positive integer $q \geq 2$, we represent $n \times m$ matrices with entries in $\mathbb{Z}_q$ by $\mathbb{Z}_q^{n \times m}$. We let $\mathbf{I}_m$ be the $m \times m$ identity matrix. The vectors are treated as column vectors, unless stated otherwise. The transpose of matrix $\mathbf{A}$ is denoted by $\mathbf{A}^\top$. The symbol "$[\cdot | \cdot]$" denotes the concatenation of two elements. For instance, let $\mathbf{A} \in \mathbb{Z}_q^{n \times m_1}$ and $\mathbf{B} \in \mathbb{Z}_q^{n \times m_2}$ be two matrices, and $[\mathbf{A}|\mathbf{B}]$ denotes a concatenated matrix in $\mathbb{Z}_q^{n \times (m_1 + m_2)}$. Let $\|\mathbf{v}\|$ be the standard Euclidean norm of vector $\mathbf{v} \in \mathbb{R}^m$. For a matrix $\mathbf{X} = [\mathbf{x}_1 | \mathbf{x}_2, \ldots | \mathbf{x}_k]$ with column vectors $\mathbf{x}_i$ in $\mathbb{R}^m$, $\|\mathbf{X}\|$ denotes the norm of matrix $\mathbf{X}$ which is the norm of its longest column, i.e. $\|\mathbf{X}\| = \max_i \|\mathbf{x}_i\|$. We denote the Gram-Schmidt orthogonalisation of $\mathbf{X}$ by $\tilde{\mathbf{X}} = \{\tilde{\mathbf{s}}_1, \tilde{\mathbf{s}}_2, \ldots, \tilde{\mathbf{s}}_k\}$ and the Gram-Schmidt norm of $\mathbf{X}$ by $\|\tilde{\mathbf{X}}\|$. For the security parameter λ, a function $\mathrm{negl}(\lambda)$ is negligible in λ if it is smaller than all polynomial fractions for a sufficiently large λ.

2.1   An Overview of Deterministic Finite Automata

A *deterministic* finite automaton M is a 5-tuple $(Q, \Sigma, \delta, s_0, F)$, where

1. Q is a finite set of states,
2. Σ is a finite set called alphabet,
3. $\delta : Q \times \Sigma \to Q$ is the transition function,
4. $s_0 \in Q$ is the start state,
5. $F \subseteq Q$ is a set of accept states.

Let $\mathcal{T}$ be the set of transitions associated with transition function δ, where $t = (s, s', b) \in \mathcal{T}$ iff $\delta(s, b) = s'$ for $s, s' \in Q$ and $b \in \Sigma$. Let $M = (Q, \Sigma, \delta, s_0, F)$ be a deterministic finite automaton, and $w = w_1 w_2 \cdots w_\ell \in \Sigma^*$ be an input string. M *accepts* w if there exists a sequence of states $r_0, r_1, \cdots, r_\ell \in Q$ with three conditions:

1. $r_0 = s_0$,
2. $\delta(r_i, w_i) = r_{i+1}$,
3. $r_\ell \in F$.

The language $L(M)$ accepted by a machine M is defined to be the set of all strings that are accepted by M: $L(M) = \{w : M \text{ accepts } w\}$. A language L is called regular if there exists a deterministic finite automaton M such that $L = L(M)$. Our scheme supports a restricted form of regular languages. In our scheme, the length of input string has a polynomial bound $\eta = \text{poly}(\lambda)$ where λ is the security parameter. Without loss of generality, we use $\Sigma = \{0, 1\}$ in our construction.

2.2 Definitions of ABE System for DFAs

The following definition follows from [21].

Definition 1 (Key-Policy ABE for DFAs). *A Key-Policy ABE scheme for DFAs consists of the following four algorithms:*

Setup($1^\lambda, \Sigma$) → (**Pub, Msk**)*: The system setup algorithm* **Setup** *takes the security parameter λ and an universal alphabet Σ as input, and outputs the public parameters* **Pub** *and master secret key* **Msk**.

KeyGen(**Pub, Msk**, M) → **Sk**$_M$*: The key generation algorithm takes the public parameters* **Pub**, *the master secret key* **Msk** *and a deterministic finite automaton M as input. It outputs a decryption key* **Sk**$_M$ *associated with M.*

Encrypt(**Pub**, w, **Msg**) → **Ctx**$_w$*: The encryption algorithm* **Encrypt** *takes as input the public parameters* **Pub**, *a string $w \in \Sigma^*$ and the message* **Msg**. *It outputs the ciphertext* **Ctx**$_w$ *associated with w (we assume w is explicitly included in* **Ctx**$_w$).

Decrypt(**Pub, Sk**$_M$, **Ctx**$_w$) → **Msg** *or $\bot$: The decryption algorithm takes as input the public parameters* **Pub**, *the decryption key which is associated with the deterministic finite automaton M and a ciphertext of message* **Msg** *that is encrypted with string w. It recovers the message* **Msg** *if $w \in L(M)$ or otherwise outputs the symbol $\bot$.*

We review the game-based selective-security definition for DFA-based ABE. The notion of ciphertext privacy, which implies both semantic security and recipient anonymity, is considered here. The selective security game between an adversary $\mathcal{A}$ and a simulator $\mathcal{B}$ is defined as follows:

- **Preparation.** The adversary $\mathcal{A}$ submits a string $w^* \in \Sigma^*$ as its challenge.
- **Setup.** $\mathcal{B}$ runs algorithm Setup to generate the public parameters Pub and master secret key Msk and passes Pub to $\mathcal{A}$.
- **Phase 1.** $\mathcal{A}$ adaptively issues the key generation queries for keys correspond to any DFA M of its choice. The only restriction is $w^* \notin L(M)$. $\mathcal{B}$ runs the algorithm KeyGen(Pub, Msk, M) and returns Sk$_M$.

- **Challenge.** $\mathcal{A}$ chooses a challenge message to be encrypted. $\mathcal{B}$ flips a random coin $\gamma \in \{0, 1\}$ bit. If $\gamma = 1$, the challenge ciphertext is returned. Otherwise, a random element in the ciphertext space is returned.
- **Phase 2.** This phase is exactly the same as **Phase 1**.
- **Guess.** Finally, $\mathcal{A}$ outputs a guess bit γ' of γ. It wins if $\gamma' = \gamma$.

The advantage of $\mathcal{A}$ in the above game is defined as $|\Pr[\gamma' = \gamma] - \frac{1}{2}|$. A KP-ABE scheme for DFAs is selectively secure if all probabilistic polynomial time (PPT) adversaries have at most negligible advantage in the above game. In the adaptive security model, the adversary dose not need to declare the challenge string w^* in the initial phase. Instead, it is able to decide the challenge string in the challenge phase.

3   Lattices

3.1   Integer Lattices

Definition 2 (Random Integer Lattice). *For a positive integer (later a prime) q, a matrix $\mathbf{A} \in \mathbb{Z}_q^{n \times m}$ and a vector $\mathbf{u} \in \mathbb{Z}_q^n$, define the m-dimensional full-rank integer lattice $\Lambda_q^{\perp}(\mathbf{A}) = \{\mathbf{e} \in \mathbb{Z}^m \text{ s.t. } \mathbf{Ae} = \mathbf{0} \mod q\}$ and its coset $\Lambda_q^{\mathbf{u}}(\mathbf{A}) = \{\mathbf{e} \in \mathbb{Z}^m \text{ s.t. } \mathbf{Ae} = \mathbf{u} \mod q\}$.*

3.2   Trapdoors of Lattices and Discrete Gaussians

In [3], Ajtai showed how to sample an essentially uniform matrix $\mathbf{A} \in \mathbb{Z}_q^{n \times m}$ along with a basis $\mathbf{B} \in \mathbb{Z}^{m \times m}$ of integer lattice $\Lambda_q^{\perp}(\mathbf{A})$ where $\mathbf{B}$ has low Gram-Schmidt norm. A further improvement was given by Alwen and Peikert [4].

Theorem 1 ([4], Theorem 3.2). *Let n, q, m be positive integer with $q \geq 2$ and $m \geq 6n \log q$. There exists a PPT algorithm TrapGen that outputs a pair $\mathbf{A} \in \mathbb{Z}_q^{n \times m}$, $\mathbf{B} \in \mathbb{Z}^{m \times m}$ such that $\mathbf{A}$ is statistically close to uniform in $\mathbb{Z}_q^{n \times m}$ and $\mathbf{B}$ is a basis of $\Lambda_q^{\perp}(\mathbf{A})$ satisfying $\|\tilde{\mathbf{B}}\| \leq O(\sqrt{n \log q})$ and $\|\mathbf{B}\| \leq O(n \log q)$ with all but negligible probability.*

Definition 3. *Let $m \in \mathbb{Z}_{>0}$ be a positive integer and $\Lambda \subset \mathbb{Z}^m$. For any vector $\mathbf{c} \in \mathbb{R}^m$ and any positive parameter $\sigma \in \mathbb{R}_{>0}$, $\forall \mathbf{y} \in \Lambda$, the discrete Gaussian distribution over Λ with center $\mathbf{c}$ and parameter σ is denoted by $\mathcal{D}_{\Lambda, \sigma, \mathbf{c}} = \rho_{\sigma, \mathbf{c}}(\mathbf{y}) / \rho_{\sigma, \mathbf{c}}(\Lambda)$ where $\rho_{\sigma, \mathbf{c}}(\mathbf{x}) = \exp\left(-\pi \|\mathbf{x} - \mathbf{c}\|^2 / \sigma^2\right)$ is the Gaussian function and $\rho_{\sigma, \mathbf{c}}(\Lambda) = \sum_{\mathbf{x} \in \Lambda} \rho_{\sigma, \mathbf{c}}(\mathbf{x})$. For notational convenience, $\rho_{\sigma, 0}$ and $\mathcal{D}_{\Lambda, \sigma, 0}$ are abbreviated as ρ_{σ} and $\mathcal{D}_{\Lambda, \sigma}$.*

For a matrix $\mathbf{U} = [\mathbf{u}_1 \mid \ldots \mid \mathbf{u}_k] \in \mathbb{Z}_q^{n \times k}$, define the $\mathcal{D}_{\Lambda_q^{\mathbf{U}}(\mathbf{A}), \sigma}$ be the discrete Gaussian distribution on matrices in $\mathbb{Z}_q^{m \times k}$ where the ith column is sampled from the distribution $\mathcal{D}_{\Lambda_q^{\mathbf{u}_i}(\mathbf{A}), \sigma}$ for $i \in [k]$.

Here, we recall several useful facts about discrete Gaussian distribution on lattices. The first fact on the bound of Gaussian vectors follows from Lemma 4.4 of [17]. The second and third fact are from Lemma 5.2 of [12]. The last two algorithms were given in [12]

Lemma 1. *Let $q > 2$ be an integer and $\mathbf{A} \in \mathbb{Z}_q^{n \times m}$ be a matrix where $m > n$. Let $\mathbf{B_A}$ be a basis of lattice $\Lambda_q^{\perp}(\mathbf{A})$ and $\sigma \geq \|\tilde{\mathbf{B}}_{\mathbf{A}}\| \omega\sqrt{\log m}$. Then for $\mathbf{c} \in \mathbb{R}^m$ and $\mathbf{u} \in \mathbb{Z}_q^n$:*

1. $\Pr[\|\mathbf{x} - \mathbf{c}\| > \sigma\sqrt{m} \;:\; \mathbf{x} \sim \mathcal{D}_{\Lambda_q^{\perp}(\mathbf{A}),\sigma,\mathbf{c}}] \leq \mathrm{negl}(n)$.
2. *Assume the columns of $\mathbf{A}$ generate the space $\mathbb{Z}_q^n$, Then for $\mathbf{e} \sim \mathcal{D}_{\mathbb{Z}^m,\sigma}$, $\mathbf{u} = \mathbf{A}\mathbf{e}$ mod q is statistically close to the uniform distribution over $\mathbb{Z}_q^n$.*
3. *For any $\mathbf{t} \in \Lambda_q^{\mathbf{u}}(\mathbf{A})$, the conditional distribution of $\mathbf{e} \sim D_{\mathbb{Z}^m,\sigma}$ given $\mathbf{A}\mathbf{e} = \mathbf{u}$ mod q is exactly $\mathbf{t} + D_{\Lambda_q^{\perp},\sigma,-\mathbf{t}}$.*
4. *There is a PPT algorithm SampleGaussian$(\mathbf{A}, \mathbf{B_A}, \sigma, \mathbf{c})$ that returns $\mathbf{x} \in \Lambda_q^{\perp}(\mathbf{A})$ drawn from a distribution statistically close to $\mathcal{D}_{\Lambda_q^{\perp}(\mathbf{A}),\sigma,\mathbf{c}}$.*
5. *There is a PPT algorithm SamplePre$(\mathbf{A}, \mathbf{B_A}, \mathbf{u}, \sigma)$ that returns a sample $\mathbf{x} \in \Lambda_q^{\mathbf{u}}(\mathbf{A})$ from a distribution statistically close to $\mathcal{D}_{\Lambda_q^{\mathbf{u}}(\mathbf{A}),\sigma}$.*

In our construction, we also need another discrete Gaussian sampling algorithm SampleLeft which is defined in [1]. Here we consider the case that the syndrome contains m vectors in $\mathbb{Z}_q^n$, i.e. a matrix in $\mathbb{Z}_q^{n \times m}$.

Lemma 2 ([1], Theorem 14). *Let $q > 2$, $m > n$. Let $\mathbf{A} \in \mathbb{Z}_q^{n \times m}$, $\mathbf{G} \in \mathbb{Z}_q^{n \times m_1}$, and $\mathbf{U} \in \mathbb{Z}_q^{n \times k}$ be three integer matrices with rank n. $\mathbf{B_A} \in \mathbb{Z}^{m \times m}$ is a basis of lattice $\Lambda_q^{\perp}(\mathbf{A})$. Let the Gaussian parameter $\sigma > \|\tilde{\mathbf{B}}_{\mathbf{A}}\| \cdot \omega(\sqrt{\log(m + m_1)})$. There is a PPT algorithm SampleLeft$(\mathbf{A}, \mathbf{G}, \mathbf{B_A}, \mathbf{U}, \sigma)$ that returns $\mathbf{T} \in \Lambda_q^{\mathbf{U}}([\mathbf{A}|\mathbf{G}]) \subset \mathbb{Z}^{(m+m_1) \times k}$ from a distribution statistically close to $\mathcal{D}_{\Lambda_q^{\mathbf{U}}([\mathbf{A}|\mathbf{G}]),\sigma}$.*

Instead of using a short basis of $\Lambda_q^{\perp}(\mathbf{A})$ to sample $\mathbf{T} \in \Lambda_q^{\mathbf{U}}([\mathbf{A}|\mathbf{G}])$ as in the above lemma, one can also use a proper short basis $\mathbf{B_G}$ of lattice $\Lambda_q^{\perp}(\mathbf{G})$ to sample $\mathbf{T}$ with the same distribution that is close to $\mathcal{D}_{\Lambda_q^{\mathbf{U}}([\mathbf{A}|\mathbf{G}]),\sigma}$ by employing the same principle as SampleLeft or the basis delegation technique of [10]. We refer to this algorithm as SolveRight. The following lemma is the mirror image of the previous lemma.

Lemma 3. *Let $q > 2$, $m_1 > n$. Let $\mathbf{A} \in \mathbb{Z}_q^{n \times m}$, $\mathbf{G} \in \mathbb{Z}_q^{n \times m_1}$, and $\mathbf{U} \in \mathbb{Z}_q^{n \times k}$ be three integer matrices with rank n. $\mathbf{B_G} \in \mathbb{Z}^{m_1 \times m_1}$ is a basis of lattice $\Lambda_q^{\perp}(\mathbf{G})$. Let the Gaussian parameter $\sigma > \|\tilde{\mathbf{B}}_{\mathbf{A}}\| \cdot \omega(\sqrt{\log(m + m_1)})$. There is a PPT algorithm SolveRight$(\mathbf{A}, \mathbf{G}, \mathbf{B_G}, \mathbf{U}, \sigma)$ that returns $\mathbf{T} \in \Lambda_q^{\mathbf{U}}([\mathbf{A}|\mathbf{G}]) \subset \mathbb{Z}^{(m+m_1) \times k}$ from a distribution statistically close to $\mathcal{D}_{\Lambda_q^{\mathbf{U}}([\mathbf{A}|\mathbf{G}]),\sigma}$.*

3.3   The LWE Hardness Assumption

The LWE (learning with errors) problem was first defined by Regev [19].

Definition 4 (($\mathbb{Z}_q, n, \chi$)-LWE Problem). *Consider a prime q, a positive integer n, and a distribution χ over $\mathbb{Z}_q$, all public. An ($\mathbb{Z}_q, n, \chi$)-LWE problem instance consists of access to an unspecified challenge oracle $\mathcal{O}$, being, either, a noisy pseudo-random sampler $\mathcal{O}_s$ carrying some constant random secret key $\mathbf{s} \in \mathbb{Z}_q^n$, or, a truly random sampler $\mathcal{O}_{\$}$, whose behaviors are respectively as follows:*

$\mathcal{O}_s$: *outputs noisy pseudo-random samples of the form* $(\mathbf{w}_i, v_i) = (\mathbf{w}_i, \mathbf{s}^\top \mathbf{w}_i + x_i) \in \mathbb{Z}_q^n \times \mathbb{Z}_q$, *where,* $\mathbf{s} \in \mathbb{Z}_q^n$ *is a uniformly distributed persistent secret key that is invariant across invocations,* $x_i \in \mathbb{Z}_q$ *is a freshly generated ephemeral additive noise component with distribution* χ, *and* $\mathbf{w}_i \in \mathbb{Z}_q^n$ *is a fresh uniformly distributed vector revealed as part of the output.*

$\mathcal{O}_\$$: *outputs truly random samples* $(\mathbf{w}_i, v_i) \in \mathbb{Z}_q^n \times \mathbb{Z}_q$, *drawn independently uniformly at random in the entire domain* $\mathbb{Z}_q^n \times \mathbb{Z}_q$.

The $(\mathbb{Z}_q, n, \chi)$-*LWE problem statement, or* LWE *for short, allows an unspecified number of queries to be made to the challenge oracle* $\mathcal{O}$, *with no stated prior bound. We say that an algorithm* $\mathcal{A}$ *decides the* $(\mathbb{Z}_q, n, \chi)$-*LWE problem if* $\left|\Pr[\mathcal{A}^{\mathcal{O}_s} = 1] - \Pr[\mathcal{A}^{\mathcal{O}_\$} = 1]\right|$ *is non-negligible for a random* $\mathbf{s} \in \mathbb{Z}_q^n$.

For the LWE problem with polynomial size q (known as the *standard* LWE problem), the average-case hardness is shown quantumly [19] and classically [9] as hard as certain standard lattice problems (e.g. the GapSVP problem). Peikert [18] showed a reduction from standard worst-case lattice problems to the LWE problem with exponentially large q (known as the *exponential* LWE problem).

Definition 5 ([1], Definition 8). *Consider a real parameter* $\alpha \in \{0, 1\}$ *and a prime* q. *Denote by* $\mathbb{T} = \mathbb{R}/\mathbb{Z}$ *the group of reals* $[0, 1)$ *with addition modulo 1. Denote by* Ψ_α *the distribution over* $\mathbb{T}$ *of a normal variable with mean 0 and standard deviation* $\alpha/\sqrt{2\pi}$ *then reduced modulo 1. Denote by* $\lfloor x \rceil = \lfloor x + \frac{1}{2} \rfloor$ *the nearest integer to the real* $x \in \mathbb{R}$. *We denote by* $\bar{\Psi}_\alpha$ *the discrete distribution over* $\mathbb{Z}_q$ *of the random variable* $\lfloor qX \rceil \bmod q$ *where the random variable* $X \in \mathbb{T}$ *has distribution* Ψ_α.

Theorem 2 ([19]). *Let* $\alpha \in \{0, 1\}$ *and let* q *be a prime such that* $\alpha q > 2\sqrt{n}$. *If there exists an efficient (possibly quantum) algorithm that solves* $(\mathbb{Z}_q, n, \chi)$-*LWE problem, then there exists an efficient quantum algorithm for approximating* SIVP *and* GapSVP *in the* ℓ_2 *norm, in the worst case, to within* $\tilde{O}(n/\alpha)$ *factors.*

The SIVP and GapSVP are both believed to be hard because the best known algorithms for 2^k-approximation of GapSVP and SIVP in k-dimensional lattices run in time $2^{\tilde{O}(n/k)}$. It follows from the above theorem that the LWE problem with noise ratio $\alpha = 2^{-n^\epsilon}$ is likely hard for some constant $\epsilon < 1$.

We will use the following lemma from [1] to show the correctness of the decryption in our scheme.

Lemma 4 ([1], Lemma 10). *Let* $\mathbf{d}$ *be some vector in* $\mathbb{Z}^m$ *and let* $\mathbf{y} \leftarrow \bar{\Psi}_\alpha^m$. *Then the quantity* $|\mathbf{y}^\top \mathbf{d}|$ *when treated as an integer in* $(-q/2, q/2]$ *satisfies*

$$|\mathbf{y}^\top \mathbf{d}| \le \|\mathbf{d}\| q\alpha \cdot \omega(\sqrt{\log m}) + \|\mathbf{d}\|\sqrt{m}/2$$

with all but negligible probability in m.

4   Attribute-Based Encryption for DFAs

4.1   Construction

- **Setup**$(1^\lambda, \Sigma = \{0,1\}, 1^\eta)$: The system setup algorithm Setup takes as input a security parameter λ, an universal alphabet $\Sigma = \{0,1\}$, and a bound $\eta \geq 0$ on the length of the input string. Then it does:

  1. Select 2η random matrices $\mathbf{G}_b^{(j)} \in \mathbb{Z}_q^{n \times m}$ for negative integers $j \in [-\eta, -1]$ and bit values $b \in \{0, 1\}$. The matrix $\mathbf{G}_b^{(j)}$ is associated with ciphertext input bit b at time position j (which is $|j|$ positions counting backwards from the end of the input that defines the time position 0).

  2. Select η random matrices $\mathbf{H}_i \in \mathbb{Z}_q^{n \times m}$ for $i \in [\eta]$. The matrix $\mathbf{H}_i$ is associated with the start state at time position $-i$ and thus also with ciphertext input strings of length i (since the accept states are acceptable only at the end of the input word or in other words time position 0).

  3. Run TrapGen to sample a matrix $\mathbf{A}_{start} \in \mathbb{Z}_q^{n \times m}$ along with a trapdoor basis $\mathbf{B}_{\mathbf{A}_{start}} \in \mathbb{Z}^{m \times m}$ of the lattice $\Lambda_q^{\perp}(\mathbf{A}_{start})$.

  4. Select a uniformly random vector $\mathbf{u} \in \mathbb{Z}_q^n$.

  5. Output the public parameters and master secret key as

$$\mathsf{Pub} = \left(\{\mathbf{G}_b^{(j)}\}_{b \in \{0,1\}, j \in [-\eta, -1]}, \ \{\mathbf{H}_i\}_{i \in [\eta]}, \ \mathbf{A}_{start}, \ \mathbf{u} \right); \ \mathsf{Msk} = \mathbf{B}_{\mathbf{A}_{start}}$$

- **KeyGen**$(\mathsf{Pub}, \mathsf{Msk}, M = (Q, \mathcal{T}, s_0, F))$: On input the public parameters Pub, the master secret key Msk, and a deterministic finite automaton M, the key generation algorithm does:

  1. For the start state $s_0 \in Q$, for each possible starting time position $j \in [-\eta, 0]$ (where s_0 at time position j is for the use with a ciphertext input string of length $|j|$):

     (a) Run the algorithm TrapGen to sample a random matrix $\mathbf{A}_{s_0}^{(j)} \in \mathbb{Z}_q^{n \times m}$ along with a respective trapdoor basis $\mathbf{B}_{\mathbf{A}_{s_0}^{(j)}} \in \mathbb{Z}^{m \times m}$ of $\Lambda_q^{\perp}(\mathbf{A}_{s_0}^{(j)})$.

     (b) Invoke the algorithm $\mathsf{SampleLeft}(\mathbf{A}_{start}, \mathbf{H}_{|j|}, \mathbf{B}_{\mathbf{A}_{start}}, \mathbf{A}_{s_0}^{(j)}, \sigma)$ to compute a low-norm Gaussian matrix $\mathbf{T}_{start}^{(j)} \in \mathbb{Z}^{2m \times m}$ such that

$$[\mathbf{A}_{start} \mid \mathbf{H}_{|j|}] \cdot \mathbf{T}_{start}^{(j)} = \mathbf{A}_{s_0}^{(j)} \pmod{q}.$$

  2. For each transition $t = (s, s', b) \in \mathcal{T}$, for each possible time position $j \in [-\eta, -1]$:

     (a) On the first occurrence of a transition to state s' with this value of j, run TrapGen to sample a matrix $\mathbf{A}_{s'}^{(j+1)} \in \mathbb{Z}_q^{n \times m}$ and a trapdoor basis $\mathbf{B}_{\mathbf{A}_{s'}^{(j+1)}} \in \mathbb{Z}^{m \times m}$ of the lattice $\Lambda_q^{\perp}(\mathbf{A}_{s'}^{(j+1)})$.

     (b) Invoke the algorithm $\mathsf{SampleLeft}(\mathbf{A}_s^{(j)}, \mathbf{G}_b^{(j)}, \mathbf{B}_{\mathbf{A}_s^{(j)}}, \mathbf{A}_{s'}^{(j+1)}, \sigma)$ to compute a low-norm Gaussian matrix $\mathbf{T}_t^{(j)} \in \mathbb{Z}^{2m \times m}$ such that

$$[\mathbf{A}_s^{(j)} \mid \mathbf{G}_b^{(j)}] \cdot \mathbf{T}_t^{(j)} = \mathbf{A}_{s'}^{(j+1)} \pmod{q}.$$

3. For each accept state $s_x \in F$, considered only such accept state(s) at time position 0:

   (a) Let $\mathbf{A}_{s_x}^{(0)}$ be the ephemeral state matrix already defined and in the previous steps (this matrix is already defined unless the automaton contains no transition into s_x).

   (b) Let $\mathbf{B}_{\mathbf{A}_{s_x}^{(0)}} \in \mathbb{Z}^{m \times m}$ be the basis of $\Lambda_q^{\perp}(\mathbf{A}_{s_x}^{(0)})$, previously obtained.

   (c) Run $\mathsf{SamplePre}(\mathbf{A}_{s_x}^{(0)}, \mathbf{B}_{\mathbf{A}_{s_x}^{(0)}}, \mathbf{u}, \sigma)$ to compute a vector $\mathbf{d}_{s_x} \sim \mathcal{D}_{\Lambda_q^{\mathbf{u}}(\mathbf{A}_{s_x}^{(0)}), \sigma}$ i.e. a $\mathbb{Z}^m$-vector with conditional discrete Gaussian distribution such that $\mathbf{A}_{s_x}^{(0)} \cdot \mathbf{d}_{s_x} = \mathbf{u} \pmod{q}$.

4. Output the decryption key for the DFA machine M as

$$\mathsf{Sk}_M = \left(\{\mathbf{T}_{start}^{(j)}\}_{j \in [-\eta, 0]}, \ \{\mathbf{T}_t^{(j)}\}_{t \in \mathcal{T}, j \in [-\eta, -1]}, \ \{\mathbf{d}_{s_x}\}_{s_x \in F} \right).$$

- **Encrypt$(\mathsf{Pub}, w, \mathsf{Msg})$**: The encryption algorithm takes as input the public parameters Pub, a binary string w with length $\ell \leq \eta$, and a message bit $\mathsf{Msg} \in \{0, 1\}$. Denote the i-th bit of w by $w[i]$. The algorithm then does:

  1. Randomly select a vector $\mathbf{s} \in \mathbb{Z}_q^n$.
  2. Select a noise scalar $\nu_0 \in \mathbb{Z}_q$ according to the distribution $\bar{\Psi}_\alpha$ and compute the scalar

$$c_0 = \mathbf{s}^\top \mathbf{u} + \nu_0 + \mathsf{Msg} \cdot \lfloor q/2 \rfloor.$$

  3. Select a noise vector $\nu_1 \in \mathbb{Z}_q^{(\ell+2)m}$, whose components are sampled independently from the distribution $\bar{\Psi}_\alpha$, and compute the vector

$$\mathbf{c}_1^\top = \mathbf{s}^\top \left[\mathbf{A}_{start} \mid \mathbf{H}_\ell \mid \mathbf{G}_{w[1]}^{(-\ell)} \mid \mathbf{G}_{w[2]}^{(-\ell+1)} \mid \cdots \mid \mathbf{G}_{w[\ell-1]}^{(-2)} \mid \mathbf{G}_{w[\ell]}^{(-1)} \right] + \nu_1^\top.$$

  4. Output the ciphertext for the attribute input string w as

$$\mathsf{Ctx}_w = (c_0, \mathbf{c}_1).$$

- **Decrypt$(\mathsf{Pub}, \mathsf{Sk}_M, \mathsf{Ctx}_w)$**: Given the public parameters Pub, a ciphertext Ctx_w, the attribute string w, and a secret key Sk_M for the DFA machine M, the decryption algorithm $\mathsf{Decrypt}$ does:

  1. If $w \notin L(M)$, return an error symbol $\perp$. Otherwise, find the execution path from the start state s_0 at time position $-\ell$ to an accept state s_x at time position 0. Collect the $\ell + 1$ transition matrices corresponding to the steps in the path. (Note, for a DFA, $w \in L(M)$ iff such path exists and is unique, and in our setup an accepting path consists of ℓ directed steps each of which consumes one ciphertext "input bit" matrix $\mathbf{G}_b^{(j)}$, plus one initial step which consumes the ciphertext "input length" matrix $\mathbf{H}_\ell$.)

  2. Use the $\ell + 1$ transition matrices $\mathbf{T}_{start}^{(-\ell)}$, $\left\{ \mathbf{T}_{t_i}^{(j)} \right\}_{j \in [-\ell, -1], i \in [\ell], t_i \in \mathcal{T}}$ in the path and the vector $\mathbf{d}_{s_x}$ associated with state-time matrix $\mathbf{A}_{s_x}^{(0)}$ to compute the decryption vector $\mathbf{d} \in \mathbb{Z}^{(\ell+2)m}$ as:

$$\mathbf{d} = \begin{bmatrix} \mathbf{T}_{start}^{(-\ell)} & & & \\ & \mathbf{I}_m & & \\ & & \mathbf{I}_m & \\ & & & \ddots & \\ & & & & \mathbf{I}_m \end{bmatrix} \times \begin{bmatrix} \mathbf{T}_{t_1}^{(-\ell)} & & & \\ & \mathbf{I}_m & & \\ & & \ddots & \\ & & & \mathbf{I}_m \end{bmatrix} \times \begin{bmatrix} \mathbf{T}_{t_2}^{(-\ell+1)} & & \\ & \ddots & \\ & & \mathbf{I}_m \end{bmatrix} \times \cdots \times \underbrace{\left[\mathbf{T}_{t_\ell}^{(-1)} \right]}_{\in \mathbb{Z}^{2m \times m}} \times \underbrace{\mathbf{d}_{s_x}}_{\in \mathbb{Z}^{m \times 1}}$$

$$\underbrace{}_{\in \mathbb{Z}^{(\ell+2)m \times (\ell+1)m}} \quad \underbrace{}_{\in \mathbb{Z}^{(\ell+1)m \times (\ell m)}} \quad \underbrace{}_{\in \mathbb{Z}^{(\ell m) \times (\ell-1)m}}$$

3. Compute the scalar $\Delta = c_0 - \mathbf{c}_1^\top \cdot \mathbf{d} \bmod q$ and output $\mathsf{Msg} = 0$ if $\|\Delta\| < q/4$, or $\mathsf{Msg} = 1$ if otherwise.

The vector $\mathbf{d}$ and the inner product $\mathbf{c}_1^\top \cdot \mathbf{d}$ can be also computed incrementally in the obvious way which does not require the full matrix product expansion in the expression of $\mathbf{d}$.

We show the correctness of decryption with properly chosen parameters in Appendix A and Lemma 5.

4.2   Proof of Security

Theorem 3. *If there exists a probabilistic polynomial-time algorithm $\mathcal{A}$ with advantage ε in attacking the above scheme in the selective security model, then there exists a probabilistic polynomial-time algorithm $\mathcal{B}$ that decides the $(\mathbb{Z}_q, n, \bar{\Psi}_\alpha)$-LWE problem with advantage ε, where α is as above (per Lemma 5).*

Proof. We show how to construct a simulation algorithm $\mathcal{B}$ to solve the LWE problem by using an efficient adversary $\mathcal{A}$ of the above scheme.

- **Preparation.** $\mathcal{A}$ outputs his challenge string $w^* \in \{0,1\}^\ell$ where $\ell \leq \eta$. Let the i-th bit of w^* be $w^*[i]$.
- **Instance.** $\mathcal{B}$ obtains $(\ell + 2)m + 1$ LWE tuples from the LWE challenge oracle $\mathcal{O}$:

$$\begin{aligned} [(\mathbf{w}, v)] &\in (\mathbb{Z}_q^n \times \mathbb{Z}_q) \\ [(\mathbf{w}_{-1}^1, v_{-1}^1), \ldots, (\mathbf{w}_{-1}^m, v_{-1}^m)] &\in (\mathbb{Z}_q^n \times \mathbb{Z}_q)^m \\ [(\mathbf{w}_0^1, v_0^1), \ldots, (\mathbf{w}_0^m, v_0^m)] &\in (\mathbb{Z}_q^n \times \mathbb{Z}_q)^m \\ [(\mathbf{w}_1^1, v_1^1), \ldots, (\mathbf{w}_1^m, v_1^m)] &\in (\mathbb{Z}_q^n \times \mathbb{Z}_q)^m \\ &\vdots \\ [(\mathbf{w}_\ell^1, v_\ell^1), \ldots, (\mathbf{w}_\ell^m, v_\ell^m)] &\in (\mathbb{Z}_q^n \times \mathbb{Z}_q)^m \end{aligned}$$

- **Setup.** $\mathcal{B}$ does the following to construct the public parameters:

   1. Set the vector $\mathbf{u} \in \mathbb{Z}_q^n$ as $\mathbf{w}$, i.e. $\mathbf{u} = \mathbf{w}$. Construct the matrix $\mathbf{A}_{start} = [\mathbf{w}_{-1}^1 \mid \ldots \mid \mathbf{w}_{-1}^m] \in \mathbb{Z}_q^{n \times m}$ by using the -1-st set of LWE tuples.
   2. To set the matrices $\mathbf{H}_i$ for $i \in [\eta]$, do:
      (a) Build the matrix $\mathbf{H}_\ell = [\mathbf{w}_0^1 \mid \ldots \mid \mathbf{w}_0^m] \in \mathbb{Z}_q^{n \times m}$ from the 0-th set of LWE tuples.

(b) Set the matrices $\mathbf{H}_i$ for $i \in \{1, 2, \ldots, \ell - 1, \ell + 1, \ldots, \eta\}$ by running TrapGen to sample each matrix $\mathbf{H}_i \in \mathbb{Z}_q^{n \times m}$ together with a short basis $\mathbf{B}_{\mathbf{H}_i} \in \mathbb{Z}_q^{m \times m}$ of the lattice $\Lambda_q^{\perp}(\mathbf{H}_i)$.

3. Set the matrices $\mathbf{G}_b^{(j)}$ for $j \in [-\eta, -\ell - 1]$ and $b \in \{0, 1\}$, by picking them uniformly at random from $\mathbb{Z}_q^{n \times m}$.

4. To set the matrices $\mathbf{G}_b^{(j)}$, for $j \in [-\ell, -1]$ and $b \in \{0, 1\}$, do:

   (a) Set $\mathbf{G}_{w^*[\ell+j+1]}^{(j)} = [\mathbf{w}_{\ell+j+1}^1 \mid \cdots \mid \mathbf{w}_{\ell+j+1}^m] \in \mathbb{Z}_q^{n \times m}$ by using the $\ell + j + 1$-th set of LWE tuples.

   (b) Set $\mathbf{G}_{1-w^*[\ell+j+1]}^{(j)}$ by invoking TrapGen to sample $\mathbf{G}_{1-w^*[\ell+j+1]}^{(j)}$ along with a short basis of $\Lambda_q^{\perp}(\mathbf{G}_{1-w^*[\ell+j+1]}^{(j)})$.

5. Publish the public parameters

$$\mathsf{Pub} = \left(\{\mathbf{G}_b^{(j)}\}_{b \in \{0,1\}, j \in [-\eta, -1]}, \ \{\mathbf{H}_i\}_{i \in [\eta]}, \ \mathbf{A}_{start}, \ \mathbf{u} \right)$$

– **Phase 1.** In this phase, $\mathcal{A}$ adaptively submits DFAs $M = (Q, \mathcal{T}, s_0, F)$ such that $w^* \notin L(M)$ to request the corresponding keys Sk_M. To construct the decryption key for a given M, $\mathcal{B}$ proceeds as follows:

1. For the start state $s_0 \in Q$, for all time positions $j \in [-\eta, 0] \setminus \{-\ell\}$, run TrapGen multiple times to sample matrices $\mathbf{A}_{s_0}^{(j)} \in \mathbb{Z}_q^{n \times m}$ with corresponding short bases $\mathbf{B}_{\mathbf{A}_{s_0}^{(j)}} \in \mathbb{Z}_q^{m \times m}$ for $\Lambda_q^{\perp}(\mathbf{A}_{s_0}^{(j)})$.

2. For the start transition at all time positions $j \in [-\eta, 0] \setminus \{-\ell\}$, $\mathcal{B}$ knows the short basis $\mathbf{B}_{\mathbf{H}_{|j|}}$ of $\mathbf{H}_{|j|}$. It computes the start transition matrix by using the algorithm SolveRight to get $\mathbf{T}_{start}^{(j)}$ such that $[\mathbf{A}_{start} \mid \mathbf{H}_{|j|}] \cdot \mathbf{T}_{start}^{(j)} = \mathbf{A}_{s_0}^{(j)} \pmod{q}$. To see that $\mathbf{T}_{start}^{(j)}$ is well-formed, by Lemma 2 and Lemma 3, the matrix $\mathbf{T}_{start}^{(j)}$ constructed from the "left-hand" trapdoor basis $\mathbf{B}_{\mathbf{A}_{start}}$ (as in the real scheme) has the same distribution as the one constructed from the "right-hand" trapdoor basis $\mathbf{B}_{\mathbf{H}_{|j|}}$ (as here in the simulation), with overwhelming probability.

3. For the start transition at time position $j = -\ell$, $\mathcal{B}$ does not have a trapdoor for the matrix $\mathbf{H}_\ell$. Instead, it runs the algorithm SampleGaussian to sample a low-norm matrix with distribution $(\mathcal{D}_{\mathbb{Z}^m, \sigma})^m$ and takes it to be the transition matrix $\mathbf{T}_{start}^{(-\ell)}$.

4. For the start state $s_0 \in Q$ at time position $j = -\ell$, using the identity matrix $\mathbf{I}_m$ as a short basis of the lattice $\mathbb{Z}^{m \times m}$, $\mathcal{B}$ computes the state-time matrix for state s_0 at time position ℓ as: $\mathbf{A}_{s_0}^{(\ell)} = [\mathbf{A}_{start}^{(-\ell)} \mid \mathbf{H}_\ell] \cdot \mathbf{T}_{start}^{(-\ell)}$ mod q. By the facts 2 and 3 of Lemma 1, matrix $\mathbf{A}_{s_0}^{(\ell)}$ has a distribution which is statistically close to the distribution output by TrapGen in the real scheme. $\mathbf{T}_{start}^{(-\ell)}$ here also has the correct Gaussian distribution.

5. For all paths starting from s_0 at the time positions apart from $-\ell$, $\mathcal{B}$ has trapdoor bases for the matrices $\mathbf{A}_{s_0}^{(j)}$ since we computed them in the first step. $\mathcal{B}$ constructs the transition matrices in the same way as it does in the real scheme. For the transition $t = (s, s', b) \in \mathcal{T}$ with time position j, the state matrix $\mathbf{A}_s^{(j)}$ must be already defined with its trapdoor $\mathbf{B}_{\mathbf{A}_s^{(j)}}$.

(a) $\mathcal{B}$ runs TrapGen to generate the ephemeral state-time matrices $\mathbf{A}_{s'}^{(j+1)}$ along with a trapdoor basis $\mathbf{B}_{\mathbf{A}_{s'}^{(j+1)}}$.

(b) Then it runs SampleLeft to compute a matrix $\mathbf{T}_t^{(j)} \in \mathbb{Z}^{2m \times m}$ such that $[\mathbf{A}_s^{(j)} \mid \mathbf{G}_b^{(j)}] \cdot \mathbf{T}_t^{(j)} = \mathbf{A}_{s'}^{(j+1)} \pmod{q}$.

With the direction of the transitions facing forward, the algorithm constructs the "forest" of all possible transitions $t \in \mathcal{T}$ that could be taken at any time position j subsequent to launching the DFA from the start state s_0 at a time position other than $-\ell$. This algorithm generates all transitions that could possibly be needed in any computation path to an accept state, except for such transitions at such time position that could only be reached when the input word has length ℓ.

6. For every computation path starting from s_0 at time position $-\ell$, since $w^* \notin L(M)$ at some time position $j^* \in [-\ell, -1]$, the input symbol $b = w[\ell + j^* + 1]$ must be such that $b = 1 - w^*[\ell + j^* + 1]$, i.e., the input w must deviate from w^* before reaching an accept state at time position 0. Otherwise w^* would be in the language. The bit where the bifurcation occurs corresponds to a ciphertext matrix $\mathbf{G}_{1-w^*[\ell+j^*+1]}^{(j^*)}$ for which $\mathcal{B}$ had constructed a trapdoor. Along every path of length ℓ, there are three cases of transition to consider, depending on whether the transition lies before, at, or after a bifurcation:

(a) Before bifurcation: this is the case of a transition $t = (s, s', b) \in \mathcal{T}$ at time position $j < j^*$: In this case, $\mathcal{A}$ started from s_0 at time position $-\ell$ and the input substring so far is a prefix of the challenge input string w^*. In this case, the state-time matrix $\mathbf{A}_s^{(j)}$ is defined without trapdoor. $\mathcal{B}$ runs algorithm SampleGaussian to sample a Gaussian matrix $\mathbf{T}_t^{(j)} \sim (\mathcal{D}_{\mathbb{Z}^m, \sigma})^m$ and computes the "next" state-time matrix along the w^*-input path: $\mathbf{A}_{s'}^{(j+1)} = [\mathbf{A}_s^{(j)} \mid \mathbf{G}_b^{(j)}] \cdot \mathbf{T}_t^{(j)} \bmod q$. (The first matrix along this path $\mathbf{A}_0^{(-\ell)}$ is previously defined.)

(b) At the bifurcation: this is the case of the transition $t = (s, s', b) \in \mathcal{T}$ at time position $j = j^*$: $\mathcal{B}$ runs TrapGen to sample a random state matrix $\mathbf{A}_{s'}^{(j^*+1)}$ with a short basis $\mathbf{B}_{\mathbf{A}_{s'}^{(j^*+1)}} \in \mathbb{Z}^{m \times m}$ for lattice $\Lambda_q^{\perp}(\mathbf{A}_{s'}^{(j^*+1)})$. Then, it computes the transition matrix $\mathbf{T}_t^{(j^*)}$ by using the algorithm SolveRight with trapdoor basis of the $\mathbf{G}$ matrix such that $[\mathbf{A}_s^{(j^*)} \mid \mathbf{G}_{1-w^*[\ell+j^*+1]}^{(j^*)}] \cdot \mathbf{T}_t^{(j^*)} = \mathbf{A}_{s'}^{(j^*+1)} \bmod q$. (The trapdoor of the $\mathbf{G}_{1-w^*[\ell+j^*+1]}^{(j^*)}$ matrix allows this transition matrix to "bridge" the current trapdoorless state-time matrix $\mathbf{A}_s^{(j^*)}$ to the next matrix $\mathbf{A}_{s'}^{(j^*+1)}$, which is already defined with a trapdoor.) Here $\mathbf{T}_t^{(j^*)}$ has the proper distribution.

(c) After the bifurcation: this is the case of a transition $t = (s, s', b) \in \mathcal{T}$ at time position $j > j^*$: In this case, the state-time matrix $\mathbf{A}_s^{(j)}$ has been defined with a trapdoor $\mathbf{B}_{\mathbf{A}_s^{(j)}}$ for the associated lattice. If the next state-time matrix has not been defined yet, $\mathcal{B}$ runs TrapGen to generate the next ephemeral state-time matrices $\mathbf{A}_{s'}^{(j+1)} \in \mathbb{Z}_q^{n \times m}$ and a "short" basis $\mathbf{B}_{\mathbf{A}_{s'}^{(j+1)}} \in \mathbb{Z}^{m \times m}$. It may also be the cases that the next matrix may already have been defined, possibly with or without a trapdoor (for the situation that it has been defined without trapdoor, see below). Once the target matrix is set up, $\mathcal{B}$ runs SampleLeft with Gaussian parameter σ to compute a low-norm Gaussian matrix $\mathbf{T}_t^{(j)} \in \mathbb{Z}^{2m \times m}$ such that $[\mathbf{A}_s^{(j)} \mid \mathbf{G}_b^{(j)}] \cdot \mathbf{T}_t^{(j)} = \mathbf{A}_{s'}^{(j+1)} \pmod{q}$. Here, $\mathbf{T}_t^{(j)}$ has the right distribution, because in this step, $\mathcal{B}$ acts the same as the KeyGen algorithms does in the real scheme.

(d) **Remark: special cases.**

A special case of (c) is when a transition $t = (s, s', b) \in \mathcal{T}$ at time position $j > j^*$ after bifurcation brings the execution back to the same state-time $(s', j + 1)$ where we would be after evaluating the challenge w^* up to time $j + 1$ and the state-time matrix $\mathbf{A}_{s'}^{(j+1)}$ has no trapdoor. When this happens, we "waste" the trapdoor that we gained from the earlier bifurcation, by using it to transition back to a target matrix $\mathbf{A}_{s'}^{(j+1)}$ that does not have a trapdoor. Similarly, special cases of (a) or (b) occur when, subsequent to a prior bifurcation, we have already returned back on the path defined by the challenge input word w^* per the previous special case. When this happens, it is as if no bifurcation had occurred yet, and we have to wait for the next bifurcation to depart (again) from the non-accept path defined by the challenge word w^* on which we have returned.

7. Per the previous steps, all accept states $s_x \in F$ at position time 0 (at least those that can be reached at all from the start state) have a defined state-time matrix $\mathbf{A}_{s_x}^{(0)}$ with a trapdoor basis $\mathbf{B}_{\mathbf{A}_{s_x}^{(0)}}$ of $\Lambda_q^\perp(\mathbf{A}_{s_x}^{(0)})$. It follows that $\mathcal{B}$ is able to compute a low-norm Gaussian decryption vector $\mathbf{d}_{s_x} \in \mathbb{Z}_q^m$ for all states $s_x \in F$ such that $\mathbf{A}_{s_x}^{(0)} \cdot \mathbf{d}_{s_x} = \mathbf{u} \pmod{q}$ by calling SamplePre.

8. Finally, $\mathcal{B}$ provides $\mathcal{A}$ with the key consisting of:

$$\mathsf{Sk}_M = \left(\{\mathbf{T}_{start}^{(j)}\}_{j \in [-\eta, 0]}, \ \{\mathbf{T}_t^{(j)}\}_{t \in \mathcal{T}, j \in [-\eta, -1]}, \ \{\mathbf{d}_{s_x}\}_{s_x \in F} \right)$$

- **Challenge.** $\mathcal{A}$ chooses a challenge message Msg^*. $\mathcal{B}$ outputs the challenge ciphertext $\mathsf{Ctx}_{w^*} = (c_0, \mathbf{c}_1)$ as:

$$c_0 = v + \mathsf{Msg}^* \cdot \lfloor q/2 \rfloor$$
$$\mathbf{c}_1^\top = [v_{-1}^1 \ldots v_{-1}^m \mid v_0^1 \ldots v_0^m \mid v_1^1 \ldots v_1^m \mid \ldots \mid v_{\ell-1}^1 \ldots v_{\ell-1}^m \mid v_\ell^1 \ldots v_\ell^m]$$

If $\mathcal{B}$'s LWE challenge comes from the oracle $\mathcal{O}_s$, it is not difficult to see this is a valid ciphertext for w^* under some unknown random encryption vector $\mathbf{s} \in \mathbb{Z}_q^n$. If $\mathcal{B}$'s challenge is from oracle $\mathcal{O}_\$$, the challenge ciphertext is uniformly random and $\mathcal{A}$ gets no advantage.

- **Phase 2.** The same as **Phase 1.**

- **Guess.** Eventually, $\mathcal{A}$ outputs the guess γ' as to whether the ciphertext is valid or not. If $\gamma' = 1$, $\mathcal{B}$ outputs "$\mathcal{O}_s$". Otherwise, $\mathcal{B}$ outputs "$\mathcal{O}_\$$". If $\mathcal{A}$ has probability $\frac{1}{2} + \varepsilon$ in guessing the validity of the ciphertext, $\mathcal{B}$ will decide the LWE oracle correctly with probability at least $\frac{1}{2} + \varepsilon$.

As shown, all the elements presented to the adversary $\mathcal{A}$ in the simulation are distributed as in the real scheme, so the simulation is indistinguishable from the real scheme.   □

Corollary 1. *Under the conditions and in the sense of Theorem 3, the scheme is secure under the standard* LWE *assumption on inputs of polylogarithmic length, i.e.* $\alpha = 1/O(poly(n))$ *when* $\eta = O(polylog(n))$.

Corollary 2. *Under the conditions and in the sense of Theorem 3, the scheme is secure under an exponential* LWE *assumption on inputs of polylogarithmic length, i.e.* $\alpha = exp(-O(poly(n)))$ *when* $\eta = O(poly(n))$.

5   Efficiency and Further Discussion

5.1   Efficiency

Firstly, we analyse the efficiency of our direct construction and other indirect constructions from lattices. To convert a deterministic finite automaton $M = (Q, \Sigma, \delta, s_0, F)$ with fixed input length ℓ into a circuit, one could get such circuit with ℓ input nodes, size (number of gates) $O(\ell \cdot |Q|)$, and depth $O(\ell \cdot \log |Q|)$. We compare the efficiency of our scheme with other circuit-based constructions based on this conversion. Since the DFAs in our scheme are polynomially bounded, one can get ABE for DFAs with bounded input length η by converting any bounded DFA machine into one circuit (handles input strings with η different lengths by one circuit), and then applying the ABE schemes for circuits from [7,13]. For this conversion, the final circuit has $\eta(\eta+1)/2$ input wires, depth $O(\eta \cdot \log |Q| + \log \eta)$ and size $O(\eta^2 \cdot |Q|)$.

Let λ be the security parameter. Let $n = n(\lambda)$ and $q = q(\lambda)$ be chosen such that the LWE problem is hard. Let $m = O(n \log q)$ be the dimension of integer lattice, and $|C|$ be the size of circuit C. For simplicity, we use m and η to express the size of parameters. We assume $|Q| \leq \eta$.

In our construction, the LWE parameter q is set to be $q = O(m^\eta)$ (see the Lemma 5 and recall in the decryption procedure noise increases exponentially). As the public parameter roughly consists of $O(\eta)$ matrices in $\mathbb{Z}_q^{n \times m}$, it has size $O(\eta^2 m^2 \log m)$. The decryption key in our construction consists of $O(\eta|Q|)$ matrices in $\mathbb{Z}_q^{2m \times m}$, and has size $O(\eta^2 |Q| m^2 \log m)$. The ciphertext in our scheme is up to a vector in $\mathbb{Z}_q^{(\eta+2)m}$. Therefore, it has size $O(\eta^2 m \log m)$.

For the generic construction from [13], the maximum depth of circuits is set to be $d_{max} = O(\eta \cdot \log |Q| + \log \eta)$ and $q = O(m^{(\eta \cdot \log |Q| + \log \eta)})$. The public parameters contain $O(\eta^2)$ matrices in $\mathbb{Z}_q^{n \times m}$ in order to handle input strings with length $\eta(\eta + 1)/2$, and thus have size $O(\eta^3 \cdot m^2 \log m)$. The decryption key roughly consists of $|C| = O(\eta^2 \cdot |Q|)$ recoding matrices in $\mathbb{Z}_q^{2m \times m}$ plus the description of C. So the decryption key in [13] is of size $O(\eta^3 |Q| \cdot m^2 \log m)$. The ciphertext in [13] has size $O(\eta^2 \cdot m \log m)$.

For the generic construction from [7], we set $q = O(m^{(\eta \cdot \log |Q| + \log \eta)})$. The decryption key consists of a matrix in $\mathbb{Z}_q^{2m \times m}$ and a description of the circuit C. So it has size $O(\eta \cdot m^2 \log m)$. The size of public parameters and ciphertext in [7] are the same as the ones in [13], i.e. $O(\eta^3 \cdot m^2 \log m)$ and $O(\eta^2 \cdot m \log m)$ respectively.

The comparison result is summarised in Table 1. Our construction enjoys increased efficiency.

Table 1. Efficiency comparison

	LWE modulus q	|Pub|	|Sk|	|Ctx|
This work	$q = O(m^\eta)$	$O(\eta^2 m^2 \log m)$	$O(\eta^2 |Q| m^2 \log m)$	$O(\eta^2 m \log m)$
[13]	$q = O(m^{(\eta \log |Q| + \log \eta)})$	$O(\eta^3 m^2 \log m)$	$O(\eta^3 |Q| m^2 \log m)$	$O(\eta^2 m \log m)$
[7]	$q = O(m^{(\eta \log |Q| + \log \eta)})$	$O(\eta^3 m^2 \log m)$	$O(\eta m^2 \log m)$	$O(\eta^2 m \log m)$

5.2   Discussion

ABE for Bounded NFAs. One natural question is how to extend the DFA-based scheme into the one that is able to handle non-deterministic finite automata (NFAs). With minor changes, our approach gives an ABE candidate for bounded NFAs that runs in polynomial time and accepts polynomial size inputs. We provide a brief discussion here. In a bounded NFA machine, one state may have multiple outgoing paths. Also, there is a special "empty" transition function $\delta(s, \$) \mapsto s'$ that shifts a DFA machine from one state s to another state s' without digesting any input symbol (we use \$ to represent this empty symbol). The candidate works as follow. For any two transitions $\delta(s, b) \mapsto s'$ and $\delta(s, b) \mapsto s''$ at a same time position, say j, we pick two state matrices for s' and s'' with trapdoors and sample the transition matrices for these two transition using the trapdoor from the "root" state s. For the special "empty" transition $\delta(s, \$) \mapsto s'$, we neglect the input $\mathbf{G}$ matrix and simply sample a transition matrix $\mathbf{T} \in \mathbb{Z}^{m \times m}$ such that $\mathbf{A}_s^{(j)} \cdot \mathbf{T} = \mathbf{A}_{s'}^{(j)} \pmod{q}$ without increasing the time positions (recall $j < 0$ and this transition equation indicates that the machine still hasn't been reading the $\ell + j + 1$'th input letter where ℓ is the length of input string). We know of no attacks to this scheme, but we can not prove it is secure. The main issue in adapting the security proof in our DFA-based construction is that there is a possibility that two uncontrolled states (the matrices defined without trapdoors) map to the same target state through the *same* challenge input letter. In such situation, the simulator has no help from the input letter. It would only be able to sample one low-norm transition matrix to define the target matrix but can not compute the low-norm transition matrix for another path without the trapdoor.

The Weak Two-to-One Recoding is Inadequate for Our Construction. One may wonder whether the weak TOR technique proposed in [13], which may potentially result in more efficient schemes (for instance, ones with smaller LWE parameter q), is applicable for our purpose. It turns out such technique is inadequate. The reason is that the weak TOR suffers from backtracking attack. In our construction, the execution of a DFA machine is depicted as a special directed acyclic graph that contains no direct cycles. Two different execution paths starting from different time positions may intersect at one state with the same time position. The adversary is able to backtrack from the state with time position $j+1$ backwardly to a state with time position j. More specifically, if we apply the weak TOR to construct the transition equation as $\mathbf{A}_s^{(j)} + \mathbf{G}_b^{(j)} \cdot \mathbf{T}_t^{(j)} = \mathbf{A}_{s'}^{(j+1)} \pmod{q}$ for a transition $t = (s, s', b)$ at time position j ($\mathbf{T}_t^{(j)}$ is sampled by using the trapdoor from $\mathbf{G}_b^{(j)}$), one can illegally create a backward transition $t' = (s', s, b)$ from state s' at time position $j+1$ to state s at time position j with transition matrix $\mathbf{T}' = -\mathbf{T}_t^{(j)}$. This leads to an insecure scheme in which adversaries can splice the fragments of two execution paths, which start from different time positions, into one illegal path by using above backward transition. We note that this does not happen with the (exponentially sized) branching programs of [13], because such branching programs retain the entire execution history in their states.

6   Conclusion

In this paper, we propose the first direct construction of attribute-based encryption for finite automata with bounded input length from lattices. Its security is based on the hardness of the learning with errors (LWE) problem.

Our construction is simple and more efficient than indirect constructions able to provide this functionality, such as key-homomorphism and two-to-one recoding. Our construction is based on a kind of two-to-one recoding technique for the direct (but simulatable) encoding of a tape as a "matrix ribbon" which can then be manipulated locally using linear key delegation operations directed by an outside ciphertext-driven logic. The main contribution is the way we encode such bounded form of DFAs economically into directed acyclic graph with high constrains.

It is an intriguing question to generalise our "ribbon" technique to be able to handle non-deterministic automata and/or more expressive tape machines such as Turing machines in the bounded form, which we were recently able to achieve. An even more challenging question is to construct ABE scheme for fully functional DFAs and NFAs, thus without a bound on the input length from lattices.

A   Parameters and Correctness of Construction

By applying the decryption algorithm, we have $\Delta = \mathsf{Msg} \cdot \lfloor q/2 \rfloor + \nu_0 - \nu_1^\top \cdot \mathbf{d}$. Let $\mathsf{Error} = \nu_0 - \nu_1^\top \cdot \mathbf{d}$. In order to correctly recover the message, we must ensure that the noise term $|\mathsf{Error}| < q/4$. The following lemma states this fact.

Lemma 5. *Suppose the parameters α and q are set as:*

$$\alpha \leq \left(\omega(\sqrt{\log m})\sigma^{\eta+2}m^{(\eta+2)/2}\right)^{-1}, \quad q = \Omega\left(\sigma^{\eta+2}m^{(\eta+3)/2}\right),$$

the quantity $|\mathsf{Error}|$ is bounded by $q/4$ with overwhelming probability.

Proof. Notice that all the transition matrices used to construct the decryption vector $\mathbf{d}$ have discrete Gaussian distribution in $\mathbb{Z}^{2m\times m}$ with parameter σ. The norm of those are all bounded by $\sigma\sqrt{m}$ according to the fact 1 of Lemma 1. Likewise, since the vector $\mathbf{d}_{s_x} \sim \mathcal{D}_{\Lambda_q^u(\mathbf{A}_{s_x}^{(0)}),\sigma}$, by the fact 1 of Lemma 1, we also have $\|\mathbf{d}_{s_x}\| \leq \beta = \sigma\sqrt{m}$.

Therefore, by using Lemma 4,

$$|\mathsf{Error}| = |\nu_0 - \nu_1^\top \cdot \mathbf{d}| \leq |\nu_0| + |\nu_1^\top \cdot \mathbf{d}|$$
$$\leq \left(|\nu_0| \leq q\alpha\omega(\sqrt{\log m}) + 1/2\right) + \left(\|\mathbf{d}\|q\alpha\omega(\sqrt{\log m}) + \|\mathbf{d}\|\sqrt{m}/2\right)$$

It now suffices to bound $\mathbf{d}$. We have $\|\mathbf{d}\|^2 \leq \sum_{i=1}^{\ell+1}(\beta^i)^2 \cdot \|\mathbf{d}_{s_x}\|^2 \leq (\eta+1)(\sigma^2 m)^{\eta+2}$. Thus $\|\mathbf{d}\| \leq \sqrt{(\eta+1)}\sigma^{\eta+2}m^{(\eta+2)/2} \leq O(\sigma^{\eta+2}m^{(\eta+2)/2})$.

Summing up, we have

$$|\mathsf{Error}| \leq \left(q\alpha\omega(\sqrt{\log m}) + 1/2\right)$$
$$+ \left(q\alpha\omega(\sqrt{\log m}) + \sqrt{m}/2\right)\sqrt{(\eta+1)}\sigma^{\eta+2}m^{(\eta+2)/2}$$
$$\leq q\alpha\omega(\sqrt{\log m})O(\sigma^{\eta+2}m^{(\eta+2)/2}) + O(\sigma^{\eta+2}m^{(\eta+3)/2})$$

To make $|\mathsf{Error}| < q/4$, it is sufficient to set $\alpha \leq \left(\omega(\sqrt{\log m})\sigma^{\eta+2}m^{(\eta+2)/2}\right)^{-1}$ and $q = \Omega\left(\sigma^{\eta+2}m^{(\eta+3)/2}\right)$. □

To set the remaining parameters, we need to ensure the conditions:

1. we be able to run the algorithm TrapGen (i.e. $m > 6n\log q$);
2. the Gaussian parameter σ be large enough for SamplePre and SampleLeft (i.e. $\sigma > \|\tilde{\mathbf{B}}\| \cdot \omega(\sqrt{\log m})$ where $\mathbf{B}$ is a basis output by TrapGen);
3. the LWE average-case to worst-case reduction apply (i.e. $q > 2\sqrt{n}/\alpha$).

One consistent selection is to set the parameters as follows:

- The maximum length of input: $\eta = O(\lambda)$
- The lattice dimensions: $m = 6n^{1+\delta}$, where $n^\delta > \lceil \log q \rceil$
- The Gaussian parameter $\sigma = m \cdot \omega(\sqrt{\log n})$
- The prime modulus $q = m^{(3\eta+5)/2} \cdot \omega(\sqrt{\log n})$
- The LWE parameter $\alpha = \left(m^{3(\eta+2)/2} \cdot \omega(\sqrt{\log n})\right)^{-1}$

References

1. Agrawal, S., Boneh, D., Boyen, X.: Efficient lattice (H)IBE in the standard model. In: Gilbert, H. (ed.) EUROCRYPT 2010. LNCS, vol. 6110, pp. 553–572. Springer, Heidelberg (2010)
2. Agrawal, S., Freeman, D.M., Vaikuntanathan, V.: Functional encryption for inner product predicates from learning with errors. In: Lee, D.H., Wang, X. (eds.) ASIACRYPT 2011. LNCS, vol. 7073, pp. 21–40. Springer, Heidelberg (2011)
3. Ajtai, M.: Generating hard instances of lattice problems (extended abstract). In: Proceedings of STOC 1996, pp. 99–108. ACM (1996)
4. Alwen, J., Peikert, C.: Generating shorter bases for hard random lattices. Theor. Comput. Syst. **48**(3), 535–553 (2011)
5. Attrapadung, N.: Dual system encryption via doubly selective security: framework, fully secure functional encryption for regular languages, and more. In: Nguyen, P.Q., Oswald, E. (eds.) EUROCRYPT 2014. LNCS, vol. 8441, pp. 557–577. Springer, Heidelberg (2014)
6. Boneh, D., Boyen, X.: Efficient selective-ID secure identity-based encryption without random oracles. In: Cachin, C., Camenisch, J.L. (eds.) EUROCRYPT 2004. LNCS, vol. 3027, pp. 223–238. Springer, Heidelberg (2004)
7. Boneh, D., Gentry, C., Gorbunov, S., Halevi, S., Nikolaenko, V., Segev, G., Vaikuntanathan, V., Vinayagamurthy, D.: Fully key-homomorphic encryption, arithmetic circuit ABE and compact garbled circuits. In: Nguyen, P.Q., Oswald, E. (eds.) EUROCRYPT 2014. LNCS, vol. 8441, pp. 533–556. Springer, Heidelberg (2014)
8. Boneh, D., Sahai, A., Waters, B.: Functional encryption: definitions and challenges. In: Ishai, Y. (ed.) TCC 2011. LNCS, vol. 6597, pp. 253–273. Springer, Heidelberg (2011)
9. Brakerski, Z., Langlois, A., Peikert, C., Regev, O., Stehlé, D.: Classical hardness of learning with errors. In: Proceedings of STOC 2013, pp. 575–584. ACM (2013)
10. Cash, D., Hofheinz, D., Kiltz, E., Peikert, C.: Bonsai trees, or how to delegate a lattice basis. In: Gilbert, H. (ed.) EUROCRYPT 2010. LNCS, vol. 6110, pp. 523–552. Springer, Heidelberg (2010)
11. Garg, S., Gentry, C., Halevi, S., Sahai, A., Waters, B.: Attribute-based encryption for circuits from multilinear maps. In: Canetti, R., Garay, J.A. (eds.) CRYPTO 2013, Part II. LNCS, vol. 8043, pp. 479–499. Springer, Heidelberg (2013)
12. Gentry, C., Peikert, C., Vaikuntanathan, V.: Trapdoors for hard lattices and new cryptographic constructions. In: Proceedings of STOC 2008, pp. 197–206. ACM (2008)
13. Gorbunov, S., Vaikuntanathan, V., Wee, H.: Attribute-based encryption for circuits. In: Proceedings of STOC 2013, pp. 545–554. ACM (2013)
14. Gorbunov, S., Vaikuntanathan, V., Wee, H.: Predicate encryption for circuits from LWE. In: Gennaro, R., Robshaw, M. (eds.) CRYPTO 2015. LNCS, vol. 9216, pp. 503–523. Springer, Heidelberg (2015)
15. Goyal, V., Pandey, O., Sahai, A., Waters, B.: Attribute-based encryption for fine-grained access control of encrypted data. In: Proceedings of CCS 2006, pp. 89–98. ACM (2006)
16. Katz, J., Sahai, A., Waters, B.: Predicate encryption supporting disjunctions, polynomial equations, and inner products. In: Smart, N.P. (ed.) EUROCRYPT 2008. LNCS, vol. 4965, pp. 146–162. Springer, Heidelberg (2008)

17. Micciancio, D., Regev, O.: Worst-case to average-case reductions based on gaussian measures. SIAM J. Comput. **37**(1), 267–302 (2007)
18. Peikert, C.: Public-key cryptosystems from the worst-case shortest vector problem: extended abstract. In: Proceedings of STOC 2009, pp. 333–342. ACM (2009)
19. Regev, O.: On lattices, learning with errors, random linear codes, and cryptography. In: Proceedings of STOC 2005, pp. 84–93. ACM (2005)
20. Waters, B.: Dual system encryption: realizing fully secure IBE and HIBE under simple assumptions. In: Halevi, S. (ed.) CRYPTO 2009. LNCS, vol. 5677, pp. 619–636. Springer, Heidelberg (2009)
21. Waters, B.: Functional encryption for regular languages. In: Safavi-Naini, R., Canetti, R. (eds.) CRYPTO 2012. LNCS, vol. 7417, pp. 218–235. Springer, Heidelberg (2012)

Functional Signcryption: Notion, Construction, and Applications

Pratish Datta, Ratna Dutta, and Sourav Mukhopadhyay[✉]

Department of Mathematics, Indian Institute of Technology Kharagpur,
Kharagpur 721302, India
{pratishdatta,ratna,sourav}@maths.iitkgp.ernet.in

Abstract. Functional encryption (FE) enables sophisticated control over decryption rights in a multi-user scenario, while functional signature (FS) allows to enforce complex constraints on signing capabilities. This paper introduces the concept of *functional signcryption* (FSC) that aims to provide the functionalities of both FE and FS in an *unified cost-effective primitive*. FSC provides a solution to the problem of achieving confidentiality and authenticity simultaneously in digital communication and storage systems involving multiple users with better efficiency compared to a sequential implementation of FE and FS. We begin by providing formal definition of FSC and formulating its security requirements. Next, we present a generic construction of this challenging primitive that supports arbitrary polynomial-size signing and decryption functions from known cryptographic building blocks, namely, *indistinguishability obfuscation* (IO) and *statistically simulation-sound non-interactive zero-knowledge proof of knowledge* (SSS-NIZKPoK). Finally, we exhibit a number of representative applications of FSC: (I) We develop the *first* construction of *attribute-based signcryption* (ABSC) supporting signing and decryption policies representable by *general polynomial-size circuits* from FSC. (II) We show how FSC can serve as a tool for building SSS-NIZKPoK system and IO, a result which in conjunction with our generic FSC construction can also be interpreted as establishing an equivalence between FSC and the other two fundamental cryptographic primitives.

Keywords: Functional signcryption · Indistinguishability obfuscation · Statistically simulation-sound non-interactive zero-knowledge proof of knowledge · Polynomial-size circuits

1 Introduction

In order to realize fine-grained control over decryption capabilities in multi-user digital communication or storage systems, the concept of *functional encryption* (FE) has been introduced [5,15]. An FE scheme includes a trusted authority which holds a master secret key and publishes system public parameters. An encrypter uses this system public parameters to encrypt a message. A decrypter may obtain a decryption key $\mathrm{DK}(g)$ for some decryption function g from the

© Springer International Publishing Switzerland 2015
M.-H. Au and A. Miyaji (Eds.): ProvSec 2015, LNCS 9451, pp. 268–288, 2015.
DOI: 10.1007/978-3-319-26059-4_15

authority if and only if the authority deems that the decrypter is entitled to possess that key. The decrypter can now use the decryption key $\mathrm{DK}(g)$ to decrypt a ciphertext encrypting some message m to obtain $g(m)$ and nothing more.

On the other hand, *functional signature* (FS), introduced in [2,3], allows managing complex signing credentials. Just like an FE scheme, an FS system also involves a trusted authority that publishes system public parameters and possesses a master signing key which can be used for signing any message and providing a constrained signing key $\mathrm{SK}(f)$ for some signing function f to a signer after verification of its signing credentials. This restricted signing key $\mathrm{SK}(f)$ can be used for producing signatures, verifiable under the system public parameters, on only those messages that are in the range of the function f.

However, given this state of the art, exercising fine-grained control over the signing and decryption rights in a multi-user confidential and authenticated digital communication or storage system would necessitate implementing both FE and FS sequentially which would entail summing up the cost incurred by both primitives. In this work, we put forward a *new* cryptographic paradigm termed as *functional signcryption* (FSC) that unifies the functionalities of both FE and FS. In other words, FSC aims to provide enhanced access control in the context of the traditional digital signcryption. FSC solves the issue of simultaneously managing signing and decryption credentials in a multi-user environment with better efficiency. More precisely, in an FSC scheme, we consider a trusted authority that holds a master secret key and publishes system public parameters. Using its master secret key, the authority can provide a signing key $\mathrm{SK}(f)$ for some signing function f to a signcrypter, as well as, a decryption key $\mathrm{DK}(g)$ corresponding to some decryption function g to a decrypter after verifying their credentials. Now such a signing key $\mathrm{SK}(f)$ enables a signcrypter to signcrypt, i.e., encrypt and authenticate simultaneously only those messages which are in the range of f, while a decryption key $\mathrm{DK}(g)$ can be utilized to unsigncrypt a ciphertext, which is the signcryption of some message m to retrieve $g(m)$ only and to verify the authenticity of the ciphertext at the same time.

We define two security notions for FSC, namely, *message confidentiality* and *ciphertext unforgeability*. Roughly speaking, message confidentiality guarantees that arbitrary collusion of decrypters cannot retrieve any additional information about the signcrypted message from a ciphertext beyond the union of what they could obtain individually. On the other hand, ciphertext unforgeability assures that collusion of signcrypters cannot help them to generate a valid signcryption of a message which none of them could have signcrypted on their own.

A motivating practical application of FSC could be the following: Suppose the government of some country is collecting complete photographs of individuals as part of the census and storing the collected data in a large server to allow utilizing it in future by other organizations for various survey purposes. For maintaining the security and improving the quality of the collected photos at the same time, the government is using some photo-processing software that edits the photos and encrypts them before storing them to the server. Now, it is desirable that the software is allowed to perform only some minor touchups of the photos such as changing the color scale or removing red eyes, but is not allowed to make more significant changes such as merging two photos or cropping a picture. FSC can naturally address this issue as follows: The government, acting as the trusted authority, would provide the photo-processing software (signcrypter) the signing keys ($\text{SK}(f)$) which allows it to signcrypt original photographs with only the allowable modifications (i.e., those in the range of f) and store the signcrypted photos in the server. Later, when some organization (decrypter) wants to access only those informations from stored photos meeting certain criteria (g), e.g., faces of individuals residing in a particular city, the government would give the organization the corresponding functional decryption key ($\text{DK}(g)$) after being fully convinced about the credentials of the organization. Now, when the organization would access that data base (i.e., signcryption of m) using the obtained decryption key, it could only obtain the face portion of the photographs of individuals living in that particular city ($g(m)$) and would be convinced that the photos obtained were undergone through only minor photo-editing modifications.

Our Contributions: We begin with formally introducing (FSC) and formalizing its security notions. We then present a *generic construction* of FSC that supports signing and decryption functions expressible as *general polynomial-size circuits*, assuming the existence of *indistinguishability obfuscation* (IO) for all polynomial-size circuits and *statistically simulation-sound non-interactive zero-knowledge proof of knowledge* (SSS-NIZKPoK) system for NP relations. Besides, we use ordinary public key encryption and digital signature schemes as building blocks for our FSC construction. We provide a rigorous security analysis of our FSC construction in our proposed security model and prove that it achieves *selective* message confidentiality against chosen plaintext attack (CPA), as well as, *selective* ciphertext unforgeability against chosen message attack (CMA).

Utilizing FSC, we further develop *attribute-based signcryption* (ABSC) supporting *arbitrary polynomial-size circuits*. ABSC is a related but weaker notion for controlling the signing and decryption capabilities in signcryption. Although in the last few years ABSC has gained a lot of attention in the literature [12–14], the class of allowable signing and decryption predicates have been restricted to *monotone Boolean formulas* or, in other words, to *circuits with fan-out one*. As noted in [6], these schemes are vulnerable to "backtracking" attack. To the best of our knowledge, our proposed ABSC scheme is the *first* to realize general polynomial-size circuits for signing and decryption policies.

Finally, we establish an equivalence between FSC and the two primitives, namely, SSS-NIZKPoK for NP relations and IO for all polynomial-size circuits. Our generic construction, described in Sect. 4.1 shows that those cryptographic tools are *sufficient* to build FSC. A natural question that arises, therefore, is that whether SSS-NIZKPoK and IO are *necessary*, i.e., whether those are implied by FSC. In Sect. 6, we address this question by exhibiting that FSC indeed implies SSS-NIZKPoK for NP relations and IO for general polynomial-size circuits.

2   Preliminaries

Here we give the necessary background on the cryptographic primitives we will be using in our FSC construction. For positive integers n, a, b (with $a < b$), we let $[n] = \{1, \ldots, n\}$ and $[a, b] = \{a, \ldots, b\}$. For any set S, $x \leftarrow S$ represents the uniform random variable on S. For a randomized algorithm $\mathcal{M}$, we denote by $\theta = \mathcal{M}(v; r)$ the random variable defined by the output of $\mathcal{M}$ on input v and randomness r, while $\theta \leftarrow \mathcal{M}(v)$ has the same meaning with the randomness suppressed. For any circuit C, $|C|$ denotes the size of C. For any two strings $s, s' \in \{0, 1\}^*$, $s\|s'$ represents the concatenation of s and s'.

2.1   Indistinguishability Obfuscation

Following formalization of indistinguishability obfuscation (IO) is due to Garg et al. [5].

Definition 1 (Indistinguishability Obfuscation: IO). *An indistinguishability obfuscator* (IO) $\mathcal{O}$ *for a circuit class* $\{\mathbb{C}_\lambda\}$ *is a probabilistic polynomial-time* (PPT) *uniform algorithm satisfying the following conditions:*

- $\mathcal{O}(1^\lambda, C)$ *preserves the functionality of the input circuit* C, *i.e., for any* $C \in \mathbb{C}_\lambda$, *if we compute* $C' = \mathcal{O}(1^\lambda, C)$, *then* $C'(v) = C(v)$ *for all inputs* v.
- *For any* λ *and any two circuits* $C_0, C_1 \in \mathbb{C}_\lambda$ *with the same functionality, the circuits* $\mathcal{O}(1^\lambda, C_0)$ *and* $\mathcal{O}(1^\lambda, C_1)$ *are computationally indistinguishable. More precisely, for all* (*not necessarily uniform*) *PPT adversaries* $\mathcal{D} = (\mathcal{D}_1, \mathcal{D}_2)$, *there exists a negligible function* ϵ *such that, if*

$$\Pr\big[(C_0, C_1, \alpha) \leftarrow \mathcal{D}_1(1^\lambda) \; : \; \forall \, v, C_0(v) = C_1(v)\big] > 1 - \epsilon(\lambda),$$
$$then \; \big|\Pr\big[\mathcal{D}_2(\alpha, \mathcal{O}(1^\lambda, C_0)) = 1\big] - \Pr\big[\mathcal{D}_2(\alpha, \mathcal{O}(1^\lambda, C_1)) = 1\big]\big| < \epsilon(\lambda).$$

When clear from the context, we will drop 1^λ as an input to $\mathcal{O}$ and λ as a subscript of $\mathbb{C}$. The circuit classes we are interested in are polynomial-size circuits, i.e., when $\mathbb{C}_\lambda$ is the collection of all circuits of size at most λ. This circuit class is denoted by P/poly. The first candidate construction of IO for P/poly was presented in [5] in a generic model of encoded matrices. Later, [7,11] have shown that IO for P/poly can be developed based on a single instance-independent assumption.

2.2   Statistically Simulation-Sound Non-interactive Zero-Knowledge Proof of Knowledge

Simulation-sound non-interactive zero-knowledge proof of knowledge have been introduced and formalized in the full version of [8]. However, here we slightly simplify the original definition following [3,5].

Definition 2 (Statistically Simulation-Sound Non-interactive Zero-Knowledge Proof of Knowledge: SSS-NIZKPoK). *Let $R \subset \{0,1\}^* \times \{0,1\}^*$ be an NP (binary) relation. For pairs $(X, W) \in R$, we call X the statement and W the witness. Let $\mathbb{L} \subset \{0,1\}^*$ be the language consisting of statements in R. An SSS-NIZKPoK system for $\mathbb{L}$ consists of the following PPT algorithms:*

SSS-NIZKPoK.Setup(1^λ): *The trusted authority takes as input a security parameter 1^λ and publishes a common reference string CRS.*

SSS-NIZKPoK.Prove(CRS, X, W): *Taking as input the common reference string CRS, a statement $X \in \mathbb{L}$ along with a witness W, a prover outputs a proof π for X.*

SSS-NIZKPoK.Verify(CRS, X, π): *On input the common reference string CRS, a statement $X \in \{0,1\}^*$, and a proof π, a verifier outputs 1, if the proof π is acceptable, or 0, otherwise.*

SSS-NIZKPoK.SimSetup(1^λ, X): *The simulator takes as input the security parameter 1^λ together with a statement $X \in \{0,1\}^*$. It produces a simulated common reference string CRS along with a trapdoor TR that enables it to simulate a proof for X without access to a witness.*

SSS-NIZKPoK.SimProve(CRS, TR, X): *Taking as input the simulated common reference string CRS, the trapdoor TR, and the statement $X \in \{0,1\}^*$ for which CRS and TR have been generated, the simulator outputs a simulated proof π for X.*

SSS-NIZKPoK.ExtSetup(1^λ): *The extractor, on input the security parameter 1^λ, outputs an extraction-enabling common reference string CRS and an extraction trapdoor $\widehat{\text{TR}}$.*

SSS-NIZKPoK.Extr(CRS, $\widehat{\text{TR}}$, X, π): *The extractor takes as input the extraction-enabling common reference string CRS, the extraction trapdoor $\widehat{\text{TR}}$, a statement $X \in \{0,1\}^*$, and a proof π. It outputs a witness W.*

An SSS-NIZKPoK system should possess the following properties:

• **Perfect Completeness**: *An SSS-NIZKPoK system is perfectly complete if for all security parameter λ, all $X, W \in R$, all CRS $\leftarrow$ SSS-NIZKPoK.Setup(1^λ), and all $\pi \leftarrow$ SSS-NIZKPoK.Prove(CRS, X, W), SSS-NIZKPoK.Verify(CRS, X, π) = 1.*

• **Statistical Soundness**: *An SSS-NIZKPoK system is statistically sound if for all non-uniform adversaries $\mathcal{A}$ there exists a negligible function ϵ such that for any security parameter λ, we have*

$$\Pr\big[\text{CRS} \leftarrow \text{SSS-NIZKPoK.Setup}(1^\lambda); \ (X, \pi) \leftarrow \mathcal{A}(\text{CRS}) \ :$$
$$\text{SSS-NIZKPoK.Verify}(\text{CRS}, X, \pi) = 1 \ \bigwedge \ X \notin \mathbb{L}\big] < \epsilon(\lambda).$$

• **Computational Zero-Knowledge**: *We define the SSS-NIZKPoK system to be computationally zero-knowledge if for all non-uniform PPT adversaries $\mathcal{A}$ there exists a negligible function ϵ such that for any security parameter λ, we have for all $X \in \mathbb{L}$*

$$\left|\Pr\left[\text{CRS} \leftarrow \text{SSS-NIZKPoK.Setup}(1^\lambda);\right.\right.$$
$$\pi \leftarrow \text{SSS-NIZKPoK.Prove}(\text{CRS}, X, W) \ : \ \mathcal{A}(\text{CRS}, X, \pi) = 1\big]$$
$$-\Pr\left[(\text{CRS}, \text{TR}) \leftarrow \text{SSS-NIZKPoK.SimSetup}(1^\lambda, X);\right.$$
$$\left.\left. \pi \leftarrow \text{SSS-NIZKPoK.SimProve}(\text{CRS}, \text{TR}, X) \ : \ \mathcal{A}(\text{CRS}, X, \pi) = 1\right]\right| < \epsilon(\lambda)$$

where W is a witness corresponding to X.

- **Knowledge Extraction**: We call an SSS-NIZKPoK system a proof of knowledge for R if for any security parameter λ the following holds: For all non-uniform adversaries $\mathcal{A}$ there exists a negligible function ϵ_1 such that

$$\left|\Pr\left[\text{CRS} \leftarrow \text{SSS-NIZKPoK.Setup}(1^\lambda) \ : \ \mathcal{A}(\text{CRS}) = 1\right]\right.$$
$$\left.-\Pr\left[(\text{CRS}, \widehat{\text{TR}}) \leftarrow \text{SSS-NIZKPoK.ExtSetup}(1^\lambda) \ : \ \mathcal{A}(\text{CRS}) = 1\right]\right| < \epsilon_1(\lambda)$$

and for all non-uniform PPT adversaries $\mathcal{A}$ there exists a negligible function ϵ_2 such that

$$\Pr\left[(\text{CRS}, \widehat{\text{TR}}) \leftarrow \text{SSS-NIZKPoK.ExtSetup}(1^\lambda);\right.$$
$$(X, \pi) \leftarrow \mathcal{A}(\text{CRS}); W^* \leftarrow \text{SSS-NIZKPoK.Extr}(\text{CRS}, \widehat{\text{TR}}, X, \pi) \ :$$
$$\left.\text{SSS-NIZKPoK.Verify}(\text{CRS}, X, \pi) = 1 \bigwedge (X, W^*) \notin R\right] < \epsilon_2(\lambda).$$

- **Statistical Simulation-Soundness**: An SSS-NIZKPoK system is statistically simulation-sound if for all non-uniform adversaries $\mathcal{A}$ there exists a negligible function ϵ such that for any security parameter λ, we have for all statements $X \in \{0,1\}^*$

$$\Pr\left[(\text{CRS}, \text{TR}) \leftarrow \text{SSS-NIZKPoK.SimSetup}(1^\lambda, X);\right.$$
$$\pi \leftarrow \text{SSS-NIZKPoK.SimProve}(\text{CRS}, \text{TR}, X); (X^*, \pi^*) \leftarrow \mathcal{A}(\text{CRS}, X, \pi) \ :$$
$$\left.X^* \neq X \bigwedge X^* \notin \mathbb{L} \bigwedge \text{SSS-NIZKPoK.Verify}(\text{CRS}, X^*, \pi^*) = 1\right] < \epsilon(\lambda).$$

Constructions of *non-interactive zero-knowledge proof of knowledge* (NIZKPoK) for NP relations are well-known [9,10]. Using any NIZKPoK together with a *non-interactive perfectly binding commitment* scheme we can construct an SSS-NIZKPoK system following the same technique as described in [5].

3   The Notion of Functional Signcryption

■ **Syntax**: A functional signcryption (FSC) scheme for a message space $\mathbb{M}$, a family of signing functions $\mathbb{F} = \{f : \mathbb{D}_f \rightarrow \mathbb{M}\}$, and a class of decryption functions $\mathbb{G} = \{g : \mathbb{M} \rightarrow \mathbb{R}_g\}$, where $\mathbb{D}_f$ and $\mathbb{R}_g$ denote the domain of the function f and range of the function g respectively, consists of the following PPT algorithms:

FSC.Setup(1^λ): The trusted authority takes as input the security parameter 1^λ and publishes the public parameters MPK, while keeps the master secret key MSK to itself.

FSC.SKeyGen(MPK, MSK, f): Taking as input the public parameters MPK, the master secret key MSK, and a signing function $f \in \mathbb{F}$ from a signcrypter, the trusted authority provides a signing key SK(f) to the signcrypter.

FSC.Signcrypt(MPK, SK(f), z): A signcrypter takes as input the public parameters MPK, its signing key SK(f) corresponding to some signing function $f \in \mathbb{F}$, and an input $z \in \mathbb{D}_f$. It produces a ciphertext CT which is a signcryption of $f(z) \in \mathbb{M}$.

FSC.DKeyGen(MPK, MSK, g): On input the public parameters MPK, the master secret key MSK, and a decryption function $g \in \mathbb{G}$ from a decrypter, the trusted authority hands the decryption key DK(g) to the decrypter.

FSC.Unsigncrypt(MPK, DK(g), CT): A decrypter, on input the public parameters MPK, its decryption key DK(g) associated with its decryption function $g \in \mathbb{G}$, and a ciphertext CT signcrypting a message $m \in \mathbb{M}$, attempts to unsigncrypt the ciphertext CT and outputs $g(m)$, if successful, or a special string $\perp$ indicating failure, otherwise.

■ **Correctness:** An FSC scheme is correct if for all $f \in \mathbb{F}$, $z \in \mathbb{D}_f$, and $g \in \mathbb{G}$,

$$\Pr\big[(\text{MPK}, \text{MSK}) \leftarrow \text{FSC.Setup}(1^\lambda) : $$
$$\text{FSC.Unsigncrypt}\big(\text{MPK}, \text{FSC.DKeyGen}(\text{MPK}, \text{MSK}, g),$$
$$\text{FSC.Signcrypt}(\text{MPK}, \text{FSC.SKeyGen}(\text{MPK}, \text{MSK}, f), z)\big) = g(f(z))\big] > 1 - \epsilon(\lambda)$$

for some negligible function ϵ.

■ **Security:** An FSC scheme has two security requirements, namely, (I) *message confidentiality* and (II) *ciphertext unforgeability* which are described below. For simplicity, we present our security definitions for the *selective* model, where the adversary must decide the challenge messages up front, before the system parameters are chosen.

(I) *message confidentiality:* We define this security notion on indistinguishability of ciphertexts against *chosen plaintext attack* (CPA) through the following game between a probabilistic adversary $\mathcal{A}$ and a probabilistic challenger $\mathcal{C}$.

Init: $\mathcal{A}$ submits two pairs $(f_0^*, z_0^*), (f_1^*, z_1^*)$ of signing functions and inputs in the respective domains that will be used to frame the challenge.

Setup: $\mathcal{C}$ performs FSC.Setup(1^λ) to obtain (MPK, MSK) and hands MPK to $\mathcal{A}$.

Query Phase 1: $\mathcal{A}$ may adaptively make any polynomial number of queries which may be of the following types to be answered by $\mathcal{C}$.

- *Signing key query:* Upon receiving a signing key query for a signing function $f \in \mathbb{F}$ from $\mathcal{A}$, $\mathcal{C}$ returns SK(f) to $\mathcal{A}$ by running FSC.SKeyGen(MPK, MSK, f).
- *Decryption key query:* When $\mathcal{A}$ queries a decryption key for a decryption function $g \in \mathbb{G}$ to $\mathcal{C}$ subject to the constraint that $g(f_0^*(z_0^*)) = g(f_1^*(z_1^*))$, $\mathcal{C}$ provides the decryption key DK(g) to $\mathcal{A}$ by running FSC.DKeyGen(MPK, MSK, g).

– *Signcryption query:* In response to a signcryption query of $\mathcal{A}$ for a signing function $f \in \mathbb{F}$ and an input $z \in \mathbb{D}_f$, $\mathcal{C}$ hands the ciphertext CT to $\mathcal{A}$, which is a signcryption of $f(z)$, by performing FSC.Signcrypt$($MPK, FSC.SKeyGen$($MPK, MSK, $f)$, $z)$.

Challenge: $\mathcal{C}$ flips a random coin $b \leftarrow \{0,1\}$ and generates the challenge ciphertext CT* by running FSC.Signcrypt$($MPK, FSC.SKeyGen$($MPK, MSK, $f_b^*)$, $z_b^*)$.

Query Phase 2: $\mathcal{A}$ may continue adaptively to make a polynomial number of queries as in **Query Phase 1**, subject to the same restriction as earlier, and $\mathcal{C}$ provides the answer to them.

Guess: $\mathcal{A}$ eventually outputs a guess b' for b and wins the game if $b' = b$.

Definition 3. *An FSC scheme is defined to be selectively message confidential against* CPA *if for all* PPT *adversaries $\mathcal{A}$ there exists a negligible function ϵ such that for any security parameter λ,* $\mathsf{Adv}_{\mathcal{A}}^{\mathsf{FSC,s\text{-}IND\text{-}CPA}}(\lambda) = |\mathsf{Pr}[b' = b] - 1/2| < \epsilon(\lambda)$.

(II) *Ciphertext Unforgeability:* This notion of security is defined on existential unforgeability against *chosen message attack* (CMA) through the following game between a probabilistic adversary $\mathcal{A}$ and a probabilistic challenger $\mathcal{C}$.

Init: $\mathcal{A}$ declares a message $m^* \in \mathbb{M}$ to $\mathcal{C}$ on which the forgery will be outputted.

Setup: $\mathcal{C}$ runs FSC.Setup(1^λ) to obtain (MPK, MSK) and hands MPK to $\mathcal{A}$.

Query Phase: $\mathcal{A}$ may adaptively make a polynomial number of queries of the following types to $\mathcal{C}$ and $\mathcal{C}$ provides the answer to those queries.

– *Signing key query:* Upon receiving a signing key query from $\mathcal{A}$ corresponding to a signing function $f \in \mathbb{F}$ subject to the constraint that there exists no $z \in \mathbb{D}_f$ such that $f(z) = m^*$, $\mathcal{C}$ returns SK(f) to $\mathcal{A}$ by executing FSC.SKeyGen$($MPK, MSK, $f)$.
– *Decryption key query:* When $\mathcal{A}$ queries a decryption key for a decryption function $g \in \mathbb{G}$, $\mathcal{C}$ gives DK(g) to $\mathcal{A}$ by running FSC.DKeyGen$($MPK, MSK, $g)$.
– *Signcryption query:* In response to a signcryption query of $\mathcal{A}$ for a signing function $f \in \mathbb{F}$ and input $z \in \mathbb{D}_f$, $\mathcal{C}$ returns the ciphertext CT, which is a signcryption of $f(z)$, to $\mathcal{A}$ by performing FSC.Signcrypt$($MPK, FSC.SKeyGen$($MPK, MSK, $f)$, $z)$.
– *Unsigncryption query:* Upon receiving an unsigncryption query from $\mathcal{A}$ for a ciphertext CT under a decryption function $g \in \mathbb{G}$, $\mathcal{C}$ performs DK$(g) \leftarrow$ FSC.DKeyGen$($MPK, MSK, $g)$ followed by FSC.Unsigncrypt$($MPK, DK(g), CT$)$ and sends the result to $\mathcal{A}$.

Forgery: $\mathcal{A}$ finally outputs a forgery CT* on m^*. $\mathcal{A}$ wins the game if CT* is indeed a valid functional signcryption of m^*, i.e., FSC.Unsigncrypt$($MPK, DK(g), CT*$) = g(m^*)$ for all $g \in \mathbb{G}$, and there does not exist any (f, z) pair such that (f, z) was a signcryption query of $\mathcal{A}$ and $m^* = f(z)$.

Definition 4. *An FSC scheme is defined to be selectively ciphertext unforgeable against* CMA *if for all* PPT *adversaries $\mathcal{A}$ there exists a negligible function ϵ such that for any security parameter λ,* $\mathsf{Adv}_{\mathcal{A}}^{\mathsf{FSC,s\text{-}UF\text{-}CMA}}(\lambda) = \mathsf{Pr}[\mathcal{A}\ wins] < \epsilon(\lambda)$.

4 Our FSC Scheme

Let λ be the underlying security parameter. The cryptographic building blocks used in our FSC construction are the following:

- $\mathcal{O}$: An indistinguishability obfuscator for P/poly.
- PKE=(PKE.KeyGen, PKE.Encrypt, PKE.Decrypt): A CPA-secure public key encryption scheme with message space $\mathbb{M} \subseteq \{0,1\}^{n(\lambda)}$, for some polynomial n.
- SIG=(SIG.KeyGen, SIG.Sign, SIG.Verify): An existentially unforgeable signature scheme with message space $\{0,1\}^{\lambda}$.
- SSS-NIZKPoK = (SSS-NIZKPoK.Setup, SSS-NIZKPoK.Prove, SSS-NIZKPoK. Verify, SSS-NIZKPoK.SimSetup, SSS-NIZKPoK.SimProve, SSS-NIZKPoK. ExtSet up, SSS-NIZKPoK.Extr): An SSS-NIZKPoK system for the NP relation R, with statements of the form $X = \left(\text{PK}_{\text{PKE}}^{(1)}, \text{PK}_{\text{PKE}}^{(2)}, \text{VK}_{\text{SIG}}, e_1, e_2\right) \in \{0,1\}^*$, witnesses of the form $W = (m, r_1, r_2, f, \sigma, z) \in \{0,1\}^*$, and

$$(X, W) \in R \iff \left(e_1 = \text{PKE.Encrypt}(\text{PK}_{\text{PKE}}^{(1)}, m; r_1) \bigwedge\right.$$
$$e_2 = \text{PKE.Encrypt}(\text{PK}_{\text{PKE}}^{(2)}, m; r_2) \bigwedge$$
$$\left.\text{SIG.Verify}(\text{VK}_{\text{SIG}}, f, \sigma) = 1 \bigwedge m = f(z)\right), \quad (1)$$

for a function family $\mathbb{F} = \{f : \mathbb{D}_f \to \mathbb{M}\} \subseteq$ P/poly (with representation in $\{0,1\}^{\lambda}$).

We build an FSC scheme for message space $\mathbb{M}$, family of signing functions $\mathbb{F}$, and the class of decryption functions $\mathbb{G} = \{g : \mathbb{M} \to \mathbb{R}_g\} \subseteq$ P/poly.

4.1 Construction

FSC.Setup(1^{λ}): The trusted authority takes in a security parameter 1^{λ} and proceeds as follows:
1. It generates $(\text{PK}_{\text{PKE}}^{(1)}, \text{SK}_{\text{PKE}}^{(1)}), (\text{PK}_{\text{PKE}}^{(2)}, \text{SK}_{\text{PKE}}^{(2)}) \leftarrow$ PKE.KeyGen(1^{λ}).
2. It obtains $(\text{VK}_{\text{SIG}}, \text{SK}_{\text{SIG}}) \leftarrow$ SIG.KeyGen(1^{λ}).
3. It generates CRS $\leftarrow$ SSS-NIZKPoK.Setup(1^{λ}).
4. It publishes the public parameters MPK $= \left(\text{PK}_{\text{PKE}}^{(1)}, \text{PK}_{\text{PKE}}^{(2)}, \text{VK}_{\text{SIG}}, \text{CRS}\right)$, while keeps the master secret key MSK $= (\text{SK}_{\text{PKE}}^{(1)}, \text{SK}_{\text{SIG}})$ to itself.

FSC.SKeyGen(MPK, MSK, f): Taking as input the public parameters MPK, the master secret key MSK, and a signing function $f \in \mathbb{F}$ from a signcrypter, the trusted authority runs SIG.Sign($\text{SK}_{\text{SIG}}, f$) to obtain a signature σ on f and return the signing key SK(f) $= (f, \sigma)$ to the signcrypter.

FSC.Signcrypt(MPK, SK(f), z): A signcrypter takes as input the public parameters MPK, its signing key SK(f) $= (f, \sigma)$ corresponding to some signing function $f \in \mathbb{F}$, and an input $z \in \mathbb{D}_f$. It prepares the ciphertext as follows:
1. It computes $e_{\ell} = \text{PKE.Encrypt}(\text{PK}_{\text{PKE}}^{(\ell)}, f(z); r_{\ell})$ for $\ell = 1, 2$, where r_{ℓ} is the randomness selected for encryption.

2. It generates a proof $\pi \leftarrow$ SSS-NIZKPoK.Prove(CRS, X, W) where $X = (\text{PK}_{\text{PKE}}^{(1)}, \text{PK}_{\text{PKE}}^{(2)}, \text{VK}_{\text{SIG}}, e_1, e_2)$ is a statement of the NP relation R defined in Eq. (1) and $W = (f(z), r_1, r_2, f, \sigma, z)$ is the corresponding witness.

3. It outputs the ciphertext CT $= (e_1, e_2, \pi)$.

FSC.DKeyGen(MPK, MSK, g): On input the public parameters MPK, the master secret key MSK, and a decryption function $g \in \mathbb{G}$ from a decrypter, the trusted authority computes the obfuscation $\mathcal{O}(P^{(g,\text{SK}_{\text{PKE}}^{(1)},\text{MPK})})$ of the program $P^{(g,\text{SK}_{\text{PKE}}^{(1)},\text{MPK})}$ using the circuit size value $\max\{|P^{(g,\text{SK}_{\text{PKE}}^{(1)},\text{MPK})}|, |\widetilde{P}^{(g,\text{SK}_{\text{PKE}}^{(2)},\text{MPK})}|\}$, where the programs $P^{(g,\text{SK}_{\text{PKE}}^{(1)},\text{MPK})}$ and $\widetilde{P}^{(g,\text{SK}_{\text{PKE}}^{(2)},\text{MPK})}$ are described in Fig. 1. It provides the decryption key DK$(g) = (g, \mathcal{O}(P^{(g,\text{SK}_{\text{PKE}}^{(1)},\text{MPK})}))$ to the decrypter.

FSC.Unsigncrypt(MPK, DK(g), CT): A decrypter, on input the public parameters MPK, its decryption key DK$(g) = (g, \mathcal{O}(P^{(g,\text{SK}_{\text{PKE}}^{(1)},\text{MPK})}))$, along with a ciphertext CT $= (e_1, e_2, \pi)$, runs the obfuscated program $\mathcal{O}(P^{(g,\text{SK}_{\text{PKE}}^{(1)},\text{MPK})})$ with input (e_1, e_2, π) and outputs the result.

Correctness: Note that the correctness of the proposed scheme follows immediately from the correctness of $\mathcal{O}$, PKE, and SIG, perfect completeness of SSS-NIZKPoK systems, as well as description of the program template $P^{(g,\text{SK}_{\text{PKE}}^{(1)},\text{MPK})}$.

Remark 1. Note that the size of the ciphertext in our FSC scheme is $\tau(\lambda, n)$ for some polynomial τ.

$P^{(g,\text{SK}_{\text{PKE}}^{(1)},\text{MPK})}$	$\widetilde{P}^{(g,\text{SK}_{\text{PKE}}^{(2)},\text{MPK})}$
Given input (e_1, e_2, π), the program proceeds as follows:	Given input (e_1, e_2, π), the program proceeds as follows:
1. Extract $\text{PK}_{\text{PKE}}^{(1)}$, $\text{PK}_{\text{PKE}}^{(2)}$, VK_{SIG}, CRS from MPK.	1. Extract $\text{PK}_{\text{PKE}}^{(1)}$, $\text{PK}_{\text{PKE}}^{(2)}$, VK_{SIG}, CRS from MPK.
2. Set $X = (\text{PK}_{\text{PKE}}^{(1)}, \text{PK}_{\text{PKE}}^{(2)}, \text{VK}_{\text{SIG}}, e_1, e_2)$.	2. Set $X = (\text{PK}_{\text{PKE}}^{(1)}, \text{PK}_{\text{PKE}}^{(2)}, \text{VK}_{\text{SIG}}, e_1, e_2)$.
3. If SSS-NIZKPoK.Verify(CRS, X, π) $= 0$, then output $\perp$ and stop. Otherwise, continue to the next step.	3. If SSS-NIZKPoK.Verify(CRS, X, π) $= 0$, then output $\perp$ and stop. Otherwise, continue to the next step.
4. Output $g(\text{PKE.Decrypt}(\text{SK}_{\text{PKE}}^{(1)}, e_1))$.	4. Output $g(\text{PKE.Decrypt}(\text{SK}_{\text{PKE}}^{(2)}, e_2))$.

Fig. 1. Programs $P^{(g,\text{SK}_{\text{PKE}}^{(1)},\text{MPK})}$ and $\widetilde{P}^{(g,\text{SK}_{\text{PKE}}^{(2)},\text{MPK})}$

4.2 Security Analysis

Theorem 1 (Message Confidentiality of FSC). *Assuming IO $\mathcal{O}$ for P/poly, CPA-secure public key encryption PKE, along with the statistical simulation-soundness and zero-knowledge properties of SSS-NIZKPoK system, the FSC scheme described in Sect. 4.1 is selectively message confidential against CPA as per the definition given in Sect. 3.*

Proof. Suppose that any adversary in the selective CPA-message confidentiality game of Sect. 3 makes at most $q = q(\lambda)$ many decryption key queries. For simplicity, we assume that the adversary always makes exactly q decryption key queries. We denote g_i for $i \in [q]$ to be the i-th decryption function for which a decryption key query is made. By the rules of the game $g_i(f_0^*(z_0^*))$ is constrained to be equal to $g_i(f_1^*(z_1^*))$ for all $i \in [q]$.

We organize our proof into a sequence of hybrids. In the first hybrid the challenger signcrypts $f_0^*(z_0^*)$. We then gradually change the signcryption in multiple hybrid steps into a signcryption of $f_1^*(z_1^*)$ in the challenge ciphertext. We show that each hybrid experiment is indistinguishable from the previous one, thus showing our FSC scheme to have selective message confidentiality against CPA.

Sequence of Hybrids:

- Hyb_0: This corresponds to the honest execution of the selective CPA-message confidentiality game introduced in Sect. 3 when the challenger signcrypts $f_0^*(z_0^*)$ in the challenge ciphertext $\mathrm{CT}^* = (e_1^*, e_2^*, \pi^*)$, i.e., $e_\ell^* = \mathsf{PKE.Encrypt}$ $\left(\mathrm{PK}_{\mathsf{PKE}}^{(\ell)}, f_0^*(z_0^*); r_\ell^*\right)$ for $\ell = 1, 2$ and $\pi^* \leftarrow \mathsf{SSS\text{-}NIZKPoK.Prove}(\mathrm{CRS}, X^*, W^*)$ where $X^* = (\mathrm{PK}_{\mathsf{PKE}}^{(1)}, \mathrm{PK}_{\mathsf{PKE}}^{(2)}, \mathrm{VK}_{\mathsf{SIG}}, e_1^*, e_2^*)$ and W^* is a valid witness corresponding to X^*.

- Hyb_1: In this hybrid, the common reference string CRS included in the public parameters MPK is formed as $(\mathrm{CRS}, \mathrm{TR}) \leftarrow \mathsf{SSS\text{-}NIZKPoK.SimSetup}(1^\lambda, X^*)$, and the proof π^* included in the challenge ciphertext CT^* is simulated as $\pi^* \leftarrow \mathsf{SSS\text{-}NIZKPoK.SimProve}(\mathrm{CRS}, \mathrm{TR}, X^*)$ where $X^* = (\mathrm{PK}_{\mathsf{PKE}}^{(1)}, \mathrm{PK}_{\mathsf{PKE}}^{(2)}, \mathrm{VK}_{\mathsf{SIG}}, e_1^*, e_2^*)$. The rest of the experiment continues as in Hyb_0 using the simulated common reference string CRS.

- Hyb_2: This hybrid is the same as the last hybrid except that the challenge ciphertext is computed as $\mathrm{CT}^* = (e_1^* = \mathsf{PKE.Encrypt}(\mathrm{PK}_{\mathsf{PKE}}^{(1)}, f_0^*(z_0^*); r_1^*), e_2^* = \mathsf{PKE.Encrypt}(\mathrm{PK}_{\mathsf{PKE}}^{(2)}, f_1^*(z_1^*); r_2^*), \pi^* \leftarrow \mathsf{SSS\text{-}NIZKPoK.SimProve}(\mathrm{CRS}, \mathrm{TR}, X^*))$ where $X^* = (\mathrm{PK}_{\mathsf{PKE}}^{(1)}, \mathrm{PK}_{\mathsf{PKE}}^{(2)}, \mathrm{VK}_{\mathsf{SIG}}, e_1^*, e_2^*)$.

- $\mathsf{Hyb}_{3,i}$ for $i \in [0, q]$: In this sequence of hybrids, we change the form of the decryption keys provided to the adversary in response to its decryption key queries. In $\mathsf{Hyb}_{3,i}$, for $i \in [0, q]$, the first i decryption keys requested by the adversary will result in decryption keys generated as $\mathrm{DK}(g_i) = \left(g_i, \mathcal{O}(\widetilde{P}^{(g_i, \mathrm{SK}_{\mathsf{PKE}}^{(2)}, \mathrm{MPK})})\right)$ while the remaining $i+1$ to q decryption keys are generated as $\mathrm{DK}(g_i) = \left(g_i, \mathcal{O}(P^{(g_i, \mathrm{SK}_{\mathsf{PKE}}^{(1)}, \mathrm{MPK})})\right)$ as in Hyb_2, where $P^{(g_i, \mathrm{SK}_{\mathsf{PKE}}^{(1)}, \mathrm{MPK})}$ and $\widetilde{P}^{(g_i, \mathrm{SK}_{\mathsf{PKE}}^{(2)}, \mathrm{MPK})}$ are depicted in Fig. 1. Observe that $\mathsf{Hyb}_{3,0}$ is equivalent to Hyb_2.

- Hyb_4: This hybrid is identical to the hybrid $\mathsf{Hyb}_{3,q}$ except that the challenge ciphertext is generated as $\mathrm{CT}^* = (e_1^*, e_2^*, \pi^*)$ where $e_1^* = \mathsf{PKE.Encrypt}(\mathrm{PK}_{\mathsf{PKE}}^{(1)}, f_1^*(z_1^*); r_1^*)$, $e_2^* = \mathsf{PKE.Encrypt}(\mathrm{PK}_{\mathsf{PKE}}^{(2)}, f_1^*(z_1^*); r_2^*)$, and the proof π^* is still simulated.

- $\mathsf{Hyb}_{5,i}$ for $i \in [0, q]$: In this sequence of hybrids, we again change the form of the decryption keys returned to the adversary in response to its decryption key queries. In $\mathsf{Hyb}_{5,i}$, for $i \in [0,q]$, the first i decryption key queries of the adversary will result in decryption keys generated as $\mathrm{DK}(g_i) = \left(g_i, \mathcal{O}(P^{(g_i,\mathrm{SK}_{\mathsf{PKE}}^{(1)},\mathrm{MPK})})\right)$ while the rest of the decryption keys $i + 1$ to q are generated as $\mathrm{DK}(g_i) = \left(g_i, \mathcal{O}(\widetilde{P}^{(g_i,\mathrm{SK}_{\mathsf{PKE}}^{(2)},\mathrm{MPK})})\right)$ as in Hyb_4, where $P^{(g_i,\mathrm{SK}_{\mathsf{PKE}}^{(1)},\mathrm{MPK})}$ and $\widetilde{P}^{(g_i,\mathrm{SK}_{\mathsf{PKE}}^{(2)},\mathrm{MPK})}$ are defined in Fig. 1. Note that $\mathsf{Hyb}_{5,0}$ is equivalent to Hyb_4.

- Hyb_6: In this hybrid, the common reference string CRS included in MPK is obtained as $\mathrm{CRS} \leftarrow \mathsf{SSS\text{-}NIZKPoK.Setup}(1^\lambda)$ and the proof π^* included in the challenge ciphertext CT^* is generated as $\pi^* \leftarrow \mathsf{SSS\text{-}NIZKPoK.Prove}(\mathrm{CRS}, X^*, W^*)$ where $X^* = (\mathrm{PK}_{\mathsf{PKE}}^{(1)}, \mathrm{PK}_{\mathsf{PKE}}^{(2)}, \mathrm{VK}_{\mathsf{SIG}}, e_1^*, e_2^*)$ and W^* is a valid witness corresponding to X^*. The remainder of the experiment continues identically as in $\mathsf{Hyb}_{5,q}$ using the honestly generated common reference string CRS. Notice that this hybrid corresponds to the selective CPA-message confidentiality game when $f_1^*(z_1^*)$ is signcrypted in the challenge ciphertext.

Proofs of Hybrid Arguments: We will present a sequence of lemmas which will demonstrate that no PPT adversary can distinguish with non-negligible advantage between any two consecutive hybrids described above, and thus security in the selective CPA-message confidentiality game follows.

Lemma 1. *Assuming* $\mathsf{SSS\text{-}NIZKPoK}$ *system is computationally zero-knowledge, no* PPT *adversary can distinguish with non-negligible advantage between* Hyb_0 *and* Hyb_1.

Proof. Suppose there is a PPT adversary $\mathcal{A}$ that can distinguish with non-negligible advantage between Hyb_0 and Hyb_1. We construct a PPT algorithm $\mathcal{C}$ that breaks the zero-knowledge property of $\mathsf{SSS\text{-}NIZKPoK}$ using $\mathcal{A}$ as a subroutine. $\mathcal{C}$ interacts with $\mathcal{A}$ as follows:

- $\mathcal{C}$ begins by initializing $\mathcal{A}$ and receiving $(f_0^*, z_0^*), (f_1^*, z_1^*)$ from $\mathcal{A}$.
- In order to setup the public parameters, $\mathcal{C}$ proceeds as follows:
  - $\mathcal{C}$ itself generates $(\mathrm{PK}_{\mathsf{PKE}}^{(1)}, \mathrm{SK}_{\mathsf{PKE}}^{(1)}), (\mathrm{PK}_{\mathsf{PKE}}^{(2)}, \mathrm{SK}_{\mathsf{PKE}}^{(2)}) \leftarrow \mathsf{PKE.KeyGen}(1^\lambda)$ and $(\mathrm{VK}_{\mathsf{SIG}}, \mathrm{SK}_{\mathsf{SIG}}) \leftarrow \mathsf{SIG.KeyGen}(1^\lambda)$.
  - After that, it computes $e_\ell^* = \mathsf{PKE.Encrypt}(\mathrm{PK}_{\mathsf{PKE}}^{(\ell)}, f_0^*(z_0^*); r_\ell^*)$ using randomness r_ℓ^*, for $\ell = 1, 2$ and $\sigma^* \leftarrow \mathsf{SIG.Sign}(\mathrm{SK}_{\mathsf{SIG}}, f_0^*)$.
  - It then submits the statement $X^* = (\mathrm{PK}_{\mathsf{PKE}}^{(1)}, \mathrm{PK}_{\mathsf{PKE}}^{(2)}, \mathrm{VK}_{\mathsf{SIG}}, e_1^*, e_2^*)$ along with the corresponding witness $W^* = (f_0^*(z_0^*), r_1^*, r_2^*, f_0^*, \sigma^*, z_0^*)$ to its *zero-knowledge challenger* $\mathcal{B}$ and receives back a common reference string CRS' together with a proof π'^* on X^* from $\mathcal{B}$.
  - $\mathcal{C}$ hands the public parameters $\mathrm{MPK} = (\mathrm{PK}_{\mathsf{PKE}}^{(1)}, \mathrm{PK}_{\mathsf{PKE}}^{(2)}, \mathrm{VK}_{\mathsf{SIG}}, \mathrm{CRS} = \mathrm{CRS}')$ to $\mathcal{A}$ and keeps $\widetilde{\mathrm{MSK}} = (\mathrm{SK}_{\mathsf{PKE}}^{(1)}, \mathrm{SK}_{\mathsf{SIG}}, e_1^*, e_2^*, \pi'^*)$.
- The signing key, decryption key, and signcryption queries of $\mathcal{A}$ are answered by $\mathcal{C}$ as described below:
  - *Signing key query*: Since $\mathcal{C}$ knows $\mathrm{SK}_{\mathsf{SIG}}$, it answers any signing key query of $\mathcal{A}$ for any signing function $f \in \mathbb{F}$ by generating $\sigma \leftarrow \mathsf{SIG.Sign}(\mathrm{SK}_{\mathsf{SIG}}, f)$ and returning $\mathrm{SK}(f) = (f, \sigma)$ to $\mathcal{A}$.

- *Decryption key query*: Using $\text{SK}_{\text{PKE}}^{(1)}$ and MPK, $\mathcal{C}$ constructs the program $P^{(g_i, \text{SK}_{\text{PKE}}^{(1)}, \text{MPK})}$ described in Fig. 1 upon receiving a decryption key query from $\mathcal{A}$ corresponding to a decryption function $g_i \in \mathbb{G}$, and provides the decryption key $\text{DK}(g_i) = \left(g_i, \mathcal{O}(P^{(g_i, \text{SK}_{\text{PKE}}^{(1)}, \text{MPK})})\right)$ to $\mathcal{A}$.
- *Signcryption query*: When $\mathcal{A}$ makes a signcryption query corresponding to a signing function $f \in \mathbb{F}$ and input $z \in \mathbb{D}_f$, $\mathcal{C}$ first computes $\sigma \leftarrow$ SIG.Sign$(\text{SK}_{\text{SIG}}, f)$, $e_\ell = $ PKE.Encrypt$(\text{PK}_{\text{PKE}}^{(\ell)}, f(z); r_\ell)$ using randomness r_ℓ, for $\ell = 1, 2$, along with a proof $\pi \leftarrow$ SSS-NIZKPoK.Prove(CRS, X, W) where $X = (\text{PK}_{\text{PKE}}^{(1)}, \text{PK}_{\text{PKE}}^{(2)}, \text{VK}_{\text{SIG}}, e_1, e_2)$ and $W = (f(z), r_1, r_2, f, \sigma, z)$. It provides the ciphertext CT $= (e_1, e_2, \pi)$ to $\mathcal{A}$.
- $\mathcal{C}$ sends the challenge ciphertext CT$^* = (e_1^*, e_2^*, \pi^* = \pi'^*)$ to $\mathcal{A}$.
- Finally, $\mathcal{A}$ outputs a bit $b' \in \{0, 1\}$. $\mathcal{C}$ also outputs b'.

Note that if $\mathcal{B}$ used the real setup algorithm SSS-NIZKPoK.Setup(1^λ) to generate CRS$'$ and real prover SSS-NIZKPoK.Prove(CRS', X^*, W^*) to generate the proof π'^*, then we are exactly in Hyb_0. On the other hand, if the common reference string and the proof are simulated, then we are in Hyb_1. Hence the lemma. $\quad\square$

Lemma 2. *Assuming* PKE *is* CPA *secure, no* PPT *adversary can distinguish with non-negligible advantage between the hybrids* Hyb_1 *and* Hyb_2.

Proof. Suppose there is a PPT adversary $\mathcal{A}$ that can distinguish with non-negligible advantage between Hyb_1 and Hyb_2. We construct a PPT algorithm $\mathcal{C}$ that breaks the CPA-security of PKE using $\mathcal{A}$ as a sub-routine. $\mathcal{C}$ interacts with $\mathcal{A}$ as follows:

- $\mathcal{C}$ begins by initializing $\mathcal{A}$ and receiving $(f_0^*, z_0^*), (f_1^*, z_1^*)$ from $\mathcal{A}$.
- To setup the public parameters, $\mathcal{C}$ proceeds as follows:
  - $\mathcal{C}$ itself generates $(\text{PK}_{\text{PKE}}^{(1)}, \text{SK}_{\text{PKE}}^{(1)}) \leftarrow$ PKE.KeyGen(1^λ).
  - It also receives a public key PK_{PKE}' for PKE from its *CPA-security challenger* $\mathcal{B}$ and sets $\text{PK}_{\text{PKE}}^{(2)} = \text{PK}_{\text{PKE}}'$.
  - Then, it computes $e_1^* = $ PKE.Encrypt$(\text{PK}_{\text{PKE}}^{(1)}, f_0^*(z_0^*); r_1^*)$ itself using randomness r_1^*.
  - Next, it sends the two messages $f_0^*(z_0^*), f_1^*(z_1^*)$ to $\mathcal{B}$ which sends back a challenge ciphertext e'^*. It designates $e_2^* = e'^*$.
  - After that, $\mathcal{C}$ itself generates $(\text{VK}_{\text{SIG}}, \text{SK}_{\text{SIG}}) \leftarrow$ SIG.KeyGen(1^λ) together with $(\text{CRS}, \text{TR}) \leftarrow$ SSS-NIZKPoK.SimSetup$(1^\lambda, X^*)$ where $X^* = (\text{PK}_{\text{PKE}}^{(1)}, \text{PK}_{\text{PKE}}^{(2)}, \text{VK}_{\text{SIG}}, e_1^*, e_2^*)$.
  - It hands the public parameters MPK $= (\text{PK}_{\text{PKE}}^{(1)}, \text{PK}_{\text{PKE}}^{(2)}, \text{VK}_{\text{SIG}}, \text{CRS})$ to $\mathcal{A}$ while keeps $\widetilde{\text{MSK}} = (\text{SK}_{\text{PKE}}^{(1)}, \text{SK}_{\text{SIG}}, \text{TR}, e_1^*, e_2^*)$.
- Using SK_{SIG} and $\text{SK}_{\text{PKE}}^{(1)}$, the signing key, decryption key, and signcryption queries of $\mathcal{A}$ are answered by $\mathcal{C}$ in an analogous fashion as in the proof of Lemma 1.
- In order to generate the challenge ciphertext, $\mathcal{C}$ computes $\pi^* \leftarrow$ SSS-NIZKPoK.SimProve$(\text{CRS}, \text{TR}, X^*)$ where $X^* = (\text{PK}_{\text{PKE}}^{(1)}, \text{PK}_{\text{PKE}}^{(2)}, \text{VK}_{\text{SIG}}, e_1^*, e_2^*)$. It sends the challenge ciphertext CT$^* = (e_1^*, e_2^*, \pi^*)$ to $\mathcal{A}$.

- Eventually, $\mathcal{A}$ outputs a bit $b' \in \{0, 1\}$. $\mathcal{C}$ also outputs b'.

Observe that, if $\mathcal{B}$ gave $e'^* \leftarrow$ PKE.Encrypt($\text{PK}'_{\text{PKE}}, f_0^*(z_0^*)$), then we are exactly in hybrid Hyb_1. On the other hand, if it gave $e'^* \leftarrow$ PKE.Encrypt($\text{PK}'_{\text{PKE}}, f_1^*(z_1^*)$), then we are in Hyb_2. Hence the lemma. $\qquad\square$

Lemma 3. *Assuming $\mathcal{O}$ is an IO for P/poly and SSS-NIZKPoK is statistically simulation-sound, no PPT adversary can distinguish with non-negligible advantage between $\text{Hyb}_{3,i}$ and $\text{Hyb}_{3,i+1}$ for $i \in [0, q-1]$.*

Proof. Suppose that there is a PPT adversary $\mathcal{A}$ that can distinguish with non-negligible advantage between $\text{Hyb}_{3,i}$ and $\text{Hyb}_{3,i+1}$. We build a PPT algorithm $\mathcal{C}$ that breaks the IO property of $\mathcal{O}$ using $\mathcal{A}$ as a subroutine. $\mathcal{C}$ interacts with $\mathcal{A}$ as follows:

- $\mathcal{C}$ starts with initializing $\mathcal{A}$ and obtaining $(f_0^*, z_0^*), (f_1^*, z_1^*)$ from $\mathcal{A}$.
- In order to setup the public parameters, $\mathcal{C}$ performs the following steps:
  - $\mathcal{C}$ first generates $(\text{PK}_{\text{PKE}}^{(1)}, \text{SK}_{\text{PKE}}^{(1)}), (\text{PK}_{\text{PKE}}^{(2)}, \text{SK}_{\text{PKE}}^{(2)}) \leftarrow$ PKE.KeyGen(1^λ) and $(\text{VK}_{\text{SIG}}, \text{SK}_{\text{SIG}}) \leftarrow$ SIG.KeyGen(1^λ).
  - After that it computes $e_1^* =$ PKE.Encrypt($\text{PK}_{\text{PKE}}^{(1)}, f_0^*(z_0^*); r_1^*$) and $e_2^* =$ PKE.Encrypt($\text{PK}_{\text{PKE}}^{(2)}, f_1^*(z_1^*); r_2^*$) using randomness r_1^* and r_2^* respectively.
  - Then it obtains $(\text{CRS}, \text{TR}) \leftarrow$ SSS-NIZKPoK.SimSetup($1^\lambda, X^*$) where $X^* = (\text{PK}_{\text{PKE}}^{(1)}, \text{PK}_{\text{PKE}}^{(2)}, \text{VK}_{\text{SIG}}, e_1^*, e_2^*)$.
  - It gives the public parameters $\text{MPK} = (\text{PK}_{\text{PKE}}^{(1)}, \text{PK}_{\text{PKE}}^{(2)}, \text{VK}_{\text{SIG}}, \text{CRS})$ to $\mathcal{A}$ while keeps $\widetilde{\text{MSK}} = (\text{SK}_{\text{PKE}}^{(1)}, \text{SK}_{\text{PKE}}^{(2)}, \text{SK}_{\text{SIG}}, \text{TR}, e_1^*, e_2^*)$ to itself.
- The signing key and signcryption key queries of $\mathcal{A}$ are answered by $\mathcal{C}$ in the same manner as in the proof of Lemma 2 using SK_{SIG}. Now consider the decryption key queries made by $\mathcal{A}$. Recall that $\mathcal{A}$ makes q decryption key queries corresponding to decryption functions $g_i \in \mathbb{G}$. The answers to these queries are provided as follows:
  - (a) For $j \leq i$, $\mathcal{C}$ forms the j-th decryption key $\text{DK}(g_j) = (g_j, \mathcal{O}$ $(\widetilde{P}^{(g_j, \text{SK}_{\text{PKE}}^{(2)}, \text{MPK})}))$. Note that $\mathcal{C}$ knows $\text{SK}_{\text{PKE}}^{(2)}$ and therefore can form the program $\widetilde{P}^{(g_j, \text{SK}_{\text{PKE}}^{(2)}, \text{MPK})}$ itself.
  - (b) For $j > i+1$, the j-th queried decryption key is created as $\text{DK}(g_j) = (g_j, \mathcal{O}$ $(P^{(g_j, \text{SK}_{\text{PKE}}^{(1)}, \text{MPK})}))$ by $\mathcal{C}$ using $\text{SK}_{\text{PKE}}^{(1)}$.
  - (c) For the $(i+1)$-th decryption key query, $\mathcal{C}$ submits $C_0 = P^{(g_{i+1}, \text{SK}_{\text{PKE}}^{(1)}, \text{MPK})}$ and $C_1 = \widetilde{P}^{(g_{i+1}, \text{SK}_{\text{PKE}}^{(2)}, \text{MPK})}$ to its IO *challenger* $\mathcal{B}$ and receives back an obfuscated circuit C'. $\mathcal{C}$ gives $\text{DK}(g_{i+1}) = (g_{i+1}, C')$ to $\mathcal{A}$.
- For the challenge ciphertext, $\mathcal{C}$ computes $\pi^* \leftarrow$ SSS-NIZKPoK.SimProve(CRS, TR, X^*) where $X^* = (\text{PK}_{\text{PKE}}^{(1)}, \text{PK}_{\text{PKE}}^{(2)}, \text{VK}_{\text{SIG}}, e_1^*, e_2^*)$. $\mathcal{C}$ sends the challenge ciphertext $\text{CT}^* = (e_1^*, e_2^*, \pi^*)$ to $\mathcal{A}$.
- Eventually, $\mathcal{A}$ outputs a bit $b' \in \{0, 1\}$. $\mathcal{C}$ also outputs b'.

We now argue that (C_0, C_1) forms a valid instance of the IO assumption by exhibiting that both the programs $P^{(g_{i+1}, \text{SK}_{\text{PKE}}^{(1)}, \text{MPK})}$ and $\widetilde{P}^{(g_{i+1}, \text{SK}_{\text{PKE}}^{(2)}, \text{MPK})}$ described in Fig. 1 produce the same output on each input. We break our argument into cases on the input to these programs.

(I) We first consider inputs (e_1, e_2, π) where e_1, e_2 are valid encryption of the same message and π is a proof of the statement $X = (\text{PK}_{\text{PKE}}^{(1)}, \text{PK}_{\text{PKE}}^{(2)}, \text{VK}_{\text{SIG}}, e_1, e_2)$ for which $\text{SSS-NIZKPoK.Verify}(\text{CRS}, X, \pi) = 1$. For these inputs both programs will reach Step 4 where they decrypt the same message, no matter whether they use $\text{SK}_{\text{PKE}}^{(1)}$ or $\text{SK}_{\text{PKE}}^{(2)}$, and compute the same function g_{i+1} on the decrypted message. Thus the output of both programs is the same on all inputs of this class.

(II) Next we consider inputs (e_1, e_2, π) for which $\text{SSS-NIZKPoK.Verify}(\text{CRS}, (\text{PK}_{\text{PKE}}^{(1)}, \text{PK}_{\text{PKE}}^{(2)}, \text{VK}_{\text{SIG}}, e_1, e_2), \pi)$ in Step 3 of both programs outputs 0. In this case both the programs output $\perp$.

(III) Finally, we consider inputs (e_1, e_2, π) for which $\text{SSS-NIZKPoK.Verify}(\text{CRS}, (\text{PK}_{\text{PKE}}^{(1)}, \text{PK}_{\text{PKE}}^{(2)}, \text{VK}_{\text{SIG}}, e_1, e_2), \pi)$ in Step 3 of both the programs outputs 1 but e_1, e_2 are not valid encryptions of the same message. Note that, due to the statistical simulation-soundness property of SSS-NIZKPoK, with all but negligible probability this can happen only when $e_1 = e_1^*$ and $e_2 = e_2^*$, and hence, decrypting e_1 gives $f_0^*(z_0^*)$ while decrypting e_2 results in $f_1^*(z_1^*)$. However, $P^{(g_{i+1}, \text{SK}_{\text{PKE}}^{(1)}, \text{MPK})}$ outputs $g_{i+1}(f_0^*(z_0^*))$ which is bound to be equal to $g_{i+1}(f_1^*(z_1^*))$ (by the rules of the game), which is the output of $\widetilde{P}^{(g_{i+1}, \text{SK}_{\text{PKE}}^{(2)}, \text{MPK})}$. Thus, we can see that both programs have the same output for this input class as well.

Now, observe that, if $\mathcal{B}$ gave $C' = \mathcal{O}(C_0)$, then we are exactly in $\text{Hyb}_{3,i}$. Whereas, if it gave $C' = \mathcal{O}(C_1)$, then we are in $\text{Hyb}_{3,i+1}$. The lemma follows. $\square$

Lemma 4. *Assuming PKE is CPA secure, no PPT adversary can distinguish with non-negligible advantage between $\text{Hyb}_{3,q}$ and Hyb_4.*

Lemma 5. *Assuming $\mathcal{O}$ is an IO for P/poly and SSS-NIZKPoK is statistically simulation-sound, no PPT adversary can distinguish with non-negligible advantage between $\text{Hyb}_{5,i}$ and $\text{Hyb}_{5,i+1}$ for $i \in [0, q]$.*

Lemma 6. *Assuming SSS-NIZKPoK is computationally zero-knowledge, no PPT adversary can distinguish with non-negligible advantage between $\text{Hyb}_{5,q}$ and Hyb_6.*

The proofs of Lemmas 4, 5, and 6 follow in a directly analogous manner to those of Lemmas 2, 3, and 1 respectively. $\square$

Theorem 2 (Ciphertext Unforgeability of FSC). *Under the assumption that SIG is existentially unforgeable against CMA and SSS-NIZKPoK is a proof of knowledge, the FSC construction of Sect. 4.1 is selectively ciphertext unforgeable against CMA as per the definition given in Sect. 3.*

The proof of Theorem 2 is available in the full version.

5 Attribute-Based Signcryption (ABSC) for General Circuits from FSC

5.1 The Notion of ABSC for General Circuits

The formal notion of *attribute-based signcryption* (ABSC) [12–14], when supporting *general polynomial-size circuits*, can be described as follows: As for other attribute-based primitives such as attribute-based encryption or signature, ABSC also has two flavors, namely, *key-policy* and *ciphertext-policy*. For definiteness of exposure, lets consider the key-policy version where the access structures, represented as circuits, are embedded in signing and decryption keys, while signing and decryption attribute sets, expressed as bit strings, are associated with signcrypted message.

Let $\mathbb{F}_{\mathsf{ABSC}} \subset \mathsf{P}/\mathsf{poly}$ and $\mathbb{G}_{\mathsf{ABSC}} \subset \mathsf{P}/\mathsf{poly}$ respectively denote the class of Boolean circuits representing the signing and decryption policies with the input strings to these circuits representing the signing and decryption attribute sets. Let $\mathbb{M}_{\mathsf{ABSC}} \subset \{0,1\}^*$ be the message space and λ be the underlying security parameter. A key-policy ABSC scheme consists of the following PPT algorithms:

ABSC.Setup(1^λ): The trusted authority publishes the public parameters $\mathrm{MPK}_{\mathsf{ABSC}}$, while keeps the master secret key $\mathrm{MSK}_{\mathsf{ABSC}}$ to itself.

ABSC.SKeyGen($\mathrm{MPK}_{\mathsf{ABSC}}, \mathrm{MSK}_{\mathsf{ABSC}}, C^{(\mathsf{SIG})}$): The authority hands a signing key $\mathrm{SK}_{\mathsf{ABSC}}(C^{(\mathsf{SIG})})$ for a signing circuit $C^{(\mathsf{SIG})} \in \mathbb{F}_{\mathsf{ABSC}}$ with input length $\mu(\lambda)$, for some polynomial μ, to a signcrypter.

ABSC.DKeyGen($\mathrm{MPK}_{\mathsf{ABSC}}, \mathrm{MSK}_{\mathsf{ABSC}}, C^{(\mathsf{DEC})}$): A decryption key $\mathrm{DK}_{\mathsf{ABSC}}(C^{(\mathsf{DEC})})$ corresponding to a decryption circuit $C^{(\mathsf{DEC})} \in \mathbb{G}_{\mathsf{ABSC}}$ having input length $\nu(\lambda)$ is given to a decrypter by the trusted authority, where ν is some polynomial.

ABSC.Signcrypt($\mathrm{MPK}_{\mathsf{ABSC}}, \mathrm{SK}_{\mathsf{ABSC}}(C^{(\mathsf{SIG})}), y, \overline{y}, M$): A signcrypter outputs a signcryption $\mathrm{CT}_{\mathsf{ABSC}}^{(y,\overline{y})}$ of a message $M \in \mathbb{M}_{\mathsf{ABSC}}$ under decryption input string $y \in \{0,1\}^\nu$ and signature input string $\overline{y} \in \{0,1\}^\mu$.

ABSC.Unsigncrypt($\mathrm{MPK}_{\mathsf{ABSC}}, \mathrm{DK}_{\mathsf{ABSC}}(C^{(\mathsf{DEC})}), \mathrm{CT}_{\mathsf{ABSC}}^{(y,\overline{y})}$): A decrypter ends up either retrieving the signcrypted message or $\perp$ if unsuccessful.

A key-policy ABSC scheme is *correct* if for all $C^{(\mathsf{SIG})} \in \mathbb{F}_{\mathsf{ABSC}}$ with input length μ, $\overline{y} \in \{0,1\}^\mu$ with $C^{(\mathsf{SIG})}(\overline{y}) = 1$, $C^{(\mathsf{DEC})} \in \mathbb{G}_{\mathsf{ABSC}}$ with input length ν, $y \in \{0,1\}^\nu$ such that $C^{(\mathsf{DEC})}(y) = 1$, and $M \in \mathbb{M}_{\mathsf{ABSC}}$,

$$\Pr\big[(\mathrm{MPK}_{\mathsf{ABSC}}, \mathrm{MSK}_{\mathsf{ABSC}}) \leftarrow \mathsf{ABSC.Setup}(1^\lambda) :$$

$$\mathsf{ABSC.Unsigncrypt}\big(\mathrm{MPK}_{\mathsf{ABSC}}, \mathsf{ABSC.DKeyGen}(\mathrm{MPK}_{\mathsf{ABSC}}, \mathrm{MSK}_{\mathsf{ABSC}}, C^{(\mathsf{DEC})}),$$

$$\mathsf{ABSC.Signcrypt}(\mathrm{MPK}_{\mathsf{ABSC}}, \mathsf{ABSC.SKeyGen}(\mathrm{MPK}_{\mathsf{ABSC}}, \mathrm{MSK}_{\mathsf{ABSC}}, C^{(\mathsf{SIG})}),$$

$$y, \overline{y}, M)\big) = M\big] > 1 - \epsilon(\lambda)$$

for some negligible function ϵ.

The two security notions for key-policy ABSC for general polynomial-size circuits, namely, (I) *message confidentiality* and (II) *ciphertext unforgeability* can be formalized by adopting those defined in [12,13] to the case of general circuits in a straightforward manner.

5.2   Our Key-Policy **ABSC** Scheme

Let λ be the underlying security parameter. We consider the family of signing circuits $\mathbb{F}_{\mathsf{ABSC}} \subset \mathsf{P/poly}$ whose members have input length $\mu(\lambda)$ and the class of decryption circuits $\mathbb{G}_{\mathsf{ABSC}} \subset \mathsf{P/poly}$ containing circuits of input length $\nu(\lambda)$ for polynomials μ and ν. The message space for our ABSC scheme is $\mathbb{M}_{\mathsf{ABSC}} = \{0,1\}^{\gamma(\lambda)}$ for some polynomial γ. Consider a FSC scheme FSC=(FSC.Setup, FSC.SKeyGen, FSC.Signcrypt, FSC.DKeyGen, FSC.Unsigncrypt) for any polynomial-size signing function family $\mathbb{F} \subseteq \mathsf{P/poly}$, decryption function class $\mathbb{G} \subseteq \mathsf{P/poly}$, and the message space $\mathbb{M} = \{0,1\}^n \cup \{\perp\}$ where $n = \nu + \mu + \gamma$. Let us now define signing and decryption functions for the FSC scheme that would instantiate ABSC. We associate a signing function $f_{C^{(\mathsf{SIG})}} \in \mathbb{F}$, where $f_{C^{(\mathsf{SIG})}} : \mathbb{D}_f = \{0,1\}^n \to \mathbb{M}$ to each signing circuit $C^{(\mathsf{SIG})} \in \mathbb{F}_{\mathsf{ABSC}}$ and a decryption function $g_{C^{(\mathsf{DEC})}} \in \mathbb{G}$, where $g_{C^{(\mathsf{DEC})}} : \mathbb{M} \to \mathbb{M}$, corresponding to each decryption circuit $C^{(\mathsf{DEC})} \in \mathbb{G}_{\mathsf{ABSC}}$, defined as follows:

$$f_{C^{(\mathsf{SIG})}}(y\|\overline{y}\|M) = \begin{cases} y\|\overline{y}\|M, & \text{if } C^{(\mathsf{SIG})}(\overline{y}) = 1 \\ \perp, & \text{otherwise} \end{cases} \tag{2}$$

$$g_{C^{(\mathsf{DEC})}}(y\|\overline{y}\|M) = \begin{cases} y\|\overline{y}\|M, & \text{if } C^{(\mathsf{DEC})}(y) = 1 \\ \perp, & \text{otherwise} \end{cases}$$

Our ABSC works as follows:

ABSC.Setup(1^λ): The trusted authority takes as input the security parameter λ and generates $(\mathsf{MPK}, \mathsf{MSK}) \leftarrow$ FSC.Setup(1^λ). It publishes the public parameters $\mathsf{MPK}_{\mathsf{ABSC}} = \mathsf{MPK}$, while keeps the master secret key $\mathsf{MSK}_{\mathsf{ABSC}} = \mathsf{MSK}$ to itself.

ABSC.SKeyGen($\mathsf{MPK}_{\mathsf{ABSC}} = \mathsf{MPK}, \mathsf{MSK}_{\mathsf{ABSC}} = \mathsf{MSK}, C^{(\mathsf{SIG})}$): The authority creates the signing key $\mathsf{SK}(f_{C^{(\mathsf{SIG})}}) \leftarrow$ FSC.SKeyGen($\mathsf{MPK}, \mathsf{MSK}, f_{C^{(\mathsf{SIG})}}$) for the signing function $f_{C^{(\mathsf{SIG})}} \in \mathbb{F}$ defined in Eq. (2) and gives $\mathsf{SK}_{\mathsf{ABSC}}(C^{(\mathsf{SIG})}) = \mathsf{SK}(f_{C^{(\mathsf{SIG})}})$ to the signcrypter.

FSC.DKeyGen($\mathsf{MPK}_{\mathsf{ABSC}} = \mathsf{MPK}, \mathsf{MSK}_{\mathsf{ABSC}} = \mathsf{MSK}, C^{(\mathsf{DEC})}$): The trusted authority forms the decryption key $\mathsf{DK}(g_{C^{(\mathsf{DEC})}}) \leftarrow$ FSC.DKeyGen($\mathsf{MPK}, \mathsf{MSK}, g_{C^{(\mathsf{DEC})}}$) for the decryption function $g_{C^{(\mathsf{DEC})}} \in \mathbb{G}$ described in Eq. (2) and gives $\mathsf{DK}_{\mathsf{ABSC}}(C^{(\mathsf{DEC})}) = \mathsf{DK}(g_{C^{(\mathsf{DEC})}})$ to the decrypter.

ABSC.Signcrypt($\mathsf{MPK}_{\mathsf{ABSC}} = \mathsf{MPK}, \mathsf{SK}_{\mathsf{ABSC}}(C^{(\mathsf{SIG})}) = \mathsf{SK}(f_{C^{(\mathsf{SIG})}}), y, \overline{y}, M$): Provided $C^{(\mathsf{SIG})}(\overline{y}) = 1$, a signcrypter computes $\mathsf{CT} \leftarrow$ FSC.Signcrypt(MPK, $\mathsf{SK}(f_{C^{(\mathsf{SIG})}}), z = y\|\overline{y}\|M$). It outputs $\mathsf{CT}_{\mathsf{ABSC}}^{(y,\overline{y})} = (y, \overline{y}, \mathsf{CT})$.

ABSC.Unsigncrypt($\mathsf{MPK}_{\mathsf{ABSC}} = \mathsf{MPK}, \mathsf{DK}_{\mathsf{ABSC}}(C^{(\mathsf{DEC})}) = \mathsf{DK}(g_{C^{(\mathsf{DEC})}}), \mathsf{CT}_{\mathsf{ABSC}}^{(y,\overline{y})} = (y, \overline{y}, \mathsf{CT})$): A decrypter runs FSC.Unsigncrypt(MPK, $\mathsf{DK}(g_{C^{(\mathsf{DEC})}}), \mathsf{CT}$) and obtains $y'\|\overline{y}'\|M'$ or $\perp$. If the decrypter gets $y'\|\overline{y}'\|M'$ and it holds that $y' = y \bigwedge \overline{y}' = \overline{y}$, then the decrypter outputs M'. Otherwise, it outputs $\perp$.

Note that the correctness of the above ABSC scheme is immediate from the correctness of the FSC scheme. The security follows from the following two theorems:

Theorem 3 (Message Confidentiality of ABSC). *If FSC is selectively message confidential against CPA as per the definition of Sect. 3, then the ABSC described above is also selectively message confidential against CPA as per the notion given in Sect. 5.1.*

Theorem 4 (Ciphertext Unforgeability of ABSC). *If the FSC scheme is selectively ciphertext unforgeable against CMA as per the definition of Sect. 3, then the ABSC scheme described above is also selectively ciphertext unforgeable against CMA according to the notion given in Sect. 5.1.*

The proofs of Theorems 3 and 4 are provided in the full version. Observe that it is also possible to instantiate ciphertext-policy ABSC from FSC employing an analogous technique as has been demonstrated above for the key-policy version.

6 Other Cryptographic Primitives from FSC

■ **SSS-NIZKPoK from FSC:** Let R be an NP relation and $\mathbb{L}$ be the associated language. Recall that for $(X, W) \in R$, we call X the statement that is contained in $\mathbb{L}$ and W an witness for X. Let κ and ρ be the upper bounds on the lengths of the statements and witnesses of R. Consider a FSC scheme FSC=(FSC.Setup, FSC.SKeyGen, FSC.Signcrypt, FSC.DKeyGen, FSC.Unsigncrypt) supporting signing function family $\mathbb{F} \subseteq$ P/poly and class of decryption functions $\mathbb{G} \subseteq$ P/poly. Let $\mathbb{M} = \{0,1\}^n \cup \{\bot\}$ be the message space of FSC where $n = \kappa + \rho + 1$. The SSS-NIZKPoK system is described as follows:

SSS-NIZKPoK.Setup(1^λ): First, the trusted authority executes (MPK, MSK) $\leftarrow$ FSC.Setup(1^λ). Next, it identifies some statement $X^* \in \mathbb{L}$. Then, it generates a signing key for FSC, SK(f) $\leftarrow$ FSC.SKeyGen(MPK, MSK, f) for the signing function $f \in \mathbb{F}$, where $f : \{0,1\}^n \to \mathbb{M}$, and a decryption key for FSC, DK(g) $\leftarrow$ FSC.DKeyGen(MPK, MSK, g) for the decryption function $g \in \mathbb{G}$, where $g : \mathbb{M} \to \{0,1\}^\kappa \cup \{\bot\}$, defined as follows:

$$f(X\|W\|\beta) = \begin{cases} X\|W\|\beta, & \text{if } (X, W) \in R \bigwedge \beta = 1 \\ \bot, & \text{otherwise} \end{cases}$$

$$g(X\|W\|\beta) = \begin{cases} X, & \text{if } [(X, W) \in R \bigwedge \beta = 1] \bigvee [X = X^* \bigwedge W = 0^\rho \bigwedge \beta = 0] \\ \bot, & \text{otherwise} \end{cases}$$

$$(3)$$

The trusted authority publishes the common reference string CRS = (MPK, SK(f), DK(g)).

SSS-NIZKPoK.Prove(CRS, X, W): A prover executes CT $\leftarrow$ FSC.Signcrypt(MPK, SK(f), $X\|W\|1$) and outputs $\pi =$ CT.

SSS-NIZKPoK.Verify(CRS, $X, \pi = $ CT): A verifier outputs 1, if $X' = X$, or 0, otherwise, where it obtains $X' \leftarrow$ FSC.Unsigncrypt(MPK, DK(g), CT).

SSS-NIZKPoK.SimSetup($1^\lambda, \widetilde{X}^*$): First, the simulator performs (MPK, MSK) $\leftarrow$ FSC.Setup(1^λ). Next it computes a signing key SK(f) $\leftarrow$ FSC.SKeyGen(MPK, MSK, f) for the signing function $f \in \mathbb{F}$ and a decryption key DK(g) $\leftarrow$ FSC.DKeyGen(MPK, MSK, g) for the decryption function $g \in \mathbb{G}$ defined in Eq. (3) where $\widetilde{X}^*$ will play the role of X^*. It also computes a signing key SK($\widetilde{f}$) $\leftarrow$ FSC.SKeyGen(MPK, MSK, $\widetilde{f}$) for the following signing function $\widetilde{f} \in \mathbb{F}$.

$$\widetilde{f}(X\|W\|\beta) = \begin{cases} X\|W\|\beta, \text{ if } [(X, W) \in R \bigwedge \beta = 1] \bigvee \\ \qquad\qquad [X = \widetilde{X}^* \bigwedge W = 0^\rho \bigwedge \beta = 0] \\ \bot, \qquad\quad \text{otheriwse} \end{cases} \quad (4)$$

It outputs the simulated common reference string CRS $=$ (MPK, SK(f), DK(g)) and its simulation trapdoor is TR $=$ SK($\widetilde{f}$).

SSS-NIZKPoK.SimProve(CRS, TR, $\widetilde{X}^*$): The simulator computes the ciphertext for FSC, $\widetilde{CT} \leftarrow$ FSC.Signcrypt(MPK, SK($\widetilde{f}$), $\widetilde{X}^*\|0^\rho\|0$) and outputs the simulated proof as $\widetilde{\pi} = \widetilde{CT}$.

SSS-NIZKPoK.ExtSetup(1^λ): The extractor forms (MPK, MSK) $\leftarrow$ FSC.Setup(1^λ). It identifies some fixed statement $X^* \in \mathbb{L}$ and computes the signing key SK(f) and decryption key DK(g) respectively for functions $f \in \mathbb{F}$ and $g \in \mathbb{G}$ defined in Eq. (3). It additionally computes a decryption key DK(g') $\leftarrow$ FSC.DKeyGen(MPK, MSK, g') for the function $g' \in \mathbb{G}$ where $g' : \{0,1\}^n \to \{0,1\}^{\rho+1}$ is defined by

$$g'(X\|W\|\beta) = W\|\beta, \text{ for } X\|W\|\beta \in \{0,1\}^n. \quad (5)$$

It outputs the common reference string CRS $=$ (MPK, SK(f), DK(g)) and its extraction trapdoor is $\widehat{TR} = $ DK(g').

SSS-NIZKPoK.Extr(CRS, $\widehat{TR}, X, \pi = $ CT): The extractor runs FSC.Unsigncrypt (MPK, DK(g'), CT). If it obtains $W\|1 \in \{0,1\}^{\rho+1}$, then it outputs W. Otherwise, it outputs $\bot$ indicating failure.

The fact that the above construction satisfies all the requirements of an SSS-NIZKPoK system if FSC is selectively secure is formally stated in the following theorem, the proof of which is given in the full version.

Theorem 5 (Security of SSS-NIZKPoK). *Assuming that* FSC *is selective message confidential against* CPA *and selective ciphertext unforgeable against* CMA *as per the definition of Sect. 3, the* SSS-NIZKPoK *system described above satisfies all the criteria of* SSS-NIZKPoK *defined in Sect. 2.2.*

■ **IO from FSC:** Note that from any selectively secure FSC scheme we can obtain a *selectively secure functional encryption* (FE) scheme (for background on FE see [5]) with the same message space and decryption function family as the underlying FSC scheme by including a signing key in the public parameters of FE for the signing function which is simply the *identity function* on the message space of FSC. Recently, Ananth et al. [1] has shown how to construct IO for P/poly from selectively secure FE. Following these, we can design an IO for P/poly from FSC. The details are omitted.

7 Conclusion

There are a number of open research directions pertaining to FSC. Firstly, in view of making FSC more practicable one may attempt to construct FSC, possibly for restricted classes of functions, from weaker and more efficient primitives rather than using IO or SSS-NIZKPoK. Secondly, it would be quite interesting to develop an FSC scheme that provides adaptive security as opposed to our selectively secure construction. Thirdly, in this work, we did not consider the simulation paradigm to define security for FSC. Formulating a simulation-based security notion for FSC and identifying the possibilities and impossibilities of that simulation-based security definition have important theoretical significance. A fourth fascinating line of research would be to develop a meaningful notion of *function privacy* in the context of FSC and find out its importance in practical scenarios. Also, it is instructive to investigate whether our non-function-private FSC construction can be extended to achieve that new definition of function privacy for FSC applying a similar transformation technique as has been employed in [4] in case of FE. Finally, we believe that FSC can be utilized as a tool for constructing many more fundamental cryptographic primitives and discovering those new applications of FSC is another interesting area of research.

References

1. Ananth, P., Jain, A., Sahai, A.: Achieving compactness generically: Indistinguishability obfuscation from non-compact functional encryption. IACR Cryptology ePrint Archive 2015, 730 (2015)
2. Bellare, M., Fuchsbauer, G.: Policy-based signatures. In: Krawczyk, H. (ed.) PKC 2014. LNCS, vol. 8383, pp. 520–537. Springer, Heidelberg (2014)
3. Boyle, E., Goldwasser, S., Ivan, I.: Functional signatures and pseudorandom functions. In: Krawczyk, H. (ed.) PKC 2014. LNCS, vol. 8383, pp. 501–519. Springer, Heidelberg (2014)
4. Brakerski, Z., Segev, G.: Function-private functional encryption in the private-key setting. In: Dodis, Y., Nielsen, J.B. (eds.) TCC 2015, Part II. LNCS, vol. 9015, pp. 306–324. Springer, Heidelberg (2015)
5. Garg, S., Gentry, C., Halevi, S., Raykova, M., Sahai, A., Waters, B.: Candidate indistinguishability obfuscation and functional encryption for all circuits. In: 2013 IEEE 54th Annual Symposium on Foundations of Computer Science (FOCS), pp. 40–49. IEEE (2013)
6. Garg, S., Gentry, C., Halevi, S., Sahai, A., Waters, B.: Attribute-based encryption for circuits from multilinear maps. In: Canetti, R., Garay, J.A. (eds.) CRYPTO 2013, Part II. LNCS, vol. 8043, pp. 479–499. Springer, Heidelberg (2013)
7. Gentry, C., Lewko, A.B., Sahai, A., Waters, B.: Indistinguishability obfuscation from the multilinear subgroup elimination assumption. IACR Cryptology ePrint Archive 2014, 309 (2014)
8. Groth, J.: Simulation-sound NIZK proofs for a practical language and constant size group signatures. In: Lai, X., Chen, K. (eds.) ASIACRYPT 2006. LNCS, vol. 4284, pp. 444–459. Springer, Heidelberg (2006)

9. Groth, J., Ostrovsky, R., Sahai, A.: Perfect non-interactive zero knowledge for NP. In: Vaudenay, S. (ed.) EUROCRYPT 2006. LNCS, vol. 4004, pp. 339–358. Springer, Heidelberg (2006)
10. Groth, J., Ostrovsky, R., Sahai, A.: New techniques for noninteractive zero-knowledge. J. ACM (JACM) **59**(3), 11 (2012)
11. Pass, R., Seth, K., Telang, S.: Indistinguishability obfuscation from semantically-secure multilinear encodings. In: Garay, J.A., Gennaro, R. (eds.) CRYPTO 2014, Part I. LNCS, vol. 8616, pp. 500–517. Springer, Heidelberg (2014)
12. Rao, Y.S., Dutta, R.: Expressive attribute based signcryption with constant-size ciphertext. In: Pointcheval, D., Vergnaud, D. (eds.) AFRICACRYPT. LNCS, vol. 8469, pp. 398–419. Springer, Heidelberg (2014)
13. Rao, Y.S., Dutta, R.: *Expressive* bandwidth-efficient attribute based signature and signcryption in standard model. In: Susilo, W., Mu, Y. (eds.) ACISP 2014. LNCS, vol. 8544, pp. 209–225. Springer, Heidelberg (2014)
14. Wang, C., Huang, J.: Attribute-based signcryption with ciphertext-policy and claim-predicate mechanism. In: 2011 Seventh International Conference on Computational Intelligence and Security (CIS), pp. 905–909. IEEE (2011)
15. Waters, B.: A punctured programming approach to adaptively secure functional encryption. IACR Cryptology ePrint Archive 2014, 588 (2014)

Privacy and Cloud

BetterTimes
Privacy-Assured Outsourced Multiplications for Additively Homomorphic Encryption on Finite Fields

Per Hallgren[1]([✉]), Martín Ochoa[2,3], and Andrei Sabelfeld[1]

[1] Chalmers University of Technology, Gothenburg, Sweden
hallgrep@chalmers.se
[2] Technische Universität München, Munich, Germany
[3] Singapore University of Technology and Design, Singapore, Singapore

Abstract. We present a privacy-assured multiplication protocol using which an arbitrary arithmetic formula with inputs from two parties over a finite field $\mathbb{F}_p$ can be jointly computed on encrypted data using an additively homomorphic encryption scheme. Our protocol is secure against malicious adversaries. To motivate and illustrate applications of this technique, we demonstrate an attack on a class of known protocols showing how to compromise location privacy of honest users by manipulating messages in protocols with additively homomorphic encryption. We evaluate our approach using a prototypical implementation. The results show that the added overhead of our approach is small compared to insecure outsourced multiplication.

1 Introduction

There has been an increase of the public awareness about the importance of privacy. This has become obvious with cases such as Snowden [37] and the Tor project [11]. Unfortunately, the current practice is not yet to address privacy concerns by design [7,27,32,36]. It is by far more common that the end consumer has to send privacy-sensitive information to service providers in order to achieve a certain functionality, rather than the service using privacy-preserving technologies. A major challenge of today's research community is to enable services to address privacy without hampering sought functionality and efficiency.

Recent years have brought much attention to secure computations distributed among several participants, a subfield of cryptography generally known as *Secure Multi-party Computation* (SMC). SMC has in recent years been brought to the brink of being widely applicable to real world scenarios [3,4], although general purpose solutions with strong security guarantees are still too slow to be widely applied in practice.

This paper proposes a novel and efficient approach to jointly compute an arbitrary arithmetic formula using certain additively homomorphic encryption schemes, while maintaining security against malicious adversaries. The solution is shown to be valuable as a vital complement to boost the security of a class

© Springer International Publishing Switzerland 2015
M.-H. Au and A. Miyaji (Eds.): ProvSec 2015, LNCS 9451, pp. 291–309, 2015.
DOI: 10.1007/978-3-319-26059-4_16

of privacy-preserving protocols [12,19,33,34,38], where *Alice* queries *Bob* for a function over their combined inputs (see Fig. 2). In such scenarios, it is common that *Bob* is intended to learn nothing at all, while still providing *Alice* with useful information such as whether a picture of a face matches a database [12,33] or whether two principals are close to each other [19,34,38]. This work allows such solutions to harden the attacker model from *honest-but-curious* to *malicious* attackers that do not necessarily follow the protocol (both attacker models are standard in SMC and are presented for instance in [17,28]).

Although some connections have been identified [19,30,34], the two communities of Privacy-preserving Services and Secure Multi-Party Computations are still largely separated. One of the goals of this paper is to contribute to bridging the gap, in particular when it comes to rigorously improving the security of efficient protocols using additively homomorphic encryption in the presence of honest-but-curious adversaries, enabling them to also protect against malicious adversaries in an efficient manner.

Problem Statement. In general in secure two-party computation [28] one considers the case where two parties, *Alice* with inputs $\overrightarrow{x}$ and *Bob* with inputs $\overrightarrow{y}$, want to compute a functionality $f(\overrightarrow{x}, \overrightarrow{y}) = (g(\overrightarrow{x}, \overrightarrow{b}), h(\overrightarrow{x}, \overrightarrow{y}))$, where the procedure f yields a tuple in which *Alice*'s output is the first item and *Bob*'s output is the second item. For the scope of this work, h is always the empty string, and the inputs of both parties are in $\mathbb{F}_p$, such that $\forall x_i \in \overrightarrow{x} : x_i \in \mathbb{F}_p$ and $\forall y_i \in \overrightarrow{y} : y_i \in \mathbb{F}_p$. That is, *Alice* obtains the result of g whereas *Bob* observes nothing (as usual when using partial or full homomorphic encryption). For this reason, in the following we will refer only to $g(\overrightarrow{x}, \overrightarrow{y})$ as the functionality.

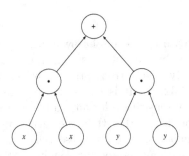

Fig. 1. Arithmetic formula computing $x^2 + y^2$.

Moreover, we set $g(\overrightarrow{x}, \overrightarrow{y})$ to be an arbitrary arithmetic formula over $\overrightarrow{x}$ and $\overrightarrow{y}$ in the operations $(\cdot, +)$ of $\mathbb{F}_p$, that is an arithmetic circuit [35] that is also a directed tree, as the one depicted in Fig. 1.

We assume as usual that both *Alice* and *Bob* want *privacy* of their inputs, as much as it is allowed by g. *Bob* is willing to reveal the final output of g, but not any intermediate results, or a different function g' that would compromise the privacy of his inputs. More precisely, we want a secure two-party computation in the malicious adversary model for a malicious *Alice* [28], as depicted in Fig. 2.

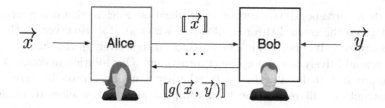

Fig. 2. High-level view of a 2-party computation based on homomorphic encryption, where $[\![\cdot]\!]$ denotes encryption under the public key of *Alice*.

Note that additions in the formula can be done correctly by *Bob* without the help of *Alice* when using an additively homomorphic encryption scheme. This holds also for all multiplications involving *Bob*'s input only, and multiplications with a ciphertext and a value known to *Bob*. The only operations outside of the scope of the additively homomorphic capabilities are multiplications involving inputs from *Alice* only. For instance in Fig. 1, *Bob* can not compute x^2 (assuming x is a private input to *Alice*). In this work therefore we focus on a protocol such that *Bob* can outsource such multiplications to *Alice* without disclosing the value of the operands, and such that if *Alice* does not cooperate, the final value of the arithmetic formula is corrupted and useless to her. This will allow us to show that our protocol is fully privacy-preserving in the malicious adversary model of SMC.

Fairness of the computation (that is, all parties receive their intended output) is out of scope for two reasons: it is impossible to guarantee this property for two-party computations in the malicious model [28], but more interestingly, note that since by construction *Bob* is allowed to observe nothing, an early abortion of the protocol by *Alice* will only hamper fairness for herself.

Contributions. The paper outlines a novel protocol *BetterTimes* which lets *Bob* outsource multiplications using an additively homomorphic encryption scheme (where he does not hold the private key) while asserting privacy of his inputs. *BetterTimes* provides *Bob* not only with the encrypted product but also the encryption of an assurance value (a field element $a \in \mathbb{F}_p$) which is a random value in $\mathbb{F}_p^*$ if *Alice* does not follow the protocol and an encryption of 0 otherwise. The assurance is added to the final output of g thus making the result useless to *Alice* if she tries to cheat. Our contribution thus brings the state-of-the art forward by efficiently giving *Bob* guarantees in the case that *Alice* is malicious.

We illustrate the usefulness of our approach for a class of protocols from the literature [12,19,33,34,38], which compute whether the distance between two vectors in the plane is less than a threshold. In the presence of malicious adversaries, leakage of private information is possible. A solution using our technique is presented for these protocols. Moreover, we make our implementation fully available to the community[1].

Relation to Zero Knowledge Proofs. An alternative solution to the presented problem would be to use a Zero Knowledge schema such that *Bob* can verify that

---

[1] https://bitbucket.org/hallgrep/bettertimes.

a ciphertext corresponds to a certain multiplication. Such a schema is guaranteed to exist given the general theorem of Goldreich et al. [18]. However, to the best of our knowledge it is not straightforward to constructively devise such a scheme for a given additively homomorphic cryptosystem. Our solution in contrast does not require *Bob* to be able to verify whether a multiplication is correct, but by construction will render the final computation result useless to malicious adversaries.

In a nutshell, the novelty as compared to zero-knowledge proofs is based on the simple realization that *Bob* does not need to know whether *Alice* is cheating or not in order to assure the correctness of the final computation and the privacy of his inputs, which decreases the number of round-trips that such a verification step implies. This is a special case of the *conditional disclosure of secrets* introduced by Gertner et al. [16], where a secret is disclosed using SMC only if some condition is met. In our case, the condition is that $z_i = x_i \cdot y_i$ for each multiplication in the formula, and the secret is the output of g.

To the best of our knowledge, there is no previous solution to accomplish secure outsourced multiplications for additively homomorphic encryption in the malicious model without the use of zero-knowledge proofs.

Outline. The paper first introduces necessary background and notation in Sect. 2. Following, in Sect. 3 the BetterTimes protocol is described, and its application to computing arbitrary arithmetic formulas is discussed. Section 4 presents the security guarantees in the malicious adversary setting. Section 5 presents benchmarks that allow one to estimate which impact the approach would have in comparison to only protecting against semi-honest adversaries. Section 6 positions this work in perspective to already published work. Finally, Sect. 7 summarizes the material presented in this paper. Before delving into details, a concrete application of the proposed solution is outlined in Sect. 1.1.

1.1   Exploits for Proximity Protocols

We illustrate the usefulness of our approach by an attack on a class of protocols from the literature [12,19,33,34,38], which compute whether the distance between two vectors in the plane is less than a threshold in a privacy-preserving manner. Popular applications of this algorithm are geometric identification and location proximity. For concreteness, this section focuses on the distance computation used in the *InnerCircle* protocol by Hallgren et al. [19]. The same attack also applies to the other representatives of the same class of protocols [12,33,34,38], but in many cases a successful exploit does not have as visible effects.

Hallgren et al. present a protocol for privacy-preserving location proximity. It is based on the fact that *Bob* can compute the euclidean distances from a point represented as three ciphertexts $[\![2x]\!]$, $[\![2y]\!]$ and $[\![x^2 + y^2]\!]$ to any other point known by *Bob* using additively homomorphic encryption (here $[\![\cdot]\!]$ stands for encryption under the public key of *Alice*). A problem with the approach is that *Bob* has no knowledge of how the ciphertexts are actually related, he sees three ciphertexts $[\![\alpha]\!]$, $[\![\beta]\!]$ and $[\![\gamma]\!]$. In the case that $\gamma \neq (\alpha/2)^2 + (\beta/2)^2$, subsequent computations may leak unwanted information. The distance is expressed as the (squared) distance as shown in Eq. (1), computed homomorphically as shown in Eq. (2) where only some of *Bob*'s inputs are needed in plaintext.

$$D = x_A^2 + y_A^2 + x_B^2 + y_B^2 - (2x_A x_B + 2y_A y_B) \tag{1}$$

$$[\![D]\!] = [\![x_A^2 + y_A^2]\!] \oplus [\![x_B^2 + y_B^2]\!] \ominus ([\![2x_A]\!] \odot x_B \oplus [\![2y_A]\!] \odot y_B) \tag{2}$$

Here, $\oplus$, $\ominus$ and $\odot$ are the homomorphic operations which in the plaintext space map to $+$, $-$ and $\cdot$ respectively (see Sect. 2). Now, by replacing the information sent by *Alice* by α, β and γ and observing that *Alice* can choose α and β arbitrarily, the expression becomes as in Eq. (3):

$$D = x_B^2 + y_B^2 + \gamma + \alpha x_B + \beta y_B \tag{3}$$

The effects of the attack are very illustrative in [19,34,38]. In these works, *Bob* wants to return a boolean $b = (r^2 > D)$ indicating whether two principals are within r from each other. Thus the result given to *Alice* is the evaluation of the function $r^2 > x_B^2 + y_B^2 + \alpha x_B + \beta y_B + \gamma$. This is equivalent to the result of $r^2 - \gamma > x_B^2 + y_B^2 + \alpha x_B + \beta y_B$. Given that *Alice* knows r, she can encode it into the manipulated variables thus forcing the evaluation of $\delta > x_B^2 + y_B^2 + \alpha x_B + \beta y_B + \eta$, with $\gamma = r^2 - \delta - \eta$. By changing α, β and η, *Alice* can move the center of the queried area, and by tweaking δ she can dictate the size of the area, causing unwanted and potentially very serious information leakage (for instance by querying in arbitrarily located and precise areas such as buildings).

Securing Affected Protocols. Based on the novel asserted multiplication presented in Sect. 3, a new structure for the protocols of Hallgren et al. can be constructed. Similar amendments can easily be constructed in similar form for other afflicted solutions [12,33,34,38]. Using the system proposed in this paper, it is possible to send only the encryption of x_A and y_A in the initial message, and securing the necessary squaring by means of *BetterTimes*.

An arithmetic formula which computes the distance directly using x_A, y_A, x_B and y_B is already defined in Eq. (1). Now remains only to model this such that it can be computed by the system presented later in this paper, after which the protocols can proceed to compute the proximity result as they would normally.

The result is an algorithm modeled using the recursive data structure *Ins*, which simply is passed to the procedure *evaluate* by *Bob*, see Sect. 3 and Fig. 6. The formula of can be depicted as a tree as in Fig. 3. The concrete instructions (instances of *Ins*) are spelled out in Appendix A.

2 Background

The solution proposed in this paper makes use of any additively homomorphic encryption scheme which provides semantic security and where the plaintext space is a field (for instance such as the DGK Scheme [9]). For a definition of semantic security see [2].

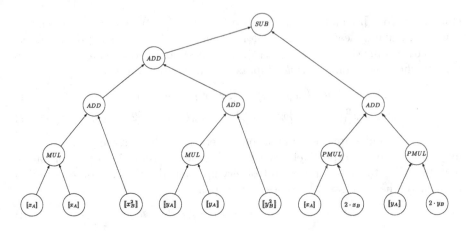

Fig. 3. Tree depicting computation of a secured version of the protocol.

Additively Homomorphic Encryption Schemes. Here and henceforth, k is the private key belonging to *Alice* and K and is the corresponding public key. Let the plaintext space $\mathcal{M}$ be isomorphic to the field $(\mathbb{Z}_p, \cdot, +)$ for some prime number p and the ciphertext space $\mathcal{C}$ such that encryption using public key K is a function $E : \mathcal{M} \to \mathcal{C}$ and decryption using a private key k is $D : \mathcal{C} \to \mathcal{M}$.

The vital homomorphic features which is used later in the paper is an addition function $\oplus : \mathcal{C} \times \mathcal{C} \to \mathcal{C}$, a unary negation function $\neg : \mathcal{C} \to \mathcal{C}$, and a multiplication function $\odot : \mathcal{C} \times \mathcal{M} \to \mathcal{C}$.

$$E(m_1) \oplus E(m_2) = E(m_1 + m_2) \tag{4}$$
$$\neg E(m_1) = E(-m_1) \tag{5}$$
$$E(m_1) \odot m_2 = E(m_1 \cdot m_2) \tag{6}$$

Note that in a finite field any non-zero element multiplied with a non-zero random element yields a non-zero uniformly distributed element. Formally:

$$E(m_1) \odot \rho = \begin{cases} E(0) & \text{if } m_1 = 0 \\ E(l) & \text{with } l \in \mathcal{M}^{\mathcal{U}} \text{ otherwise} \end{cases}, \text{ with } \rho \in \mathcal{M}^{\mathcal{U}} \tag{7}$$

where $m_1 \in \mathcal{M}$, $m_2 \in \mathcal{M}$ and $\mathcal{M}^{\mathcal{U}}$ is a uniformly random distribution of all elements in $\mathcal{M} \setminus \{0\}$.

Syntax and Conventions. For readability, the operations $\oplus$, $\odot$, $\neg$, E and D do not have a key associated to them, we assume they all use the usual k, K pair where *Alice* holds k. The $\ominus$ symbol is used in the following to represent addition by a negated term. That is, $c_1 \oplus \neg c_2$ is written as $c_1 \ominus c_2$. For further brevity, a ciphertext c encrypting a plaintext p under the public key of *Alice* is denoted as $[\![p]\!]$.

The protocol description in Figs. 5 and 6 is given in the language pWHILE [1]. For the convenience of the reader a few constructs used in the paper are outlined here, but for details the reader is directed to [1]. $a \leftarrow b$ means assigning a value b to a variable a, while $a \xleftarrow{\$} [0..n]$ means assigning a random value between 0 and n to a.

Security Concepts. In the following we briefly recall some fundamental concepts from SMC that will be useful for the security guarantees discussion of Sect. 4.

Definition 1 (Negligible functions). *A function $\epsilon : \mathbb{N} \to \mathbb{R}$ is said to be negligible if*

$$\forall\, c \in \mathbb{N}.\ \exists\, n_c \in \mathbb{N}.\ \forall_{n \geq n_c}\ |\epsilon(n)| \leq n^{-c}$$

That is, ϵ decreases faster than the inverse of any polynomial.

Definition 2 (Indistinguishability). *The two random variables $X(n, a)$ and $Y(n, a)$ (where n is a security parameter and a represents the inputs to the protocol) are called computationally indistinguishable and denoted $X \overset{c}{\equiv} Y$ if for a probabilistic polynomial time (PPT) adversary $\mathcal{A}$ the following function is negligible:*

$$\delta(n) = |\Pr[\mathcal{A}(X(n, a)) = 1] - \Pr[\mathcal{A}(Y(n, a)) = 1]|$$

3   Arithmetic Formulas Through Assured Multiplication

As previously discussed, our goal is a system which can compute any arithmetic formula in the presence of a malicious *Alice* (who holds the private key), without leaking any information derived from *Bob*'s inputs except the result of g. To show how to reach this, we first outline the primary building block, *BetterTimes*.

3.1   Privacy-Assured Outsourced Multiplication

The core of the solution is a novel outsourced multiplication protocol with privacy guarantees, *BetterTimes*. The protocol is visualized in Fig. 4 and detailed in Fig. 5. *BetterTimes* allows *Bob* to calculate a multiplication by outsourcing to *Alice*, while retaining an attestation value with which it is possible to make sure that *Alice* can learn no unintended information.

The principals interact once during BetterTimes, where *Bob* contacts *Alice* through the procedure *OS* (for outsource), defined in Fig. 5. As a result of this interaction, *Bob* can compute a value $[\![z]\!]$ which corresponds to the encryption of the multiplication $x \cdot y$ if *Alice* is honest and an attestation value a which will be uniformly random if *Alice* does not comply with the protocol. *Alice* can only deviate from the protocol by using $OS' \neq OS$.

BetterTimes contains several random variables, here follows a brief explanation of their names to make the procedures easier to follow. The first two, c_a and c_m, serve to construct the challenge c used in the attestation. c_a and c_m are an additive and multiplicative component, respectively. The second pair, b_x and b_y, are used to blind the operands x and y, respectively, when outsourcing the

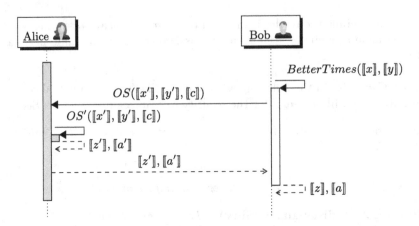

Fig. 4. Visualization of the attested multiplication protocol

Proc. $BetterTimes(\llbracket x \rrbracket, \llbracket y \rrbracket)$:
$c_a \xleftarrow{\$} \{0..p\}; c_m \xleftarrow{\$} \{1..p\};$
$b_x \xleftarrow{\$} \{0..p\}; b_y \xleftarrow{\$} \{0..p\};$
$\rho \xleftarrow{\$} \{1..p\};$
// *Blind operands*
$\llbracket x' \rrbracket \leftarrow \llbracket x \rrbracket \oplus \llbracket b_x \rrbracket; \llbracket y' \rrbracket \leftarrow \llbracket y \rrbracket \oplus \llbracket b_y \rrbracket;$
// *Create challenge*
$\llbracket c \rrbracket \leftarrow (\llbracket x' \rrbracket \oplus \llbracket c_a \rrbracket) \odot c_m;$
// *Outsource multiplication*
$(\llbracket z' \rrbracket, \llbracket a' \rrbracket) \leftarrow OS(\llbracket x' \rrbracket, \llbracket y' \rrbracket, \llbracket c \rrbracket);$
// *Compute assurance value*
$\llbracket a \rrbracket \leftarrow (\llbracket a' \rrbracket \ominus \llbracket z' \rrbracket \odot c_m \ominus \llbracket y' \rrbracket \odot (c_a \cdot c_m)) \odot \rho;$
// *Un-blind multiplication*
$\llbracket z \rrbracket \leftarrow \llbracket z' \rrbracket \ominus (\llbracket x' \rrbracket \odot b_y \oplus \llbracket y' \rrbracket \odot b_x \oplus \llbracket b_x \cdot b_y \rrbracket);$
return $(\llbracket a \rrbracket, \llbracket z \rrbracket);$

Proc. $OS(\llbracket x \rrbracket, \llbracket y \rrbracket, \llbracket c \rrbracket)$:
return $((E(D(\llbracket x \rrbracket) \cdot D(\llbracket y \rrbracket),$
$E(D(\llbracket c \rrbracket) \cdot D(\llbracket y \rrbracket)));$

Fig. 5. The attested multiplication protocol

multiplication. Finally ρ is used to make sure that an attestation which doesn't match the supplied product causes a random offset of the final result.

Note that the attestation is only needed when outsourcing a multiplication. The blinding used in BetterTimes has also been presented and used by, among others, Kolesnikov et al. [22]. The construction using the challenges c_a and c_m yield the following computations in the plaintext, starting with the attestation value a in Eq. (8). Through the procedure OS, *Alice* replies with (in the plaintexts) as in Eq. (9). Thus, assuming *Alice* is honest, we see that Eq. (10) must hold.

$$a = (a' - z' \cdot c_m - y' \cdot c_a \cdot c_m) \cdot \rho = (a' - z' - y' \cdot c_a) \cdot c_m \cdot \rho \tag{8}$$

$$a' = ((x' + c_a) \cdot c_m) \cdot y' = (x' \cdot y' + y' \cdot c_a) \cdot c_m \tag{9}$$

$$a = (x' \cdot y' - z') \cdot c_m \cdot \rho \tag{10}$$

Since by assumption *Alice* is honest, $z' = x' \cdot y' \implies a = 0$. To see that this is the case if and only if *Alice* honest, see Sect. 4.

3.2   Privacy-Assured Arithmetic Formulas

Using *BetterTimes* as described above, the following discusses how to construct arbitrary arithmetic formulas. The general idea is to accumulate any errors caused by misbehavior by *Alice* using attestations a_j, one for each outsourced multiplication. The other operations require no attestations as they can be calculated locally by *Bob*. If *Alice* is dishonest during an outsourced multiplication, the corresponding attestation a_j is a uniformly random variable. Once an arithmetic formula has been fully evaluated, and the result obtained as $[\![result]\!]$, *Bob* instead returns the value $[\![result]\!] \oplus \sum a_i$. The returned value is $[\![result]\!]$ if and only if *Alice* is honest, and the encryption of a uniformly random field element if she is dishonest.

Given an arbitrary arithmetic formula g, the system is designed using a recursive data structure **Ins**, modeling an *instruction* representing g. An instruction either contains an operation and two operands or a scalar. Formally, **Ins** $\in \{[o, l, r] \| x\}$, where o is the operator, l and r are the left- and right-hand side operands, and x is a scalar. The operands are nested instances of **Ins**. The operator is an enum-like variable, with four possible values $\{ADD, SUB, MUL, PMUL\}$. The scalar member holds a ciphertext or a plaintext. An instance *ins* of **Ins** is created using either $Ins(scalar)$, or $Ins(op, ins1, ins2)$. An instruction to compute the addition of two encrypted values $[\![x]\!]$ and $[\![y]\!]$ thus looks like as e.g.: $Ins(ADD, Ins([\![x]\!]), Ins([\![y]\!]))$. At the start of the protocol, *Bob* must collect *Alice*'s encrypted inputs, and hard-wire them into the algorithm. For an example, see Appendix A.

The core of the setup is the recursive procedure *binOp*, defined in Fig. 6, which recursively computes an instruction including any nested instructions. The *binOp* return value has the same structure as that of *BetterTimes*, but the attestation in the first part of the return value is now an accumulated value over all nested instructions.

The main function, wrapping all functionality, is the *evaluate* procedure, see Fig. 6. It takes as parameter an algorithm, which is modeled using an instruction with nested instructions. Evaluate adds the attestation values and the result of the instructions, creating the final result – which is the output of g if and only if *Alice* is honest. For a visualization of messages exchanged and actions taken by each principal, see Appendix B.

4   Security Guarantees

The goal of this section is to show that the result of *evaluate* as defined above is secure in the malicious adversary model for *Alice* (as depicted in Fig. 2), following standard SMC security definitions. We have already introduced the fundamental notion of computational indistinguishability in Sect. 2.

Proc. $binOp(ins)$:
if $isScalar(ins)$ **then** :
    return $(\llbracket 0 \rrbracket, ins)$;
else :
    $(a_1, x) \leftarrow binOp(ins[1])$;
    $(a_2, y) \leftarrow binOp(ins[2])$;
    switch$(ins[0])$:
        case ADD :
            return $(a_1 \oplus a_2, x \oplus y)$;
        case SUB :
            return $(a_1 \oplus a_2, x \ominus y)$;
        case $PMUL$:
            return $(a_1 \oplus a_2, x \odot y)$;
        case MUL :
            $(a_3, z) \leftarrow BetterTimes(x, y)$
            return $(a_1 \oplus a_2 \oplus a_3, z)$;

Proc. $evaluate(alg)$:
  $(a, result) \leftarrow binOp(alg)$;
  return $result \oplus a$;

Fig. 6. The procedures to evaluate recursive instructions.

Malicious Adversary. Recall that a malicious *Alice* in possession of the private key can attack the privacy of the inputs of *Bob* by deviating from the original protocol (as discussed in Sect. 1.1 for a proximity calculation protocol). Intuitively, a malicious *Alice* will deviate from the protocol every time it fails to answer to the outsourced multiplication with the expected values z' and a' as defined in Fig. 5. A deviation would be for example failing to multiply x' with y', in order to change the intended jointly computed arithmetic formula. Formally, we set out to prove the following theorem, which is an instance of the general definition of [28] where the concrete SMC protocol π will depend on the arithmetic formula g to be jointly computed. In the following indistinguishability will be established with respect to the size p of the field $\mathbb{F}_p$ (p is thus the security parameter).

Theorem 1. *For a fixed but arbitrary arithmetic formula* $g(\overrightarrow{x}, \overrightarrow{y})$ *represented by a recursive instruction* $\iota \in \textbf{Ins}$, *for every adversary* $\mathcal{A}$ *against the protocol* π *resulting from* $evaluate(\iota)$, *there exist a simulator* $\mathcal{S}$ *such that:*

$$\{\text{IDEAL}_{g, \mathcal{S}(s)}(\overrightarrow{x}, \overrightarrow{y})\} \stackrel{c}{\equiv} \{\text{REAL}_{\pi, \mathcal{A}(s)}(\overrightarrow{x}, \overrightarrow{y})\}$$

where $\stackrel{c}{\equiv}$ *denotes computational indistinguishability of distributions.*

Here the IDEAL function gives the distribution of the output of a simulator $\mathcal{S}$ that interacts with an idealized implementation of the functionality g on behalf of *Alice*, where both parties give their inputs to a trusted third party that computes g and gives it back to $\mathcal{S}$. Recall that in our setting *Bob* receives no output from the ideal functionality. Therefore, it does not make sense for the adversary to abort the protocol. Also, this means that fairness guarantees for *Bob* are out of scope, so we do not account for abortions of the protocol by the simulator.

On the other hand REAL stands for the distribution of the output of a real adversary $\mathcal{A}$ against concrete executions of the protocol π. The parameter s stands for extra information known to the attacker, in this case we assume that the adversary knows the abstract arithmetic formula g and therefore knows how many multiplications it contains.

Before proceeding with the proof, we introduce the following Lemma.

Lemma 1. *In the outsourced multiplication protocol BetterTimes the attestation value* **a** *is equal to 0 if the protocol is followed, and is indistinguishable from a randomly distributed non-zero element otherwise.*

Proof. First recall the calculations from Fig. 5:

$$[\![a]\!] \leftarrow ([\![a']\!] \ominus [\![z']\!] \odot c_m \ominus [\![y']\!] \odot (c_a \cdot c_m)) \odot \rho; \tag{11}$$

$$[\![z]\!] \leftarrow [\![z']\!] \ominus ([\![x']\!] \odot b_y \oplus [\![y']\!] \odot b_x \oplus [\![b_x \cdot b_y]\!]) \tag{12}$$

Which in the plaintexts corresponds to:

$$a = (a' - (z' + y' \cdot c_a) \cdot c_m) \cdot \rho \tag{13}$$

$$z = z' - (x' \cdot b_y + y' \cdot b_x + b_x \cdot b_y) \tag{14}$$

where a' and z' are produced by *Alice*. It is easy to see that if a' and z' are computed following the protocol, then $a = 0$ by construction.

To see that if *Alice* does not comply with the protocol then a is a randomly distributed non-zero element with very high probability, first note that there are three cases for non-compliance, either $z' \neq x' \cdot y'$, $a' \neq y' \cdot c$ or both. In any case of non-compliance, the goal of *Alice* is to construct a' and z' such that:

$$a' - (z' + y' \cdot c_a) \cdot c_m = 0$$

since otherwise by construction a will be random. Then it must hold:

$$a' = (z' + y' \cdot c_a) \cdot c_m$$

Note that given $(x' + c_a) \cdot c_m$ (which is known by *Alice*), the probability of guessing c_m is at most $\epsilon = \frac{1}{2^p}$ where p is the size of the field, since multiplication is a random permutation and c_a is unknown and uniformly distributed.

Now by contradiction, lets assume that the probability of *Alice* of computing $a' = (z' + y' \cdot c_a) \cdot c_m$ with $z' \neq x' \cdot y'$ is bigger than ϵ. If this holds, then she can also compute:

$$\alpha = a' - (x' + c_a) \cdot c_m \cdot y' = (z' - x' \cdot y') \cdot c_m$$

But then she could also compute $c_m = \alpha(z' - x' \cdot y')^{-1}$ with probability bigger than ϵ, since by hypothesis $z' \neq x' \cdot y'$ and thus $(z' - x' \cdot y') \in \mathbb{F}_p^*$ is invertible, which contradicts the fact that the probability of guessing c_m is smaller than ϵ. $\square$

Now, for the proof of Theorem 1:

Proof (Theorem 1). Without loss of generality, we assume that $\iota \in \mathbf{Ins}$ has m instructions of type MUL. We will distinguish two cases.

$\mathcal{A}$ *follows the protocol* It is easy to see that all m intermediate messages sent from *Bob* appear uniformly random to *Alice* (and independent) due to the fact that they are all of the type $r_i = (x', y', c)$ where each value is blinded. In the case when $\mathcal{A}$ complies with the protocol, the last message contains the correct output g, since *Bob* is an honest party. This implies that the output of $\mathcal{A}$ depends exclusively on $r_0, \ldots, r_m$ uniformly distributed triples and $g(\overrightarrow{x}, \overrightarrow{y})$, so we can simulate an adversary as:

$$\mathcal{S} := \mathcal{A}(r_0, \ldots, r_m, g(\overrightarrow{x}, \overrightarrow{y}))$$

$\mathcal{A}$ *does not follow the protocol* Note that independently of the cheating strategy of $\mathcal{A}$, all m intermediate messages sent from *Bob* appear uniformly random to $\mathcal{A}$ since the blinding is done by *Bob* locally with randomization independent from $\mathcal{A}$'s inputs. Now, as a consequence of Lemma 1, if $\mathcal{A}$ does not follow the protocol for at least one of the outsourced multiplications, the final message will be blinded by the accumulated attestation value, which is indistinguishable from random. Therefore, the last message will contained the encryption of a random value, denoted r_{m+1}. Therefore we can simulate this in the ideal model as:

$$\mathcal{S} := \mathcal{A}(r_0, \ldots, r_m, r_{m+1})$$

for pairwise independent and random variables r_i. $\qquad\square$

Rings. Note that additively homomorphic schemes are commonly defined over groups where when multiplying a non zero element γ with a uniformly chosen ρ, the result is not necessarily uniformly distributed, thus potentially affecting the blinding of $g(x, y)$. For instance, in groups such as $\mathbb{Z}_n$ for composite $n = p \cdot q$ (as used by the Paillier [31] encryption scheme) when multiplying a non invertible element with random ρ, the result stays in the subgroup of non-invertible elements. In that setting is thus possible to show a counterexample to the theorem above, which motivates our restriction to constructions over fields.

5   Evaluation

The approach has been implemented in Python using the GMP [13] arithmetic library. The implementation as been benchmarked to show the impact of using our approach compared to the more common approach of naive outsourced multiplications. In the naive approach, *Alice* is honest-but-curious, and the operands are therefore only blinded. For this implementation, the DGK [9] cryptosystem was used.

Table 1 shows time in milliseconds for different sizes of plaintexts and keys for the two cases when outsourced multiplication is performed using BetterTimes, or naively. The difference between the two approaches is a small factor of about

Table 1. Benchmarks for outsourced multiplication

Plaintext space	Time (in milliseconds)					
	1024 bits			2048 bits		
	This approach	Naive approach	Extra work	This approach	Naive approach	Extra work
2^2	6.286	4.016	56.52 %	29.686	19.458	52.56 %
2^8	6.400	4.017	59.32 %	30.052	19.484	54.24 %
2^{16}	6.432	4.148	55.06 %	30.188	19.574	54.22 %
2^{24}	6.538	4.100	59.46 %	30.578	19.801	54.43 %

1.5 for both key sizes, though slightly smaller for the larger keys. The factor is only marginally increasing as the plaintext space grows from 2^2 to 2^{24}.

The benchmarked time shows only the processing time for each multiplication, the communication overhead is exactly twice for our approach as compared to the naive solution.

6 Related Work

There are three current approaches to compute an arbitrary formula in the two-party setting in the presence of malicious adversaries, Fully Homomorphic Encryption, Enhanced Garbled Circuits and Zero-knowledge proofs.

FHE is by far the most inefficient approach, and its use is often considered not feasible due to the heavy resource consumption. We do not consider FHE a viable alternative to additively homomorphic encryption for practical applications. Garbled Circuits is an excellent tool for boolean circuits, but has been found to not perform as well for arithmetic circuits as approaches built on homomorphic encryption. Zero-knowledge proofs could be used instead of the proposed approach, but at the cost of more computations and/or round trips.

Zero-Knowledge Proofs. The technique which most resembles *BetterTimes* is that of *Zero-Knowledge* (ZK) proofs. Any statement in NP can be proven using generic, though inefficient, ZK (Goldreich et al. [18]). However, to the best of our knowledge, there is no ad-hoc proof for correct multiplications that directly applies to the setting of additively homomorphic encryption without significantly more overhead than the proposed approach, by e.g. introducing more round trips.

Some protocols in the literature can be used efficiently for proving correct multiplications, with only one additional round trip. One such is the Chaum-Pedersen protocol [6], which however is not trivially applicable to an arbitrary encryption scheme. Another interesting solution was introduced by Damgård and Jurik [10], but which is constructed specifically for the Damgård-Jurik cryptosystem.

Secure Multi-party Computations. There are two main categories for private remote computations: Homomorphic Encryption and Garbled Circuits. Through recent research they are both near practical applicability (see [20,24,25] and [5, 15,20]). However, which of the two approaches to choose is typically application-dependent [23,26]. Our approach brings state-of-the-art SMC solutions based on additively homomorphic cryptographic systems forward by protecting against malicious adversaries when outsourcing multiplications, while remaining strongly competitive to the efficient though less secure approaches which currently are popular examples.

There are several works that combine the use of an additively homomorphic scheme with secret sharing, to compute multiplications securely using threshold encryption. This line of work stems from the SMC schemes developed by Cramer et al. [8]. Note that such approaches are secure only against malicious *minorities*, and are not directly applicable in scenarios with only two parties.

To compare against GC-solutions which can compute arbitrary formulas, some experiments using FastGC, a Garbled Circuit framework by Huang et al. [20] were conducted. Any arithmetic circuit can be expressed as a binary circuit, and vice versa [14]. In this framework for arbitrary computations, integer multiplication of 24-bit numbers needed 332 ms to finish, approximately 5078 % slower than BetterTimes. Note however that FastGC is only secure in the honest-but-curious model, and thus not as secure as the approach presented in this paper. Further work exists in the direction of efficiently providing security against malicious adversaries by the authors of FastGC [21], however where one bit of the input is leaked. Moreover, work on optimizing garbled-circuits in the honest-but-curious model also exists, e.g. recently [29], but so far without enough speedup that it can compare to additively homomorphic encryption for privately computing arithmetic formulas.

7 Conclusions

We have presented a protocol for outsourcing multiplications and have shown how to use it construct a system for computation of arbitrary arithmetic formulas with strong privacy guarantees. We have shown that the construction is secure in the malicious adversary model and that the overhead of using the approach is a small constant factor.

The need for such a protocol is justified by the format attacks we have unveiled in known protocols, and presented a concrete exploit targeting [38] where we can alter the format of a message and gain more than the intended amount of location information. We have made a case for using a more realistic attacker model and identified examples from the literature which are vulnerable to this stronger attacker, while also showing how to amend such vulnerabilities. Moreover, we make our implementation fully available to the community.

As future work we plan to investigate the non-trivial task of applying closely related primitives (such as Zero-Knowledge constructions [6] and Threshold Encryption [8]) to achieve the same security guarantees, and benchmark those solutions to compare them to *BetterTimes*.

Acknowledgments. Thanks are due to Allen Au for the useful comments. This work was funded by the European Community under the ProSecuToR project and the Swedish research agencies SSF and VR.

A   A Concrete Instantiation to Secure Hallgren et al.

To make the protocol from Hallgren et al., and other afflicted solutions, secure against format attacks from *Alice*, the distance can be computed directly on the coordinates instead of using several correlated values. The secured algorithm could be modeled as follows:

$$
\begin{aligned}
&Ins(SUB, \\
&\quad Ins(ADD, \\
&\qquad Ins(ADD, Ins(MUL, Ins([\![x_A]\!]), Ins([\![x_A]\!])), Ins([\![x_B^2]\!])), \\
&\qquad Ins(ADD, Ins(MUL, Ins([\![y_A]\!]), Ins([\![y_A]\!])), Ins([\![y_B^2]\!])) \\
&\quad), \\
&\quad Ins(ADD, \\
&\qquad Ins(PMUL, Ins([\![x_A]\!]), Ins(2 \cdot x_B)), \\
&\qquad Ins(PMUL, Ins([\![y_A]\!]), Ins(2 \cdot y_B)) \\
&\quad), \\
&)
\end{aligned}
$$

B   Visualization of Privacy-Preserving Arithmetic Formula

Figure 7 depicts the system for privacy-preserving arithmetic formulas presented in this paper, during an execution where *Alice* is honest. *Alice* is the initiating party, and starts by sending her inputs to *Bob*. *Bob* then hardwires both is and *Alice*'s inputs into a instruction of nested operations, forming a tree like in Fig. 3. Depending on g, *Bob* computes any local operations and executes BetterTimes as necessary, with as many iterations as necessary. Finally, he computes the ciphertext $[\![result]\!]$. Since *Alice* by assumption is honest, $[\![result]\!]$ will hold the output of g (and would hold the encryption of a random element in $\mathbb{F}_p$ if *Alice* was dishonest). BetterTimes is simplified here, for a more complete visualization see Fig. 4.

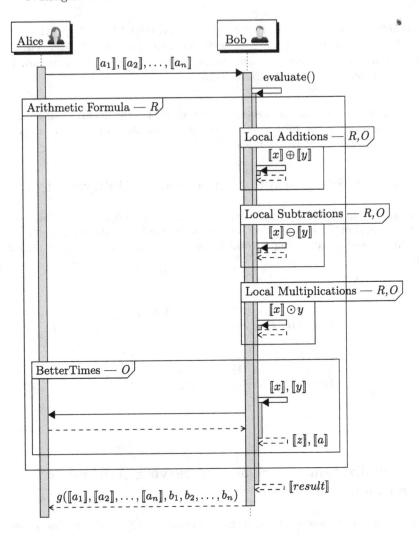

Fig. 7. Visualization of actions by each principal, where R and O means repeatable and optional, respectively.

References

1. Barthe, G., Grégoire, B., Béguelin, S.Z.: Formal certification of code-based cryptographic proofs. In: Shao, Z., Pierce, B.C. (eds.) Proceedings of the 36th ACM SIGPLAN-SIGACT Symposium on Principles of Programming Languages, POPL 2009, Savannah, GA, USA, January 21–23, pp. 90–101. ACM (2009)
2. Bellare, M., Boldyreva, A., Micali, S.: Public-key encryption in a multi-user setting: security proofs and improvements. In: Preneel, B. (ed.) EUROCRYPT 2000. LNCS, vol. 1807, pp. 259–274. Springer, Heidelberg (2000)

3. Bogdanov, D., Laur, S., Willemson, J.: Sharemind: a framework for fast privacy-preserving computations. In: Jajodia, S., Lopez, J. (eds.) ESORICS 2008. LNCS, vol. 5283, pp. 192–206. Springer, Heidelberg (2008)

4. Bogetoft, P., et al.: Secure multiparty computation goes live. In: Dingledine, R., Golle, P. (eds.) FC 2009. LNCS, vol. 5628, pp. 325–343. Springer, Heidelberg (2009)

5. Brakerski, Z., Gentry, C., Vaikuntanathan, V.: Fully homomorphic encryption without bootstrapping. In: Electronic Colloquium on Computational Complexity (ECCC), vol. 18, p. 111 (2011)

6. Chaum, D., Pedersen, T.P.: Wallet databases with observers. In: Brickell, E.F. (ed.) CRYPTO 1992. LNCS, vol. 740, pp. 89–105. Springer, Heidelberg (1993)

7. Coldewey, D.: "Girls Around Me" Creeper App Just Might Get People To Pay Attention To Privacy Settings. TechCrunch, March 2012

8. Cramer, R., Damgård, I.B., Nielsen, J.B.: Multiparty computation from threshold homomorphic encryption. In: Pfitzmann, B. (ed.) EUROCRYPT 2001. LNCS, vol. 2045, pp. 280–299. Springer, Heidelberg (2001)

9. Damgård, I.B., Geisler, M., Krøigaard, M.: Efficient and secure comparison for on-line auctions. In: Pieprzyk, J., Ghodosi, H., Dawson, E. (eds.) ACISP 2007. LNCS, vol. 4586, pp. 416–430. Springer, Heidelberg (2007)

10. Damgård, I.: A generalisation, a simplification and some applications of Paillier's probabilistic public-key system. In: Kim, K. (ed.) PKC 2001. LNCS, vol. 1992, pp. 119–136. Springer, Heidelberg (2001)

11. Dingledine, R., Mathewson, N., Syverson, P.F.: Tor: The second-generation onion router. In: USENIX Security Symposium, pp. 303–320. USENIX (2004)

12. Erkin, Z., Franz, M., Guajardo, J., Katzenbeisser, S., Lagendijk, I., Toft, T.: Privacy-preserving face recognition. In: Goldberg, I., Atallah, M.J. (eds.) PETS 2009. LNCS, vol. 5672, pp. 235–253. Springer, Heidelberg (2009)

13. Free Software Foundation. The gnu multiple precision arithmetic library (1991–2013). http://gmplib.org/

14. Gentry, C.: Fully homomorphic encryption using ideal lattices. In: Mitzenmacher, M. (ed.) STOC, pp. 169–178. ACM (2009)

15. Gentry, C., Sahai, A., Waters, B.: Homomorphic encryption from learning with errors: conceptually-simpler, asymptotically-faster, attribute-based. In: Canetti, R., Garay, J.A. (eds.) CRYPTO 2013, Part I. LNCS, vol. 8042, pp. 75–92. Springer, Heidelberg (2013)

16. Gertner, Y., Ishai, Y., Kushilevitz, E., Malkin, T.: Protecting data privacy in private information retrieval schemes. J. Comput. Syst. Sci. **60**(3), 592–629 (2000)

17. Goldreich, O.: The Foundations of Cryptography, vol. 2. Cambridge University Press, Basic Applications (2004)

18. Goldreich, O., Micali, S., Wigderson, A.: Proofs that yield nothing but their validity or all languages in np have zero-knowledge proof systems. J. ACM **38**(3), 690–728 (1991)

19. Hallgren, P., Ochoa, M., Sabelfeld, A.: InnerCircle: a parallelizable decentralized privacy-preserving location proximity protocol. In: International Conference on Privacy, Security and Trust (PST), July 2015. http://dblp.uni-trier.de/rec/bibtex/conf/pst/HallgrenOS15

20. Huang, Y., Evans, D., Katz, J., Malka, L.: Faster secure two-party computation using garbled circuits. In: USENIX Security Symposium, USENIX Association (2011)

21. Huang, Y., Katz, J., Evans, D.: Quid-pro-quo-tocols: Strengthening semi-honest protocols with dual execution. In: IEEE Symposium on Security and Privacy, SP 2012, 21–23 May 2012, San Francisco, California, USA, pp. 272–284. IEEE Computer Society (2012)

22. Kolesnikov, V., Sadeghi, A.-R., Schneider, T.: From dust to dawn: Practically efficient two-party secure function evaluation protocols and their modular design. IACR Cryptology ePrint Archive 2010, 79 (2010)

23. Kolesnikov, V., Sadeghi, A.-R., Schneider, T.: A systematic approach to practically efficient general two-party secure function evaluation protocols and their modular design. J. Comput. Secur. 21(2), 283–315 (2013)

24. Kolesnikov, V., Schneider, T.: Improved garbled circuit: free XOR gates and applications. In: Aceto, L., Damgård, I., Goldberg, L.A., Halldórsson, M.M., Ingólfsdóttir, A., Walukiewicz, I. (eds.) ICALP 2008, Part II. LNCS, vol. 5126, pp. 486–498. Springer, Heidelberg (2008)

25. Kreuter, B., Shelat, A., Shen, C.: Billion-gate secure computation with malicious adversaries. In: Kohno, T. (ed.) Proceedings of the 21st USENIX Security Symposium, 8–10 August, 2012, Bellevue, WA, USA, pp. 285–300. USENIX Association (2012)

26. Lagendijk, R.L., Erkin, Z., Barni, M.: Encrypted signal processing for privacy protection: Conveying the utility of homomorphic encryption and multiparty computation. IEEE Signal Process. Mag. 30(1), 82–105 (2013)

27. Li, M., Zhu, H., Gao, Z., Chen, S., Yu, L., Hu, S., Ren, K.: All your location are belong to us: breaking mobile social networks for automated user location tracking. In: MobiHoc, pp. 43–52 (2014)

28. Lindell, Y., Pinkas, B.: Secure multiparty computation for privacy-preserving data mining. IACR Cryptology ePrint Archive 2008, 197 (2008)

29. Liu, C., Wang, X.S., Nayak, K., Huang, Y., Shi, E.: Oblivm: A programming framework for secure computation. In: 2015 IEEE Symposium on Security and Privacy, SP 2015, 17–21 May, 2015, San Jose, CA, USA, pp. 359–376. IEEE Computer Society (2015)

30. Narayanan, A., Thiagarajan, N., Lakhani, M., Hamburg, M., Boneh, D.: Location privacy via private proximity testing. In: Proceedings of the Network and Distributed System Security Symposium, NDSS 2011, 6–9 February 2011, San Diego, California, USA. The Internet Society (2011)

31. Paillier, P.: Public-key cryptosystems based on composite degree residuosity classes. In: Stern, J. (ed.) EUROCRYPT 1999. LNCS, vol. 1592, pp. 223–238. Springer, Heidelberg (1999)

32. Polakis, I., Argyros, G., Petsios, T., Sivakorn, S., Keromytis, A.D.: Where's wally? precise user discovery attacks in location proximity services. In: ACM Conference on Computer and Communications Security, October 2015. http://dblp.uni-trier.de/rec/bibtex/conf/ccs/PolakisAPSK15

33. Sadeghi, A.-R., Schneider, T., Wehrenberg, I.: Efficient privacy-preserving face recognition. In: Lee, D., Hong, S. (eds.) ICISC 2009. LNCS, vol. 5984, pp. 229–244. Springer, Heidelberg (2010)

34. Sedenka, J., Gasti, P.: Privacy-preserving distance computation and proximity testing on earth, done right. In: Moriai, S., Jaeger, T., Sakurai, K. (eds.) 9th ACM Symposium on Information, Computer and Communications Security, ASIA CCS 2014, 03–06 June, 2014, Kyoto, Japan, pp. 99–110. ACM (2014)

35. Shpilka, A., Yehudayoff, A.: Arithmetic circuits: A survey of recent results and open questions. Found. Trends Theo. Comput. Sci. 5(3–4), 207–388 (2010)

36. Veytsman, M.: How I was able to track the location of any Tinder user, February 2014. http://blog.includesecurity.com/
37. Wachs, M., Schanzenbach, M., Grothoff, C.: On the feasibility of a censorship resistant decentralized name system. In: Danger, J.-L., Debbabi, M., Marion, J.-Y., Garcia-Alfaro, J., Heywood, N.Z. (eds.) FPS 2013. LNCS, vol. 8352, pp. 19–30. Springer, Heidelberg (2014)
38. Zhong, G., Goldberg, I., Hengartner, U.: Louis, Lester and Pierre: three protocols for location privacy. In: Borisov, N., Golle, P. (eds.) PET 2007. LNCS, vol. 4776, pp. 62–76. Springer, Heidelberg (2007)

Provably Secure Identity Based Provable Data Possession

Yong Yu[1,2]([✉]), Yafang Zhang[1], Yi Mu[3], Willy Susilo[3], and Hongyu Liu[1]

[1] School of Computer Science and Engineering, University of Electronic Science
and Technology of China, Chengdu 611731, China
yuyong@uestc.edu.cn, zyfg908@63.com, 38386969@qq.com
[2] State Key Laboratory of Information Security, Institute of Information
Engineering, Chinese Academy of Sciences, Beijing 100093, China
[3] Center for Computer and Information Security Research,
School of Computing and Information Technology, University of Wollongong,
Wollongong, NSW 2522, Australia
{ymu,wsusilo}@uow.edu.au

Abstract. Provable Data Possession (PDP), which enables cloud users to verify the integrity of their outsourced data without retrieving the entire file from cloud servers, is highly essential in secure cloud storage. A majority of the existing PDP schemes rely on the expensive Public Key Infrastructure (PKI). In this paper, we eliminate the complex certificate management of PDP by presenting a generic construction of identity-based PDP (ID-PDP) protocol, derived from identity-based signatures (IBS) and traditional PDP protocols. We formalize the security model of ID-PDP and prove that the soundness of the generic construction depends on the security of the underlying PDP protocols and the IBS. Then, a concrete ID-PDP protocol is described as an instance of the generic construction to a state-of-the-art PDP protocol due to Shacham and Waters. The implementation shows that our ID-PDP protocol is efficient and practical.

1 Introduction

Cloud computing, which offers dynamically scalable resources provisioned as a service over the Internet, has been emerged as a service over the Internet's evolution. Major advantages of cloud computing include, to name a few, less maintenance, ubiquitous network access, location independent resource pooling, usage-based pricing and rapid resource elasticity [1,2]. With these appealing features, it has become an inevitable trend that individuals and IT enterprises store data remotely to the cloud in a flexible on-demand manner, which is a popular way of data outsourcing [3–5]. Cloud storage service, which allows cloud users to migrate data from their local storage systems to remote cloud servers, is one of the most important services provided by cloud computing. Cloud storage relieves the burden of storage management and maintenance. In addition, cloud storage is cost-effective since it makes data owners avoid the initial investment of

© Springer International Publishing Switzerland 2015
M.-H. Au and A. Miyaji (Eds.): ProvSec 2015, LNCS 9451, pp. 310–325, 2015.
DOI: 10.1007/978-3-319-26059-4_17

expensive infrastructure setup, and the expenditure of maintenance. Meanwhile, the cloud users can enjoy the flexibility of accessing their outsourced files at anytime and from anywhere.

Despite a long list of merits that cloud storage can provide, it does trigger numerous security challenges since the cloud servers are not regarded as fully trusted. According to the white paper [7] released by the Cloud Vulnerabilities Working Group of the cloud security alliance (CSA), the top three threats were "Insecure Interfaces & APIs", "Data Loss & Leakage" and "Hardware Failure". These three threats counted for 64 % of all cloud outage incidents. Since data owners lose physical control over their data once the data are outsourced to cloud, data integrity and leakage becomes a primary concern of data owners [6]. There have been a lot of incidents of data loss or leakage in the past few years. For example, it was reported that "Amazon's huge EC2 cloud services crash permanently destroyed some data. The data loss was apparently small relative to the total data stored, but anyone who runs a website can immediately understand how terrifying a prospect any data loss is"[1]. Moreover, it is not mandatory for cloud servers to report these incidents. Indeed, to maintain a good reputation or gain more monetary benefit, the cloud server has an incentive to hide data loss accidents or reclaim storage space by discarding data that are rarely accessed. As a consequence, providing strong guarantee of data integrity is of prime importance for data owners.

Unfortunately, traditional data integrity checking mechanisms (e.g. MAC, digital signature) are not applicable for the cloud storage scenario, because the verifiers lack a local copy of the original data in the verification phase. To solve this challenging problem, in 2007, Ateniese et al. [8,9] presented the model of Provable Data Possession (PDP) that provides probabilistic proofs of possession and proposed two provably-secure and practical PDP schemes from the RSA assumption. Meanwhile, Juels et al. [10] proposed the notion of Proof of Retrievability (PoR), which enables a prover to produce a concise proof that a verifier could retrieve a target file in its entirety. Subsequently, Shacham and Waters [11,12] described two efficient and compact PoR schemes. The first one, built from BLS signature [13], is publicly verifiable and provably secure in the random oracle model; the second one allows private verification based on pseudo-random functions (PRFs) and is secure in the standard model. With the proliferation of cloud storage, a variety of cloud auditing protocols and their variants [14–24] were proposed for catering some specific properties, such as public verification, dynamic operations and privacy preserving. A majority of the proposals consider the single cloud-only scenario; however, in some cases, data users might store their data on the infrastructures owned by multiple cloud vendors according to the different requirements of the stored data and various properties of cloud storage services. For example, Spideroak [25] is a good solution for security and privacy, which might be particularly appealing if a user would like to store sensitive data; Dropbox [25], as one of the first online storage services, is useful, reliable and works across multiple platforms; Microsoft OneDrive and Google

---

[1] http://www.businessinsider.com.au/amazon-lost-data-2011-4.

Drive [25] are both excellent choices when a user wants an added dimension of productivity thanks to their associated web-based suites. When the existing auditing protocols are expanded to support multi-cloud auditing, the overhead of communication and computation at the verifier's side will be huge. In addition, almost all the PDP and PoR schemes are based on the PKI-based framework, where a complex and expensive key management procedure is involved. This kind of infrastructure would lead to low efficiency in computation since it is mandatory for the verifier to validate the certificates before checking the proof of possession each time.

To improve the efficiency of PDP constructions, Zhu et al. [26] proposed a cooperative PDP protocol for distributed data integrity verification in multi-cloud storage. In their protocol, one of the cloud vendors acts as an organizer whose work is to initiate and organize the auditing process. Unfortunately, Wang and Zhang [27] demonstrated the cooperative PDP scheme [26] fails to achieve the security goal of knowledge soundness because a malicious server is able to generate a valid response even all the stored data have been discarded. In order to remove the public key infrastructure from PDP schemes, recently, Wang [28] introduced the notion of identity-based distributed PDP scheme, ID-DPDP in short, for multi-cloud storage. In this new primitive, digital certificates are removed and a *Combiner* is involved to distribute block-tag pairs and challenges to various cloud servers, and combine the proofs from different servers and forward them to the verifier. As claimed in [28], a distinctive feature of ID-DPDP is to support private verification, delegated verification and public verification simultaneously.

Contributions. It is straightforward to see that the ID-DPDP scheme in [28] fails to achieve the property of soundness, the most desirable property a PDP protocol should provide. Specifically, a malicious cloud server could deceive a verifier to believe that it is maintaining the entire file intact using only hash values of data blocks and the corresponding tags, instead of the file itself. In this paper, we give a simple but adequate approach to remedy the drawbacks. Specifically, we present a generic construction of identity-based PDP (ID-PDP) by combing identity-based signatures (IBS) and standard PDP protocols, and prove the security of the generic approach. To the best of our knowledge, this is the first formal treatment to ID-PDP. Our contributions are summarized as follows.

1. We formalize the security model of soundness for ID-PDP protocols for the first time.
2. We propose a generic approach to building ID-PDP protocols that connect identity-based signatures with traditional PDP protocols.
3. We prove soundness of the generic construction in our new security model.
4. We describe a practical instantiation of ID-PDP protocol following our generic approach, along with its implementation.

Roadmap. The rest of the paper is organized as follows. In Sect. 2, we introduce the system model and security model for identity-based PDP protocols. Section 3 proposes a generic construction of ID-PDP and its security proof.

Section 4 gives a concrete ID-PDP construction and its performance analysis. Section 5 concludes our work.

2 Models and Assumptions

We describe the system model and give the security model for ID-PDP in this section.

2.1 System Model for ID-PDP

As shown in Fig. 1, four major entities namely, the cloud server, data owners or cloud users, a verifier and PKG are involved in an identity-based PDP protocol. The cloud server has huge storage space and computational resources. It provides data storage service and charges cloud users according to pay-per-use regulation. The users rent data storage service and interact with the server to upload, access and update their stored data. The verifier can be a cloud user, a delegated party, or a third party auditor (TPA), whose work is to check the integrity of the data stored on the cloud. The PKG is responsible for generating keys for cloud users using their identity information. Assume users' data are stored in form of files which are divided into a number of blocks, and each block is further split into some sectors. For integrity checking, each block will have a tag attached, which was generated by the user when he or she uploads the file to a cloud.

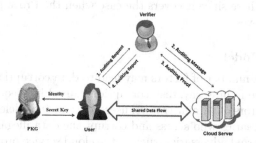

Fig. 1. System components of ID-PDP

An ID-PDP system is composed of three algorithms, namely Setup, Extract, Store and an interactive protocol Prove. The details are as follows.

- Setup (1^k) is a probabilistic algorithm run by the PKG. It takes a security parameter k as input and outputs the system parameters $param$, the master secret key msk and the master public key mpk.
- Extract (mpk, msk, ID) is a probabilistic algorithm run by the PKG. It takes the system parameters $param$, the master secret key msk and a user's identity $ID \in \{0,1\}^*$ as input, outputs the secret key sk_{ID} that corresponds to this identity ID.

- Store $(param, sk_{ID}, F)$ is a randomized file-storing algorithm run by the data owner. It takes the system parameters $param$, the secret key of the user sk_{ID} and a file $F \in \{0, 1\}^*$ to store as input and process F to produce and output F^*, which will be stored on the cloud and a file tag σ output by the Store algorithm. The tag contains information that names the file being outsourced; it could also contain additional information for the future data checking. We also assume Store outputs a file handle η that can be used to refer to file F uniquely.
- Prove $(param, mpk, ID, \eta)$ is an interactive protocol between a verifier $\mathcal{V}$ and the cloud server or prover $\mathcal{P}$, defining a protocol for proving the data integrity of a file with handle η. The common input to both parties are $param$, mpk, ID and η. The cloud server has additional input, the file F^* and the tag σ. Upon completion of the protocol, the verifier outputs 1 or 0. We denote a run of two machines executing the algorithms as $\{0, 1\} \leftarrow (\mathcal{V}(param, mpk, ID, \eta) \rightleftharpoons \mathcal{P}(param, mpk, ID, \eta, \sigma, F^*))$.

Remarks on Protocol Prove. In many of the existing PDP schemes, the Prove protocol is of two moves only. In that case, it can be defined as three algorithms, namely, Challenge, ProofGen, Verify, which together constituted the Proof protocol as follows. In the first move, the verifier invokes the Challenge algorithm to generate a challenge *chal*, which is sent to the cloud server. Taking as input the file, the corresponding tag and *chal*, the cloud server invokes the ProofGen algorithm to generate a proof P, which is returned to the verifier. The verifier invokes the Verify algorithm to validates the proof P. We employ a more general definition (Prove) here since it covers the case when the Prove protocol involves more than two moves.

2.2 Security Model

In cloud storage, a number of factors may lead to data corruption, including, (1) Hardware/software failure, say, disk corruption caused by frequent data access; (2) Operational errors of administrators, users' data may be deleted accidentally; (3) External adversaries who access and corrupt the data illegally stored on the cloud; and (4) Internal adversaries, such as the cloud service provider. Therefore, an ID-PDP scheme should be both correct and sound. Correctness states that the probability of the Prove protocol returns 0 is negligible if the proof of possession P is generated from valid data blocks and tags by a valid prover. Soundness [11] means that if Prove protocol returns 1, the prover is actually storing that file with overwhelming probability. This is formally defined by the existence of an extractor that is able to extract the file through interacting with the server using the ID-PDP protocol. Specifically, the extractor algorithm takes as input the identity ID and its corresponding private key k_{ID} and the description of an interactive Turning machine implementing the prover's role in the ID-PDP protocol, the output of the algorithm is the outsourced file F.

Wang [28] proposed a security notion called *unforgeability* for ID-DPDP protocols to capture the property of soundness and provided a concrete security model. In this model, the challenged data blocks are not allowed for TagGen queries, which indicates that the adversary cannot access the tags of these blocks. However, this requirement is not consistent with the cloud storage environment in reality where the cloud server is in fact storing the tags of all data blocks as well. We borrow the ideas of Ateniese [9] and Shacham, Waters [12] and propose a new security model called soundness for ID-PDP protocols, which is described using the data possession game below between an adversary $\mathcal{A}$ and an environment.

- Setup: The environment runs Setup algorithm to obtain system parameters $param$, master secret key msk and master public key mpk. The environment forwards $param$ and mpk to the adversary, while keeps msk confidential.
- Queries: The adversary makes a number of extract queries and store queries to the environment adaptively.
  1. Extract Queries: The adversary can ask for the private key of any identity ID_i. The environment computes the private key sk_i by running the Extract algorithm and forwards it to the adversary.
  2. Store Queries: The adversary can make queries to a store oracle, providing, for each query, some file F and an identity ID_i. The environment computes the secret key sk_i and $(F^*, t, \eta) \leftarrow Store(param, sk_i, F)$, then returns both F^*, t and η to the adversary.
- Prove: For a file F of which a Store query has been made, the adversary can undertake executions of the ID-PDP protocol by specifying the identity ID of the data owner and the file handle η. The environment plays the role of the verifier $\mathcal{V}$ and the adversary $\mathcal{A}$ behaves as the prover during the protocol execution, that is, $\mathcal{V}(param, mpk, ID, \eta) \rightleftharpoons \mathcal{A}$. The adversary can get the output of $\mathcal{V}$ when a protocol execution completes.
- Output: Finally, the adversary chooses a file handle $\eta^\dagger$ and a user's identity $ID^\dagger$. $ID^\dagger$ must not have appeared in any key extraction query and that there exists a Store query with input $F^\dagger$ and $ID^\dagger$ whose output is $\eta^\dagger$ and $t^\dagger$. The adversary also outputs the description of a prover $P^\dagger$ which is ϵ-admissible defined below.

We say the cheating prover $P^\dagger$ is ϵ-admissible if it convincingly answers an ϵ fraction of integrity challenges, that is if $\Pr[(\mathcal{V}(param, mpk, ID^\dagger, \eta^\dagger) \rightleftharpoons \mathcal{P}^\dagger) = 1] \geq \epsilon$. The probability here is over the coins of the verifier and the prover.

An ID-PDP scheme is called ϵ-sound if there exists an extraction algorithm Extr such that, for every adversary $\mathcal{A}$, whenever $\mathcal{A}$, playing the soundness game, outputs an ϵ-admissible cheating prover $P^\dagger$ on identity $ID^\dagger$ and file handle $\eta^\dagger$, Extr recovers $F^\dagger$ from $P^\dagger$, i.e., $Extr(param, mpk, ID^\dagger, \eta^\dagger, P^\dagger) = F$, except possibly with negligible probability.

3   A Generic Construction of ID-PDP

In this section, we show how to build an ID-PDP by describing a generic construction of ID-PDP from traditional PDP protocols and secure ID-based signature (IBS) algorithms. Our construction is inspired by the idea of Galindo,

Herranz and Kiltz [31], who gave generic constructions of identity-based signature schemes with additional properties, including identity-based proxy signatures, identity-based blind signatures and identity-based undeniable signatures etc. Our construction can be viewed as an extension of Galindo-Herranz-Kiltz's method [31], from identity-based digital signature schemes to identity-based PDP schemes. The security of the proposed ID-PDP protocols can be reduced to that of the underlying PDP protocols and IBS schemes.

3.1   A Generic Construction

We describe a framework of ID-PDP protocols that is publicly verifiable based on standard PDP schemes and IBS [29–32]. A standard PDP scheme [8,9] consists of the following polynomial-time algorithms, (sk, pk) ←PDP.KeyGen(1^k), (σ, η) ←PDP.Store(F, sk, pk), P ← PDP.ProofGen (pk, F, σ, η, $chal$) where $chal$ ← PDP.Challenge (pk, η) is a challenge from the verifier and $(1/0)$ ←PDP.Verify (pk, P, η, $chal$).

Analogously, an ID-based signature scheme involves a triple of entities, the PKG, a signer with identity ID and a verifier respectively, and is composed of four (probabilistic polynomial-time) algorithms [29]. The **Setup** algorithm takes a security parameter k as input and outputs system public parameters mpk as well as a master secret key msk. We denote an execution of this process as (msk, mpk) ←IBS.Setup(1^k). The key extraction algorithm, run by the PKG, takes the master secret key msk and a user's identity ID as input and outputs a secret key sk_{ID} for the user. We denote an execution of this process as sk_{ID} ←IBS.Extract(msk, ID). The **Sign** algorithm takes the public parameter mpk, the secret key sk_{ID} of the user and a message m to be signed as input, and outputs a signature φ on m. To refer to an execution of this phase, we use notation φ ←IBS.Sign(m, mpk, k_{ID}). The remaining algorithm, verification, takes the system public parameter mpk, the identity ID, the signed message m and the signature φ as input, and returns 1 if the signature is valid, and 0 otherwise. We use notation $(1/0)$ ←IBS.Verify(mpk, ID, m, φ) to refer to an execution of this protocol. According to the previous work [31,32], the widely accepted security notion of IBS is existentially unforgeable under adaptive-chosen identity and message attacks.

In the following, we propose a generic construction of ID-PDP protocol from an IBS scheme and a standard PDP infrastructure. The intuitive idea is after generating a secret key for a user with identity ID, the user signs a temporary public key using an ID-based signature to authenticate it. We then include the temporary public key and its signature as a part of the tag of the file such that the verifier can check the validity of the public key via ID-based signature verification algorithm directly. Upon validating the temporary public key, it can be used in the verification of the traditional PDP scheme. The details of the generic construction are below.

– ID-PDP.Setup (1^k): The PKG runs the **IBS.Setup** algorithm to obtain the key pair (msk, mpk) of the ID-PDP scheme, i.e., (msk, mpk) ←IBS.Setup(1^k), where k is a security parameter. PKG publishes mpk while keeps msk secret.

- ID-PDP.Extract (ID, mpk, msk): Given an identity $ID \in \{0,1\}^*$, the PKG runs the key extract algorithm of the IBS scheme **IBS.Extract**, i.e., $k_{ID} \leftarrow$ IBS.Extract(mpk, msk, ID) to get a secret key k_{ID}. PKG then forwards k_{ID} to the data owner in a secure manner.

- ID-PDP.Store (F, ID, mpk, k_{ID}): Given a file F, for the data owner who stores files to cloud for the first time, the user generates a fresh key pair (pk, sk) by running the **PDP.KeyGen** algorithm, namely $(pk, sk) \leftarrow$ PDP.KeyGen(1^k). The user computes an identity-based signature on pk by running IBS.Sign(k_{ID}, pk) $\rightarrow$ s. Note that (pk, sk, s) can be reused in the future storage. Finally, the user runs the **PDP.Store(F, sk, pk)** to obtain a processed file $F*$, the corresponding tag σ and file handle η. Finally, the user stores $(\eta, F*, \sigma, pk, s)$ to the cloud.

- ID-PDP.Proof (mpk, ID, η): The verifier challenges the cloud server on behalf of the data owner with identity ID for the file with handle η using the following interactive protocol. Note that the cloud server has additional input $(F*, \sigma, pk, s)$.
  - The cloud server sends (pk, s) to the verifier.
  - The verifier checks if s is a valid ID-based signature on pk by running IBS.Verify(mpk, ID, pk, s). If it is invalid, abort and output 0. Otherwise, the verifier runs PDP.Challenge(pk, η) to obtain $chal$ and sends $chal$ to the cloud server.
  - The cloud server runs PDP.ProofGen $(pk, F*, \sigma, \eta, chal)$ to generate a proof P and forwards it to the verifier.
  - The verifier runs PDP.Verify $(pk, P, \eta, chal)$ to obtain the checking result, 0 or 1.

3.2 Soundness Proof

Intuitively, we prove that the ID-PDP protocol described above can be proven secure under the security model described in Sect. 2, assuming that the IBS scheme and the standard PDP protocol are secure.

Theorem 1. If the underlying identity-based signature scheme is unforgeable and the underlining PDP scheme is sound, the proposed ID-PDP scheme is sound.

Proof. Assume there exits an adversary $\mathcal{A}$ that can break the soundness of the ID-PDP scheme, we can build another algorithm $\mathcal{B}$, who takes $\mathcal{A}$ as a subroutine, can violate the unforgeability of the underlining identity-based signature scheme or break the soundness of the underlining PDP scheme.

- Setup: Algorithm $\mathcal{B}$ initially receives a master public key $mpk*$ of an IBS scheme and a $pk*$ of a PDP scheme. $\mathcal{B}$ sets the IBS scheme and the PDP scheme as those used in the ID-PDP protocol. $mpk*$ is given to $\mathcal{A}$ as the master public key. Without loss of generality, we assume $\mathcal{A}$ invokes queries (extract and store) for N different identities, say, $ID_1, \ldots, ID_N$. $\mathcal{B}$ picks an index $i* \in \{1, \ldots, N\}$.

- Queries: The adversary $\mathcal{A}$ is allowed to make the following queries to $\mathcal{B}$ adaptively.

    1. Extract Queries: When $\mathcal{A}$ queries the private key for an identity ID_i of its choice, $\mathcal{B}$ invokes the simulator of IBS simulator by inputting ID_i to the Extract query of the IBS scheme, and obtains the private key k_{ID_i}. $\mathcal{B}$ returns k_{ID_i} to $\mathcal{A}$ as the answer of his query.

    2. Store Queries: $\mathcal{A}$ requests a store query for file F_j of user ID_i. If $i \neq i*$, $\mathcal{B}$ invokes the Extract query of the IBS simulator, and obtains the private key k_{ID_i} of ID_i (if it has not done so). $\mathcal{B}$ also invokes PDP.KeyGen to obtain (pk_i, sk_i) (again, if it has not done so). With k_{ID_i}, $\mathcal{B}$ can follow the protocol to store the file F_j of user ID_i.
    For $i = i*$, $\mathcal{B}$ queries the IBS simulator with input $pk*$ and ID_{i*} and receives an identity-based signature s on $pk*$. $\mathcal{B}$ invokes the Store Query of the PDP simulator with input (F) and obtains the processed file $F*$, the corresponding tag σ and file handle η. $\mathcal{B}$ returns $(F*, \sigma, \eta, pk*, s)$ to $\mathcal{A}$. For notational convenience, we use pk_{i*} to denote $pk*$.

    3. Prove: $\mathcal{B}$ behaves as the verifier and $\mathcal{A}$ acts as the prover. $\mathcal{A}$ can specific a file handle η which is an output of a Store query on some identity ID_i and file F_j and act as a prover. $\mathcal{B}$ acts as a verifier and follows the protocol honestly. The result is also forwarded to $\mathcal{A}$.

- Output: Finally, the adversary $\mathcal{A}$ outputs an identity $ID^\dagger$ and a file handle $\eta^\dagger$ such that there exists a Store query with input F and $ID^\dagger$ and the output file handle is $\eta^\dagger$. $\mathcal{A}$ also has to output the description of a prover $P^\dagger$ that is ϵ-admissible.

- Analysis: It remains to argue that given $P^\dagger$, there exists an extractor which can recover the file F with non-negligible probability. Recall that N is the number of identities presented by $\mathcal{A}$. With probability $1/N$, $ID^\dagger = ID_{i*}$. Thus, with probability $1/N$, the first move of the interaction with $P^\dagger$ involves it outputting (pk, s) where s is a valid ID-based signature on pk and identity ID_{i*}. If $pk \neq pk*$, (pk, s) corresponds to a forged identity-based signature and happens with negligible probability if the underlying IBS is secure. Taking away the first move, $P^\dagger$'s behaviour is exactly the same as an ϵ-admissible prover of the underlying PDP. Based on the security of the underlying PDP scheme, any ϵ-admissible results in the extraction of the underlying file F and thus we could recovers the file F from $P^\dagger$.

4   An Instantiation and Performance

In this section, we firstly apply our generic construction to the state-of-the-art PDP scheme due to shacham and Waters [12] and the IBS scheme proposed by Cha and Cheon [29] to obtain a concrete construction of an ID-PDP scheme for cloud storage. We then analyze its security and implement the scheme to assess its efficiency.

4.1 Scheme Description

ID-PDP.Setup: Let $\mathbb{G}, \mathbb{G}_T$ be multiplicative groups of prime order p and $e : \mathbb{G} \times \mathbb{G} \to \mathbb{G}_T$ be a bilinear map. g is a generator of $\mathbb{G}$. Define three hash functions: $H : \{0,1\}^* \to \mathbb{G}$, $H_1 : \{0,1\}^* \to \mathbb{G}$ and $H_2 : \mathbb{G} \times \mathbb{G} \to Z_q$. Define a pseudo-random function $f : Z_q^* \times \{1, \cdots, n\} \to Z_q^*$ and a pseudo-random permutation $\pi : Z_q \times \{1, \cdots, n\} \to \{1, \cdots, n\}$. PKG picks a random $x \in Z_q$ and computes $y = g^x$. The public parameters are $\{\mathbb{G}, \mathbb{G}_T, e, q, g, H, H_1, H_2, f, \pi, y\}$ and the master key of PKG is x.

ID-PDP.Extract: Given an identity $ID \in \{0,1\}^*$, PKG computes the private key associated to this identity as $k_{ID} = H(ID)^x$ and forwards it to the user via a secure channel.

ID-PDP.Store: When a user with identity ID would like to store a file F to the cloud, the user will perform the following steps.

1. Generate a random signing keypair (spk, ssk).
2. Pick a random $\alpha \in Z_p$ and compute $v = g^\alpha$.
3. Apply the erasure code to F and obtain F'. Split F' into n blocks, each s sectors long; that is, $F' = m_{ij} (1 \le i \le n, 1 \le j \le s)$.
4. Choose a file name $name$ for F and s random elements $u_1, \cdots, u_s \in \mathbb{G}$.
5. Let $\tau_0 = name||n||u_1|| \cdots ||u_s$ and the file tag $\tau = \tau_0 || SSig_{ssk}(\tau_0)$.
6. For each $i, 1 \le i \le n$, compute $\sigma = \{\sigma_i\}$

$$\sigma_i = (H_1(name||i) \cdot \prod_{j=1}^{s} u_j^{m_{ij}})^\alpha.$$

7. Pick a random $r \in Z_q$ and compute an identity based signature $\sigma_{pk} = (U, V)$ on the temporary key (spk, v) as $U = H(ID)^r$, $h = H_2(spk, v, U)$ and $V = k_{ID}^{r+h}$.
8. Store $(F', \tau, \sigma, spk, v, \sigma_{pk})$ to the cloud.

ID-PDP.Proof: The verifier and the cloud server interactive to generate a ID-PDP proof with identity ID as follows.

1. Upon receiving a proof request from the verifier, the cloud server sends (spk, v, U, V) to the verifier.
2. The verifier computes $h = H_2(spk, v, U)$ and checks if

$$e(g, V) = e(y, U)e(y, H(ID)^h)$$

holds. If it does not hold, reject by emitting 0 and halting. Otherwise, go to the next step.
3. The verifier verifies if the file tag τ is a valid signature on τ_0 using spk. If it does not hold, reject by emitting 0 and halting. Otherwise, go to the next step.

4. The verifier picks a random c-element set I, a subset of $[1, n]$, and for each $i \in I$, chooses a random $v_i \in Z_p$. The verifier sends the challenge set $Q = \{(i, v_i)\}$ to the cloud server.
5. The cloud server calculates $\mu_j = \sum_{(i,v_i)\in Q} v_i m_{ij}$ for $1 \le j \le s$, and $\sigma = \prod_{(i,v_i)\in Q} \sigma_i^{v_i}$, and responds $\{\mu_1, \cdots, \mu_s, \sigma\}$ to the verifier.
6. The verifier checks if the following equation holds,

$$e(g, \sigma) = e(\prod_{(i,v_i)\in Q} H_1(name||i)^{v_i} \cdot \prod_{i=1}^{c} u_j^{\mu_j}, v).$$

If the verification holds, the **ID-PDP.Proof** outputs 1; otherwise, output 0.

4.2   Correctness and Soundness

We can verify the correctness of scheme by a straightforward calculation via the useful property of bilinear pairing. Regarding the soundness of the scheme, we have the following theorem.

Theorem 2: In the random oracle model, if the digital signature scheme used for generating the file tag τ is existentially unforgeable and the CDH problem is intractable in bilinear groups, except with negligible probability, no adversary could break the soundness of the proposed ID-PDP.

Proof: In the proposed ID-PDP, we leverage the identity based signature scheme due to Hess [30] to generate a valid signature to authenticate the temporary public key (spk, v). Hess proved that in the random oracle model, the unforgeability of the identity based signature depends on the CDH assumption. The underlining PDP scheme used in our ID-PDP comes from compact proofs of retrievability due to Shacham and Waters. The soundness proof of this scheme was provided in [11,12]. Since our concrete ID-PDP scheme follows our generic construction strictly, the proof of the scheme can go through following the framework of the proof of our generic construction and the security proofs in [11,12,30]. Thus, the proposed ID-PDP instantation has the property of soundness according to the security conclusion in Sect. 3.

4.3   Probabilistic Checking

The proposed ID-PDP protocol utilized spot checking technique due to Ateniese et al. [8], which can significantly reduce the workload on the cloud server. The cloud server hosts an n-block file, out of which x blocks are corrupted. The verifier checks the integrity of the entire file containing n blocks by randomly sampling c different blocks. X denotes a discrete random variable defined as the number of blocks selected by the verifier that match those blocks corrupted by the cloud server. P_X denotes the probability that at least one block chosen by the verifier matches one of the blocks corrupted by the server. Clearly we have

$$P_X = 1 - \frac{n-x}{n} \times \frac{n-x-1}{n-1} \times \cdots \times \frac{n-x-c+1}{n-c+1}.$$

Thus, P_X denotes the probability of the server misbehavior detection. That is, the probability that if the cloud server corrupts x blocks of the file, the verifier is able to detect the server's misbehavior when challenging c blocks of the file. Figure 4 plots P_X for different choices of n and c. That is, we show P_X as a function of n and c for $x = 1\,\%n$, $x = 5\,\%n$, $x = 10\,\%n$ and $x = 20\,\%n$ respectively (Fig. 2).

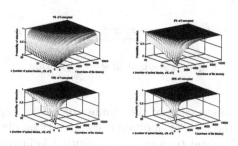

Fig. 2. The probability of server misbehavior detection

4.4   Evaluation

The implementation was conducted on a notebook with Intel Core $i5 - 4200UCPU@1.6GHz$, 2.29 GHz and the memory is 4.00 GB. In our implementation, we made use of the MIRACL library to implement number-theoretic based algorithms of cryptography. The parameter p is approximately 1024 bits and q is 160 bits. Our tests aim to mainly determine the overheads of the following algorithms involved in our protocol, namely Store and Prove. Note that the computation cost of Setup and Extract is nearly negligible since there is no any expensive operations in these algorithms. There is only one exponentiation operation in these two algorithms and the average running time of the algorithm is 1.13 ms with repeated 100 trials.

To observe the impact of block size on the time cost of the store algorithm, we proceed our test as follows: we use a file with fixed size, namely 1M, in our test. As each sector is of 160 bits, thus, we can change the block size by changing the number of blocks, from 1 to 51200. The time cost of the store algorithm corresponding to these number of blocks can be recorded. Specifically, Fig. 3 illustrates the results of our tests in details. The store procedure is efficient in general. It costs less than 48 s to pre-process the file using the store algorithm for future secure storage. In more details, it shows that the total time overhead for store is almost constant when the number of blocks is less than 2048, that is, each block is less than $0.5k$ containing 4 sectors. This is in accordance with the empirical analysis since for a file with constant size, the number of sectors is fixed. As a result, the overhead of the most expensive computation $\prod u_j{}^{m_{ij}}$ for the entire file is constant. Different number of blocks implies different number of exponentiation operations. Compared with the time cost of $\prod u_j{}^{m_{ij}}$ for the whole file, the increased cost is almost negligible when the number of blocks is not large.

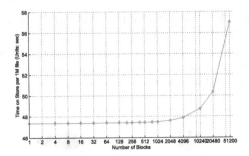

Fig. 3. Time cost of store algorithm

With the continuous increasing of the number of blocks, especially when it is greater than 4096, the cost of additional computations obviously affect that of $\prod u_j{}^{m_{ij}}$. Thus, the total time of store algorithm is increasing dramatically. One may argue that keeping the entire file as one block is the best solution. However, we have to consider the balance of the communication overhead and the computation overhead at the meantime. The response of a challenge from the server is $\{\mu_1, \cdots, \mu_s, \sigma\}$ where σ is constant size of 160 bits, while $\mu_j = \sum v_i m_{ij}$ for $1 \leq j \leq s$. That is, the number of μ_j totally depends on the number of sectors. For a file with constant size, with the increment number of sectors in a block, the number of blocks decreases. From the experimental results, we suggest the best size of the block is between 1KB to 4KB in the real-world applications, which delivers the best performance for our implementation.

Figure 4 shows the time cost for the verifier and prover during the ID-PDP.Proof. We proceed our test by employing a file of 10000 blocks. According to our suggestion from store experiment, we set each block 4KB. We test the time overhead of both participants by challenging the prover with an increasing number of randomly selected blocks, from 1 to 1024. We can see the prove protocol is highly efficient for both the prover and the verifier. It costs the verifier nearly 1.1 s and the prover 0.6 s when challenging 256 blocks. According to the probability analysis [9], assuming that the server corrupts at least 100 blocks, then the verifier is able to detect server's misbehavior with probability over 99 % by asking proof for 460 randomly selected blocks. In this situation, the time cost in both the verifier and the prover is less than 1.5 s. With the increment of the challenged blocks, the time cost of both sides increases. This is in accordance with the empirical analysis since with the increasing number of challenged blocks, the cloud server has an increasing number of exponentiations and multiplications in $\prod \sigma_i^{v_i}$ while the verifier has an increasing number of exponentiations and multiplications in $H_1(name\|i)^{v_i} \cdot \prod u_j^{\mu_j}$. Our implementation results are consistent with that of the benchmark of [33] for exponentiations where it shows that an exponentiation costs almost 1 ms in prime-order elliptic curve groups.

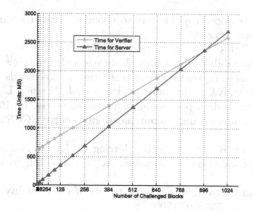

Fig. 4. Time cost of prove protocol

5   Conclusion

This paper revisited the identity-based distributed provable data possession scheme in multi-cloud storage [28] and demonstrated that even all the original data have been discarded, the server is still able to generate a valid proof to cheat the verifier that the data are well accommodated. To remedy this weakness, for a further investment of ID-PDP, we proposed a generic construction of ID-PDP protocols by using IBS schemes and traditional PDP protocols and proved its security. In addition, we built a concrete ID-PDP protocol and an extended version which is suitable for the multi-cloud storage. The implementation demonstrates that the new proposal is practical.

Acknowledgements. This work is supported by the NSFC of China under Grant Number 61300213, 61272436.

References

1. Mell, P., Grance, T.: Draft NIST working definition of cloud computing, Referenced on June 3rd (2009). http://csrc.nist.gov/groups/SNS/cloud-computing/index.html
2. Wang, X., Cao, J., Xiang, Y.: Dynamic cloud service selection using an adaptive learning mechanism in multi-cloud computing. J. Syst. Softw. **100**, 195–210 (2015)
3. Yi, X., Bertino, E., Vaidya, J., Xing, C.: Private searching on streaming data based on keyword frequency. IEEE Trans. Dependable Sec. Comput. **11**(2), 155–167 (2014)
4. Li, J., Huang, X., Li, J., Chen, X., Xiang, Y.: Securely outsourcing attribute-based encryption with checkability. IEEE Trans. Parallel Distrib. Syst. **25**(8), 2201–2210 (2014)
5. Chen, X., Li, J., Huang, X., Li, J., Xiang, Y., Wong, D.: Secure outsourced attribute-based signatures. IEEE Trans. Parallel Distrib. Syst. **25**(12), 3285–3294 (2014)

6. Cloud Security Alliance. Top Threats to Cloud Computing (2010). http://www. cloudsecurityalliance.org

7. Cloud Vulnerabilities Working Group of the cloud security alliance. Cloud Computing Vulnerability Incidents: A Statistical Overview (2011). https:// cloudsecurityalliance.org/research/vulnerabilities/#_downloads

8. Ateniese, G., Burns, R.C., Curtmola, R., Herring, J., Kissner, L., Peterson, Z.N.J., Song, D.X.: Provable data possession at untrusted stores. In: Processing of ACM Conference on Computer and Communications Security (CCS2007), pp. 598–609 (2007)

9. Ateniese, G., Burns, R., Curtmola, R., Herring, J., Kissner, L., et al.: Remote data checking using provable data possession. ACM Trans. Inf. Syst. Secur. **14**, 1–34 (2011)

10. Juels, A., Burton, J., Kaliski, S.: Pors: proofs of retrievability for large files. In: ACM CCS 2007, pp. 584–597 (2007)

11. Shacham, H., Waters, B.: Compact proofs of retrievability. In: Pieprzyk, J. (ed.) ASIACRYPT 2008. LNCS, vol. 5350, pp. 90–107. Springer, Heidelberg (2008)

12. Shacham, H., Waters, B.: Compact proofs of retrievability. J. Cryptology **26**(3), 442–483 (2013)

13. Boneh, D., Lynn, B., Shacham, H.: Short signatures from the weil pairing. In: Boyd, C. (ed.) ASIACRYPT 2001. LNCS, vol. 2248, pp. 514–532. Springer, Heidelberg (2001)

14. Wang, C., Ren, K., Lou, W., Li, J.: Toward public auditable secure cloud data storage services. IEEE Netw. **24**(4), 19–24 (2010)

15. Zhu, Y., Hu, H., Ahn, G.J., Stephen, Y.S.: Efficient audit service outsourcing for data integrity in clouds. J. Syst. Softw. **85**(5), 1083–1095 (2012)

16. Wang, C., Wang, Q., Ren, K., Lou, W.: Privacy-preserving public auditing for data storage security in cloud computing. In: Processing of INFOCOM 2010, pp. 525–533 (2010)

17. Yang, K., Jia, X.: An efficient and secure dynamic auditing protocol for data storage in cloud computing. IEEE Trans. Parallel Distrib. Syst. **24**(9), 1717–1726 (2013)

18. Lier, S., Wörsdörfer, D., Gesing, J.: Business models and product service systems for transformable, modular plants in the chemical process industry. In: Meier, H. (ed.) Product-Service Integration for Sustainable Solutions. LNPE, vol. 6, pp. 227–238. Springer, Heidelberg (2013)

19. Wang, B., Li, B., Li, H.: Public auditing for shared data with efficient user revocation in the cloud. In: Proceeding of IEEE Conference on Computer Communications (IEEE INFOCOM 2013), Turin, Italy, pp. 2904–2912, 14–19 April 2013

20. Wang, B., Li, B., Li, H.: Panda: Public Auditing for Shared Data with Efficient User Revocation in the Cloud. IEEE Trans. Serv. Comput. **8**(1), 92–106 (2015). doi:10.1109/TSC.2013.2295611

21. Yu, Y., Zhang, Y., Ni, J., Au, M.H., et al.: Remote data possession checking with enhanced security for cloud storage. Future Gener. Comput. Syst. **52**, 77–85 (2015)

22. Yu, Y., Au, M.H., Mu, Y., Tang, S., Ren, J., Susilo, W., Dong, L.: Enhanced privacy of a remote data integrity checking protocol for secure cloud storage. Int. J. Inf. Secur. **14**(4), 307–318 (2014). doi:10.1007/s10207-014-0263-8

23. Yu, Y., Ni, J., Au, M.H., Mu, Y., Wang, B.Y., Li, H.: Comments on a public auditing mechanism for shared cloud data service. IEEE Trans. Serv. Comput. (2014). doi:10.1109/TSC.2014.2355201

24. Yu, Y., Ni, J., Au, M.H., Xu, C.X., et al.: Improved security of a dynamic remote data possession checking protocol for cloud storage. Expert Syst. Appl. **41**(17), 7789–7796 (2014)

25. Casserly, M.: 7 best cloud storage services-2014's best online storage sites revealed, 14 March 2014. http://www.pcadvisor.co.uk/features/internet/3506734/best-cloud-storage-services-review/
26. Zhu, Y., Hu, H., Ahn, G., Yu, M.: Cooperative provable data possession for integrity verification in multi-cloud storage. IEEE Trans. Parallel Distrib. Syst. **23**(12), 2231–2243 (2011)
27. Wang, H., Zhang, Y.: On the knowledge soundness of a cooperative provable data possession scheme in multicloud storage. IEEE Trans. Parallel Distrib. Syst. **25**(1), 264–267 (2014)
28. Wang, H.: Identity-based distributed provable data possession in multi-cloud storage. IEEE Trans. Serv. Comput. **8**(2), 328–340 (2015). doi:10.1109/TSC.2014.1
29. Cha, J.C., Cheon, J.H.: An identity-based signature from gap Diffie-Hellman groups. In: Desmedt, Y.G. (ed.) Public Key Cryptography – PKC 2003. LNCS, vol. 2567, pp. 18–30. Springer, Heidelberg (2003)
30. Hess, F.: Efficient identity based signature schemes based on pairings. In: Nyberg, K., Heys, H. (eds.) Selected Areas in Cryptography. LNCS, vol. 2595, pp. 310–324. Springer, Heidelberg (2003)
31. Galindo, D., Herranz, J., Kiltz, E.: On the generic construction of identity-based signatures with additional properties. In: Lai, X., Chen, K. (eds.) ASIACRYPT 2006. LNCS, vol. 4284, pp. 178–193. Springer, Heidelberg (2006)
32. Bellare, M., Namprempre, C., Neven, G.: Security proofs for identity-based identification and signature schemes. In: Cachin, C., Camenisch, J.L. (eds.) EUROCRYPT 2004. LNCS, vol. 3027, pp. 268–286. Springer, Heidelberg (2004)
33. Guillevic, A.: Comparing the pairing efficiency over composite-order and prime-order elliptic curves?, Cryptology ePrint Archive, Technical report. 2013/218 (2013). http://eprint.iacr.org/

Efficient Private Set Intersection Cardinality in the Presence of Malicious Adversaries

Sumit Kumar Debnath$^{(\boxtimes)}$ and Ratna Dutta

Department of Mathematics, Indian Institute of Technology Kharagpur,
Kharagpur 721302, India
sd.iitkgp@gmail.com, ratna@maths.iitkgp.ernet.in

Abstract. In this paper, we study Private Set Intersection Cardinality (PSI-CA) protocols and propose *two* new constructions of PSI-CA. While one of these constructions is secure in the standard model, the other one is secure in the random oracle model (ROM). The security is under the Decisional Diffie-Hellman (DDH) assumption against malicious adversaries. Our proposed PSI-CA protocols are the *first* to achieve *linear communication and computation complexities* and secure against *malicious adversaries*. Furthermore, each of our PSI-CA constructions can be converted to PSI without losing any of the above stated properties.

Keywords: PSI-CA · PSI · Semi-honest adversary · Malicious adversary · Bloom filter

1 Introduction

Private Set Intersection (PSI) enables two parties to secretly compute the intersection of their respective private sets without revealing any information about items that are not in the intersection. PSI has many potential applications in privacy preserving location-based services, data mining, social networks, testing of fully sequenced human genomes, collaborative botnet detection, on-line gaming and so on. The recent research community has considered PSI quite extensively due to its importance and wide applications.

On the other hand, *Private Set Intersection Cardinality* (PSI-CA) allows the client to learn only the cardinality rather than the contents of the intersection. As for example, in DNA matching, PSI-CA can be utilized to realize private computation of Hamming Distance between two strings on an arbitrarily large alphabet as follows: two parties may use PSI-CA by treating each symbol in the alphabet together with its position in the string as a unique set element, such that the client privately learns the number of elements (symbols) in common, thereby obtaining the Hamming Distance. PSI-CA has widespread applications in role-based association rule mining, location sharing, affiliation-hiding authentication, genomic operations etc.

Our Contribution: We concentrate mainly on designing the cardinality version of PSI. We summarize below our main findings:

© Springer International Publishing Switzerland 2015
M.-H. Au and A. Miyaji (Eds.): ProvSec 2015, LNCS 9451, pp. 326–339, 2015.
DOI: 10.1007/978-3-319-26059-4_18

We start with presenting our first construction PSI-CA-I which is a PSI-CA protocol and is proven to be secure under the DDH assumption in standard model against malicious adversaries, incurring linear complexity. Utilizing Bloom filter, we construct our second scheme PSI-CA-II retaining all the properties of PSI-CA-I with significant communication complexity. However, the security is in the ROM instead of standard. To the best of our knowledge, [1,6,7,14,16,18] are the only works on PSI-CA available in the literature and [6,16] are the only PSI-CA secure in the malicious model, both of which incur quadratic computation complexity. In contrast to [6], the input need not be certified for our constructions. Although the constructions of [7] are the most efficient, the security proofs are in the ROM under non-standard cryptographic assumption. The PSI protocols designed by Dong et al. [8] and Pinkas et al. [17] are very efficient. However, extending these works to PSI-CA seems to be a non-trivial task. As far as we are aware of, there has been no prior work with linear complexity while achieving security in the malicious model. Our work is the first to capture these two features together. More interestingly, unlike most of the existing works, our PSI-CA-I and PSI-CA-II are easily extendable to PSI constructions with the same security level and no significant increased cost in the efficiency. We refer to Table 1 for a comparative summary of PSI-CA.

We propose PSI-I, PSI-II respectively by transforming PSI-CA-I and PSI-CA-II to PSI setup making the security and the other properties to remain invariant. We emphasize that, PSI-I works favorably over the most effi-

Table 1. Comparison of PSI-CA protocols

Protocol	Security model	Adv. model	Security assumption	Comm.	Comp.	Based on
[1]	ROM	SH	DDH	$O(w+v)$	$O(w\log w + v\log v)$	CE
[11]	Std	SH	HE	$O(w+v)$	$O(w\log\log v)$	OPE
[16]	Std	Mal	HE	$O(t^2v)$	$O(v^2)$	OPE
[14]	Std	SH	SD and SC	$O(w+v)$	$O(w\log\log v)$	OPE
[18]	ROM	SH	DLP	$O(t^2v)$	$O(tv)$	COWHF
Sch. 1 of [7]	ROM	SH	DDH and GOMDH	$O(w+v)$	$O(w+v)$	
Sch. 2 of [7]	ROM	MS SHC	GOMDH	$O(w+v)$	$O(w+v)$	
PSI-CA-I	Std	Mal	DDH	$O(w+v)$	$O(w+v)$	
PSI-CA-II	ROM	Mal	DDH	$O(w+v)$	$O(w+v)$	BF

BF= Bloom Filter, OPE= Oblivious Polynomial Evaluation, Std= Standard,
SH= Semi-honest,
SHC= Semi-honest, Client, MS= Malicious Server, HE= Homomorphic Encryption,
DDH=Decisional Diffie-Hellman, Mal=Malicious, ROM= Random Oracle Model,
SC: Subgroup
Computation, SD: Subgroup Decision, DLP: Discrete Logarithm Problem, GOMDH:
Gap-One-More-Diffie-Hellman, CE= Commutative Encryption,
COWHF= Commutative One-way
Hash Function, t= number of parties, v,w are the sizes of the input sets

cient PSI protocols [13,15] in *standard* model secure against the *malicious* parties under *standard* cryptographic assumptions with *linear* complexity in the following sense:

- The main shortcoming of the protocol of [15] is that it is secure in the common reference string (CRS) model, where the CRS includes a safe RSA composite that determines the group order and implies high overhead when mutually produced. Besides, for the security purpose, the inputs must be encoded in a polynomially-sized domain. Our construction does not have these kind of drawbacks.
- Unlike the PSI protocol of [13], we do not use hybrid model to prove security and the complexity does not depend on efficient choice of Pseudorandom Function (PRF). Apart from, we require only two communication rounds while [13] requires more.

The most efficient Bloom filter based PSI protocol secure against *malicious* parties is the scheme 2 of [8]. Similar to [8], our PSI-II uses Bloom filter, thereby includes a false positive rate. However, our PSI-II requires only two communication rounds whereas [8] requires more.

2   Preliminaries

Throughout the paper the notations κ, $a \leftarrow A$, $x \hookleftarrow X$ and $\{\mathcal{X}_t\}_{t\in\mathcal{N}} \equiv^c \{\mathcal{Y}_t\}_{t\in\mathcal{N}}$ are used to represent "security parameter", "a is output of the procedure A", "variable x is chosen uniformly at random from set X"and "the distribution ensemble $\{\mathcal{X}_t\}_{t\in\mathcal{N}}$ is computationally indistinguishable from the distribution ensemble $\{\mathcal{Y}_t\}_{t\in\mathcal{N}}$" respectively. Informally, $\{\mathcal{X}_t\}_{t\in\mathcal{N}} \equiv^c \{\mathcal{Y}_t\}_{t\in\mathcal{N}}$ means for all probabilistic polynomial time (PPT) distinguisher $\mathcal{Z}$, there exists a negligible function $\epsilon(t)$ such that $|Prob_{x\leftarrow\mathcal{X}_t}[\mathcal{Z}(x) = 1] - Prob_{x\leftarrow\mathcal{Y}_t}[\mathcal{Z}(x) = 1]| \leq \epsilon(t)$.

Definition 1 Negligible Function: *A function $\epsilon : \mathbb{N} \to \mathbb{R}$ is said to be negligible function of κ if for each constant $c > 0$, we have $\epsilon(\kappa) = o(\kappa^{-c})$ for all sufficiently large κ.*

Definition 2. *A functionality, computed by two parties A and B with inputs X_A and X_B respectively by running a protocol Θ, is denoted as $\mathcal{F}_\Theta : X_A \times X_B \to Y_A \times Y_B$, where Y_A and Y_B are the outputs of A and B respectively after completion of the protocol Π between A and B.*

Definition 3 Decisional Diffie-Hellman (DDH) Assumption [4]: *Let the algorithm $gGen$ generates a modulus n and a generator g of a multiplicative group $\mathbb{G}$ of order n on the input 1^κ. Suppose $a, b, c \hookleftarrow \mathbb{Z}_n$. Then the DDH assumption states that no PPT algorithm $\mathcal{A}$ can distinguish between the two distributions $\langle g^a, g^b, g^{ab}\rangle$ and $\langle g^a, g^b, g^c\rangle$ i.e., $|Prob[\mathcal{A}(g, g^a, g^b, g^{ab}) = 1] - Prob[\mathcal{A}(g, g^a, g^b, g^c) = 1]|$ is negligible function of κ.*

2.1 Security Model

Informally speaking the basic security requirements of any multi-party protocol are

(a) *Correctness.* At the end of the protocol an honest party should receive the correct output.
(b) *Privacy.* After completion of the protocol, no party should learn more than its prescribe output.
(c) *Fairness.* A dishonest party should receive its output if and only if the honest party also receives its output.

In this work, we focus on the malicious model when the adversary can behave arbitrarily. The security is formalized by an ideal process that involves an incorruptible trusted third party, who receives the inputs of the involved parties, computes the functionality on the receiving inputs and sends outputs back to the parties. A protocol is said to be secure if any adversary in the real protocol can be simulated by an adversary in the ideal world.

Security Model for Malicious Adversary [12]: The formal security framework of a two-party protocol in malicious model is described below:

The Real World: In the real world a protocol Θ is executed. An honest party follows the instructions of Θ, but an adversary $\mathcal{A}_i$, controlling the party P_i, can behave arbitrarily. Let the party P_1 has the private input X, the party P_2 has the private input Y and the adversary $\mathcal{A}_i$ has auxiliary input Z. At the end of the execution an honest party outputs whatever prescribed in the protocol, a corrupted party outputs nothing and an adversary outputs its view which consists of the transcripts available to the adversary. The joint output in the real world is denoted by $\mathsf{REAL}_{\Theta,\mathcal{A}_i(Z)}(X,Y)$.

The Ideal Process: Let $\mathcal{SIM}_i$ be the ideal process adversary that corrupts a party $P_i, i \in \{1,2\}$. The ideal process involves an incorruptible trusted third party.

Input: Let X and Y be the inputs of parties P_1 and P_2 respectively, $\mathcal{SIM}_i$ gets P_i's input and an auxiliary input Z.
Sending inputs to the trusted party: An honest party always sends his original input to the trusted party whereas a corrupted party may send "abort" or an arbitrary input. Let the trusted party receives $(\widetilde{X},\widetilde{Y})$, where $\widetilde{X},\widetilde{Y}$ may be different from X,Y respectively. If anyone of $\widetilde{X},\widetilde{Y}$ is "abort", then the trusted party sends $\perp$ to both the parties.
The trusted party answers the adversary: The trusted party computes the functionality $\mathcal{F}:(\widetilde{X},\widetilde{Y}) \rightarrow (F_1(\widetilde{X},\widetilde{Y}),F_2(\widetilde{X},\widetilde{Y}))$ and sends $F_i(\widetilde{X},\widetilde{Y})$ to $\mathcal{SIM}_i$. Then $\mathcal{SIM}_i$ sends "abort" or "continue" to the trusted party.
The trusted party answers the honest party: If the trusted party receives "continue" from $\mathcal{SIM}_i$, then the trusted party sends $F_j(\widetilde{X},\widetilde{Y})$ to the honest party $P_j, j \in \{1,2\} \setminus \{i\}$. Otherwise, the trusted party sends $\perp$ to the honest party.

Output: An honest party always outputs the output value it obtained from the trusted party. The corrupted party outputs nothing. The adversary outputs his view. The joint output of the ideal process is denoted by $\mathsf{IDEAL}_{\mathcal{F},\mathcal{SIM}_i(Z)}(X, Y)$.

Definition 4 Simulatability: *Let* Θ *be a protocol and* $\mathcal{F}$ *be a functionality. Then protocol* Θ *is said to securely compute* $\mathcal{F}$ *in the malicious model if for every PPT adversary* $\mathcal{A}_i$ *in the real world, there exists a PPT adversary* $\mathcal{SIM}_i$ *in the ideal model, such that for every* $i \in \{1, 2\}$, $\mathsf{IDEAL}_{\mathcal{F},\mathcal{SIM}_i(Z)}(X, Y) \equiv^c$ $\mathsf{REAL}_{\Theta,\mathcal{A}_i(Z)}(X, Y)$.

2.2 Homomorphic Encryption [5]

The ElGamal encryption [9] is a multiplicatively homomorphic encryption $\mathcal{EL}$ $= (\mathcal{EL}.\mathsf{Setup}, \mathcal{EL}.\mathsf{KGen}, \mathcal{EL}.\mathsf{Enc}, \mathcal{EL}.\mathsf{Dec})$ which works as follows:

$\mathcal{EL}.\mathsf{Setup}(1^\kappa)$ – On input 1^κ, a trusted third party outputs a public parameter par=(p, q, g), where p, q are primes such that q divides $p - 1$ and g is a generator of the unique cyclic subgroup $\mathbb{G}$ of $\mathbb{Z}_p^*$ of order q.

$\mathcal{EL}.\mathsf{KGen}(\mathsf{par})$ – User U chooses $x \hookleftarrow \mathbb{Z}_q$, computes $y = g^x$, reveals $pk_U = y$ as his public key and keeps $sk_U = x$ secret to himself.

$\mathcal{EL}.\mathsf{Enc}(m, pk_U, \mathsf{par}, r)$ – Encryptor encrypts a message $m \in \mathbb{G}$ using the public key $pk_U = y$ by computing ciphertext tuple $E_{pk_U}(m) = (\alpha, \beta) = (g^r, my^r)$, where $r \hookleftarrow \mathbb{Z}_q$.

$\mathcal{EL}.\mathsf{Dec}(E_{pk_U}(m), sk_U)$ – On receiving ciphertext tuple $E_{pk_U}(m) = (\alpha, \beta) = (g^r, my^r)$, decryptor U decrypts it using the secret key $sk_U = x$ by computing $\frac{\beta}{\alpha^x} = \frac{m(g^x)^r}{(g^r)^x} = m$.

The ElGamal encryption is semantically secure encryption scheme provided DDH problem is hard in $\mathbb{G}$.

2.3 Bloom Filter [3]

Bloom filter (BF) is a data structure that represents a set $X = \{s_1, s_2, ..., s_v\}$ of v elements by an array of m bits and uses k independent hash functions $H = \{h_0, h_1, ..., h_{k-1}\}$ with $h_i : \{0, 1\}^* \to \{0, 1, ..., m - 1\}$ for $i = 0, 1, ..., k - 1$. Let $\mathsf{BF}_X \in \{0, 1\}^m$ represents a Bloom filter for the set X and $\mathsf{BF}_X[i]$ represents the bit at the index i in BF_X. We describe below a Bloom filter [3] that completes in three steps- Initialization, Add, Check.

Initialization: Set 0 to all the bits of an m-bit array, which is an empty Bloom filter with no element in that array.

Add(s): To add an element $s \in X \subseteq \{0, 1\}^*$ into a Bloom filter, s is hashed with the k hash functions $\{h_0, h_1, ..., h_{k-1}\}$ to get k indices $h_0(s), h_1(s), ..., h_{k-1}(s)$. Set 1 to the indices $h_0(s), h_1(s), ..., h_{k-1}(s)$ of the Bloom filter. Each $s \in X$ needs to be added to get $\mathsf{BF}_X \in \{0, 1\}^m$.

Check($\hat{s}$): To check if an element $\hat{s}$ belongs to X or not, $\hat{s}$ is hashed with the k hash functions $\{h_0, h_1, ..., h_{k-1}\}$ to get k indices $h_0(\hat{s}), h_1(\hat{s}), ..., h_{k-1}(\hat{s})$. Now if at least one of $\mathsf{BF}_X[h_0(\hat{s})], ..., \mathsf{BF}_X[h_{k-1}(\hat{s})]$ is 0 then $\hat{s}$ is not in X, otherwise $\hat{s}$ is *probably* in X.

Bloom filter allows false positive whereby an element that has not been inserted in the filter can mistakenly pass the set membership test. This happens due to the fact that an element $\hat{s}$ may not belong to X but $\mathsf{BF}_X[h_i(\hat{s})] = 1$ for all $i = 0, 1, ..., k-1$. On the contrary, Bloom filter never yields false negative i.e., an element that has been inserted in the filter will always pass the test. This is because if $\hat{s}$ belongs to X, then each of $\mathsf{BF}_X[h_0(\hat{s})], ..., \mathsf{BF}_X[h_{k-1}(\hat{s})]$ is 1.

Theorem 1. *Given the number v of elements to be added and a desired maximum false positive rate $\frac{1}{2^k}$, the optimal size m of the Bloom filter is $m = \frac{vk}{\ln 2}$.*

2.4 Zero-Knowledge Proof of Knowledge [2]

We describe below a general construction of zero-knowledge proofs of knowledge, denoted by

$$\mathsf{PoK}\{(\alpha_1, ..., \alpha_l) \mid \wedge_{i=1}^{m} X_i = f_i(\alpha_1, ..., \alpha_l)\}, \tag{1}$$

where the prover wants to prove the knowledge of $(\alpha_1, ..., \alpha_l)$ to the verifier by sending the commitments $X_i = f_i(\alpha_1, ..., \alpha_l), i = 1, ..., m$ such that extracting $(\alpha_1, ..., \alpha_l)$ from $X_1, ..., X_m$ is infeasible for anyone. For each $i = 1, ..., m$, f_i is publicly computable linear function from $\mathcal{X}^l$ to $\mathcal{Y}$, where $\mathcal{X}$ is *additive* set and $\mathcal{Y}$ is *multiplicative* set. The verification of the proof is done by executing the following steps:

1. The prover chooses $v_1, ..., v_l$ and sends the commitments $\overline{X}_i = f_i(v_1, ..., v_l)$, $i = 1, ..., m$ to the verifier.
2. The verifier sends a challenge $c \in \mathcal{X}$ to the prover.
3. For each $j = 1, ..., l$, prover sets $r_j = v_j + c\alpha_j$ and sends the response $(r_1, ..., r_l)$ to the verifier.
4. The verifier checks whether the relations $f_i(r_1, ..., r_l) = \overline{X}_i X_i^c$, $i = 1, ..., m$ hold or not. If all of them hold, then the verifier accepts it, otherwise rejects it.

Non-interactive Version: Using Fiat-Shamir method [10], the proof system represented by Eq. 1 can be converted to non-interactive zero-knowledge proof.

3 Protocol

We now describe our constructions PSI-CA-I and PSI-CA-II. Each of our protocols executes between two parties – a client C with private input set $X = \{x_1, ..., x_v\}$ and a server S with private input set $Y = \{y_1, ..., y_w\}$. We start with PSI-CA-I (see Fig. 1) before going to PSI-CA-II (see Fig. 2). The interactive zero-knowledge proofs as discussed in the Sect. 2.4 are to be used in

Input: The client C has the private input set $X = \{x_1, ..., x_v\}$, the server has the private input set $Y = \{y_1, ..., y_w\}$ and $\mathsf{par} = (p, q, g)$ is their common input.

Auxiliary Inputs: Auxiliary inputs include the security parameter κ, v (the size of X), w (the size of Y).

Step 1. The client C generates $(pk_C = h = g^{a_1}, sk_C = a_1) \leftarrow \mathcal{EL}.\mathsf{KGen}(\mathsf{par})$ and proceeds as follows:

   (i) chooses $r_{x_1}, ..., r_{x_v} \hookleftarrow \mathbb{Z}_q$ and encrypts each element $x_i \in X$ with his public key pk_C to generate

$$E_{pk_C}(x_i) = (c_{x_i} = g^{r_{x_i}}, d_{x_i} = x_i h^{r_{x_i}}) \leftarrow \mathcal{EL}.\mathsf{Enc}(x_i, pk_C, \mathsf{par}, r_{x_i});$$

   (ii) constructs the proof

$$\pi_1 = \mathsf{PoK}\{(r_{x_1}, ..., r_{x_v}) | \wedge_{i=1}^{v} (c_{x_i} = g^{r_{x_i}})\};$$

   (iii) sends $R_1 = \langle \{E_{pk_C}(x_1), ..., E_{pk_C}(x_v)\}, \pi_1 \rangle$ to S.

Step 2. On receiving $R_1 = \langle \{E_{pk_C}(x_1), ..., E_{pk_C}(x_v)\}, \pi_1 \rangle$ from C, the server S interacts with C to checks the validity of the proof π_1 using the similar technique as described in section 2.4. The server S aborts if verification fails, else does the following:

   (i) chooses $r \hookleftarrow \mathbb{Z}_q$ and computes

$$\widehat{Y} = \{t_1 = (y_1)^r, ..., t_w = (y_w)^r\},$$
$$(E_{pk_C}(x_i))^r = (\hat{c}_{x_i} = (c_{x_i})^r, \hat{d}_{x_i} = (d_{x_i})^r) \text{ for } i = 1, ..., v;$$

   (ii) shuffles the set $\{(E_{pk_C}(x_1))^r, ..., (E_{pk_C}(x_v))^r\}$ using a random permutation Perm such that

$$\mathsf{Perm}\{(E_{pk_C}(x_1))^r, ..., (E_{pk_C}(x_v))^r\} = \{(E_{pk_C}(\bar{x}_1))^r, ..., (E_{pk_C}(\bar{x}_v))^r\} = \overline{X},$$

where the set $\{\bar{x}_1, ..., \bar{x}_v\}$ is same as $\{x_1, ..., x_v\}$ in some order. Note that S keeps Perm secret to himself;

   (iii) constructs the proof

$$\pi_2 = \mathsf{PoK}\{(r) | (\Pi_{i=1}^{v} \hat{c}_{\bar{x}_i} = (\Pi_{i=1}^{v} c_{x_i})^r) \wedge (\Pi_{i=1}^{v} \hat{d}_{\bar{x}_i} = (\Pi_{i=1}^{v} d_{x_i})^r)\};$$

   (iv) sends $R_2 = \langle \widehat{Y} = \{t_1, ..., t_w\}, \overline{X} = \{(E_{pk_C}(\bar{x}_1))^r, ..., (E_{pk_C}(\bar{x}_v))^r\}, \pi_2 \rangle$ to C.

Step 3. The client C, on receiving $R_2 = \langle \widehat{Y} = \{t_1, ..., t_w\}, \overline{X} = \{(E_{pk_C}(\bar{x}_1))^r, ..., (E_{pk_C}(\bar{x}_v))^r\}, \pi_2 \rangle$ form S, verifies the validity of the proof π_2 utilizing the similar approach as explained in section 2.4. If the verification does not succeed then C aborts. Otherwise, C proceeds as follows:

   (i) for $i = 1, ..., v$, runs the decryption algorithm for $\mathcal{EL}$ to compute

$$s_i = (\bar{x}_i)^r \leftarrow \mathcal{EL}.\mathsf{Dec}((E_{pk_C}(\bar{x}_i))^r, sk_C);$$

   (ii) sets the cardinality of the intersection $X \cap Y$ as

$$|X \cap Y| = |\{s_1, ..., s_v\} \cap \{t_1, ..., t_w\}|$$

Fig. 1. Description of our PSI-CA-I

Input: The client C has the private input set $X = \{x_1, ..., x_v\}$, the server has the private input set $Y = \{y_1, ..., y_w\}$ and they have the common input $\mathsf{par} = (p, q, g)$.

Auxiliary Inputs: Auxiliary inputs consist of the security parameter κ, v (the size of X) and w (the size of Y), and the optimal Bloom filter parameters m, H and k.

Step 1. The client C generates $(pk_C = h = g^{a_1}, sk_C = a_1) \leftarrow \mathcal{EL}.\mathsf{KGen}(\mathsf{par})$ and does the following:

(i) chooses $r_{x_1}, ..., r_{x_v} \hookleftarrow \mathbb{Z}_q$ and encrypts each member $x_i \in X$ with his public key pk_C to generate

$$E_{pk_C}(x_i) = (c_{x_i} = g^{r_{x_i}}, d_{x_i} = x_i h^{r_{x_i}}) \leftarrow \mathcal{EL}.\mathsf{Enc}(x_i, pk_C, \mathsf{par}, r_{x_i});$$

(ii) constructs the proof

$$\pi_1 = \mathsf{PoK}\{(r_{x_1}, ..., r_{x_v}) | \wedge_{i=1}^{v} (c_{x_i} = g^{r_{x_i}})\};$$

(iii) sends $R_1 = \langle \{E_{pk_C}(x_1), ..., E_{pk_C}(x_v)\}, \pi_1 \rangle$ to S.

Step 2. On receiving $R_1 = \langle \{E_{pk_C}(x_1), ..., E_{pk_C}(x_v)\}, \pi_1 \rangle$ from C, the server S checks the validity of the proof π_1 using the similar procedure as discussed in section 2.4. The server S aborts if verification fails, else does the following:

(i) chooses $r \hookleftarrow \mathbb{Z}_q$ and computes $\widehat{Y} = \{t_1 = (y_1)^r, ..., t_w = (y_w)^r\}$ and

$$(E_{pk_C}(x_i))^r = (\hat{c}_{x_i} = (c_{x_i})^r, \hat{d}_{x_i} = (d_{x_i})^r) \text{ for } i = 1, ..., v;$$

(ii) constructs a Bloom filter $\mathsf{BF}_{\widehat{Y}} \in \{0, 1\}^m$ for the set $\widehat{Y}$ following the procedure explained in section 2.3;

(iii) shuffles the set $\{(E_{pk_C}(x_1))^r, ..., (E_{pk_C}(x_v))^r\}$ using a permutation Perm such that

$$\mathsf{Perm}\{(E_{pk_C}(x_1))^r, ..., (E_{pk_C}(x_v))^r\} = \{(E_{pk_C}(\bar{x}_1))^r, ..., (E_{pk_C}(\bar{x}_v))^r\} = \overline{X},$$

where the set $\{\bar{x}_1, ..., \bar{x}_v\}$ is same as $\{x_1, ..., x_v\}$ in some order. Note that S keeps Perm secret to himself;

(iv) generates the proof

$$\pi_2 = \mathsf{PoK}\{(r) | (\Pi_{i=1}^{v} \hat{c}_{\bar{x}_i} = (\Pi_{i=1}^{v} c_{x_i})^r) \wedge (\Pi_{i=1}^{v} \hat{d}_{\bar{x}_i} = (\Pi_{i=1}^{v} d_{x_i})^r)\};$$

(v) sends $R_2 = \langle \mathsf{BF}_{\widehat{Y}}, \overline{X} = \{(E_{pk_C}(\bar{x}_1))^r, ..., (E_{pk_C}(\bar{x}_v))^r\}, \pi_2 \rangle$ to C.

Step 3. On receiving $R_2 = \langle \mathsf{BF}_{\widehat{Y}}, \overline{X} = \{(E_{pk_C}(\bar{x}_1))^r, ..., (E_{pk_C}(\bar{x}_v))^r\}, \pi_2 \rangle$ form S, the client C verifies the proof π_2 following the procedure similar to that described in section 2.4. If the verification fails then C aborts. Otherwise, C sets $\mathsf{card} = 0$ and proceeds as follows:

(i) for $i = 1, ..., v$, runs the decryption algorithm for $\mathcal{EL}$ to generate

$$s_i = (\bar{x}_i)^r \leftarrow \mathcal{EL}.\mathsf{Dec}((E_{pk_C}(\bar{x}_i))^r, sk_C);$$

(ii) for $i = 1, ..., v$, checks that whether s_i satisfies the set membership test for the Bloom filter $\mathsf{BF}_{\widehat{Y}}$, if s_i satisfies the set membership test then increments card by 1 i.e., $\mathsf{card} = \mathsf{card} + 1$;

(iii) finally, sets card as the cardinality of the intersection $X \cap Y$.

Fig. 2. Description of our PSI-CA-II

PSI-CA-I. On the other hand, the non-interactive zero-knowledge proofs as discussed in the Sect. 2.4 are to be used in PSI-CA-II. This is because the security of PSI-CA-I is to be proven in standard model but PSI-CA-II is already in ROM due to the use of Bloom filter. We use the multiplicative homomorphic property of ElGamal encryption $(\mathcal{EL})$ i.e.,

$$(E_{pk}(m))^l = E_{pk}(m^l) \text{ for some } l \in \mathbb{Z}_q$$

In the rest of our discussion, k represents number of hash functions for Bloom filter, H denotes the set $\{h_0, h_1, ..., h_{k-1}\}$ of k hash functions with $h_i : \{0,1\}^* \to \{0, 1, ..., m-1\}$ for $i = 0, 1, ..., k-1$, m stands for optimal size of Bloom filter.

Correctness of PSI-CA-I: As the set $\{\bar{x}_1, ..., \bar{x}_v\}$ is same as $\{x_1, ..., x_v\}$ in some order, the set $\{\bar{x}_1^r, ..., \bar{x}_v^r\}$ is same as $\{x_1^r, ..., x_v^r\}$ in that order. Thus we have the following:

$$\begin{aligned}
|\{s_1, ..., s_v\} \cap \{t_1, ..., t_w\}| &= |\{\bar{x}_1^r, ..., \bar{x}_v^r\} \cap \{y_1^r, ..., y_w^r\}| \\
&= |\{x_1^r, ..., x_v^r\} \cap \{y_1^r, ..., y_w^r\}| \\
&= |\{x_1, ..., x_v\} \cap \{y_1, ..., y_w\}| \\
&= |X \cap Y|
\end{aligned}$$

Correctness of PSI-CA-II: As the set $\{\bar{x}_1, ..., \bar{x}_v\}$ is same as $\{x_1, ..., x_v\}$ in some order, the set $\{\bar{x}_1^r, ..., \bar{x}_v^r\}$ is same as $\{x_1^r, ..., x_v^r\}$ in that order. Thus we can conclude that $s_i = \bar{x}_i^r$ satisfies the set membership test for the Bloom filter $\mathsf{BF}_{\widehat{Y}}$ implies there exists $x_j^r \in \{x_1^r, ..., x_v^r\}$ which satisfies the set membership test for the Bloom filter $\mathsf{BF}_{\widehat{Y}}$. In other words, $x_j^r \in \widehat{Y}$ which implies $x_j \in Y$ except with negligible probability $\frac{1}{2^k}$. Note that the variable card is incremented only if an element of $\{\bar{x}_1^r, ..., \bar{x}_v^r\}$ satisfies the set membership test for the Bloom filter $\mathsf{BF}_{\widehat{Y}}$ i.e., an element of $X = \{x_1, ..., x_v\}$ belongs to $Y = \{y_1, ..., y_w\}$. Hence card gives the cardinality of the intersection $X \cap Y$ except with negligible probability $\frac{1}{2^k}$.

Complexity: The computation overhead of our constructions is measured by modular exponentiation, modular inversion and hash computation. On the other hand, the number of group elements transmitted publicly by the users in our protocols incurs the communication cost. Let Exp denotes total number of modular exponentiations, GE stands for total number of group elements, Inv represents total number of modular inversions and H stands for total number of hash queries. Our PSI-CA-I requires at most $8v + w + 7$ Exp, $6v + w + 5$ GE and v Inv. On the other hand, PSI-CA-II requires at most $8v + w + 7$ Exp, $5v + 4$ GE, v Inv and $k(v + w)$ H.

Remark 1. Our PSI-CA-I and PSI-CA-II can be converted to PSI protocols: PSI-I and PSI-II respectively by removing the associated permutations. Due to limited space PSI-I and PSI-II will appear in the full version.

4   Security

We describe the security of PSI-CA-I followed by the security of PSI-CA-II. Both the protocols are proven to be secure in the malicious model. We consider $\mathcal{A}_c(\mathcal{A}_s)$ as real world adversary who corrupts $C(S)$ and $\mathcal{SIM}_c(\mathcal{SIM}_s)$

as the corresponding ideal process adversary. Let $\bar{C}$ and $\bar{S}$ be the honest client and honest server in ideal process. In real world, a trusted third party generates the public parameter par $= (p, q, g)$ whereas in ideal process $\mathcal{SIM}_c(\mathcal{SIM}_s)$ does those things. We denote the join output of $C, S, \mathcal{A}_c(\mathcal{A}_s)$ as $\mathsf{REAL}_{\Theta, \mathcal{A}_c(Z)(\mathcal{A}_s(Z))}(X, Y)$ in real world and the joint output of $\bar{C}, \bar{S}$, $\mathcal{SIM}_c(\mathcal{SIM}_s)$ as $\mathsf{IDEAL}_{\mathcal{F}_{card}, \mathcal{SIM}_c(Z)(\mathcal{SIM}_s(Z))}(X, Y)$ in ideal process.

Theorem 2. *If the encryption scheme $\mathcal{EL}$ is semantically secure, the associated proof protocols are zero knowledge proof and the associated permutation is random, then our PSI-CA-I presented in Sect. 3 is a secure computation protocol for the functionality $\mathcal{F}_{card} : (X, Y) \rightarrow (|X \cap Y|, \bot)$ in the security model described in Sect. 2.1.*

Proof. To prove the security of PSI-CA-I, we first consider the case when the client C is corrupted then we will go for the case when the server S is corrupted.

1. **$\mathcal{A}_c$ corrupts the client C:** Let Z be a distinguisher that controls $\mathcal{A}_c$, feeds the input of the receiver S, and also sees the output of S. We now prove that Z's view in real world ($\mathcal{A}_c$'s view + S's output) is indistinguishable from its view in ideal process ($\mathcal{A}_c$'s view + $\bar{S}$'s output). This is proven by considering a series of games $Game_0, Game_1, Game_2$, where $Game_{i+1}$ modifies $Game_i$ slightly for $i = 0, 1$. We consider $Prob[i]$ as the probability that Z distinguishes its view in $Game_i$ from its view in real protocol. Further, we assume that S_i is the simulator in $Game_i$.

   $Game_0$: This game corresponds to the real world protocol, where the simulator S_0 has full knowledge of S and interacts with $\mathcal{A}_c$. Hence

   $$Prob[\mathsf{REAL}_{\Theta, \mathcal{A}_c(z)}(X, Y)] = Prob[Game_0].$$

   $Game_1$: $Game_1$ is same as $Game_0$ except that if the proof π_1 is valid then the simulator S_1 runs the extractor algorithm for π_1 with C to extract the exponents $\{r_{x_1}, ..., r_{x_v}\}$. The simulator S_1 then constructs $X = \{x_1, ..., x_v\}$ by using $\{r_{x_1}, ..., r_{x_v}\}$, extracting $\{d_{x_1} = x_1 h^{r_{x_1}}, ..., d_{x_v} = x_v h^{r_{x_v}}\}$ from $\{E_{pk_C}(x_1), ..., E_{pk_C}(x_v)\}$ in R_1, h from pk_C and computing $\{x_1 = \frac{d_{x_1}}{h^{r_{x_1}}}, ..., x_v = \frac{d_{x_v}}{h^{r_{x_v}}}\}$. Z's views in $Game_0$ and $Game_1$ are indistinguishable due to the simulation soundness property of the proof π_1. Therefore,

   $$|Prob[Game_1] - Prob[Game_0]| \leq \epsilon_1(\kappa), \text{ where } \epsilon_1(\kappa) \text{ is a negligible function.}$$

   $Game_2$: $Game_2$ is same as $Game_1$ except that after constructing $X = \{x_1, ..., x_v\}$, the simulator S_2 does the following:
   - computes $|X \cap Y|$,
   - constructs a set $\overline{Y} = \{\bar{y}_1, ..., \bar{y}_w)\}$ by including $|X \cap Y|$ many random elements of X together with $w - |X \cap Y|$ many random elements of $\mathbb{G}$,
   - chooses $r \hookleftarrow \mathbb{Z}_q$,
   - computes $\{(\bar{y}_1)^r, ..., (\bar{y}_w)^r\}, \{(E_{pk_C}(x_1))^r, ..., (E_{pk_C}(x_v))^r\}$,
   - chooses a random permutation Perm and permutes the set $\{(E_{pk_C}(x_1))^r, ..., (E_{pk_C}(x_v))^r\}$ such that

   $$\mathsf{Perm}\{(E_{pk_C}(x_1))^r, ..., (E_{pk_C}(x_v))^r\} = \{(E_{pk_C}(\bar{x}_1))^r, ..., (E_{pk_C}(\bar{x}_v))^r\},$$

where the set $\{\bar{x}_1, ..., \bar{x}_v\}$ is same as $\{x_1, ..., x_v\}$ in some order and keeps Perm secret to himself,

– sends $\langle\{(\bar{y}_1)^r, ..., (\bar{y}_w)^r\}, \{(E_{pk_C}(\bar{x}_1))^r, ..., (E_{pk_C}(\bar{x}_v))^r\}\rangle$ as $\langle\{(y_1)^r, ..., (y_w)^r\}, \{(E_{pk_C}(\bar{x}_1))^r, ..., (E_{pk_C}(\bar{x}_v))^r\}\rangle$ and simulates the proof π_2.

Since the associated encryption scheme $\mathcal{EL}$ is semantically secure, the distributions of $\langle\{(y_1)^r, ..., (y_w)^r\}, \{(E_{pk_C}(\bar{x}_1))^r, ..., (E_{pk_C}(\bar{x}_v))^r\}\rangle$ in $Game_1$ and $Game_2$ are identical. By the zero-knowledge simulatability of the proof π_2 and indistinguishablity of $\langle\{(y_1)^r, ..., (y_w)^r\}, \{(E_{pk_C}(\bar{x}_1))^r, ..., (E_{pk_C}(\bar{x}_v))^r\}\rangle$ in $Game_1$ and $Game_2$ the views of $\mathcal{Z}$ in these two games are indistinguishable. Hence, there exists a negligible function $\epsilon_2(\kappa)$ such that

$$|Prob[Game_2] - Prob[Game_1]| \leq \epsilon_2(\kappa).$$

Now we construct the ideal world adversary $\mathcal{SIM}_c$ that uses $\mathcal{A}_c$ as subroutine, simulates the honest party S and incorporates all steps from $Game_2$.

(i) $\mathcal{SIM}_c$ first plays the role of the trusted third party by generating the public parameter par $= (p, q, g)$. $\mathcal{SIM}_c$ then invokes $\mathcal{A}_c$ with the input $X = \{x_1, ..., x_v\}$ and the auxiliary input z.

(ii) On receiving $\langle\{E_{pk_C}(x_1), ..., E_{pk_C}(x_v)\}, \pi_1\rangle$ from $\mathcal{A}_c$, $\mathcal{SIM}_c$ verifies the validity of the proof π_1 utilizing the similar approach as discussed in Sect. 2.4. If the verification succeeds then $\mathcal{SIM}_c$ extracts the exponents $\{r_{x_1}, ..., r_{x_v}\}$ by running the extractor algorithm. The simulator $\mathcal{SIM}_c$ then extracts $x_i = \frac{d_{x_i}}{h^{r_{x_i}}}$ by extracting $d_{x_i} = x_i h^{r_{x_i}}$ from $E_{pk_C}(x_i)$ in R_1, h from pk_C and using the exponent r_{x_i} for $1 \leq i \leq v$. Thereby, $\mathcal{SIM}_c$ extracts the set $\{x_1, ..., x_v\}$. Otherwise, $\mathcal{SIM}_c$ sends $\perp$ to the trusted party T who computes the functionality $\mathcal{F}_{card}$ and terminates the execution.

(iii) $\mathcal{SIM}_c$ sends X and $\bar{S}$ sends Y to T who in turn computes the functionality $\mathcal{F}_{card}$ for inputs X and Y and returns $|X \cap Y|$ to $\mathcal{SIM}_c$.

(iv) On receiving $|X \cap Y|$ from T, the simulator does the following:
   – $\mathcal{SIM}_c$ constructs a set $\overline{Y} = \{\bar{y}_1, ..., \bar{y}_w\}$ by including $|X \cap Y|$ many random elements of X together with $w - |X \cap Y|$ many random elements of $\mathbb{G}$,
   – chooses $r \leftarrow \mathbb{Z}_q$,
   – computes $\{(\bar{y}_1)^r, ..., (\bar{y}_w)^r\}, \{(E_{pk_C}(x_1))^r, ..., (E_{pk_C}(x_v))^r\}$,
   – selects a random permutation Perm and permutes the set $\{(E_{pk_C}(x_1))^r, ..., (E_{pk_C}(x_v))^r\}$ such that

$$\mathsf{Perm}\{(E_{pk_C}(x_1))^r, ..., (E_{pk_C}(x_v))^r\} = \{(E_{pk_C}(\bar{x}_1))^r, ..., (E_{pk_C}(\bar{x}_v))^r\},$$

where the set $\{\bar{x}_1, ..., \bar{x}_v\}$ is same as $\{x_1, ..., x_v\}$ in some order and keeps Perm secret to himself,
   – sends $\langle\{(\bar{y}_1)^r, ..., (\bar{y}_w)^r\}, \{(E_{pk_C}(\bar{x}_1))^r, ..., (E_{pk_C}(\bar{x}_v))^r\}\rangle$ as $\langle\{(y_1)^r, ..., (y_w)^r\}, \{(E_{pk_C}(\bar{x}_1))^r, ..., (E_{pk_C}(\bar{x}_v))^r\}\rangle$ and simulates the proof π_2.

Thus the simulator SIM_c provides $\mathcal{A}_c$ the same simulation as the simulator S_2 as in $Game_2$. Hence $Prob[\text{IDEAL}_{\mathcal{F}_{card},SIM_c(z)}(X,Y)] = Prob[Game_2]$ and

$$|Prob[\text{IDEAL}_{\mathcal{F}_{card},SIM_c(z)}(X,Y)] - Prob[\text{REAL}_{\Theta,\mathcal{A}_c(z)}(X,Y)]|$$
$$= |Prob[Game_2] - Prob[Game_0]|$$
$$\leq \Sigma_{i=0}^{1}(|Prob[Game_{i+1}] - Prob[Game_i]|)$$
$$\leq \epsilon_2(\kappa) + \epsilon_1(\kappa) = \rho(\kappa),$$

where $\rho(\kappa)$ is a negligible function. Therefore we have

$$\text{IDEAL}_{\mathcal{F}_{card},SIM_c(z)}(X,Y) \equiv^c \text{REAL}_{\Theta,\mathcal{A}_c(z)}(X,Y).$$

2. $\mathcal{A}_s$ **corrupts the server** S: Let us consider $\mathcal{Z}$ as a distinguisher that controls $\mathcal{A}_s$, feeds the input of the client C, and also sees the output of C. A series of games $Game_0, Game_1, Game_2$ is presented to show that $\mathcal{Z}$'s view in real world ($\mathcal{A}_c$'s view + C's output) is indistinguishable form its view in ideal process ($\mathcal{A}_c$'s view + $\bar{C}$'s output). Each $Game_{i+1}$ modifies $Game_i$ slightly for $i = 0, 1$. Let $\mathcal{Z}$ distinguishes its view in $Game_i$ from its view in real protocol with the probability $Prob[i]$ and S_i be the simulator in $Game_i$.
$Game_0$: This game is same as the real world protocol, where the simulator S_0 has full knowledge of C and interacts with $\mathcal{A}_s$. Hence

$$Prob[\text{REAL}_{\Pi,\mathcal{A}_s(z)}(X,Y)] = Prob[Game_0].$$

$Game_1$: $Game_1$ is same as $Game_0$ except that S_1 simulates π_1 instead of proving it as in $Game_0$ and generates $(pk_C, sk_C) \leftarrow \mathcal{EL}.\text{KGen}(par)$. $\mathcal{Z}$'s view in $Game_0$ is indistinguishable form its view in $Game_1$ because of zero-knowledge (simulatability) of the proof π_1. Therefore,

$$|Prob[Game_1] - Prob[Game_0]| \leq \epsilon_1(\kappa), \text{ where } \epsilon_1(\kappa) \text{ is a negligible function.}$$

$Game_2$: This game is same as $Game_0$ except the following:
– if the verification of the proof π_2 fails then S_2 outputs $\perp$ as the final output of C.
– if the verification of the proof π_2 succeeds then S_2 runs the extractor algorithm for π_2 to extract the exponent r,
– constructs the set $Y = \{y_1, ..., y_w\}$ from the set $\widehat{Y} = \{t_1 = (y_1)^r, ..., t_w = (y_w)^r\}$ by computing $(t_j)^{r^{-1}} = (y_j)^{rr^{-1}} = y_j$,
– computes $|X \cap Y|$ and outputs $|X \cap Y|$ as the final output of C,
By simulation soundness property of π_2, $\mathcal{Z}$'s views in $Game_1$ and $Game_2$ are indistinguishable. Consequently, there exists a negligible function $\epsilon_2(\kappa)$ such that

$$|Prob[Game_2] - Prob[Game_1]| \leq \epsilon_2(\kappa).$$

Now we construct the ideal world adversary SIM_c that uses $\mathcal{A}_s$ as subroutine, simulates the honest party C and incorporates all steps from $Game_2$.

(i) $\mathcal{SIM}_s$ first plays the role of the trusted third party by generating the public parameter $\mathsf{par} = (p, q, g)$. $\mathcal{SIM}_c$ then invokes $\mathcal{A}_s$ with the input $Y = \{y_1, ..., y_w\}$ and the auxiliary input z.

(ii) Now $\mathcal{SIM}_s$ acts the role of honest client C as follows:
   - generates $(pk_C, sk_C) \leftarrow \mathcal{EL}.\mathsf{KGen}(\mathsf{par})$,
   - constructing a set $\tilde{X} = \{\tilde{x}_1, ..., \tilde{x}_v\}$,
   - encrypts each member $\tilde{x}_i \in \tilde{X}$
   - finally sends $\{E_{pk_C}(\tilde{x}_1), ..., E_{pk_C}(\tilde{x}_v)\}$ as $\{E_{pk_C}(x_1), ..., E_{pk_C}(x_v)\}$ to $\mathcal{A}_s$ and simulates the proof π_1.

(iii) On receiving $\langle \{t_1, ..., t_w\}, \overline{X}, \pi_2 \rangle$ form $\mathcal{A}_s$, $\mathcal{SIM}_s$ checks the verification of the proof π_2 using the similar technique as discussed in Sect. 2.4. If the verification fails then $\mathcal{SIM}_s$ sends $\perp$ to T who computes the functionality $\mathcal{F}_{\mathsf{card}}$ and terminates. Otherwise, $\mathcal{SIM}_s$ runs the extractor algorithm for π_2 to extract the exponent r. $\mathcal{SIM}_s$ then constructs the set $Y = \{y_1, ..., y_w\}$ from the set $\tilde{Y} = \{t_1 = (y_1)^r, ..., t_w = (y_w)^r\}$ by computing $(t_j)^{r^{-1}} = (y_j)^{rr^{-1}} = y_j$.

(iv) $\mathcal{SIM}_s$ sends Y and $\bar{C}$ sends X to T who in turn computes the functionality $\mathcal{F}_{\mathsf{card}}$ for inputs X and Y and returns $|X \cap Y|$ to $\bar{C}$.

Therefore the simulator $\mathcal{SIM}_s$ provides $\mathcal{A}_s$ the same simulation as the simulator S_2 as in $Game_2$. Thus $Prob[\mathsf{IDEAL}_{\mathcal{F}_{\mathsf{card}}, \mathcal{SIM}_s(z)}(X, Y)] = Prob[Game_2]$ and

$$|Prob[\mathsf{IDEAL}_{\mathcal{F}_{\mathsf{card}}, \mathcal{SIM}_s(z)}(X, Y)] - Prob[\mathsf{REAL}_{\Theta, \mathcal{A}_s(z)}(X, Y)]|$$
$$= |Prob[Game_2] - Prob[Game_0]| \leq \Sigma_{i=0}^{1}(|Prob[Game_{i+1}] - Prob[Game_i]|)$$
$$\leq \epsilon_2(\kappa) + \epsilon_1(\kappa) = \rho(\kappa),$$

where $\rho(\kappa)$ is a negligible function. Hence we have

$$\mathsf{IDEAL}_{\mathcal{F}_{\mathsf{card}}, \mathcal{SIM}_s(z)}(X, Y) \equiv^c \mathsf{REAL}_{\Theta, \mathcal{A}_s(z)}(X, Y).$$

Theorem 3. *If the encryption scheme $\mathcal{EL}$ is semantically secure, the associated proof protocols are zero knowledge proof and the associated permutation is random, then our PSI-CA-II presented in Sect. 3 is a secure computation protocol for the functionality $\mathcal{F}_{\mathsf{card}} : (X, Y) \rightarrow (|X \cap Y|, \perp)$ in the security model described in Sect. 2.1 except with negligible probability $\frac{1}{2^k}$.*

Due to limited space proof of Theorem 3 will appear in the full version.

5   Conclusion

This paper consists of two flavors of PSI-CA, one is secure in standard model and the other one is secure in ROM. Both are secure against malicious parties with linear computation and communication complexities under DDH assumption. Till now, the constructions of [7] are the most efficient PSI-CA to the best of our knowledge. However, the security proofs are in the random oracle model (ROM) under non-standard cryptographic assumption and the adversaries models are not fully malicious. In particular, our PSI-CA constructions are the *first* to achieve *linear complexity* in the presence of *malicious* adversaries.

References

1. Agrawal, R., Evfimievski, A., Srikant, R.: Information sharing across private databases. In: Proceedings of the 2003 ACM SIGMOD International Conference on Management of Data, pp. 86–97. ACM (2003)
2. Bellare, M., Goldreich, O.: On defining proofs of knowledge. In: Brickell, E.F. (ed.) CRYPTO 1992. LNCS, vol. 740, pp. 390–420. Springer, Heidelberg (1993)
3. Bloom, B.H.: Space/time trade-offs in hash coding with allowable errors. Commun. ACM **13**(7), 422–426 (1970)
4. Boneh, D.: The decision Diffie-Hellman problem. In: Buhler, J.P. (ed.) ANTS 1998. LNCS, vol. 1423, pp. 48–63. Springer, Heidelberg (1998)
5. Camenisch, J.L., Shoup, V.: Practical verifiable encryption and decryption of discrete logarithms. In: Boneh, D. (ed.) CRYPTO 2003. LNCS, vol. 2729, pp. 126–144. Springer, Heidelberg (2003)
6. Camenisch, J., Zaverucha, G.M.: Private intersection of certified sets. In: Dingledine, R., Golle, P. (eds.) FC 2009. LNCS, vol. 5628, pp. 108–127. Springer, Heidelberg (2009)
7. De Cristofaro, E., Gasti, P., Tsudik, G.: Fast and private computation of cardinality of set intersection and union. In: Pieprzyk, J., Sadeghi, A.-R., Manulis, M. (eds.) CANS 2012. LNCS, vol. 7712, pp. 218–231. Springer, Heidelberg (2012)
8. Dong, C., Chen, L., Wen, Z.: When private set intersection meets big data: An efficient and scalable protocol. In: Proceedings of the 2013 ACM SIGSAC Conference on Computer & Communications Security, pp. 789–800. ACM (2013)
9. El Gamal, T.: A public key cryptosystem and a signature scheme based on discrete logarithms. In: Blakely, G.R., Chaum, D. (eds.) CRYPTO 1984. LNCS, vol. 196, pp. 10–18. Springer, Heidelberg (1985)
10. Fiat, Amos, Shamir, Adi: How to prove yourself: practical solutions to identification and signature problems. In: Odlyzko, Andrew M. (ed.) CRYPTO 1986. LNCS, vol. 263, pp. 186–194. Springer, Heidelberg (1987)
11. Freedman, M.J., Nissim, K., Pinkas, B.: Efficient private matching and set intersection. In: Cachin, C., Camenisch, J.L. (eds.) EUROCRYPT 2004. LNCS, vol. 3027, pp. 1–19. Springer, Heidelberg (2004)
12. Goldreich, O.: Foundations of cryptography: vol. 2, basic applications. Cambridge University Press (2004)
13. Hazay, C.: Oblivious polynomial evaluation and secure set-intersection from algebraic prfs. IACR Cryptology ePrint Archive **2015**, 4 (2015)
14. Hohenberger, S., Weis, S.A.: Honest-verifier private disjointness testing without random oracles. In: Danezis, G., Golle, P. (eds.) PET 2006. LNCS, vol. 4258, pp. 277–294. Springer, Heidelberg (2006)
15. Jarecki, S., Liu, X.: Efficient oblivious pseudorandom function with applications to adaptive OT and secure computation of set intersection. In: Reingold, O. (ed.) TCC 2009. LNCS, vol. 5444, pp. 577–594. Springer, Heidelberg (2009)
16. Kissner, L., Song, D.: Privacy-preserving set operations. In: Shoup, V. (ed.) CRYPTO 2005. LNCS, vol. 3621, pp. 241–257. Springer, Heidelberg (2005)
17. Pinkas, B., Schneider, T., Zohner, M.: Faster private set intersection based on ot extension. USENIX Security **14**, 797–812 (2014)
18. Vaidya, J., Clifton, C.: Secure set intersection cardinality with application to association rule mining. J. Comput. Secur. **13**(4), 593–622 (2005)

A Formal Dynamic Verification
of Choreographed Web Services Conversations

Karim Dahmani, Mahjoub Langar$^{(\boxtimes)}$, and Riadh Robbana

LIP2 Research Laboratory, Faculté des Sciences de Tunis, Tunis, Tunisia
mahjoub.langar@gmail.com

Abstract. Performing runtime verification of composite web services is one of the actual main research challenges. This paper presents a formal approach for dynamically enforcing security policies on web services choreographies. We define a security framework for monitoring choreographed web services by inlining a monitor that checks whether a choreography adheres to some constraints dictated by a security policy. Therefore, this monitor prohibits the execution of undesirable behaviors during runtime and does not change the original behavior of the choreography until an action is about to violate the security policy.

Keywords: Monitoring · Choreography · Formal verification · Web service composition · Security policy enforcement · Runtime verification

1 Introduction

Nowadays, web services technology is widely used to integrate heterogeneous systems and develop new applications. Web services are loosely-coupled applications that are accessible through the Web and that offer a set of functionalities to individuals or businesses. Therefore, individual Web services are conceptually limited to offer simple functionalities that, in some cases, are not sufficient to satisfy requirements needed by a consumer. This yields to compose web services together in order to fulfill complex user requirements. There are mainly two approaches to web services composition: orchestration and choreography. In the web service orchestration approach, a web service is added to composed web services and has the role of coordinating between several web services in order to achieve a particular goal. The added web service is called orchestrator, hence the name of web service orchestration. However the web service choreography is a technique that composes web services in a decentralized manner, without the exploitation of a central coordinator. The intuition behind the name of choreography is the following: *Dancers dance following a global scenario without a single point of control.* Indeed, a choreography defines complex tasks via the definition of the conversation that should be undertaken by each participant. Then, each participant will execute its proper role according to other participants' behaviors. The most important proposals for composing web services are Business Process Execution Language (BPEL) [1] used for the orchestration technique and Web

© Springer International Publishing Switzerland 2015
M.-H. Au and A. Miyaji (Eds.): ProvSec 2015, LNCS 9451, pp. 340–353, 2015.
DOI: 10.1007/978-3-319-26059-4_19

Service Choreography Description Language (WS-CDL) [2]. Due to the lack of research efforts in securing web service choreographies, this paper addresses a security framework for monitoring choreographed web services.

One of the current and promising avenues of researches in web services programming paradigms is the development of security frameworks for enforcing security policies on choreographies of web services. Formal verification of choreographies of web services is the process of checking whether a participant's behavior satisfies some security requirements using mathematical reasoning. The literature records various techniques for enforcing security policies belonging to mainly two principal classes: static approaches including typing theory [3], Proof Carrying Code [4], and dynamic approaches including reference monitors [5,6] and Java stack inspection [7]. Verifying statically a web services choreography conformance to security properties consists on examining the behavior of each involved participant before its execution. However, a dynamic analysis of a choreography of web services consists on verifying the execution of participants' behaviors during runtime by intercepting critical events and halting the latter whenever an action is attempting to violate a security policy. Nevertheless, a web service that has been demonstrated to conform to some security requirements before deployment using static verification methods could violate these constraints after runtime. This is due to the evolution of the execution environment of the service itself and of other services involved in the choreography. So, if security cannot be achieved statically, one should establish trustworthiness dynamically by monitoring the execution of the web service. Such a monitor can be either in-lined into the program code or integrated into the runtime environment.

In this paper, we formally define an in-lined monitor that checks whether a choreography of web services adheres to constraints specified by some security properties. When a participant in the choreography is going to violate a security property then the monitor halts its evolution. More precisely, we define an operator that takes as input a process describing a participant's behavior involved in a choreography and a security property and produces as output a secured version of the process. This secured process will ensure a behavior of the concerned participant that is similar to the original behavior and that respects the enforced security property. We remind that the class of security policies dynamically enforceable are safety properties. By safety, we mean that something bad will never happen during the execution of the choreography.

The rest of the paper is structured as follows. First, we present a running case-study in Sect. 2. Section 3 presents the End-Point Calculus, a formal language used to describe behaviors of choreographed services. In Sect. 4, we present the logic used to specify security policies. In Sect. 5, we introduce the Secured End-Point Calculus, an extension of the End-Point Calculus that holds the monitoring process. In Sect. 6, we discuss related work while the conclusion and perspectives for future work are in Sect. 7. The proof of the correctness of the present approach has been removed for the sake of space.

2   Scenario and Motivation

Consider a buyer that wants to purchase some goods on-line. He establishes a communication with a seller service then requests for a quote of a chosen product. The seller responds with the corresponding quote. At this stage, the buyer has the choice between accepting the quote or rejecting it. If he rejects the quote then the protocol terminates. Otherwise, he should notify the seller for his acceptance. In this case, the seller asks the buyer for an order confirmation then the buyer confirms his command. After that, the seller establishes a communication with a shipper service and requests for delivery details of the chosen product. The shipper responds with delivery details and finally, the seller transfers the delivery details to the buyer and the protocol terminates.

This is a choreography composed of three agents: a buyer, a seller and a shipper service. The buyer is considered as a service requester. The shipper is a service provider. However, the seller is a service provider from the viewpoint of the buyer and a service requester from the viewpoint of the shipper. The security property that will be enforced on this choreography says: *the seller should not send delivery details to the buyer until he receives a confirmation of the command to be delivered.*

We remind that the goal of this work is to inline a monitor that enforces a security property into the concerned participant's process. The security property mentioned above concerns the seller service. So, throughout this paper, we will encapsulate the seller's process within a monitor whose intent is to compel the seller to perform all operations except the invocation of delivery details operation. Once the seller has received a confirmation for the purchased product, then all operations will be permitted without exception.

3   Choreography Specification Language

A collaboration between W3C WS-CDL working group and a team of π-calculus experts led by R. Milner [8] has introduced a formal theory of end-point projection. For this purpose, the authors use two typed calculi for describing interactions, a distilled version of WS-CDL (Global Calculus) and an applied π-calculus (End-Point Calculus) and define a mapping from the former to the latter. The Global Calculus describes the global flow of interactions between participants. The end-point calculus (EPC) is based on a process calculus in the style of the π-calculus. More precisely, EPC is a calculus with locations linked by channel names. Each location identifies a participant in a choreography. The mapping defined by [8] is based on three principles for global descriptions. These principles enunciate general disciplines for well-structured global descriptions. Reasons behind the choice of EPC as a formal language for describing web services behaviors are:

1. The end-point projection [8] that maps the global calculus to EPC allows us to describe a choreography in a natural way using the global calculus then project the obtained specification into local processes describing the behaviors of the involved participants.

2. EPC is a session-based calculus. Session-based languages are highly suited for programming web service communications since they guarantee the correctness of process interactions (represented by sessions) taking place between web services.
3. EPC is the π-calculus [9] extended with session [10] as well as locations [11] and store [12].

3.1 Syntax of EPC

EPC specifies local behaviors of end-points and their composition. Its syntax is given by the BNF grammar in Table 1. The main syntactic terms are processes $(P, Q, ...)$ and networks $(N, M, ...)$. Below $ch, ch_A, ch_B, ...$ range over service channels, $s, s', ...$ range over session channels, $x, y, ...$ range over variables, $X, Y, ...$ range over term variables and $e_1, e_2, ...$ range over expressions which can be atomic values (such as a natural number or a boolean value) or a function (such as arithmetic functions and boolean operators) or a variable. The symbol "!" in $!ch(\tilde{s}).P$ indicates replication, which says that the service channel is available for an unbounded number of invocations.

Table 1. Syntax of EPC.

$$P ::= !ch(\tilde{s}).P \mid \overline{ch}(\nu\tilde{s}).P \mid s \triangleright \sum_{i \in I} op_i(x_i).P_i \mid \bar{s} \triangleleft op\langle e \rangle.P \mid$$
$$x := e.P \mid \text{if } e \text{ then } P \text{ else } Q \mid P \oplus Q \mid P \mid Q \mid$$
$$(\nu s)P \mid \mu X.P \mid 0$$
$$N ::= A[P]_\sigma \mid N \mid M \mid (\nu s)N \mid \epsilon$$

The two first constructs are dual operations used for session initiation. The process $!ch(\tilde{s}).P$ is embodying a repeatedly available service accessible via the public service channel ch. After invocation, the service offers interactions described in process P through freshly generated session channels s from $\tilde{s}$. The process $\overline{ch}(\nu\tilde{s}).P$ is requesting a service ch with session channels $\tilde{s}$. After freshly generated session channels have been shared between two participants, they can communicate through these channels using the standard in-session communication operations. The process $s \triangleright \sum_i op_i(x_i).P_i$ offers one of operators op_i through the session channel s. When op_i is invoked, then it assigns a communicated value to its local variable x_i and behaves as described in P_i. For instance, a seller service receives a confirmation or a cancellation for a purchase:

$$s \triangleright confPurchase(x_{conf}).P + s \triangleright cancPurchase(x_{canc}).0$$

The process $\bar{s} \triangleleft op\langle e \rangle.P$ invokes the operator op through session channel s and communicates the result of the evaluation of the expression e, then behaves as P. For example, the buyer service requests for a quote from the seller service:

$$\bar{s} \triangleleft quoteRequest\langle e_{product} \rangle.P$$

Another prefix operator is the assignment operator: $x := e.P$, which assigns the result of the evaluation of e to a local variable x and then behaves as P. The term $\oplus$ denotes internal choice. The rest is standard. Networks are parallel compositions of participants. A participant A with its behavior P at a local state σ is called a network and denoted by $A[P]_\sigma$. The local state σ is interpreted as a function from variables to values.

3.2   Semantics of EPC

In order to minimize the number of reduction rules, we define first the structural congruence for EPC.

Definition 1 (End-Point Structural Congruence). The structural congruence $\equiv$ is defined as the least congruence on processes such that $(\equiv, 0, \oplus)$ and $(\equiv, 0, |)$ are commutative monoids and such that it satisfies:

- $(\nu s)0 \equiv 0$,
- $(\nu s_1)(\nu s_2)P \equiv (\nu s_2)(\nu s_1)P$,
- $((\nu s)P)|Q \equiv (\nu s)(P|Q)$ where s is not a free session channel of Q.

We extend $\equiv$ to networks such that $(\equiv, \epsilon, |)$ is a commutative monoid and:

- $A[P]_\sigma \equiv A[Q]_\sigma \ (P \equiv Q)$ - $(\nu s)\epsilon \equiv \epsilon$
- $A[(\nu s)P]_\sigma \equiv (\nu s)A[P]_\sigma$ - $(\nu s_1)(\nu s_2)M \equiv (\nu s_2)(\nu s_1)M$

- $((\nu s)M)|N \equiv (\nu s)(M|N)$ where s is not a free session channel of N.

The evolution of processes and networks via communication and other actions is given as a binary relation over networks, written $N \to M$. The operational semantics of EPC are given in Table 2. The first rule (INIT) initiates a communication session via the public service channel ch. Participants A and B share new freshly generated session channels $\tilde{s}$ through which they will communicate. These session channels are restricted to these two participants using the binding operator ν. The communication rule (COM) shows how a communication is established between two participants. When B invokes the operation op_j, which is one of the operations offered by A, then the local state σ_A of A evaluates the received expression e to value v and assigns it $(\sigma_A[x_j \mapsto v])$ to its local variable x_j, then behaves as described in P_j and B behaves as in Q. The symbol $\sigma_A \vdash e \Downarrow v$ is an evaluation judgment. It says that expression e is evaluated to value v at the local state σ_A. The assignment rule (ASSIGN) is a local operation, it evaluates an expression e to a value v and assigns v to the local variable x. (IFTRUE) and (IFFALSE) express a choice based on the evaluation of a boolean expression e. The recursion rule (REC) says that when we substitute each free X in P for $\mu X.P$, denoted by $P[\mu X.P/P]$, the process P evolves to P' then $\mu X.P$ evolves to P'. (STRUCT) says that we take the reductions up to the structural rule. The rest is standard.

Example. In the buyer-seller example, the choreography will be written using EPC as follows:

$$Seller[P]_{\sigma_P} \mid Buyer[Q]_{\sigma_Q} \mid Shipper[R]_{\sigma_R}$$

where

$P = !ch_S(s).\overline{s} \triangleleft ack\langle e\rangle.s \triangleright \underline{reqQ(x)}.\overline{s} \triangleleft resQ\langle e\rangle.(s \triangleright accQ(x).$
$\overline{s} \triangleleft order\langle e\rangle.s \triangleright conf(x).\overline{ch_{Sh}}(\nu s').s' \triangleright ack(x).\overline{s'} \triangleleft req\langle e\rangle.$
$s' \triangleright dd(x).\overline{s} \triangleleft dd\langle e\rangle.0 \ ) + (s \triangleright rejQ(x).0),$
$Q = \overline{ch_S}(\nu s).s \triangleright ack(x).\overline{s} \triangleleft reqQ\langle e\rangle.s \triangleright resQ(x).\text{if } v_Q < 1000$
then $\overline{s} \triangleleft accQ\langle e\rangle.s \triangleright order(x).\overline{s} \triangleleft conf\langle e\rangle.s \triangleright dd(x).0$ else
$\overline{s} \triangleleft rejQ\langle e\rangle.0$ and
$R = !ch_{Sh}(s').\overline{s'} \triangleleft ack\langle e\rangle.s' \triangleright req(x).\overline{s'} \triangleleft dd\langle e\rangle.0$

4 Security Policy Specification Language

The purpose of this section is to define a logic for the specification of security policies. It is recalled that the class of security properties that can be enforced dynamically are safety properties. Safety properties are properties that ensure that something bad will never happen during the execution of the choreography. Hence, to formally describe security properties, we define a new linear temporal logic from the class of regular languages called L_φ Logic.

In EPC, a process P located within a participant A can evolve into another process P' either by evaluating a boolean expression using *ifthenelse* rules or by executing one of the following atomic actions:

Table 2. Semantics of EPC.

$$\frac{}{A[!ch(\tilde{s}).P|P']_{\sigma_A} \mid B[\overline{ch}(\nu\tilde{s}).Q \mid Q']_{\sigma_B} \to (\nu\tilde{s})(A[!ch(\tilde{s}).P|P|P']_{\sigma_A} \mid B[Q|Q']_{\sigma_B})} \ (\text{INIT})$$

$$\frac{\sigma_A \vdash e\Downarrow v}{A[s\triangleright\Sigma_i op_i(x_i).P_i|P']_{\sigma_A} \mid B[\overline{s}\triangleleft op_j\langle e\rangle.Q|Q']_{\sigma_B} \to A[P_j|P']_{\sigma_A[x_j\mapsto v]} \mid B[Q|Q']_{\sigma_B}} \ (\text{COM})$$

$$\frac{\sigma_A \vdash e\Downarrow tt}{A[\text{if } e \text{ then } P \text{ else } Q|R]_{\sigma_A} \to A[P|R]_{\sigma_A}} \ (\text{IFTRUE}) \qquad \frac{\sigma_A \vdash e\Downarrow ff}{A[\text{if } e \text{ then } P \text{ else } Q|R]_{\sigma_A} \to A[Q|R]_{\sigma_A}} \ (\text{IFFALSE})$$

$$\frac{\sigma_A \vdash e\Downarrow v}{A[x:=e.P|P']_{\sigma_A} \to A[P|P']_{\sigma_A[x\mapsto v]}} \ (\text{ASSIGN}) \qquad \frac{A[P_1|P']_{\sigma_A} \to A[P_1'|P']_{\sigma_A'}}{A[P_1|P_2|P']_{\sigma_A} \to A[P_1'|P_2|P']_{\sigma_A'}} \ (\text{PAR})$$

$$\frac{A[P]_{\sigma_A} \to A[P']_{\sigma_A'}}{A[(\nu s)P]_{\sigma_A} \to A[(\nu s)P']_{\sigma_A'}} \ (\text{RES}) \qquad \frac{A[P_1|P']_{\sigma_A} \to A[P_1'|P']_{\sigma_A'}}{A[P_1\oplus P_2|P']_{\sigma_A} \to A[P_1'|P']_{\sigma_A'}} \ (\text{SUM})$$

$$\frac{A[P[\mu X.P/X]]_{\sigma_A} \to A[P']_{\sigma_A'}}{A[\mu X.P]_{\sigma_A} \to A[P']_{\sigma_A'}} \ (\text{REC}) \qquad \frac{M\to M'}{M|N\to M'|N} \ (\text{PAR-NET})$$

$$\frac{M\to M'}{(\nu s)M\to(\nu s)M'} \ (\text{RES-NET}) \qquad \frac{M\equiv M' \quad M'\to N' \quad N'\equiv N}{M\to N} \ (\text{STRUCT})$$

- $ch(\tilde{s})$ offers a new communication session through $\tilde{s}$.
- $\overline{ch}(\nu\tilde{s})$ invokes a new communication session through $\tilde{s}$.
- $\overline{s} \lhd op\langle e\rangle$ is an output interaction.
- $s \rhd op(x)$ is an input interaction.
- $x := e$ is an assignment.

Communication actions $(s \rhd op(x), \overline{s} \lhd op\langle e\rangle)$ are the type of actions that will be monitored during the execution of the choreography. These actions are identified by three parameters:

- the session channel s that is shared between exactly two participants,
- the operation op to be invoked,
- and the direction of the interaction. $s \rhd \ldots$ stands for an input interaction and $\overline{s} \lhd \ldots$ for an output.

We present hereafter the syntax and trace semantics of L_φ.

4.1 Syntax of L_φ

The syntax of the logic L_φ is presented by the BNF grammar in Table 3, where tt is the boolean constant *true*, 1 denotes an empty sequence of actions, $\vee$ is the disjunction operator, "." is the temporal operator, $\neg$ is the negation operator, s range over session channels, op range over operations, e range over expressions and finally $\varphi_1^* \varphi_2$ is the Kleene operator [13] that allows us to describe infinite properties. By this logic, we can perfectly express control access security properties. Indeed, the role of an L_φ formula is to prohibit the access to some operations offered by participants. However, information flow security properties can not be expressed using L_φ since there are no control on exchanged data. Indeed, we do not control what an operation, when invoked, should receive as data. The extension of L_φ for supporting information flow security policies is the topic of a future work. We show hereafter some examples of security properties written using the logic L_φ.

Table 3. Syntax of L_φ.

$$\varphi_1, \varphi_2 ::= tt \mid 1 \mid a \mid \varphi_1.\varphi_2 \mid \varphi_1 \vee \varphi_2 \mid \neg\varphi \mid \varphi_1^*\varphi_2$$
$$a \quad ::= \overline{s} \lhd op\langle e\rangle \mid s \rhd op(x)$$

Example. In the buyer-seller protocol, the seller should not send to the buyer the delivery details for his purchase until the seller gets confirmation. So, the security property will be enforced on the seller's process and will be written as follows:

$$\varphi = \neg(\overline{s} \lhd dd\langle e\rangle \vee s \rhd conf(x))^* s \rhd conf(x).tt$$

Table 4. Trace semantics of L_φ.

$$[\![tt]\!] = \mathcal{T}$$
$$[\![1]\!] = \{\epsilon\}$$
$$[\![a]\!] = \{a\}$$
$$[\![\varphi_1.\varphi_2]\!] = \{\xi_1.\xi_2 : \xi_1 \in [\![\varphi_1]\!] \ and \ \xi_2 \in [\![\varphi_2]\!]\}$$
$$[\![\varphi_1 \vee \varphi_2]\!] = [\![\varphi_1]\!] \cup [\![\varphi_2]\!]$$
$$[\![\varphi_1^*\varphi_2]\!] = \begin{cases} [\![\varphi_1]\!]^* \cup \{\xi_1.\xi_2|\xi_1 \in [\![\varphi_1]\!]^* and \ \xi_2 \in [\![\varphi_2]\!]\} \ If \ [\![\varphi_2]\!] \neq \emptyset \\ [\![\varphi_1]\!]^\omega \ elsewhere \end{cases}$$
$$[\![\neg\varphi]\!] = \mathcal{T} \backslash [\![\varphi]\!]$$

4.2   Semantics of L_φ

We denote by $\tilde{S}$ the set of all session channels used in a given choreography and op the set of all operations that can be invoked. The set of communication actions $\mathcal{A}$ is given formally by:

$$\mathcal{A} = \bigcup_{\substack{s \in \tilde{S} \\ op \in Op}} \overline{s} \triangleleft op\langle e \rangle \cup s \triangleright op(x).$$

Let $\mathcal{T}$ be the monoid $(\mathcal{A}, ., \epsilon)$ where ϵ denotes the empty trace. The trace semantics of L_φ are defined by the function $[\![\ ]\!] : L_\varphi \longmapsto \mathcal{T}$ as shown in Table 4. Intuitively, any trace respects the formula tt and only the empty trace ϵ respects the formula 1. Furthermore, traces that respect the formula $\varphi_1.\varphi_2$ are traces that have prefixes respecting φ_1 and suffixes respecting φ_2. Besides, only traces that respect φ_1 or φ_2 respect $\varphi_1 \vee \varphi_2$. For the Kleene operator, we say that a trace respects $\varphi_1^*\varphi_2$ if either it respects φ_2 or it has a prefix that respects φ_1 and a suffix that respects $\varphi_1^*\varphi_2$. Finally, a trace respects $\neg\varphi$ if it does not respect φ.

Example. The trace semantics of the security property of the buyer-seller example are:

$$[\![\neg(\overline{s} \triangleleft dd\langle e \rangle \vee s \triangleright conf(x))^* s \triangleright conf(x).tt]\!] = E^* \cup F$$

where
$E = \mathcal{T} \backslash \{\overline{s} \triangleleft dd\langle e \rangle, s \triangleright conf(x)\}$ and
$F = \{\xi_1.s \triangleright conf(x).\xi_2 : \xi_1 \in E^* \ and \ \xi_2 \in \mathcal{T}\}$.

4.3   Satisfaction Notion

Hereafter, we will define the satisfaction notion for formulas of L_φ. Intuitively, a trace ξ of communication actions of EPC may satisfy a formula φ of L_φ, denoted by $\xi \hspace{0.1em}\vdash\!\!\sim \varphi$, when this trace is a prefix of a trace that satisfies the formula. We formally define the satisfaction notion for traces by:

Definition 1 (Satisfaction Notion for Traces). Let φ be a formula of L_φ and ξ a trace in $\mathcal{T}$.

- We say that ξ satisfies the formula φ, denoted by $\xi \vDash \varphi$, iff $\xi \in [\![\varphi]\!]$.
- We say that a trace ξ prefix-satisfies the formula φ, denoted by $\xi \mathrel{\mkern-5mu\vdash\mkern-5mu\sim} \varphi$, iff there exists a trace ξ' such that $\xi.\xi' \vDash \varphi$.

Example. The trace
$$\xi = \overline{s} \lhd quoteResp\langle e\rangle.s \rhd conf(x).\overline{s} \lhd dd\langle e\rangle \mathrel{\mkern-5mu\vdash\mkern-5mu\sim} \varphi$$
where $\varphi = \neg(\overline{s} \lhd dd\langle e\rangle \vee s \rhd conf(x))^* s \rhd conf(x).tt$

5   Secured End-Point Calculus

The secured EPC, denoted by EPC^φ, is an extension of EPC in which we have added an enforcement operator responsible for the monitoring of the execution of a web service.

5.1   Syntax

$$\partial_\varphi^\xi(P)$$

In addition to the operators of EPC, the syntax of EPC^φ is extended by this operator. The enforcement operator takes as input a security policy, a process describing the behavior of a participant in a choreography and the environment ξ in which P evolves. It returns a secured version of the participant's behavior. The environment ξ saves the trace of communication actions that P has executed. Hence, the choreography will respect the security policy since each participant concerned by the security policy respects it. This new version behaves exactly like the original one and does not violate the enforced security policy.

5.2   Semantics

Before defining semantics of the operator $\partial_\varphi^\xi(P)$, we need first to define a simulation transition. Indeed, a participant can execute a communication action by synchronizing with an another participant. Since monitoring consists on intercepting each communication action before its execution, we need to simulate interactions locally without synchronization. We will first introduce a natural order over processes of EPC then we define the simulation transition.

Proposition (Normal form of a process). Every process P from EPC representing the local behavior of a participant can be written as a sum of processes, which we call the normal form of a process:

$$\forall P \in \mathcal{P}, \ P = \sum_{i \in I} a_i P_i$$

where $\mathcal{P}$ denotes the set of processes, a_i range over atomic actions and P_i range over processes in $\mathcal{P}$.

Proof. The normal form of processes P and Q are denoted by:

$$P = \sum_{i \in I} a_i.P_i, \qquad Q = \sum_{j \in J} b_j.Q_j.$$

We give hereafter an algorithm that determines the normal form of each process of EPC^Σ.

$$
\begin{aligned}
!ch(\tilde{s}).P &\rightarrow !ch(\tilde{s}).P \\
\overline{ch}(\nu\tilde{s}).P &\rightarrow \overline{ch}(\nu\tilde{s}).P \\
\overline{s} \lhd op\langle e\rangle.P &\rightarrow \overline{s} \lhd op\langle e\rangle.P \\
s \rhd \Sigma_i op_i(x_i).P_i &\rightarrow \Sigma_i s \rhd op_i(x_i).P_i \\
x := e.P &\rightarrow x := e.P \\
P \oplus Q &\rightarrow \sum_{i \in I} a_i.P_i + \sum_{j \in J} b_j.Q_j \\
P|Q &\rightarrow \sum_{i \in I} a_i.(P_i|Q) + \sum_{j \in J} b_j.(P|Q_j) \\
(\nu s)P &\rightarrow \sum_{i \in I} a_i.((\nu s)P_i) \\
\mu X.P &\rightarrow \sum_{i \in I} a_i.P_i[\mu X.P/X] \\
0 &\rightarrow 0
\end{aligned}
$$

The normal form of if e then P else Q is $\sum_{i \in I}(e \downarrow)a_i.P_i + \sum_{j \in J}(e \downarrow)b_j.Q_j$ where $(e \downarrow) = \begin{cases} tt \\ ff \end{cases}$, $ff.P = ff$ and $tt.P = P$.

Definition 2 (Simulation Transition). We define a simulation transition over processes, denoted by $P \stackrel{a}{\leadsto} P'$, which says that the process P is able to execute the action a and reduce to P'. The simulation relation is defined following this rule

$$\frac{P = \bigoplus_{i \in I} a_i P_i \quad \exists j \in I : a = a_j}{P \stackrel{a}{\leadsto} P_j}$$

This rule says that when P is written in its normal form and one of the constituting processes is prefixed by an action a then P is able to do it.

Semantics. Next, we will show how does our enforcement operator behave when applied to different processes of EPC. Reduction rules related to the enforcement operator are given in Table 5. Rules ∂-COMIN and ∂-COMOUT show how the enforcement operator controls the execution of communication actions. ∂-COMIN says that when a participant is able to receive an invocation of one of its offered operations op_i, and when this action prefixed with the trace already executed by this participant may satisfy the security property, then $A[\partial^\xi_\varphi(P)]$ executes it and becomes $A[\partial^{\xi.s \rhd op(x)}_\varphi(P')]$. ∂-COMOUT says that when a participant is able to invoke an operation op and this action, when prefixed with the trace already executed by this participant, satisfies the security property φ then $A[\partial^\xi_\varphi(P)]$ invokes it and evolves to $A[\partial^{\xi.\overline{s} \lhd op\langle e\rangle}_\varphi(P')]$. In the two cases, we do update the execution environment of P by concatenating the action executed with ξ.

Table 5. Semantics of EPC.

$$\frac{-}{A[\partial_\varphi^\xi(!ch(\tilde{s}).P)|P']_{\sigma_A}|B[\overline{ch}(\nu\tilde{s}).Q|R]_{\sigma_B}\to(\nu\tilde{s})(A[\partial_\varphi^\xi(P)|\partial_\varphi^\xi(!ch(\tilde{s}).P)|P']_{\sigma_A}|B[Q|R])}\ (\partial\text{-INITIN})$$

$$\frac{-}{A[\partial_\varphi^\xi(\overline{ch}(\nu\tilde{s}).P)|P']_{\sigma_A}|B[!ch(\tilde{s}).Q|R]_{\sigma_B}\to(\nu\tilde{s})(A[\partial_\varphi^\xi(P)|P']_{\sigma_A}|B[!ch(\tilde{s}).Q|R]_{\sigma_B})}\ (\partial\text{-INITOUT})$$

$$\frac{P\overset{s\triangleright op(x)}{\leadsto}P'\quad\xi.s\triangleright op(x)\models\varphi\quad\sigma_A\vdash e\Downarrow v}{A[\partial_\varphi^\xi(P)|P'']_{\sigma_A}|B[s\triangleleft op\langle e\rangle.Q|R]_{\sigma_B}\to A[\partial_\varphi^{\xi.s\triangleright op(x)}(P')|P'']_{\sigma_A[x\mapsto v]}|B[Q|R]_{\sigma_B}}\ (\partial\text{-COMIN})$$

$$\frac{P\overset{\tilde{s}\triangleleft op_j\langle e\rangle}{\leadsto}P'\quad\xi.\tilde{s}\triangleleft op_j\langle e\rangle\models\varphi\quad\sigma_B\vdash e\Downarrow v\quad j\in I}{A[\partial_\varphi^\xi(P)|P'']_{\sigma_A}|B[s\triangleright\underset{i\in I}{\Sigma}op_i(x_i).Q_i|R]_{\sigma_B}\to A[\partial_\varphi^{\xi.\tilde{s}\triangleleft op_j\langle e\rangle}(P')|P'']_{\sigma_A}|B[Q_j|R]_{\sigma_B[x_j\mapsto v]}}\ (\partial\text{-COMOUT})$$

$$\frac{\sigma\vdash e\Downarrow v}{A[\partial_\varphi^\xi(x:=e.P)|P']_\sigma\to A[\partial_\varphi^\xi(P)|P']_{\sigma[x\mapsto v]}}\ (\partial\text{-ASSIGN})\qquad\frac{A[\partial_\varphi^\xi(P_1)|R]_\sigma\to A[\partial_\varphi^{\xi'}(P_1')|R]_{\sigma'}}{A[\partial_\varphi^\xi(P_1|P_2)|R]_\sigma\to A[\partial_\varphi^{\xi'}(P_1'|P_2)|R]_{\sigma'}}\ (\partial\text{-PAR})$$

$$\frac{\sigma\vdash e\Downarrow tt}{A[\partial_\varphi^\xi(if\ e\ then\ P_1\ else\ P_2)|P]_\sigma\to A[\partial_\varphi^\xi(P_1)|P]_\sigma}\ (\partial\text{-IFTRUE})$$

$$\frac{\sigma\vdash e\Downarrow ff}{A[\partial_\varphi^\xi(if\ e\ then\ P_1\ else\ P_2)|P]_\sigma\to A[\partial_\varphi^\xi(P_2)|P]_\sigma}\ (\partial\text{-IFFALSE})$$

$$\frac{A[\partial_\varphi^\xi(P)]_\sigma\to A[\partial_\varphi^\xi(P')]_{\sigma'}}{A[(\nu\tilde{s})(\partial_\varphi^\xi(P))]_\sigma\to A[(\nu\tilde{s})(\partial_\varphi^\xi(P'))]_{\sigma'}}\ (\partial\text{-RES})\qquad\frac{A[\partial_\varphi^\xi(P_1)|P']_\sigma\to A[\partial_\varphi^{\xi'}(P_1')|P']_{\sigma'}}{A[\partial_\varphi^\xi(P_1\oplus P_2)|P']_\sigma\to A[\partial_\varphi^{\xi'}(P_1')|P']_{\sigma'}}\ (\partial\text{-SUM})$$

$$\frac{A[\partial_\varphi^\xi(P[\mu X.P/X])]_\sigma\to A[\partial_\varphi^{\xi'}(P')]_{\sigma'_A}}{A[\partial_\varphi^\xi(\mu X.P)]_{\sigma_A}\to A[\partial_\varphi^{\xi'}(P')]_{\sigma'}}\ (\partial\text{-REC})$$

Example. The secured choreography of the buyer-seller protocol is given by:

$$Seller[\partial_\varphi^\epsilon(P)]_{\sigma_S}\ |\ Buyer[Q]_{\sigma_B}\ |\ Shipper[R]_{\sigma_{Sh}}$$

where P, Q and R are respectively behaviors of the seller, the buyer and the shipper depicted in previous examples as well as the security policy φ. ϵ is the empty trace. In this example, the security policy is enforced on the seller's process. Indeed, the concerned participant by these security requirements is the seller. $\partial_\varphi^\epsilon(P)$ will not be able to send delivery details before receiving confirmation. We note that, in the beginning of a choreography, the environment ξ of the enforcement operator is empty since no communication action has already occurred.

6   Related Work

Formal verification of compositions of web services has been a subject of interest of several research efforts. Major contributions offer a security framework for orchestrated web services despite the lack of efforts spent in ensuring security of choreographed services, in particular dynamic verification of web service choreographies. The key novelty of the present work is the introduction of a formal dynamic verification of a choreography of web services. Some of the relevant contributions in ensuring secure web service compositions are cited in this section. Dumez et al. [14] proposed an approach for specifying, verifying and implementing composite services according to the principles of Model-Driven Architecture. They elaborate a specification model of the composition using business process modeling languages such as UML. Then, they translate the specification model into a formal specification using the LOTOS formal specification language. This formalization is then verified statically using the CADP toolset and implemented using BPEL. W. Tan et al. [15] have proposed an approach to analyze the compatibility of two services. They translated their BPEL descriptions into Colored Petri Net then checked statically if their composition violates the constraints imposed by either side. The previous cited approaches do not concern dynamic verification. They are static approaches for analyzing web services behaviors. D. Dranidis et al. [16] introduced an approach to verify the conformance of a web service implementation against a behavioral specification, through the application of testing. The Stream X-machines are used as an intuitive modeling formalism for constructing the behavioral specification of a stateful web service and a method for deriving test cases from that specification in an automated way. The test generation method produces complete sets of test cases that, under certain assumptions, are guaranteed to reveal all non-conformance faults in a service implementation under test. However, this approach only returns non-conformance faults and does not react dynamically against these errors. Moreover, L. Ardissono et al. [17] proposed a monitoring framework of a choreographed service that supports the early detection of faults and decides whether it is still possible to continue the service. However, authors do not use formal methods to prove the correctness of the proposed approach. R. Gay et al. [18] have proposed service automata as a framework for enforcing security policies in distributed systems. They encapsulate the program in a service automaton composed of the monitored program, an interceptor, an enforcer, a coordinator and a local policy. The interceptor intercepts critical actions and passes them to the coordinator. The latter determines whether the action complies the security policy or not and decides upon possible countermeasures. Then, the enforcer implements these decisions. However, authors do not precise how to detect critical actions. W. She et al. [19] have developed an innovative security-aware service composition protocol with composition-time information flow control that can reduce the execution-time failure rate of the composed composite services due to information flow control violations. This approach only guarantees that there are no access control violations at execution time but do not guarantee that there are not access control violations at runtime. Jose A. Martin et al. [20] developed a framework based on the partial model checking technique for statically verifying whether a composition of web services satisfies cryptographic properties such as secrecy and authenticity.

7   Conclusion and Future Work

In this paper, we have extended an existing calculus with an enforcement operator $\partial_\varphi^\xi(P)$ having the role of an IRM that mediates the execution of a choreography of web services by controlling the behavior of each involved participant. Hence, $\partial_\varphi^\xi(P)$ intercepts communication actions of P and verifies whether their execution adheres to security constraints defined by the formula φ. Future work consists on extending L_φ for supporting information flow control. It is intended also to optimize this security framework by making $\partial_\varphi^\xi(P)$ intercept only security-relevant communication actions.

References

1. Corporation, I.: Business process execution language for web services bpel-4ws (2002). http://www.ibm.com/developerworks/library/ws-bpel/
2. Kavantzas, N., Burdett, D., Ritzinger, G., Fletcher, T., Lafon, Y.: Web services choreography description language version 1.0. W3C Working Draft, December 2004
3. Morrisett, G., Walker, D., Crary, K., Glew, N.: From system f to typed assembly language. ACM Trans. Program. Lang. Syst. **21**(3), 527–568 (1999)
4. Necula, G.C.: Proof-carrying code. In: Proceedings of the 24th ACM SIGPLAN-SIGACT Symposium on Principles of Programming Languages. POPL '97, pp. 106–119. ACM, New York, NY, USA (1997)
5. Ligatti, J., Bauer, L., Walker, D.: Edit automata: enforcement mechanisms for run-time security policies. Int. J. Inf. Secur. **4**(1–2), 2–16 (2005)
6. Martinell, F., Matteucci, I.: Through modeling to synthesis of security automata. In: Proceedings of the Second International Workshop on Security and Trust Management (STM 2006). Electronic Notes in Theoretical Computer Science, vol. 179, pp. 31–46 (2007)
7. Erlingsson, Schneider, F.: Irm enforcement of java stack inspection. In: 2000 Proceedings of IEEE Symposium on Security and Privacy, 2000. S P 2000, pp. 246–255 (2000)
8. Carbone, M., Honda, K., Yoshida, N.: Theoretical aspects of communication-centred programming. Electr. Notes Theor. Comput. Sci. **209**, 125–133 (2008)
9. Milner, R., Parrow, J., Walker, D.: A calculus of mobile processes. I. Inf. Comput. **100**(1), 1–40 (1992)
10. Honda, K., Vasconcelos, V.T., Kubo, M.: Language primitives and type discipline for structured communication-based programming. In: Hankin, C. (ed.) ESOP 1998. LNCS, vol. 1381, pp. 122–138. Springer, Heidelberg (1998)
11. Hennessy, M., Riely, J.: Resource access control in systems of mobile agents. Electr. Notes Theor. Comput. Sci. **16**(3), 174–188 (1998)
12. Carbone, M., Nielsen, M., Sassone, V.: A calculus for trust management. In: Lodaya, K., Mahajan, M. (eds.) FSTTCS 2004. LNCS, vol. 3328, pp. 161–173. Springer, Heidelberg (2004)
13. Kozen, D.: Kleene algebra with tests. ACM Trans. Program. Lang. Syst. **19**(3), 427–443 (1997)
14. Dumez, C., Bakhouya, M., Gaber, J., Wack, M., Lorenz, P.: Model-driven approach supporting formal verification for web service composition protocols. J. Netw. Comput. Appl. **36**(4), 1102–1115 (2013)

15. Tan, W., Fan, Y., Zhou, M.: A petri net-based method for compatibility analysis and composition of web services in business process execution language. IEEE Trans. Autom. Sci. Eng. **6**(1), 94–106 (2009)
16. Dranidis, D., Ramollari, E., Kourtesis, D.: Run-time verification of behavioural conformance for conversational web services. In: ECOWS, pp. 139–147 (2009)
17. Ardissono, L., Furnari, R., Goy, A., Petrone, G., Segnan, M.: Monitoring choreographed services. In: Sobh, T. (ed.) Innovations and Advanced Techniques in Computer and Information Sciences and Engineering, pp. 283–288. Springer, Netherlands (2007)
18. Gay, R., Mantel, H., Sprick, B.: Service automata. In: Barthe, G., Datta, A., Etalle, S. (eds.) FAST 2011. LNCS, vol. 7140, pp. 148–163. Springer, Heidelberg (2012)
19. She, W., Yen, I., Thuraisingham, B.M., Bertino, E.: Security-aware service composition with fine-grained information flow control. IEEE Trans. Serv. Comput. **6**(3), 330–343 (2013)
20. Martín, J.A., Martinelli, F., Matteucci, I., Pimentel, E., Turuani, M.: On the synthesis of secure services composition. In: Heisel, M., Joosen, W., Lopez, J., Martinelli, F. (eds.) Engineering Secure Future Internet Services and Systems. LNCS, vol. 8431, pp. 140–159. Springer, Heidelberg (2014)

Efficient Unconditionally Secure Comparison and Privacy Preserving Machine Learning Classification Protocols

Bernardo David[1], Rafael Dowsley[2]([✉]), Raj Katti[3],
and Anderson C.A. Nascimento[3]

[1] Aarhus University, Aarhus, Denmark
bernardo@cs.au.dk
[2] Karlsruhe Institute of Technology, Karlsruhe, Germany
rafael.dowsley@kit.edu
[3] University of Washington Tacoma, Tacoma, USA
{rajkatti,andclay}@uw.edu

Abstract. We propose an efficient unconditionally secure protocol for privacy preserving comparison of ℓ-bit integers when both integers are shared between two semi-honest parties. Using our comparison protocol as a building block, we construct two-party generic private machine learning classifiers. In this scenario, one party holds an input while the other holds a model and they wish to classify the input according to the model without revealing their private information to each other. Our constructions are based on the setup assumption that there exists pre-distributed correlated randomness available to the computing parties, the so-called commodity-based model. The protocols are storage and computationally efficient, consisting only of additions and multiplications of integers.

Keywords: Secure comparison · Private machine learning · Unconditional security · Commodity based model

1 Introduction

We propose protocols for privacy preserving machine learning classification. Our protocols are information theoretically secure and work in the commodity-based cryptographic model [3,5], where a trusted center pre-distributes correlated randomness to Alice and Bob during a setup phase. The trusted initializer never knows the players's inputs, as the pre-distributed data is independent from the actual inputs to the protocol. Moreover, the trusted initializer never engages in

Bernardo David was supported by European Research Council Starting Grant 279447. The author acknowledges support from the Danish National Research Foundation and The National Science Foundation of China (under the grant 61061130540) for the Sino-Danish Center for the Theory of Interactive Computation, and also from the CFEM research centre (supported by the Danish Strategic Research Council) within which part of this work was performed.

© Springer International Publishing Switzerland 2015
M.-H. Au and A. Miyaji (Eds.): ProvSec 2015, LNCS 9451, pp. 354–367, 2015.
DOI: 10.1007/978-3-319-26059-4_20

the protocol execution after the setup phase. Our main technique is to reduce all the fundamental building blocks used in privacy preserving machine learning classification (a comparison protocol and a previously proposed protocol to compute the inner-product [23]) to protocols that can be efficiently computed in the commodity-based cryptography model. In the case a trusted initializer is not available or desirable, we sketch how to substitute the TI by a pre-processing phase where Alice and Bob engage in a protocol for emulating the trusted initializer behavior. The resulting protocol is computationally secure in this case.

Comparison Protocols. In a secure comparison protocol, Alice and Bob hold inputs x and y, respectively, and would like to know weather $y > x$ while leaking no information on their private inputs besides what is already leaked by the output itself. Given an active trusted third party, secure comparisons (or any other secure computation) are trivially implementable: Alice and Bob give their inputs to the trusted third party who computes the desired function of the inputs and announces the result. In cryptography, we are interested in emulating this *ideal* protocol without a trusted third party actively engaging and computing with Alice and Bob. Computing secure comparisons finds diverse applications, such as solving the classic Millionaires Problem [44], implementing secure auctions [18], computing the median [1] and solving minimum spanning tree and a variant of shortest paths [12]. In this work, we are interested in applying secure comparisons to perform privacy preserving machine learning [11,13,34].

Private Machine Learning Classification. We use our secure comparison computations to provide protocols for private machine learning classification. Supervised machine learning algorithms usually have two phases: training and classification. We focus on the privacy issues that arise during the classification phase [11,28]. In this phase, Alice holds an input vector v that represents, for example, her personal health records. Bob (a health care provider) holds a classifier C and a model w so that $C(w, v)$ represents, for example, Alice's estimated health care related expenses for the current year. For obvious reasons, Alice does not want to reveal her complete personal health records to Bob, while Bob worries that knowledge about the model might reveal something about the training dataset used to obtain w (e.g., previously stored personal health records).

Commodity Based Cryptography. We obtain our results based on the existence of pre-distributed correlated data to Alice and Bob, the so-called commodity-based model. This model was introduced by Beaver [3,5] and is inspired by the client-server distributed computation model. It is an alternative for obtaining efficient secure multi-party computation. In this model a trusted initializer (TI) distributes values (i.e., the commodities) to the parties before the start of the protocol execution (possibly long before the inputs are known), requiring no subsequent communication. The values are correlated and distributed according to a joint probability distribution. Since complex operations can be delegated to the TI (the parties need only to de-randomize the pre-distributed computations to match the actual inputs which are not known to the TI), it is possible to obtain very efficient protocols in this model. In cases where the presence of a trusted initializer is undesirable (or infeasible), it can be substituted by a secure two-party computation protocol that generates the necessary correlated randomness. For example, there are a number of known approaches [20–22,36] for generating multiplicative triples that are used for performing secure multiplication [4].

1.1 Related Works

Clearly, assumptions are needed in order to perform secure comparisons. Computationally secure protocols assume, for example, that adversaries are computationally bounded and that some specific cryptographic related computational problems are intractable. Most of the previously proposed protocols for secure comparison are computationally secure. Secure comparison protocols in the plain model (without assuming correlated randomness) have been implemented using Yao's garbled circuits [31], using encryption of bits as quadratic and non-quadratic residues modulo an RSA modulus [25], homomorphic encryption [18,19,26,30], and other adhoc techniques [7,8]. In all of these protocols modular exponentiations, public key operations or computations of comparable complexity are required.

Information-theoretically secure (or unconditionally secure) protocols do not make any assumptions whatsoever on the computing power of an adversary. In the plain model (without correlated randomness or other setup assumptions) it is necessary to consider the multiparty setting with an honest majority in order to build unconditionally secure protocols. In this setting, a secure comparison protocol with $O(\log(\ell))$ rounds (for ℓ bit values) was introduced in [10]. A constant round protocol requiring $O(\ell log(\ell))$ secure multiplications was introduced in [17]. An improvement of this protocol requiring $O(\ell \log^*(\ell))$ secure multiplications (where $\log^*$ is the iterated logarithm) was introduced by Toft [39]. Since this protocol information-theoretically reduces the task of secure comparison to that of secure multiplication, instantiating it with a suitable secure multiplication protocol [4] yields unconditionally secure comparisons in the commodity based cryptography model.

In [11], protocols for computing $C(w,v)$ privately for the case of some general classifiers were proposed. These protocols are computationally secure and require many modular exponentiations. In [28] computationally secure privacy preserving procedures for both training and classification phases are constructed from somewhat homomorphic encryption (SHE). The SHE scheme proposed by the authors incurs in high computational and communication overheads, requiring expensive operations (*e.g.* modular exponentiations) and that ciphertexts grow with the number of multiplications performed.

Many protocols were designed in the commodity based cryptography model for functionalities such as commitments [9,32,38], oblivious transfer [2,3], distributed inner product [23], verifiable secret sharing [24,33], proximity testing [40] and oblivious polynomial evaluation [41]. For recent and fundamental results on the power of pre-distributed correlated randomness, see [29].

1.2 Our Contributions

In this paper we propose a new two-party unconditionally secure comparison protocol in the commodity based cryptography model. Our protocol is computationally efficient requiring solely a linear number of additions and multiplications of integers. On the other hand, most previous protocols for secure comparison [7,8,18,19,25,26,31] require computationally expensive operations (*e.g.* modular exponentiations) and only achieve computational security. As in previous approaches that achieve unconditional security and comparable efficiency (requiring solely additions and multiplications of integers) [17,39], we use an underlying protocol for secure multiplications [4]. However, while the protocol of [39] requires $O(\ell \log^*(\ell))$ calls to the secure multiplications protocol, our protocol requires exactly $O(\ell)$ calls. Moreover, our approach requires multiplications and additions modulo a prime $q > 2^{\ell+2}$ achieving low storage and communication overheads, whereas in [18] 1024-bit prime moduli are required in order to guarantee the security of the underlying homomorphic cryptosystem.

Additionally, we also propose new, efficient and unconditionally secure protocols for private machine learning classification [11] based on our secure comparison protocol. Here, we show that, in the commodity-based model, we can obtain very efficient protocols for two general classifiers: (i) hyperplane decision and (ii) Naïve Bayes classifiers. Our protocols are computationally efficient (requiring solely additions and multiplications of integers) and also efficient in terms of the amount of data that has to be pre-distributed. On the other hand, previous results [11,28] require computationally expensive operations (*e.g.* modular exponentiations) and incur in higher communication overhead.

We also point out that the trusted initializer can be replaced by a secure two-party computation protocol (though at the cost of unconditional security, since such protocols require computational assumptions). Most of the correlated randomness needed in our protocols is used by the underlying multiplicaiton protocol [4] and consists of multiplicative triples, which can be generated through known protocols [22,36]. Notice that the techniques used for computing multiplicative triples can also be directly used for computing correlated randomness required by the vector inner product protocol used in the classifiers [23]. The remaining correlated data is of the form $z \in \mathbb{Z}_q^*, r \in \mathbb{Z}_q, z_A = r, z_B = z - r$, which can be trivially computed with an additively homomorphic encryption scheme, *e.g.* Paillier [35]. We outline the techniques for substituting the trusted initializer in our protocols but leave a full description, security proof and performance analysis as a future work.

Security Model. Our proposed protocols are sequentially composable in the simulation based definition by Canetti's [14] assuming honest-but-curious behavior. Honest-but-curious behavior is assumed in most of the previous results in secure comparisons and private machine learning. In the full version of this paper we show that our comparison protocol can be simply enhanced in order to achieve security in the stronger framework of universal composability [15].

2   Commodity Based Cryptography

In the commodity based cryptography [2,3] model a trusted initializer (TI) distributes values (i.e., correlated randomness which are the commodities) to the parties before the start of the protocol execution, possibly long before the inputs are known. This pre-distributed data can be obtained in many different settings: (1) it can pre-distributed by a single trusted center that is active during a setup phase. Alice and Bob contact the trusted center during a setup phase, receive their correlated data and no further communication is necessary between Alice and Bob and the center. Note that the center does not engage in the execution of the protocol itself nor is aware of Alice and Bob's input; (2) it can be pre-distributed by many centers that do not interact with each other. A secure protocol is possible if a majority of the servers is honest [3,5]; (3) it can be pre-computed by players that do communicate through private channels with each other and emulate a trusted center by running a general MPC protocol (given that a majority of them is honest and a broadcast channel is available).

The TI has no access to the parties' secret inputs and does not communicate with the parties except for delivering the pre-distributed values during the setup. One main advantage of this model is the already mentioned high computational efficiency that arises from the fact that the parties only need to derandomize the pre-computed instances to match their own inputs. Another advantage is the fact that since the computations are pre-distributed by a trusted initializer, most protocols yield perfect security. In this work we model the trusted initializer as an ideal functionality that generates the correlated randomness that is distributed to the parties.

Beaver [4] proposed a very efficient protocol for secure distributed (modular) multiplication in the commodity-based model which will be used as a building block in this work. The protocol description is omitted due to the lack of space, see the references for details.

Eliminating the Trusted Initializer. In this multiplication protocol, the trusted initializer can be substituted by a two-party protocol that computes the required multiplicative triples (t, a_A, b_A) for A and $(a_B, b_B, I = (a_A b_B + a_B b_A - t))$ for B. Since generating this specific correlated data finds several applications, it is a well studied problem. Well known protocols for general purpose multiparty computation [20,21] introduced a pre-processing phase protocol where multiplication triples are generated using additively homomorphic encryption schemes (*e.g.* Paillier [35]), which can be adapted to the two-party case as described in [36]. A different approach builds on oblivious transfer to perform the necessary secure multiplications [27]. Recent implementation results [22,36] show that both techniques achieve good performance. In particular, [22] shows that an OT based protocol requires only tens of milliseconds per triple. However, we remark that using such protocols for computing correlated randomness implies the loss of unconditional security guarantees, since they are based on computational assumptions. Comprehensive surveys of different methods for generating multiplicative triples and their concrete efficiency can be found in [22,36].

3   Secure Distributed Comparison Protocol

Using the protocol for secure distributed multiplication presented in [4] as a sub-protocol we build our secure distributed comparison protocol. It implements the distributed comparison functionality $\mathcal{F}_{DC}^{\mathcal{R}}$, which takes the ℓ-bit integers x, y to be compared in form of shares, reconstruct them from the shares, performs the comparison and then distributes shares of zero (in the field $\mathbb{Z}_q$) if $y > x$ and shares of an uniformly random $w \in \mathbb{Z}_q^*$ if $y \leq x$. More specifically, upon receiving A's shares of the inputs, x_A, y_A, and B's shares of the inputs, x_B, y_B, $\mathcal{F}_{DC}^{\mathcal{R}}$ proceeds as follows: (1) runs the algorithm $\mathcal{R}$ to reconstruct the inputs x and y from the shares x_A, y_A, x_B, y_B; (2) picks a random $r \in \mathbb{Z}_q$ and sends it to A; (3) if $y > x$, sends $-r \mod q$ to B; (4) if $y \leq x$, picks a random $w \in \mathbb{Z}_q^*$ and sends $w - r \mod q$ to B.

The protocol that implements it follows the lines of Damgård, Geisler and Krøigaard [18], which is one of the most efficient known solutions for the secure comparison problem. But due to our usage of pre-distributed, correlated randomness it is possible to eliminate the use of (homomorphic) encryption and the computation of the XOR of the shared inputs bits, which are both computationally intensive steps.

Let the ℓ-bit integers being compared be $x = (x_\ell, \ldots, x_1)$ and $y = (y_\ell, \ldots, y_1)$. Let q be a prime such that $q > 2^{\ell+2}$ (all operations are modulo q). The parties A and B have additive shares of each bit of x and y. A has $x_A = (x_{\ell A}, \ldots, x_{1A})$ and $y_A = (y_{\ell A}, \ldots, y_{1A})$ and B has $x_B = (x_{\ell B}, \ldots, x_{1B})$ and $y_B = (y_{\ell B}, \ldots, y_{1B})$ such that $x_{iA}, x_{iB}, y_{iA}, y_{iB} \in \mathbb{Z}_q$, $x_i, y_i \in \{0,1\}$, $x_i = x_{iA} + x_{iB} \mod q$ and $y_i = y_{iA} + y_{iB} \mod q$. We write $[y_i]$ to denote the shares of y_i, i.e., y_{iA} and y_{iB} such that $y_i = y_{iA} + y_{iB} \mod q$. The distributed comparison protocol uses these shares and proceeds as follows:

1. The trusted initializer chooses uniformly random $z \in \mathbb{Z}_q^*$ and $r \in \mathbb{Z}_q$ and distributes the shares $z_A = r$ to A and $z_B = z - r$ to B. It also pre-distributes the correlated randomness necessary for the execution of ℓ instances of the distributed multiplication protocol.
2. For $i = 1, \ldots, \ell$, A and B locally compute shares $[d_i]$ where $d_i = x_i - y_i$, i.e., A computes $d_{iA} = x_{iA} - y_{iA} \mod q$ and B computes $d_{iB} = x_{iB} - y_{iB} \mod q$. Note that $d_i \in \{0, 1, -1\}$.
3. For $i = 1, \ldots, \ell$, A and B locally compute shares $[c_i]$ where $c_i = x_i - y_i + 1 + \sum_{j=i+1}^{\ell} d_j 2^{\ell-j+2}$ (the shares of 1 are fixed a priori, lets say A's share is 1 and B's is 0). Let the shares of c_i that A has be $c_A = (c_{\ell A}, \ldots, c_{1A})$ and those of B be $c_B = (c_{\ell B}, \ldots, c_{1B})$.
4. A and B use ℓ times the distributed multiplication protocol in order to compute shares of $w = z \prod_{i=1}^{\ell} c_i$. Let the final shares be w_A and w_B, such that $w = (w_A + w_B) \mod q$. A outputs w_A and Bob outputs w_B.

Note that if one of the parties, lets say A, is supposed to learn the result of the comparison, this can be easily accomplished by having B sending his share w_B to A, who can then reconstruct w and test whether $w = 0 \mod q$ and so $y > x$ or $w \neq 0 \mod q$ and so $y \leq x$.

Theorem 1. *Let q be a prime such that $q > 2^{\ell+2}$ and let $\mathcal{R}$ be the recovering algorithm that takes the additives shares modulo q of each bit x_i of x and y_i of y and returns x and y. The distributed comparison protocol is correct and securely implements the distributed comparison functionality $\mathcal{F}_{DC}^{\mathcal{R}}$ against honest but curious adversaries in the commodity based model.*

Proof. **Correctness:** We have that $y > x$ if and only if there exists i such that all the bits $(x_\ell, \dots, x_{i+1})$ are identical to the bits $(y_\ell, \dots, y_{i+1})$ and $x_i - y_i + 1 = 0$. Equivalently, $y > x$ if and only if there exists i such that all $d_\ell = \dots = d_{i+1} = 0$ and $d_i + 1 = 0$. We first prove the following useful lemmas.

Lemma 2. *Let $S_i = \sum_{j=i+1}^{\ell} d_j 2^{\ell-j+2}$, where $d_j \in \{0, 1, -1\}$. If $d_\ell = \dots = d_{i+1} = 0$, then $S_i = 0$; otherwise $S_i \notin \{-3, -2, -1, 0, 1, 2, 3\}$ modulo q.*

Proof. If all $d_\ell = \dots = d_{i+1} = 0$ then it follows trivially that $S_i = 0$. Now we show that if $S_i \in \{-3, -2, -1, 0, 1, 2, 3\}$ modulo q then all $d_\ell = \dots = d_{i+1} = 0$. Suppose that there are some d_j which are not 0 and let $k \in \{i+1, \dots, \ell\}$ be smallest value such that $d_k \in \{1, -1\}$. Since the operations are modulo $q > 2^{\ell+2}$, the sum of the powers $\sum_{j=k+1}^{\ell} 2^{\ell-j+2} \le 2^{\ell-k+2} - 4$ and the power of 2 associated with d_k is $2^{\ell-k+2} \le 2^{\ell+1}$, it follows that $S_i \notin \{-3, -2, -1, 0, 1, 2, 3\}$ modulo q if d_k is non-zero. Therefore all $d_\ell = \dots = d_{i+1} = 0$ if $S_i \in \{-3, -2, -1, 0, 1, 2, 3\}$ modulo q.

Lemma 3. *For any $i \in \{1, \dots, \ell\}$, $c_i = 0$ if and only if $d_\ell = \dots = d_{i+1} = 0$ and $d_i + 1 = 0$.*

Proof. It is trivial that if $d_\ell = \dots = d_{i+1} = 0$ and $d_i + 1 = 0$, then $c_i = 0$, so lets prove the other direction. Since $d_i \in \{0, 1, -1\}$, it implies that $d_i + 1 \in \{0, 1, 2\}$. But by Lemma 2, $S_i = \sum_{j=i+1}^{\ell} d_j 2^{\ell-j+2}$ is such that $S_i \in \{-3, -2, -1, 0, 1, 2, 3\}$ modulo q only if $d_\ell = \dots = d_{i+1} = 0$, which imply that $c_i = d_i + 1 + S_i$ will be different from zero if $d_i + 1 \ne 0$ or any $d_\ell, \dots, d_{i+1}$ is different from 0.

Hence we have that $y > x$ if and only if there exists i such that $c_i = 0$. Since z is uniformly random in $\mathbb{Z}_q^*$ and $w = z \prod_{i=1}^{\ell} c_i \mod q$, we have that $w = 0$ if and only if there exists i such that $c_i = 0$; otherwise it is uniformly distributed in $\mathbb{Z}_q^*$. And thus the correctness of the protocol is proved.

Security: Note that the first and second steps of the protocol do not require message exchanging (the shares of the constant 1 in the second step can be fixed a priori). So the only messages exchanged are those for the execution of the distributed multiplication protocol and therefore the real protocol transcript can be perfectly simulated as explained in [4].

Note that even if one of the parties, lets say A, is supposed to learn the result of the comparison and so B sends w_B to A as a last step, this does not affect the security of the protocol since this last message can also be perfectly simulated by a simulator that only learns A's inputs and outputs. This is due to the fact that either $y > x$ and so some $c_i = 0$, $w = 0 \mod q$ and $w_B = -w_A \mod q$ or $y \le x$ and so all $c_i \ne 0 \mod q$ and w is uniformly random in $\mathbb{Z}_q^*$ since z is uniformly distributed in $\mathbb{Z}_q^*$.

4   Argmin and Argmax

Suppose that the parties A and B have shares of a tuple of values $(v_1, \ldots, v_k)$ and they want to learn the value $m \in \{1, \ldots, k\}$ such that $v_m \leq v_i$ for all $i \in \{1, \ldots, k\}$, but no party should learn any v_i or the relative order between the elements. I.e., the parties just want to learn $m = \mathrm{argmin}_{i \in \{1,\ldots,k\}} v_i$. Using our protocol for secure distributed comparison it is possible to give a practical, secure solution for this problem. The main idea is that for such m we have that $v_m \leq v_i$ for all other v_i. Hence if we compare v_m with each v_i using our distributed comparison protocol with v_m playing the role of y and v_i in the role of x, then all the output values that are shared between A and B will be uniformly random in $\mathbb{Z}_q^*$, so the product of them all is also uniformly random in $\mathbb{Z}_q^*$. On the other hand, for any j, if there is some i such that $v_j > v_i$, then the result of comparing v_j playing the role of y with v_i in the role of x will be 0, and so the product of the outputs is also 0.

The argmin functionality $\mathcal{F}_{\mathrm{argmin}}^{\mathcal{R}}$ is parametrized by the size q of the field in which the operations are done, the bit-length ℓ of the values being compared and the algorithm $\mathcal{R}$ that reconstructs the inputs from the shares. Upon receiving A's inputs shares, $(v_{1A}, \ldots, v_{kA})$, and B's inputs shares, $(v_{1B}, \ldots, v_{kB})$, $\mathcal{F}_{\mathrm{argmin}}^{\mathcal{R}}$ proceeds as follows: (1) runs $\mathcal{R}$ to reconstruct the inputs $(v_1, \ldots, v_k)$ from the shares; (2) computes $m = \mathrm{argmin}_{i \in \{1,\ldots,k\}} v_i$; (3) sends m to A.

The argmin protocol works as follows. Let ℓ be the bit length of the values v_i and let q be a prime such that $q > 2^{\ell+2}$. All operations are modulo q. The trusted initializer pre-distributes all the correlated randomness necessary for the execution of the instances of the distributed multiplication protocol and of the distributed comparison protocol (with the same field size q). A has shares of the inputs $(v_{1A}, \ldots, v_{kA})$ and B also has shares of the inputs $(v_{1B}, \ldots, v_{kB})$. For $j = 1, \ldots, k$, the protocol then proceeds as follows:

1. For all $i \in \{1, \ldots, k\} \setminus j$, A and B execute the distributed comparison protocol with inputs v_j in the role of y and v_i in the role of x. Let w_i denote the shared output obtained by A and B.
2. A and B use $k - 2$ times the distributed multiplication protocol in order to compute shares of $w = \prod_{i \in \{1,\ldots,k\} \setminus j} w_i$. Let the final shares be w_A and w_B. B sends his share w_B to A.
3. A recovers $w = (w_A + w_B) \bmod q$. If $w \neq 0 \bmod q$, append j to the value to be output by A in the end.

Theorem 4. *Let q be a prime such that $q > 2^{\ell+2}$ and let $\mathcal{R}$ be the recovering algorithm that takes the additives shares modulo q of each bit of v_i and returns v_i. The* argmin *protocol is correct and securely implements the* argmin *functionality $\mathcal{F}_{\mathrm{argmin}}^{\mathcal{R}}$ against honest but curious adversaries in the commodity based model.*

Proof. **Correctness:** Let m be a value such that $v_m \leq v_i$ for all $i \in \{1, \ldots, k\} \setminus m$. Each comparison of v_m playing the role of y and v_i ($i \in \{1, \ldots, k\} \setminus m$) in the role of x will result in a shared output value w_i which is uniformly random in $\mathbb{Z}_q^*$, and so $w = \prod_{i \in \{1,\ldots,k\} \setminus j} w_i$ is also uniformly random in $\mathbb{Z}_q^*$ and m is appended to A's output. On the other hand, for any j such that there is some i with $v_j > v_i$, the result of comparing v_j playing the role of y with v_i in the role of x will be 0, and so the product of the outputs is also 0 and j is not appended to A's output.

Security: As explained in the previous sections the messages involved in the distributed comparison and the distributed multiplication protocols can be straightforwardly and perfectly simulated by the simulator. The share sent in the third step only reveal 1 bit of information, either $w = 0$ if the value is not the argmin or w is completely random in $\mathbb{Z}_q^*$ if the value is the argmin. This can be trivially simulated given the output of the argmin functionality.

The complementary problem is to compute the value $m = \mathrm{argmax}_{i \in \{1,\dots,k\}} v_i$. From the secure argmin protocol it is trivial to obtain a secure argmax protocol by simply running the argmin protocol with inputs $(2^\ell - 1 - v_1, \dots, 2^\ell - 1 - v_k)$.

5   Applications

Practical secure protocols for distributively computing the comparison have many applications such as: auctions, private machine learning classifiers, benchmarking and secure extraction of statistical data from databases. In this section, we show that our previously proposed protocol for comparison can be used directly to obtain secure auctions and that our protocol for secure computing the argmax function can be used to obtain private machine learning classifiers.

5.1   Auctions

As already mentioned by Damgård et al. [18] a secure comparison protocol can be used to execute an auction protocol in which no party learns the value of the highest bid until the auction is finished. Lets say that A is the auction house and B is the accounting company. A and B hold shares of the biggest bid x done so far, x_A and x_B respectively. Now if a new participant wants to bid y, he creates shares y_A and y_B of his bid and send them to A and B respectively. Then A and B can compare the bids without discovering their values. This is particularly useful in the scenario of online auctions where the participants can submit a maximum bid to the system, which will them automatically bid for the participant until it wins the bid with the minimum possible bid or its maximum bid is achieved. Notice that the knowledge of the maximum bid in such case should be kept confidential from the other participants and from the auction house since they could otherwise exploit such knowledge. Using the secure comparison protocol A and B can keep track of both the highest bid so far, x, and the maximum bid y that was still not achieved (there is either none or one such value) without either A or B learning x or y. Then when a new bid z arrives, they can securely compare z to y and to x in order to update the values of the highest bid and of the maximum bid not yet achieved.

5.2   Private Machine Learning

In machine learning the supervised learning algorithms should given an input v output a guess of what class $c \in \{1, \ldots, k\}$ it belongs to. They are divided in two phases: the training and the classification. In the training phase, given labeled samples (i.e., inputs and the corresponding classes) the algorithm learns a model w. Then in the classification phase, the algorithm takes the model w and an input v and should output the guess c of which class v belongs to. Here we focus on obtaining privacy-preserving classifiers.

Imagine for instance the scenario where a health care provider has a model w to predict the occurrence of certain diseases which was built using the medical profile of several persons and a patient wants to obtain the prediction $C(w, v)$ of what diseases he is likely to have given his medical profile v. On one hand, the model w can leak sensitive information about the medical profile of the patients whose medical profiles were used as labeled samples, and therefore should be kept confidential (this can even be required by law depending on the jurisdiction). On the other hand, the patient does not want do reveal his sensitive medical profile v. Hence the patient and the health care provider should ideally be able to interact in a protocol in which the patient learns $C(w, v)$ in the end, but nothing else; while the health care provider does not learn anything.

As pointed out by Bost et al. [11], the core building blocks for designing many private classifiers are secure comparison, argmax and inner product protocols. In this paper we developed practical, unconditionally secure solutions for computing the comparison and the argmax with a trusted initializer. A practical and unconditionally secure inner product protocol with a trusted initializer was already presented by Dowsley et al. [23], so combining these protocols (and making the necessary conversions to the bit-wise shares) we are able to obtain practical private classifiers. One example of a classifier which is used in many learning algorithms is the hyperplane decision classifier. In this classifier the model w consists of k vectors $w_1, \ldots, w_k$ and the classification of the input v is done by computing

$$C(w, v) = \arg\max_{i \in \{1, \ldots, k\}} \langle v, w_i \rangle.$$

This can be straightforwardly implemented using the inner product protocol from Dowsley et al. [23] (which shares the result between the parties), a conversion to bit-wise shares (techniques from [43] or [39] can be used) and our argmax protocol. Another classifier that can be implemented in a privacy-preserving way using these building blocks is the Naïve Bayes classifier. In this classifier the model consists of the probability that each class c_i, $\{p(C = c_i)\}_{i=1}^{k}$, happens and the probability that each element v_j of the input v happens in a certain class c_i. The classification using a maximum a posteriori decision rule is computed as

$$C(w, v) = \arg\max_{i \in \{1, \ldots, k\}} \left\{ \log p(C = c_i) + \sum_j \log p(V_j = v_j | C = c_i) \right\}.$$

Note that our protocols work with integers, so we first need to convert the log of the probabilities to integers by multiplying by a large number T. For details about this issue please refer to [11,42]. The converted value of $\log p(C = c_i)$ can be shared by the model owner. To produce shares of $\log p(V_j = v_j | C = c_i)$ without revealing v_j to the model owner, the parties, for each possible value v_k in the domain of V_j, compute a distributed multiplication of the converted value of $\log p(V_j = v_k | C = c_i)$ (with the shares distributed by the model owner) and either 0 if $v_k \neq v_j$ or 1 if $v_k = v_j$ (the shares of this second number to be multiplied are distributed by the user). The shared results of these multiplications are then added to produce the shares of the converted value of $\log p(V_j = v_j | C = c_i) = 1 \log p(V_j = v_j | C = c_i) + \sum_{k \neq j} 0 p(V_j = v_k | C = c_i)$ without revealing v_j. From there the remaining additions can be done locally by the parties and then the argmax protocol is used to generate the output.

Eliminating the Trusted Initializer. In order to substitute the trusted initializer in our private classifiers, we need to construct secure two party protocols that generate the correlated randomness for both the vector inner product protocol [23] and the comparison protocol of Sect. 3. As we have pointed out in Sect. 2, there exist a number of highly efficient methods [22,36] for generating the correlated data used by the underlying multiplication protocol [4]. The same techniques can be applied in a straightforward way to generate the correlated randomness used in the vector inner product protocol [23].

The only remaining data that must be generated is $z \in \mathbb{Z}_q^*, r \in \mathbb{Z}_q, z_A = r, z_B = z - r$, which is used by the comparison protocol. These values can be trivially computed using an additively homomorphic cryptosystem such as the one by Paillier [35]. Let such cryptosystem be described by the following algorithms: Key Generation $\mathsf{Gen}(1^\lambda) \to (sk, pk)$, Encryption $Enc(pk, m) \to c$ and Decryption $Dec(sk, c) \to m$, with $m_1 + m_2 = Dec(sk, c_1 \cdot c_2)$ for $c_1 = Enc(pk, m_1)$ and $c_2 = Enc(pk, m_2)$. To generate z_A, z_B, B runs $\mathsf{Gen}(1^\lambda) \to (sk, pk)$, uniformly samples $z_1 \in \mathbb{Z}_q^*$ and sends $(pk, \hat{z}_1 = Enc(pk, z_1))$ to A. A uniformly samples $z_2 \in \mathbb{Z}_q^*, r \in \mathbb{Z}_q$, computes $\hat{z}_2 = Enc(pk, z_2), \hat{r} = Enc(pk, r), \hat{z} = \hat{z}_1 \cdot \hat{z}_2$, sends $\hat{z}_B = \hat{z} \cdot \hat{r}^{-1}$ to B and sets $z_A = r$. B decrypts $\hat{z}_B$ and sets $z_B = Dec(sk, \hat{z}_B)$. This protocol's security follows from the IND-CPA security of Paillier's cryptosystem.

Notice that the efficiency of both the multiplication protocol of [4] and the protocols introduced in this paper is independent from the efficiency of the trusted initializer, since the correlated randomness provided by it can be precomputed independently from our protocol execution. In fact, the trusted initializer (or a substitute two-party protocol) can compute the necessary correlated randomness at any given time before the actual protocol inputs are known. Hence, a large amount of correlated randomness can be pre-computed and stored for future protocol executions.

As we remarked before, such two-party protocols for generating correlated randomness require computational assumptions. In fact, it is well known that any two-party protocol that computes multiplications cannot achieve unconditional security in the plain model (*i.e.* without setup assumptions) [6,16,37]. Hence, substituting the trusted initializer implies the loss of unconditional security guarantees. We leave a full description, security proof and performance analysis of protocols for substituting the trusted initializer as a future work.

6   Conclusion

In this paper we proposed an unconditionally secure protocol for secure comparison of integers. We also proposed protocols for computing the *argmin* and *argmax* functions and show how they can be used to obtain generic private machine learning algorithms, namely the hyperplane based and Naïve Bayes classifiers. We proved that our protocols are secure against honest-but-curious adversaries. Our protocols are very efficient from a storage and computational point of view. In many real-world scenarios it does make sense to assume the existence of trusted initializers. Therefore, we see commodity-based cryptography as a realistic model for obtaining efficient secure computation protocols. On the other hand, we also outline alternatives to the trusted initializer for situations where its existence might be considered an issue.

References

1. Aggarwal, G., Mishra, N., Pinkas, B.: Secure computation of the kth-ranked element. In: Cachin, C., Camenisch, J.L. (eds.) EUROCRYPT 2004. LNCS, vol. 3027, pp. 40–55. Springer, Heidelberg (2004)
2. Beaver, D.: Precomputing oblivious transfer. In: Coppersmith, D. (ed.) CRYPTO 1995. LNCS, vol. 963, pp. 97–109. Springer, Heidelberg (1995)
3. Beaver, D.: Commodity-based cryptography (extended abstract). In: 29th ACM STOC, pp. 446–455. ACM Press (1997)
4. Beaver, D.: One-time tables for two-party computation. In: Hsu, W.-L., Kao, M.-Y. (eds.) COCOON 1998. LNCS, vol. 1449, pp. 361–370. Springer, Heidelberg (1998)
5. Beaver, D.: Server-assisted cryptography. In: NSPW 1998, pp. 92–106. ACM, New York (1998)
6. Ben-Or, M., Goldwasser, S., Wigderson, A.: Completeness theorems for non-cryptographic fault-tolerant distributed computation (extended abstract). In: 20th ACM STOC, pp. 1–10. ACM Press (1988)
7. Blake, I.F., Kolesnikov, V.: Strong conditional oblivious transfer and computing on intervals. In: Lee, P.J. (ed.) ASIACRYPT 2004. LNCS, vol. 3329, pp. 515–529. Springer, Heidelberg (2004)
8. Blake, I.F., Kolesnikov, V.: Conditional encrypted mapping and comparing encrypted numbers. In: Di Crescenzo, G., Rubin, A. (eds.) FC 2006. LNCS, vol. 4107, pp. 206–220. Springer, Heidelberg (2006)
9. Blundo, C., Masucci, B., Stinson, D.R., Wei, R.: Constructions and bounds for unconditionally secure non-interactive commitment schemes. Des. Codes Crypt. **26**(1–3), 97–110 (2002)
10. Bogetoft, P., Christensen, D.L., Damgård, I., Geisler, M., Jakobsen, T., Krøigaard, M., Nielsen, J.D., Nielsen, J.B., Nielsen, K., Pagter, J., Schwartzbach, M., Toft, T.: Secure multiparty computation goes live. In: Dingledine, R., Golle, P. (eds.) FC 2009. LNCS, vol. 5628, pp. 325–343. Springer, Heidelberg (2009)
11. Bost, R., Popa, R.A., Tu, S., Goldwasser, S.: Machine learning classification over encrypted data. Cryptology ePrint Archive, Report 2014/331 (2014). http://eprint.iacr.org/2014/331
12. Brickell, J., Shmatikov, V.: Privacy-preserving graph algorithms in the semi-honest model. In: Roy, B. (ed.) ASIACRYPT 2005. LNCS, vol. 3788, pp. 236–252. Springer, Heidelberg (2005)

13. Brickell, J., Shmatikov, V.: Privacy-preserving classifier learning. In: Dingledine, R., Golle, P. (eds.) FC 2009. LNCS, vol. 5628, pp. 128–147. Springer, Heidelberg (2009)

14. Canetti, R.: Security and composition of multiparty cryptographic protocols. J. Cryptol. **13**(1), 143–202 (2000)

15. Canetti, R.: Universally composable security: a new paradigm for cryptographic protocols. In: 42nd FOCS, pp. 136–145. IEEE Computer Society Press (2001)

16. Chaum, D., Crépeau, C., Damgård, I.: Multiparty unconditionally secure protocols (extended abstract). In: 20th ACM STOC, pp. 11–19. ACM Press (1988)

17. Damgård, I.B., Fitzi, M., Kiltz, E., Nielsen, J.B., Toft, T.: Unconditionally secure constant-rounds multi-party computation for equality, comparison, bits and exponentiation. In: Halevi, S., Rabin, T. (eds.) TCC 2006. LNCS, vol. 3876, pp. 285–304. Springer, Heidelberg (2006)

18. Ivan, D., Martin, G., Mikkel, K.: Homomorphic encryption and secure comparison. IJACT **1**(1), 22–31 (2008)

19. Damgård, I., Geisler, M., Krøigaard, M.: A correction to 'efficient and secure comparison for on-line auctions'. IJACT **1**(4), 323–324 (2009)

20. Damgård, I., Keller, M., Larraia, E., Pastro, V., Scholl, P., Smart, N.P.: Practical covertly secure MPC for dishonest majority – or: breaking the SPDZ limits. In: Crampton, J., Jajodia, S., Mayes, K. (eds.) ESORICS 2013. LNCS, vol. 8134, pp. 1–18. Springer, Heidelberg (2013)

21. Damgård, I., Pastro, V., Smart, N., Zakarias, S.: Multiparty computation from somewhat homomorphic encryption. In: Safavi-Naini, R., Canetti, R. (eds.) CRYPTO 2012. LNCS, vol. 7417, pp. 643–662. Springer, Heidelberg (2012)

22. Demmler, D., Schneider, T., Zohner, M.: ABY - a framework for efficient mixed-protocol secure two-party computation. In: NDSS 2015. The Internet Society (2015)

23. Dowsley, R., van de Graaf, J., Marques, D., Nascimento, A.C.A.: A two-party protocol with trusted initializer for computing the inner product. In: Chung, Y., Yung, M. (eds.) WISA 2010. LNCS, vol. 6513, pp. 337–350. Springer, Heidelberg (2011)

24. Dowsley, R., Müller-Quade, J., Otsuka, A., Hanaoka, G., Imai, H., Nascimento, A.C.A.: Universally composable and statistically secure verifiable secret sharing scheme based on pre-distributed data. IEICE Trans. **94–A**(2), 725–734 (2011)

25. Fischlin, M.: A cost-effective pay-per-multiplication comparison method for millionaires. In: Naccache, D. (ed.) CT-RSA 2001. LNCS, vol. 2020, pp. 457–471. Springer, Heidelberg (2001)

26. Garay, J.A., Schoenmakers, B., Villegas, J.: Practical and secure solutions for integer comparison. In: Okamoto, T., Wang, X. (eds.) PKC 2007. LNCS, vol. 4450, pp. 330–342. Springer, Heidelberg (2007)

27. Gilboa, N.: Two party RSA key generation (extended abstract). In: Wiener, M. (ed.) CRYPTO 1999. LNCS, vol. 1666, p. 116. Springer, Heidelberg (1999)

28. Graepel, T., Lauter, K., Naehrig, M.: ML confidential: machine learning on encrypted data. In: Kwon, T., Lee, M.-K., Kwon, D. (eds.) ICISC 2012. LNCS, vol. 7839, pp. 1–21. Springer, Heidelberg (2013)

29. Ishai, Y., Kushilevitz, E., Meldgaard, S., Orlandi, C., Paskin-Cherniavsky, A.: On the power of correlated randomness in secure computation. In: Sahai, A. (ed.) TCC 2013. LNCS, vol. 7785, pp. 600–620. Springer, Heidelberg (2013)

30. Katti, R.S., Ababei, C.: Secure comparison without explicit XOR. In: CoRR, abs/1204.2854 (2012)

31. Naor, M., Pinkas, B., Sumner, R.: Privacy preserving auctions and mechanism design. In: 1st ACM Conference on Electronic Commerce, pp. 129–139, New York, NY, USA (1999)
32. Nascimento, A.C.A., Müller-Quade, J., Otsuka, A., Hanaoka, G., Imai, H.: Unconditionally secure homomorphic pre-distributed bit commitment and secure two-party computations. In: Boyd, C., Mao, W. (eds.) ISC 2003. LNCS, vol. 2851, pp. 151–164. Springer, Heidelberg (2003)
33. Nascimento, A.C.A., Müller-Quade, J., Otsuka, A., Hanaoka, G., Imai, H.: Unconditionally non-interactive verifiable secret sharing secure against faulty majorities in the commodity based model. In: Jakobsson, M., Yung, M., Zhou, J. (eds.) ACNS 2004. LNCS, vol. 3089, pp. 355–368. Springer, Heidelberg (2004)
34. Nikolaenko, V., Weinsberg, U., Ioannidis, S., Joye, M., Boneh, D., Taft, N.: Privacy-preserving ridge regression on hundreds of millions of records. In: 2013 IEEE Symposium on Security and Privacy, pp. 334–348. IEEE Computer Society Press (2013)
35. Paillier, P.: Public-key cryptosystems based on composite degree residuosity classes. In: Stern, J. (ed.) EUROCRYPT 1999. LNCS, vol. 1592, pp. 223–238. Springer, Heidelberg (1999)
36. Pullonen, P.: Actively secure two-party computation: efficient beaver triple generation. Master's thesis, University of Tartu (2013)
37. Rabin, T., Ben-Or, M.: Verifiable secret sharing and multiparty protocols with honest majority (extended abstract). In: 21st ACM STOC, pp. 73–85. ACM Press (1989)
38. Rivest, R.L.: Unconditionally secure commitment and oblivious transfer schemes using private channels and a trusted initializer (1999). http://people.csail.mit.edu/rivest/Rivest-commitment.pdf
39. Toft, T.: Constant-rounds, almost-linear bit-decomposition of secret shared values. In: Fischlin, M. (ed.) CT-RSA 2009. LNCS, vol. 5473, pp. 357–371. Springer, Heidelberg (2009)
40. Tonicelli, R., David, B.M., de Morais Alves, V.: Universally composable private proximity testing. In: Boyen, X., Chen, X. (eds.) ProvSec 2011. LNCS, vol. 6980, pp. 222–239. Springer, Heidelberg (2011)
41. Tonicelli, R., Nascimento, A.C., Dowsley, R., Müller-Quade, J., Imai, H., Hanaoka, G., Otsuka, A.: Information-theoretically secure oblivious polynomial evaluation in the commodity-based model. Int. J. Inf. Secur. 14(1), 73–84 (2015)
42. Tschiatschek, S., Reinprecht, P., Mücke, M., Pernkopf, F.: Bayesian network classifiers with reduced precision parameters. In: Flach, P.A., De Bie, T., Cristianini, N. (eds.) ECML PKDD 2012, Part I. LNCS, vol. 7523, pp. 74–89. Springer, Heidelberg (2012)
43. Veugen, T.: Linear round bit-decomposition of secret-shared values. IEEE Trans. Inf. Forensics Secur. 10(3), 498–506 (2015)
44. Yao, A.C.-C.: Protocols for secure computations (extended abstract). In: 23rd FOCS, pp. 160–164. IEEE Computer Society Press (1982)

Leakage-Resilient Cryptography and Lattice Cryptography

Attribute-Based Encryption Resilient to Auxiliary Input

Zhiwei Wang[1,2]($\boxtimes$) and Siu Ming Yiu[2]

[1] College of Computer, Nanjing University of Posts and Telecommunications,
Nanjing 210003, Jiangsu, China
zhwwang@njupt.edu.cn
[2] University of Hong Kong, Pokfulam, Hong Kong

Abstract. The *auxiliary input* model defines a class of computationally uninvertible function families $\mathcal{F}$ to simulate a large class of leakage. Such a function $f \in \mathcal{F}$ can information-theoretically reveal the entire secret key SK, but it is still computationally infeasible to recover SK from $f(SK)$. That means SK can be used for multiple tasks, since SK doesn't need to be continually refreshed. We propose the first CP-ABE scheme based on linear secret sharing schemes, that can tolerate leakage on master key and attribute-based secret keys with *auxiliary input*(AI). For the security proof of our scheme, we present three modified assumptions in composite order bilinear groups, and prove their hardness. Under these modified assumptions, our scheme can be proved AI-CPA secure in the standard model. Finally, we devise a key-policy ABE scheme also resilient to *auxiliary input*.

Keywords: Leakage resilience · Attribute-based encryption · Auxiliary input · Linear secret sharing scheme

1 Introduction

With the development of cloud computing, there is a trend for users to store their data on the cloud server. It is inefficient to distribute these encrypted data to a specific set of users in traditional cryptosystems, e.g., PKI, ID-based cryptosystem, since the cipher-text size and computational cost of encryption/decryption algorithms are linear with the number of receivers. For this reason, Sahai and Waters [1] firstly proposed the concept of attribute-based encryption. In attribute-based encryption, cipher-texts and keys are associated with sets of attributes and access structure over attributes. Only when the attributes of the cipher-text match those of the users' key, the corresponding cipher-text can be decrypted. There are two kinds of ABE systems: The first one is ciphertext-policy ABE (CP-ABE), where cipher-texts are associated with access structures and keys are associated with sets of attributes; the second one is key-policy ABE (KP-ABE), where keys are associated with access structure and cipher-texts are associated with sets of attributes.

How to achieve a more expressive access policy over many attributes is an important problem in ABE. Sahai and Waters's [1] scheme was limited to specify

© Springer International Publishing Switzerland 2015
M.-H. Au and A. Miyaji (Eds.): ProvSec 2015, LNCS 9451, pp. 371–390, 2015.
DOI: 10.1007/978-3-319-26059-4_21

as threshold access policies with one threshold gate. After then, Lewko et al. [5] used monotone span programs (MSPs) as access structure to devise a CP-ABE and a KP-ABE, which are proved secure in composite bilinear groups. However, their schemes are very inefficient, since the length of cipher-texts and keys, and the number of pairings in decryption are all polynomial in the size of MSPs. In order to improve the efficiency, some ABE systems make use of linear secret sharing scheme (LSSS) or boolean formulas as access structure. Waters [10] employed LSSS matrix as access structure to realize CP-ABE under concrete and noninteractive cryptographic assumptions. In [6], Goyal et al. provided a mapping from a universal access tree to formulas consisting of threshold gates. They used this technique to construct a bounded CP-ABE scheme. There is a close relation between LSSS and MSP access structure. Beimel et al. [7] proved that the existence of a LSSS for a specific MSP access structure is equivalent to a smallest MSP. Pandit et al. [8] used minimal sets to realize the smallest MSP for describing general access structure in ABE systems. Recently, Zhang et al. [12] proposed a CP-ABE and a KP-ABE resilient to continual leakage by minimal sets.

In practice, many cryptosystems are difficult to avoid the side-channel attacks, which allow attackers to learn partial information about secret by observing physical properties of a cryptographic execution such as timing, power assumption, temperature, radiation, etc. [14–18]. The concept of leakage resilient cryptography has been proposed, which has led to construction of many cryptographic primitives which can be proved secure even against adversaries who can obtain partial information of secret keys and other initial state. Leakage resilience has been studied in many previous work under a variety of leakage models. We review these leakage models as follows:

Exposure-resilient: This model addressed adversaries who could learn a subset of the bits of the secret key or internal state [19,20].

Only computation leaks information: In this model, it is assumed that leakage occurs every time the device performs a computation, but any part of the memory not involved in computation does not leak [21,22].

Bounded retrieval model: In this model, the total number of bits leaked over the lifetime of system is significantly less than the bit-length of the key, and hope the attack is detected and stopped before the whole secret is leaked. This model has been employed successfully in many constructions of cryptographic primitives [23–25].

Continual leakage model: In this model, it is assumed the leakage between consecutive updates is bounded in term of a fraction of the secret key size, and the secret key should be refreshed continually. There is no leakage during the update process. Dodis et al. [26] constructed one-way relations, signatures, identification schemes, and authenticated key agreement protocols resilient to continual leakage. Lewko et al. [27], proposed fully secure IBE, HIBE, ABE systems which are be realized as resilience against continual leakage. Zhang et al. [12] also proposed a CP-ABE system and a KP-ABE system resilient to continual leakage.

Auxiliary input model: Auxiliary input model is developed from the *relative leakage* model [14], which allows any uninvertible function f that no PPT adversary can compute the actual pre-image with non-negligible probability[1]. That is to say, although such a function information-theoretically reveals the entire secret key SK, it still computationally infeasible to recover SK from $f(SK)$. If an encryption scheme is secure w.r.t. any auxiliary input, then user's secret and public key pair can be used for multiple tasks. Dodis et al. [13] firstly introduced the notion of *auxiliary input*, and proposed the public key encryption schemes in this model. Yuen et al. [3] proposed the first IBE scheme that is proved secure even when the adversary is equipped with auxiliary input. In [3], they also propose the model of *continual auxiliary leakage* that combines the concepts of auxiliary inputs with continual memory leakage.

Recently, Waters [9] introduced a new technique for security proof called *dual system encryption*, in which there are two kinds of keys and cipher-texts: *normal* and *semi-functional*[2]. Normal keys can decrypt both forms of cipher-texts, while semi-functional keys can only decrypt normal cipher-texts. In the real game, keys and cipher-texts are all normal, but they will be transformed into semi-functional one by one in the security proof. We must prove that the adversary cannot distinguish these transformations. In the final game, all keys and cipher-texts are semi-functional, which cannot be decrypted correctly. Lewko et al. [27] showed that the technique of dual system encryption and leakage resilience are highly compatible, their combination not only improves the leakage tolerance of cryptographic primitives, but also no sacrifices of efficiency.

Our Contribution. In this work, we propose the first CP-ABE scheme that is secure in presence of *auxiliary input*. After extension, our scheme can be transformed to a CP-ABE scheme resilient to *continual auxiliary leakage*. Our construction is based on Waters' most efficient construction of CP-ABE [10]. Our scheme in Sect. 4 preserves the nice features of Waters' scheme: security in the standard model, and based on static assumptions. In order to resist the leakage in form of auxiliary input and continual auxiliary leakage, we use the *GL Theorem for Large Fields*. The key point for using the *GL Theorem for Large Fields* is how to split the secret key into m pieces, since the *GL Theorem for Large Fields* states that if the pieces of secret key α_i belongs to a subgroup H of $\mathbb{Z}_{p_1}$ (p_1 is a λ-bit prime.), then the running time of inverter is $poly(|H|)$. Thus, if H is a large field, and close to $\mathbb{Z}_{p_1}$ (λ is a security parameter.), then the running time is close to $poly(2^\lambda)$, which is undesirable for the inverter. Our scheme also can be extended to an ABE scheme resilient to *continual auxiliary leakage*, if it doesn't allow leakage during the setup phase.

Lewko et al. [4] proposed three static assumptions in composite order groups, which has been used in many constructions [3,12,27]. However, they cannot

---

[1] "non-negligible probability" means that the probability cannot be ignored.
[2] The definitions of *normal* and *semi-functional* are only for proof, and they are not concerned with construction.

be directly used in the security proof of our constructions. We propose three modified assumptions and prove their hardness by using the two theorems in [9]. Another technical difficulty in our security proof is the form of attribute. If we use 2-SDP assumption to prove the Lemma 1, each attribute should be a integer number in $\mathbb{Z}_N$. Thus, we must pre-define an injective map from the attributes space to $\mathbb{Z}_N$. Since attributes space can be public, this map also can be public, and has no impact to the security level of ABE scheme.

Organization. In Sect. 2, we propose three modified complexity assumptions, and their proofs are provided in Appendix A. In Sect. 3, we provide the security model of CP-ABE resilient to auxiliary input. In Sect. 4, we devise a concrete CP-ABE scheme resilient to auxiliary input based on LSSS scheme. In Sect. 5, we prove our scheme by using the technique of dual system encryption. In Sect. 6, we design a KP-ABE scheme resilient to auxiliary input. In Sect. 7, we conclude our paper.

2 Background

In this section, we firstly give the definitions and proofs to our modified hard assumptions. Secondly, we provide the formal definitions for access structures and Linear Secret Sharing Scheme (LSSS).

2.1 Hardness Assumptions

Bilinear groups of composite order are groups introduced by [2], where the group order is product of two or more distinct primes. In our construction, we use the group order of $N = p_1 p_2 p_3$, where p_1, p_2, p_3 are three distinct prime numbers. We denote this group as $\mathbb{G}$, and admit an efficient bilinear map $\hat{e} : \mathbb{G} \times \mathbb{G} \to \mathbb{G}_T$, where $\mathbb{G}_T$'s order is the same as $\mathbb{G}$'s. Any element of $\mathbb{G}$ can be denoted as $g_1^{a_1} g_2^{a_2} g_3^{a_3}$, where g_i is the generator of subgroup $\mathbb{G}_{p_i}$. Each $\mathbb{G}_{p_i}$ has the order p_i, and $a_i \in \mathbb{Z}_{p_i}$. We denote $\mathbb{G}_{p_i p_j}$ as the subgroup of order $p_i p_j$ in $\mathbb{G}$. For all $T \in \mathbb{G}_{p_i p_j}$, T can be defined as the product of an element in $\mathbb{G}_{p_i}$ and an element in $\mathbb{G}_{p_j}$. For all $v \in \mathbb{G}_{p_i}$ and $w \in \mathbb{G}_{p_j}$, $\hat{e}(v, w) = 1$ if $i \neq j$. The following three hardness assumptions, which have been analyzed in [4,5], have been used in many constructions [3,12,27].

Definition 1 (1-SDP assumption). *Given* $\Theta = (N = p_1 p_2 p_3, \mathbb{G}, \mathbb{G}_T, \hat{e})$, *if for all PPT algorithm* $\mathfrak{A}$, *there exists a negligible probability* ϵ *such that*

$$|Pr[\mathfrak{A}(\Theta, g_1, X_3, T_0) = 1] - Pr[\mathfrak{A}(\Theta, g_1, X_3, T_1) = 1]| \leq \epsilon,$$

where the probabilities are taken over the choice of $g_1 \in \mathbb{G}_{p_1}, X_3 \in \mathbb{G}_{p_3}, T_0 \in \mathbb{G}_{p_1 p_2}, T_1 \in \mathbb{G}_{p_1}$.

Definition 2 (2-SDP assumption). *Given* $\Theta = (N = p_1 p_2 p_3, \mathbb{G}, \mathbb{G}_T, \hat{e})$, *if for all PPT algorithm* $\mathfrak{A}$, *there exists a negligible probability* ϵ *such that*

$$|Pr[\mathfrak{A}(\Theta, g_1, X_1 X_2, X_3, Y_2 Y_3, T_0) = 1] - Pr[\mathfrak{A}(\Theta, g_1, X_1 X_2, X_3, Y_2 Y_3, T_1) = 1]| \leq \epsilon,$$

where the probabilities are taken over the choice of $g_1 \in \mathbb{G}_{p_1}, X_2, Y_2 \in \mathbb{G}_{p_2}, X_3, Y_3 \in \mathbb{G}_{p_3}, T_0 \in \mathbb{G}_{p_1p_3}, T_1 \in \mathbb{G}.$

Definition 3 (BSDP assumption). *Given* $\Theta = (N = p_1p_2p_3, \mathbb{G}, \mathbb{G}_T, \hat{e})$, *if for all PPT algorithm* $\mathfrak{A}$, *there exists a negligible probability* ϵ *such that*

$$|Pr[\mathfrak{A}(\Theta, g_1, g_1^\alpha X_2, X_3, g_1^s Y_2, Z_2, T_0) = 1] - Pr[\mathfrak{A}(\Theta, g_1, g_1^\alpha X_2, X_3, g_1^s Y_2, Z_2, T_1) = 1]| \le \epsilon,$$

where the probabilities are taken over the choice of $s, \alpha \in \mathbb{Z}_N, g_1 \in \mathbb{G}_{p_1}, X_2, Y_2, Z_2 \in \mathbb{G}_{p_2}, X_3 \in \mathbb{G}_{p_3}, T_0 = \hat{e}(g_1^\alpha, g_1^s), T_1 \in \mathbb{G}_T.$

However, our construction in Sect. 4 should be proved secure under the following three modified assumptions. Let $[m]$ denote $\{1, \cdots, m\}$.

Definition 4 (modified 1-SDP assumption). *Given* $\Theta = (N = p_1p_2p_3, \mathbb{G}, \mathbb{G}_T, \hat{e})$, *if for all PPT algorithm* $\mathfrak{A}$, *there exists negligible probabilities* $\epsilon_1, \cdots, \epsilon_m$ *such that*

$$|Pr[\mathfrak{A}(\Theta, g_1, X_3, T_{01}) = 1] - Pr[\mathfrak{A}(\Theta, g_1, X_3, T_{11}) = 1]| \le \epsilon_1,$$

$$\vdots$$

$$|Pr[\mathfrak{A}(\Theta, g_1, X_3, T_{0m}) = 1] - Pr[\mathfrak{A}(\Theta, g_1, X_3, T_{1m}) = 1]| \le \epsilon_m,$$

where the probabilities are taken over the choice of $g_1 \in \mathbb{G}_{p_1}, X_3 \in \mathbb{G}_{p_3}, T_{0i} \in \mathbb{G}_{p_1p_2}, T_{1i} \in \mathbb{G}_{p_1}.$

Definition 5 (modified 2-SDP assumption). *Given* $\Theta = (N = p_1p_2p_3, \mathbb{G}, \mathbb{G}_T, \hat{e})$, *if for all PPT algorithm* $\mathfrak{A}$, *there exists a negligible probability* ϵ *such that*

$$|Pr[\mathfrak{A}(\Theta, g_1, (X_{1i}X_{2i})_{i \in [m]}, X_3, Y_2Y_3, T_0) = 1]$$
$$-Pr[\mathfrak{A}(\Theta, g_1, (X_{1i}X_{2i})_{i \in [m]}, X_3, Y_2Y_3, T_1) = 1]| \le \epsilon,$$

where the probabilities are taken over the choice of $g_1 \in \mathbb{G}_{p_1}, X_{2i}, Y_2 \in \mathbb{G}_{p_2}, X_3, Y_3 \in \mathbb{G}_{p_3}, T_0 \in \mathbb{G}_{p_1p_3}, T_1 \in \mathbb{G}.$

Definition 6 (modified BSDP assumption). *Given* $\Theta = (N = p_1p_2p_3, \mathbb{G}, \mathbb{G}_T, \hat{e})$, *if for all PPT algorithm* $\mathfrak{A}$, *there exists a negligible probability* ϵ *such that*

$$|Pr[\mathfrak{A} \ (\Theta, g_1, (g_1^{1/b_i})_{i \in [m]}, (B_i^{\alpha_i} X_2)_{i \in [m]}, X_3, (B_i^{s_i} Y_2)_{i \in [m]}, Z_2, T_0) = 1]$$
$$-Pr[\mathfrak{A}(\Theta, g_1, (g_1^{1/b_i})_{i \in [m]}, (B_i^{\alpha_i} X_2)_{i \in [m]}, X_3, (B_i^{s_i} Y_2)_{i \in [m]}, Z_2, T_1) = 1]| \le \epsilon,$$

where the probabilities are taken over the choice of $s_i, \alpha_i, b_i \in \mathbb{Z}_N, g_1, B_i = g_1^{b_i} \in \mathbb{G}_{p_1}, X_2, Y_2, Z_2 \in \mathbb{G}_{p_2}, X_3 \in \mathbb{G}_{p_3}, T_0 = \prod_{i=1}^m \hat{e}(g_1, B_i)^{\alpha_i s_i}, T_1 \in \mathbb{G}_T.$

We prove the hardness of three modified assumptions in **Appendix A**.

2.2   Access Structure and Linear Secret Sharing Scheme

We adapt our definitions which are given by [11]. However, the role of parties is taken by the attributes in our definitions.

Definition 7 (Access Structure). *Let $\{S_1, \cdots, S_n\}$ be a set of attributes. An authorized collection $\mathbb{A} \subset 2^{\{S_1, \cdots, S_n\}}$ is monotone, if $\forall B, C$, $B \in \mathbb{A}$ and $B \subseteq C$ then $C \in \mathbb{A}$. A monotone access structure is a monotone collection $\mathbb{A}$ of non-empty of subsets of $\{S_1, \cdots, S_n\}$. The sets not in $\mathbb{A}$ are called the unauthorized sets.*

Definition 8 (Linear Secret Sharing Scheme (LSSS)). *A secret sharing scheme Π over a set of attributes S is called linear on the two conditions that: 1) The shares for each attributes form a vector from $\mathbb{Z}_N$. 2) There exists an $l \times n$ matrix $\mathcal{A}$ called sharing-generating matrix for Π. For all $i = 1, \cdots, l$, the function ρ maps the i-th row of $\mathcal{A}$ to an attribute labeling $\rho(i)$. Then, we selects a random column vector $v = (\mu, r_2, \cdots, r_n)$ where $\mu \in \mathbb{Z}_N$ is the secret to be shared, and $\mathcal{A}v$ is the vector of l shares of the secret μ according to Π. The share $(\mathcal{A}v)_i$ belongs to the attribute $\rho(i)$.*

From the discussion in [11], each LSSS scheme Π for the access structure $\mathbb{A}$ has a property of *linear reconstruction*. Let $\mathcal{C} \in \mathbb{A}$ be any authorized set, and let $I \subset \{1, \cdots, l\}$ be defined as $I = \{i : \rho(i) \in \mathcal{C}\}$. Then, there exists constant $\{\omega_i \in \mathbb{Z}_N\}_{i \in I}$ such that, if $\{\lambda_i\}$ are valid shares of any μ in Π, then $\sum_{i \in I} \omega_i \lambda_i = \mu$. These $\{\omega_i\}$ can be found in polynomial time in the size of matrix $\mathcal{A}$.

3   Attribute Based Encryption with Auxiliary Inputs

In this section, we give the security model of cipher-text-policy ABE resilient to auxiliary input (AI-CP-ABE), where the access structure is monotonic. In Sect. 6, we will provide the concrete scheme of key-policy ABE resilient to auxiliary input (AI-KP-ABE).

A CP-ABE for a general monotone access structure $\mathbb{A}$ over the monotone attribute universe space Σ is composed of four probabilistic polynomial time algorithms:

1. **Setup($1^\lambda, \Sigma$):** The setup algorithm takes as input a security parameter λ and an attribute set Σ, and outputs system public key MPK and master key MSK.
2. **KeyGen($MSK, \mathbb{S}$):** This algorithm takes as input an attribute set $\mathbb{S}$, and the master secret key MSK, and outputs a private key $SK_\mathbb{S}$.
3. **Encrypt($M, \mathbb{A}$):** The encryption algorithm takes as input a monotone access structure $\mathbb{A}$ and a message M, and outputs a cipher-text CT.
4. **Decrypt(CT, SK):** This algorithm takes as input a cipher-text CT for an access structure $\mathbb{A}$ and a private key SK for a set $\mathbb{S}$, and outputs M if and only if the attribute set $\mathbb{S}$ satisfies the monotone access structure $\mathbb{A}$.

Let Σ and $\mathcal{M}$ be the monotone attribute space and the message space respectively. $\forall M \in \mathcal{M}$, $\forall \mathbb{A}^3 \in 2^\Sigma$ and $\forall \mathbb{S} \in \mathbb{A}$, $M \leftarrow$ Decrypt(SK,

---

[3] The access structure $\mathbb{A}$ is a monotone collection of non-empty of subsets of Σ.

Encrypt($MPK, M, \mathbb{A}$)), where (MPK, MSK) $\leftarrow$ Setup($1^\lambda, \Sigma$), SK $\leftarrow$ $KeyGen(MSK, \mathbb{S})$.

3.1 Security Model of AI-CP-ABE

In this section, we provide the security model of ciphertext-policy attribute based encryption for semantic security with leakage in form of auxiliary input (AI-CP-ABE). Let $\mathcal{F}$ denote a polynomial time computable function family. We define the security model by an indistinguishable game between a challenger $\mathfrak{C}$ and an adversary $\mathfrak{A}$. In order to record the queried and leaked keys, we set two empty lists: $\mathfrak{R} = \langle \bar{j}, \mathbb{S} \rangle$ and $\mathfrak{Q} = \langle \bar{j}, \mathbb{S}, SK_\mathbb{S} \rangle$, where $\bar{j}$ is a handle index[4].

Setup. The challenger $\mathfrak{C}$ runs the Setup algorithm to generate MPK and MSK, and sends MPK to $\mathfrak{A}$.

Query 1. The adversary $\mathfrak{A}$ can perform the following queries:
  - **Key extraction query($\mathcal{Q}_E$):** When $\mathfrak{A}$ makes a key extraction query on an attribute set $\mathbb{S} \subset \Sigma$, $\mathfrak{C}$ checks the list $\mathfrak{Q}$ for the tuple with the form $\langle \bar{j}, \mathbb{S}, SK_\mathbb{S} \rangle$. If there is no such tuple, then $\bar{j}$ is set to 1, and $\mathfrak{C}$ answers $SK_\mathbb{S} \leftarrow KeyGen(MSK, \mathbb{S})$. Then, $\mathfrak{C}$ puts $\langle \bar{j}, \mathbb{S}, SK_\mathbb{S} \rangle$ into the list $\mathfrak{Q}$. Otherwise, $\mathfrak{C}$ returns $SK_\mathbb{S}$ from the tuple $\langle \bar{j}, \mathbb{S}, SK_\mathbb{S} \rangle$, and set $\bar{j} = \bar{j} + 1$.
  - **Key leakage query($\mathcal{Q}_L$):** When $\mathfrak{A}$ makes a key leakage query on an attribute set $\mathbb{S} \subset \Sigma$ with a function $f \in \mathcal{F}$, $\mathfrak{C}$ returns $f(MSK, \mathfrak{Q}, MPK, \mathbb{S})$.
  - **Key update query($\mathcal{Q}_U$):** This query is useful for schemes with probabilistic attribute based private key generation, where a user of attribute set $\mathbb{S}$ may request for another attribute based private key after obtained the first copy. When $\mathfrak{A}$ makes a key update query for another attribute-based secret key after obtained the first copy. $\mathfrak{C}$ checks the list $\mathfrak{Q}$ for the tuple with the form $\langle \bar{j}, \mathbb{S}, SK_\mathbb{S} \rangle$. If there is no such tuple, then $\hat{j}$ is set to 1, and returns null. Otherwise, $\hat{j}$ is set to $\bar{j} + 1$, and returns $\hat{SK}_\mathbb{S} \leftarrow KeyGen(MSK, \mathbb{S})$. $\mathfrak{C}$ puts $\langle \hat{j}, \mathbb{S}, \hat{SK}_\mathbb{S} \rangle$ into the list $\mathfrak{Q}$, and returns the update times $\hat{j}$.

Challenge. $\mathfrak{A}$ outputs two messages $M_0, M_1 \in \mathcal{M}$ and a monotone access structure $\mathbb{A}^*$ such that $\forall \mathbb{S} \in \mathfrak{R}$ doesn't satisfy $\mathbb{A}^*$. $\mathfrak{C}$ randomly choose a bit $b \in \{0, 1\}$, and returns the cipher-text $CT^* \leftarrow Encrypt(M_b, \mathbb{A}^*)$.

Query 2. $\mathfrak{A}$ can make the key extraction queries like Query 1 except the queries on the attribute sets which satisfies $\mathbb{A}^*$.

Response. Finally, $\mathfrak{A}$ outputs a guess b' of b. $\mathfrak{A}$'s advantage of this game can be defined as $ADV_\mathfrak{A}(1^\lambda, \Sigma) = |2Pr[b = b'] - 1|$.

We say that a CP-ABE is AI-CPA secure w.r.t. auxiliary inputs from $\mathcal{F}$ on the condition that $ADV_\mathfrak{A}$ is negligible for any PPT adversary $\mathfrak{A}$ in the above game.

---

[4] $\bar{j}$ is used to index the attributes set and the secret key.

We consider the definition of function families $\mathcal{F}$. To parameterize $\mathcal{F}$, the min-entropy $k_A{}^5$ of attribute-based secret key is an important parameter. $\mathcal{F}$ can be denoted as $\mathcal{F}(g(k_A))$. Let q_l denote the times of $\mathfrak{A}$'s key leakage queries, and let q_e denote the times of $\mathfrak{A}$'s key extraction queries. Let Δ denote a set of q_e attribute-based secret keys. Then, for $\forall i \in [q_l]$, given $\{MPK, \mathbb{A}^*, \Delta, \{f_i(MSK, \mathfrak{Q}, MPK, \mathbb{S})\}_{i \in [q_l]}\}$, where all $f_i \in \mathcal{F}(g(k_A))$, no PPT algorithm can find a valid secret key $SK_{\mathbb{S}^*}$ such that attribute set $\mathbb{S}^* \in \mathbb{A}^*$ with a non-negligible probability greater than $g(k_A)^6$, where $g(k_A) \geq 2^{-k_A}$ is the hardness parameter. Our goal is to make $g(k_A)$ as close to $\mathrm{negl}(k_A)$ as possible[7]. Thus, we have the following definition:

Definition 9 (AI-CPA-CP-ABE). *If a ciphertext-policy attribute-based encryption is CPA secure w.r.t. auxiliary input families $\mathcal{F}(g(k_A))$, then it is said to be $g(k_A)$ auxiliary input CPA secure ($g(k_A)$-AI-CPA).*

4   Construction of CP-ABE Resilient to Auxiliary Input Model

4.1   Preparation

Let Λ be a monotone universal attribute space. In the security proof of this construction, we should convert each attribute to a random number belonging to $\mathbb{Z}_N$, where N is a product of three distinct prime numbers p_1, p_2, p_3. Thus, an injection map χ should be pre-defined, and $\chi(S_i) \in \mathbb{Z}_N$ for all $S_i \in \Lambda$. Let $\Sigma = \chi(\Lambda)$, which is a subset of $\mathbb{Z}_N$. For simplicity, we denote the number set Σ as an universal attribute space in the following, and U denotes the cardinality of $U = |\Sigma|$.

Our construction should be resorted to the Goldreich-Levin Theorem for large fields. Let's review it according to [3,13].

Theorem 1 (GL Theorem for Large Fields). *Let q be a big prime, and let H be a subset of $GF(q)$. Let f mapping from H^m to $\{0,1\}^*$ be any function. Randomly chooses a vector s from H^m, and compute $y = f(s)$. Then, randomly selects a vector r from $GF(q)^m$. If a PPT distinguisher $\mathfrak{D}$ runs in time t, and there exists a probability ϵ such that*

$$|Pr[\mathfrak{D}(y, r, <r, s>) = 1] - Pr[u \leftarrow GF(q) : \mathfrak{D}(y, r, u) = 1]| = \epsilon,$$

then given $y \leftarrow f(s)$, there exists an inverter $\mathfrak{A}$ who can compute s from y in time $t' = t \cdot poly(m, |H|, 1/\epsilon)$ with the probability

$$Pr[s \leftarrow H^m, y \leftarrow f(s) : \mathfrak{A}(y) = s] \geq \frac{\epsilon^3}{512 \cdot m \cdot q^2}.$$

---

[5] If the key is generated randomly, then k_A equals the length of secret key.

[6] $g(k_A)$ is a non-negligible probability function.

[7] In the auxiliary model, any hard-to-invert function $f \in \mathcal{F}$ can hardly recover a secret key SK even the min-entropy of SK is 0.

4.2   Construction

Our construction is based on Waters' most efficient cipher-text-policy ABE scheme [10]. In our construction, we try to construct the public key as in the Yuen et al.'s scheme [3], then the master public key becomes $y_i = e(g_1, B_i)^{\alpha_i}$ (B_i, α_i are defined in the Setup algorithm.), and the master secret key becomes m pieces $(g_1^{\alpha_1}, \cdots, g_1^{\alpha_m})$ in order to use the GL Theorem for large fields.

Setup($1^\lambda, \Sigma$): The setup algorithm takes as input a security parameter λ, a monotone universal attribute space Σ. This algorithm runs the bilinear group generator to produce $\Theta = (N = p_1 p_2 p_3, \mathbb{G}, \mathbb{G}_T, \hat{e})$, where p_1, p_2, p_3 are three distinct λ-bit primes. Then, it selects random generators $g_1, h_1, \cdots, h_U \in G_{p_1}$ and $g_3 \in G_{p_3}$. Let $m = (3\lambda)^{1/\epsilon}$, where the security is w.r.t. auxiliary inputs that are hard to invert with probability 2^{-m^ϵ}. It picks $a, \alpha_1, \cdots, \alpha_m, b_1, \cdots, b_m \in \mathbb{Z}_N$, and sets $B_1 = g_1^{b_1}, \cdots, B_m = g_1^{b_m}$. It selects $g_3 \in \mathbb{G}_{p_3}$ and $u_1, \cdots, u_m \in \mathbb{Z}_{p_3}$. The master public key is

$$MPK : \{\Theta, g_1, g_3, (g_1^{a/b_i})_{i \in [m]}, B_1, \cdots, B_m, h_1, \cdots, h_U, (y_i = e(g_1, B_i)^{\alpha_i})_{i \in [m]}\},$$

and the master secret key is $MSK = (g_1^{\alpha_i} \cdot g_3^{u_i})_{i \in [m]}$.

KeyGen($MSK, MPK, \mathbb{S}$): This algorithm takes as input an attribute set $\mathbb{S}$[8], the master public key MPK and the master secret key MSK. It first chooses $y_{11}, \cdots, y_{1m}, y_2, y_{31}, \cdots, y_{3U}, t \in \mathbb{Z}_N$, and creates the private key as

$$SK_\mathbb{S} = \{(K_{1i})_{i \in [m]}, K_2, (K_{3x})_{x \in \mathbb{S}}\}$$
$$= \{(g_1^{\alpha_i} g_1^{at/b_i} \cdot g_3^{y_{1i}} g_3^{u_i})_{i \in [m]}, g_1^t g_3^{y_2}, (h_x^t g_3^{y_{3x}})_{x \in \mathbb{S}}\}.$$

Encrypt(M, Π, MPK): The encryption algorithm takes as input an LSSS scheme $\Pi = (\mathcal{A}, \rho)$ for a monotone access structure $\mathbb{A}$, a message M and the master public key MPK. Here, $\mathcal{A}$ is an $l \times n$ matrix. The function ρ associates the rows of $\mathcal{A}$ to the attributes[9]. The algorithm first chooses random $s_1, \cdots, s_m \in \mathbb{Z}_N$ and a random vector $\boldsymbol{v} = (\sum_{i=1}^m s_i, v_2, \cdots, v_n) \in \mathbb{Z}_N^n$. For $i = 1$ to l, it computes $\lambda_i = \boldsymbol{v} \cdot \mathcal{A}_i$, where $\mathcal{A}_i$ is the vector corresponding to the ith row of $\mathcal{A}$. In addition, the algorithm chooses random $r_1, \cdots, r_l \in \mathbb{Z}_N$. The generated cipher-text CT is

$$\{C = M \cdot \prod_{i=1}^m y_i^{s_i}, (C_i' = B_i^{s_i})_{i \in [m]}, (C_i = g_1^{a\lambda_i} h_{\rho(i)}^{-r_i}, D_i = g_1^{r_i})_{i \in [l]}\}.$$

Decrypt(CT, SK, MPK): This algorithm takes as input a cipher-text CT for an LSSS scheme $\Pi = (\mathcal{A}, \rho)$ on the monotone access structure $\mathbb{A}$, a private key SK for a set $\mathbb{S}$ and the master public key MPK. If $\mathbb{S} \in \mathbb{A}$ is an authorized

---

[8] $\mathbb{S}$ is a subset of number set Σ.

[9] Since each attribute is mapped to a random number in $\mathbb{Z}_N$, ρ can be defined as $\rho : \mathbb{Z}_N^l \to \Sigma$.

set, then let $I \subset [l]$ be defined as $I = \{i : \rho(i) \in \mathbb{S}\}$. Then, it computes a set $\{\omega_i \in \mathbb{Z}_N\}_{i \in I}$ such that $\sum_{i \in I} \omega_i \lambda_i = \sum_{i=1}^{m} s_i$, if $\{\lambda_i\}$ are valid shares according to $\mathcal{A}$. Then, the decryption algorithm computes

$$\frac{\prod_{i=1}^{m} \hat{e}(C_i', K_{1i})}{\prod_{i \in I}(\hat{e}(C_i, K_2)\hat{e}(D_i, K_{3\rho(i)}))^{\omega_i}} = \prod_{i=1}^{m} y_i^{s_i}.$$

Finally, it can obtain the message M from C.

Correctness: The correctness of decryption is described as follows:

$$\frac{\prod_{i=1}^{m} \hat{e}(C_i', K_{1i})}{\prod_{i \in I}(\hat{e}(C_i, K_2)\hat{e}(D_i, K_{3\rho(i)}))^{\omega_i}}$$

$$= \frac{\prod_{i=1}^{m} \hat{e}(B_i^{s_i}, g_1^{\alpha_i} \cdot g_1^{at/b_i} \cdot g_3^{y_{1i}+u_i})}{\prod_{i \in I}(\hat{e}(g_1^{a\lambda_i} h_{\rho(i)}^{-r_i}, g_1^t g_3^{y_2})\hat{e}(g_1^{r_i}, h_{\rho(i)}^t g_3^{y_{3\rho(i)}}))^{\omega_i}}$$

$$= \frac{(\prod_{i=1}^{m} \hat{e}(g_1, B_i)^{\alpha_i s_i}) \cdot \hat{e}(g_1, g_1)^{at \cdot (\sum_{i=1}^{m} s_i)}}{\prod_{i \in I}(\hat{e}(g_1^{a\lambda_i}, g_1^t) \cdot \hat{e}(h_{\rho(i)}^{-r_i}, g_1^t) \cdot \hat{e}(g_1^{r_i}, h_{\rho(i)}^t))^{\omega_i}}$$

$$= \frac{(\prod_{i=1}^{m} \hat{e}(g_1, B_i)^{\alpha_i s_i}) \cdot \hat{e}(g_1, g_1)^{at \cdot (\sum_{i=1}^{m} s_i)}}{\hat{e}(g_1, g_1)^{at \cdot \sum_{i \in I} \lambda_i \omega_i}}$$

$$= \prod_{i=1}^{m} \hat{e}(g_1, B_i)^{\alpha_i s_i} = \prod_{i=1}^{m} y_i^{s_i}.$$

4.3   Performance Comparison

In this section, we provide the performance comparison with Lewko et al.'s scheme [27], Zhang et al.'s scheme [12] and our scheme. These three schemes are all ciphertext-policy attribute-based encryption schemes in the presence of key leakage model. Lewko et al.'s scheme and our scheme use LSSS to denote the access structure, while Zhang et al.'s scheme uses the minimal set to denote the access structure.

Let Pr denote the computation cost of pairing, Ex denote the exponent cost, and Mu denote the point multiplication. For [27] and our scheme, we assume that the LSSS matrix is $l \times n$. For [12,27], we assume that the leakage parameter is denoted as ϖ, the allowable leakage probability parameter is denoted as ς and the leakage bound of a key is denoted as ζ. For [12], let κ denote the number of minimal sets. In decryption, we only evaluate the computational costs of pairing, since the pairing operation is very time-consuming compared to other the other operations.

From the Table 1, we can see that the computational cost of Lewko et al.'s scheme [4] and Zhang et al.'s scheme [12] are mainly dependent on the leakage parameter ϖ, while the computational cost of our scheme is mainly dependent on the number of pieces m. However, Our scheme resilient to auxiliary input haven't the limitation of leakage bound.

Table 1. Performance comparison

Schemes	Lewko [27]	Zhang [12]	Our scheme
Encrypt	$2(\varpi + 2l)Mu$	$(\varpi + 2\kappa)Mu$	$(2l + m + 1)Ex$
Decrypt	$(\varpi + 2l + 1)Pr$	$(\varpi + 3)Pr$	$(m + 2|I|)Pr$
Leakage bound	$\zeta = 2 + (\varpi - 1 - 2\varsigma)\log p_2$	$\zeta = 2 + (\varpi - 1 - 2\varsigma)\log p_2$	No
Leakage model	Bounded leakage	Continuous leakage	Auxiliary input

5 Security Proof

Our security proof employs the dual system encryption mechanism, which requires three semi-functional(SF) structures. Let g_2 be the generator of $\mathbb{G}_{p_2}$.

SF master secret key: $(g_1^{\alpha_i} \cdot g_2^{\theta_i} \cdot g_3^{u_i})_{i \in [m]}$, where $\theta_1, \cdots, \theta_m \in \mathbb{Z}_N$.

SF attribute-based secret key: $\{(g_1^{\alpha_i + at/b_i} \cdot g_2^{z_i} g_3^{y_{1i}})_{i \in [m]}, g_1^t g_2^d g_3^{y_2}, (h_x^t g_3^{y_{3x}})_{x \in \mathbb{S}}\}$, where $z_1, \cdots, z_m, d \in \mathbb{Z}_N$.

SF cipher-text: $\{C = M \cdot \prod_{i=1}^m y_i^{s_i}, (\tilde{C}_i' = B_i^{s_i} g_2^{\delta_i})_{i \in [m]}, (\tilde{C}_i = g_1^{a\lambda_i} h_{\rho(i)}^{-r_i} g_2^{\tau_i}, \tilde{D}_i = g_1^{r_i})_{i \in [l]}\}$, where $\delta_1, \cdots, \delta_m, \tau_1, \cdots, \tau_l \in \mathbb{Z}_N$.

When a SF attribute-based secret key is used to decrypt a SF cipher-text, we will obtain an extra term $\hat{e}(g_2, g_2)^{\sum_{i=1}^m \delta_i z_i - d \sum_{i \in I} \tau_i \omega_i}$. If $\sum_{i=1}^m \delta_i z_i - d \sum_{i \in I} \tau_i \omega_i = 0$, we call a *SF attribute-based secret key* is a *nominally semi-functional(NSF) attribute-based secret key*. An NSF attribute-based secret key is a special kind of SF attribute-based secret key, which can be used to decrypt SF cipher-text, that means $\sum_{i=1}^m \delta_i z_i = d \sum_{i \in I} \tau_i \omega_i$. If an attribute-based secret key is generated from a SF master secret key, then it is also semi-functional. If we use it to decrypt a SF cipher-text, we will obtain another extra term $\hat{e}(g_2, g_2)^{\sum_{i=1}^m \delta_i \theta_i - d \sum_{i \in I} \tau_i \omega_i}$. Similarly, if $\sum_{i=1}^m \delta_i \theta_i = d \sum_{i \in I} \tau_i \omega_i$, then decryption still works and the SF attribute-based secret key is an NSF attribute-based secret key.

Theorem 2. *Our CP-ABE scheme is (2^{-m^ϵ})-AI-CPA leakage secure under the modified assumptions 1,2 and 3.*

Proof: We prove this theorem by a series of games. In the first real $Game_{rl}$, the key and cipher-text are normal forms. Let $\mathbb{A}^*$ denote the challenge access structure, which is a monotone collection. The second game $Game_{rt}$ is the same as $Game_{rl}$ except that the adversary cannot ask for any attribute set belonging to the collection $\mathbb{A}^*$. Then, we convert the challenge cipher-text into semi-functional, and convert the keys into semi-functional forms one by one. Finally, we also prove that the message is distinguishable from a random message in the challenge cipher-text.

Lemma 1. *If $Adv_A^{Game_{rl}} - Adv_A^{Game_{rt}} \geq \epsilon$, then Assumption 2 is broken.*

Lemma 2. *If $Adv_A^{Game_{rt}} - Adv_A^{Game_0} \geq \epsilon$, then modified Assumption 1 is broken.*

Lemma 3. *If* $Adv_A^{Game_{k+1}} - Adv_A^{Game_k} \geq \epsilon$, *then modified Assumption 2 is broken.*

Lemma 4. *If* $Adv_A^{Game_Q} - Adv_A^{Game_f} \geq \epsilon$, *then modified Assumption 3(modified BSDP assumption) is broken.*

We prove **Lemma 1–4** in **Appendix** B. From **Lemma 1–4**, if modified assumptions 1,2,3 hold, then $Game_{rl}$ is indistinguishable from $Game_f$. Obviously, the adversary can win the $Game_{rl}$ with negligible probability. Thus, our CP-ABE scheme is (2^{-m^ϵ})-AI-CPA leakage secure.   □

Note: Our scheme can be easily extended to an ABE scheme secure in the *continual auxiliary leakage* model [3], if the extended scheme does not allow leakage during the setup phase. It only adds two update algorithms for MSK and attribute-based secret key, and the proof is similar to the above, since the updates all used random elements in $\mathbb{G}_{p3}$, which has no impact to the previous proof.

6   KP-ABE Resilient to Auxiliary Input

In this section, we construct key-policy attribute-based encryption leakage resilient to auxiliary input model. In KP-ABE, a key is associated with an access structure and a cipher-text is associated with a set of attributes. The construction has the similar security proof with AI-CP-ABE. In this construction, we encode a monotone universal attribute space as an index numbers set, which is still monotone. Let Σ be the universal attribute space, and $U = |\Sigma|$. We use a function I to map each attribute to its index number. Let $I_\mathbb{S}$ denote the index numbers set of attributes set $\mathbb{S}$. It means that $I_\mathbb{S} \subset \{1, \cdots, U\}$. Let $\mathbb{A} = \{\mathbb{S}_1, \cdots, \mathbb{S}_n\}$ be a monotone access structure, and all $\mathbb{S}_i$s are authorized attribute sets. Then, $I_\mathbb{A} = \{I_{\mathbb{S}_1}, \cdots, I_{\mathbb{S}_n}\}$ is a monotone collection of index numbers sets corresponding to $\mathbb{A}$.

Setup($1^\lambda, \Sigma$): The setup algorithm takes as input a security parameter λ, a monotone universal attributes set Σ. This algorithm runs the bilinear group generator to produce $\Theta = (N = p_1 p_2 p_3, \mathbb{G}, \mathbb{G}_T, \hat{e})$. Then, it selects random generators $g_1, h_1, \cdots, h_u \in G_{p1}$ and $g_3 \in G_{p3}$. Let $m = (3\lambda)^{1/\epsilon}$. It picks $a, \alpha_1, \cdots, \alpha_m b_1, \cdots, b_m \in \mathbb{Z}_{p1}$, and sets $B_1 = g_1^{b_1}, \cdots, B_m = g_1^{b_m}$. It selects $g_3 \in \mathbb{G}_{p3}$ and $u \in \mathbb{Z}_{p3}$. The master public key is

$$MPK : \{\Theta, g_1, g_1^a, g_3, B_1, \cdots, B_m, h_1, \cdots, h_U, (H_i = h_i^{b_1}, \cdots, H_i = h_i^{b_m})_{i \in [U]},$$

$$(y_i = e(g_1, B_i)^{\alpha_i})_{i \in [m]}\},$$

and the master secret key is $MSK = (g_1^{\alpha_i} g_3^{u_i})_{i \in [m]}$.

KeyGen($MSK, \mathbb{A}$): This algorithm takes as input a monotone access structure $\mathbb{A}$ and the master secret key MSK. It first chooses

$$y_{11}, \cdots, y_{1m}, y_2, y_{31}, \cdots, y_{3U}, t, r_1, \cdots, r_U \in \mathbb{Z}_N,$$

and creates the private key as

$$SK = \{(K_{1i})_{i \in [m]}, (K_{2i})_{i \in I_A}, (K_{3i})_{i \in [U]}\}$$
$$= \{(g_1^{\alpha_i + at} \cdot g_3^{y_{1i} + u_i})_{i \in [m]}, (g_1^{-at}(\prod_{j \in I_{S_i}} h_j^{r_j}) g_3^{y_2})_{i \in I_A}, (g_1^{r_i} g_3^{y_{3i}})_{i \in [U]}\}.$$

Encrypt$(M, \mathbb{S})$: The encryption algorithm takes as input an attributes set $\mathbb{S}$ and a message M. The algorithm firstly transforms $\mathbb{S}$ to its corresponding index set $I_\mathbb{S}$. Then, it chooses random $s_1, \cdots, s_m \in \mathbb{Z}_N$, and outputs the cipher-text CT as

$$< C = M \cdot \prod_{i=1}^m y_i^{s_i}, (C_i' = B_i^{s_i})_{i \in [m]}, (C_i = \prod_{j=1}^m H_{ij}^{s_j})_{i \in I_\mathbb{S}} > .$$

Decrypt(CT, SK): This algorithm takes as input a cipher-text CT for an attribute set $\mathbb{S}_k$ and a private key SK associated with a monotone access structure $\mathbb{A}$. If $\mathbb{S}_k \in \mathbb{A}$ is an authorized set, then $I_{\mathbb{S}_k} \in I_\mathbb{A}$. The decryption algorithm computes

$$\frac{\prod_{i=1}^m \hat{e}(C_i', K_{1i}) \cdot \hat{e}(K_{2k}, \prod_{i=1}^m C_i')}{\prod_{i \in I_{\mathbb{S}_k}} \hat{e}(C_i, K_{3i})} = \prod_{i=1}^m y_i^{s_i}.$$

Finally, it can obtain the message M from C.

7 Conclusions

In this paper, we propose a security model of CP-ABE leakage resilient to auxiliary input, and a concrete construction based on linear secret sharing schemes. Our scheme can tolerate leakage on master key and attribute-based secret key with auxiliary input. For the security proof of our scheme, we present three modified static assumptions in composite order bilinear groups, and prove them in detail. Our scheme also can be easily extended to an ABE scheme resilient to continual auxiliary leakage, if it doesn't allow leakage in setup phase. Finally, we also propose a KP-ABE scheme resilient to auxiliary input.

Acknowledgments. This research is partially supported by the National Natural Science Foundation of China under Grant No.61373006, NSFC/RGC Joint Research Scheme of Hong Kong and China (N-HKU 729/13) and seed funding projects of HKU (201311159040 and 201411159142).

A Proofs of Three Modified Assumptions

We adopt the notion of [4] to denote an element $g_1^{a_1} g_2^{a_2} g_3^{a_3}$ of $\mathbb{G}$ as (a_1, a_2, a_3). The element $\hat{e}(g_1, g_1)^{a_1} \hat{e}(g_2, g_2)^{a_2} \hat{e}(g_3, g_3)^{a_3}$ in $\mathbb{G}_T$ will be denoted by $[a_1, a_2, a_3]$.

We use capital letter to denote the random variables. For example, $X = (X_1, Y_1, Z_1)$ is denoted as a random element of $\mathbb{G}$. We say that X is dependent on $\{A_i\}$, if there exists values $\lambda_i \in \mathbb{Z}_N$ such that $X = \sum_i \lambda_i A_i$. Otherwise, X is independent on $\{A_i\}$. For the security proof, we should review the following two theorems from [9].

Theorem 3 *(Theorem A.1 in [9]). Let $N = \prod_{i=1}^m p_i$ be a product of distinct primes, each greater than 2^λ. Let $\{A_i\}$ be a random variables set over $\mathbb{G}$, and let $\{B_i\}, T_0, T_1$ be random variables over $\mathbb{G}_T$, where all variables have the degree greater than t. The following game between an adversary $\mathfrak{A}$ and a challenger $\mathfrak{C}$ is in generic group model.*

Given $N, \{A_i\}, \{B_i\}, \mathfrak{C}$ chooses a random bit b, and sends T_b to $\mathfrak{A}$. $\mathfrak{A}$ outputs a bit b', and succeeds the game if $b' = b$.

If the following conditions are satisfied, then $\mathfrak{C}$ can find a nontrivial factor of N by using $\mathfrak{A}$ in time polynomial in λ with probability at least $\delta - \mathcal{O}(q^2 t/2^\lambda)$.

1. *Each of T_0 and T_1 is independent of $\{B_i\} \cup \{e(A_i, A_j)\}$.*
2. *$\mathfrak{A}$ issuing at most q queries and having advantage δ in the above game.*

Theorem 4 *(Theorem A.2 in [9]). Let $N = \prod_{i=1}^m p_i$ be a product of distinct primes, each greater than 2^λ. Let $\{A_i\}$ be a random variables set over $\mathbb{G}$, and let $\{B_i\}, T_0, T_1$ be random variables over $\mathbb{G}_T$, where all variables have the degree greater than t. The game between an adversary $\mathfrak{A}$ and a challenger $\mathfrak{C}$ is the same as above.*

Let $S := \{i | \hat{e}(T_0, A_i) \neq \hat{e}(T_1, A_i)\}$. If the following conditions are satisfied, then $\mathfrak{C}$ can find a nontrivial factor of N by using $\mathfrak{A}$ in time polynomial in λ with probability at least $\delta - \mathcal{O}(q^2 t/2^\lambda)$.

1. *Each of T_0 and T_1 is independent of $\{A_i\}$.*
2. *For all $k \in S$, $\hat{e}(T_0, A_k)$ and $\hat{e}(T_1, A_k)$ are independent of $\{B_i\} \cup \{\hat{e}(A_i, A_j)\} \cup \{\hat{e}(T_1, A_i)\}_{i \neq k}$.*
3. *$\mathfrak{A}$ issuing at most q queries and having advantage δ in the above game.*

We apply these two theorems to prove the hardness of our modified assumptions in generic group model.

modified 1-SDP assumption. To prove this assumption, we will use **Theorem 4**. Firstly, we can express this assumption as:

$$A_1 = (1, 0, 0), A_2 = (0, 0, X_3)$$
$$\{T_{0i} = (X_{1i}, X_{2i}, 0)\}_{i \in [m]}, \{T_{1i} = (X_{1i}, 0, 0)\}_{i \in [m]}$$

Since $\hat{e}(T_{0i}, A_1) = [X_{1i}, 0, 0] = \hat{e}(T_{1i}, A_1) = [X_{1i}, 0, 0]$ and $\hat{e}(T_{0i}, A_2) = [0, 0, 0] = \hat{e}(T_{1i}, A_2) = [0, 0, 0]$, we can note that $S = \emptyset$, and for all $i \in [m]$, T_{0i} and T_{1i} are independent of $\{A_1, A_2\}$ since X_{1i} does not exist in both A_1 and A_2. Then, in the game of Theorem 4, if $\exists i \in [m]$, the adversary $\mathfrak{A}$ can distinguish T_{0i} and T_{1i} with probability δ, then N can be factored with probability less than δ. Since it is hard to find a nontrivial factor of N, then the modified 1-SDP assumption is secure.

modified 2-SDP assumption. To prove this assumption, we will also use **Theorem 4**. Firstly, we can express this assumption as:

$$A_1 = (1,0,0), \{A_{2i} = (X_{1i}, X_{2i}, 0)\}_{i \in [m]}, A_3 = (0,0,X_3), A_4 = (0, Y_2, Y_3)$$

$$T_0 = (Z_1, Z_2, Z_3), T_1 = (Z_1, 0, Z_3)$$

We note that $S = \{\{2i\}_{i \in [m]}, 4\}$ in this case. It is clear that

1. Both T_0 and T_1 are independent of $\{A_i\}$, since Z_1 cannot be found in A_i's.
2. Since $\hat{e}(T_0, A_{2i}) = [X_{1i}Z_1, X_{2i}Z_2, 0]$,

$$\{\hat{e}(T_0, A_i)\}_{i \in \{1,3,4\}} = \{[Z_1, 0, 0], [0, 0, X_3Z_3], [0, Y_2Z_2, Y_3Z_3]\}$$

and

$$\{\hat{e}(T_0, A_{2j})\}_{j \in [m], j \neq i} = \{X_{1j}Z_1, X_{2j}Z_2, 0\}_{j \in [m], j \neq i}$$

$\hat{e}(T_0, A_{2i})$ is independent of $\{\hat{e}(A_i, A_j)\} \cup \{\hat{e} = (T_0, A_i)\}_{i \in \{1,3,4\}} \cup \{\hat{e} = (T_0, A_{2j})\}_{j \in [m], j \neq i}$. We can find that it is impossible to obtain $X_{1i}Z_1$ in the first coordinate of a combination of elements of $\{\hat{e}(A_i, A_j)\} \cup \{\hat{e} = (T_0, A_i)\}_{i \in \{1,3,4\}} \cup \{\hat{e} = (T_0, A_{2j})\}_{j \in [m], j \neq i}$. Obviously, $\hat{e}(T_1, A_{2i})$ is also independent of $\{\hat{e}(A_i, A_j)\} \cup \{\hat{e} = (T_0, A_i)\}_{i \in \{1,3,4\}} \cup \{\hat{e} = (T_0, A_{2j})\}_{j \in [m], j \neq i}$ due to the same reason.
3. From $\hat{e}(T_0, A_4) = [0, Y_2Z_2, Y_3Z_3]$ and $\hat{e}(T_1, A_4) = [0, 0, Y_3Z_3]$, we can conclude that $\hat{e}(T_0, A_4)$ and $\hat{e}(T_1, A_4)$ are both independent of $\{\hat{e}(A_i, A_j)\} \cup \{\hat{e} = (T_0, A_i)\}_{i \neq 4}$, since we cannot obtain Y_3Z_3 in the third coordinate of a combination of elements of $\{\hat{e}(A_i, A_j)\} \cup \{\hat{e} = (T_0, A_i)\}_{i \neq 4}$.

Thus, from Theorem 4, modified 2-SDP assumption is generically secure on the condition that it is hard to factor N.

modified BSDP assumption. We use **Theorem 3.** to prove this assumption. Firstly, we can express this assumption as:

$$A_1 = (1,0,0), \{A_{2i} = (1/b_i, 0, 0)\}_{i \in [m]}, \{A_{3i} = (b_i\alpha_i, X_2, 0)\}_{i \in [m]}, A_4 = (0, 0, X_3),$$

$$\{A_{5i} = (b_is_i, Y_2, 0)\}_{i \in [m]}, A_6 = (0, Z_2, 0), T_0 = [\sum_{i=1}^{m} \alpha_ib_is_i, 0, 0], T_1 = [Z_1, Z_2, Z_3].$$

We note that

1. It is clear that the only way to obtain $\sum_{i=1}^{m} \alpha_ib_is_i$ is to compute $\prod_{i=1}^{m} \hat{e}(A_{3i}, A_{5i})$. However, $\prod_{i=1}^{m} \hat{e}(A_{3i}, A_{5i}) = [\sum_{i=1}^{m} \alpha_ib_is_i, (X_2Y_2)^m, 0]$, then $(X_2Y_2)^m$ are left in the second coordinate that cannot be canceled. So T_0 is independent of $\{\hat{e}(A_i, A_j)\}$.
2. T_1 is independent of $\{\hat{e}(A_i, A_j)\}$, because Z_1, Z_2, Z_3 cannot be found in $\{A_i\}$.

From the discussion above, we can conclude that the modified BSDP assumption is generically secure under Theorem 3.

B Proofs of Lemma 1–4

Lemma 1. *If $Adv_A^{Game_{rl}} - Adv_A^{Game_{rt}} \geq \epsilon$, then Assumption 2 is broken.*

Proof: Let $\mathbb{A}^*$ denote the challenge access structure. For every $\mathcal{S}^* \in \mathbb{A}^*$, assuming that $\mathcal{S}^* = \{S_1, \cdots, S_n\}$ has n attributes[10], we define a superset of $\mathcal{S}^*$ as $\mathbb{S}^* = \{S_1'|S_1' = S_1 \mod p_2\} \cup \cdots \cup \{S_n'|S_n' = S_n \mod p_2\}$. Let Ω^* denote the collection of all $\mathbb{S}^*$s. If adversary $\mathfrak{A}$ makes key query on an attribute set $\Xi \notin \mathbb{A}^*$, for $\forall S_i' \in \Xi$, the challenger $\mathfrak{C}$ answers as follows:

- If $S_i' \notin \mathbb{S}^*$, for $\forall \mathbb{S}^* \in \Omega^*$, then $\mathfrak{C}$ responses by using MSK and the **KeyGen** algorithm.
- If $S_i' \in \mathbb{S}^*$, for $\exists \mathbb{S}^* \in \Omega^*$, then $S_i' \neq S_i$ and $S_i' = S_i \mod p_2$. $\mathfrak{C}$ computes $a = \gcd(S_i - S_i^*, N)$. We denote $b = N/a$, where $N = p_1 p_2 p_3$. We assume that $(g, X_1 X_2, X_3, Y_2 Y_3, T)$ is an instance from 2-SDP assumption.
  1. If $a = p_1 p_2$ and $b = p_3$, then $\mathfrak{C}$ can check whether $a = p_1 p_2$ from $(X_1 X_2)^a = 1$. If the equation holds, then $\mathfrak{C}$ can distinguish between $T \in \mathbb{G}_{p_1 p_3}$ and $T \in \mathbb{G}$ by using $\hat{e}(Y_2 Y_3, T)^b \overset{?}{=} 1$.
  2. If $a = p_2 p_3$ and $b = p_1$, then $\mathfrak{C}$ checks whether $a = p_2 p_3$ from $(Y_2 Y_3)^a = 1$. $\mathfrak{C}$ also can distinguish between $T \in \mathbb{G}_{p_1 p_3}$ and $T \in \mathbb{G}$ by using $\hat{e}(X_1 X_2, T)^b \overset{?}{=} 1$.
  3. If $a = p_2$ and $b = p_1 p_3$, then $\mathfrak{C}$ can distinguish between $T \in \mathbb{G}_{p_1 p_3}$ and $T \in \mathbb{G}$ by using $T^b \overset{?}{=} 1$. □

Then, the challenge ciphertext is converted into semi-functional in $Game_0$.

Lemma 2. *If $Adv_A^{Game_{rt}} - Adv_A^{Game_0} \geq \epsilon$, then modified Assumption 1 is broken.*

Proof: Given an instance $(N, g_1, X_3, \mathbb{G}, \mathbb{G}_T, (T_i)_{i \in [m]})$ of modified 1-SDP assumption, $\mathfrak{C}$ constructs the master public key MPK as

$$< g_1, X_3, (g_1^{a/b_i})_{i \in [m]}, B_1, \cdots, B_m, h_1, \cdots, h_U, (y_i = \hat{e}(g_1, B_i)^{\alpha_i})_{i \in [m]} >,$$

where $a, \alpha_i, b_i \in \mathbb{Z}_N$. The master secret key $MSK = (g_1^{\alpha_i} X_3^{u_i})_{i \in [m]}$. $\mathfrak{C}$ can answer the key extraction queries, key leakage queries and key update queries from $\mathfrak{A}$. In the challenge phase, $\mathfrak{A}$ provides the challenge message and access structure as $(M_0, M_1, \mathbb{A}^*)$. Then, $\mathfrak{C}$ randomly chooses values $\tilde{\lambda}_1, \cdots, \tilde{\lambda}_l, r_1, \cdots, r_l \in \mathbb{Z}_N$, and outputs the ciphertext CT^* as

$$< M_b \cdot \prod_{i=1}^{m} \hat{e}(g_1^{\alpha_i}, T_i), (T_i)_{i \in [m]}, (C_i = T_i^{a\tilde{\lambda}_i} h_{\rho(i)}^{-r_i}, D_i = g_1^{r_i})_{i \in [l]} >$$

If $T_i = g_1^{b_i s_i} g_2^{c_i} \in \mathbb{G}_{p_1 p_2}$, then CT^* is

$$< M_b \cdot \prod_{i=1}^{m} \hat{e}(g_1^{\alpha_i}, B_i^{s_i}), (B_i^{s_i} g_2^{\delta_i})_{i \in [m]}, (C_i = g_1^{a\lambda_i} h_{\rho(i)}^{-r_i} g_2^{\tau_i}, D_i = g_1^{r_i})_{i \in [l]} >,$$

---

[10] Here, each attribute is mapped to a random number in $\mathbb{Z}_N$.

where $\delta_i = c_i, \lambda_i = b_i \cdot s_i \cdot \tilde{\lambda}_i, \tau_i = ac\tilde{\lambda}_i$. This is a semi-functional ciphertext, and $\mathfrak{C}$ simulates $Game_0$. If $T_i \in \mathbb{G}_{p_1}$, $\mathfrak{C}$ can simulate a normal ciphertext game $Game_{rt}$. Thus, if $\mathfrak{A}$ can distinguish between a semi-functional ciphertext and a normal ciphertext with a non-negligible probability, then $\mathfrak{C}$ can use $\mathfrak{A}$'s output to break the modified Assumption 1. $\square$

Let Q denote the times of queries that $\mathfrak{A}$ issues when the challenge ciphertext is semi-functional. We set two types of attribute-based private key as follows:

Type I: $< (g_1^{\alpha_i + at/b_i} \cdot g_2^{z_i} g_3^{y_{1i}+u_i})_{i\in[m]}, g_1^t g_2^d g_3^{y_2}, (h_x^t g_3^{y_{3x}})_{x\in\mathbb{S}} >$
Type II: $< (g_1^{\alpha_i + at/b_i} \cdot g_3^{y_{1i}+u_i})_{i\in[m]}, g_1^t g_2^d g_3^{y_2}, (h_x^t g_3^{y_{3x}})_{x\in\mathbb{S}} >$

For $k = 1, \cdots, Q-1$, in $Game_k$, the first $k-1$ keys are semi-functional of type II, the k-th key is semi-functional of type I, and the rest keys are normal. Thus, in $Game_Q$, all keys are semi-functional of type II.

Lemma 3. *If* $Adv_A^{Game_{k+1}} - Adv_A^{Game_k} \geq \epsilon$, *then modified Assumption 2 is broken.*

Proof: Provided an instance $(g_1, (X_{1i}X_{2i})_{i\in[m]}, X_3, Y_2Y_3, T)$ of modified 2-SDP assumption, $\mathfrak{C}$ constructs the master public key

$$MPK :<\Theta, g_1, g_3, (g_1^{a/b_i})_{i\in[m]}, B_1, \cdots, B_m, h_1, \cdots, h_U, (y_i = e(g_1, B_i)^{\alpha_i})_{i\in[m]} >,$$

and the master secret key $MSK = (g_1^{\alpha_i} g_3^{u_i})_{i\in[m]}$. In the first $k-1$ key queries, $\mathfrak{C}$ answers with $< (g_1^{\alpha_i + at/b_i} \cdot g_3^{y_{1i}+u_i})_{i\in[m]}, g_1^t (Y_2Y_3)^h g_3^{y_2}, (h_x^t g_3^{y_{3x}})_{x\in\mathbb{S}} >$, which is a type II semi-functional key. For $k+1$-th to Q-th queries, $\mathfrak{C}$ answers with normal keys.

For the k-th query, $\mathfrak{C}$ answers the key as follows:

1. $< (g_1^{\alpha_i} \cdot T^a \cdot g_3^{y_{1i}+u_i})_{i\in[m]}, T \cdot g_3^{y_2}, (h_x^t g_3^{y_{3x}})_{x\in\mathbb{S}} >$
2. $< (g_1^{\alpha_i} \cdot T^a \cdot g_3^{y_{1i}+u_i})_{i\in[m]}, T \cdot g_3^{y_2} \cdot (Y_2Y_3)^h, (h_x^t g_3^{y_{3x}})_{x\in\mathbb{S}} >$

In case 1, if $T = g_1^t g_2^r g_3^s \in \mathbb{G}$, then the k-th key is a semi-functional key of type I. If $T = g_1^t g_3^s \in \mathbb{G}_{p_1 p_3}$, the k-th key is a normal form key.

In case 2, if $T = g_1^t g_2^r g_3^s \in \mathbb{G}$, then the k-th key is a semi-functional key of type I. However, if $T = g_1^t g_3^s \in \mathbb{G}_{p_1 p_3}$, the k-th key is a type II semi-functional key.

When $\mathfrak{A}$ makes a key leakage query, $\mathfrak{C}$ returns $f(MSK', \mathfrak{Q}, MPK, \mathbb{S})$, where MSK' is semi-functional, and for the last entry $< \cdot, \mathbb{S}, SK'_{\mathbb{S}} >\in \mathfrak{Q}$, $SK'_{\mathbb{S}}$ is a type II semi-functional key.

When $\mathfrak{A}$ makes a key update query, $\mathfrak{C}$ returns a type II semi-functional key $SK'_{\mathbb{S}}$ and the update times j', then puts $< j', \mathbb{S}, SK'_{\mathbb{S}} >$ to $\mathfrak{Q}$.

In the challenge phase, $\mathfrak{C}$ randomly chooses $\tilde{\lambda}_1, \cdots, \tilde{\lambda}_l \in \mathbb{Z}_N$, and returns the ciphertext as

$$C = M_b \prod_{i=1}^m \hat{e}(g_1^{\alpha_i}, X_{1i}X_{2i}), (C_i' = X_{1i}X_{2i})_{i\in[m]}, (C_i = (X_{1i}X_{2i})^{a\tilde{\lambda}_i} h_{\rho(i)}^{-r_i}, D_i = g_1^{r_i})_{i\in[l]}.$$

If we let $X_{1i}X_{2i} = g_1^{b_i s_i} g_2^{c_i}$, then

$$C = M_b \prod_{i=1}^{m} \hat{e}(g_1^{\alpha_i}, B_i^{s_i}), (C_i' = B_i^{s_i} g_2^{\delta_i})_{i \in [m]}, (C_i = g_1^{a\lambda_i} h_{\rho(i)}^{-r_i} g_2^{\tau_i}, D_i = g_1^{r_i})_{i \in [l]},$$

where $\delta_i = c_i, \lambda_i = b_i \cdot s_i \cdot \tilde{\lambda}_i, \tau_i = ac\tilde{\lambda}_i$. This is a semi-functional ciphertext.

We can thus conclude that, if $T \in \mathbb{G}$, $\mathfrak{C}$ can simulate $Game_{k+1}$. Otherwise, $\mathfrak{C}$ can simulate $Game_k$. From the above analysis, $\mathfrak{A}$ cannot distinguish between type I semi-functional key and normal form key in case 1, and $\mathfrak{A}$ also cannot distinguish between type I semi-functional key and type II semi-functional key in case 2. Thus, if an adversary has a non-negligible probability in $Adv_A^{Game_{k+1}} - Adv_A^{Game_k}$, then $\mathfrak{C}$ can break the modified 2-SDP assumption. $\square$

The final game $Game_f$ is the same as $Game_Q$ except that the message is masked with a random element in $\mathbb{G}_T$, instead of M_0, M_1. That is to say, the value of b is information theoretically hidden from $\mathfrak{A}$.

Lemma 4. If $Adv_A^{Game_Q} - Adv_A^{Game_f} \geq \epsilon$, then modified Assumption 3(modified BSDP assumption) is broken.

Proof: Given an instance $(g_1, (g_1^{1/b_i})_{i \in [m]}, (B_i^{\alpha_i} X_2)_{i \in [m]}, X_3, (B_i^{s_i} Y_2)_{i \in [m]}, Z_2, T)$ of modified BSDP assumption, $\mathfrak{C}$ sets $g_3 = X_3, g_2 = Z_2, y_i = \hat{e}(g_1, B_i^{\alpha_i} X_2) = \hat{e}(g_1, B_i)^{\alpha_i}$. $\mathfrak{C}$ constructs the master public key MPK and the master secret key $MSK = (B_i^{\alpha_i} X_2 \cdot g_3^{u_i})_{i \in [m]}$.

In key extraction phase, $\mathfrak{C}$ can answer all key queries as

$$SK_{\mathbb{S}} = < (K_{1i})_{i \in [m]}, K_2, (K_{3x})_{x \in \mathbb{S}} >$$
$$= < ((B_i^{\alpha_i} X_2) \cdot g_1^{at/b_i} \cdot g_3^{y_{1i}+u_i})_{i \in [m]}, g_1^t g_3^{y_2}, (h_x^t g_3^{y_{3x}})_{x \in \mathbb{S}} > .$$

$\mathfrak{C}$ also can answer the key leakage queries and key update queries from $\mathfrak{A}$, since it knows MSK.

In the challenge phase, $\mathfrak{C}$ randomly chooses $\tilde{\lambda}_1, \cdots, \tilde{\lambda}_l, r_1, \cdots, r_l \in \mathbb{Z}_N$ returns the ciphertext CT^* as

$$< M_b \cdot T, (B_i^{s_i} Y_2)_{i \in [m]}, (C_i = (B_i^{s_i} Y_2)^{a\tilde{\lambda}_i} h_{\rho(i)}^{-r_i}, D_i = g_1^{r_i})_{i \in [l]} >,$$

where T is the assumption term. Let $B_i^{s_i} Y_2 = B_i^{s_i} g_2^{c_i}$, then

$$< M_b \cdot T, (B_i^{s_i} g_2^{\delta_i})_{i \in [m]}, (C_i = g_1^{a\lambda_i} h_{\rho(i)}^{-r_i} g_2^{\tau_i}, D_i = g_1^{r_i})_{i \in [l]} >,$$

where $\delta_i = c_i, \lambda_i = b_i \cdot s_i \cdot \tilde{\lambda}_i, \tau_i = ac\tilde{\lambda}_i$. If $T = \prod_{i=1}^{m} \hat{e}(g_1, B_i)^{\alpha_i s_i}$, then CT^* is a semi-functional ciphertext and $\mathfrak{C}$ can simulate $Game_Q$ in this case. However, if $T \in \mathbb{G}_T$ is random element, then $\mathfrak{C}$ can simulate $Game_f$. Thus, if the adversary $\mathfrak{A}$ has non-negligible for distinguishing between $Game_f$ and $Game_Q$, then $\mathfrak{C}$ can break the modified BSDP assumption by using $\mathfrak{A}$'s output with the same probability. $\square$

References

1. Sahai, A., Waters, B.: Fuzzy identity-based encryption. In: Cramer, R. (ed.) EURO-CRYPT 2005. LNCS, vol. 3494, pp. 457–473. Springer, Heidelberg (2005)
2. Boneh, D., Goh, E.-J., Nissim, K.: Evaluating 2-DNF formulas on ciphertexts. In: Kilian, J. (ed.) TCC 2005. LNCS, vol. 3378, pp. 325–341. Springer, Heidelberg (2005)
3. Yuen, T.H., Chow, S.S.M., Zhang, Y., Yiu, S.M.: Identity-based encryption resilient to continual auxiliary leakage. In: Pointcheval, D., Johansson, T. (eds.) EURO-CRYPT 2012. LNCS, vol. 7237, pp. 117–134. Springer, Heidelberg (2012)
4. Lewko, A., Waters, B.: New techniques for dual system encryption and fully secure HIBE with short ciphertexts. In: Micciancio, D. (ed.) TCC 2010. LNCS, vol. 5978, pp. 455–479. Springer, Heidelberg (2010)
5. Lewko, A., Okamoto, T., Sahai, A., Takashima, K., Waters, B.: Fully secure functional encryption: attribute-based encryption and (hierarchical) inner product encryption. In: Gilbert, H. (ed.) EUROCRYPT 2010. LNCS, vol. 6110, pp. 62–91. Springer, Heidelberg (2010)
6. Goyal, V., Jain, A., Pandey, O., Sahai, A.: Bounded ciphertext policy attribute based encryption. In: Aceto, L., Damgård, I., Goldberg, L.A., Halldórsson, M.M., Ingólfsdóttir, A., Walukiewicz, I. (eds.) ICALP 2008, Part II. LNCS, vol. 5126, pp. 579–591. Springer, Heidelberg (2008)
7. Beimel, A., Gal, A., Paterson, M.: Lower bounds for monotone span programs. Comput. Complex. 6(1), 29–45 (1997)
8. Pandit, T., Barua, R.: Efficient fully secure attribute-based encryption schemes for general access structures. In: Takagi, T., Wang, G., Qin, Z., Jiang, S., Yu, Y. (eds.) ProvSec 2012. LNCS, vol. 7496, pp. 193–214. Springer, Heidelberg (2012)
9. Waters, B.: Dual system encryption: realizing fully secure IBE and HIBE under simple assumptions. In: Halevi, S. (ed.) CRYPTO 2009. LNCS, vol. 5677, pp. 619–636. Springer, Heidelberg (2009)
10. Waters, B.: Ciphertext-policy attribute-based encryption: an expressive, efficient, and provably secure realization. In: Catalano, D., Fazio, N., Gennaro, R., Nicolosi, A. (eds.) PKC 2011. LNCS, vol. 6571, pp. 53–70. Springer, Heidelberg (2011)
11. Beimel, A.: Secure schemes for secret sharing and key distribution. Ph.D. thesis, Israel Institute of Technology, Technion, Haifa, Israel (1996)
12. Zhang, M., Shi, W., Wang, C., Chen, Z., Mu, Y.: Leakage-resilient attribute-based encryption with fast decryption: models, analysis and constructions. In: Deng, R.H., Feng, T. (eds.) ISPEC 2013. LNCS, vol. 7863, pp. 75–90. Springer, Heidelberg (2013)
13. Dodis, Y., Goldwasser, S., Tauman Kalai, Y., Peikert, C., Vaikuntanathan, V.: Public-key encryption schemes with auxiliary inputs. In: Micciancio, D. (ed.) TCC 2010. LNCS, vol. 5978, pp. 361–381. Springer, Heidelberg (2010)
14. Akavia, A., Goldwasser, S., Vaikuntanathan, V.: Simultaneous hardcore bits and cryptography against memory attacks. In: Reingold, O. (ed.) TCC 2009. LNCS, vol. 5444, pp. 474–495. Springer, Heidelberg (2009)
15. Alwen, J., Dodis, Y., Naor, M., Segev, G., Walfish, S., Wichs, D.: Public-key encryption in the bounded-retrieval model. In: Gilbert, H. (ed.) EUROCRYPT 2010. LNCS, vol. 6110, pp. 113–134. Springer, Heidelberg (2010)
16. Dodis, Y., Lewko, A., Waters, B., Wichs, D.: Storing secrets on continually leaky devices. In: FOCS 2011, pp. 688–697 (2011)

17. Yang, B., Zhang, M.: LR-UESDE: a continual-leakage resilient encryption with unbounded extensible set delegation. In: Takagi, T., Wang, G., Qin, Z., Jiang, S., Yu, Y. (eds.) ProvSec 2012. LNCS, vol. 7496, pp. 125–142. Springer, Heidelberg (2012)

18. Zhang, M., Yang, B., Takagi, T.: Bounded leakage-resilient funtional encryption with hidden vector predicate. Comput. J. **56**(4), 464–477 (2013). Oxford

19. Canetti, R., Dodis, Y., Halevi, S., Kushilevitz, E., Sahai, A.: Exposure-resilient functions and all-ornothing transforms. In: EUROCRYPT, pp. 453–469 (2000)

20. Kamp, J., Zuckerman, D.: Deterministic extractors for bit- xing sources and exposure-resilient cryptography. In: FOCS, pp. 92–101 (2003)

21. Dziembowski, S., Pietrzak, K.: Leakage-resilient cryptography. In: FOCS, pp. 293–302 (2008)

22. Faust, S., Kiltz, E., Pietrzak, K., Rothblum, G.N.: Leakage-resilient signatures. In: Micciancio, D. (ed.) TCC 2010. LNCS, vol. 5978, pp. 343–360. Springer, Heidelberg (2010)

23. Alwen, J., Dodis, Y., Naor, M., Segev, G., Walfish, S., Wichs, D.: Public-key encryption in the bounded-retrieval model. In: Gilbert, H. (ed.) EUROCRYPT 2010. LNCS, vol. 6110, pp. 113–134. Springer, Heidelberg (2010)

24. Alwen, J., Dodis, Y., Wichs, D.: Leakage-resilient public-key cryptography in the bounded-retrieval model. In: Halevi, S. (ed.) CRYPTO 2009. LNCS, vol. 5677, pp. 36–54. Springer, Heidelberg (2009)

25. Di Crescenzo, G., Lipton, R.J., Walfish, S.: Perfectly secure password protocols in the bounded retrieval model. In: Halevi, S., Rabin, T. (eds.) TCC 2006. LNCS, vol. 3876, pp. 225–244. Springer, Heidelberg (2006)

26. Dodis, Y., Haralambiev, K., Lopez-Alt, A., Wichs, D.: Cryptography against continuous memory attacks. In: FOCS, pp. 511–520 (2010)

27. Lewko, A., Rouselakis, Y., Waters, B.: Achieving leakage resilience through dual system encryption. In: Ishai, Y. (ed.) TCC 2011. LNCS, vol. 6597, pp. 70–88. Springer, Heidelberg (2011)

On Provable Security of wPRF-Based Leakage-Resilient Stream Ciphers

Maciej Skórski[✉]

Cryptology and Data Security Group, University of Warsaw, Warsaw, Poland
maciej.skorski@mimuw.edu.pl

Abstract. Weak pseudorandom functions (wPRFs) found an important application as main building blocks for leakage-resilient ciphers (EURO-CRYPT'09 and later works). Several security bounds, based on different techniques and different assumptions, were given to those stream ciphers. The aim of this paper is twofold. First, we present a clear comparison of quantitatively different security bounds in the literature, obtained by means of *time-to-success ratio* analysis. Second, we revisit the current proof techniques and answer the natural question of how far we are from meaningful and provable security guarantees, when instantiating weak PRFs with standard primitives (block ciphers or hash functions). In particular, we attempt to fix some flaws in the recent analysis of the EURO-CRYPT'09 stream cipher (TCC'14), applying new proof techniques to the problem of *simulating auxiliary inputs*. For one bit of leakage, for the first time, we achieve meaningful security of 60 bits when the cipher is build on the AES.

Keywords: Leakage-resilient cryptography · Stream ciphers · Simulating side information · Convex approximation

1 Introduction

1.1 Leakage-Resilient Cryptography

Leakage Resilience. Traditional security notions in cryptography consider adversaries who can interact with a primitive only in a black-box manner, observing its input/output behavior. Unfortunately, this assumption is unrealistic in practice. In fact, information might leak from cryptograms at the *physical implementation* layer. The attacks that capture information this way are called *side-channel attacks*, and include power consumption analysis [KJJ99], timing attacks [Koc96], fault injection attacks [BBKN12] or memory attacks [HSH+08]. Searching for countermeasures against side-channel attacks, one can try to prevent them modifying software or further secure hardware. However, these techniques are more ad-hoc than generic. A completely different viewpoint is to

M. Skórski—This work was partly supported by the WELCOME/2010-4/2 grant founded within the framework of the EU Innovative Economy Operational Programme.

M.-H. Au and A. Miyaji (Eds.): ProvSec 2015, LNCS 9451, pp. 391–411, 2015.
DOI: 10.1007/978-3-319-26059-4_22

provide primitives which are *provably secure against leakage*. The research field following this paradigm is called *leakage-resilient cryptography*, and has become very popular in recent years. A lot of work and progress has been done in this topic so far, since the breakthrough paper on resilient stream ciphers [DP08], much more than we could mention here. We refer the reader to [ADW09] and [Mol10] for good surveys.

Modeling Leakage. A number of ways to capture the leakage has been proposed. Very first works focused on strongly restricting the type of leakage. Here we briefly discuss most important ones, referring interested readers to surveys.

- *exposure resilient cryptography.* In this line of work, the type of leakage is restricted so that adversaries learn subsets of the bits of the secret state key [CDH+00,DSS01].
- *continuous bounded computational leakage.* Perhaps the most popular line of research restricting the leakage type, based on the "only computation leaks information" axiom introduced Micali and Reyzin [MR04]. In this modeling approach the overal execution of a cryptographic protocol is divided into time frames, and in every round leakage comes only from the parts of the internal state which are touched by computations. The amount of leakage is bounded in every round but unbounded overall. This model successfully captures side-channels attacks resulting from computation [Mol10], however memory attacks are more problematic as they are possible even if no computation is performed [HSH+08]. Nonetheless, leakage-resilient constructions under the "only computation leaks information" assumption, are of big interest [DP08,Pie09,DP10,FPS12,YS13], to mention only stream-ciphers related works. We also note that in specific cases, in particular for stream ciphers we will be interested in, the authors argue that their security models go beyond the "only computation leaks information" assumption and actually capture memory attacks (cf. [Pie09]).
- *probing attacks.* In this approach, initiated in [ISW03], adversaries can learn or influence the values at some wires, during the evaluation of a cicuit.
- *auxiliary inputs.* The works [DKL09,DGK+10] study a setting where adversaries can learn a function of the secret state, which is hard to invert. It allows leaking information larger than the size of the secret state and is believed to be most practical. However, it is also considered very challenging to proving security of constructions in this model.

Being interested in leakage-resilient stream ciphers, we follow the related works and focus on continuous computational leakage through this paper (see Sect. 2 for a formal definition in the concrete setting).

1.2 Leakage-Resilient Stream Ciphers

What Are Atream Ciphers? The purpose of stream ciphers is to efficiently encrypt data streams of arbitrary length. The most popular construction mimics the one-time pad encryption, by deploying a generator which stretches the initial randomness into a keystream. Such a generator, when initialized with a secret state, recursively computes a sequence of output blocks, where the security requirement is that the last block looks random given the previous outputs. Note that one block of input data can be encrypted with a key stretched by a pseudorandom generator. However, it determines the maximum size of the input block and the key. To generate the long keystream, not just one fixed-length key, one replaces the PRG with pseudorandom or weak-pseudorandom functions, which are designed to work with many inputs. For more details and the formal definition see Definition 2.

Leakage-Resilient Design. The main concern in proving leakage-resilience is that the keystream generator must be secure against leakages, which appear in every round (in the continuous leakage model). Such a generator could be deployed either with a pseudorandom generator and extractor [DP08], or a weak pseudorandom functions [Pie09, YSPY10, FPS12, YS13]. In any case, the idea is to refresh the secret state (key) in every round, to make compromising it possibly difficult. Below we briefly discuss some advantages of the second approach, and return to a more detailed discussion of the concrete designs in Sect. 3.

Why wPRFs-Based Design? Informally, pseudorandom functions look random on many adversarialy chosen inputs (under a uniform secret key), whereas weak pseudorandom functions look random only on random inputs. Below we elaborate more on why weak pseudorandom functions are of special interests for leakage-resilient stream cipher constructions.

(a) From a high-level viewpoint, we have at least two very good reasons to build leakage-resilient stream ciphers using weak PRFs, as proposed in [Pie09]. First, this approach is simple and thus more efficient to implement and much easier to analyze than the original proposal [DP08], which combines a pseudorandom generator and an extractor. Second, and most important, it less vurnelable to side-channel attacks and more reliable from a practical viewpoint. This is because the construction can be instantiated with only one component - a weak PRF. Mounting an attack against one component is less likely, as opposed to the original construction [Sta10, MS11, MSJ12]. Moreover, this construction is more reliable from a practical viewpoint when instantiated with block ciphers understood as weak PRFs (like AES), because their security against side-channel attacks has been carefully analyzed.

(b) From a technical viewpoint, weak pseudorandom functions are primitives very pleasurable to deal with in the context of leakage. As opposed to (strong) pseudorandom functions they can be shown to remain secure with weak keys (that is when keys are not uniform but have some entropy deficiency) [DY13, Pie09], which is the key ingredient of the cipher resilience proof. Security with weak keys can be proven either by a computational variant of the Dense Model Theorem [Pie09] or by a recent techniques involving the square-security notion [DY13].

1.3 Reductions Quality Issues

The security of leakage-resilient stream ciphers is always proven by a reduction to underlying more standard components, as pseudorandom generators, extractors, pseudorandom functions, whose security is generally better understood. Proving these bounds is challenging and still we can only prove quite poor bounds, unless we impose strong idealistic assumptions. Below we elaborate more on this topic.

(a) *Significant security losses in the standard model.* Reduction proofs yield quite weak bounds, and this is common for all related works. For leakage-resilient stream ciphers we have to lose a constant fraction of the security compared to its original level, even if the leakage is just one bit!

(b) *No provable security with standard building bricks.* When we aim for the (provable) security level recommended nowadays, which is at least 80 bits, we need primitives (like block ciphers) whose security is bigger than 400 bits, given current knowledge. This is a direct consequence of the issue with weak reductions we mentioned above.

(c) *Different bounds are hard to compare.* Depending on the technique, different bounds are obtained. Formulas offer security against different adversarial profiles - running time, success probability, leakage length.

1.4 Problem and Results, Informally

The aim of this paper is to understand *limitations* of proofs for leakage resilient stream ciphers. Motivated in this, we state our problem as a series of questions concerning *what can and what can't be achieved* for resilient stream ciphers given the current state of the art in the standard model. We briefly answer them, announcing our results informally, and discuss in the next section in more detail.

Q1: How tight are reduction-based security proofs for leakage-resilient stream ciphers?

We revisit the best known bounds and analyze the tightness of reductions using time-success ratios. We discuss these tools in more detail in the next section.

A1: All results loses more than 75 % of the original security (measured in bits), paying for the resilience feature. This holds even for one bit of leakage per computation!

The second issue we address is how far we really are from having provable security for constructions instantiated from practically used components.

Q2: Can we instantiate a leakage-resilient stream cipher, provable secure in the standard model, with a standard (128 or 256-bit) block cipher as a weak PRF?

The most serious attempt to achieve meaningful security using standard 256-bit block ciphers is due to Pietrzak and Jetchev [JP14]. They improved and simplified bounds for the EUROCRYPT'09 stream cipher. However, as we will explain later, the better of the two claimed bounds doesn't apply because of a flaw in the proof [Pie15].

A2: In general no, given the current state of art. The recent analysis from TCC'14 which gives an affirmative answer, contains a flaw (we will discuss it in Sect. 4.3). However, we can provide meaningful security bounds of ~ 60 bits for one bit of leakage, with a slightly different proof technique. See Table 1 in Sect. 5.

Because of the lack of a positive answer above, it is natural to ask how strong our starting primitive needs to be, given current proof techniques. We believe that it is of interests to know how far we are with provable secure bounds from the idealized bounds, given that this approach seems to be relatively rarely taken.

Q3: How strong a weak PRF has to be, to achieve the recommended security level of 80 bits, given the known constructions?

Using our time-success ratio analysis we give an answer

A3: At least with 512 bits of security (and assuming small leakage). We therefore propose to instantiate with SHA512 as a weak PRF.

1.5   Results and Techniques in Details

Flaws in the Recent Analysis of the EUROCRYPT'09 Stream Cipher. Jetchev and Pietrzak came up with an elegant idea to simplify the security proof of the EUROCRYPT'09 stream cipher built from a weak PRF. To this end, they prove a theorem about simulating auxiliary inputs, giving two alternative proofs [JP14]. One of them would imply good security in the standard model, with the AES as a weak PRF (for the first time). Unfortunately, as we point out in Sect. 4.3 in this paper, the proof of this stronger bound is wrong. For this reason, only the second much weaker bound applies so we cannot prove meaningful security instantiating the stream cipher with a standard 256 block cipher, like AES.

An Improved Simulator for Auxiliary Inputs and Better Security for the EURO-CRYPT'09 Stream Cipher. We don't know how to completely fix the issue with the flawed analysis in [JP14]. However, we come up with two new ideas:

(a) we can improve the min-max based alternative proof of the simulating lemma by a significant factor, which gives a better analysis of the stream cipher than the [JP14] but not better than the result of Vadhan and Zheng [VZ13].
(b) by a boosting technique we prove much better security than already known, for the special case of 1 bit of leakage.

We refer the reader to Theorems 4 and 5 in Sect. 4.3 for more details.

A Framework to Compare Different Reductions. Bellare and Rogaway [BR96] were first who emphasized the importance of studying the tightness of security proofs in practical applications. Following the approach proposed by Luby [LM94], based on time-success ratio (see Sect. 2.2), we provide a general tool for determining the security of every stream cipher reducing to a weak PRF. Technically, by constrained optimization we determine the time-success ratio of a stream cipher from the security of its main building component. This approach is used in different area of provable security (cf. [BL13] and many similar works), but to our knowledge has never been taken with respect to leakage-resilient stram ciphers (in particular in all the works we cite).

A Clear Security Loss Formula. We abstract the "typical form" for the loss in most reductions from a stream cipher to the underlying weak PRF. Namely the time/advantage pairs, describing adversarial resources and success probability, for the original primitive (s, ϵ) and for the cipher (s', ϵ') are related as $\epsilon' = \epsilon^A$ and $s' = s \cdot \epsilon^C - \epsilon^{-B}$ for some *explicit constants* A, B, C in the exponents. Extending slightly this model to capture leakage-depended factors, we actually cover all related works. We solve the related optimization program and show how *explicitly* the time-success ratio degradation depends on these constants (see Sect. 4.2). It turns out that what remains is a fraction of $\sim \frac{A}{B+C+1}$ of the original security (in bits). For all constructions, this is smaller than 25 %.

A Survey of Known Results. We present the time-success ratio analysis of wPRF-based leakage-resilient stream ciphers. The lack of such results is perhaps partially because of complicated formulas, and partially because in folklore these bounds are considered mainly of theoretical interests. Yet, we believe that comparing these bounds is interesting, in particular with respect to the "dream bounds" corresponding to the flawed analysis in [JP14], which - if can be proven - gives a much better security level than other techniques. For more details, see Sect. 5.

2 Preliminaries

2.1 Leakage Resilient Cryptography

We start with the definition of weak pseudorandom functions, which are *computationaly indistinguishable* from random functions, when queried on random inputs and fed with iniform secret key.

Definition 1 (Weak pseudorandom functions). *A function* $F : \{0,1\}^k \times \{0,1\}^n \to \{0,1\}^m$ *is an* (ϵ, s, q)*-secure weak PRF if its outputs on* q *random inputs are indistinguishable from random, that is when for any distinguisher (probabilistic circuit)* D *of size* s *it holds that*

$$|\Pr[D((X_i)_{i=1}^q, F((K, X_i)_{i=1}^q) = 1] - \Pr[D((X_i)_{i=1}^q, (R_i)_{i=1}^q) = 1]| \leqslant \epsilon$$

where the probability is over the choice of the random $X_i \leftarrow \{0,1\}^n$*, the choice of a random key* $K \leftarrow \{0,1\}^k$ *and* $R_i \leftarrow \{0,1\}^m$ *conditioned on* $R_i = R_j$ *if* $X_i = X_j$ *for some* $j < i$.

Stream ciphers generate a keystream in a recursive manner. The security requires the output stream should be indistinguishable from uniform[1].

---

[1] We note that in a more standard notion the entire stream $X_1, \ldots, X_q$ is indistinguishable from random. This is implied by the notion above by a standard hybrid argument, with a loss of a multiplicative factor of q in the distinguishing advantage.

Definition 2 (Stream ciphers). *A stream-cipher* $\mathsf{SC} : \{0,1\}^k \to \{0,1\}^k \times \{0,1\}^n$ *is a function that need to be initialized with a secret state* $S_0 \in \{0,1\}^k$ *and produces a sequence of output blocks* $X_1, X_2, \ldots$ *computed as*

$$(S_i, X_i) := \mathsf{SC}(S_{i-1}).$$

A stream cipher SC *is* (ϵ, s, q)-*secure if for all* $1 \leqslant i \leqslant q$, *the random variable* X_i *is* (s, ϵ)-*indistinguishable from random given* $X_1, \ldots, X_{i-1}$ *(the probability is also over the choice of the initial random key* S_0*).*

Now we define the security of leakage resilient stream ciphers, which follows the "only computation leaks" assumption. Note that leakage is modeled as arbitrary information of specified length, not necessarily efficiently computable.

Definition 3 (Leakage-resilient stream ciphers [JP14]). *A leakage-resilient stream-cipher is* $(\epsilon, s, q, \lambda)$-*secure if it is* (ϵ, s, q)-*secure as defined above, but where the distinguisher in the j-th round gets* λ *bits of arbitrary deceptively chosen leakage about the secret state accessed during this round. More precisely, for* $j = 1, \ldots, q$ *before* $(S_j, X_j) := \mathsf{SC}(S_{j-1})$ *is computed, the distinguisher D in Definition 2 can choose any leakage function* f_j *with range* $\{0,1\}^\lambda$, *and then not only get* X_j, *but also* $\Lambda_j := f_j(\hat{S}_{j-1})$, *where* $\hat{S}_{j1}$ *denotes the part of the secret state that was modified (i.e., read, overwritten) in the computation* $\mathsf{SC}(S_{j-1})$.

2.2 Time-Success Ratio

The running time (circuit size) s and success probability ϵ of attacks against a particular primitive or protocol may vary. For this reason Luby [LM94] introduced the time-success ratio $\frac{t}{\epsilon}$ as a universal measure of security. This model widely used to analyze security, cf. [BL13] and related works.

Definition 4 (Security by Time-Success Ratio [LM94]). *A primitive P is said to be* 2^k-*secure if for every adversary with time resources (circuit size in the nonuniform model)* s, *the success probability in breaking P (advantage) is at most* $\epsilon < s \cdot 2^{-k}$. *We also say that the time-success ratio of P is* 2^k, *or that is has k bits of security.*

For example, the AES with a 256-bit random key is believed to have 256 bits of security as a *weak* PRF[2].

3 Leakage-Resilient Stream Ciphers Design

In this section we briefly discuss the known constructions of leakage-resilient stream ciphers in the standard model (without random-oracle assumptions).

---

[2] We consider the security of AES256 as a weak PRF, and not a standard PRF, because of non-uniform attacks which show that no PRF with a k bit key can have $s/\epsilon \approx 2^k$ security [DTT09], at least unless we additionally require $\epsilon \gg 2^{-k/2}$.

3.1 The Very First Idea (FOCS'08)

The first construction of leakage-resilient stream cipher was proposed by Dziembowski and Pietrzak in [DP08]. It has the characteristic *alternating structure* which allows for proving security against *adaptively chosen leakage*.

3.2 A Construction Based on a wPRF (EUROCRYPT'09)

On Fig. 1 below we present a simplified version of this cipher [Pie09] based on a weak pseudorandom function (wPRF). A weak pseudorandom function is a primitive which "looks" like a random function when queried on random inputs, see Sect. 2 for a formal definition.

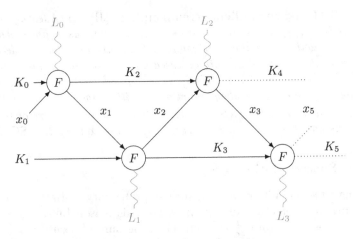

Fig. 1. The EUROCRYPT'09 stream cipher (adaptive leakage). F denotes a weak PRF. By K_i and x_i we denote, respectively, values of the secret state and keystream bits. Leakages are denoted in gray with L_i.

3.3 Saving Key Randomness (CSS'10, CHES'12)

A slightly different approach is proposed in [YSPY10]. The authors argue that side-channel attacks in practice are mounted against a specific target, and require specific measurements equipment; thus adaptive security is somewhat an overkill. The second observation is that the cipher in [Pie09] seems to waste lots of randomness, because the security in best case is only comparable to the length of one secret key, whereas the cipher is initialized with two random keys (denoted with K_0, K_1 on Fig. 1). They remove the alternating structure and use only one key and two alternating public random values, aiming at (weaker) non-adaptive security. Unfortunately, the proof that these two alternating public values are enough were wrong, as pointed out in [FPS12]. However one gets provable non-adaptive security, assuming that every round uses fresh randomness [FPS12].

Such a big amount of randomness makes the cipher inpractical, but the authors show how to reduce it further. Summing up, one gets only non-adaptive security but saves secret randomness replacing the "wasted" key by a public string. The scheme is illustrated in Fig. 2 below.

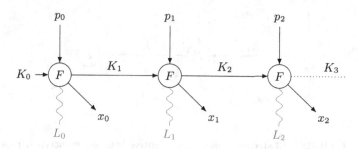

Fig. 2. The CSS'10/CHES'12 stream cipher. F denotes a waek PRF. By K_i and x_i we denote, respectively, the values of secret state and keystream bits. Leakages are denoted in gray with L_i. The cipher requires public independent random values p_i.

3.4 Saving Public Randomness (CT-RSA'13)

The problem with large public randomness, required for the last cipher, was addressed in [YSPY10]. The public values, required in the previous construction, are generated on-the-fly from a single public value, by running a strong PRF in counter mode on it. For an illustration, see Fig. 3 below. The result is only conditional and holds in the hypothetical world minicrypt, where one-way functions exist, but there is no public-key cryptography. Still, it may be a good clue on what we should expect in the standard model.

4 Results

4.1 The Time-Success Ratio Under Reductions

We consider first a very abstract setting, where a primitive P' is built from P. Assume, that the security of P' reduces to the security of P in the following quantitative way:

R: If P is secure against an adversary (s, ϵ), then P' is secure against any adversary (s', ϵ'), where

$$s' = p(s, \epsilon),$$
$$\epsilon' = q(s, \epsilon) \tag{1}$$

for some functions $p(\cdot), q(\cdot)$.

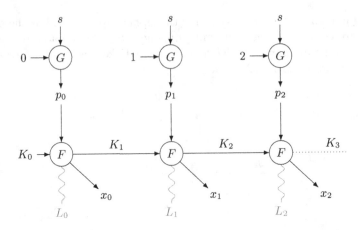

Fig. 3. The CTR-RSA'13 stream cipher (nonadaptive leakage, minicrypt). F is a weak PRF and G is a strong PRF. By K_i and x_i we denote, respectively, the values of secret state and keystream bits. Leakages are denoted in gray with L_i. The function F generating the keystream is re-randomized using values p_i, produced by G in counter mode from the single public seed s.

In the simplest case, the functions $p(\cdot)$ and $q(\cdot)$ are algebraic functions of original parameters, like $\epsilon' = \epsilon^{1/2}$ or $s' = s\epsilon^2$ (the second case appears particularly often as a result of the Chernoff Bounds). In leakage-resilient cryptography these formulas are more complicated and typically involve some additional parameters, like the leakage length or the number of queries. The natural question here is how the security, understood as in Definition 4, of P and P' are related to each other. Before we give the general answer (the proof appears in Appendix A).

Theorem 1 (The time-success ratio as min-max optimization). *Let security of P' reduces to security of P as in Eq. (1). If P has k bits of security then P' has k' bits of security where k' is the maximal value such that the following program*

$$\underset{(s',\epsilon')}{\text{minimize}} \ \underset{(s,\epsilon)}{\text{maximize}} \quad \frac{s'}{\epsilon'}$$

$$\text{s.t.} \quad \frac{s'}{\epsilon'} \leqslant 2^{k'}, 1 \leqslant s', \ 0 \leqslant \epsilon' \tag{2}$$

$$\frac{s}{\epsilon} \leqslant 2^{k}, \ 1 \leqslant s, \ 0 \leqslant \epsilon$$

$$s' \leqslant p(s,\epsilon), \ \epsilon' \geqslant q(s,\epsilon)$$

has a positive finite value.

Remark 1. If we cannot find a pair (s,ϵ) corresponding to (s',ϵ') then the feasible set in Eq. (2) is empty, so that the value of the program becomes $-\infty$.

4.2 The Time-Success Ratio Under Algebraic Transformations

In the most typical case we can solve Eq. (2) explicitly, as shown by Theorem 2 below.

Theorem 2 (Time-success ratio for algebraic transformations). *Let* a, b, c *and* A, B, C *be positive constants. Suppose that* P' *is secure against adversaries* (s', ϵ'), *whenever* P *is secure against adversaries* (s, ϵ), *where*

$$s' = s \cdot c \epsilon^C - b \epsilon^{-B}$$
$$\epsilon' = a \epsilon^A. \tag{3}$$

In addition, suppose that the following condition is satisfied

$$A \leqslant C + 1. \tag{4}$$

Then the following is true: if P *is* 2^k*-secure, then* P' *is* $2^{k'}$*-secure where*

$$k' = \begin{cases} \frac{A}{B+C+1}k + \frac{A}{B+C+1}(\log c - \log b) - \log a, & b \geqslant 1 \\ \frac{A}{C+1}k + \frac{A}{C+1}\log c - \log a, & b = 0 \end{cases} \tag{5}$$

The proof is elementary though not immediate. It appears in Appendix B.

Remark 2 (On the technical condition (4)). This condition is satisfied in almost all applications, at in the reduction proof typically ϵ' cannot be better (meaning higher exponent) than ϵ. Thus, quite often we have $A \leqslant 1$.

4.3 Towards Fixing the Flaw in the Recent EUROCRYPT'09 Stream Cipher Analysis (TCC'13)

Simulating Auxiliary Inputs. The work [JP14] studied the problem of approximately computing (simulating) short information Z from correlated X. This problem is motivated by applications in leakage-resilient cryptography, where it is convenient to represent leakage Z from some secret state X as the function $Z = h(X)$. Since perfect equality means that h is inefficient, one considers computational relaxations (making h efficient at the cost of accepting some errors). The answer is given below (here we state the corrected version [Pie15]):

Lemma 1 (Simulating auxiliary inputs [JP14]). *For any random variable* $X \in \{0,1\}^n$, *any correlated* $Z \in \{0,1\}^\lambda$ *and every choice of parameters* (ϵ, s) *there is a randomized function* $\mathsf{Sim} : \{0,1\}^n \to \{0,1\}^\lambda$ *of complexity* $O\left(s \cdot 2^{4\lambda} \epsilon^{-4}\right)$ *such that* Z *and* $\mathsf{Sim}(X)$ *are* (ϵ, s)*-indistinguishable given* X.

This theorem is the core of the improved analysis of the EUROCRYPT'09 stream cipher. Using it, as described in [JP14], one proves the resilience of the cipher if the underlying weak PRF is (s, ϵ)-secure against two queries on random inputs.

Theorem 3 (Security of the EC'09 stream cipher, depending on the simulator complexity). *If F is an $(\epsilon_F, s_F, 2)$-secure weak PRF then the EC'09 stream cipher* SC^F *is a* $(\epsilon', s', q, \lambda)$*-secure leakage resilient stream cipher where*

$$\epsilon' = 4q\sqrt{\epsilon_F 2^\lambda}, \quad s' = \Theta(1) \cdot \frac{s_F \epsilon'^4}{2^{4\lambda}}.$$

Remark 3 (The exact complexity loss). The inspection of the proof shows that in general s' is such that s_F equals the complexity of the simulator in Lemma 1 applied to the class of all circuits of size $s = s'$ and the advantage $\epsilon = \epsilon'$.

More on the Flaws. In the claimed better bound $O\left(s \cdot 2^{3\lambda} \epsilon^{-2}\right)$ there is a mistake on page 18 (eprint version). The argument given is a boosting algorithm: whenever we find some "bad" distinguisher D of size s, we can improve the current simulator towards the direction pointed by D. The authors enforce the obtained signed measure to be a probability measure by a mass shifting argument applied to the function D. However the number M defined there is in fact a hard-to-compute function of x, not a constant independent on x. For this reason, we actually build the simulator from functions much more complicated than of size s; the final complexity would be bigger than polynomial in ϵ^{-1} [Pie15].

In the alternative bound $O\left(s \cdot 2^{3\lambda} \epsilon^{-4}\right)$ a fixable flaw is a missing factor of 2^λ in the complexity (page 16 in the eprint version), which is because what is constructed in the proof is only a probability mass function, not yet a sampler [Pie15].

Our Improvements

Our Improvement. We don't know how to reduce the exponent in ϵ in general. However, we offer improvements in two special cases: a better min-max based proof and a much better boosting proof for one bit of leakage. For proofs, see Appendixes C and D. For a comparison with related works [JP14, VZ13] we refer to Table 1.

Theorem 4 (Simulating auxiliary inputs, better min-max proof). *For every joint distribution (X, Z) on $\mathcal{X} \times \{0, 1\}^\lambda$ and every ϵ, s there exists a "simulator" $h : \mathcal{X} \to \{0, 1\}^\lambda$ such that (a) the distributions of $(X, h(X))$ and (X, Z) are (s, ϵ)-indistinguishable and (b) h is of complexity $s_h = O\left(s \cdot 2^{2\lambda} \epsilon^{-4}\right)$.*

The proof technique utilizes a variant of the Baron-Maurey convex approximation theorem, combined with the standard min-max argument (we start by showing how to construct a simulator for every single D which is much easier).

Theorem 5 (Simulating auxiliary inputs, much better boosting proof for $\lambda = 1$ bit of leakage). *For every joint distribution (X, Z) on $\mathcal{X} \times \{0, 1\}^\lambda$ and every s, ϵ there exists a simulator $h : \mathcal{X} \to \mathcal{Z}$ such that (a) (X, Z) and $(X, h(X))$ are (s, ϵ)-indistinguishable and (b) h is of complexity at most $s_h = O\left(s \cdot \epsilon^{-2}\right)$*

The proof goes by a boosting argument where as long as we find D which contradicts property (a), we can use it to improve the current simulator by a shifting argument. The technical problems are to guarantee that the loop terminates and that the corrected simulator is still a valid probability measure.

5 Survey of Security Bounds

In Table 1 below we present the comparison of different bounds for leakage-resilient stream ciphers built from weak PRFs. We assume that the number of blocks q is constant. Without loosing generality, we assume that the time-advantage ratio for our PRF is constant, that is $s/\epsilon \approx 2^k$ where k is the key length. This corresponds to the assumption that the best attack is a brute-force search[3]. This assumption is reasonable, for example best block ciphers like AES are believed to have such security as PRFs. The security is computed by putting the bounds from the related works to Theorem 2 (we omit computations). Note that for the simulator technique we use Theorem 3 with Remark 3.

Table 1. Different bounds for wPRF-based leakage-resilient stream ciphers. k is the security level of the wPRF. The value k' is the security level for the cipher, understood in terms of time-success ratio. The numbers denote: (1) the EUROCRYPT'09 cipher, (2) the CSS'10/CHES'12 cipher, (3) the CT-RSA'13 cipher. The *Dream Bound* is related to the conjecture that best simulator complexity loss in Lemma 1 is by a factor of $O(2^\lambda \epsilon^{-2})$ (the best of [JP14] and [VZ13]).

Cipher	Analysis	Proof techniques	Security level	Comments
(1)	[Pie09]	Pseudoentropy chain rules	$k' \ll \frac{1}{8}k$	large number of blocks
(1)	[JP14]	Aux. Inputs Simulator (corr.)	$k' \approx \frac{k}{6} - \frac{5}{6}\lambda$	
(1)	[VZ13]	Aux. Inputs Simulator	$k' \approx \frac{k}{6} - \frac{1}{3}\lambda$	
(1)	**this work**	Aux. Inputs Simulator (impr.)	$k' \approx \frac{k}{6} - \frac{1}{2}\lambda$	
(1)	**this work**	Aux. Inputs Simulator	$k' \approx \frac{k}{4}$	only for $\lambda = 1$
(1)	*Dream bound*	Aux. Inputs Simulator (impr.)	$k' \approx \frac{k}{4} - \lambda$	unproven (the flaw)
(2)	[FPS12]	Pseudoentropy chain rules	$k' \approx \frac{k}{5} - \frac{3}{5}\lambda$	large public seed
(3)	[YS13]	Square-friendly apps	$k' \approx \frac{k}{4} - \frac{3}{4}\lambda$	only in minicrypt

It seems that the best cipher (in the standard model) is the EUROCRYPT'09 cipher. It provides the adaptive security in the standard model and loses about $\frac{5}{6}$ of its original security (the best analysis is due to Vadhan, the second best is this paper). The CSS'10/CHES'12 loses about $\frac{4}{5}$ of its original security but requires large public randomness.

---

[3] This is not the case of asymmetric primitives: consider e.g. RSA, here given our current understanding of the hardness of factoring, ϵ goes from basically 0 to 1 as the running time s reaches the time required to run the best factoring algorithms.

A   Proof of Theorem 1

We notice that we are looking for the biggest value k' such that for *every* (s', ϵ') satysfying $s' \geqslant 1$, $\epsilon' \geqslant 0$, $2^{k'} \geqslant s'/\epsilon'$ there exist *some* values (s, ϵ) such that $s \geqslant 1$, $\epsilon \geqslant 0$, $s' \leqslant p(s, \epsilon)$, $\epsilon' \geqslant q(s, \epsilon)$ and $2^k \geqslant s/\epsilon$. For given values (s', ϵ') we can choose (s, ϵ) so that the ratio s'/ϵ' is possibly maximal, provided that the constraint $s/\epsilon \leqslant 2^k$ is satisfied. Next, we chose the worst (s', ϵ') to obtain the worst-case guarantees as in Definition 4. Thuss, we maximize over the choice of profiles (s, ϵ) for P, and then minimize over profiles (s', ϵ') for P'.

B   Proof of Theorem 2

Proof. Consider the program in Theorem 1. In our setting we have

$$p(s, \epsilon) = s \cdot c\epsilon^C - b\epsilon^{-B}$$
$$q(s, \epsilon) = a\epsilon^A$$

The constraint $s' \geqslant 1$ is equivalent to

$$s \geqslant c^{-1}(1 + b\epsilon^{-B})\epsilon^{-C} \tag{6}$$

Thus, the all constraints on s can be written as

$$c^{-1}(1 + b\epsilon^{-B})\epsilon^{-C} \leqslant s, \quad s \leqslant 2^k \epsilon, \quad s' \leqslant p(s, \epsilon).$$

By definition $p(\cdot)$ is increasing in s. Therefore we can assume that

$$s\epsilon^{-1} = 2^k. \tag{7}$$

The constraint $\epsilon' \geqslant 0$ reduces to $\epsilon \geqslant 0$. Thus, the all constraints with ϵ are

$$0 \leqslant \epsilon, \quad s \leqslant 2^k \epsilon, \quad q(s, \epsilon) \leqslant \epsilon'$$

Since $q(\cdot)$ is increasing, we can assume that $\epsilon' = q(s, \epsilon)$, or in other words that

$$\epsilon' = a\epsilon^A. \tag{8}$$

Given Eqs. (7) and (8) the maximum part of the optimization is eliminated. Our task reduces to minimizing the following expression

$$\frac{s'}{\epsilon'} = s \cdot \frac{c}{a}\epsilon^{C-A} - \frac{b}{a}\epsilon^{-B-A} = \epsilon^{-A}\left(\frac{c}{a} \cdot 2^k \epsilon^{C+1} - \frac{b}{a}\epsilon^{-B}\right).$$

over (s', ϵ') or equivalenty over s, ϵ (given the equalities (7) and (8)), provided that Eq. (6) is satisfied. Thus we obtain the following problem

$$\underset{\epsilon}{\text{minimize}} \quad a^{-1}\epsilon^{-A}\left(2^k c \cdot \epsilon^{C+1} - b\epsilon^{-B}\right)$$
$$\text{s.t.} \quad 2^k c \cdot \epsilon^{C+1} - b\epsilon^{-B} \geqslant 1. \tag{9}$$

Now everything depends on the behavior of the objective function

$$f(u) = \frac{2^k c}{a} \cdot u^{C+1-A} - \frac{b}{a} \cdot u^{-B-A}$$

However the condition (4) implies that $f(u)$ is increasing. Thus, it attains its minimum on the boundary point, which is given by

$$2^k c \cdot \epsilon^{C+1} - b\epsilon^{-B} = 1. \tag{10}$$

The objective function evaluated at this point gives us

$$f(\epsilon) = a^{-1}\epsilon^{-A} \tag{11}$$

Note that from Eq. (10) it follows that

$$2^k c \cdot \epsilon^{B+C+1} = b + \epsilon^B$$

If $b \geqslant 1$ we obtain $\epsilon^{B+C+1} \approx 2^{-k}bc^{-1}$ (up to a multiplicative factor of at most 2). If $b = 0$ then $\epsilon^{C+1} \approx 2^{-k}c^{-1}$.

C   Proof of Theorem 4

We give a proof for real-valued circuits of size s. This class can be simulated by probabilistic boolean distinguishers of size $\approx s$.

Proof. We first show how to build a simulator $h = h^D$ for one circuit D.

Claim 1 (A perfect simulator for any fixed real-valued distinguisher). For any $[0,1]$-valued D of size s there exists a function $h_D : \mathcal{X} \to \{0,1\}^\lambda$ of complexity $O\left(s \cdot 2^\lambda\right)$ such that $\mathbb{E}\, D(X, Z) = \mathbb{E}\, D(X, h(X))$.

Proof (of Claim 1). Let h_D^+ and h_D^- be functions such that

$$D(x, h_D^-(x)) = \min_z D(x, z), \quad D(x, h_D^+(x)) = \max_z D(x, z)$$

Both functions can be computed by enumerating over all $z \in \{0,1\}^\lambda$, using $2 \cdot 2^\lambda$ calls to D. For any X, Z we have

$$\mathop{\mathbb{E}}_{x \leftarrow X} D(x, h_D^-(x)) \leqslant \mathbb{E}\, D(X, Z) \leqslant \mathop{\mathbb{E}}_{x \leftarrow X} D(x, h_D^+(x))$$

Therefore there exists a number $\gamma_D \in [0, 1]$ such that

$$\mathbb{E}\, D(X, Z) = \gamma_D \mathop{\mathbb{E}}_{x \leftarrow X} D(x, h_D^-(x)) + (1 - \gamma_D) \mathop{\mathbb{E}}_{x \leftarrow X} D(x, h_D^+(x)).$$

We define $h(x) = h_D(x)$ as follows: sample $r \in [0,1]$; if $r \leqslant \gamma$ then we output $h_D^-(x)$ else we output $h_D^+(x)$.

Now we apply the min-max theorem in a standard way, changing quantifiers.

Claim 2 (One simulator for all distinguishers). There exists a distribution $\bar{h}$ on functions h of complexity $O\left(s \cdot 2^\lambda\right)$ such that $|\mathbb{E}\, \mathrm{D}(X, Z) - \mathbb{E}_{h \leftarrow \bar{h}}\, \mathrm{D}(X, h(X))| \leqslant \epsilon$ for all D of size $s\epsilon^2$.

Proof. By a standard application of the min-max theorem combined with the Chernoff Bound (see [BSW03] for this technique) we get that there is a distribution $\bar{h}$ such that for all D of size $s\epsilon^2$ we have $\mathbb{E}\, \mathrm{D}(X, Z) - \mathbb{E}_{h \leftarrow \bar{h}}\, \mathrm{D}(X, h(X)) \leqslant \epsilon$. Since this holds for D and D^c for any D of size s, the result follows.

In the last step we approximate this possibly inefficient simulator.

Claim 3 (One efficient simulator for all distinguishers). There exists a simulator h of complexity $O\left(s \cdot 2^{2\lambda}\epsilon^{-2}\right)$ such that $|\mathbb{E}\, \mathrm{D}(X, Z) - \mathbb{E}\, \mathrm{D}(X, h(X))| \leqslant 2\epsilon$ for all D of size $s\epsilon^2$.

Proof (Proof of Claim 3). Let h_0 be the inefficient simulator guaranteed by Claim 2. We know that h_0 for every pair (x, z) satisfies

$$\mathbf{P}_{X,h_0(X)}(x, z) = \mathop{\mathbb{E}}_{h \leftarrow \bar{h}} \mathbf{P}_{X,h(X)}(x, z) \tag{12}$$

Fix a number t and sample $h_j \leftarrow \bar{h}$ for $j = 1, \ldots, t$. For a fixed choice of $h_1, \ldots, h_t$ we define the randomized function $\tilde{h}(x)$ as follows: $\mathbf{P}_{\tilde{h}(x)}(z) = t^{-1} \sum_{j=1}^{t} \mathbf{P}_{h_j(x)}(z)$ (it simply takes $i \leftarrow \{1, \ldots, t\}$ and outputs h_i). Below we assume that x is sampled according to X. Let us compute

$$\mathop{\mathbb{E}}_{\{h_j\}_{j=1}^t} \mathop{\mathbb{E}}_{x} \left\| \mathbf{P}_{\tilde{h}(x)}(\cdot) - \mathbf{P}_{\bar{h}(x)}(\cdot) \right\|_2^2 = t^{-2} \mathop{\mathbb{E}}_{x} \mathop{\mathbb{E}}_{\{h_i\}_{i=1}^t} \left\| \sum_{j=1}^{t} \left(\mathbf{P}_{h_j(x)}(\cdot) - \mathbf{P}_{\bar{h}(x)}(\cdot) \right) \right\|_2^2$$

$$= t^{-2} \mathop{\mathbb{E}}_{x} \left[\sum_{j=1}^{t} \mathop{\mathbb{E}}_{h_j} \left\| \mathbf{P}_{h_j(x)}(\cdot) - \mathbf{P}_{\bar{h}(x)}(\cdot) \right\|_2^2 \right]$$

$$= t^{-1} \left(\mathop{\mathbb{E}}_{h \leftarrow \bar{h}} \mathop{\mathbb{E}}_{x} \left\| \mathbf{P}_{h(x)}(\cdot) \right\|_2^2 - \mathop{\mathbb{E}}_{x} \left\| \mathbf{P}_{\bar{h}(x)}(\cdot) \right\|_2^2 \right).$$

Therefore for some choice of $h_1, \ldots, h_t$ we have

$$\mathop{\mathbb{E}}_{x} \left\| \mathbf{P}_{\tilde{h}(x)}(\cdot) - \mathbf{P}_{\bar{h}(x)}(\cdot) \right\|_2^2 \leqslant \frac{1}{t} \tag{13}$$

Note that the simple probabilistic proof of Eq. (13) resembles the proof of Maurey-Jones-Barron Theorem (see Lemma 1 in [Bar93]) on approximating convex hulls in Hilbert spaces. Using the triangle inequality, the fact that $|\mathrm{D}(\cdot, \cdot)| \leqslant 1$ and inequality between the first and the second norm

$$\left| \mathbb{E}\, \mathrm{D}(X, \tilde{h}(X)) - \mathbb{E}\, \mathrm{D}(X, \bar{h}(X)) \right| \leqslant \mathop{\mathbb{E}}_{x} \left| \mathbb{E}\, \mathrm{D}(x, \tilde{h}(x)) - \mathbb{E}\, \mathrm{D}(x, \bar{h}(x)) \right|$$

$$\leqslant \mathop{\mathbb{E}}_{x} \left\| \mathbf{P}_{\tilde{h}(x)}(\cdot) - \mathbf{P}_{\bar{h}(x)}(\cdot) \right\|_1$$

$$\leqslant 2^{\lambda/2} \cdot \left(\mathop{\mathbb{E}}_{x} \left\| \mathbf{P}_{\tilde{h}(x)}(\cdot) - \mathbf{P}_{\bar{h}(x)}(\cdot) \right\|_2 \right)^{\frac{1}{2}} \tag{14}$$

Combining Eqs. (13) and (14) we get for some choices of $h_1, \ldots, h_t$

$$\left| \mathbb{E} \, D(X, \tilde{h}(X)) - \mathbb{E} \, D(X, \bar{h}(X)) \right| \leqslant (2^\lambda t^{-1})^{\frac{1}{2}} \qquad (15)$$

Setting $t = 2^\lambda \epsilon^{-2}$ we finish the proof.

The result follows now directly from Claim 3.

D   Proof of Theorem 5

Below we prove our Theorem 5. The claimed security of the EUROCRYPT'09 stream cipher follows by Remark 3. For technical convenience, we will prove that for every $g : \mathcal{X} \times \mathcal{Z} \to [0, 1]$ satisfying $\sum_z g(x, z) = 1$ for every x, and for every distinguisher class $\mathcal{D}$ there exists h satisfying the same restrictions as g, being of complexity $O(\epsilon^{-2})$ with respect to $\mathcal{D}$, and such that

$$\left| \sum_z \mathop{\mathbb{E}}_{x \sim X} [D(x, z) \cdot (g(x, z) - h(x, z))] \right| \leqslant \epsilon \qquad (16)$$

for every $D \in \mathcal{D}$. To this end, it suffices to prove

$$\sum_z \mathop{\mathbb{E}}_{x \sim X} [D(x, z) \cdot (g(x, z) - h(x, z))] \leqslant \epsilon \qquad (17)$$

for every $D \in \mathcal{D} \cup -\mathcal{D}$ (where the class $-\mathcal{D}$ contains all the functions from $\mathcal{D}$ taken with the negative sign). Given this, the result follows by taking g to be a randomized function such that $\Pr[g(x) = z] = \Pr[X = x | Z = z]$. The sketch of the construction is shown in Algorithm 1

Proof. Consider h^t. Denote for shortness $\overline{D}^t(x, z) = D^t(x, z) - \mathbb{E}_{z' \leftarrow U_z} D(x, z')$ and $\tilde{h}^{t+1}(x, z) \stackrel{def}{=} h^t(x, z) + \gamma \cdot \overline{D}^{t+1}(x, z)$. According to Algorithm 1, we have

$$h^{t+1}(x, z) = h^t(x, z) + \gamma \cdot \overline{D}^{t+1}(x, z) + \theta^{t+1}(x, z) \qquad (18)$$

with the correction term $\theta^{t+1}(x, z)$ computed as (see Line 13 in Algorithm 1)

$$\begin{aligned} \theta^{t,0}(x, z) &= 0 \\ \theta^{t+1}(x, z) &= \begin{cases} -\min\left(h^t(x, z) + \gamma \cdot \overline{D}^{t+1}(x, z), 0\right), & \text{if } z = z^t_{\min}(x) \\ \min\left(h^t(x, z^t_{\min}(x)) + \gamma \cdot \overline{D}^{t+1}(x, z^t_{\min}(x)), 0\right) & \text{if } z \neq z^t_{\min}(x) \end{cases} \qquad t = 0, 1, \ldots \end{aligned} \qquad (19)$$

where $z^t_{\min}(x)$ is one of the points z minimizing $h^t(x, z) + \overline{D}^{t+1}(x, z)$. For the sake of concreteness we can choose it to have the smallest Hamming weight

$$z^t_{\min}(x) \in \mathrm{argmin}_z \left\{ h^t(x, z) + \gamma \cdot \overline{D}^{t+1}(x, z) \right\} \qquad (20)$$

Algorithm 1. Simulator for auxiliary 1-bit input

---

input : A function $g : \{0,1\}^n \times \{0,1\} \to [0,1]$, a class $\mathcal{D}$ of distinguishers, non-negative numbers γ, ϵ

output: A function h which is indistinguishable from g by $\mathcal{D}$

1 $t = 0$
2 $h^0(x,z) = \frac{1}{2}$
3 **while** *exists* $\mathrm{D} \in \mathcal{D} \cup -\mathcal{D}$ *such that*
$$\mathbb{E}_{x \sim X}\left[\sum_{z \in \{0,1\}}\left(\mathrm{D}(x,z) - \frac{\mathrm{D}(x,0)+\mathrm{D}(x,1)}{2}\right) \cdot \left(g(x,z) - h^t(x,z)\right)\right] \geqslant \epsilon$$ **do**
   /* while the simulator is not good enough */
4 $\quad$ $\mathrm{D}^{t+1} \leftarrow \mathrm{D}$
5 $\quad$ **for** $z' \in \{0,1\}$ **do**   /* improve the simulator towards the distinguisher direction */
6 $\quad\quad$ $h^{t+1}(x,z') \leftarrow h^t(x,z') + \gamma\left(\mathrm{D}^{t+1}(x,z') - \frac{\mathrm{D}^{t+1}(x,0)+\mathrm{D}^{t+1}(x,1)}{2}\right)$
7 $\quad$ $t \leftarrow t+1$
8 $\quad$ $m \leftarrow 0$
9 $\quad$ **for** $z' \in \{0,1\}$ **do**   /* locate the negative point mass */
10 $\quad\quad$ **if** $h^t(x,z') < m$ **then**
11 $\quad\quad\quad$ $m \leftarrow h^t(x,z')$

12 $\quad$ **for** $z' \in \{0,1\}$ **do**
13 $\quad\quad$ **if** $h^t(x,z') = m$ **then**   /* correct the negative point mass */
14 $\quad\quad\quad$ $h^t(x,z') = 0$
15 $\quad\quad$ **else**
16 $\quad\quad\quad$ $h^t(x,z') \leftarrow h^t(x,z') + m$

17 **return** $h^t(x,z)$

In particular

$$h^t(x, z^t_{\min}(x))) + \gamma\overline{\mathrm{D}}^{t+1}(x, z^t_{\min}(x)) < 0 \iff \exists z : \ h^t(x,z) + \gamma\overline{\mathrm{D}}^{t+1}(x,z) < 0 \tag{21}$$

Notation. For notational convenience we indenify the functions $\overline{\mathrm{D}}^t(x,z)$, $\theta^t(x,z)$, $\tilde{h}^t(x,z)$ and $h^t(x,z)$ with matrices where x are columns and z are rows.

Claim 4 (Complextity of Algorithm 1). T executions of the "while loop" can be realized with time $O\left(T \cdot \mathrm{size}(\mathcal{D})\right)$ and memory $O(1)$.[4]

Claim 5 (Energy function). Define the auxiliary function

$$\Delta^t = \sum_{i=0}^{t-1} \mathbb{E}_{x \sim X}\left[\overline{\mathrm{D}}^{i+1}_x \cdot \left(g_x - h^i_x\right)\right]. \tag{22}$$

---

[4] This is easy to see in the RAM model. The equivalent circuit complexity equals $O\left(T \cdot \mathrm{size}(\mathcal{D})\right) \cdot O(1)$, that is remains the same.

Then we have $\Delta^t = E_1 + E_2$ where

$$E_1 = \frac{1}{\gamma} \mathbb{E}_{x \sim X} \left[\left(h_x^t - h_x^0 \right) \cdot g_x + \frac{1}{2} \sum_{i=0}^{t-1} \left(h_x^{i+1} - h_x^i \right)^2 - \frac{1}{2} \left(\left(h_x^t \right)^2 - \left(h_x^0 \right)^2 \right) \right]$$
$$E_2 = \frac{1}{\gamma} \mathbb{E}_{x \sim X} \left[-\sum_{i=0}^{t-1} \theta_x^{i+1} \cdot \left(g_x - h_x^{i+1} \right) - \sum_{i=0}^{t-1} \theta_x^{i+1} \cdot \left(h_x^{i+1} - h_x^i \right) \right]$$

$$(23)$$

The proof is based on simple algebraic manipulations and is ommited.

Remark 4 (Technical issues and intuitions). From Eq. (23) it is clear that we need two important properties

(a) *Boundness of correction terms,* that is $|\theta^i(x.z)| = O(\gamma)$.
(b) *Acute angle between the correction and error vectors,* that is $\theta_x^i \cdot (g_x - h_x^i) \geqslant 0$.

Indeed, with these assumptions we can prove that

$$E_1 + E_2 = O\left(t\gamma + \gamma^{-1} \right).$$

Since in the other hand we have $t\epsilon \leqslant \Delta^t$, setting $\gamma = \epsilon$ we get that the algorithm terminates after $T = O(\epsilon^{-2})$ steps. We stress that it outputs a *probability measure*, because in the final round the (only) negative mass is corrected. We also note that condition (b) means that mass cuts should go in the right direction, as it is much simpler to prove that Algorithm 1 terminates when there are no correction terms θ^t; thus we don't want to go in a wrong direction and ruin the energy gain. Property (a) is trivial, concrete bounds on (b) are given in Claim 6.

Claim 6 (The angle formed by the correction and the difference vector is acute). For every x, t we have $\text{Angle} \left(\theta_x^{t+1}, g_x - h_x^{t+1} \right) \in \left[-\frac{\pi}{2}, \frac{\pi}{2} \right]$.

Proof (of Claim 6). If $\theta^{t+1}(x, z) = 0$ then there is nothing to prove. Suppose that $\theta^{t+1}(x, z) < 0$. Let $z_0 = z_{\min}^t(x)$ (see Eq. (20)) and $z_1 = 1 - z_0$. According to Eq. (19) we have $\theta^{t+1}(x, z_0) = -\tilde{h}^{t+1}(x, z_0)$ and $\theta^{t+1}(x, z_1) = \tilde{h}^{t+1}(x, z_0)$. Therefore

$$\theta_x^{t+1} \cdot \left(g_x - \tilde{h}_x^{t+1} \right) = -\tilde{h}^{t+1}(x, z_0) \left(g(x, z_0) - \tilde{h}^{t+1}(x, z_0) \right)$$
$$+ \tilde{h}^{t+1}(x, z_0) \left(g(x, z_1) - \tilde{h}^{t+1}(x, z_1) \right)$$
$$= -2\tilde{h}^{t+1}(x, z_0) \left(g(x, z_0) - \tilde{h}^{t+1}(x, z_0) \right). \quad (24)$$

and

$$-\theta_x^{t+1} \cdot \theta_x^{t+1} = -2\tilde{h}^{t+1}(x, z_0) \cdot \tilde{h}^{t+1}(x, z_0). \quad (25)$$

Adding Eqs. (24) and (25) by sides we obtain

$$\theta_x^{t+1} \cdot \left(g_x - h_x^{t+1} \right) = \theta_x^{t+1} \cdot \left(g_x - \tilde{h}_x^{t+1} \right) - \theta_x^{t+1} \cdot \theta_x^{t+1} = -2\tilde{h}^{t+1}(x, z_0) \cdot g(x, z_0)$$

which is non-negative because $\tilde{h}^{t+1}(x, z_0) < 0$ and $g(x, z_0) \geqslant 0$. This proves Claim 6.

Proof. The result follows now by combining the claims, as discussed. The problem with extending the algorithm to many bits is the complexity of the correction term. Having two points we have only one way to rearrange the mass.

References

ADW09. Alwen, J., Dodis, Y., Wichs, D.: Survey: leakageresilience and the bounded retrieval model (2009)

Bar93. Barron, A.R.: Universal approximation bounds for superpositions of a sigmoidal function. IEEE Trans. Inf. Theory **39**, 930–945 (1993)

BBKN12. Barenghi, A., Breveglieri, L., Koren, I., Naccache, D.: Fault injection attacks on cryptographic devices: theory, practice, and countermeasures. In: Proceedings of the IEEE (2012)

BL13. Buldas, A., Laanoja, R.: Security proofs for hash tree time-stamping using hash functions with small output size. In: Boyd, C., Simpson, L. (eds.) ACISP. LNCS, vol. 7959, pp. 235–250. Springer, Heidelberg (2013)

BR96. Bellare, M., Rogaway, P.: The exact security of digital signatures - how to sign with RSA and rabin. In: Maurer, U.M. (ed.) EUROCRYPT 1996. LNCS, vol. 1070, pp. 399–416. Springer, Heidelberg (1996)

BSW03. Barak, B., Shaltiel, R., Wigderson, A.: Computational analogues of entropy. In: Arora, S., Jansen, K., Rolim, J.D.P., Sahai, A. (eds.) RANDOM 2003 and APPROX 2003. LNCS, vol. 2764, pp. 200–215. Springer, Heidelberg (2003)

CDH+00. Canetti, R., Dodis, Y., Halevi, S., Kushilevitz, E., Sahai, A.: Exposureresilient functions and all-or-nothing transforms. In: Preneel, B. (ed.) EUROCRYPT 2000. LNCS, vol. 1807, p. 453. Springer, Heidelberg (2000)

DGK+10. Dodis, Y., Goldwasser, S., Tauman Kalai, Y., Peikert, C., Vaikuntanathan, V.: Public-key encryption schemes with auxiliary inputs. In: Micciancio, D. (ed.) TCC 2010. LNCS, vol. 5978, pp. 361–381. Springer, Heidelberg (2010)

DKL09. Dodis, Y., Kalai, Y.T., Lovett, S.: On cryptography with auxiliary input. In: STOC (2009)

DP08. Dziembowski, S., Pietrzak, K.: Leakage-resilient cryptography. In: FOCS (2008)

DP10. Dodis, Y., Pietrzak, K.: Leakage-resilient pseudorandom functions and side-channel attacks on feistel networks. In: Rabin, T. (ed.) CRYPTO 2010. LNCS, vol. 6223, pp. 21–40. Springer, Heidelberg (2010)

DSS01. Dodis, Y., Sahai, A., Smith, A.: On perfect and adaptive security in exposure-resilient cryptography. In: Pfitzmann, B. (ed.) EUROCRYPT 2001. LNCS, vol. 2045, pp. 301–324. Springer, Heidelberg (2001)

DTT09. De, A., Trevisan, L., Tulsiani, M.: Non-uniform attacks against one-way functions and prgs. In: ECCC, vol. 16, p. 113 (2009)

DY13. Dodis, Y., Yu, Y.: Overcoming weak expectations. In: Sahai, A. (ed.) TCC 2013. LNCS, vol. 7785, pp. 1–22. Springer, Heidelberg (2013)

FPS12. Faust, S., Pietrzak, K., Schipper, J.: Practical leakage-resilient symmetric cryptography. In: Prouff, E., Schaumont, P. (eds.) CHES 2012. LNCS, vol. 7428, pp. 213–232. Springer, Heidelberg (2012)

HSH+08. Halderman, J.A., Schoen, S.D., Heninger, N., Clarkson, W., Paul, W., Cal, J.A., Feldman, A.J., Felten, E.W.: Least we remember: cold boot attacks on encryption keys. USENIX (2008)

ISW03. Ishai, Y., Sahai, A., Wagner, D.: Private circuits: securing hardware against probing attacks. In: Boneh, D. (ed.) CRYPTO 2003. LNCS, vol. 2729, pp. 463–481. Springer, Heidelberg (2003)

JP14. Jetchev, D., Pietrzak, K.: How to fake auxiliary input. In: Lindell, Y. (ed.) TCC 2014. LNCS, vol. 8349, pp. 566–590. Springer, Heidelberg (2014)

KJJ99. Kocher, P.C., Jaffe, J., Jun, B.: Differential power analysis. In: Wiener, M. (ed.) CRYPTO 1999. LNCS, vol. 1666, pp. 388–397. Springer, Heidelberg (1999)

Koc96. Kocher, P.C.: Timing attacks on implementations of Diffie-Hellman, RSA, DSS, and other systems. In: Koblitz, N. (ed.) CRYPTO 1996. LNCS, vol. 1109, pp. 104–113. Springer, Heidelberg (1996)

LM94. Luby, M.G., Michael, L.: Pseudorandomness and Cryptographic Applications. Princeton University Press, Princeton (1994)

Mol10. Mol, P.: Leakage-resilient cryptography: a survey of recent advances 2010. http://cseweb.ucsd.edu/~pmol/Documents/RE.pdf

MR04. Micali, S., Reyzin, L.: Physically observable cryptography. In: Naor, M. (ed.) TCC 2004. LNCS, vol. 2951, pp. 278–296. Springer, Heidelberg (2004)

MS11. Medwed, M., Standaert, F.-X.: Extractors against side-channel attacks: weak or strong? In: Preneel, B., Takagi, T. (eds.) CHES 2011. LNCS, vol. 6917, pp. 256–272. Springer, Heidelberg (2011)

MSJ12. Medwed, M., Standaert, F.-X., Joux, A.: Towards super-exponential side-channel security with efficient leakage-resilient PRFs. In: Prouff, E., Schaumont, P. (eds.) CHES 2012. LNCS, vol. 7428, pp. 193–212. Springer, Heidelberg (2012)

Pie09. Pietrzak, K.: A leakage-resilient mode of operation. In: Joux, A. (ed.) EUROCRYPT 2009. LNCS, vol. 5479, pp. 462–482. Springer, Heidelberg (2009)

Pie15. Pietrzak, K.: Private communication (2015)

Sta10. Standaert, F.-X.: How leaky is an extractor? In: Abdalla, M., Barreto, P.S.L.M. (eds.) LATINCRYPT 2010. LNCS, vol. 6212, pp. 294–304. Springer, Heidelberg (2010)

VZ13. Vadhan, S., Zheng, C.J.: A uniform min-max theorem with applications in cryptography. In: Canetti, R., Garay, J.A. (eds.) CRYPTO 2013, Part I. LNCS, vol. 8042, pp. 93–110. Springer, Heidelberg (2013)

YS13. Yu, Y., Standaert, F.-X.: Practical leakage-resilient pseudorandom objects with minimum public randomness. In: Dawson, E. (ed.) CT-RSA 2013. LNCS, vol. 7779, pp. 223–238. Springer, Heidelberg (2013)

YSPY10. Yu, Y., Standaert, F.-X., Pereira, O., Yung, M.: Practical leakage-resilient pseudorandom generators. In: CCS (2010)

Tighter Security for Efficient Lattice Cryptography via the Rényi Divergence of Optimized Orders

Katsuyuki Takashima[1] and Atsushi Takayasu[2]([✉])

[1] Mitsubishi Electric, Kamakura, Japan
Takashima.Katsuyuki@aj.MitsubishiElectric.co.jp
[2] The University of Tokyo, Kashiwa, Japan
a-takayasu@it.k.u-tokyo.ac.jp

Abstract. In security proofs of lattice based cryptography, to bound the closeness of two probability distributions is an important procedure. To measure the closeness, the Rényi divergence has been used instead of the classical statistical distance. Recent results have shown that the Rényi divergence offers security reductions with better parameters, e.g. smaller deviations for discrete Gaussian distributions. However, since previous analyses used a fixed order Rényi divergence, i.e., order two, they lost tightness of reductions. To overcome the deficiency, we *adaptively* optimize the orders based on the advantages of the adversary for several lattice-based schemes. The optimizations enable us to prove the security with both improved efficiency and tighter reductions. Indeed, our analysis offers security reductions with smaller parameters than the statistical distance based analysis and the reductions are tighter than that of previous Rényi divergence based analysis. As applications, we show tighter security reductions for sampling discrete Gaussian distributions with smaller precomputed tables for BLISS signatures, and variants of learning with errors (LWE) problem and small integer solution (SIS) problem called k-LWE and k-SIS.

Keywords: Lattice based cryptography · Tight reduction · Rényi divergence · Sampling discrete Gaussian · BLISS · LWE · SIS

1 Introduction

Background. The security of currently used cryptographic schemes relies on the hardness of factorization/RSA problem and (elliptic curve) discrete logarithm problem. Solving these problems becomes feasible when quantum computers are available. Though inventions of quantum computers may not be soon, a research for next candidate cryptographic constructions is worth devoting. Lattice based cryptographic schemes have become a central candidate for the post-quantum world. While some papers have theoretical flavors, there are several

© Springer International Publishing Switzerland 2015
M.-H. Au and A. Miyaji (Eds.): ProvSec 2015, LNCS 9451, pp. 412–431, 2015.
DOI: 10.1007/978-3-319-26059-4_23

papers which discuss practical implementations of the schemes and the appropriate parameter selections [4,5,9,14]. For example, one of the bottlenecks for the efficiency is the discrete Gaussian sampling with large deviations.

In security proofs of lattice based cryptography, to bound the closeness of two probability distributions (e.g. zero centered and non-zero centered discrete Gaussian distributions) is an important procedure. To measure the closeness, the classical statistical distance (SD) is naturally used. However, several papers [2,8,10,12] used the Rényi divergence (RD) [6,16] instead of the SD. These works showed that the RD offers better security reductions for lattice based cryptographic schemes. More concretely, the RD enables security reductions with better parameters (e.g. smaller deviations for discrete Gaussian distributions) which cannot be handled via the SD.

Briefly speaking, the SD denotes differences of two probability distributions, in contrast, the RD denotes ratios of the distributions. Hence, some properties of the SD expressed by additions are replaced by multiplications in the RD. For the SD based security proofs to be relevant, the quantity of the SD has to be smaller than a probability for an adversary to break the scheme. To satisfy the restriction, inefficient parameters (e.g. large deviations for discrete Gaussian distributions) have to be used. On the other hand, for the RD based security proofs to be relevant, the quantity of the RD can be permitted to larger bounds, e.g. logarithm of the probability for an adversary to break the scheme. In some cases, the latter requirement (for the RD) is weaker than the former requirement (for the SD). Indeed, there have been several reports when the RD based analysis offers a significant saving of parameters.

However, there is a drawback for the RD based analysis which cannot be ignored. The RD based security reductions lose the tightness. If the quantity of the SD is significantly small, the SD based security reduction becomes tight, and probabilities for an adversary to break the real scheme and the simulated scheme are almost the same. However, even if the quantity of the RD is significantly small, the probability for an adversary to break the real scheme is at least larger than a square root of the probability for the adversary to break the simulated scheme. Therefore, for the probability to break the real scheme to be sufficiently small, the RD based analysis requires the smaller probability to break the simulated scheme than the SD based analysis. As a result, the RD based analysis sacrifices the tightness to achieve the parameter saving compared with the SD based analysis.

Previous Results of the RD Based Security Proofs. Suppose instances of a real cryptographic scheme are sampled from one distribution and those of a simulated scheme are sampled from the other distribution. We define the former (resp. latter) distribution *real* (resp. *ideal*) distribution. If the two distributions are statistically close, then an adversary which breaks the real scheme is also an adversary which breaks the simulated scheme. Then, if the simulated scheme is assumed to be secure, the real scheme is also secure.

The Bimodal Lattice Signature Scheme (BLISS) was proposed by Ducas et al. [5] (Crypto 2013) which is comparably efficient as RSA and ECDSA. For signing a signature, about several hundreds independent integers should be sampled from one-dimensional discrete Gaussian distributions. To implement BLISS signature scheme over constrained devices, they also proposed an efficient algorithm for the discrete Gaussian sampling. At first, to sample an integer from a discrete Gaussian distribution, several integers are sampled from Bernoulli distributions independently. Using these Bernoulli random integers and a rejection sampling technique, a discrete Gaussian distribution is sampleable. Sampling from Bernoulli distributions is efficiently performed with a precomputed table which stores the probabilities. Since the probabilities are not rational, each stored value is truncated with some precisions. Required precisions to maintain the security of BLISS are analyzed by measuring the statistical closeness between truncated Bernoulli distributions (*real distribution*) and untruncated Bernoulli distributions (*ideal distribution*). Though two distributions become close with large precisions, that makes the scheme inefficient since the table storage becomes large. Ducas et al. analyzed the precisions using the SD, and Pöppelmann et al. [14] (CHES 2014) gave alternative analysis using the Kullback-Leibler divergence (KLD). The KLD based analysis reduces the required precisions which lead to lower the table storage. Recently, Bai et al. [2] (Asiacrypt 2015) further improved the analysis based on the RD though the reduction is no longer tight.

Boneh and Freeman [3] (PKC 2011) introduced the k-SIS problem which is a variant of the small integer solution (SIS) problem [13]. In short, the k-SIS problem is defined as follows: given k hint vectors which are solutions of the original SIS problem and the goal of the problem is to compute a short vector which is orthogonal to the k hint vectors. Based on the hardness of the k-SIS problem, they constructed lattice based linearly homomorphic signatures, k time signatures, and proved that the k time GPV signature scheme [7] is secure in the standard model. However, for the k-SIS problem to be no easier than the SIS problem, the solution bound of the SIS problem becomes exponential of k. Hence, the k-SIS problem is as hard as the worst case standard lattice problems only when $k = O(1)$. Ling et al. [10] (Crypto 2014) introduced the dual problem, k-LWE problem which is a variant of the learning with errors (LWE) problem [15]. Based on the hardness of the k-LWE problem, they proposed the first algebraic construction of a traitor tracing scheme from lattices. Moreover, Ling et al. considered more efficient reduction than [3]. Their reduction enables the quantity of k to be a polynomial of the lattice dimension and the technique used in the reduction is applicable to the k-SIS problem. Ling et al.'s reduction consists of two subreductions. In the first subreduction, they reduce LWE to k-LWE where k hint vectors are sampled from non-zero centered discrete Gaussian distributions (*real distribution*). In the second subreduction, they reduce the former k-LWE to k-LWE where k hint vectors are sampled from zero centered discrete Gaussian distributions (*ideal distribution*). To bound the closeness of two distributions, the RD is used. Though the analyses can handle smaller Gaussian deviations than the SD based analysis, the reduction is not tight.

Our Contributions. In this paper, we show improved security reductions for several lattice based cryptographic schemes. Our analysis offers security reductions with *smaller parameters* than the SD and KLD based analyses and the

Table 1. Comparison of required precisions p and success probabilities ε for adversaries $\mathcal{A}$ to break BLISS signatures where each Bernoulli variable is sampled with truncated probabilities (*real distribution*). Each signature is generated by sampling $2n$ discrete Gaussian variables, and each discrete Gaussian variable is produced by sampling ℓ Bernoulli variables. Adversaries $\mathcal{A}$ are allowed q_s signing queries and break BLISS signatures with probabilities ε' where each Bernoulli variable is sampled with untruncated probabilities (*ideal distribution*). In the last column for ε, $\approx$ means approximate equivalence when $-\ln(\varepsilon') \gg \ell \cdot n \cdot q_s \cdot 2^{-2p}$, which holds for practical numerical examples given in the right parameter of Table 4.

Disc. Gauss. Sampling	Stat. measure	Precision p	ε
DDLL13 [5]	SD	$\log(\ell \cdot 2n \cdot q_s/\varepsilon)$	$\leq \varepsilon' + \ell \cdot 2n \cdot q_s \cdot 2^{-p-1} \approx \varepsilon'$
PDG14 [14]	KLD	$\log(\ell \cdot 2n \cdot q_s/\varepsilon^2)/2 +1/2$	$\leq \varepsilon' + \sqrt{\ell \cdot 2n \cdot q_s} \cdot 2^{-2p} \approx \varepsilon'$
BLL+15 [2]	RD, $\alpha = +\infty$	$\log(\ell \cdot 2n \cdot q_s)$	$\leq \varepsilon' \cdot (1 + 2^{-p})^{\ell \cdot 2n \cdot q_s} \approx \varepsilon'$
BLL+15 [2]	RD, $\alpha = 2$	$\log(\ell \cdot 2n \cdot q_s)/2$	$\leq \varepsilon'^{1/2} \cdot (1 + 2^{-2p})^{\ell \cdot 2n \cdot q_s/2} \approx \varepsilon'^{1/2}$
Proposed	RD, $\alpha = \sqrt{\dfrac{-\ln(\varepsilon')}{\ell \cdot n \cdot q_s \cdot 2^{-2p}}}$	$\log(-\ln(\varepsilon') \cdot \ell \cdot n \cdot q_s)/2$	$\leq \exp\left(-\left(\sqrt{-\ln(\varepsilon')} - \sqrt{\ell \cdot n \cdot q_s \cdot 2^{-2p}}\right)^2\right) \approx \varepsilon'$

Table 2. Comparison of Gaussian deviations $\sigma_{m'}(S)$ and success probabilities ε for adversaries $\mathcal{A}$ to solve LWE. The quantity of γ has a negative correlation with standard deviations of discrete Gaussian distributions. Adversaries $\mathcal{A}$ solve k-LWE with advantage ε'. λ denotes a security parameter and k denotes the number of hint vectors. In the last column for ε, $\approx$ means approximate equivalence when $-\ln(\varepsilon') \gg \kappa\gamma$.

LWE to k-LWE reduction	Stat. measure	$\sigma_{m'}(S)$	ε
	SD	2^λ	$\leq \varepsilon' + \mathrm{negl}(\lambda) \approx \varepsilon'$
LPSS14 [10]	RD, $\alpha = 2$	$poly(\lambda)$	$\leq \exp\left(\ln\left(\varepsilon'\right)/3 + 2k\gamma/3\right) \approx \varepsilon'^{1/3}$
Proposed	RD, $\alpha = \left(1 + \sqrt{1 - \dfrac{2\ln(\varepsilon')}{k\gamma}}\right)/2$	$poly(\lambda)$	$\leq \exp\left(\ln\left(\varepsilon'\right)/2 + k\gamma\sqrt{1 - \dfrac{2\ln(\varepsilon')}{k\gamma}}/2\right)$ $\approx \varepsilon'^{1/2}$

Table 3. Comparison of Gaussian deviations $\sigma_{m'}(S)$ and success probabilities ε for adversaries $\mathcal{A}$ to solve SIS. The quantity of γ has a negative correlation with standard deviations of discrete Gaussian distributions. Adversaries $\mathcal{A}$ solve k-SIS with advantage ε'. λ denotes a security parameter and k denotes the number of hint vectors. In the last column for ε, $\approx$ means approximate equivalence when $-\ln(\varepsilon') \gg \kappa\gamma$.

SIS to k-SIS reduction	Stat. measure	$\sigma_{m'}(S)$	ε
	SD	2^λ	$\leq \varepsilon' + \mathrm{negl}(n) \approx \varepsilon'$
LPSS14 [10]	RD, $\alpha = 2$	$poly(\lambda)$	$\leq \exp\left(\ln\left(\varepsilon'\right)/2 + k\gamma\right) \approx \varepsilon'^{1/2}$
Proposed	RD, $\alpha = \sqrt{-\ln(\varepsilon')/(k\gamma)}$	$poly(\lambda)$	$\leq \exp\left(-\left(\sqrt{-\ln(\varepsilon')} - \sqrt{k\gamma}\right)^2\right) \approx \varepsilon'$

reductions are *tighter* than that of previous RD based analyses. Especially, when we analyze specific parameter selections, the improvement of the tightness becomes significant. Our results are as follows:

- Sampling discrete Gaussian distributions for the BLISS signature scheme (Theorem 1 in Sect. 3) with *both* less table storages and tight reduction. In particular, our analysis shows that the sampling can be performed with 1276 bits table for BLISS-I scheme with 128 bit security. Table 1 compares the required precisions p (which affect the table storages), and the probabilities ε' (which represent the tightness) for an adversary to break the BLISS signature scheme with idealized distributions. Our reduction is as tight as SD [5], KLD [14], and RD of order $+\infty$ [2] based analyses with less table storages. Though our table requires slightly larger storages than those of RD of order 2 based analysis [2], the reduction is tighter. See Table 4 in Sect. 3 for detailed comparisons.
- LWE to k-LWE reduction (Theorem 2 in Sect. 4) with *both* small Gaussian deviations to sample hint vectors and tighter reduction. Table 2 compares the Gaussian deviations $\sigma_{m'}(S)$, and the probabilities ε' (which represent the tightness) for an adversary to solve k-LWE. Our reduction is as tight as SD based analysis with smaller Gaussian deviations, and the deviations are as small as previous RD based analysis [10] with tighter reductions.
- SIS to k-SIS reduction (Theorem 4 in Sect. 5) with *both* small Gaussian deviations to sample hint vectors and tighter reduction. Table 3 compares the Gaussian deviations $\sigma_{m'}(S)$, and the probabilities ε' (which represent the tightness) for an adversary to solve k-SIS. Our reduction is as tight as SD based analysis with smaller Gaussian deviations, and the deviations are as small as previous RD based analysis with tighter reductions.

Our improved results are obtained with the RD as previous works [2,10]. In previous RD based analyses, the order is fixed to $\alpha = 2$. However, we *adaptively* optimize the order based on the scheme parameters and probabilities for an adversary to break the simulated scheme. In Tables 1, 2 and 3, ε (resp. ε') denotes advantage for an adversary to break the real (resp. simulated) scheme. As the tables show, the RD based analyses (including previous works) offer security reductions with smaller parameters (p for Table 1 and $\sigma_{m'}(S)$ for Tables 2 and 3) than the SD based analyses. In addition, our optimizations of the order offer tighter reductions than previous RD based analyses with fixed orders. Briefly speaking, though upper bounds of ε for search problems (resp. distinguishing problems) are at least larger than $\varepsilon'^{1/2}$ (resp. $\varepsilon'^{1/3}$) when the order is fixed to $\alpha = 2$, our improvements offer tighter upper bounds which are almost ε' (resp. $\varepsilon'^{1/2}$). For appropriate choices of parameters, our results offer almost the same tightness as the SD based analyses. Therefore, efficient parameters and tight reductions are compatible in our improved analyses.

Adaptive Optimization of α. We briefly summarize the point of our improvements; *adaptive* optimizations of the order. Let P and P' be two computing problems where the problem P (resp. P') is defined as follows: given

$X = \{x_i : x_i \leftarrow \Phi\}_{i=1,\dots,k}$ (resp. $X' = \{x'_i : x'_i \leftarrow \Phi'\}_{i=1,\dots,k}$) and the goal of the problem is to compute $f(X)$ (resp. $f(X')$). In cryptographic security proofs, P (resp. P') can be viewed as the real (resp. simulated) cryptographic schemes, and Φ (resp. Φ') is the *real* (resp. *ideal*) distribution. We should handle as many number of samples k as possible since the number relates to cryptographic security or functionality, e.g., the number of signing queries in BLISS signatures. Let γ be some constant which satisfies[1] $R_\alpha(\Phi\|\Phi') \leq \exp(\alpha \cdot \gamma)$. We should handle as large γ as possible since the quantity relates to cryptographic efficiency, e.g., the size of table storages for sampling discrete Gaussian distribution for BLISS signatures. By the definition and the properties of the RD, if there is an adversary $\mathcal{A}$ against the problem P with run-time T and advantage ε, then $\mathcal{A}$ is also an adversary against the problem P' with run-time $T' = T$ and advantage ε' where

$$\varepsilon \leq \left(\varepsilon' \cdot R_\alpha(\Phi\|\Phi')^k\right)^{\frac{\alpha-1}{\alpha}} \leq \exp\left(\frac{\alpha-1}{\alpha} \cdot \ln(\varepsilon') + (\alpha-1) \cdot k\gamma\right). \tag{1}$$

We say that the reduction is tight when the right hand side of the inequality (1) is approximately equivalent to ε', i.e., $\approx \varepsilon'$. When the order is fixed to $\alpha = 2$ as previous works, the inequality (1) becomes $\varepsilon \leq \exp(\ln(\varepsilon')/2 + k\gamma)$. Hence, the upper bound of ε becomes larger than $\varepsilon'^{1/2}$ and the reduction is not tight. That is the bottleneck of previous RD based analyses which always lose the tightness.

To overcome the issue, we *adaptively* optimize the order α which enables the reduction to be tighter. At first, we analyze the inequality (1) with a general $\alpha \in (1, +\infty]$. For the fixed analysis with $\alpha = 2$, the tightness is lost by the existence of the exponent of ε', $\frac{\alpha-1}{\alpha}$. If we use larger α, the exponent becomes close to 1. Therefore, the reduction is expected to be tighter. However, we cannot use infinitely large α since $R_\alpha(\Phi\|\Phi')$ becomes exponentially large which results in the loss of the tightness. Hence, we optimize the order α to minimize the right hand side of the inequality (1). The right hand side is lower bounded as

$$\exp\left(\ln(\varepsilon') - k\gamma + (-\ln(\varepsilon')/\alpha + \alpha \cdot k\gamma)\right) \geq \exp\left(\ln(\varepsilon') - k\gamma + 2\sqrt{-\ln(\varepsilon') \cdot k\gamma}\right)$$

by the inequality of arithmetic mean and geometric mean, in which the equality holds if and only if $-\ln(\varepsilon')/\alpha = \alpha \cdot k\gamma$, i.e., $\alpha = \sqrt{-\ln(\varepsilon')/(k\gamma)}$. Then, we set the order $\alpha = \sqrt{-\ln(\varepsilon')/(k\gamma)}$ and the inequality (1) becomes

$$\varepsilon \leq \exp\left(\ln(\varepsilon') - k\gamma + 2\sqrt{-\ln(\varepsilon') \cdot k\gamma}\right) = \exp\left(-\left(\sqrt{-\ln(\varepsilon')} - \sqrt{k\gamma}\right)^2\right). \tag{2}$$

The right hand side of the inequality (2) is always smaller than that of the inequality (1) with fixed $\alpha = 2$. Hence, our optimization always offers tighter reduction than previous analyses [2,10]. Since we only use the order $\alpha \in (1, +\infty]$, it holds $\alpha = \sqrt{-\ln(\varepsilon')/(k\gamma)} > 1$, i.e., $-\ln(\varepsilon') > k\gamma$. Moreover, when $-\ln(\varepsilon') \gg$

---

[1] Though there are no assurance for the upper bound of $R_\alpha(\Phi\|\Phi')$ to be $O(\exp(\alpha))$ for arbitrary distributions Φ and Φ', it holds for the distributions which we study in this paper.

$k\gamma$, the right hand side of the inequality (2) is approximately equivalent to ε', that is, the ideal P' to the real P reduction is almost tight.

The above analysis captures security reductions for computing problems, a security proof for discrete Gaussian sampling and SIS to k-SIS reduction in our results. Though the result of LWE to k-LWE reduction, which are distinguishing problems, does not follow the inequality (1), the spirit of the improvement is the same.

2   Preliminaries

Notation. Let $\ln(x)$ (resp. $\log(x)$) denote the natural logarithm (resp. the base 2 logarithm) of x. Let $\mathbb{T}$ denote the additive group $\mathbb{R}/\mathbb{Z}$. For an integer q, we let $\mathbb{Z}_q$ denote the ring of integers modulo q. Vectors are denoted in bold and are column representations. For $\boldsymbol{b} \in \mathbb{R}^n$, we let $\|\boldsymbol{b}\|$ denote its Euclidean norm. We let $\langle \cdot, \cdot \rangle$ denote the canonical inner product. If A is a matrix, we denote by a_{ij} the entries. For two matrices A, B of compatible dimensions, we let $(A|B)$ (resp. $(A\|B)$) denote the horizontal (resp. vertical) concatenations of A and B. For $A \in \mathbb{Z}_q^{m \times n}$, we define $\mathrm{Im}(A) = \{A\boldsymbol{s} : \boldsymbol{s} \in \mathbb{Z}_q^n\} \subseteq \mathbb{Z}_q^m$. For $X \subseteq \mathbb{Z}_q^m$, we let $\mathrm{Span}(X)$ denote the set of all linear combinations of elements of X. We let $X^\perp$ denote the linear subspace $\{\boldsymbol{b} \in \mathbb{Z}_q^m : \forall \boldsymbol{c} \in X, \langle \boldsymbol{b}, \boldsymbol{c} \rangle = 0\}$. For a matrix $S \in \mathbb{Z}^{m \times n}$, we let $\|S\|$ denote the norm of its largest column. The smallest (resp. largest) singular value of S is denoted by $\sigma_n(S) = \inf(\|S\boldsymbol{u}\|)$ (resp. $\sigma_1(S) = \sup(\|S\boldsymbol{u}\|)$) where $\boldsymbol{u} \in \mathbb{R}^n$ and $\|\boldsymbol{u}\| = 1$.

If D is a probability distribution, we let $\mathrm{Supp}(D) = \{x : D(x) \neq 0\}$ denote its support. The uniform distribution on a finite set X is denoted by $U(X)$. The statistical distance (SD) between two distributions D_1 and D_2 over a countable support X is $\Delta(D_1, D_2) = \frac{1}{2} \sum_{x \in X} |D_1(x) - D_2(x)|$. For a function $f : X \to \mathbb{R}$ over a countable domain X, we let $f(X) = \sum_{x \in X} f(x)$. Let ν_β denote the one-dimensional Gaussian distribution on $\mathbb{T}$ with center 0 and standard deviation β.

Lattices and Discrete Gaussian Distributions. Lattice Λ is an additive discrete subgroup of $\mathbb{R}^n$. An n-dimensional lattice $\Lambda \subseteq \mathbb{R}^n$ is the set of all integer linear combinations $\sum_{j=1}^k c_j \boldsymbol{b}_j, c_j \in \mathbb{Z}$ of some linearly independent vectors $\boldsymbol{b}_1, \ldots, \boldsymbol{b}_k \in \mathbb{R}^n$ for some $k \leq n$. The rank of Λ is k. The determinant $\det(\Lambda)$ is defined as $\sqrt{\det(B^T B)}$, where $B = (\boldsymbol{b}_i)_i$ is any such basis of Λ. For a matrix $A \in \mathbb{Z}_q^{m \times n}$, define $\Lambda^\perp(A) = \{\boldsymbol{x} \in \mathbb{Z}^m : \boldsymbol{x}^T \cdot A = 0 \mod q\}$. The dual Λ^* of a lattice Λ is defined as $\Lambda^* = \{x \in \mathbb{R}^n : \forall y \in \Lambda, \langle x, y \rangle \in \mathbb{Z}\}$.

For a rank-n matrix $S \in \mathbb{R}^{m \times n}$ and a vector $\boldsymbol{c} \in \mathbb{R}^n$, the ellipsoid discrete Gaussian distribution with parameter S and center $\boldsymbol{c}$ is defined as $\forall \boldsymbol{x} \in \mathbb{R}^n, \rho_{S,\boldsymbol{c}}(x) = \exp\left(-\pi(\boldsymbol{x} - \boldsymbol{c})^T \left(S^T S\right)^{-1} (\boldsymbol{x} - \boldsymbol{c})\right)$. Note that $\rho_{S,\boldsymbol{c}}(x) = \exp(-\pi\|(S^T)^\dagger(\boldsymbol{x} - \boldsymbol{c})\|^2)$, where $X^\dagger$ denotes a pseudo-inverse of X. The ellipsoid discrete Gaussian distribution over a coset $\Lambda + \boldsymbol{z}$ of a lattice Λ, with parameter S and center $\boldsymbol{c}$ is defined as: $\forall \boldsymbol{x} \in \Lambda + \boldsymbol{z}, D_{\Lambda+\boldsymbol{z},S,\boldsymbol{c}} = \rho_{S,\boldsymbol{c}}(\boldsymbol{x})/\rho_{S,\boldsymbol{c}}(\Lambda)$. For $S = sI_m$, we write $\rho_{s,\boldsymbol{c}}$ and $D_{\Lambda+\boldsymbol{z},s,\boldsymbol{c}}$. When $\boldsymbol{c} = 0$, the subscript $\boldsymbol{c}$ is omitted.

Smoothing Parameter. The smoothing parameter [13] $\eta_\varepsilon(\Lambda)$ of an n-dimensional lattice Λ and a real $\varepsilon > 0$ is defined as the smallest s such that $\rho_{1/s}(\Lambda^* \setminus \{0\}) \leq \varepsilon$. When the deviation of the discrete Gaussian distribution is larger than the smoothing parameter, the following results are known.

Lemma 1 (Lemma 2.5 of [8]). *Let Λ be an n-dimensional lattice and $\varepsilon \in (0,1)$. Then for any $c \in \mathbb{R}^n$ and $s \geq \eta_\varepsilon(\Lambda)$ we have $\rho_{s,c}(\Lambda) \in [1-\varepsilon, 1+\varepsilon] \cdot \det(\Lambda)^{-1}$.*

Lemma 2 (Lemma 3 of [1]). *For a rank-n lattice Λ, a constant $0 < \varepsilon < 1$, a vector c and a matrix S with $\sigma_n(S) \geq \eta_\varepsilon(\Lambda)$, if x is sampled from $D_{\Lambda,S,c}$ then $\|x\| \leq \sigma_1(S)\sqrt{n}$ with probability $\leq \frac{1+\varepsilon}{1-\varepsilon} \cdot 2^{-n}$.*

Lemma 3 (Lemma 1 of [10]). *Let q be a prime and m,n integers with $m \geq 2n$ and $\varepsilon > 0$, then $\eta_\varepsilon(\Lambda^\perp(A)) \leq 4q^{n/m}\sqrt{\log(2m(1+1/\varepsilon))/\pi}$, for all except a fraction $2^{-\Omega(n)}$ of $A \in \mathbb{Z}_q^{m \times n}$.*

Rényi Divergence. For any two discrete probability distributions P and Q such that $\mathrm{Supp}(P) \subseteq \mathrm{Supp}(Q)$ and $\alpha \in (1,\infty]$, we define Rényi divergence (RD) of order α by

$$R_\alpha(P\|Q) = \left(\sum_{x \in \mathrm{Supp}(P)} \frac{P(x)^\alpha}{Q(x)^{\alpha-1}} \right)^{\frac{1}{\alpha-1}} \quad \text{for } \alpha \in (1,\infty),$$

$$R_\infty(P\|Q) = \max_{x \in \mathrm{Supp}(P)} \frac{P(x)}{Q(x)}.$$

We summarize the basic properties of RD which we use in this paper.

Lemma 4 (Lemma 4.1 of [8]). *Let P_1, P_2, P_3 and Q_1, Q_2 denote discrete distributions on a domain X. Let $\alpha \in (1, +\infty]$. Then the following properties hold:*

- *Log. Positivity: $R_\alpha(P_1\|Q_1) \geq R_\alpha(P_1\|P_1) = 1$,*
- *Data Processing Inequality: $R_\alpha\left(P_1^f\|Q_1^f\right) \leq R_\alpha(P_1\|Q_1)$ for any function f, where P_1^f (resp. Q_1^f) denotes the distribution of $f(y)$ induced by sampling $y \leftarrow P_1$ (resp. $y \leftarrow Q_1$).*
- *Multiplicativity: Let P and Q denote any two distributions of a pair of random variables (Y_1, Y_2) on $X \times X$. For $i \in \{1,2\}$, let P_i(resp. Q_i) denote the marginal distribution of Y_i under P (resp. Q), and $P_{(2|1)}(\cdot|y_1)$ (resp. $Q_{(2|1)}(\cdot|y_1)$) denote the conditional distribution of Y_2 given that $Y_1 = y_1$. Then we have $R_\alpha(P\|Q) = R_\alpha(P_1\|Q_1) \cdot R_\alpha(P_2\|Q_2)$ if Y_1 and Y_2 are independent, and $R_\alpha(P\|Q) \leq R_\infty(P_1\|Q_1) \cdot \max_{y_1 \in X} R_\alpha(P_{2|1}(\cdot|y_1)\|Q_{2|1}(\cdot|y_1))$.*
- *Weak Triangle Inequality: We have $R_\alpha(P_1\|P_3) \leq R_\alpha(P_1\|P_2) \cdot R_\infty(P_2\|P_3)$, and $R_\alpha(P_1\|P_3) \leq R_\infty(P_1\|P_2)^{\alpha/(\alpha-1)} \cdot R_\alpha(P_2\|P_3)$.*
- *R_∞ Triangle Inequality: If $R_\infty(P_1\|P_2)$ and $R_\infty(P_2\|P_3)$ are defined, then $R_\infty(P_1\|P_3) \leq R_\infty(P_1\|P_2) \cdot R_\infty(P_2\|P_3)$.*

– *Probability Preservation:* Let $E \subseteq X$ be an arbitrary event. Then $Q_1(E) \geq P_1(E)^{\alpha/(\alpha-1)}/R_\alpha(P_1\|Q_1)$.

The divergence R_1 is the exponential of the KLD, $R_1(P\|Q) = \exp\left(\sum_{x\in\mathrm{Supp}(P)} P(x)\log\frac{P(x)}{Q(x)}\right)$. The probability preservation property of the KLD can be written as $Q(E) \geq P(E) - \sqrt{\ln R_1(P\|Q)/2}$.

In this paper, we use the following results[2] which is essential for our improvements in Sects. 4 and 5.

Lemma 5. *For any n-dimensional lattice $\Lambda \subseteq \mathbb{R}^n$ and inversible rank-n matrix $S \in \mathbb{R}^{m\times n}$ for $m \geq n$, set $P = D_{\Lambda,S,c}$ and $Q = D_{\Lambda,S,c'}$ for some fixed $c, c' \in \mathbb{R}^n$. If $c, c' \in \Lambda$, let $\varepsilon = 0$. Otherwise, fix $\varepsilon \in (0,1)$ and assume that $\sigma_n(S) \geq \eta_\varepsilon(\Lambda)$. Then $R_\alpha(P\|Q) \leq \left(\frac{1+\varepsilon}{1-\varepsilon}\right)^{\frac{\alpha}{\alpha-1}} \cdot \exp\left(\alpha\pi\frac{\|c-c'\|^2}{\sigma_n(S)^2}\right).$*

3 Tighter Analysis for Discrete Gaussian Sampling with Small Precomputed Tables

In this section, we study Ducas et al.'s discrete Gaussian sampling [5] with precomputed tables. By adaptively optimizing the order of RD, we show that the sampling for BLISS signature scheme can be securely performed with less table storages.

Discrete Gaussian Sampling. In the BLISS signature scheme [5], signing a signature requires to sample $2n$ independent integers from one-dimensional discrete Gaussian distributions $D_{\mathbb{Z},s}$, where s is the standard deviation parameter. See Appendix A for detailed algorithms. In [5], an efficient sampling algorithm for $D_{\mathbb{Z},s}$ is presented. Let B_c be the Bernoulli distribution which outputs 1 with probability c and 0 otherwise. At first, the algorithm samples ℓ Bernoulli random variables of the form B_{c_i} for $i = 0, \ldots, \ell-1$ where $c_i = \exp(-\pi 2^i/s^2)$. By using a rejection sampling [7], these ℓ Bernoulli samples produce a sample from $D_{\mathbb{Z},s}$. Hence, to sign a signature, we sample $\ell \cdot 2n$ Bernoulli variables. For the detailed algorithm, see Table 3 in [5]. In this paper, we focus on sampling from Bernoulli distributions. To sample the Bernoulli random variables efficiently, a precomputed table which stores the probabilities c_i for $i = 0, \ldots, \ell-1$ is used. The algorithm samples x from a uniform distribution over $(0,1)$, and outputs 1 if $x < c_i$ and 0 otherwise. Since the exact quantities of c_i are real, the truncated $\tilde{c}_i = c_i + \varepsilon_i$ are stored. Here, $|\varepsilon_i| \leq 2^{-p}c_i$ denote truncation errors where p is a bit precision. When $c_i > 1/2$, we store truncated probabilities for $1 - c_i$ with bit precisions p. Hence, the table storage becomes $\ell \cdot p$ bits whose size affects the efficiency.

---

[2] In [2], Bai et al. showed a slightly better bound for our Lemma 5. However, we do not know the proof and we prove the lemma in this paper. See the full version of this paper.

Previous Analyses. As in [2], we analyze the security of BLISS when an adversary is allowed up to q_s signing queries. Then, $\ell \cdot 2n \cdot q_s$ Bernoulli random variables should be sampled since we should sample $\ell \cdot 2n$ Bernoulli random variables to sign a signature. Let Φ (resp. Φ') be a distribution of signatures in the view of the adversary where all $\ell \cdot 2n \cdot q_s$ variables are sampled from the truncated (resp. untruncated) Bernoulli distribution $B_{\tilde{c}_i}$ (resp. B_{c_i}). The distribution Φ (resp. Φ') is regarded as the *real* (resp. *ideal*) distribution. We will show that the BLISS signature scheme by sampling from the real distribution Φ is secure with smaller parameters, i.e., more signing queries q_s and less bit precision p, and the reduction from the scheme by sampling from the ideal distribution Φ' is tight, i.e., ε becomes small with larger ε'.

To examine the security, Ducas et al. [5] and Pöppelmann et al. [14] used SD and KLD, respectively. Though we omit details, the SD becomes $\Delta(\Phi, \Phi') = \ell \cdot 2n \cdot q_s \cdot 2^{-p-1}$ which leads to $\varepsilon \le \varepsilon' + \ell \cdot 2n \cdot q_s \cdot 2^{-p-1}$. Hence, when $p \ge \log(\ell \cdot 2n \cdot q_s/\varepsilon)$, the reduction becomes almost tight, i.e., $\varepsilon \le 2 \cdot \varepsilon'$. The KLD becomes $\ln R_1(\Phi\|\Phi') \le \ell \cdot 2n \cdot q_s \cdot 2^{-2p}$ which leads to $\varepsilon \le \varepsilon' + \sqrt{\ell \cdot 2n \cdot q_s \cdot 2^{-2p}}$. Hence, when $p \ge \log(\ell \cdot 2n \cdot q_s/\varepsilon^2)/2 + 1/2$, the reduction becomes almost tight, i.e., $\varepsilon \le 2 \cdot \varepsilon'$. See [2] for detailed analyses. Notice that the required precisions p depend on ε for both SD and KLD based analyses.

Bai et al. [2] used RD of orders $\alpha = +\infty, 2$ and showed that the sampling algorithm becomes secure with less table storages $\ell \cdot p$ which do not depend on ε. From the multiplicativity property over $i = 0, \ldots, \ell-1$ and data processing inequality of RD, $R_\alpha(\Phi\|\Phi') \le (\max_{i \in [1,\ell]} R_\alpha(B_{\tilde{c}_i}\|B_{c_i}))^{\ell \cdot 2n \cdot q_s}$. Let ε (resp. ε') be advantage for an adversary to break BLISS whose instances are sampled from Φ (resp. Φ'). From the probability preservation property of RD, $\varepsilon \le (\varepsilon' \cdot R_\alpha(\Phi\|\Phi'))^{\frac{\alpha-1}{\alpha}}$.

Using symmetry, we assume that $c_i \le 1/2$. Otherwise, we exchange c_i and $1 - c_i$ in the following calculations. First, Bai et al. used RD of $\alpha = +\infty$. By definition,

$$R_\infty(B_{\tilde{c}_i}\|B_{c_i}) = \max\left\{\frac{c_i + \varepsilon_i}{c_i}, \frac{1 - c_i - \varepsilon_i}{1 - c_i}\right\} = 1 + \frac{|\varepsilon_i|}{c_i} \le 1 + 2^{-p}.$$

Then, $R_\infty(\Phi\|\Phi') \le (1 + 2^{-p})^{\ell \cdot 2n \cdot q_s}$ from the multiplicativity property over $i = 0, \ldots, \ell-1$ and data processing inequality of RD. The RD bound leads to $\varepsilon \le \varepsilon' \cdot (1 + 2^{-p})^{\ell \cdot 2n \cdot q_s}$ from the probability preservation property of RD. Hence, when $p \ge \log(\ell \cdot 2n \cdot q_s)$, the reduction becomes almost tight, i.e., $\varepsilon \le 2 \cdot \varepsilon'$. Since the probability preservation property of the RD is multiplicative, the required precisions do not depend on ε which results in the less table storages. The required precision is less than previous SD and KLD based analyses [5,14].

Next, they used RD of $\alpha \in (1, +\infty)$. By definition,

$$(R_\alpha(B_{\tilde{c}_i}\|B_{c_i}))^{\alpha-1} = c_i \left(\frac{c_i + \varepsilon_i}{c_i}\right)^\alpha + (1 - c_i)\left(\frac{1 - c_i - \varepsilon_i}{1 - c_i}\right)^\alpha. \tag{3}$$

In particular, they focused on the case $\alpha = 2$, that is, $R_2(B_{\tilde{c}_i}\|B_{c_i}) = 1 + \frac{\varepsilon_i^2}{c_i(1 - c_i)} \le 1 + 2^{-2p}$. The last inequality holds by using the fact that $|\varepsilon_i| \le 2^{-p}c_i$ and the assumption $c_i \leq 1/2$. Then, $R_2(\Phi \| \Phi') \leq (1 + 2^{-2p})^{\ell \cdot 2n \cdot q_s}$ from the multiplicativity property over $i = 0, \dots, \ell - 1$ and data processing inequality of RD. The RD bound leads to $\varepsilon \leq \varepsilon'^{1/2} \cdot (1 + 2^{-2p})^{\ell \cdot 2n \cdot q_s}$ from the probability preservation property of RD. Hence, they concluded the precision as $p \geq \log(\ell \cdot 2n \cdot q_s)/2$. The required precision of R_2 based analysis becomes half compared with R_∞ based analysis. The improvements are derived from the exponent of $R_2(B_{\tilde{c}_i} \| B_{c_i})$ becomes $-2p$, though that of R_∞ is $-p$. Though the required precision is less than R_∞ based analysis, R_2 based analysis offers the reduction which is no longer tight, i.e., $\varepsilon \leq 2 \cdot \varepsilon'^{1/2}$ from the probability preservation property of RD. The deficiency comes from the preservation property of R_2, i.e., $\varepsilon \leq \varepsilon'^{1/2} \cdot R_2(\Phi \| \Phi')$. The exponent of ε' never allows tight reductions even if the precisions become infinitely large.

Tighter RD Based Analysis with Smaller Table Storages. In the rest of this section, we show that R_α based analysis offers both less required precision and tighter reduction when the order α is appropriately determined. At first, we bound the RD of the inequality (3) for general α as follows.

Lemma 6. *Let probability distributions $B_{\tilde{c}_i}$ and B_{c_i} be defined as above. If the order α be an integer with $\alpha < 2^p$, then $(R_\alpha(B_{\tilde{c}_i} \| B_{c_i}))^{\alpha-1} = \exp\left(\frac{\alpha(\alpha-1)}{2} \cdot 2^{-2p}\right) + O((\alpha 2^{-p})^3)$.*

The proof of Lemma 6 is given in Appendix B. Since we only use RD of order α which is much smaller than 2^p, we ignore the small term and assume $(R_\alpha(B_{\tilde{c}_i} \| B_{c_i}))^{\alpha-1} = \exp\left(\frac{\alpha(\alpha-1)}{2} \cdot 2^{-2p}\right)$ which leads to $(R_\alpha(\Phi \| \Phi'))^{\alpha-1} \leq (R_\alpha(B_{\tilde{c}_i} \| B_{c_i}))^{(\alpha-1) \cdot \ell \cdot 2n \cdot q_s} = \exp\left(\alpha(\alpha-1) \cdot \ell \cdot n \cdot q_s \cdot 2^{-2p}\right)$ from the multiplicativity property over $i = 0, \dots, \ell - 1$ and data processing inequality of RD. Since the exponent is $-2p$, the analysis needs small precision as R_2 based analysis. In addition, since $\varepsilon \leq (\varepsilon' \cdot R_\alpha(\Phi \| \Phi'))^{\frac{\alpha-1}{\alpha}} = \varepsilon'^{\frac{\alpha-1}{\alpha}} \cdot \exp\left((\alpha-1) \cdot \ell \cdot n \cdot q_s \cdot 2^{-2p}\right)$ holds from the probability preservation property of RD, the reduction becomes almost tight when α is large. When the order α is appropriately determined, the sampling can be performed with small table storages with almost tight reduction. As a result, we obtain the following Theorem 1.

For the condition in Theorem 1, we define the minimal key recovery advantage $\hat{\varepsilon}$: in Appendix A of [5], known attacks for BLISS are summarized including lattice reduction attacks for the underlying SIS, primal and dual lattice reduction key recovery. The most primitive brute-force key recovery is also analyzed, in which an adversary guesses a random secret vector g and check whether $f = a_q^{-1}(2g + 1) \mod q$ is a legitimate secret polynomial or not for public polynomial a_q. (Otherwise, the adversary aborts.) The advantage is estimated as[3] $\hat{\varepsilon} = 2^{-d_1 - d_2} \cdot \binom{n}{d_1}^{-1} \cdot \binom{n-d_1}{d_2}^{-1}$ where d_1 and d_2 are defined in key generation of BLISS. For example, $\hat{\varepsilon} \approx 2^{-600}$ for BLISS-I parameter $n = 512, d_1 \approx 153, d_2 \approx 0$.

---

[3] While in [5], the *brute-force* adversary for all key candidates is considered, we consider the corresponding *one-time* guessing adversary. Hence, the advantage of the guessing adversary is the inverse of the computation time of the brute-force adversary.

In Theorem 1, we consider powerful adversaries with signing query number $q_s \approx 2^{64}$. For such a powerful adversary, it holds that $\ell \cdot n \cdot q_s \gg -\ln(\hat{\varepsilon})$. For example, for practical BLISS-I parameters ($n = 512, \ell = 29$), the left (resp. right) hand side $\approx 2^{78}$ (resp. ≈ 600), then the above inequality holds.

Theorem 1. *Let parameters p, ℓ, n, q_s, probability distributions $B_{\tilde{c}_i}$ and B_{c_i} be defined as above. Then, if there is an adversary $\mathcal{A}$ against the BLISS signature scheme where Bernoulli random variables are sampled from $B_{\tilde{c}_i}$ with run-time T and advantage ε, then $\mathcal{A}$ is also an adversary against the BLISS signature scheme where Bernoulli random variables are sampled from B_{c_i} with run-time $T' = T$ and advantage ε' which satisfies $-\ln(\varepsilon') > \ell \cdot n \cdot q_s \cdot 2^{-2p}$ and*

$$\varepsilon \leq \exp\left(-\left(\sqrt{-\ln(\varepsilon')} - \sqrt{\ell \cdot n \cdot q_s \cdot 2^{-2p}}\right)^2\right). \tag{4}$$

Proof. As we showed, $\varepsilon \leq (\varepsilon' \cdot R_\alpha(\Phi \| \Phi'))^{\frac{\alpha-1}{\alpha}} = \varepsilon'^{\frac{\alpha-1}{\alpha}} \cdot \exp\left((\alpha-1) \cdot \ell \cdot n \cdot q_s \cdot 2^{-2p}\right)$ which leads to

$$\varepsilon \leq \exp\left(\frac{\alpha-1}{\alpha}\ln(\varepsilon') + (\alpha-1) \cdot \ell \cdot n \cdot q_s \cdot 2^{-2p}\right).$$

The inequality is equivalent to the inequality (1) in Sect. 1. The right hand side of the inequality is lower bounded as

$$\exp\left(\ln(\varepsilon') - \ell \cdot n \cdot q_s \cdot 2^{-2p} + \left(-\ln(\varepsilon')/\alpha + \alpha \cdot \ell \cdot n \cdot q_s \cdot 2^{-2p}\right)\right)$$
$$\geq \exp\left(\ln(\varepsilon') - \ell \cdot n \cdot q_s \cdot 2^{-2p} + 2\sqrt{-\ln(\varepsilon') \cdot \ell \cdot n \cdot q_s \cdot 2^{-2p}}\right)$$

by the inequality of arithmetic mean and geometric mean, in which the equality holds if and only if $-\ln(\varepsilon')/\alpha = \alpha \cdot \ell \cdot n \cdot q_s \cdot 2^{-2p}$, i.e., $\alpha = \sqrt{\frac{-\ln(\varepsilon')}{\ell \cdot n \cdot q_s \cdot 2^{-2p}}}$. Then, we set the order $\alpha = \sqrt{\frac{-\ln(\varepsilon')}{\ell \cdot n \cdot q_s \cdot 2^{-2p}}}$ and the above inequality becomes

$$\varepsilon \leq \exp\left(-\left(\sqrt{-\ln(\varepsilon')} - \sqrt{\ell \cdot n \cdot q_s \cdot 2^{-2p}}\right)^2\right).$$

The inequality is equivalent to the inequality (2) in Sect. 1 as required. The order $\alpha = \sqrt{\frac{-\ln(\varepsilon')}{\ell \cdot n \cdot q_s \cdot 2^{-2p}}}$ which we use satisfies $\alpha \in (1, +\infty]$ since $-\ln(\varepsilon') > \ell \cdot n \cdot q_s \cdot 2^{-2p}$. □

For the BLISS signature scheme to be secure (ε to be small) with *smaller* $-\ln(\varepsilon')$ (larger ε', i.e., tighter reduction), *more* signing queries q_s (i.e., for powerful adversaries), and *larger* 2^{-p} (less precision p, i.e., more efficiency), the inequality (4) shows an appropriate tradeoff. The upper bound of ε based on our analysis is lower than that of Bai et al.'s R_2 based analysis for all $\varepsilon', \ell, n, q_s$ and p. In particular, from the inequality (4)

$$\varepsilon \le \exp\left(-\left(\sqrt{-\ln(\varepsilon')} - \sqrt{\ell \cdot n \cdot q_s \cdot 2^{-2p}}\right)^2\right)$$
$$= \varepsilon' \cdot \exp\left(2\sqrt{-\ln(\varepsilon') \cdot \ell \cdot n \cdot q_s \cdot 2^{-2p}} - \ell \cdot n \cdot q_s \cdot 2^{-2p}\right),$$

when $-\ln(\varepsilon') \cdot \ell \cdot n \cdot q_s \cdot 2^{-2p} \le 1$, then $\varepsilon \le \varepsilon' \cdot O(1)$ holds whose upper bound cannot be obtained by R_2 based analysis. The condition leads to the precision requirement $p \ge \log(-\ln(\varepsilon') \cdot \ell \cdot n \cdot q_s)/2$ which is less than SD, KLD, and R_∞ based analyses for powerful adversaries, i.e., $\ell \cdot n \cdot q_s \gg -\ln(\hat{\varepsilon})$.

Table 4. Comparison of required precisions p, table bit-size and upper bounds of $-\log\varepsilon'$. The left table is the summary of previous analyses which are the same as in Table 1 of [2]. The right table is based on our analysis.

statistical measure	p	Table bit-size	$-\log\varepsilon'$
SD [6]	207	6003	≤ 129
KLD [15]	168	4872	≤ 129
RD, $\alpha = +\infty$ [3]	79	2291	≤ 129
RD, $\alpha = 2$ [3]	40	1160	256.45

α	p	Table bit-size	$-\log\varepsilon'$
2.48	36	1044	418.66
6.94	38	1102	184.97
24.76	40	1160	141.26
96.07	42	1218	131.25
381.30	44	1276	128.80

Numerical Examples. Table 4 shows the numerical examples which compare required precisions p, table bit-size $\ell \cdot p$, and upper bounds of $-\log(\varepsilon')$ between previous analyses [2,5,14] and our analysis. As Table 1 in [2], an adversary is allowed $q_s = 2^{64}$ sign queries and breaks BLISS-I with probability $\varepsilon = 2^{-128}$ with parameters $n = 512, \ell = 29$. The quantities of $-\log(\varepsilon')$ are calculated by

$$-\log(\varepsilon') \le \log\left(\exp\left(\left(\sqrt{-\ln(\varepsilon)} + \sqrt{\ell \cdot n \cdot q_s \cdot 2^{-2p}}\right)^2\right)\right)$$

which is equivalent to the inequality (4). The table clarifies our improvement which is briefly summarized in Table 1. Though Bai et al.'s R_2 based analysis [2] requires less precision p than SD, KLD, and R_∞ based analyses [2,5,14], the reduction is no longer tight, $-\log(\varepsilon')$ becomes much larger than $-\log(\varepsilon) = 128$. Theorem 1 shows better tradeoff than previous analyses. As the right table shows, the larger bit precisions p are used, the smaller $-\log(\varepsilon')$ becomes and the tighter the reduction becomes. In particular, the upper bound of $-\log(\varepsilon')$ for $p = 40$ based on our analysis is smaller that of R_2 based analysis by Bai et al. [2]. As a result[4], when $p \ge 44$, the reduction becomes almost tight,

---

[4] In [2], Bai et al. analyzed the precisions by measuring the closeness between $B_{\tilde{c}_i}$ and B_{c_i} depending on i. The analysis further reduces the required precisions for SD and KLD based analyses, i.e., 4598 and 3893 bits tables respectively. Though our analysis also offers lower precisions, we omit the analysis in this paper.

i.e., $-\log(\varepsilon') \leq 129$. Notice that the orders α are always much smaller than 2^p which we assume to bound the quantity of RD.

4   Tighter Analysis for LWE to k-LWE Reduction

In this section, we study LWE to k-LWE reduction [10]. By adaptively optimizing the order of RD, the reduction becomes tighter.

First, we introduce a variant of LWE problem where the number of samples m produced by the oracle is a priori bounded.

Definition 1 (LWE$_{\beta,m}$ Problem). *Given $A \leftarrow U\left(\mathbb{Z}_q^{m \times n}\right)$, the goal of LWE$_{\beta,m}$ problem is to distinguish between the distributions (over $\mathbb{T}^m$)*

$$\frac{1}{q}U\left(\mathrm{Im}(A)\right) + \nu_\beta^m \text{ and } \frac{1}{q}U\left(\mathbb{Z}_q^m\right) + \nu_\beta^m.$$

Next, we introduce k-LWE problem defined in [10].

Definition 2 ((k, S, C)-LWE$_{\beta,m}$ Problem, Definition 7 of [10]). *Let $k \leq m$, $S \in \mathbb{R}^{m \times m}$ invertible and $C = (c_1 \| \cdots \| c_k) \in \mathbb{R}^{k \times m}$. Given $A \leftarrow U\left(\mathbb{Z}_q^{m \times n}\right)$, and $x_i \leftarrow D_{\Lambda^\perp(A),S,c_i}$ for $i \leq k$, the goal of (k, S, C)-LWE$_{\beta,m}$ problem ((k, S)-LWE$_{\beta,m}$ problem when $C = 0$) is to distinguish between the distributions (over $\mathbb{T}^m$)*

$$\frac{1}{q}U\left(\mathrm{Im}\left(A\right)\right) + \nu_\beta^m \text{ and } \frac{1}{q}U\left(\mathrm{Span}_{i \leq k}\left(x_i\right)^\perp\right) + \nu_\beta^m.$$

The k vectors $x_1, \ldots, x_k$ can be used to solve the original LWE$_{\beta,m}$. When we obtain a vector y from the left distribution, $\langle x_i, y \rangle$ becomes much smaller than 1 for standard parameter setting since $x_i \in \Lambda^\perp(A)$ and orthogonal to $\mathrm{Im}(A)$. On the other hand, when we obtain a vector y from the right distribution, $\langle x_i, y \rangle$ should be uniform. However, (k, S, C)-LWE$_{\beta,m}$ becomes non-trivial and seems to be hard since the right distribution $\frac{1}{q}U\left(\mathbb{Z}_q^m\right)$ is replaced by $\frac{1}{q}U\left(\mathrm{Span}_{i \leq k}\left(x_i\right)^\perp\right)$.

Ling et al. [10] proved the security reduction for the (k, S)-LWE$_{\beta,m}$ problem; an adversary which solves the (k, S)-LWE$_{\beta',m+2n}$ problem in Definition 2 is also an adversary which solves the LWE$_{\beta,m}$ problem for Definition 1. However, their reduction is not tight since they fixed the order of RD as $\alpha = 2$. We show the tighter security reduction as follows by *adaptively* optimizing the order.

Theorem 2. *There exists $c > 0$ such that the following holds for $k = n/(c \log n)$. Let m, q, σ, σ' be such that $\sigma \geq \Omega(n), \sigma' \geq \Omega\left(n^3 \sigma^2 / \log n\right), q \geq \Omega\left(\sigma' \sqrt{\log m}\right)$ is prime, and $m \geq \Omega(n \log q)$ (e.g., $\sigma = \Theta(n), \sigma' = \Theta(n^5 / \log n), q = \Theta(n^5)$ and $m = \Theta(n \log n)$). If there exists a distinguisher $\mathcal{A}$ against (k, S)-LWE$_{\beta',m+2n}$ in dimension $4n$, with $\beta' = \Omega\left(mn^{3/2}\sigma\sigma'\beta\right)$ and S is a diagonal matrix where $a_{ii} = \sigma$ for $1 \leq i \leq m+n$ and $a_{ii} = \sigma'$ for $m+n+1 \leq i \leq m+2n$ with run-time T and advantage ε. Then there exists a distinguisher $\mathcal{A}'$ for LWE$_{\beta,m}$ in dimension*

n *with run-time* $T' = O(poly(m) \cdot (\varepsilon - 2^{-\Omega(n/\log n)})^{-2} \cdot (T + poly(m)))$ *and advantage* ε' *where*

$$\varepsilon \le \exp\left(\frac{\ln\left(\varepsilon' + 2^{-\Omega(n)}\right)}{2} + \frac{\sqrt{-1 - 2n\ln(\varepsilon' + 2^{-\Omega(n)})}}{2n}\right) \cdot 2^{O(k \cdot 2^{-n})}$$
$$+ 2^{-\Omega(n/\log n)}.$$

Proof. The proof of Theorem 2 consists of Lemma 7 and Theorem 3. That is, the required reduction of Theorem 2 consists of two subreductions as in [10]. The first is the LWE to (k, S, C)-LWE reduction, and the second is the (k, S, C)-LWE to (k, S)-LWE reduction. We follow the first subreduction[5] from [10].

Lemma 7 ([10]). *Let parameters* $k, n, m, q, \sigma, \sigma', \beta'$ *and a matrix* S *as in Theorem 2. Let a matrix* $C \in \mathbb{R}^{k \times (m+2n)}$ *whose* i-*th row is the unit vector* $c_i = (0^{m+n}|\delta_i)$ *where* δ_i *denotes the* i-*th canonical unit vector. If there exists a distinguisher* $\mathcal{A}$ *against* (k, S, C)-LWE$_{\beta', m+2n}$ *in dimension* $4n$ *with run-time* T *and advantage* ε, *then* $\mathcal{A}$ *is also a distinguisher against* LWE$_{\beta, m}$ *in dimension* n *with run-time* $T' = T + poly(m)$ *and advantage* $\varepsilon' = \varepsilon - 2^{-\Omega(n/\log n)}$.

Next, we analyze the second subreduction. Though our analysis is similar to that in [10], the following Theorem 3 is obtained as an application of our optimized selection of the order α.

Theorem 3. *Let* $m' = m + 2n, n' = 4n$, *and assume that* $\sigma_{m'}(S) \ge \omega(\sqrt{n})$. *Let* γ *be a constant which satisfies* $\sigma_{m'}(S) \ge \sqrt{\pi/\gamma} \cdot \|C\|$. *If there exists a distinguisher* $\mathcal{A}$ *against* (k, S)-LWE$_{\beta', m+2n}$ *in dimension* n' *with run-time* T *and advantage* ε, *then* $\mathcal{A}$ *is also a distinguisher against* (k, S, C)-LWE$_{\beta', m+2n}$ *with run-time* $T' = O\left(poly(m') \cdot (\varepsilon - 2^{-\Omega(n)})^{-2} \cdot T\right)$ *and advantage* ε' *which satisfies* $-\ln\left(\varepsilon' + 2^{-\Omega(n)}\right) \ge k\gamma$, *and*

$$\varepsilon \le \exp\left(\frac{\ln\left(\varepsilon' + 2^{-\Omega(n)}\right)}{2} + \frac{k\gamma\sqrt{-1 - 2\ln(\varepsilon' + 2^{-\Omega(n)})/(k\gamma)}}{2}\right) \cdot 2^{O(k \cdot 2^{-n})}$$
$$+ 2^{-\Omega(n)}.$$

The proof of Theorem 3 is given in the full version of this paper. Based on SD, the deviations to sample k hint vectors become exponential of the security parameter. Since Ling et al. used RD, the deviations become smaller. In addition, we optimize the order α and obtain a tighter reduction.

Note that in the above reduction from LWE$_{\beta, m}$ to (k, S, C)-LWE$_{\beta', m+2n}$, $\|C\| = 1, \sigma_{m'}(S) = \sigma = \Omega(n)$. Hence, we set $\gamma = O(1/n^2)$ and using the fact that $k < n$, we can obtain the required inequality of Theorem 2. □

---

[5] In a very recent version [11], Ling et al. proposed improved results for the first subreduction. We can incorporate the improvements into our Theorems 2 and 4.

Analogous to Theorem 3, the inequality in [10] can be written as

$$\varepsilon \leq \exp\left(\frac{\ln\left(\varepsilon' + 2^{-\Omega(n)}\right)}{3} + \frac{2k\gamma}{3}\right) \cdot 2^{O(k \cdot 2^{-n})} + 2^{-\Omega(n)}.$$

The inequality can be obtained via R_2. The right hand side of the inequality becomes the same as ours only when $\alpha = 2$. Otherwise, our analysis always offers a tighter reduction since the right hand side of the inequality in Theorem 3 is always smaller than that in Ling et al.'s.

5 Tighter Analysis for SIS to k-SIS Reduction

In this section, we study SIS to k-SIS reduction [3,10]. By adaptively optimizing the order of RD, the reduction becomes tighter.

First, we introduce the SIS problem.

Definition 3 ($SIS_{\beta,m}$ Problem). *Given $A \leftarrow U\left(\mathbb{Z}_q^{m \times n}\right)$, the goal of $SIS_{\beta,m}$ problem is to find nonzero vector $b \in \mathbb{Z}^m$ such that*

- $\|b\| \leq \beta$,
- $b^T \cdot A = 0 \mod q$.

Next, we introduce k-SIS problem. The definition follows from Definition 2 rather than the original one from [3].

Definition 4 ((k, S, C)-$SIS_{\beta,m}$ Problem, Adapted from Definition 4.1 of [3]). *Let $k \leq m$, $S \in \mathbb{R}^{m \times m}$ invertible and $C = (c_1 \| \cdots \| c_k) \in \mathbb{R}^{k \times m}$. Given $A \leftarrow U\left(\mathbb{Z}_q^{m \times n}\right)$ and $x_i \leftarrow D_{\Lambda^\perp(A),S,c_i}$ for $i \leq k$, the goal of (k, S, C)-$SIS_{\beta,m}$ problem ((k, S)-$SIS_{\beta,m}$ problem when $C = 0$) is to find nonzero vector $b \in \mathbb{Z}^m$ such that*

- $\|b\| \leq \beta$,
- $b^T \cdot A = 0 \mod q$,
- $b \in \mathrm{Span}_{i \leq k}\left(x_i\right)^\perp$.

The k vectors $x_1, \ldots, x_k$ for (k, S)-$SIS_{\beta,m}$ can be used to solve the original $SIS_{\beta,m}$. The vectors satisfy the second condition of $SIS_{\beta,m}$ by definition. Since the vectors are sampled from Gaussian distributions, the norms are small and the vectors are expected to satisfy the first condition of $SIS_{\beta,m}$. However, (k, S, C)-$SIS_{\beta,m}$ is non-trivial and seems to be hard since there is an additional condition $b \in \mathrm{Span}_{i \leq k}\left(x_i\right)^\perp$. The integer linear combinations of the k hint vectors cannot be solutions of (k, S, C)-$SIS_{\beta,m}$.

Ling et al. [10] briefly summarize the SIS to k-SIS reduction. As the $LWE_{\beta,m}$ to (k, S)-$LWE_{\beta,m}$ reduction, they showed that an adversary which solves the (k, S)-$SIS_{\beta',m}$ problem for Definition 4 is also an adversary which solves the $SIS_{\beta,m}$ problem for Definition 3. However, their reduction is not tight since they fixed the order of RD as $\alpha = 2$. We show the tighter security reduction as follows by *adaptively* optimizing the order.

Theorem 4. *Let parameters $k, n, m, q, \sigma, \sigma', \beta'$ and a matrix S as in Theorem 2. If there exists an adversary $\mathcal{A}$ against (k, S)-SIS$_{\beta', m+2n}$ in dimension n, with run-time T and advantage ε, then $\mathcal{A}'$ is also an adversary against SIS$_{\beta, m}$ in dimension n and $\beta = \Omega(m^{1/2} n^{3/2} \sigma \sigma' \beta')$ with run-time $T' = T + poly(m)$ and advantage ε' where*

$$\varepsilon \leq \exp\left(-\left(\sqrt{-\ln\left(\varepsilon' + 2^{-\Omega(n)}\right)} - \sqrt{k\gamma}\right)^2\right) \cdot 2^{O\left(k \cdot 2^{-n}\right)} + 2^{-\Omega(n)}.$$

Proof. As LWE to (k, S)-LWE reduction, the reduction consists of two subreductions. The first is the SIS to (k, S, C)-SIS reduction, and the second is the (k, S, C)-SIS to (k, S)-SIS reduction. The first subreduction is almost the same as that for LWE to (k, S, C)-LWE reduction as suggested in [10].

Lemma 8 (Adapted from [10]). *Let k, m, q, σ, σ' be the same as Theorem 2. If there exists an adversary against (k, S, C)-SIS$_{\beta', m+2n}$ in dimension n, with S as in Theorem 2, with run-time T and advantage ε, then there exists an adversary against SIS$_{\beta, m}$ in dimension n with $\beta = \Omega(m^{1/2} n^{3/2} \sigma \sigma' \beta')$ with run-time $T' = T + poly(m)$ and advantage $\varepsilon' = \varepsilon - 2^{-\Omega(n/\log n)}$.*

The proof of Lemma 8 is given in the full version of this paper.

Next, we analyze the second subreduction. The following Theorem 5 is obtained as an application of our optimized selection of the order α. We cannot obtain the same tightness when we fix the order $\alpha = 2$ as in [10].

Theorem 5. *Assume that $\sigma_{m'}(S) \geq \omega(\sqrt{n})$. Let γ be a constant which satisfies $\sigma_{m'}(S) \geq \sqrt{\pi/\gamma} \cdot \|C\|$. If there exists an adversary $\mathcal{A}$ against (k, S)-SIS$_{\beta, m'}$ in dimension n with run-time T and advantage ε, then $\mathcal{A}$ is also an adversary against (k, S, C)-SIS$_{\beta, m'}$ with run-time $T' = T$ and advantage ε' which satisfies $-\ln\left(\varepsilon' + 2^{-\Omega(n)}\right) \geq k\gamma$, and*

$$\varepsilon \leq \exp\left(-\left(\sqrt{-\ln\left(\varepsilon' + 2^{-\Omega(n)}\right)} - \sqrt{k\gamma}\right)^2\right) \cdot 2^{O\left(k \cdot 2^{-n}\right)} + 2^{-\Omega(n)}.$$

The proof of Theorem 5 is given in the full version of this paper. Based on SD, the deviations to sample k hint vectors become exponential of the security parameter. Since Ling et al. used RD, the deviations become smaller. In addition, we optimize the order α and obtain a tighter reduction.

Note that in the above reduction from SIS$_{\beta, m}$ to (k, S, C)-SIS$_{\beta', m+2n}$, $\|C\| = 1, \sigma_{m'}(S) = \sigma = \Omega(n)$. Hence, we set $\gamma = O(1/n^2)$ and using the fact that $k < n$, we can obtain the required inequality of Theorem 4.   □

Analogous to Theorem 5, the inequality can be written as

$$\varepsilon \leq \exp\left(\frac{\ln\left(\varepsilon' + 2^{-\Omega(n)}\right)}{2} + k\gamma\right) \cdot 2^{O\left(k \cdot 2^{-n}\right)} + 2^{-\Omega(n)}.$$

when we fix the order $\alpha = 2$. The right hand side of the inequality becomes the same as ours only when $\alpha = 2$. Otherwise, our analysis always offers tighter reduction since the right hand side of the inequality in Theorem 5 is always smaller than that of R_2 based analysis.

A BLISS Signature Scheme

BLISS signature algorithm proceed as follows:

- Key generation algorithm, KeyGen():
  - Choose f, g as uniform polynomials with exactly $d_1 = \lceil \delta_1 n \rceil$ entries in $\{\pm 1\}$ and $d_2 = \lceil \delta_2 n \rceil$ entries in $\{\pm 2\}$
  - $S = (s_1, s_2)^T \leftarrow (f, 2g + 1)^T$
  - If $N_\kappa(S) \geq C^2 \cdot 5 \cdot (\lceil \delta_1 n \rceil + 4 \lceil \delta_2 n \rceil) \cdot \kappa$ then restart
  - $a_q = (2g + 1)/f \mod q$ (restart if f is not invertible)
  - Return $(pk = A, sk = S)$ where $A = (2a_q, q - 2) \mod 2q$.
- Signature Algorithm, Sign($\mu, pk = A, sk = S$):
  - $y_1, y_2 \leftarrow D_{\mathbb{Z}^n, s}$
  - $u = \zeta \cdot a_1 \cdot y_1 + y_2 \mod 2q$
  - $c \leftarrow H(\lfloor u \rceil_d \mod p, \mu)$
  - Choose a random bit b
  - $z_1 \leftarrow y_1 + (-1)^b s_1 c$
  - $z_2 \leftarrow y_2 + (-1)^b s_2 c$
  - Continue with probability $1 / \left(M \exp \left(-\frac{\|Sc\|^2}{s^2/\pi} \right) \cosh \left(\frac{\langle z, Sc \rangle}{s^2/\pi} \right) \right)$ otherwise restart
  - $z_2^\dagger \leftarrow (\lfloor u \rceil_d - \lfloor u - z_2 \rceil_d) \mod p$
  - Return $(z_1, z_2^\dagger, c)$
- Verification Algorithm, Verify($\mu, pk = A, (z_1, z_2^\dagger, c)$):
  - if $\|(z_1 | 2^d \cdot z_2^\dagger)\|_2 \geq B_2$, then reject
  - if $\|(z_1 | 2^d \cdot z_2^\dagger)\|_\infty \geq B_\infty$, then reject
  - Accept if and only if $c = H(\lfloor \zeta \cdot a_1 \cdot z_1 + \zeta \cdot q \cdot c \rceil_d + z_2^\dagger \mod p, \mu)$

For the detailed definitions of parameters, see Table 3 in [5].

B Proof of Lemma 6 in Sect. 3

From an equality (3),

$$
(R_\alpha(B_{\tilde{c}_i} \| B_{c_i}))^{\alpha-1} = c_i \sum_{j=0}^\alpha \binom{\alpha}{j} \left(\frac{\varepsilon_i}{c_i} \right)^j + (1 - c_i) \sum_{j=0}^\alpha \binom{\alpha}{j} \left(-\frac{\varepsilon_i}{1 - c_i} \right)^j
$$

$$
= \sum_{j=0}^\alpha \binom{\alpha}{j} \left(\frac{\varepsilon_i^j}{c_i^{j-1}} + \frac{(-\varepsilon_i)^j}{(1 - c_i)^{j-1}} \right)
$$

$$
= 1 + \frac{\alpha(\alpha - 1)}{2} \cdot \frac{\varepsilon_i^2}{c_i(1 - c_i)} + \sum_{j=3}^\alpha \binom{\alpha}{j} \left(\frac{\varepsilon_i^j}{c_i^{j-1}} + \frac{(-\varepsilon_i)^j}{(1 - c_i)^{j-1}} \right).
$$

The first two terms satisfy

$$1 + \frac{\alpha(\alpha-1)}{2} \cdot \frac{\varepsilon_i^2}{c_i(1-c_i)} \le \left(1 + \frac{|\varepsilon_i|^2}{c_i(1-c_i)}\right)^{\frac{\alpha(\alpha-1)}{2}}$$

$$\le \left(1 + 2^{-2p} \cdot \frac{c_i}{1-c_i}\right)^{\frac{\alpha(\alpha-1)}{2}} \le \left(1 + 2^{-2p}\right)^{\frac{\alpha(\alpha-1)}{2}}$$

by using the fact that $c_i \le 1/2$ and $|\varepsilon_i| \le c_i 2^{-p}$. Since $\ln(1 + 2^{-2p}) \le 2^{-2p}$,

$$\left(1 + 2^{-2p}\right)^{\frac{\alpha(\alpha-1)}{2}} \le \exp\left(\frac{\alpha(\alpha-1)}{2} \cdot 2^{-2p}\right).$$

Then, all we have to prove is the remaining terms to be $O((\alpha 2^{-p})^3)$. The terms are upper bounded as

$$\sum_{j=3}^{\alpha} \binom{\alpha}{j} \left(\frac{(-\varepsilon_i)^j}{(1-c_i)^{j-1}} + \frac{\varepsilon_i^j}{c_i^{j-1}}\right) \le \sum_{j=3}^{\alpha} \frac{\alpha^j}{j!} \left(\frac{(-\varepsilon_i)^j}{(1-c_i)^{j-1}} + \frac{\varepsilon_i^j}{c_i^{j-1}}\right)$$

$$\le \sum_{j=3}^{\alpha} \frac{\alpha^j}{j!} \cdot 2 \cdot \frac{|\varepsilon_i|^j}{c_i^j} \cdot c_i \le \sum_{j=3}^{\alpha} \frac{(\alpha 2^{-p})^j}{j!}$$

by using the fact that $c_i \le 1/2$ and $|\varepsilon_i| \le c_i 2^{-p}$. Then, the terms are upper bounded as

$$\le (\alpha 2^{-p})^3 \cdot \sum_{j=0}^{\alpha-3} \frac{(\alpha 2^{-p})^j}{j!} \le (\alpha 2^{-p})^3 \cdot \sum_{j=0}^{\infty} \frac{(\alpha 2^{-p})^j}{j!} = (\alpha 2^{-p})^3 \cdot \exp(\alpha 2^{-p})$$

$$= O((\alpha 2^{-p})^3)$$

by using the fact that $\alpha 2^{-p} \le 1$.

Acknowledgements. K. Takashima is supported by the JSPS Fellowship for Young Scientists.

References

1. Agrawal, S., Gentry, C., Halevi, S., Sahai, A.: Discrete Gaussian Leftover Hash Lemma over Infinite Domains. In: Sako, K., Sarkar, P. (eds.) ASIACRYPT 2013, Part I. LNCS, vol. 8269, pp. 97–116. Springer, Heidelberg (2013)
2. Bai, S., Langois, A., Lepoint, T., Stehlé, D., Steinfeld, R.: Improved security proofs in lattice-based cryptography: using the Rényi divergence rather than the statistical distance. In: IACR Cryptology ePrint Archive: Report 2015/483, Asiacrypt 2015 (2015, to appear)
3. Boneh, D., Freeman, D.M.: Linearly homomorphic signatures over binary fields and new tools for lattice-based signatures. In: Catalano, D., Fazio, N., Gennaro, R., Nicolosi, A. (eds.) PKC 2011. LNCS, vol. 6571, pp. 1–16. Springer, Heidelberg (2011)

4. Chen, Y., Nguyen, P.Q.: BKZ 2.0: better lattice security estimates. In: Lee, D.H., Wang, X. (eds.) ASIACRYPT 2011. LNCS, vol. 7073, pp. 1–20. Springer, Heidelberg (2011)

5. Ducas, L., Durmus, A., Lepoint, T., Lyubashevsky, V.: Lattice signatures and bimodal gaussians. In: Canetti, R., Garay, J.A. (eds.) CRYPTO 2013, Part I. LNCS, vol. 8042, pp. 40–56. Springer, Heidelberg (2013)

6. van Erven, T., Harremoës, P.: Rényi divergence and Kullback-Leibler divergence. In: CoRR, abs/1206.2459 (2012)

7. Gentry, C., Peikert, C., Vaikuntanathan, V.: Trapdoors for hard lattices and new cryptographic constructions. In: Proceedings of STOC 2008, pp. 197–206. ACM (2008)

8. Langlois, A., Stehlé, D., Steinfeld, R.: GGHLite: more efficient multilinear maps from ideal lattices. In: Nguyen, P.Q., Oswald, E. (eds.) EUROCRYPT 2014. LNCS, vol. 8441, pp. 239–256. Springer, Heidelberg (2014)

9. Lindner, R., Peikert, C.: Better key sizes (and attacks) for LWE-based encryption. In: Kiayias, A. (ed.) CT-RSA 2011. LNCS, vol. 6558, pp. 319–339. Springer, Heidelberg (2011)

10. Ling, S., Phan, D.H., Stehlé, D., Steinfeld, R.: Hardness of k-LWE and applications in traitor tracing. In: Garay, J.A., Gennaro, R. (eds.) CRYPTO 2014, Part I. LNCS, vol. 8616, pp. 315–334. Springer, Heidelberg (2014)

11. Ling, S., Phan, D.H., Stehlé, D., Steinfeld, R.: Hardness of k-LWE and applications in traitor tracing. In: IACR Cryptology ePrint Archive: Report 2014/494 (2015). Accessed 5 August 2015

12. Lyubashevsky, V., Peikert, C., Regev, O.: On ideal lattices and learning with errors over rings. J. ACM **60**(6), 43 (2013)

13. Micciancio, D., Regev, O.: Worst-case to average-case reductions based on gaussian measures. SIAM J. Comput. **37**(1), 267–302 (2007)

14. Pöppelmann, T., Ducas, L., Güneysu, T.: Enhanced lattice-based signatures on reconfigurable hardware. In: Batina, L., Robshaw, M. (eds.) CHES 2014. LNCS, vol. 8731, pp. 353–370. Springer, Heidelberg (2014)

15. Regev, O.: On lattices, learning with errors, random linear codes, and cryptography. J. ACM **56**(6), 34 (2009)

16. Rényi, A.: On measures of entropy and information. Proc. Fourth Berkeley Symp. Math. Stat. Probab. **1**, 547–561 (1961)

Signature and Broadcast Encryption

Black-Box Separations of Hash-and-Sign Signatures in the Non-Programmable Random Oracle Model

Zongyang Zhang[1], Yu Chen[2,3]([⊠]), Sherman S.M. Chow[3], Goichiro Hanaoka[1], Zhenfu Cao[4], and Yunlei Zhao[5]

[1] National Institute of Advanced Industrial Science and Technology (AIST),
Tsukuba, Japan
{zongyang.zhang,hanaoka-goichiro}@aist.go.jp
[2] State Key Laboratory of Information Security (SKLOIS), Institute of Information
Engineering, Chinese Academy of Sciences, Beijing, China
chenyu@iie.ac.cn
[3] Department of Information Engineering, Chinese University of Hong Kong,
Shatin, Hong Kong
sherman@ie.cuhk.edu.hk
[4] East China Normal University, Shanghai, China
zfcao@sei.ecnu.edu.cn
[5] Software School, Fudan University, Shanghai, China
ylzhao@fudan.edu.cn

Abstract. A popular methodology of designing cryptosystems with practical efficiency is to give a security proof in the random oracle (RO) model. The work of Fischlin and Fleischhacker (Eurocrypt '13) investigated the case of Schnorr signature (and generally, Fiat-Shamir signatures) and showed the reliance of RO model is inherent.

We generalize their results to a large class of "malleable" hash-and-sign signatures, where one can efficiently "maul" any two valid signatures between two signature instances with different public keys if it can get the difference between the secret keys. We follow the technique of Fischlin and Fleischhacker to show that the security of malleable hash-and-sign signature cannot be reduced to its related hard cryptographic problem without programming the RO. Our proof assumes the hardness of a one-more cryptographic problem (depending on the signature instantiation). Our result applies to single-instance black-box reductions, subsuming those reductions used in existing proofs.

Our framework not only encompasses Fiat-Shamir signatures as special cases, but also covers Γ-signature (Yao and Zhao, IEEE Transactions on Information Forensics and Security '13), and other schemes which implicitly used malleable hash-and-sign signatures, including Boneh-Franklin identity-based encryption, and Sakai-Ohgishi-Kasahara non-interactive identity-based key exchange.

Keywords: Black-box separations · Hash-and-sign signatures · Random oracle model · Meta-reduction

© Springer International Publishing Switzerland 2015
M.-H. Au and A. Miyaji (Eds.): ProvSec 2015, LNCS 9451, pp. 435–454, 2015.
DOI: 10.1007/978-3-319-26059-4_24

1   Introduction

The random oracle model (ROM), introduced by Fiat and Shamir [13] and refined by Bellare and Rogaway [4], is formalized as a methodology for designing and analyzing cryptographic schemes that offers a trade-off between provable security and practical efficiency. The ROM methodology is generally conducted in the following way: first design and analyze a scheme by idealizing a hash function as a publicly accessible random function (random oracle), then instantiate the random oracle (RO) using a SHA-like cryptographic hash function in practice. The heuristic is that if cryptographic hash functions are "close enough" to random oracles, the scheme should remain "secure" even under this substitution. The ROM methodology has been widely used to argue the security of various cryptographic schemes, and it has led to many simple and efficient designs in practice (such as Schnorr signature [29], Boneh-Boyen-Shacham short group signature [7], RSA-OAEP [5], and Boneh-Franklin identity-based encryption [8]).

It is known that provable security in the ROM only serves as a heuristic argument, since it does not guarantee security in the standard model. There exist several artificial schemes [23] that are provably secure in the ROM, but completely insecure when the RO is instantiated with any function. However, the ROM still appears to be a good test bed for security analysis since no real attacks have been found against any practical scheme secure in the ROM. This motivates the research on understanding more about RO, namely, which properties of RO are inherently needed to prove security for these schemes for which no security proof exists in the standard model.

For many cryptographic schemes, security reductions exploit full programmability of RO. Roughly speaking, such property allows the reduction to arbitrarily program the output of RO within the specified range as long as the output distribution is consistent. Full programmability is a strong property since it does not quite match with the features provided by cryptographic hash functions. Consequently, several weaker models which constrain the ability of the reduction to program the RO are proposed. The randomly programming ROM [15] (RPROM) allows the reduction to program the RO with random instead of arbitrary values. The non-programmable random oracle model (NPROM) forbids the reduction to program the RO at all. Fischlin et al. [15] studied the role of the above three levels of programmability in provable security. They proved that no black-box reductions can be given for full domain hash signatures [4] in the RPROM. They also showed that Shoup's trapdoor-permutation-based key-encapsulation [32] is provably CCA-secure in RPROM, but no black-box reduction succeeds in the NPROM.

Recently, Fischlin and Fleischhacker [14] showed that the security of Schnorr signature cannot be proven equivalent to the discrete logarithm (DL) problem in the NPROM. They mainly used a special kind of meta-reduction technique (FF technique for short) in which the unbounded adversary depends on the reduction itself. Inspired by their work, and considering that the NPROM is the weakest and closest to the standard model among the above three models, we ask ourselves the following questions.

Is there any other (well-known) result in the ROM which could not have been established in the NPROM by the FF technique? Can we find a more general framework to cover as many negative results as possible in the NPROM, which are not only restricted to signatures, but also shed light on existing encryption and key-exchange schemes?

1.1 Our Results

We answer the above problems positively by proposing a general framework to analyze the security of a class of malleable hash-and-sign signature schemes in the NPROM. Informally, a hash-and-sign signature SS is *malleable* if it satisfies the following three properties: (1) the set PK of public keys and the set SK of secret keys constitute finite groups; (2) there exists a group homomorphism $\psi : PK \rightarrow SK$, which is generally inefficient to compute but can be efficiently computed given an oracle to resolve some hard cryptographic problem (referred to as P_2 later); and (3) there exists an efficient algorithm to "maul"two valid signatures between two signature instances using different public keys given the difference between their secret keys. In the following, for brevity, we sometimes say malleable signature instead of malleable hash-and-sign signature.

Suppose that the existential unforgeability of SS against chosen message attacks (EUF − CMA) in the ROM is based on the hardness of some cryptographic problem (call it P_1). We use meta-reduction to show that the security of SS cannot be reduced to problem P_1 without programming the RO, assuming the hardness of a related (and possibly new) one-more cryptographic problem (P_1, P_2). (P_1, P_2) is defined as the problem which asks an adversary to solve two randomly and independently chosen P_1 instances with at most one call to an oracle solving P_2. It might not be so straightforward to imagine the relation between P_1 and (P_1, P_2); we can take the discrete-logarithm problem and one-more discrete-logarithm problem [2] for example, and the above two problems become DL and (DL, DL). Our result works for *single-instance* black-box reduction $\mathcal{R}$ which initiates only a single instance of the adversary $\mathcal{A}$ such that it can reset $\mathcal{A}$ arbitrarily to the point after having handed over the public key (from the fixed group). Note that the existing security reductions in ROM are of this kind, except that they can control the behavior of RO.

Our main result is summarized in the following theorem.

Theorem 1 (Informal). *Let SS be a malleable hash-and-sign signature scheme which is secure in the ROM assuming the hardness of problem P_1. Then there is no polynomial-time non-programming single-instance black-box reduction for basing the EUF − CMA security of SS on the problem (P_1, P_2) (or else, (P_1, P_2) could be solved efficiently.)*

One may wonder whether the (newly) introduced problem (P_1, P_2) is hard or not, since it is meaningless if the problem is easy. Unfortunately, we are not able to directly prove the hardness of the problem (P_1, P_2) in known models, such as the generic group model.[1] The difficulty of showing the hardness of the problem (P_1, P_2) is demonstrated in a recent work [35], which relies on concurrent rewinding technique to argue that no black-box reduction can be used to base its hardness on any weaker non-interactive cryptographic assumption. We will explain more about it in Sect. 2.1.

The malleable signature is general enough to cover many known results. As a corollary, we get the followings.

Fiat-Shamir signatures: The class of Fiat-Shamir (FS) signatures comprises all signature schemes transformed from three-move identification and was shown secure in the ROM [27]. Our result shows that it is hard to base its $EUF - CMA$ security on the hardness of the DL problem in the NPROM if we consider single-instance black-box reductions and the one-more DL problem is hard (e.g., discrete log case).

Identity-based encryption (IBE): Boneh and Franklin [8,9] proposed the first practical identity-based encryption (BF-IBE). They presented two versions of BF-IBE, which are called BasicIdent and FullIdent. The FullIdent is obtained by applying Fujisaki-Okamoto transformation [18] to BasicIdent. The BasicIdent/FullIdent is secure against chosen plaintext attacks / chosen ciphetext attacks in the ROM under the hardness of the computational bilinear Diffie-Hellman (CBDH) problem [9,20].

Since there are generic methods for transforming any IBE into a signature [8,12], we further show the implicit signature from BF-IBE is also malleable. By applying our generic framework, the BF-IBE scheme cannot be proven equivalent to the CBDH problem without programming the RO. Our result is based on a new problem called one-more CBDH problem (i.e., problem (CBDH, DL)), and applies to single-instance black-box reductions, which cover all existing reductions for BF-IBE scheme. In addition, our result works even for the one-way security against chosen plaintext attacks.

Identity-based non-interactive key exchange (IB-NIKE): Sakai, Ohgishi and Kasahara [28] proposed the first efficient identity-based non-interactive key exchange (SOK IB-NIKE) in the ROM. It was later shown to be fully adaptive secure in the ROM based on the hardness of the CBDH problem [10,26].

It is easy to see the SOK IB-NIKE and the BF-IBE share common structures, and the SOK IB-NIKE also implicitly implies a malleable signature scheme. (This does not mean their exists generic methods for transforming any IB-NIKE into a signature scheme.) We show that the fully adaptive security of SOK IB-NIKE cannot be proven equivalent to the CBDH problem

---

[1] In the generic group model [31], the underlying group is considered as a generic one, where an adversary only has access to random encodings of group elements, and the operation on group elements is done in a black-box way. The problem (P_1, P_2) requires the existence of a P_2 solution oracle, which in essence contradicts the idea of the generic group since one can know the relation between two random encodings. Though it is possible to model this P_2 oracle in the generic group model, it is hard to argue that the encodings do not leak too much useful information to an adversary.

without programming the RO. Our result is based on the hardness of the one-more CBDH problem, and applies to single-instance black-box reductions. Note the single-instance reduction is general enough to cover the existing reductions [10, 26]. Moreover, our result holds even for selective semi-static one-way security. Our framework covers the existing direct proof [10].[2]

Γ-Signature: Yao and Zhao [34] first introduced the notion of Γ-signature scheme, which is especially suitable for low-power devices, like smart cards, wireless sensors, and RFID tags. It is designed through a new variant of the Fiat-Shamir transformation, called Γ-transformation. They also gave secure constructions in the ROM. We consider malleable Γ-signature and show its EUF − CMA security cannot be proven equivalent to the underlying one-way function without programming the RO. Our result is based on the hardness of the related one-more one-way function, and applies to single-instance black-box reductions, which cover the existing reductions citeYao:2013:OOS.

Interpretation of our Results: To sum up, we have shown that the above schemes are hard to prove in the NPROM. In addition, our impossibility result is based on a new assumption that is defined by the signature scheme in question. In particular, for most schemes, these assumptions are entirely unstudied, which seems to result in low confidence of our results. Although the difficulty of proving the hardness of these new assumptions is partially shown by a recent work [35], our results are only meaningful if these assumptions are hard. At first sight, this sounds like bad news. Yet, we make clear what assumptions we need to break. In particular, one might use this negative result to look out for particular schemes where the assumption is false. That would be an interesting use of our result.

Overview of Technique: Our main technique is FF technique [14] which belongs to the meta-reduction technique. We believe it is meaningful to explore more black-box separations for a larger class of signatures beyond Fiat-Shamir signatures, which help us to understand the role of programmability in ROM deeper. Moreover, our framework can also be used to analyze the security of several known schemes beyond signatures.

We show that if there is a reduction $\mathcal{R}$ which successfully solves the problem P_1 given black-box access to any successful adversary $\mathcal{A}$ against the malleable hash-and-sign signature, then there exists an efficient meta-reduction $\mathcal{M}$ which can solve the problem (P_1, P_2). Once we present a successful unbounded adversary $\mathcal{A}$, which $\mathcal{M}$ can efficiently simulate for $\mathcal{R}$, we conclude that the existence of reduction $\mathcal{R}$ would already contradict the hardness of problem (P_1, P_2). Just as the notable characteristic of the FF technique, our unbounded adversary $\mathcal{A}$ is also dependent on $\mathcal{R}$.

Concurrent Work: A concurrent and independent work [19] showed the impossibility of proving the security of any FS-type signature (under some constraints) in the NPROM. Roughly, this work is different from ours in two aspects. First,

---

[2] We remark that a previous version of this work actually predates [10].

they considered a slightly stronger reduction, called key-preserving reduction. This reduction is limited to invoke an adversary with the same public key as the one given to the reduction, whereas our reduction invokes the adversary with a public key containing the same group description as that given to the reduction. Second, they required the underlying identification (ID) protocol related to the FS transformation is secure against impersonation under the active attack, which is satisfied by many existing ID protocols, whereas we require the signature being malleable. To summarize, our result is stronger in comparison [19] in covering schemes beyond signatures, but weaker in excluding some special FS-type signatures that are not malleable.

1.2   Other Related Work

Nielsen [24] first formally investigated the role of programmability of RO, and showed that it is impossible to construct a non-committing non-interactive encryption in an ROM-like model that strictly prohibits programming of RO outputs. Wee [33] showed impossibility results in the context of zero-knowledge. Fischlin et al. [15] considered how to weaken the standard ROM by limiting the programmability of RO.

Recently, Ananth and Bhaskar [1] considered the observability property of ROM and discussed non-observing non-programming reductions. Freire et al. [17] constructed programmable hash functions in a setting where multilinear map is available [11,21], used them to replaced RO in the BF-IBE scheme, and obtained a variant of BF-IBE in the standard model based on ideal lattice over the integers. This result is somehow orthogonal to our result since underlying groups and assumptions are different. The most recent work [6] introduced the notion of non-adaptive programmability of RO, where the reduction can program the RO only in the pre-processing phase. They showed that non-adaptively-programmable ROM is equivalent to the NPROM. They also presented weak-non-adaptively-programmable ROM and showed similar possibility/impossibility results as in [15].

Another line of the research investigated tightness of the security reductions for Schnorr signatures [16,30]. As these results consider reductions in the programmable ROM, they are orthogonal to our result.

2   Preliminaries

If $\mathcal{A}$ is a deterministic algorithm, then $y \leftarrow \mathcal{A}(x)$ denotes the assignment to y of the output of running $\mathcal{A}$ on x. If $\mathcal{A}$ is a probabilistic algorithm, then $y \leftarrow_\$ \mathcal{A}(x)$ denotes the assignment to y of the output of $\mathcal{A}$ on input x with a set of uniformly random coins. We write $y := \mathcal{A}(x; r)$ to denote the assignment to y of the output of $\mathcal{A}$ on input x and random coins r.

Let $\{0,1\}^n$ be the set of n-bit strings. For a random variable X, we use notation $x \leftarrow X$ to denote that a value x is sampled according to X. For a finite set S, we write $s \leftarrow_\$ S$ to denote the assignment to s of a uniformly randomly chosen element of S. We write $|S|$ to denote the cardinality of S. Throughout this paper, we use κ as the security parameter. A function $\mu(\cdot)$, where $\mu : \mathbb{N} \rightarrow [0,1]$ is called *negligible* if for every positive polynomial $p(\cdot)$, for all sufficiently large $\kappa \in \mathbb{N}$, $\mu(\kappa) < 1/p(\kappa)$.

Definition 1 (Random Oracle $\mathcal{O}$). *All the parties (and the adversary) are allowed to evaluate values $x \in \{0,1\}^{\ell(\kappa)}$ and receive the value $y \in \{0,1\}^{k(\kappa)}$ chosen uniformly at random independent of previous evaluations, except for the evaluation on the same value x, in which $\mathcal{O}$ returns y again.*

The standard ROM implicitly captures two other properties, called *observability* [1] and *programmability*. The observability means that a reduction can see all the queries to the RO. The programmability means that a reduction can choose answers to these queries. Since we focus on programmability in this work, we divide the reductions according to programmability.

Programming Reduction: This formalizes the standard concept of black-box reductions in the ROM. It captures the fact that the reduction has full control of all the answers of RO queries.

Non-Programming Reduction: This captures the fact that the reduction has no control on the answers of RO queries. Namely, the queries are answered by an RO which is chosen once, independently from the reduction $\mathcal{B}$ and its inputs, and remains the same for every execution of an adversary $\mathcal{A}$ initiated by $\mathcal{B}$. While $\mathcal{B}$ can learn all of the RO queries issued by $\mathcal{A}$, $\mathcal{B}$ has no influence on the distributions of answers. Intuitively, this models the fact that the reduction can be run with an external RO.

2.1 Cryptographic Problems

Definition 2 (Cryptographic Problem). *A cryptographic problem* P $=$ (PGen, IGen, Orcl, Vrfy) *is defined as follows:*

- *PGen(1^κ): the parameter generator takes as input 1^κ, outputs a public parameter* par, *which specifies the instance space $\mathcal{Y}$ and the solution space $\mathcal{X}$.*
- *IGen(par): the instance generator takes as input the public parameter* par, *and outputs an instance $y \in \mathcal{Y}$.*
- *Orcl(par, q): the stateful oracle algorithm takes as input a query $q \in \{0,1\}^*$, and outputs a response r for q or a special symbol $\perp$ if q is an invalid query.*
- *Vrfy(par, y, x) the deterministic verification algorithm takes as inputs a public parameter* par, *an instance $y \in \mathcal{Y}$ and a candidate solution $x \in \mathcal{X}$, outputs a single bit b, where $b = 1$ if x is a correct solution of y, or $b = 0$ otherwise.*

Throughout this paper, we implicitly assume it is efficient to determine whether an element y (resp. x) is in $\mathcal{Y}$ (resp. $\mathcal{X}$).

Definition 3 (Hard Cryptographic Problem). *The cryptographic problem* P $=$ (PGen, IGen, Orcl, Vrfy) *is said to be hard with respect to a threshold function $\nu(\kappa)$, if for all PPT algorithm $\mathcal{A}$, its advantage function is negligible in κ:*

$$\mathrm{Adv}_{\mathrm{P},\mathcal{A}}^{hcp}(\kappa) := \Pr\left[\mathrm{Vrfy}(\mathrm{par}, y, x) = 1 \,\middle|\, \begin{array}{l} \mathrm{par} \leftarrow_\$ \mathrm{PGen}(1^\kappa); y \leftarrow_\$ \mathrm{IGen}(\mathrm{par}); \\ x \leftarrow_\$ \mathcal{A}^{\mathrm{Orcl}(\mathrm{par},\cdot)}(\mathrm{par}, y) \end{array} \right] - \nu(\kappa).$$

Usually, $\nu(\kappa) = 0$ for computational problems (e.g., DL, CDH, n-DL), and $\nu(\kappa) = 1/2$ for decisional problems (e.g., DDH, DBDH). A hard cryptographic problem is said to be *t-round* if the number of the messages exchanged between Orcl and $\mathcal{A}$ is at most t.

We sometimes require some additional properties of cryptographic problems, summarized as follows.

Definition 4 (Specific Cryptographic Problems). *Let* P = (PGen, IGen, Orcl, Vrfy) *be a cryptographic problem.*

Non-interactivity: *the problem is said to be* non-interactive *iff the algorithm* Orcl *always outputs* $\perp$ *and never change the shared state. In this case, we will remove* Orcl *in the notations.*

Efficient generation: *the problem is said to be* efficiently generatable *iff both* PGen *and* IGen *are PPT algorithms.*

Efficient verifiability: *the problem is said to be* efficiently verifiable *iff the algorithm* Vrfy *runs in polynomial-time.*

We then present a generalization of one-more type problems [35], called generalized "one-more" problems. Suppose P_1 = (PGen, IGen$_1$, Vrfy$_1$) and P_2 = (PGen, IGen$_2$, Vrfy$_2$) are two non-interactive cryptographic problems with the same parameter generator PGen, and let $\mathcal{T}$ be a family of PPT algorithms which can be used to solve one P_1 instance by only using one query to an oracle solving P_2 problem. We have the following definition.

Definition 5 (Generalized "One-More" Cryptographic Problems [35]). *For any integer $n \geq 0$, the generalized "one-more" cryptographic problem n-(P_1, P_2) = (PGen, IGen, Orcl, Vrfy) associated with two subproblems P_1 and P_2 is defined as follows:*

- *PGen(1^κ): the parameter generator takes as input 1^κ and returns a public parameter* par *for P_1 and P_2. The parameter* par *also specifies the instance/solution space $(\mathcal{Y}_1, \mathcal{X}_1)$ and $(\mathcal{Y}_2, \mathcal{X}_2)$ for P_1 and P_2 respectively.*
- *IGen(par): the instance generator independently runs IGen$_1$(par) $n + 1$ times to generate $(n + 1)$ P_1 instances $\{y_i\}_{0 \leq i \leq n}$, and outputs an instance $\mathbf{y}:=(y_0, \ldots, y_n)$. It also initializes a shared counter variable* cnt$:=0$.
- *Orcl(par, y): the stateful oracle algorithm takes as inputs a public parameter* par, *and a P_2 instance y, increments* cnt$:=$cnt$ + 1$, *and outputs a solution x of y or a special symbol $\perp$ if y is an invalid query.*
- *Vrfy(par, $\mathbf{y}$, $\mathbf{x}$): the verification algorithm takes the public parameter* par, *an instance $\mathbf{y} := (y_0, \ldots, y_n)$, and a candidate solution $\mathbf{x}:=(x_0, \ldots, x_n)$ as inputs, and outputs a single bit b, where $b = 1$ if* cnt $\leq n$ *and* Vrfy$_1$(par, y_i, x_i) $= 1$ *for all $0 \leq i \leq n$; $b = 0$ otherwise.*

In particular, if $n = 1$, we just use n-(P_1, P_2) to denote (P_1, P_2). If $P_1 = P_2$, we denote n-(P_1, P_2) by n-P_1. The problem n-(P_1, P_2) is said to be hard if for any PPT adversary $\mathcal{A}$, the advantage $\mathsf{Adv}^{hcp}_{n-(P_1,P_2),\mathcal{A}}(\kappa)$ of $\mathcal{A}$ in solving all the $n + 1$ P_1 instances in $\mathbf{y}$ with at most n P_2 queries to the oracle Orcl is negligible.

This class of problems subsumes the traditional one-more problems (e.g., n-RSA, n-DL). Recently, Zhang et al. [35] also clarified several important properties of T which are needed in the security proof. Roughly, they defined a *promise reduction* T which satisfies the following two properties.

- T solves one P_1 instance by using at most γ (non-adaptive) queries to a P_2 solving oracle, where γ is a constant;
- T always correctly solves its input P_1 instance after obtaining γ correct responses from the P_2 oracle, or outputs "$\perp$" with overwhelming probability if one of γ responses is incorrect.

Next, the following theorem shows that it is hard to reduce the hardness of the problem n-(P_1, P_2) to the hardness of standard hard problems.

Theorem 2 (*[35]*). *Let problem n-(P_1, P_2) be defined as in Definition 5. If P_1 has unique solution, P_2 is randomly self-reducible, and there exists a promise reduction T from P_1 to P_2 with at most γ queries, then there is no black-box reduction R for basing the hardness of the problem n-(P_1, P_2) (Definition 5) on any $t(\kappa)$-round hard problem C (or else C could be solved efficiently), where κ is the security parameter and $n = \gamma \cdot \omega(\kappa + t + 1)$.*

The algorithms PGen, IGen$_1$, IGen$_2$ are not required to be PPT algorithms in Theorem 2. If only single-instance black-box reductions are considered, we can get a tight separation result for $n \geq \gamma \cdot (t+1)$. Note that for the traditional n-DL, n-RSA, and the new problem (CBDH, DL), there is a natural reduction T with $\gamma = 1$. According to Theorem 2, there is no single-instance black-box reduction for basing the hardness of problem (CBDH, DL) on any non-interactive hard problem. Therefore, in order to show the hardness of problem (CBDH, DL), we might have to resort to non-black-box techniques. Considering the one-more one-way function for the Γ-signature, if the one-way function has unique solution and is randomly self-reducible, and there is a promise reduction, then the above theorem also applies.

2.2   Digital Signature Scheme

Definition 6 (Hash-and-Sign   Signature). *A   hash-and-sign   signature scheme* SS = (PGen, SGen, SSig, SVer) *is defined as follows:*

- PGen(1^κ): *on input 1^κ, the parameter generator outputs a public parameter* par *which includes a description of message space* Msg *and a randomness space* Rnd *for signing, and a hash function* H : Msg × Rnd → Int, *where* Int *is the space of intermediate value. For simplicity, we omit* H *in the following algorithms. We require* $|\mathsf{Msg}| = \kappa^{\omega(1)}$.
- SGen(par): *on input a public parameter* par, *the key generation algorithm outputs a public/secret key pair* (pk, sk).
- SSig(par, sk, m): *on input a public parameter* par, *a secret key sk, and a message $m \in$* Msg, *the signing algorithm chooses a random coin $r \in$* Rnd, *and outputs* $\sigma :=$ SInner(sk, H(m, r); r) *by using another PPT algorithm* SInner.[3]

---

[3] We use an inner algorithm SInner to clarify that the input of H does not include the public key. For brevity, we allow H to use whole r. In explicit constructions, H might only use part of the randomness r. In this case, H just neglects the rest part of r.

– SVer(par, pk, m, σ): *on input a public parameter* par, *a public key* pk, *a message m, and a candidate signature* σ, *the verification algorithm outputs a bit* b, *with* $b = 1$ *signifying "accept" or* $b = 0$ *signifying "reject".*

It satisfies the correctness *property, i.e., for all* $\kappa \in \mathbb{N}$, *all* $(par, H) \leftarrow_\$ PGen(1^\kappa)$, *all* $(pk, sk) \leftarrow_\$ SGen(par)$, *all* $m \in Msg$, *and all* $\sigma \leftarrow_\$ SSig(par, sk, m)$, *it holds that* SVer(par, pk, m, σ) $= 1$.

In Definition 6, the inputs of function H are a message and the randomness used to sign. This means that H is forbidden be dependent on the public/secret key.

Definition 7 (Existential Unforgeability). *A hash-and-sign signature scheme* SS $=$ (PGen, SGen, SSig, SVer) *is said to be* existential unforgeable under adaptive chosen-message attacks *(EUF – CMA)* iff *for all PPT adversaries* $\mathcal{A}$, *its advantage* $\text{Suc}_{SS,\mathcal{A}}^{euf\text{-}cma}(\cdot)$ *is negligible in the security parameter* κ, *where* $\text{Suc}_{SS,\mathcal{A}}^{euf\text{-}cma}(\cdot)$ *is defined as:*

$$\text{Suc}_{SS,\mathcal{A}}^{euf\text{-}cma}(\kappa) := \Pr \left[\begin{array}{c} SVer(par, pk, m^*, \sigma^*) = 1 \\ \wedge m^* \notin M \end{array} \middle| \begin{array}{l} (par, H) \leftarrow_\$ PGen(1^\kappa); \\ (pk, sk) \leftarrow_\$ SGen(par); \\ (m^*, \sigma^*) \leftarrow_\$ \mathcal{A}^{SSig(par, sk, \cdot)}(par, pk) \end{array} \right].$$

Here, M *is the set of all messages queried by* $\mathcal{A}$ *to the signing oracle.*

2.3 Malleable Hash-and-Sign Signature

Roughly speaking, a hash-and-sign signature is malleable if there exists an efficient algorithm to "maul" two valid signatures between two signature instances with different public keys as long as it can obtain the "difference" between the secret keys. Here, the difference comes from the algebraic structure of the key, i.e., both its public key set and secret key set compose a group and there is a group homomorphism ψ from public key set to secret key set.

Definition 8 (Malleability). *Suppose* SS $=$ (PGen, SGen, SSig, SVer) *is a hash-and-sign signature scheme, in which* PK *is the set of public keys, and* SK *is the set of secret keys. Suppose* SS *is proven to be secure in the* ROM *based on some hard non-interactive cryptographic problem* P_1. *We say* SS *is* malleable, if *for all* $(par, H) \leftarrow_\$ PGen(1^\kappa)$, *it satisfies the following properties:*

– *Both* PK *and* SK *are finite groups. We denote them by* $\langle PK, \times \rangle$ *and* $\langle SK, + \rangle$, *respectively. In particular, we explicitly require the group operation together with the inverse operation in* PK *and* SK *can be efficiently done without any secret information.*
– *There exists a group homomorphism* $\psi : PK \to SK$, *which is defined by the* SGen *algorithm.*[4] *For any* $(pk_0, sk_0) \leftarrow_\$ SGen(par)$ *and* $(pk_1, sk_1) \leftarrow_\$ SGen(par)$, *we have* $\psi(pk_0 \times pk_1) = \psi(pk_0) + \psi(pk_1)$. *Obviously, the group homomorphism is generally inefficient to compute. However, it could be efficiently computed by only querying an oracle* $\mathcal{O}$ *once, which solves a hard non-interactive cryptographic problem* P_2.

---

[4] This implies that each public key is corresponding to only one secret key.

– For $b = 0, 1$, given a signature σ_b of message m_b under private key sk_b, together with $sk' = sk_0 - sk_1$, one can efficiently compute a signature of m_b under secret key sk_{1-b}. That is, there exists an efficient algorithm ReSign such that for $b = 0, 1$, for all $(pk_b, sk_b) \leftarrow_\$ \mathsf{SGen}(\mathsf{par})$, all messages $m_b \in \mathsf{Msg}$, all signatures $\sigma_b \leftarrow_\$ \mathsf{SSig}(\mathsf{par}, sk_b, m_b)$, we have

$$\mathsf{SVer}(\mathsf{par}, pk_0, m_1, \mathsf{ReSign}(\mathsf{par}, pk_0, pk_1, sk', m_1, \sigma_1)) = 1$$
$$\mathsf{SVer}(\mathsf{par}, pk_1, m_0, \mathsf{ReSign}(\mathsf{par}, pk_1, pk_0, -sk', m_0, \sigma_0)) = 1$$

Definition 8 implicitly implies a new problem (P_1, P_2). The definition is meaningful when both problems P_1 and (P_1, P_2) are hard. In fact, the group homomorphism ψ is dependent on the reduction $\mathcal{T}$ from problem P_1 to P_2. We also require that $\mathcal{T}$ always correctly solves one P_1 instance by using at most one query to a P_2 solving oracle (i.e., set $\gamma := 1$, see Sect. 2.1). In the following, we omit $\mathcal{T}$ for brevity.

3   Security of Malleable Signature in the NPROM

We then use the FF technique to analyze the security of malleable signature in the NPROM. Henceforth, we borrow the existing notations and follow the existing proof structure [14] We define the meaning of breaking EUF − CMA security of the scheme, and the meaning of basing EUF − CMA security of the scheme on the hardness of some specific cryptographic problem.

Definition 9 (Breaking EUF − CMA). Let $\mathsf{SS} = (\mathsf{PGen}, \mathsf{SGen}, \mathsf{SSig}, \mathsf{SVer})$ be a malleable hash-and-sign signature scheme. We say that $\mathcal{A}$ breaks the EUF − CMA security of SS with probability $\mu(\cdot)$ if for every $\kappa \in \mathbb{N}$, $\mathsf{Suc}^{euf\text{-}cma}_{\mathsf{SS}, \mathcal{A}}(\kappa) \geq \mu(\kappa)$.

Definition 10 (Basing EUF − CMA Security on the Hardness of P_1). We say that $\mathcal{R}$ is a Time$(\cdot)$-black-box reduction for basing the EUF − CMA security of SS on the hardness of non-interactive cryptographic problem P_1 w.r.t threshold $\nu(\cdot)$ if $\mathcal{R}$ is a time-Time$(\cdot)$ probabilistic oracle algorithm and there exists a polynomial $p(\cdot, \cdot)$ such that, for every probabilistic algorithm $\mathcal{A}$ (not necessarily efficient) that breaks EUF − CMA security of SS with probability $\mu(\cdot)$, for every $\kappa \in \mathbb{N}$, $\mathcal{R}^{\mathcal{A}}$ breaks P_1 w.r.t ν with advantage $\mathsf{Adv}^{hcp}_{P_1, \mathcal{R}^{\mathcal{A}}}(\kappa) = p(\mu(\kappa), 1/\kappa)$.

Then we show that a malleable hash-and-sign signature scheme cannot be proven EUF − CMA secure in the NPROM by a restricted type of reductions, called *single-instance* black-box reduction [14], which is still general enough to cover existing proofs. Such reductions can only invoke a single instance of the adversary and rewind the adversary, but it cannot be rewound to a point before it got the public key for the first time. In the proof, we will consider the adversary as a family $\mathbb{A}$ of adversaries $\mathcal{A}_{\mathcal{R}, a}$ depending on the reduction $\mathcal{R}$ and some randomness a. Sometimes, we will omit these sub-indices for convenience.

Theorem 3. *Let* $\mathsf{SS} = (\mathsf{PGen}, \mathsf{SGen}, \mathsf{SSig}, \mathsf{SVer})$ *be a malleable hash-and-sign signature scheme. If there exists a non-programming single-instance* $\mathsf{Time}_{\mathcal{R}}(\cdot)$-*black-box reduction* $\mathcal{R}$ *for basing* $\mathsf{EUF} - \mathsf{CMA}$ *security of* SS *on the non-interactive hard cryptographic problem* P_1 *w.r.t threshold* $\nu = \nu(\cdot)$ *with advantage* $\mathsf{Adv}^{hcp}_{\mathrm{P}_1, \mathcal{R}^{\mathcal{A}}}(\cdot)$, *then there exists a family* $\mathbb{A}$ *of successful (but possibly inefficient) adversaries* $\mathcal{A}_{\mathcal{R},a} \in \mathbb{A}$ *and a* $\mathsf{Time}_{\mathcal{M}}(\cdot)$-*meta-reduction* $\mathcal{M}$ *such that for infinitely many* $\kappa \in \mathbb{N}$, $\mathcal{M}$ *breaks* $(\mathrm{P}_1, \mathrm{P}_2)$ *with advantage* $\mathsf{Adv}^{hcp}_{(\mathrm{P}_1, \mathrm{P}_2), \mathcal{M}}(\kappa) \geq$ $(\mathsf{Adv}^{hcp}_{\mathrm{P}_1, \mathcal{R}^{\mathcal{A}_{\mathcal{R},a}}}(\kappa) + \nu)^2 \cdot (1 - 1/|\mathsf{Msg}|) + \nu^2 - \nu$ *for random* $\mathcal{A}_{\mathcal{R},a} \in \mathbb{A}$ *and runtime* $\mathsf{Time}_{\mathcal{M}}(\kappa) = 2 \cdot \mathsf{Time}_{\mathcal{R}}(\kappa) + \mathsf{poly}(\kappa).$[5]

Before presenting the proof idea, we briefly explain the implications of Theorem 3. If ν equals 0 (resp. 1/2), which covers the cases for most computational (resp. decisional) cryptographic problems, the advantage $\mathsf{Adv}^{hcp}_{(\mathrm{P}_1, \mathrm{P}_2), \mathcal{M}}(\kappa)$ is non-negligible, and our results shows SS (e.g., the DDH-based signature [22]) is unlikely to be proved in the NPROM based on the hardness of P_1. Moreover, if ν equals 0, the message space can be shrunk to only two. Similar results hold for $1/2 < \nu < 1$. However, for values of $0 < \nu < 1/2$, $\mathsf{Adv}^{hcp}_{(\mathrm{P}_1, \mathrm{P}_2), \mathcal{M}}(\kappa)$ might not be non-negligible or even be negative and our technique may fail.

Next we give the detailed proof which is adapted to our case partially verbatim from the existing proof [14] for easier comparison.

Proof (of Theorem 3). We first design a family of computationally unbounded adversaries $\mathcal{A}_{\mathcal{R},a}$ that breaks the $\mathsf{EUF} - \mathsf{CMA}$ security of SS.

A Family of Adversaries $\mathcal{A}_{\mathcal{R},a}$: Let Ω be defined as the set $\mathsf{Msg}^2 \times \mathcal{Y}_1^2 \times \{0,1\}^{\mathsf{poly}(\kappa)}$. For every $a = (m_0, m_1, y_0, y_1, \varpi) \in \Omega$ such that m_0, m_1 are messages, y_0, y_1 are P_1 instances, and ϖ is a random tape describing a random function, for every reduction $\mathcal{R}$, $\mathcal{A}_{\mathcal{R},a}$ internally runs a copy of $\mathcal{R}$ (denoted by $\mathcal{R}^*$) and proceeds as follows. As the reduction works for any adversary, it also works for a randomly chosen $a \leftarrow_\$ \Omega$ and thus a randomly chosen adversary $\mathcal{A}_{\mathcal{R},a}$ from $\mathbb{A}$. Note that once a is fixed, $\mathcal{A}_{\mathcal{R},a}$ is deterministic.

$\mathcal{A}_{\mathcal{R},a}$ (described in Fig. 1) internally runs a copy of $\mathcal{R}$ denoted by $\mathcal{R}^*$ and externally interacts with a challenger (or reduction). Upon receiving pk_0 from outside, $\mathcal{A}_{\mathcal{R}}$ submits a query m_0 to its signing oracle and verifies the reply σ_0. If σ_0 is not a valid signature for m_0, $\mathcal{A}_{\mathcal{R}}$ aborts. Otherwise, $\mathcal{A}_{\mathcal{R}}$ interacts with $\mathcal{R}^*$ on input y and random tape ϖ. When $\mathcal{R}^*$, which invokes a forger in his own view, outputs a public key pk_1, $\mathcal{A}_{\mathcal{R}}$ queries m_1 to $\mathcal{R}^*$ and receives the reply σ_1. If σ_1 is not a valid signature for m_1, then $\mathcal{A}_{\mathcal{R}}$ aborts. Otherwise, $\mathcal{A}_{\mathcal{R}}$ aborts $\mathcal{R}^*$ and proceeds to forge a signature.

$\mathcal{A}_{\mathcal{R}}$ then computes $sk' := \psi(pk_0/pk_1)$ by exhaustive search. According to the homomorphic property of ψ, we get $sk' = \psi(pk_0/pk_1) = \psi(pk_0) - \psi(pk_1) =$

---

[5] Recall that SS is malleable, according to Definition 8, the homomorphism $\psi(\cdot)$ is computable with a P_2 solving oracle. Moreover, a problem P_1 instance can also be correctly solved by using at most one query to a P_2 solving oracle (with the help of reduction $\mathcal{T}$).

Global public parameters: $(\mathsf{par}, \mathsf{H}) \leftarrow_\$ \mathsf{PGen}(1^\kappa)$

$\mathcal{A}_{\mathcal{R},(m_0, m_1, y, \varpi)}$

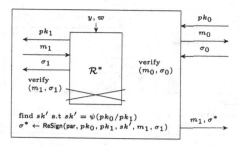

Fig. 1. For each reduction $\mathcal{R}$, the associated unbounded adversary $\mathcal{A}_\mathcal{R}$ works by choosing two messages m_0, m_1, an instance y of the P_1 problem, and a random tape ϖ for $\mathcal{R}$. It proceeds to forge a signature by internally simulating an instance of $\mathcal{R}$ on instance y and the random tape ϖ, and using its unbounded computational power to adapt the resulting signature.

$sk_0 - sk_1$. Since SS is malleable, there is an efficient algorithm ReSign such that with the knowledge of sk', it generate a valid signature $\sigma^* \leftarrow$ ReSign(par, $pk_0, pk_1, sk', m_1, \sigma_1$) for m_1 under public key pk_0. Finally, $\mathcal{A}_\mathcal{R}$ outputs (m_1, σ_1^*) as a forgery.

$\mathcal{A}_\mathcal{R}$ forwards all RO queries by $\mathcal{R}^*$ and itself to the external random oracle. As the following meta-reduction has to simulate $\mathcal{A}_\mathcal{R}$, the RO queries by $\mathcal{A}_\mathcal{R}$ also have to be simulated in the same manner. These queries are exactly those required for verifying (m_0, σ_0), those asked by $\mathcal{R}^*$ up to the point where $\mathcal{R}^*$ answers the signature query for m_1, those required for verifying (m_1, σ_1), and those queried by ReSign.

Note that $\mathcal{A}_{\mathcal{R},a}$ is fully deterministic even if it is rewound since the randomness used in the simulation is already fixed in a. As we focus on single-instance black-box reduction, the reduction is allowed to invoke one instance of the adversary and is forbidden to rewind the adversary to a point before the public key generation. If the external reduction tries to rewind the adversary $\mathcal{A}_{\mathcal{R},a}$, $\mathcal{A}_{\mathcal{R},a}$ keeps on making signature query for m_0 externally and m_1 internally, and adapting the signature.

Finally, denote by $\xi := \xi(\kappa)$ the probability that $\mathcal{A}_\mathcal{R}$ (with random a) breaks the EUF $-$ CMA property of SS. Denote by $\xi_1 := \xi_1(\kappa)$ the probability that the reduction $\mathcal{R}^*$ succeeds in answering a signature query for a random message. According to the assumption on $\mathcal{R}$, ξ_1 is non-negligible. If the two messages are equal, then $\mathcal{A}_\mathcal{R}$ fails. We then get $\xi = \xi_1 - 1/|\mathsf{Msg}| = \xi_1 - 1/\kappa^{\omega(1)} \geq \xi_1/2$. Therefore, we conclude that $\mathcal{R}^{\mathcal{A}_\mathcal{R}}$ solves P_1 with non-negligible probability.

Description of $\mathcal{M}$: The meta-reduction $\mathcal{M}$ (depicted in Fig. 2) takes input $y_0, y_1 \in \mathcal{Y}_1$ and invokes two instances $\mathcal{R}_0$ and $\mathcal{R}_1$ of $\mathcal{R}$ with independently random tapes, which get inputs y_0 and y_1 respectively. All RO queries by $\mathcal{R}_0$ and $\mathcal{R}_1$ are answered by forwarding them to the external random oracle and returning the answer. Both instances can invoke the adversary $\mathcal{A}$ at most once.

Global public parameters: $(\mathsf{par}, \mathsf{H}) \leftarrow_\$ \mathsf{PGen}(1^\kappa)$

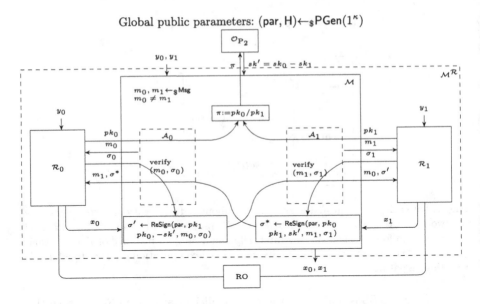

Fig. 2. The meta-reduction $\mathcal{M}$ invokes two instances of $\mathcal{R}$ and simulates the adversary $\mathcal{A}$ by obtaining the difference between the secret keys and adapting the signature output by $\mathcal{R}$ to generate a new signature under the other key, respectively.

To simulate $\mathcal{A}$ for both reductions $\mathcal{R}_0$ and $\mathcal{R}_1$, $\mathcal{M}$ then proceeds as follows.

1. Choose $m_0, m_1 \leftarrow_\$ \mathsf{Msg}$. Abort if $m_0 = m_1$.
2. Obtain pk_b from $\mathcal{R}_b$ for $b = 0, 1$.
3. Query m_b to $\mathcal{R}_b$ for $b = 0, 1$ and receive signature σ_b. Verify both signatures.
4. If either $\mathcal{R}_0$ or $\mathcal{R}_1$ was unable to provide a valid signature, abort.
5. Let $Q_{\mathsf{H},b}$ be the sequence of random oracle queries issued by $\mathcal{R}_b$ up to, and including, step 4. Query $Q_{\mathsf{H},b}$ to the random oracle interface provided by $\mathcal{R}_{1-b}$ for $b = 0, 1$, emulating the same hash queries the adversary instance for each reduction would issue.
6. Query an oracle that solves P_2 to get $sk' = \psi(pk_0/pk_1) = \psi(pk_0) - \psi(pk_1) = sk_0 - sk_1$. (Recall that according to the Definition 8, sk' can be computed by querying at most once to P_2.)
7. Compute $\sigma' \leftarrow \mathsf{ReSign}(\mathsf{par}, pk_1, pk_0, -sk', m_0, \sigma_0)$ and let $\tilde{Q}_{\mathsf{H},0}$ be the sequence of RO queries issued by ReSign. Compute $\sigma^* \leftarrow \mathsf{ReSign}(\mathsf{par}, pk_0, pk_1, sk', m_1, \sigma_1)$ and let $\tilde{Q}_{\mathsf{H},1}$ be the sequence of RO queries issued by ReSign.
8. Query $\tilde{Q}_{\mathsf{H},b}$ to the RO interface provided by $\mathcal{R}_{1-b}$ for $b = 0, 1$, emulating the same hash queries the adversary instance for each reduction would issue.
9. Return (m_1, σ^*) as a forgery to $\mathcal{R}_0$ and (m_0, σ') as a forgery to $\mathcal{R}_1$.

In the above simulation, we implicitly assume that the reduction $\mathcal{R}_b$ will use the attacking ability of the simulated adversary $\mathcal{A}_b$. However, if $\mathcal{R}_b$ never invokes $\mathcal{A}_b$ or directly outputs a solution, the meta-reduction $\mathcal{M}$ then would have one of the solutions to the instances y_0 and y_1 without invoking the oracle of P_2.

Therefore, it could just abort the other reduction instance, solve the other P_1 instance by querying the oracle P_2, and output the solutions. In the following, we omit this simple case and assume the reductions rely on the attacking ability of the adversary.

It remains to describe the simulation for $\mathcal{A}$ when the reduction rewinds $\mathcal{A}$. If $\mathcal{R}_b$ for $b = 0, 1$ tries to rewind the adversary, $\mathcal{M}$ keeps on making signature query for m_b, issuing Q_{1-b} as RO queries, adapting the signature, and issuing $\tilde{Q}_{1-b}$ as RO queries. After both reductions invoked at most one instance of $\mathcal{A}$ and possibly rewound a polynomial number of times, each outputs a candidate solution x_0 and x_1, respectively. Finally, $\mathcal{M}$ outputs x_0 and x_1.

Running Time. $\mathcal{M}$ consists of two executions of $\mathcal{R}$, several RO queries, and a constant number of modular inversions, multiplications, and additions. Therefore, it holds that $\mathsf{Time}_{\mathcal{M}}(\kappa) = 2 \cdot \mathsf{Time}_{\mathcal{R}}(\kappa) + \mathsf{poly}(\kappa)$.

Correctness. Next we show that for each reduction $\mathcal{R}_b$ for $b = 0, 1$, the simulation of $\mathcal{M}$ ("virtual" $\mathcal{A}_b$) is indistinguishable from $\mathcal{A}_{\mathcal{R}}$.

Claim 1. *The simulation of $\mathcal{M}$ is perfectly indistinguishable from $\mathcal{A}_{\mathcal{R}}$ from $\mathcal{R}_b$'s point of view.*

Proof of Claim 1. We have to argue that the messages and RO queries received from $\mathcal{M}$ are indistinguishable from those received from $\mathcal{A}_{\mathcal{R},a}$ for a random $a \in \mathsf{A}$. Recall that the adversary $\mathcal{A}_{\mathcal{R},a}$ might invoke a reduction $\mathcal{R}^*$ with a random P_1 instance y and a random tape ϖ. Moreover, $\mathcal{R}_b$ is invoked with random input y_b and an independent random tape ϖ_b. $\mathcal{M}$ simulates $\mathcal{A}_b$ as follows: (1) issue a signature query for a message m_b of its choice, and check the validity of the signature; (2) obtain a new signature for message m_{1-b} on a different public key pk_{1-b}; (3) adapt the signature using ReSign with the difference of sk_0 and sk_1. We then consider the oracle queries of $\mathcal{M}$. It issues exactly those oracles queries needed to verify (m_0, σ_0), those asked by $\mathcal{R}_{1-b}$ up to the point where $\mathcal{R}_{1-b}$ answers the signature query for m_1, those required for verifying (m_1, σ_1), and those queried by ReSign. When rewound, the execution of $\mathcal{M}$ and $\mathcal{A}_{\mathcal{R},a}$ remains the same. According to the above analysis, the behavior of $\mathcal{M}$ is consistent with the behavior of $\mathcal{A}_{\mathcal{R},a}$ where a equals $(m_b, m_{1-b}, y_{1-b}, \varpi_{1-b})$. Therefore, $\mathcal{M}$ and $\mathcal{A}_{\mathcal{R}}$ are perfectly indistinguishable from $\mathcal{R}_b$'s point of view and thus the probability that $\mathcal{R}$ with $\mathcal{M}$ breaks P_1 is the same as that of $\mathcal{R}$ with $\mathcal{A}_{\mathcal{R}}$, i.e., $\mathsf{Adv}^{hcp}_{P_1,\mathcal{R}\mathcal{M}}(\kappa) = \mathsf{Adv}^{hcp}_{P_1,\mathcal{R}^{\mathcal{A}_{\mathcal{R}}}}(\kappa)$. $\square$

We then analyze the probability of $\mathcal{M}$ in resolving the two instances y_0 and y_1. $\mathcal{M}$ succeeds in the following two cases: 1) $\mathcal{R}_0$ resolves y_0 and $\mathcal{R}_1$ resolves y_1. This means that both $\mathcal{R}_0$ and $\mathcal{R}_1$ do not abort during the simulation. 2) Both y_0 and y_1 are solved by trivial attacks. Therefore, we get

$$\mathsf{Adv}^{hcp}_{(P_1,P_2),\mathcal{M}}(\kappa) = (\mathsf{Adv}^{hcp}_{P_1,\mathcal{R}\mathcal{M}}(\kappa) + \nu)^2 \cdot (1 - 1/|\mathsf{Msg}|) + \nu \cdot \nu - \nu$$

$$= (\mathsf{Adv}^{hcp}_{P_1,\mathcal{R}^{\mathcal{A}_{\mathcal{R}}}}(\kappa) + \nu)^2 \cdot (1 - 1/|\mathsf{Msg}|) + \nu^2 - \nu$$

$\square$

Remark 1. The meta-reduction $\mathcal{M}$ does not explicitly verify the correctness of x_0 and x_1. Recall that the assumption on the existence of an efficient reduction $\mathcal{R}$ means for every adversary $\mathcal{A}$ that breaks the $\mathsf{EUF} - \mathsf{CMA}$ of SS with non-negligible probability, $\mathcal{R}$ breaks the problem P_1 with non-negligible probability. For the above unbounded $\mathcal{A}_{\mathcal{R}}$, $\mathcal{R}_b$ also works. Moreover, $\mathcal{M}$ perfectly simulates the unbounded adversary $\mathcal{A}_{\mathcal{R}}$ (as $\mathcal{A}_{\mathcal{R}_{1-b}}$) for $\mathcal{R}_b$, and always issues the same queries during the rewinding by $\mathcal{R}_b$. Therefore, $\mathcal{R}_b$ outputs a correct solution with the same probability as that with the unbounded adversary $\mathcal{A}_{\mathcal{R}_{1-b}}$ even when the solution is not efficiently verifiable.

Remark 2. The meta-reduction $\mathcal{M}$ actually mounts a related-key attack to the underlying signature. Recall that in the definition of related-key attack (RKA) security [3], an adversary can make signature queries in the form of (ϕ, m) where ϕ is some function, and a signature for a message m under a related secret key $\phi(sk)$ is returned. In our proof, the meta-reduction $\mathcal{M}$ in fact mounts an RKA to reduction $\mathcal{R}_b$ by querying (ϕ_{1-b}, m_{1-b}) $(b = 0, 1)$ for a linear function $\phi_{1-b}(x) = (x - sk_{1-b})$.

Remark 3. Our meta-reduction-based proof relies on a hard problem (P_1, P_2). A natural question is whether it is inherent. Fischlin and Fleischhacker [14] showed that finding a non-programming black-box meta-reduction to a non-interactive cryptographic problem is at least as hard as finding an adversary against the $\mathsf{EUF} - \mathsf{CMA}$ security of the scheme. A key requirement in their proof is that the signature has reconstructible hash queries, i.e., the signature allows determination of the hash queries which the signer has made given the signature only. We can also apply their technique to malleable hash-and-sign *randomized* signatures that have reconstructible hash queries.

4   Applications

Our framework for malleable signature is more general than the existing framework [14]. It not only encompasses many FS-type signature (e.g., Schnorr signature), but also can be used to analyze Boneh-Franklin IBE [9], Sakai-Ohgishi-Kasahara non-interactive identity-based key exchange [28], and Γ-signature [34]. For page limits, the latter two results are shown in the full version.

As the first practical IBE, BF-IBE has great influence on later design of IBE and other identity-based primitives, and initiated the study of pairing-based cryptography. Below we briefly review some directly related to their schemes.

Boneh and Franklin presented two versions of BF-IBE, which are called BasicIdent and FullIdent. FullIdent is obtained by applying Fujisaki-Okamoto transformation to BasicIdent [18]. BasicIdent/FullIdent is secure against chosen plaintext attacks $(\mathsf{IND} - \mathsf{ID} - \mathsf{CPA})$ / chosen ciphetext attacks $(\mathsf{IND} - \mathsf{ID} - \mathsf{CCA})$ in the ROM under the computational bilinear Diffie-Hellman (CBDH) assumption. Galindo [20] found a flaw in the original reduction from the $\mathsf{IND} - \mathsf{ID} - \mathsf{CCA}$-security of FullIdent to the CBDH assumption, and remedied the flaw by giving a new reduction, which is further refined by Nishioka [25]. Zhang and Imai [36] proposed another reduction without some intermediate steps. All these existing security reductions of BF-IBE heavily rely on the ability to re-program the RO.

Boneh and Franklin [8] described a generic method for transforming any IBE scheme into a signature scheme. Cui et al. [12] further explored the sufficient condition for designing an EUF − CMA secure signature in the above transformation, and showed OW − ID − CPA security is sufficient.

We show that the transformed signature resulting from the BF-IBE is a malleable hash-and-sign signature. By applying Theorem 3, the BF-IBE scheme cannot be proven equivalent to the CBDH problem without programming the random oracle. Our result is based on a new problem called one-more CBDH problem, i.e., (CBDH, DL), and applies to single-instance black-box reductions, which covers all existing reductions for the BF-IBE scheme. In addition, our result works even for the one-way security against chosen plaintext attacks (OW − ID − CPA).

Definition 11 ([9]). *Boneh-Franklin IBE scheme works as follows:*

- Setup(1^κ): *run the algorithm* $\mathcal{G}(1^\kappa)$ *to generate* $(q, \mathbb{G}_1, \mathbb{G}_2, e)$, *choose a random generator* $g\leftarrow_\$ \mathbb{G}_1^*$, *and then pick a random* $s\leftarrow_\$ \mathbb{Z}_q^*$ *and set* $P_{pub} = g^s$. *Choose two cryptographic hash functions* $H_1 : \{0,1\}^* \rightarrow \mathbb{G}_1^*$ *and* $H_2 : \mathbb{G}_2 \rightarrow \{0,1\}^n$ *for some* n. *The identity space* ID *is* $\{0,1\}^*$. *The message space is* $\mathsf{Msg}:=\{0,1\}^n$. *The ciphertext space is* $C:=\mathbb{G}_1^* \times \{0,1\}^n$. *The randomness space* Rnd *for encryption is* $\mathbb{Z}_q^*$. *The master public key is* $mpk:=P_{pub}$. *The master secret key is* $msk:=s$. *Output* (mpk, msk).
- Keygen(mpk, msk, id): *output a private key* $sk_{id}:=Q_{id}^s$ *where* $Q_{id}:=H_1(id)$.
- Encrypt(mpk, id, m): *compute* $Q_{id} = H_1(id)$, *choose* $r\leftarrow_\$ \mathbb{Z}_q^*$, *and output the ciphertext* $c:=(g^r, m \oplus H_2(e(Q_{id}, P_{pub})^r))$.
- Decrypt(mpk, c, sk_{id}): *parse* c *as* (c_1, c_2), *compute* $m:=c_2 \oplus H_2(e(sk_{id}, c_1))$, *and output* m.

Definition 12 (Breaking OW − ID − CPA Security). *Let* $\mathcal{E}$ *be an IBE scheme. We say that* $\mathcal{A}$ *breaks the* OW − ID − CPA *security of* $\mathcal{E}$ *with probability* $\mu(\cdot)$ *if for every* $\kappa \in \mathbb{N}$, *the advantage* $\mathsf{Adv}_{\mathcal{E},\mathcal{A}}^{ow\text{-}id\text{-}cpa}(\kappa)$ *of* $\mathcal{A}$ *is at least* $\mu(\kappa)$.

Definition 13 (Basing OW − ID − CPA Security on the CBDH Assumption). *We say that* $\mathcal{R}$ *is a* Time$(\cdot)$*-black-box reduction for basing the* OW − ID − CPA *security of IBE scheme* $\mathcal{E}$ *on the CBDH assumption if* $\mathcal{R}$ *is a time-*Time$(\cdot)$ *probabilistic oracle algorithm and there exists a polynomial* $p(\cdot, \cdot)$ *such that, for every* $\kappa \in \mathbb{N}$ *and every probabilistic algorithm* $\mathcal{A}$ *that breaks* OW − ID − CPA *security of* $\mathcal{E}$ *with probability* $\mu(\cdot)$, $\mathcal{R}^\mathcal{A}$ *breaks the CBDH assumption with advantage* $\mathsf{Adv}_{\mathsf{CBDH}, \mathcal{R}^\mathcal{A}}^{hcp}(\kappa) = p(\mu(\kappa), 1/\kappa)$.

Theorem 4. *Let* $\mathcal{E}$ *be the BF-IBE scheme. If there exists a non-programming single-instance* Time$_\mathcal{R}(\cdot)$*-black-box reduction* $\mathcal{R}$ *for basing the* OW − ID − CPA *security of $\mathcal{E}$ on the* CBDH *assumption with probability* $\mathsf{Adv}^{hcp}_{\mathrm{CBDH},\mathcal{R}^{\mathcal{A}}}(\kappa)$, *then there exists a family* $\mathbb{A}$ *of successful (but possibly inefficient) adversaries* $\mathcal{A}_{\mathcal{R},a}$ *and a* $\mathsf{Time}_{\mathcal{M}}(\cdot)$*-meta-reduction* $\mathcal{M}$ *such that for infinitely many* $\kappa \in \mathbb{N}$, $\mathcal{M}$ *breaks the* (CBDH, DL) *assumption with probability* $\mathsf{Adv}^{hcp}_{(\mathrm{CBDH,DL}),\mathcal{M}}(\kappa) \geq (\mathsf{Adv}^{hcp}_{\mathrm{CBDH},\mathcal{R}^{\mathcal{A}_{\mathcal{R},a}}}(\kappa))^2$ *for a random* $\mathcal{A}_{\mathcal{R},a} \in \mathbb{A}$ *and runtime* $\mathsf{Time}_{\mathcal{M}}(\kappa) = 2 \cdot \mathsf{Time}_{\mathcal{R}}(\kappa) + \mathsf{poly}(\kappa)$.

Proof (of Theorem 4). Recall that it has been shown [12] that the BF-IBE scheme can be transformed to a signature scheme. To apply Theorem 3, we have to show that it is a malleable hash-and-sign signature scheme.

We first roughly describe the transformed signature scheme. The system parameter is the global system parameter except the master public key. The public key (resp. secret key) for the signature scheme is the master public key mpk (resp. master secret key msk) for the IBE scheme. The signature on a message m is the IBE private key for $id := m$. To verify a signature, one chooses a random message r, encrypts r using the identity $id := m$, and then attempts to decrypt the ciphertext using the given signature on m as the decryption key. To instantiate with the BF-IBE scheme, there is a simper way to verify a signature. Suppose that σ is the signature for m. One just checks whether $e(H_1(m), P_{pub}) = e(\sigma, g)$.

We then show the transformed signature scheme is malleable. By applying Theorem 3, we conclude the theorem.

1. It is easy to verify that the set $PK = \mathbb{G}_1$ of public keys and the set $SK = \mathbb{Z}_q$ of secret keys are finite groups (for simplicity, we add $sk = 0$).
2. The group homomorphism is defined as $\psi : g^x \mapsto x$. If the DL problem is hard in $\mathbb{G}_1$, then there is no efficient algorithm to compute ψ. However, it is easy to compute once we have a solving oracle for DL. For each $y_1, y_2 \in \mathbb{G}_1$, it is straightforward that $\psi(y_1 y_2) = \psi(y_1) + \psi(y_2)$.
3. Given a signature sk_{m_0} of message m_0 under secret key msk_0, a signature sk_{m_1} of message m_1 under secret key msk_1, as well as $msk' = msk_0 - msk_1$, the algorithm ReSign works as follows: on inputs $(\mathsf{par}, mpk_0, mpk_1, msk', m_1, sk_{m_1})$, it computes $sk'_{m_1} = sk_{m_1} H(m_1)^{msk'}$, and outputs sk'_{m_1} as a signature of message m_1 under the secret key msk_0. Similarly, on inputs $(\mathsf{par}, mpk_1, mpk_0, -msk', m_0, \sigma_0)$, it computes $sk'_{m_0} = sk_{m_0} H(m_0)^{-msk'}$, and outputs sk'_{m_0} as a signature of message m_0 under the secret key msk_1. $\square$

Acknowledgments. Zongyang Zhang is an International Research Fellow of JSPS and is supported by NSFC under grant No. 61303201. Yu Chen is supported by NSFC under Grant Nos. 61303257, 61379141, the IIE's Cryptography Research Project, the Strategic Priority Research Program of CAS under Grant No. XDA06010701. Sherman S. M. Chow is supported by the Early Career Award and grants (CUHK 439713, 14201914) from the Research Grants Council, Hong Kong. Zhenfu Cao is supported by NSFC under Nos. 61411146001, 61321064, 61371083. Yunlei Zhao is supported by NSFC under Grant Nos.61272012, 61472084.

References

1. Ananth, P., Bhaskar, R.: Non observability in the random oracle model. In: Susilo, W., Reyhanitabar, R. (eds.) ProvSec 2013. LNCS, vol. 8209, pp. 86–103. Springer, Heidelberg (2013)
2. Bellare, M., Namprempre, C., Pointcheval, D., Semanko, M.: The one-more-RSA-inversion problems and the security of Chaum's blind signature scheme. J. Cryptol. 16(3), 185–215 (2003)
3. Bellare, M., Paterson, K.G., Thomson, S.: RKA security beyond the linear barrier: IBE, encryption and signatures. In: Wang, X., Sako, K. (eds.) ASIACRYPT 2012. LNCS, vol. 7658, pp. 331–348. Springer, Heidelberg (2012)
4. Bellare, M., Rogaway, P.: Random oracles are practical: a paradigm for designing efficient protocols. In: Denning, D.E., Pyle, R., Ganesan, R., Sandhu, R.S., Ashby, V. (eds.) ACM CCS, pp. 62–73. ACM (1993)
5. Bellare, M., Rogaway, P.: Optimal asymmetric encryption. In: De Santis, A. (ed.) EUROCRYPT 1994. LNCS, vol. 950, pp. 92–111. Springer, Heidelberg (1995)
6. Bhattacharyya, R., Mukherjee, P.: Non-adaptive programmability of random oracle. Theoret. Comput. Sci. 592, 97–114 (2015)
7. Boneh, D., Boyen, X., Shacham, H.: Short group signatures. In: Franklin, M. (ed.) CRYPTO 2004. LNCS, vol. 3152, pp. 41–55. Springer, Heidelberg (2004)
8. Boneh, D., Franklin, M.: Identity-based encryption from the weil pairing. In: Kilian, J. (ed.) CRYPTO 2001. LNCS, vol. 2139, pp. 213–229. Springer, Heidelberg (2001)
9. Boneh, D., Franklin, M.K.: Identity-based encryption from the Weil pairing. SIAM J. Comput. 32(3), 586–615 (2003)
10. Chen, Y., Huang, Q., Zhang, Z.: Sakai-ohgishi-kasahara identity-based non-interactive key exchange scheme, revisited. In: Susilo, W., Mu, Y. (eds.) ACISP 2014. LNCS, vol. 8544, pp. 274–289. Springer, Heidelberg (2014)
11. Coron, J.-S., Lepoint, T., Tibouchi, M.: Practical multilinear maps over the integers. In: Canetti, R., Garay, J.A. (eds.) CRYPTO 2013, Part I. LNCS, vol. 8042, pp. 476–493. Springer, Heidelberg (2013)
12. Cui, Y., Fujisaki, E., Hanaoka, G., Imai, H., Zhang, R.: Formal security treatments for IBE-to-signature transformation: relations among security notions. IEICE Trans. Fundam. Electron. Commun. Comput. Sci. 92(1), 53–66 (2009)
13. Fiat, A., Shamir, A.: How to prove yourself: practical solutions to identification and signature problems. In: Odlyzko, A.M. (ed.) CRYPTO 1986. LNCS, vol. 263, pp. 186–194. Springer, Heidelberg (1987)
14. Fischlin, M., Fleischhacker, N.: Limitations of the meta-reduction technique: the case of schnorr signatures. In: Johansson, T., Nguyen, P.Q. (eds.) EUROCRYPT 2013. LNCS, vol. 7881, pp. 444–460. Springer, Heidelberg (2013)
15. Fischlin, M., Lehmann, A., Ristenpart, T., Shrimpton, T., Stam, M., Tessaro, S.: Random oracles with(out) programmability. In: Abe, M. (ed.) ASIACRYPT 2010. LNCS, vol. 6477, pp. 303–320. Springer, Heidelberg (2010)
16. Fleischhacker, N., Jager, T., Schröder, D.: On tight security proofs for schnorr signatures. In: Sarkar, P., Iwata, T. (eds.) ASIACRYPT 2014. LNCS, vol. 8873, pp. 512–531. Springer, Heidelberg (2014)
17. Freire, E.S.V., Hofheinz, D., Paterson, K.G., Striecks, C.: Programmable hash functions in the multilinear setting. In: Canetti, R., Garay, J.A. (eds.) CRYPTO 2013, Part I. LNCS, vol. 8042, pp. 513–530. Springer, Heidelberg (2013)
18. Fujisaki, E., Okamoto, T.: Secure integration of asymmetric and symmetric encryption schemes. In: Wiener, M. (ed.) CRYPTO 1999. LNCS, vol. 1666, pp. 537–554. Springer, Heidelberg (1999)

19. Fukumitsu, M., Hasegawa, S.: Black-box separations on fiat-shamir-type signatures in the non-programmable random oracle model. In: López, J., Mitchell, C.J. (eds.) ISC 2015. LNCS, vol. 9290, pp. 3–20. Springer, Heidelberg (2015)

20. Galindo, D.: Boneh-franklin identity based encryption revisited. In: Caires, L., Italiano, G.F., Monteiro, L., Palamidessi, C., Yung, M. (eds.) ICALP 2005. LNCS, vol. 3580, pp. 791–802. Springer, Heidelberg (2005)

21. Garg, S., Gentry, C., Halevi, S.: Candidate multilinear maps from ideal lattices. In: Johansson, T., Nguyen, P.Q. (eds.) EUROCRYPT 2013. LNCS, vol. 7881, pp. 1–17. Springer, Heidelberg (2013)

22. Goh, E.J., Jarecki, S., Katz, J., Wang, N.: Efficient signature schemes with tight reductions to the Diffie-Hellman problems. J. Cryptol. **20**(4), 493–514 (2007)

23. Goldwasser, S., Kalai, Y.T.: On the (in)security of the Fiat-Shamir paradigm. In: FOCS, pp. 102–113. IEEE Computer Society (2003)

24. Nielsen, J.B.: Separating random oracle proofs from complexity theoretic proofs: the non-committing encryption case. In: Yung, M. (ed.) CRYPTO 2002. LNCS, vol. 2442, pp. 111–126. Springer, Heidelberg (2002)

25. Nishioka, M.: Reconsideration on the security of the boneh-franklin identity-based encryption scheme. In: Maitra, S., Veni Madhavan, C.E., Venkatesan, R. (eds.) INDOCRYPT 2005. LNCS, vol. 3797, pp. 270–282. Springer, Heidelberg (2005)

26. Paterson, K.G., Srinivasan, S.: On the relations between non-interactive key distribution, identity-based encryption and trapdoor discrete log groups. Des. Codes Crypt. **52**(2), 219–241 (2009)

27. Pointcheval, D., Stern, J.: Security arguments for digital signatures and blind signatures. J. Cryptol. **13**(3), 361–396 (2000)

28. Sakai, R., Ohgishi, K., Kasahara, M.: Cryptosystems based on pairing. In: The 2000 Symposium on Cryptography and Information Security, vol. 45, pp. 26–28, Japan (2000)

29. Schnorr, C.-P.: Efficient identification and signatures for smart cards. In: Brassard, G. (ed.) CRYPTO 1989. LNCS, vol. 435, pp. 239–252. Springer, Heidelberg (1990)

30. Seurin, Y.: On the exact security of schnorr-type signatures in the random oracle model. In: Pointcheval, D., Johansson, T. (eds.) EUROCRYPT 2012. LNCS, vol. 7237, pp. 554–571. Springer, Heidelberg (2012)

31. Shoup, V.: Lower bounds for discrete logarithms and related problems. In: Fumy, W. (ed.) EUROCRYPT 1997. LNCS, vol. 1233, pp. 256–266. Springer, Heidelberg (1997)

32. Shoup, V.: A proposal for an ISO standard for public key encryption. In: Cryptology ePrint Archive, Report 2001/112 (2001). http://eprint.iacr.org/

33. Wee, H.: Zero knowledge in the random oracle model, revisited. In: Matsui, M. (ed.) ASIACRYPT 2009. LNCS, vol. 5912, pp. 417–434. Springer, Heidelberg (2009)

34. Yao, A.C.C., Zhao, Y.: Online/offline signatures for low-power devices. IEEE Trans. Inf. Forensics Secur. **8**(2), 283–294 (2013)

35. Zhang, J., Zhang, Z., Chen, Y., Guo, Y., Zhang, Z.: Black-box separations for one-more (Static) CDH and its generalization. In: Sarkar, P., Iwata, T. (eds.) ASIACRYPT 2014, Part II. LNCS, vol. 8874, pp. 366–385. Springer, Heidelberg (2014)

36. Zhang, R., Imai, H.: Improvements on security proofs of some identity based encryption schemes. In: Feng, D., Lin, D., Yung, M. (eds.) CISC 2005. LNCS, vol. 3822, pp. 28–41. Springer, Heidelberg (2005)

Rethinking Privacy for Extended Sanitizable Signatures and a Black-Box Construction of Strongly Private Schemes

David Derler[(✉)] and Daniel Slamanig

IAIK, Graz University of Technology, Graz, Austria
{david.derler,daniel.slamanig}@tugraz.at

Abstract. Sanitizable signatures, introduced by Ateniese et al. at ESOR-ICS'05, allow to issue a signature on a message where certain predefined message blocks may later be changed (sanitized) by some dedicated party (the sanitizer) without invalidating the original signature. With sanitizable signatures, replacements for modifiable (admissible) message blocks can be chosen *arbitrarily* by the sanitizer. However, in various scenarios this makes sanitizers *too powerful*. To reduce the sanitizers power, Klonowski and Lauks at ICISC'06 proposed (among others) an extension that enables the signer to limit the allowed modifications per admissible block to a well defined set each. At CT-RSA'10 Canard and Jambert then extended the formal model of Brzuska et al. from PKC'09 to additionally include the aforementioned and other extensions. We, however, observe that the privacy guarantees of their model do not capture privacy in the sense of the original definition of sanitizable signatures. That is, if a scheme is private in this model it is not guaranteed that the sets of allowed modifications remain concealed. To this end, we review a stronger notion of privacy, i.e., (strong) unlinkability (defined by Brzuska et al. at EuroPKI'13), in this context. While unlinkability fixes this problem, no efficient unlinkable scheme supporting the aforementioned extensions exists and it seems to be hard to construct such schemes. As a remedy, in this paper, we propose a notion stronger than privacy, but weaker than unlinkability, which captures privacy in the original sense. Moreover, it allows to easily construct efficient schemes satisfying our notion from secure existing schemes in a black-box fashion.

1 Introduction

Digital signatures are an important cryptographic tool to assert the authenticity (source) and integrity of digital content. By virtue of these desired properties, every alteration of signed data necessarily yields an invalidation of the original signature. If one, however, considers handwritten signatures on paper documents, there are various scenarios where the handwritten signature is still

The authors have been supported by EU Horizon 2020 through project Pris-macloud, grant agreement number 644962. An extended version of this paper is available in the IACR Cryptology ePrint Archive.

M.-H. Au and A. Miyaji (Eds.): ProvSec 2015, LNCS 9451, pp. 455–474, 2015.
DOI: 10.1007/978-3-319-26059-4_25

visible (source authentication is still given), but the document contains several blacked-out sections. These sections are not readable anymore and thus remain confidential. Examples for such sanitized documents are the public release of previously classified governmental documents, legal subpoenas for documents in court trials or documents for medical or biomedical research [1,13,15].

It is clear that conventional digital signatures can not be used as a means for source authentication in such scenarios for the obvious reason. A naive solution would be to issue a fresh signature on a sanitized version of the respective document. However, this is often not possible (e.g., the signing key has already expired or is not available) or it is even undesirable (e.g., due to time or cost constraints).

1.1 Background on Sanitizable Signatures

To realize a controlled and limited sanitization of digitally signed content without signer-interaction, various approaches to so called sanitizable signatures have been introduced and refined over the years. Today, there are essentially two flavors of sanitizable signatures. The first one focuses on removal (blacking-out) of designated parts not necessarily conducted by a designated party (could be everyone) and it covers redactable signatures [20], content-extraction signatures [29] and the sanitizable signatures in [23]. The second one focuses on replacement of designated parts conducted only by a designated party (the sanitizer) and covers sanitizable signatures as defined in [2] and follow up work [4–8,26]. For a separation of these flavors we refer the reader to [22].

In addition to the motivating examples in the beginning, sanitizable signatures have shown to be a useful tool in various scenarios. Their applications include customizing authenticated multicast transmissions, database outsourcing (combating software piracy and unauthorized content distribution), remote integrity checking of outsourced data [14] and secure routing [2]. Moreover, they find applications in the context of public sector (open government) data [30], DRM licensing for digital content protection [11,32], privacy protection in smart grids [24], privacy-aware management of audit-log data [19], health record disclosure [3] and anonymization [27], as well as identity management [28,33]. On the more theoretical side, it has been shown how to build attribute-based anonymous credential systems from sanitizable signatures in a black-box fashion [12].

In this paper, we focus on sanitizable signatures in the vein of Ateniese et al. [2]. The basic idea behind such a scheme is that a message is split into fixed and modifiable (admissible) blocks, where each admissible block is replaced by a chameleon hash (a trapdoor collision resistant hash) of this block, and the concatenation of all blocks is then signed. A sanitizer being in possession of the trapdoor, can then change each admissible block arbitrarily by computing collisions. Such a sanitizable signature scheme needs to satisfy (1) *unforgeability*, which says that no one except the honest signer and sanitizer can create valid signatures and sanitizations respectively, (2) *immutability*, which says that a malicious sanitizer must not be able to modify any part of the message which has not been specified as admissible by the signer, (3) *privacy*, which says that all sanitized information is unrecoverable for anyone except signer and sanitizer, (4) *transparency*, which says that signatures created by the signer or the sanitizer are indistinguishable, and (5) *accountability*, which requires that a malicious signer or sanitizer is not able to deny authorship. These security properties have later been rigorously defined in [4], where it is also shown that accountability implies unforgeability, transparency implies privacy[1] and all other properties are independent. Later, the property of (strong) unlinkability [6,8] as an even stronger privacy property has been introduced. Additionally, other properties such as (blockwise) non-interactive public accountability [7] have been proposed and the model has also been extended to cover several signers and sanitizers simultaneously [10].

1.2 Motivation for this Work

With sanitizable signatures, admissible blocks can be replaced *arbitrarily* by the sanitizer. However, this often makes sanitizers *too powerful* and thus may limit their applicability in various scenarios severely. To reduce the sanitizers' power, Klonowski and Lauks [21] introduced several extensions for sanitizable signatures, which allow to limit the power of a sanitizer in several ways and thus eliminate the aforementioned concerns. In particular, they have introduced extensions (1) limiting the set of possible modifications for an admissible block (LimitSet), (2) forcing the sanitizer to make the same changes in logically linked admissible blocks (EnforceModif), (3) limiting the sanitizer to modify at most k out of n admissible blocks (LimitNbModif) and (4) forcing the sanitizer to construct less than ℓ versions of a message (LimitNbSanit). Later, Canard and Jambert [9] extended the security model of Brzuska et al. [4] to cover the afore-mentioned extensions (as [21] did not provide any model or proofs).

The LimitSet Extension. Although all of the aforementioned features improve the applicability of sanitizable signatures, we deem the LimitSet extension to be the generally most useful one (besides, it is the only extension that is related to the privacy property). Thus, in the remainder of this paper, we only consider the LimitSet extension and refer to schemes that implement this extension as *extended sanitizable signature schemes* (ESSS). In existing constructions, LimitSet is realized by using cryptographic accumulators, a primitive that allows to succinctly represent a set (as a so called accumulator) and to compute witnesses certifying membership for elements in the set. Basically, the set of admissible changes for such a block is accumulated and the admissible block is replaced by the respective accumulator. Loosely speaking, the signer initially provides an element together with the witness and sanitizing simply requires the sanitizer to exchange this element and the witness.

How to Define Privacy? Recall that for sanitizable signatures without extensions, privacy means that it should not be possible to recover the original message

---

[1] We note that the implication of privacy by transparency [6] only holds in the proof-restricted case (cf. Sect. 3).

from a sanitized version. Now, what is the most reasonable definition for privacy given the LimitSet extension? It seems to be most natural to require that, given a (sanitized) signature, a LimitSet block does not leak any information about the remaining elements in the respective set (and thus no information about the original message). By carefully inspecting the security model for ESSS in [9], we, however, observe that their privacy definition *does not* capture this. In fact, an ESSS that reveals *all* elements of the sets corresponding to LimitSet blocks *will be private* in their model. One motivation for a weak definition of privacy in [9] might have been to preserve the implication from (proof-restricted) transparency (as in the original model from [4]). However, as it totally neglects any privacy guarantees for the LimitSet extension, a stronger privacy notion seems advantageous and often even required. In [6,8] a stronger notion of privacy for sanitizable signatures—called (strong) unlinkability—has been introduced. This notion, when adapted to ESSS, indeed guarantees what we want to achieve. Yet, unlinkability induces a significant overhead for constructions supporting the LimitSet extension. As we will see later, the only unlinkable construction that supports the LimitSet extension [12] is rather inefficient and is only proven secure in a customized model which *does not* consider all security requirements of sanitizable signatures and thus does not represent an ESSS. In general, as we will show later, efficient unlinkable constructions of ESSS seem hard to achieve. Taking all together we conclude that, while the notion of privacy in [9] seems to be too weak, unlinkability seems to be too strong. Subsequently, we motivate why a stronger privacy notion (inbetween these two notions) that still allows to obtain efficient instantiations is however important for practical applications.

Motivating Applications. We consider use cases where it is required to limit the sanitizers abilities, while at the same time providing privacy with respect to verifiers. For instance, consider authenticity preserving workflows that span multiple enterprises. Using ESSS they can be modeled as illustrated in Fig. 1, with a signer and a sanitizer per enterprise. Then, employees can—within some well defined boundaries—act (in the role of the sanitizer) on behalf of their company, while also being accountable for their actions. However, companies do not disclose sensitive business internals. As a concrete example for such a workflow, envision that a bank signs a document containing a LimitSet block with authorized financial transactions for some company once every day. An employee of this company is then able to demonstrate the authorization of single transactions

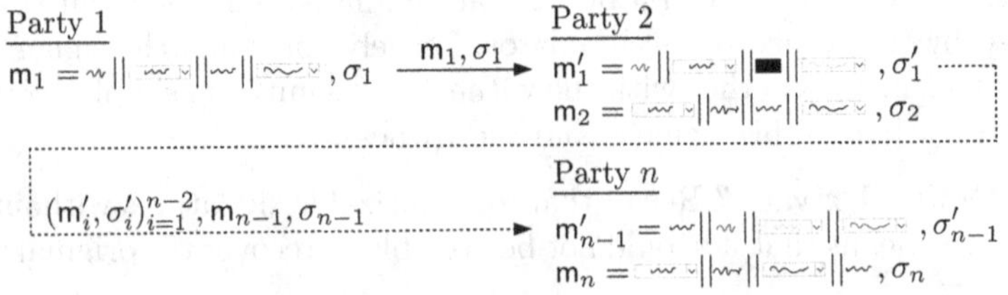

Fig. 1. Modeling a workflow using ESSS

to subsequent enterprises via sanitization, while not being able to maliciously introduce new transactions. The company will definitely want that employees can be held accountable for revealing certain transactions and that transactions which were never revealed by sanitized versions of the orignal document remain concealed. Observe, that an ESSS being private according to [9] could reveal sensitive business internals upon signature verification (i.e., the unused transaction information). Another use case is the anonymization of (medical) data before publishing it, e.g., instead of removing the entire address information of some individual, one can replace the precise address with some larger region. To do so, one could define an admissible set with two elements being the precise address and the region. This would greatly help to automate the sanitization and to reduce errors, which, in turn, improves the quality of sanitized documents[2]. Likewise to the previous example, an ESSS which is private according to the definition in [9] would allow to reconstruct the precise address from a sanitized document.

1.3 Contribution

In this paper we take a closer look at the privacy definition for ESSS in [9] as well as the unlinkability definitions in [6,8] when applied to the security model for ESSS. We conclude that these notions are either not strict enough to cover the requirements outlined in the previous section or too strict to obtain practical schemes. To this end, we introduce a stronger notion of privacy—denoted *strong privacy*—which explicitly considers privacy issues related to the LimitSet extension. More precisely, our strengthened notion guarantees that the sets of allowed modifications remain concealed, while still allowing efficient instantiations. We show that *privacy* is strictly weaker than *strong privacy* and that *unlinkability* is strictly stronger than *strong privacy*. Most importantly, we show that efficient and secure ESSS providing strong privacy can be constructed in a *black-box way* from *any* sanitizable signature scheme that is secure in the models of [4,18]. We do so by proposing (1) a generic conversion of sanitizable signatures to ESSS which support the LimitSet extension and (2) showing that instantiating the LimitSet extension in this generic conversion with indistinguishable accumulators (as introduced in [16]) yields constructions that provide strong privacy.

2 Preliminaries and Notation

For the sake of compact notation, we often use the concatenation operator, e.g., $(a_i)_{i=1}^{n} \| (b_i)_{i=1}^{m} := (a_1, \ldots, a_n, b_1, \ldots, b_m)$ and assume that concatenated sequences can later be uniquely decomposed (even when concatenating elements of different types and lengths). Let $x \xleftarrow{R} X$ denote the operation that picks an element x uniformly at random from a finite set X. A function $\epsilon : \mathbb{N} \to \mathbb{R}^+$ is called negligible if for all $c > 0$ there is a k_0 such that $\epsilon(k) < 1/k^c$ for all $k > k_0$. In the remainder of this paper, we use ϵ to denote such a negligible function.

---

[2] Such sets could be obtained and standardized by using concepts from k-anonymity [31] or t-plausibility [1] with the help of domain expert knowledge.

2.1   (Indistinguishable) Accumulators

Accumulators allow to represent a finite set $\mathcal{X}$ of values as a single succinct accumulator $\text{acc}_{\mathcal{X}}$. For each value $x \in \mathcal{X}$, one can efficiently obtain a membership witness wit_x that certifies the membership of x in $\text{acc}_{\mathcal{X}}$, while this is infeasible for values $y \notin \mathcal{X}$ (collision freeness). Indistinguishable accumulators [16] additionally require that neither the accumulator nor corresponding witnesses leak information about the accumulated set. Subsequently, we use the basic model for static accumulators from [16] and note that in general a trusted setup is assumed (i.e., AGen is run by a TTP that discards the trapdoor sk_{acc}). However, if the party maintaining $\text{acc}_{\mathcal{X}}$ is trusted, as it is the case within sanitizable signatures, using sk_{acc} may be useful as it typically supports more efficient computations (the parameter $\widetilde{\text{sk}}_{\text{acc}}$ denotes the optional trapdoor, i.e., using the trapdoor does not influence the output distributions of the algorithms and all algorithms also run without sk_{acc}).

Definition 1 (Accumulator [16]). *An accumulator is a tuple of PPT algorithms* (AGen, AEval, AWitCreate, AVerify) *which are defined as follows:*

AGen($1^\kappa, t$): *This algorithm takes a security parameter κ and a parameter t. If $t \neq \infty$, then t is an upper bound for the number of accumulated elements. It returns a key pair* $(\text{sk}_{\text{acc}}, \text{pk}_{\text{acc}})$, *where $\text{sk}_{\text{acc}} = \emptyset$ if no trapdoor exists.*

AEval(($\widetilde{\text{sk}}_{\text{acc}}, \text{pk}_{\text{acc}}$), $\mathcal{X}$): *This (probabilistic)[3] algorithm takes a key pair* $(\widetilde{\text{sk}}_{\text{acc}}, \text{pk}_{\text{acc}})$ *and a set $\mathcal{X}$ to be accumulated and returns an accumulator $\text{acc}_{\mathcal{X}}$ together with some auxiliary information* aux.

AWitCreate(($\widetilde{\text{sk}}_{\text{acc}}, \text{pk}_{\text{acc}}$), $\text{acc}_{\mathcal{X}}$, aux, x): *This algorithm takes a key pair* $(\widetilde{\text{sk}}_{\text{acc}}, \text{pk}_{\text{acc}})$, *an accumulator $\text{acc}_{\mathcal{X}}$, auxiliary information* aux *and a value x. It returns $\bot$, if $x \notin \mathcal{X}$, and a witness wit_x for x otherwise.*

AVerify(pk_{acc}, $\text{acc}_{\mathcal{X}}$, wit_x, x): *This algorithm takes a public key pk_{acc}, an accumulator $\text{acc}_{\mathcal{X}}$, a witness wit_x and a value x. It returns* true *if wit_x is a witness for $x \in \mathcal{X}$ and* false *otherwise.*

A secure indistinguishable accumulator is correct, collision free and indistinguishable. We recall the definitions for collision freeness and indistinguishability below[4].

Definition 2 (Collision Freeness). *An accumulator is* collision-free, *if for all PPT adversaries $\mathcal{A}$ there is a negligible function $\epsilon(\cdot)$ such that:*

$$\Pr \left[\begin{array}{c} (\text{sk}_{\text{acc}}, \text{pk}_{\text{acc}}) \leftarrow \text{AGen}(1^\kappa, t), \ \mathcal{O} \leftarrow \{\mathcal{O}^{\text{E}(\cdot, \cdot, \cdot)}, \mathcal{O}^{\text{W}(\cdot, \cdot, \cdot, \cdot)}\}, \\ (\text{wit}_x^*, x^*, \mathcal{X}^*, r^*) \leftarrow \mathcal{A}^{\mathcal{O}}(\text{pk}_{\text{acc}}) : \\ (\text{AVerify}(\text{pk}_{\text{acc}}, \text{acc}^*, \text{wit}_x^*, x^*) = \text{true} \ \wedge \ x^* \notin \mathcal{X}^*) \end{array} \right] \leq \epsilon(\kappa),$$

---

[3] If AEval is probabilistic, the internally used randomness is denoted as r. AEval$_r$ is used to make the randomness explicit.

[4] Note that, even though $\mathcal{A}$ can run AEval and AWitCreate itself, they are modeled as oracles to emphasize that $\mathcal{A}$ sees arbitrary accumulators and witnesses.

where $\mathsf{acc}^* \leftarrow \mathsf{AEval}_{r^*}((\mathsf{sk}_{\mathsf{acc}}, \mathsf{pk}_{\mathsf{acc}}), \mathcal{X}^*)$. *Here,* $\mathcal{O}^{\mathsf{E}}$ *and* $\mathcal{O}^{\mathsf{W}}$ *represent the oracles for the algorithms* AEval *and* $\mathsf{AWitCreate}$, *respectively. In case of randomized accumulators the adversary outputs randomness* r^*, *which is omitted for deterministic accumulators. Likewise, the adversary can control the randomness* r *used by* $\mathcal{O}^{\mathsf{E}}$ *for randomized accumulators. Thus* $\mathcal{O}^{\mathsf{E}}$ *takes an additional input* r.

Definition 3 (Indistinguishability). *An accumulator is* indistinguishable, *if for all PPT adversaries* $\mathcal{A}$ *there is a negligible function* $\epsilon(\cdot)$ *such that:*

$$\Pr\left[\begin{array}{c} (\mathsf{sk}_{\mathsf{acc}}, \mathsf{pk}_{\mathsf{acc}}) \leftarrow \mathsf{AGen}(1^\kappa, t),\ b \xleftarrow{R} \{0,1\},\ (\mathcal{X}_0, \mathcal{X}_1, \\ \mathsf{state}) \leftarrow \mathcal{A}(\mathsf{pk}_{\mathsf{acc}}), (\mathsf{acc}_{\mathcal{X}_b}, \mathsf{aux}) \leftarrow \mathsf{AEval}((\widetilde{\mathsf{sk}}_{\mathsf{acc}}, \mathsf{pk}_{\mathsf{acc}}), \mathcal{X}_b), \\ \mathcal{O} \leftarrow \{\mathcal{O}^{\mathsf{E}(\cdot,\cdot,\cdot)}, \mathcal{O}^{\mathsf{W}(\cdot,\cdot,\mathsf{aux},\cdot)}\},\ b^* \leftarrow \mathcal{A}^{\mathcal{O}}(\mathsf{pk}_{\mathsf{acc}}, \mathsf{acc}_{\mathcal{X}_b}, \mathsf{state}) : \\ b = b^* \end{array}\right] \leq \frac{1}{2} + \epsilon(\kappa),$$

where $\mathcal{X}_0$ *and* $\mathcal{X}_1$ *are two distinct subsets of the accumulation domain. Here,* $\mathcal{O}^{\mathsf{E}}$ *is defined as before, whereas* $\mathcal{O}^{\mathsf{W}}$ *is restricted to queries for values* $x \in \mathcal{X}_0 \cap \mathcal{X}_1$. *Furthermore, the input parameter* aux *for* $\mathcal{O}^{\mathsf{W}}$ *is kept up to date and is provided by the environment, since* $\mathcal{A}$ *could trivially distinguish using* aux.

It is obvious, that the notion of indistinguishability requires a randomized AEval algorithm. We stress that [16] also provide a variant of indistinguishability, which adds this non-determinism to accumulators with a deterministic AEval algorithm. To do so, an additional random value x_r from the accumulation domain is inserted into the accumulator upon AEval. This notion is called collision-freeness weakening (cfw) indistinguishability, since collision freeness only holds for $\mathcal{X} \cup \{x_r\}$ and not $\mathcal{X}$.

3   Formalizing Extended Sanitizable Signatures

In this section, we present a formal model for ESSS. Our model can thereby be seen as a rigorous formalization of the model for ESSS presented in [9]. Additionally, we include the suggestions from [18], i.e., additionally consider forgeries where one only tampers with ADM. We stress that, when omitting the extensions regarding LimitSet and ADM, it is equivalent to the model of [4], which is generally considered as the standard model for sanitizable signature schemes.

Definition 4 (Message). *A* message $\mathsf{m} = (\mathsf{m}_i)_{i=1}^n$ *is a sequence of* n *bitstrings (message blocks).*

Henceforth, we use ℓ_i to refer to the (maximum) length of message block m_i and assume an encoding that allows to derive $(\ell_i)_{i=1}^n$ from m.

Definition 5 (Admissible Modifications). *Admissible modifications* ADM *with respect to a message* $\mathsf{m} = (\mathsf{m}_i)_{i=1}^n$ *are represented as a sequence* $\mathsf{ADM} = (\mathsf{B}_i)_{i=1}^n$, *with* $\mathsf{B}_i \in \{\mathtt{fix}, \mathtt{var}, \mathtt{lim}\}$.

Here $B_i = \texttt{fix}$ indicates that no changes are allowed, $B_i = \texttt{var}$ indicates that arbitrary replacements are allowed, and $B_i = \texttt{lim}$ indicates that the replacements are limited to a predefined set ($\texttt{LimitSet}$).

Definition 6 (Set Limitations). *Set limitations* V *with respect to a message* $m = (m_i)_{i=1}^n$ *and admissible modifications* $\mathsf{ADM} = (B_i)_{i=1}^n$ *are represented by a set* $V = \{(i, M_i) : B_i = \texttt{lim} \wedge M_i \subset \bigcup_{j=0}^{\ell_i} \{0, 1\}^j\}$.

We use $m' \overset{(\mathsf{ADM},V)}{\preceq} m$ to denote that m' can be derived from m under ADM and V.

Definition 7 (Witnesses). *Witnesses* $W = \{(i, W_i)\}_{i=1}^t$, *with* $W_i = \{(m_{i_1}, \mathsf{wit}_{i_1}), \ldots, (m_{i_k}, \mathsf{wit}_{i_k})\}$, *are derived from set limitations* $V = \{(i, M_i)\}_{i=1}^t$, *with* $M_i = \{m_{i_1}, \ldots, m_{i_k}\}$. *Thereby,* wit_{i_j} *attests that its corresponding message block* m_{i_j} *is contained in the set* M_i.

With $V \overset{(m,\mathsf{ADM})}{\longleftarrow} W$, we denote the extraction of the set of witnesses V corresponding to a message m from the set W.

Definition 8 (Modification Instructions). *Modification instructions* MOD, *with respect to a message* $m = (m_i)_{i=1}^n$, *admissible modifications* ADM *and set limitations* V *are represented by a set* $\mathsf{MOD} = \{(i, m_i')\}_{i=1}^t$ *with* $t \leq n$, *where* i *refers to the position of the message block in* m, *and* m_i' *is the new content for message block* m_i.

With $\mathsf{MOD} \preceq (\mathsf{ADM}, V)$, we denote that the modification instructions in MOD are compatible with ADM and V. Furthermore, with $(m_0, \mathsf{MOD}_0, \mathsf{ADM}, V) \equiv (m_1, \mathsf{MOD}_1, \mathsf{ADM}, V)$, we denote that after applying the changes in MOD_0 and MOD_1 to m_0 and m_1 respectively, the resulting messages m_0' and m_1' are identical.

3.1 The Model

An ESSS is a tuple of PPT algorithms ($\mathsf{KeyGen}_{\mathsf{sig}}$, $\mathsf{KeyGen}_{\mathsf{san}}$, Sign, Sanit, Verify, Proof, Judge) which are defined as follows:

$\mathsf{KeyGen}_{\mathsf{sig}}(1^\kappa)$: This algorithm takes as input a security parameter κ and outputs a keypair ($\mathsf{sk}_{\mathsf{sig}}$, $\mathsf{pk}_{\mathsf{sig}}$) for the signer.

$\mathsf{KeyGen}_{\mathsf{san}}(1^\kappa)$: This algorithm takes as input a security parameter κ and outputs a keypair ($\mathsf{sk}_{\mathsf{san}}$, $\mathsf{pk}_{\mathsf{san}}$) for the sanitizer.

Sign $(m, \mathsf{ADM}, V, (\mathsf{sk}_{\mathsf{sig}}, \mathsf{pk}_{\mathsf{sig}}), \mathsf{pk}_{\mathsf{san}})$: This algorithm takes as input a message m, corresponding admissible modifications ADM and set limitations V, as well as the keypair ($\mathsf{sk}_{\mathsf{sig}}$, $\mathsf{pk}_{\mathsf{sig}}$) of the signer and the verification key $\mathsf{pk}_{\mathsf{san}}$ of the sanitizer. It computes the set W from V, obtains $V \overset{(m,\mathsf{ADM})}{\longleftarrow} W$ and outputs a signature $\sigma = (\hat{\sigma}, V)$ together with some auxiliary sanitization information $\mathsf{san} = (\mathsf{aux}, W)$[5]. In case of an error, $\perp$ is returned. As in [4], we assume that ADM can be recovered from a signature σ.

---

[5] While san is not required for plain sanitizable signature schemes, ESSS additionally return san to pass auxiliary information, which is only relevant for the sanitizer.

Sanit $((m, \sigma), \text{MOD}, \text{san}, \text{pk}_{\text{sig}}, \text{sk}_{\text{san}})$:This algorithm takes as input a valid message-signature pair (m, σ), modification instructions MOD, some auxiliary sanitization information san and the verification key pk_{sig} of the signer and the signing key sk_{san} of the sanitizer. It modifies m and σ according to MOD and outputs an updated message-signature pair (m', σ') and $\perp$ if $m' \overset{(\text{ADM}, \text{V})}{\npreceq} m$. We assume that V can be reconstructed from san.

Verify $((m, \sigma), \text{pk}_{\text{sig}}, \text{pk}_{\text{san}})$: This algorithm takes as input a message-signature pair (m, σ) and the public verification keys of the signer pk_{sig} and the sanitizer pk_{san}. It returns true if σ is a valid signature on m under pk_{sig} and pk_{san}, and false otherwise.

Proof $((m, \sigma), \{(m_j, \sigma_j)\}_{j=1}^q, (\text{sk}_{\text{sig}}, \text{pk}_{\text{sig}}), \text{pk}_{\text{san}})$: This algorithm takes as input a message-signature pair (m, σ), q message-signature pairs $\{(m_j, \sigma_j)\}_{j=1}^q$ created by the signer, the keypair $(\text{sk}_{\text{sig}}, \text{pk}_{\text{sig}})$ of the signer and the public key pk_{san} of the sanitizer and outputs a proof π.

Judge $((m, \sigma), \text{pk}_{\text{sig}}, \text{pk}_{\text{san}}, \pi)$: This algorithm takes as input a message-signature pair (m, σ), the verification keys of the signer pk_{sig} and the sanitizer pk_{san} and a proof π. It outputs a decision $d \in \{\text{sig}, \text{san}\}$, indicating whether the signature has been produced by the signer or the sanitizer.

3.2 Security Properties

For security, an ESSS is required to fulfill the following properties.

Definition 9 (Correctness). *An ESSS is correct, if*

$\forall \kappa, \forall m, \forall \text{ADM}, \forall V, \forall \text{MOD} \preceq (\text{ADM}, V),$
$\forall (\text{sk}_{\text{sig}}, \text{pk}_{\text{sig}}) \leftarrow \text{KeyGen}_{\text{sig}}(1^\kappa), \forall (\text{sk}_{\text{san}}, \text{pk}_{\text{san}}) \leftarrow \text{KeyGen}_{\text{san}}(1^\kappa),$
$\forall (\sigma, \text{san}) \leftarrow \text{Sign}(m, \text{ADM}, V, (\text{sk}_{\text{sig}}, \text{pk}_{\text{sig}}), \text{pk}_{\text{san}}),$
$\forall (m', \sigma') \leftarrow \text{Sanit}((m, \sigma), \text{MOD}, \text{san}, \text{pk}_{\text{sig}}, \text{sk}_{\text{san}}),$
$\forall \{(m_1, \text{ADM}_1, V_1), \ldots, (m_q, \text{ADM}_q, V_q)\} \supseteq (m, \text{ADM}, V) :$
$\text{Verify}((m, \sigma), \text{pk}_{\text{sig}}, \text{pk}_{\text{san}}) = \text{true} \wedge \text{Verify}((m', \sigma'), \text{pk}_{\text{sig}}, \text{pk}_{\text{san}}) = \text{true} \wedge$
$(((\sigma_j, \cdot) \leftarrow \text{Sign}(m_j, \text{ADM}_j, V_j, (\text{sk}_{\text{sig}}, \text{pk}_{\text{sig}}), \text{pk}_{\text{san}}))_{j=1}^q \wedge \pi \leftarrow \text{Proof}((m', \sigma'),$
$\{(m_j, \sigma_j)\}_{j=1}^q, (\text{sk}_{\text{sig}}, \text{pk}_{\text{sig}}), \text{pk}_{\text{san}}) \wedge \text{Judge}((m', \sigma'), \text{pk}_{\text{sig}}, \text{pk}_{\text{san}}, \pi) = \text{san}).$

Definition 10 (Unforgeability). *An ESSS is unforgeable, if for all PPT adversaries $\mathcal{A}$ there is a negligible function $\epsilon(\cdot)$ such that:*

$$\Pr \left[\begin{array}{l} (\text{sk}_{\text{sig}}, \text{pk}_{\text{sig}}) \leftarrow \text{KeyGen}_{\text{sig}}(1^\kappa), (\text{sk}_{\text{san}}, \text{pk}_{\text{san}}) \leftarrow \text{KeyGen}_{\text{san}}(1^\kappa), \\ \mathcal{O} \leftarrow \{\mathcal{O}^{\text{Sign}}(\cdot, \cdot, \cdot, (\text{sk}_{\text{sig}}, \text{pk}_{\text{sig}}), \cdot), \mathcal{O}^{\text{Sanit}}(\cdot, \cdot, \cdot, \cdot, \text{sk}_{\text{san}}), \\ \mathcal{O}^{\text{Proof}}(\cdot, \cdot, (\text{sk}_{\text{sig}}, \text{pk}_{\text{sig}}), \cdot)\}, (m^*, \sigma^*) \leftarrow \mathcal{A}^{\mathcal{O}}(\text{pk}_{\text{sig}}, \text{pk}_{\text{san}}) : \\ \text{Verify}(m^*, \sigma^*, \text{pk}_{\text{sig}}, \text{pk}_{\text{san}}) = \text{true} \wedge \\ (m^*, \text{ADM}^*, V^*, \text{pk}_{\text{san}}) \notin L^{\text{Sign}} \wedge ((m^*, \sigma^*), \text{ADM}^*, \text{pk}_{\text{sig}}) \notin L^{\text{Sanit}} \end{array} \right] \leq \epsilon(\kappa),$$

where $\mathcal{O}^{\text{Sign}}$, $\mathcal{O}^{\text{Sanit}}$ and $\mathcal{O}^{\text{Proof}}$ simulate the Sign, Sanit and Proof algorithms, respectively. The environment keeps track of the queries to $\mathcal{O}^{\text{Sign}}$ using L^{Sign}. Furthermore, it maintains a list L^{Sanit} containing the answers of $\mathcal{O}^{\text{Sanit}}$ extended with pk_{sig} and ADM from the respective oracle query.

Definition 11 (Immutability). *An* ESSS *is immutable, if for all PPT adversaries* $\mathcal{A}$ *there is a negligible function* $\epsilon(\cdot)$ *such that:*

$$\Pr\left[\begin{array}{l} (\mathsf{sk_{sig}}, \mathsf{pk_{sig}}) \leftarrow \mathsf{KeyGen_{sig}}(1^\kappa), \mathcal{O} \leftarrow \{\mathcal{O}^{\mathsf{Sign}}(\cdot, \cdot, \cdot, (\mathsf{sk_{sig}}, \mathsf{pk_{sig}}), \cdot), \\ \mathcal{O}^{\mathsf{Proof}}(\cdot, \cdot, (\mathsf{sk_{sig}}, \mathsf{pk_{sig}}), \cdot)\}, (\mathsf{pk_{san}^*}, m^*, \sigma^*) \leftarrow \mathcal{A}^{\mathcal{O}}(\mathsf{pk_{sig}}) : \\ \mathsf{Verify}(m^*, \sigma^*, \mathsf{pk_{sig}}, \mathsf{pk_{san}^*}) = \mathbf{true} \ \wedge \ \left((\cdot, \cdot, \cdot, \mathsf{pk_{san}^*}) \notin L^{\mathsf{Sign}} \ \vee \right. \\ \left. \nexists m^* \overset{(\mathsf{ADM}^*, \mathsf{V}^*)}{\preceq} m : (m, \mathsf{ADM}^*, \mathsf{V}^*, \mathsf{pk_{san}^*}) \in L^{\mathsf{Sign}}\right) \end{array}\right] \leq \epsilon(\kappa),$$

where the oracles and the environment variables are as in Definition 10.

Definition 12 (Privacy). *An* ESSS *is private, if for all PPT adversaries* $\mathcal{A}$ *there is a negligible function* $\epsilon(\cdot)$ *such that:*

$$\Pr\left[\begin{array}{l} (\mathsf{sk_{sig}}, \mathsf{pk_{sig}}) \leftarrow \mathsf{KeyGen_{sig}}(1^\kappa), (\mathsf{sk_{san}}, \mathsf{pk_{san}}) \leftarrow \mathsf{KeyGen_{san}}(1^\kappa), \\ b \overset{R}{\leftarrow} \{0, 1\}, \mathcal{O} \leftarrow \{\mathcal{O}^{\mathsf{Sign}}(\cdot, \cdot, \cdot, (\mathsf{sk_{sig}}, \mathsf{pk_{sig}}), \cdot), \\ \mathcal{O}^{\mathsf{Sanit}}(\cdot, \cdot, \cdot, \cdot, \mathsf{sk_{san}}), \mathcal{O}^{\mathsf{Proof}}(\cdot, \cdot, (\mathsf{sk_{sig}}, \mathsf{pk_{sig}}), \cdot), \mathcal{O}^{\mathsf{LoRSanit}}(\cdot, \cdot, \cdot, \\ (\mathsf{sk_{sig}}, \mathsf{pk_{sig}}), (\mathsf{sk_{san}}, \mathsf{pk_{san}}), b)\}, b^* \leftarrow \mathcal{A}^{\mathcal{O}}(\mathsf{pk_{sig}}, \mathsf{pk_{san}}) : b = b^* \end{array}\right] \leq \frac{1}{2} + \epsilon(\kappa),$$

where $\mathcal{O}^{\mathsf{Sign}}$, $\mathcal{O}^{\mathsf{Sanit}}$ *and* $\mathcal{O}^{\mathsf{Proof}}$ *are as in Definition 10.* $\mathcal{O}^{\mathsf{LoRSanit}}$ *is defined as follows:*

$\mathcal{O}^{\mathsf{LoRSanit}}((m_0, \mathsf{MOD}_0), (m_1, \mathsf{MOD}_1), \mathsf{ADM}, (\mathsf{sk_{sig}}, \mathsf{pk_{sig}}), (\mathsf{sk_{san}}, \mathsf{pk_{san}}), b):$

1: *Randomly choose* V *(compatible with* MOD_0 *and* MOD_1*).*
2: *If* $\mathsf{MOD}_0 \not\preceq (\mathsf{ADM}, \mathsf{V}) \ \vee \ \mathsf{MOD}_1 \not\preceq (\mathsf{ADM}, \mathsf{V})$*, return* $\perp$*.*
3: *If* $(m_0, \mathsf{MOD}_0, \mathsf{ADM}, \mathsf{V}) \not\equiv (m_1, \mathsf{MOD}_1, \mathsf{ADM}, \mathsf{V})$*, return* $\perp$*.*
4: *Compute* $(\sigma_b, \mathsf{san}_b) \leftarrow \mathsf{Sign}(m_b, \mathsf{ADM}, \mathsf{V}, (\mathsf{sk_{sig}}, \mathsf{pk_{sig}}), \mathsf{pk_{san}}).$
5: *Return* $(m_b', \sigma_b') \leftarrow \mathsf{Sanit}((m_b, \sigma_b), \mathsf{MOD}_b, \mathsf{san}_b, \mathsf{pk_{sig}}, \mathsf{sk_{san}}).$

Observe that since V is internally chosen (and, thus, independent of the bit b) in $\mathcal{O}^{\mathsf{LoRSanit}}$, privacy holds independent of the adversaries capability to reconstruct the set limitations. Clearly, this *contradicts* a definition of privacy in a sense that sanitized signatures do not reveal the original message.

Definition 13 (Transparency). *An* ESSS *is transparent, if for all PPT adversaries* $\mathcal{A}$ *there is a negligible function* $\epsilon(\cdot)$ *such that:*

$$\Pr\left[\begin{array}{l} (\mathsf{sk_{sig}}, \mathsf{pk_{sig}}) \leftarrow \mathsf{KeyGen_{sig}}(1^\kappa), (\mathsf{sk_{san}}, \mathsf{pk_{san}}) \leftarrow \mathsf{KeyGen_{san}}(1^\kappa), \\ b \overset{R}{\leftarrow} \{0, 1\}, \mathcal{O} \leftarrow \{\mathcal{O}^{\mathsf{Sign}}(\cdot, \cdot, \cdot, (\mathsf{sk_{sig}}, \mathsf{pk_{sig}}), \cdot), \mathcal{O}^{\mathsf{Sanit}}(\cdot, \cdot, \cdot, \cdot, \\ \mathsf{sk_{san}}), \mathcal{O}^{\mathsf{Proof}}(\cdot, \cdot, (\mathsf{sk_{sig}}, \mathsf{pk_{sig}}), \cdot), \mathcal{O}^{\mathsf{Sanit/Sign}}(\cdot, \cdot, \cdot, \cdot, \cdot, (\mathsf{sk_{sig}}, \mathsf{pk_{sig}}), \\ (\mathsf{sk_{san}}, \mathsf{pk_{san}}), b)\}, b^* \leftarrow \mathcal{A}^{\mathcal{O}}(\mathsf{pk_{sig}}, \mathsf{pk_{san}}) : b = b^* \end{array}\right] \leq \frac{1}{2} + \epsilon(\kappa),$$

where $\mathcal{O}^{\mathsf{Sign}}$, $\mathcal{O}^{\mathsf{Sanit}}$ *and* $\mathcal{O}^{\mathsf{Proof}}$ *are as in Definition 10. In addition,* $\mathcal{O}^{\mathsf{Proof}}$ *does not respond to queries for messages-signature pairs obtained using* $\mathcal{O}^{\mathsf{Sanit/Sign}}$*.* $\mathcal{O}^{\mathsf{Sanit/Sign}}$ *is defined as follows:*

$\mathcal{O}^{\mathsf{Sanit/Sign}}(m, \mathsf{ADM}, \mathsf{V}, \mathsf{MOD}, (\mathsf{sk}_{\mathsf{sig}}, \mathsf{pk}_{\mathsf{sig}}), (\mathsf{sk}_{\mathsf{san}}, \mathsf{pk}_{\mathsf{san}}), b):$

1: *If* $\mathsf{MOD} \not\preceq (\mathsf{ADM}, \mathsf{V})$, *return* $\perp$.
2: *Compute* $(\sigma, \mathsf{san}) \leftarrow \mathsf{Sign}(m, \mathsf{ADM}, \mathsf{V}, (\mathsf{sk}_{\mathsf{sig}}, \mathsf{pk}_{\mathsf{sig}}), \mathsf{pk}_{\mathsf{san}}).$
3: *Compute* $(m', \sigma_0) \leftarrow \mathsf{Sanit}((m, \sigma), \mathsf{MOD}, \mathsf{san}, \mathsf{pk}_{\mathsf{sig}}, \mathsf{sk}_{\mathsf{san}}).$
4: *Compute* $(\sigma_1, \mathsf{san}) \leftarrow \mathsf{Sign}(m', \mathsf{ADM}, \mathsf{V}, (\mathsf{sk}_{\mathsf{sig}}, \mathsf{pk}_{\mathsf{sig}}), \mathsf{pk}_{\mathsf{san}}).$
5: *Return* $(m', \sigma_b).$

Proof-Restricted Transparency [6]: $\mathcal{O}^{\mathsf{Proof}}$ does not answer queries for messages returned by $\mathcal{O}^{\mathsf{Sanit/Sign}}$. In the proof for the implication of privacy by transparency [4], $\mathcal{O}^{\mathsf{Sanit/Sign}}$ is used to simulate the $\mathcal{O}^{\mathsf{LoRSanit}}$ queries. Thus, note that the implication only holds if the privacy-adversary is restricted to $\mathcal{O}^{\mathsf{Proof}}$ queries for messages which do not originate from $\mathcal{O}^{\mathsf{LoRSanit}}$. To additionally rule out even stronger adversaries against privacy, i.e., such that privacy also holds after seeing proofs for the messages in question, one would need to prove privacy directly.

Definition 14 (Sanitizer-Accountability). *An* ESSS *is sanitizer-accountable, if for all PPT adversaries $\mathcal{A}$ there is a negligible function $\epsilon(\cdot)$ such that:*

$$\Pr\left[\begin{array}{l} (\mathsf{sk}_{\mathsf{sig}}, \mathsf{pk}_{\mathsf{sig}}) \leftarrow \mathsf{KeyGen}_{\mathsf{sig}}(1^\kappa), \mathcal{O} \leftarrow \{\mathcal{O}^{\mathsf{Sign}}(\cdot, \cdot, \cdot, (\mathsf{sk}_{\mathsf{sig}}, \mathsf{pk}_{\mathsf{sig}}), \cdot), \\ \mathcal{O}^{\mathsf{Proof}}(\cdot, \cdot, (\mathsf{sk}_{\mathsf{sig}}, \mathsf{pk}_{\mathsf{sig}}), \cdot)\}, (\mathsf{pk}^*_{\mathsf{san}}, m^*, \sigma^*) \leftarrow \mathcal{A}^{\mathcal{O}}(\mathsf{pk}_{\mathsf{sig}}), \\ \pi \leftarrow \mathsf{Proof}((m^*, \sigma^*), \mathsf{SIG}, (\mathsf{sk}_{\mathsf{sig}}, \mathsf{pk}_{\mathsf{sig}}), \mathsf{pk}^*_{\mathsf{san}}) : \mathsf{Verify}(m^*, \sigma^*, \mathsf{pk}_{\mathsf{sig}}, \\ \mathsf{pk}^*_{\mathsf{san}}) = \mathtt{true} \ \wedge \ (m^*, \mathsf{ADM}^*, \mathsf{V}^*, \mathsf{pk}^*_{\mathsf{san}}) \notin L^{\mathsf{Sign}} \ \wedge \\ \mathsf{Judge}((m^*, \sigma^*), \mathsf{pk}_{\mathsf{sig}}, \mathsf{pk}^*_{\mathsf{san}}, \pi) = \mathsf{sig} \end{array}\right] \le \epsilon(\kappa),$$

where the oracles are as in Definition 10. The environment maintains a list SIG, *containing all message-signature tuples obtained from* $\mathcal{O}^{\mathsf{Sign}}$.

Definition 15 (Signer-Accountability). *An* ESSS *is signer-accountable, if for all PPT adversaries $\mathcal{A}$ there is a negligible function $\epsilon(\cdot)$ such that:*

$$\Pr\left[\begin{array}{l} (\mathsf{sk}_{\mathsf{san}}, \mathsf{pk}_{\mathsf{san}}) \leftarrow \mathsf{KeyGen}_{\mathsf{san}}(1^\kappa), \mathcal{O} \leftarrow \{\mathcal{O}^{\mathsf{Sanit}}(\cdot, \cdot, \cdot, \cdot, \mathsf{sk}_{\mathsf{san}})\}, \\ (\mathsf{pk}^*_{\mathsf{sig}}, m^*, \sigma^*, \pi^*) \leftarrow \mathcal{A}^{\mathcal{O}}(\mathsf{pk}_{\mathsf{san}}) : \mathsf{Verify}(m^*, \sigma^*, \mathsf{pk}^*_{\mathsf{sig}}, \\ \mathsf{pk}_{\mathsf{san}}) = \mathtt{true} \ \wedge \ ((m^*, \sigma^*), \mathsf{ADM}^*, \mathsf{pk}^*_{\mathsf{sig}}) \notin L^{\mathsf{Sanit}} \ \wedge \\ \mathsf{Judge}((m^*, \sigma^*), \mathsf{pk}^*_{\mathsf{sig}}, \mathsf{pk}_{\mathsf{san}}, \pi) = \mathsf{san} \ \wedge \end{array}\right] \le \epsilon(\kappa),$$

where $\mathcal{O}^{\mathsf{Sanit}}$ as well as L^{Sanit} are as in Definition 10.

4   Rethinking Privacy for ESSS

In the following, we consider alternatives to the standard privacy property, i.e., (strong) unlinkability, and finally come up with a notion denoted as strong privacy which captures privacy for ESSS in the original sense of sanitizable signatures.

4.1 Revisiting Unlinkability

The notion of unlinkability for sanitizable signatures has been introduced in [6] as a stronger notion of privacy (which implies the usual privacy property). In [8], an even stronger notion, i.e., strong unlinkability, has been proposed. It requires that unlinkability must even hold for signers. The notions defined in [6,8] can easily be adapted to the model for ESSS and we do so below.

Definition 16 (Unlinkability). *An ESSS is unlinkable, if for all PPT adversaries $\mathcal{A}$ there is a negligible function $\epsilon(\cdot)$ such that:*

$$\Pr\left[\begin{array}{c}(\mathsf{sk_{sig}}, \mathsf{pk_{sig}}) \leftarrow \mathsf{KeyGen_{sig}}(1^\kappa), (\mathsf{sk_{san}}, \mathsf{pk_{san}}) \leftarrow \mathsf{KeyGen_{san}}(1^\kappa), \\ b \xleftarrow{R} \{0,1\}, \mathcal{O} \leftarrow \{\mathcal{O}^{\mathsf{Sign}}(\cdot, \cdot, \cdot, (\mathsf{sk_{sig}}, \mathsf{pk_{sig}}), \cdot), \mathcal{O}^{\mathsf{Sanit}}(\cdot, \cdot, \cdot, \cdot, \\ \mathsf{sk_{san}}), \mathcal{O}^{\mathsf{Proof}}(\cdot, \cdot, (\mathsf{sk_{sig}}, \mathsf{pk_{sig}}), \cdot), \mathcal{O}^{\mathsf{LoRSanit}}(\cdot, \cdot, \cdot, (\mathsf{sk_{sig}}, \mathsf{pk_{sig}}), \\ (\mathsf{sk_{san}}, \mathsf{pk_{san}}), b)\}, b^* \leftarrow \mathcal{A}^{\mathcal{O}}(\mathsf{pk_{sig}}, \mathsf{pk_{san}}) \; : \; b = b^*\end{array}\right] \leq \frac{1}{2} + \epsilon(\kappa),$$

where $\mathcal{O}^{\mathsf{Sign}}$, $\mathcal{O}^{\mathsf{Sanit}}$ and $\mathcal{O}^{\mathsf{Proof}}$ are as in Definition 10 and $\mathcal{O}^{\mathsf{LoRSanit}}$ operates as follows:

$\mathcal{O}^{\mathsf{LoRSanit}}((\mathsf{m}_0, \mathsf{MOD}_0, \mathsf{san}_0, \sigma_0), (\mathsf{m}_1, \mathsf{MOD}_1, \mathsf{san}_1, \sigma_1), \mathsf{ADM}, (\mathsf{sk_{sig}}, \mathsf{pk_{sig}}), (\mathsf{sk_{san}}, \mathsf{pk_{san}}), b)$:

1: *If* $\mathsf{MOD}_0 \not\preceq (\mathsf{ADM}, \mathsf{V}_0) \vee \mathsf{MOD}_1 \not\preceq (\mathsf{ADM}, \mathsf{V}_1)$, *return* $\bot$.
2: *If* $(\mathsf{m}_0, \mathsf{MOD}_0, \mathsf{ADM}, \mathsf{V}_0) \not\equiv (\mathsf{m}_1, \mathsf{MOD}_1, \mathsf{ADM}, \mathsf{V}_1)$, *return* $\bot$.
3: *If for any* $i \in \{0,1\}$, $\mathsf{Verify}((\mathsf{m}_i, \sigma_i), \mathsf{pk_{sig}}, \mathsf{pk_{san}}) = \mathtt{false}$, *return* $\bot$
4: *Return* $(\mathsf{m}'_b, \sigma'_b) \leftarrow \mathsf{Sanit}((\mathsf{m}_b, \sigma_b), \mathsf{MOD}_b, \mathsf{san}_b, \mathsf{pk_{sig}}, \mathsf{sk_{san}})$.

Note that V_0 and V_1 can be reconstructed from san_0 and san_1, respectively. Furthermore, note that for answers from the oracle $\mathcal{O}^{\mathsf{LoRSanit}}$, the oracle $\mathcal{O}^{\mathsf{Sanit}}$ is restricted to queries for modifications which are covered by both set limitations V_0 and V_1, which were initially submitted to $\mathcal{O}^{\mathsf{LoRSanit}}$.

Definition 17 (Strong Unlinkability). *An ESSS is strongly unlinkable, if for all PPT adversaries $\mathcal{A}$ there is a negligible function $\epsilon(\cdot)$ such that:*

$$\Pr\left[\begin{array}{c}(\mathsf{sk_{san}}, \mathsf{pk_{san}}) \leftarrow \mathsf{KeyGen_{san}}(1^\kappa), b \xleftarrow{R} \{0,1\}, \\ \mathcal{O} \leftarrow \{\mathcal{O}^{\mathsf{Sanit}}(\cdot, \cdot, \cdot, \cdot, \mathsf{sk_{san}}), \mathcal{O}^{\mathsf{LoRSanit}}(\cdot, \cdot, \cdot, \cdot, (\mathsf{sk_{san}}, \mathsf{pk_{san}}), b)\}, \\ b^* \leftarrow \mathcal{A}^{\mathcal{O}}(\mathsf{pk_{san}}) \; : \; b = b^*\end{array}\right] \leq \frac{1}{2} + \epsilon(\kappa),$$

where the oracles are as in Definition 16, except that $\mathcal{A}$ controls $(\mathsf{sk_{sig}}, \mathsf{pk_{sig}})$.

While (strong) unlinkability covers privacy for the LimitSet extension in the original sense of privacy[6], it seems very hard to construct efficient (strongly) unlinkable schemes that support the LimitSet extension. Unfortunately, it is not possible to simply extend existing (strongly) unlinkable constructions [6,8,17] by the LimitSet extension. To illustrate why, we revisit the design principle of such schemes. Here, upon Sign, the signer issues two signatures. The first signature,

---

[6] Note, that the ability to reconstruct the set limitations for σ'_b obtained via $\mathcal{O}^{\mathsf{LoRSanit}}$ would imply a trivial distinguisher for the unlinkability game.

σ_{FIX}, only covers the fixed message blocks and the public key of the sanitizer, whereas the second signature, σ_{FULL}, covers the whole message together with the public key of the signer (and the public key of the sanitizer [8]). Upon Sanit, the sanitizer simply issues a new signature σ_{FULL}, whereas the signature σ_{FIX} remains unchanged. Finally, upon Verify, one verifies whether σ_{FIX} is valid under $\mathsf{pk}_{\mathsf{sig}}$ and σ_{FULL} is either valid under $\mathsf{pk}_{\mathsf{sig}}$ or $\mathsf{pk}_{\mathsf{san}}$ for a given message m and ADM. Thereby, the signature scheme used for σ_{FIX} is a deterministic signature scheme, while the scheme used for σ_{FULL} can either also be a deterministic signature scheme [8], a group/ring signature scheme [6], or a signature scheme with rerandomizable keys [17].

When extending these schemes to also support the LimitSet extension, it is clear that the set limitations need to be fixed by the signer and must not be modifiable by the sanitizer. One simple way to realize the LimitSet extension would be to additionally include some unique encoding of the limitations V in σ_{FIX} and check whether the message is consistent with the defined limitations upon Verify. Obviously, this extension does not influence unforgeability and immutability and the scheme is still (publicly) accountable. Furthermore also privacy holds, since the set limitations which are included in the challenge tuple in the privacy game are randomly chosen inside the $\mathcal{O}^{\mathsf{LoRSanit}}$ oracle. However, unlinkability can not hold for the following reason: When querying the oracle $\mathcal{O}^{\mathsf{LoRSanit}}$ in the unlinkability game, the adversary can choose set limitations V_0 and V_1 such that $\mathsf{MOD}_0 \preceq (\mathsf{ADM}, V_0)$, $\mathsf{MOD}_1 \preceq (\mathsf{ADM}, V_1)$ and $(m_0, \mathsf{MOD}_0, \mathsf{ADM}, V_0) \equiv (m_1, \mathsf{MOD}_1, \mathsf{ADM}, V_1)$, but $V_0 \neq V_1$. For the corresponding signatures $\sigma_0 = (\sigma_{FIX_0}, \sigma_{FULL_0})$, $\sigma_1 = (\sigma_{FIX_1}, \sigma_{FULL_1})$ submitted to the oracle, this means that $\sigma_{FIX_0} \neq \sigma_{FIX_1}$ which yields a trivial distinguisher for the unlinkability game.

As an alternative, one may think of separately signing each message contained in the limited sets (using a deterministic signature scheme), where only the signatures corresponding to the chosen messages are revealed. However, to prevent forgeries where message blocks are re-used in other signatures (i.e., mix-and-match like attacks [5]), it would be required to also include some message-specific identifier in each signature. Again, it is easy to see that this would provide a trivial distinguisher for the (strong) unlinkability game.

Clearly, the requirement that the limited sets are fixed by the signer and cannot be modified later is not only specific to the aforementioned constructions, but is inherent to all constructions of such schemes. To circumvent the aforementioned issues, one could make use of more sophisticated primitives, which, however, come at the cost of significant computational overhead and complexity of the scheme. This is confirmed by the only known unlinkable construction supporting LimitSet [12]. It is computationally very expensive due to a high number of bilinear map applications and the use of non-interactive zero-knowledge proofs of knowledge in the computationally expensive target group of the bilinear map. Moreover, it is proven secure only in a model which does not consider all security requirements of sanitizable signatures (as it is tailored to their black-box construction of anonymous credentials) and thus does not represent an ESSS.

4.2   A Strengthened Notion for Privacy

Surprisingly, our requirement that the set limitations remain concealed can be met by a simple extension of the conventional privacy property. We call the extended property *strong privacy*[7]. As we will see, this modification allows to obtain efficient implementations from secure existing ones in a black-box fashion. We modify the privacy game such that the set limitations in $\mathcal{O}^{\mathsf{LoRSanit}}$ can be submitted per message, i.e., $\mathcal{O}^{\mathsf{LoRSanit}}$ takes $(m_0, \mathsf{MOD}_0, V_0), (m_1, \mathsf{MOD}_1, V_1)$, ADM. This means that V_0 and V_1 can be different and only need an overlap such that after applying MOD_0 and MOD_1 the messages m'_0 and m'_1 are identical. More formally, the game is defined as follows:

Definition 18 (Strong Privacy). *An ESSS is strongly private, if for all PPT adversaries $\mathcal{A}$ there is a negligible function $\epsilon(\cdot)$ such that:*

$$\Pr\left[\begin{array}{l} (\mathsf{sk}_{\mathsf{sig}}, \mathsf{pk}_{\mathsf{sig}}) \leftarrow \mathsf{KeyGen}_{\mathsf{sig}}(1^\kappa), (\mathsf{sk}_{\mathsf{san}}, \mathsf{pk}_{\mathsf{san}}) \leftarrow \mathsf{KeyGen}_{\mathsf{san}}(1^\kappa), \\ b \xleftarrow{R} \{0,1\}, \mathcal{O} \leftarrow \{\mathcal{O}^{\mathsf{Sign}}(\cdot, \cdot, \cdot, (\mathsf{sk}_{\mathsf{sig}}, \mathsf{pk}_{\mathsf{sig}}), \cdot), \mathcal{O}^{\mathsf{Sanit}}(\cdot, \cdot, \cdot, \cdot, \\ \mathsf{sk}_{\mathsf{san}}), \mathcal{O}^{\mathsf{Proof}}(\cdot, \cdot, (\mathsf{sk}_{\mathsf{sig}}, \mathsf{pk}_{\mathsf{sig}}), \cdot), \mathcal{O}^{\mathsf{LoRSanit}}(\cdot, \cdot, \cdot, (\mathsf{sk}_{\mathsf{sig}}, \mathsf{pk}_{\mathsf{sig}}), \\ (\mathsf{sk}_{\mathsf{san}}, \mathsf{pk}_{\mathsf{san}}), b)\}, b^* \leftarrow \mathcal{A}^{\mathcal{O}}(\mathsf{pk}_{\mathsf{sig}}, \mathsf{pk}_{\mathsf{san}}) \ : \ b = b^* \end{array}\right] \leq \frac{1}{2} + \epsilon(\kappa),$$

where the oracles $\mathcal{O}^{\mathsf{Sign}}$, $\mathcal{O}^{\mathsf{Sanit}}$ and $\mathcal{O}^{\mathsf{Proof}}$ are defined as in Definition 10. The oracle $\mathcal{O}^{\mathsf{LoRSanit}}$ is defined as follows:

$\mathcal{O}^{\mathsf{LoRSanit}}((m_0, \mathsf{MOD}_0, V_0), (m_1, \mathsf{MOD}_1, V_1), \mathsf{ADM}, (\mathsf{sk}_{\mathsf{sig}}, \mathsf{pk}_{\mathsf{sig}}), (\mathsf{sk}_{\mathsf{san}}, \mathsf{pk}_{\mathsf{san}}), b):$

    1: *If* $\mathsf{MOD}_0 \not\preceq (\mathsf{ADM}, V_0) \ \lor \ \mathsf{MOD}_1 \not\preceq (\mathsf{ADM}, V_1)$, *return* $\bot$.
    2: *If* $(m_0, \mathsf{MOD}_0, \mathsf{ADM}, V_0) \not\equiv (m_1, \mathsf{MOD}_1, \mathsf{ADM}, V_1)$, *return* $\bot$.
    3: *Compute* $(\sigma_b, \mathsf{san}_b) \leftarrow \mathsf{Sign}(m_b, \mathsf{ADM}, V_b, (\mathsf{sk}_{\mathsf{sig}}, \mathsf{pk}_{\mathsf{sig}}), \mathsf{pk}_{\mathsf{san}})$.
    4: *Return* $(m'_b, \sigma'_b) \leftarrow \mathsf{Sanit}((m_b, \sigma_b), \mathsf{MOD}_b, \mathsf{san}_b, \mathsf{pk}_{\mathsf{sig}}, \mathsf{sk}_{\mathsf{san}})$.

Note that for answers from the oracle $\mathcal{O}^{\mathsf{LoRSanit}}$, the oracle $\mathcal{O}^{\mathsf{Sanit}}$ is restricted to queries for modifications which are covered by both set limitations V_0 and V_1, which were initially submitted to $\mathcal{O}^{\mathsf{LoRSanit}}$.

Theorem 1. *Privacy is strictly weaker than strong privacy, while (strong) unlinkability is strictly stronger than strong privacy.*

As mentioned in [9], the extension of the model regarding `LimitSet` does not influence the relations of the properties shown in [4]. That is, *unforgeability* is implied by *accountability*, *(proof-restricted) privacy* is implied by *(proof-restricted) transparency* and *immutability* is still independent of the other properties. What remains for the proof of Theorem 1 is to unveil the relations of *strong privacy* to the other privacy related notions. We subsequently prove a number of lemmas to finally obtain the desired result.

---

[7] In [22], a security notion called strong privacy has been introduced for *plain* sanitizable signatures. Our notion of strong privacy is unrelated to their notion and does not conflict with their notion as ours is only meaningful in context of ESSS.

Lemma 1. *Not every transparent ESSS is strongly private.*

We prove Lemma 1 by counterexample.

Proof. Let us consider an instantiation of Scheme 1 with a *correct, unforgeable, immutable, private, (proof-restricted) transparent* and *accountable* sanitizable signature scheme. Further, assume that the accumulator scheme is distinguishable. Then, an adversary against the indistinguishability implies an adversary against strong privacy. □

From this proof, we can straight forwardly derive:

Corollary 1. *Not every private ESSS is strongly private.*

To show that strong privacy is a strictly stronger notion than privacy, we additionally need to show that the following lemma holds.

Lemma 2. *Every strongly private ESSS is also private.*

To prove this, we show that we can construct an efficient adversary $\mathcal{A}^{SP}$ against strong privacy using an efficient adversary $\mathcal{A}^{P}$ against privacy.

Proof. $\mathcal{A}^{SP}$ simply forwards the calls to the oracles $\mathcal{O}^{Sign}, \mathcal{O}^{Sanit}, \mathcal{O}^{Proof}$, whereas the oracle $\mathcal{O}^{LoRSanit}$ is simulated as follows: Upon every query (m_0, MOD_0), (m_1, MOD_1), ADM of $\mathcal{A}^{P}$, $\mathcal{A}^{SP}$ internally chooses random set limitations V such that $MOD_0 \preceq (ADM, V)$, $MOD_1 \preceq (ADM, V)$. Then $\mathcal{A}^{SP}$ forwards the query (m_0, MOD_0, V), (m_1, MOD_1, V), ADM to its own $\mathcal{O}^{LoRSanit}$ oracle and returns the result to $\mathcal{A}^{P}$. Eventually, $\mathcal{A}^{P}$ outputs a bit b which is forwarded by $\mathcal{A}^{SP}$. It is easy to see that the winning probability of $\mathcal{A}^{SP}$ is identical to that of $\mathcal{A}^{P}$. □

Subsequently, we show that unlinkability is strictly stronger than strong privacy.

Lemma 3. *Not every strongly private ESSS is (strongly) unlinkable.*

We prove Lemma 3 by counterexample.

Proof. Let us consider an instantiation of Scheme 1 with a *correct, unforgeable, immutable, private, (proof-restricted) transparent* and *accountable* sanitizable signature scheme which does *not* fulfill unlinkability. By Theorem 3, we can extend it to be strongly private by using an indistinguishable accumulator. □

Lemma 4. *Every unlinkable ESSS is also strongly private.*

To prove Lemma 4, we show that we can construct an efficient adversary $\mathcal{A}^{U}$ against unlinkability using an efficient adversary $\mathcal{A}^{SP}$ against strong privacy.

Proof. Likewise to the proof of Lemma 2, $\mathcal{A}^{U}$ simply forwards the calls to the oracles $\mathcal{O}^{Sign}, \mathcal{O}^{Sanit}, \mathcal{O}^{Proof}$, whereas the oracle $\mathcal{O}^{LoRSanit}$ is simulated as follows: Upon every query (m_0, MOD_0, V_0), (m_1, MOD_1, V_1), ADM of $\mathcal{A}^{SP}$, $\mathcal{A}^{U}$ obtains $(\sigma_0, san_0) \leftarrow \mathcal{O}^{Sign}(m_0, ADM, V_0)$, $(\sigma_1, san_1) \leftarrow \mathcal{O}^{Sign}(m_1, ADM, V_1)$ using its own $\mathcal{O}^{Sign}$ oracle. Then $\mathcal{A}^{U}$ forwards the query $(m_0, MOD_0, san_0, \sigma_0)$, $(m_1, MOD_1, san_1, \sigma_1)$, ADM to its own $\mathcal{O}^{LoRSanit}$ oracle and returns the result to $\mathcal{A}^{SP}$. Eventually, $\mathcal{A}^{SP}$ outputs a bit b which is forwarded by $\mathcal{A}^{U}$. It is easy to see that the winning probability of $\mathcal{A}^{U}$ is identical to that of $\mathcal{A}^{SP}$. □

Taking all the above results together, Theorem 1 follows.

5   Black-Box Extension of Sanitizable Signatures

Provably secure existing constructions of ESSS build up on concrete existing sanitizable signature schemes. As it turns out, we can even obtain a more general result, i.e., we obtain an ESSS that only makes black-box use of sanitizable signatures in the model of [4,18] and secure accumulators. The so obtained black-box construction of an ESSS then fulfills all the security notions of the underlying sanitizable signature scheme.

Before we continue, we recall the general paradigm for instantiating LimitSet (cf. [9,21]).

Paradigm 1. *For each* LimitSet *block, use a secure accumulator* ACC *to accumulate the set of admissible replacements. The respective message blocks are then replaced with the corresponding accumulator value, i.e., the accumulators are included in the same way as fixed message blocks. Conversely, the actually chosen message blocks for each* LimitSet *block are included in the same way as variable message blocks (since they change on every sanitization). Finally, the signature is augmented by the witnesses corresponding to the actual message blocks, while the remaining witnesses are only known to the signer and the sanitizer.*

We introduce our generic construction (that follows Paradigm 1) in Scheme 1, where we use $(\mathbf{KeyGen_{sig}}, \mathbf{KeyGen_{san}}, \mathbf{Sign}, \mathbf{Sanit}, \mathbf{Verify}, \mathbf{Proof}, \mathbf{Judge})$ to denote the algorithms of the underlying sanitizable signature scheme. We define two operators ϕ and ψ to manipulate sets $S = \{(k_1, v_1), \ldots, (k_n, v_n)\}$ of key-value pairs. Thereby, we assume the keys $k_1, \ldots, k_n$ to be unique. The operator $\phi(\cdot, \cdot)$ takes a key k and a set S, obtains the tuple (k_i, v_i) with $k = k_i$ from S, and returns v_i. If no such tuple exists, $\bot$ is returned. Similarly, the operator $\psi(\cdot, \cdot, \cdot)$, takes a key k, a value v'_i and a set S and obtains the tuple (k_i, v_i) with $k = k_i$ from S. It returns $(S \setminus \{(k_i, v_i)\}) \cup \{(k_i, v'_i)\}$ and $\bot$ if no such tuple exists.

We will prove the security of Scheme 1 using similar arguments as in [9], but relying on the abstract model of [4,18], instead of specific properties of the used sanitizable signature scheme.

Theorem 2. *When instantiating Scheme 1 with a sanitizable signature scheme that provides security properties Σ in the model of [4, 18] and a secure accumulator scheme, one obtains an ESSS that provides security properties Σ.*

We prove Theorem 2 in the extended version of this paper. Furthermore, we emphasize that—while our model includes the extensions regarding ADM from [18]—the proof does not rely on these extensions. This means that our black-box construction is also applicable to schemes in the model of [4].

Now, we discuss some observations related to the instantiation of the Limit-Set extension using accumulators. As discussed in the previous section, it seems to be hard to design generic extensions that also preserve unlinkability [6,8]. Furthermore, the abstract model does not consider the signer as an adversary, which gives some freedom regarding the implementations of certain algorithms

$\mathsf{KeyGen_{sig}}(1^\kappa)$: Given a security parameter κ, run $(\mathsf{sk_{sig}}, \mathsf{pk_{sig}}) \leftarrow \mathbf{KeyGen}(1^\kappa)$, choose an accumulator scheme and run $(\mathsf{sk_{acc}}, \mathsf{pk_{acc}}) \leftarrow \mathsf{AGen}(1^\kappa)$. Finally, return $(\mathsf{sk_{sig}}, \mathsf{pk_{sig}}) \leftarrow ((\mathsf{sk_{sig}}, \mathsf{sk_{acc}}), (\mathsf{pk_{sig}}, \mathsf{pk_{acc}}))$.

$\mathsf{KeyGen_{san}}(1^\kappa)$: Given a security parameter κ, return $(\mathsf{sk_{san}}, \mathsf{pk_{san}}) = (\mathsf{sk_{san}}, \mathsf{pk_{san}}) \leftarrow \mathbf{KeyGen_{san}}(1^\kappa)$.

$\mathsf{Sign}\,(m, \mathsf{ADM}, V, (\mathsf{sk_{sig}}, \mathsf{pk_{sig}}), \mathsf{pk_{san}})$: Given $m = (m_i)_{i=1}^n$, $\mathsf{ADM} = (B_i)_{i=1}^n$, $V = \{(i, M_i) : B_i = \mathtt{lim} \,\wedge\, M_i \subset \bigcup_{j=0}^{l_i} \{0,1\}^j\}$, $(\mathsf{sk_{sig}}, \mathsf{pk_{sig}})$ and $\mathsf{pk_{san}}$, this algorithm sets $\mathcal{V}, \mathcal{W} \leftarrow \emptyset$ and computes

    for $i = 1 \ldots n$ if $B_i = \mathtt{lim}$ do:
        $M_i \leftarrow \phi(i, V)$, $\mathsf{acc}_i \leftarrow \mathsf{AEval}((\mathsf{sk_{acc}}, \mathsf{pk_{acc}}), M_i)$, $\mathcal{W}_i \leftarrow \emptyset$,
        $\forall v_j \in M_i : \mathsf{wit}_{i_j} \leftarrow \mathsf{AWitCreate}((\mathsf{sk_{acc}}, \mathsf{pk_{acc}}), \mathsf{acc}_i, M_i, v_j), \mathcal{W}_i \leftarrow \mathcal{W}_i \cup \{(v_j, \mathsf{wit}_{i_j})\}$
        $\mathcal{V}_i \leftarrow (i, (\phi(m_i, \mathcal{W}_i), \mathsf{acc}_i)), \mathcal{V} \leftarrow \mathcal{V} \cup \mathcal{V}_i, \mathcal{W} \leftarrow \mathcal{W} \cup \{(i, \mathcal{W}_i)\}$,
        $B_i \leftarrow \mathtt{var}, m \leftarrow m||(\mathsf{acc}_i, i), \mathsf{ADM} \leftarrow \mathsf{ADM}||(\mathtt{fix})$.
    endfor.

Next, it computes $\hat{\sigma} \leftarrow \mathbf{Sign}(m, \mathsf{ADM}, (\mathsf{sk_{sig}}, \mathsf{pk_{sig}}), \mathsf{pk_{san}})$. Finally it sets $\sigma \leftarrow (\hat{\sigma}, \mathcal{V})$ and $\mathsf{san} \leftarrow (\emptyset, \mathcal{W})$ and returns (σ, san), or $\perp$ if any of the calls to ϕ, ψ or $\mathbf{Sign}$ fails.

$\mathsf{Sanit}\,((m, \sigma), \mathsf{MOD}, \mathsf{san}, \mathsf{pk_{sig}}, \mathsf{sk_{san}})$: Given $(m, \sigma) = ((m_i)_{i=1}^n, \sigma)$, $\mathsf{MOD} = \{(i, m'_i)\}^t$, san, $\mathsf{pk_{sig}}$ and $\mathsf{sk_{san}}$, this algorithm computes

    for $i = 1 \ldots n$ if $B_i = \mathtt{var} \,\wedge\, \perp \neq \phi(i, \mathcal{W})$ do:
        $\mathcal{W}_i \leftarrow \phi(i, \mathcal{W}), \mathsf{wit} \leftarrow \phi(m'_i, \mathcal{W}_i), (\mathsf{wit}_{i_j}, \mathsf{acc}_i) \leftarrow \phi(i, V), V' \leftarrow \psi(i, (\mathsf{wit}, \mathsf{acc}_i), V)$.
    endfor.

Finally, it computes $\hat{\sigma} \leftarrow \mathbf{Sanit}(Ext(m, \sigma), \mathsf{MOD}, \mathsf{pk_{sig}}, \mathsf{sk_{san}})$ and returns $\sigma = (\hat{\sigma}, \mathcal{V})$, or $\perp$ if any of the calls to ϕ, ψ or $\mathbf{Sanit}$ fails.

$\mathsf{Verify}\,((m, \sigma), \mathsf{pk_{sig}}, \mathsf{pk_{san}})$: Given $(m, \sigma) = ((m_i)_{i=1}^n, \sigma)$, $\mathsf{pk_{sig}}$ and $\mathsf{pk_{san}}$, this algorithm verifies whether $\mathbf{Verify}(Ext(m, \sigma), \mathsf{pk_{sig}}, \mathsf{pk_{san}}) = \mathtt{false}$ and returns $\mathtt{false}$ if so. Otherwise, it computes

    for $i = 1 \ldots n$ if $B_i = \mathtt{var} \,\wedge\, \perp \neq \phi(i, V)$ do:
        $(\mathsf{wit}_{i_j}, \mathsf{acc}_i) \leftarrow \phi(i, V), \mathtt{if}\,[\mathsf{AVerify}(\mathsf{pk_{acc}}, \mathsf{acc}_i, \mathsf{wit}_{i_j}, m_i) = \mathtt{false}]\,\{\,\mathtt{return\ false}\,\}$.
    endfor.

Finally, it returns $\mathtt{true}$.

$\mathsf{Proof}\,((m, \sigma), \{(m_j, \sigma_j)\}_{j=0}^q, (\mathsf{sk_{sig}}, \mathsf{pk_{sig}}), \mathsf{pk_{san}})$: Return $\mathbf{Proof}(Ext(m, \sigma), \{Ext(m_j, \sigma_j)\}_{j=0}^q, (\mathsf{sk_{sig}}, \mathsf{pk_{sig}}), \mathsf{pk_{san}})$.

$\mathsf{Judge}\,((m, \sigma), \mathsf{pk_{sig}}, \mathsf{pk_{san}}, \pi)$: Return $\mathbf{Judge}(Ext(m, \sigma), \mathsf{pk_{sig}}, \mathsf{pk_{san}}, \pi)$.

$Ext\,(m, \sigma)$: On input $(m, \sigma) = ((m_i)_{i=1}^n, \sigma)$,
    for $i = 1 \ldots n$ do:
        $(\mathsf{wit}_{i_j}, \mathsf{acc}_i) \leftarrow \phi(i, V), \mathtt{if}\,[(\mathsf{wit}_{i_j}, \mathsf{acc}_i) \neq \perp]\,\{\,\mathtt{set}\ m \leftarrow m||(\mathsf{acc}_i, i)\,\}$.
    endfor.
    Return (m, σ).

Scheme 1. Black-box construction of ESSS from any sanitizable signature scheme.

and the choice of the accumulator scheme. As mentioned in Sect. 2.1, the abstract model of accumulators assumes a trusted setup. It is, however, beneficial that the signer runs the AGen algorithm to be able to perform more efficient updates using the trapdoor. As a side effect, this also means that the signer is later able to extend the limited sets by making use of the trapdoor in the fashion of [25]. If this feature is unwanted, a TTP can run the AGen algorithm and publish $\mathsf{pk_{acc}}$ as a common reference string.

5.1 Obtaining Strong Privacy via a Black-Box Construction

Now we show how strongly private ESSS can be constructed from private sanitizable signature schemes in a black-box fashion. Basically, this can be achieved by applying the conversion in Scheme 1 and instantiating LimitSet using an accumulator that provides the indistinguishability property.

Theorem 3. *Let* ESSS *obtained using Scheme 1 be private and* (AGen, AEval, AWitCreate, AVerify) *be an indistinguishable accumulator, then* ESSS *is strongly private.*

Proof. We prove the theorem above by using a sequence of games. Thereby, we denote the event that the adversary wins Game i by S_i.

Game 0: The original strong privacy game.
Game 1: As in the original game, but we modify the oracle $\mathcal{O}^{\text{LoRSanit}}$ to firstly compute $V \leftarrow V_0 \cap V_1$ and to set $V_0 \leftarrow V$, $V_1 \leftarrow V$.

Transition Game 0 → Game 1: A distinguisher between Game 0 and Game 1 is a distinguisher for the indistinguishability game of the accumulator.

In Game 1, the signatures are computed with respect to $V_0 \cap V_1$ in $\mathcal{O}^{\text{LoRSanit}}$. This means that the LimitSet related values are independent of the bit b (similar as when randomly choosing V). Thus, from the adversary's viewpoint, Game 1 is equivalent to the conventional privacy game, meaning that $\Pr[S_1] \leq \frac{1}{2} + \epsilon_{\text{priv}}(\kappa)$. Furthermore, we know that the distinguishing probability between Game 0 and Game 1 is equivalent to the indistinguishability advantage of the accumulators, i.e., $|\Pr[S_0] - \Pr[S_1]| = k \cdot \epsilon_{\text{ind}}(\kappa)$, where k is the number of LimitSet blocks.[8] In further consequence, this shows that the advantage of an adversary to win the strong privacy game is negligible and bounded by $\Pr[S_0] \leq \frac{1}{2} + \epsilon_{\text{priv}}(\kappa) + k \cdot \epsilon_{\text{ind}}(\kappa)$. □

We also note that it might be an option to use cfw-indistinguishable accumulators instead of indistinguishable accumulators if the accumulation domain is large enough that the chosen random value x_r can not be efficiently guessed. This would resemble the suggestion of [21], who informally mentioned that additionally accumulating a random value might prevent the adversary from guessing the set limitations.

6   Conclusion

In this paper we propose the notion of strong privacy for ESSS, which, in contrast to the privacy notion for ESSS of [9] covers privacy for the LimitSet extension in the original sense of sanitizable signatures. From a practical perspective, our black-box constructions nicely combine with existing schemes in the model of [4,18]. Thus, existing implementations of schemes in these models directly yield a basis to instantiate our proposed extensions with relatively low effort, while preserving the efficiency of the underlying schemes. Conversely, it is still an open issue to construct efficient (strongly) unlinkable ESSS or to come up with a generic extension to construct such schemes from existing unlinkable sanitizable signature schemes.

---

[8] For compactness, we exchange all accumulators in a single game change and note that it is straight forward to unroll the exchange of the accumulators to k simple game changes.

References

1. Anandan, B., Clifton, C., Jiang, W., Murugesan, M., Pastrana-Camacho, P., Si, L.: *t*-Plausibility: generalizing words to desensitize text. Trans. Data Priv. **3**, 505–534 (2012)
2. Ateniese, G., Chou, D.H., de Medeiros, B., Tsudik, G.: Sanitizable signatures. In: di Vimercati, S.C., Syverson, P.F., Gollmann, D. (eds.) ESORICS 2005. LNCS, vol. 3679, pp. 159–177. Springer, Heidelberg (2005)
3. Bauer, D., Blough, D.M., Mohan, A.: Redactable signatures on data with dependencies and their application to personal health records. In: ACM WPES 2009 (2009)
4. Brzuska, C., Fischlin, M., Freudenreich, T., Lehmann, A., Page, M., Schelbert, J., Schröder, D., Volk, F.: Security of sanitizable signatures revisited. In: Jarecki, S., Tsudik, G. (eds.) PKC 2009. LNCS, vol. 5443, pp. 317–336. Springer, Heidelberg (2009)
5. Brzuska, C., Fischlin, M., Lehmann, A., Schröder, D.: Santizable signatures: how to partially delegate control for authenticated data. In: BIOSIG 2009 (2009)
6. Brzuska, C., Fischlin, M., Lehmann, A., Schröder, D.: Unlinkability of sanitizable signatures. In: Nguyen, P.Q., Pointcheval, D. (eds.) PKC 2010. LNCS, vol. 6056, pp. 444–461. Springer, Heidelberg (2010)
7. Brzuska, C., Pöhls, H.C., Samelin, K.: Non-interactive public accountability for sanitizable signatures. In: De Capitani di Vimercati, S., Mitchell, C. (eds.) EuroPKI 2012. LNCS, vol. 7868, pp. 178–193. Springer, Heidelberg (2013)
8. Brzuska, C., Pöhls, H.C., Samelin, K.: Efficient and perfectly unlinkable sanitizable signatures without group signatures. In: Katsikas, S., Agudo, I. (eds.) EuroPKI 2013. LNCS, vol. 8341, pp. 12–30. Springer, Heidelberg (2014)
9. Canard, S., Jambert, A.: On extended sanitizable signature schemes. In: Pieprzyk, J. (ed.) CT-RSA 2010. LNCS, vol. 5985, pp. 179–194. Springer, Heidelberg (2010)
10. Canard, S., Jambert, A., Lescuyer, R.: Sanitizable signatures with several signers and sanitizers. In: Mitrokotsa, A., Vaudenay, S. (eds.) AFRICACRYPT 2012. LNCS, vol. 7374, pp. 35–52. Springer, Heidelberg (2012)
11. Canard, S., Laguillaumie, F., Milhau, M.: *Trapdoor* sanitizable signatures and their application to content protection. In: Bellovin, S.M., Gennaro, R., Keromytis, A.D., Yung, M. (eds.) ACNS 2008. LNCS, vol. 5037, pp. 258–276. Springer, Heidelberg (2008)
12. Canard, S., Lescuyer, R.: Protecting privacy by sanitizing personal data: a new approach to anonymous credentials. In: ASIA CCS 2013 (2013)
13. Chakaravarthy, V.T., Gupta, H., Roy, P., Mohania, M.K.: Efficient techniques for document sanitization. In: ACM CIKM 2008 (2008)
14. Chang, E.-C., Xu, J.: Remote integrity check with dishonest storage server. In: Jajodia, S., Lopez, J. (eds.) ESORICS 2008. LNCS, vol. 5283, pp. 223–237. Springer, Heidelberg (2008)
15. Chow, R., Oberst, I., Staddon, J.: Sanitization's slippery slope: the design and study of a text revision assistant. In: SOUPS 2009. ACM (2009)
16. Derler, D., Hanser, C., Slamanig, D.: Revisiting cryptographic accumulators, additional properties and relations to other primitives. In: Nyberg, K. (ed.) CT-RSA 2015. LNCS, vol. 9048, pp. 127–144. Springer, Heidelberg (2015)
17. Fleischhacker, N., Krupp, J., Malavolta, G., Schneider, J., Schröder, D., Simkin, M.: Efficient unlinkable sanitizable signatures from signatures with rerandomizable keys. Cryptology ePrint Archive, Report 2015/395 (2015)

18. Gong, J., Qian, H., Zhou, Y.: Fully-secure and practical sanitizable signatures. In: Lai, X., Yung, M., Lin, D. (eds.) Inscrypt 2010. LNCS, vol. 6584, pp. 300–317. Springer, Heidelberg (2011)
19. Haber, S., Hatano, Y., Honda, Y., Horne, W.G., Miyazaki, K., Sander, T., Tezoku, S., Yao, D.: Efficient signature schemes supporting redaction, pseudonymization, and data deidentification. In: ACM Symposium on Information, Computer and Communications Security, ASIACCS 2008 (2008)
20. Johnson, R., Molnar, D., Song, D., Wagner, D.: Homomorphic signature schemes. In: Preneel, B. (ed.) CT-RSA 2002. LNCS, vol. 2271, p. 244. Springer, Heidelberg (2002)
21. Klonowski, M., Lauks, A.: Extended sanitizable signatures. In: Rhee, M.S., Lee, B. (eds.) ICISC 2006. LNCS, vol. 4296, pp. 343–355. Springer, Heidelberg (2006)
22. de Meer, H., Pöhls, H.C., Posegga, J., Samelin, K.: On the relation between redactable and sanitizable signature schemes. In: Jürjens, J., Piessens, F., Bielova, N. (eds.) ESSoS. LNCS, vol. 8364, pp. 113–130. Springer, Heidelberg (2014)
23. Miyazaki, K., Iwamura, M., Matsumoto, T., Sasaki, R., Yoshiura, H., Tezuka, S., Imai, H.: Digitally signed document sanitizing scheme with disclosure condition control. IEICE Trans. Fundam. Electron. Commun. Comput. Sci. 1, 239–246 (2005)
24. Brzuska, C., Fischlin, M., Lehmann, A., Schröder, D.: Redactable signatures to control the maximum noise for differential privacy in the smart grid. In: Nguyen, P.Q., Pointcheval, D. (eds.) SmartGridSec 2014. LNCS, vol. 8448, pp. 79–93. Springer, Heidelberg (2014)
25. Pöhls, H.C., Samelin, K.: On updatable redactable signatures. In: Boureanu, I., Owesarski, P., Vaudenay, S. (eds.) ACNS 2014. LNCS, vol. 8479, pp. 457–475. Springer, Heidelberg (2014)
26. Pöhls, H.C., Samelin, K., Posegga, J.: Sanitizable signatures in XML Signature — performance, mixing properties, and revisiting the property of transparency. In: Lopez, J., Tsudik, G. (eds.) ACNS 2011. LNCS, vol. 6715, pp. 166–182. Springer, Heidelberg (2011)
27. Slamanig, D., Rass, S.: Generalizations and extensions of redactable signatures with applications to electronic healthcare. In: De Decker, B., Schaumüller-Bichl, I. (eds.) CMS 2010. LNCS, vol. 6109, pp. 201–213. Springer, Heidelberg (2010)
28. Slamanig, D., Stranacher, K., Zwattendorfer, B.: User-centric identity as a service-architecture for eids with selective attribute disclosure. In: ACM SACMAT 2014 (2014)
29. Steinfeld, R., Bull, L., Zheng, Y.: Content extraction signatures. In: Kim, K. (ed.) ICISC 2001. LNCS, vol. 2288, p. 285. Springer, Heidelberg (2002)
30. Stranacher, K., Krnjic, V., Zefferer, T.: Trust and reliability for public sector data. In: ICBG (2013)
31. Sweeney, L.: Achieving k-anonymity privacy protection using generalization and suppression. Int. J. Uncertainty Fuzziness Knowl. Based Syst. 10(5), 571–588 (2002)
32. Yum, D.H., Seo, J.W., Lee, P.J.: Trapdoor sanitizable signatures made easy. In: Zhou, J., Yung, M. (eds.) ACNS 2010. LNCS, vol. 6123, pp. 53–68. Springer, Heidelberg (2010)
33. Zwattendorfer, B., Slamanig, D.: On privacy-preserving ways to porting the austrian eID system to the public cloud. In: Janczewski, L.J., Wolfe, H.B., Shenoi, S. (eds.) SEC 2013. IFIP AICT, vol. 405, pp. 300–314. Springer, Heidelberg (2013)

Unique Signature with Short Output from CDH Assumption

Shiuan-Tzuo Shen[(✉)], Amir Rezapour[(✉)], and Wen-Guey Tzeng

Department of Computer Science, National Chiao Tung University,
Hsinchu, Taiwan
{vink,rezapour,wgtzeng}@cs.nctu.edu.tw

Abstract. We give a simple and efficient construction of unique signature on groups equipped with bilinear map. In contrast to prior works, our proof of security is based on *computational Diffie-Hellman* problem in the random oracle model. Meanwhile, the resulting signature consists of only one group element. Due to its simplicity, security and efficiency, our scheme is suitable for those situations that require to overcome communication bottlenecks. Moreover, the unique signature is a building block for designing chosen-ciphertext secure cryptosystems and verifiable random functions, which have found many interesting applications in cryptographic protocol design.

Keywords: Unique signature · Strongly unforgeable signature · Verifiable unpredictable function · Verifiable random function · Bilinear map · Random oracle model

1 Introduction

Unlike traditional signature schemes, unique signature, a.k.a. verifiable unpredictable function (VUF), is a function from the message space to the signature space under the given public key. This particular property ensures that each message would have only "one" possible signature. From the security perspective, unique signature is not only existentially unforgeable against the chosen message attack, but also strongly unforgeable against the chosen message attack. The latter property assures that the adversary cannot even produce a valid signature for an earlier signed message.

Intuitively, unique signatures are very fascinating objects, as there is no reason to verify a signature on the same message twice. For instance, if one has verified a signature on one particular message, it is unnecessary to verify the message again unless the signature is changed. Another situation includes the signature scheme with a very efficient signer to generate many signatures for one particular message. This may simply lead to overload a verifier to verify many signatures on the same message. Above all, Unique signatures are a building block for constructing an *adaptive CCA-secure* IBE encryption scheme from a *selective-identity CPA-secure* IBE scheme [2].

© Springer International Publishing Switzerland 2015
M.-H. Au and A. Miyaji (Eds.): ProvSec 2015, LNCS 9451, pp. 475–488, 2015.
DOI: 10.1007/978-3-319-26059-4_26

Unique signature has significant implication for constructing verifiable random functions (VRFs). VRF has found many interesting applications, such as non-interactive zero-knowledge proofs, micropayment schemes, verifiable transaction escrow schemes, compact e-cash, adaptive oblivious transfer protocols, and keyword search as discussed in [11].

1.1   Contribution

The primary objective of this study is to find a unique signature scheme with a weaker assumption and a signature of only one group element. This is always an appealing task for cryptographers. In contrast to earlier findings, we come up with a new provable scheme under the computational Diffie-Hellman (CDH) problem. In addition to using a weaker assumption, our unique signature consists of only one group element, which results in a fixed and small signature on any arbitrary input message length. Therefore, our unique signature enjoys a shorter signature than Boneh et al. [5] and Lysyanskaya [14].

Boneh et al. proposed the BLS signature [4] and proved existential unforgeablility based on CDH assumption in the random oracle model. However, it is easy to see that their scheme also achieves strongly existential unforgeability. BLS signature outputs a signature of one element, and its signing and verification key also consist of one element respectively. Therefore, it is relatively more efficient than our construction. Nevertheless, it still has some efficiency issues as the output length of the hash function grows. Informally, in BLS construction, the purpose of the hash function is to map a given message m into a group element. However, to ensure the security of the hash function, we may need to employ an elliptic curve of larger group size[1]. This affects the performance of BLS signature and leads to a larger signature. In contrast to BLS signature, we hash a message to determine the signing key of the signature. Therefore, the group size in our construction is independent of the output length of the hash function. There is another difference between BLS signature and our unique signature. Although the two signatures are all provable in the random oracle model, they rely on different level of programmability of random oracle. BLS signature needs a random oracle for embedding the challenge instance of some hard problem, while our unique signature needs a random oracle for random outputs only.

Strongly Existential Unforgeability. Our construction is based on the result of Lysyanskaya [14], where the signature on an n_0-bit message consists of $\theta(n_0)$ group elements. Lysyanskaya proves the existential unforgeability based on the l-CDH problem. She embeds the challenge instance in ℓ independent indexes of the public key. Therefore, she can employ an error correcting code to bound the success probability of the reduction. In contrast with Lysyanskaya, we aim to give a signature of a single group element on an n_0-bit message, and prove the

---

[1] NIST [8] recommends SHA-256, SHA-384, and SHA-512 for minimum security of digital signatures, but the recommended group size of an elliptic curve is 256 bits.

existential unforgeability based on the CDH problem. The challenging part is to give a non-negligible lower bound for the success probability of our reduction. Therefore, we cannot use the proof technique of Lysyanskaya because the error correcting code that we need does not exist. We use a different technique to bound the success probability. Our strategy is to inject variability into the signature. Therefore, we design a dynamic pattern for the signature, where the combination of secret exponents is determined by the hash output of the signed message. Meanwhile, the signature that contains the solution of the CDH problem has a specific pattern. Hence, we can reduce the failure probability and obtain a non-negligible lower bound for the success probability of our reduction.

Malicious Signer Resistance. Lysyanskaya [14] achieves malicious signer resistance. She implicitly represents each codeword symbol by an element of the signature. If two messages are different, then their signatures are also different. In contrast with Lysyanskaya, we compress our signature into one group element. It is possible that two distinct messages result in the same signature. To prove that our signature achieves malicious signer resistance, we first work on giving an upper bound for the number of hash outputs which result in the same signature. We propose the notion of the equivalent set for a signature and show that the size of an equivalent set is in a negligible proportion. Then, we can prove malicious signer resistance in the random oracle model. The next task is to relax the requirement of the random oracle due to the fact that a malicious signer may be able to choose the hash function. The difficulty is that most of the cryptographic protocols rely on a trusted source of randomness. An honest signer will choose his secret key randomly, but in contrast a malicious signer would not necessarily do that. We propose the H-F-H structure to resist a malicious signer, where H stands for a hash function and F stands for a one-way permutation. The H-F-H structure has the following properties:

- To evaluate an output of the H-F-H structure, a malicious signer has to decide his public key first. Thus, he cannot choose his secret key to force two hash outputs to be in the same equivalent set. This makes the malicious signer to guess a message that results in the same signature.
- The H-F-H structure is one-way. Therefore, a malicious signer cannot compute a message from an equivalent set. More precisely, the probability of finding an input of the F-layer for a given output is negligible. Even if the malicious signer can find an input of the F-layer, the input has to pass the verification of the H-layer.
- The design of double hash layers makes a malicious signer hard to find a candidate for the hash function. The two H-layers employ the same hash function. In addition, the output of the first H-layer will determine the input of the second H-layer. Even if the malicious signer can find a candidate for first H-layer, the candidate has to pass the verification of the second H-layer or vise-versa.

2   Related Work

Unique signature has been known to exist in the random oracle model. Until the result in [15], there was no construction for such schemes in the standard model. In addition to the seminal work of Micali et al. [15], which is based on the strong RSA assumption, there are few unique signatures in the standard model. Lysyanskaya in [14] proposed such a scheme based on the many-DH assumption. This differs from that of Micali et al., in both the underlying assumptions and signature size. In contrast, Lysyanskaya provided a signature of n elements. Dodis proposed a unique signature scheme based on a much stronger assumption, sum-free l-decisional Diffie-Hellman assumption (SF-l-DDH). The key size is half of Lysyanskaya [14]'s. Dodis et al. [7] introduced another unique signature scheme based on l-Diffie-Hellman inversion assumption (l-DHI). The signature consists of only one element. Kuchta and Manulis [13] proposed a generic construction for unique aggregate signatures, which can be converted to distributed verifiable random functions. Jager [12] proposed a nearly identical unique signature scheme to that proposed by Lysyanskaya, but a new construction of VRF without having to resort to the Goldreich-Levin transformation [9]. The VRF presented in [12] is a relatively simple and efficient with large input space and full adaptive security using l-decisional Diffie-Hellman assumption in the standard model. Abdalla et al. [1] provided a methodology to construct a VRF by showing some connections to identity-based encryption. Moreover, they considered a few constructions without pairings in a more limited setting in which the number of queries was upper-bounded. They also showed that the Boneh-Franklin ID-KEM [3] can lead to a very efficient VRF in the random oracle model. Boneh et al. [4] proposed the BLS signature, which produces a signature of only one group element. The signing key and verification key are also short. Their security proof is based on the *computational Diffie-Hellman* (CDH) problem in the random oracle model.

3   Definition

We first recall some standard notations and definitions that will be used throughout the paper. Let k be a security parameter. We model the participants in the cryptographic model by probabilistic polynomial-time Turing machines (PPTMs), whose running time is at most polynomial in k. In the rest of the paper, complexity classes are with respect to k, unless there is an explicit specification.

We say that a function $\mu : \mathbb{N} \to \mathbb{R}^+$ is negligible if for every positive polynomial $P(\cdot)$ and all sufficiently large k, it holds that $0 < \mu(k) < \frac{1}{P(k)}$. For instance, $\mu(k) = 2^{-k}$ is a negligible function.

The number of elements in a set $\mathcal{X}$ is denoted as $|\mathcal{X}|$, and the bit length of an element $x \in \mathcal{X}$ is denoted as $|x|$. Choosing an element x from set $\mathcal{X}$ randomly and uniformly is denoted as $x \in_R \mathcal{X}$. The value of $x \mod n$ is denoted as $[x]_n$.

A binary string of length n consists of n symbols, where each symbol has two possible values. The set of all binary strings of length n is denoted as $\{0,1\}^n$, and the set of all binary strings of arbitrary length is denoted as $\{0,1\}^* = \bigcup_{n=0}^{\infty}\{0,1\}^n$. The i-th symbol of a string $x \in \{0,1\}^n$ is denoted as $x(i-1)$, where the index $i-1$ is between 0 and $n-1$. The concatenation of two strings $x \in \{0,1\}^n$ and $y \in \{0,1\}^n$ is denoted as $x\|y$.

3.1 Unique Signature

The notation of a unique signature was introduced by Goldwasser and Ostrovsky [10][2]. A unique signature must be a strongly unforgeable signature, but a strongly unforgeable signature [5] is not necessarily a unique signature. Unique signature is also known as verifiable unpredictable function. A verifiable unpredictable function may not be a verifiable random function, but a verifiable random function [15] must be a verifiable unpredictable function. A unique signature scheme consists of four polynomial-time algorithms Setup, KeyGen, Sign, and Verify, which are defined as follows:

- Setup(1^k) $\rightarrow \pi$: It is a probabilistic algorithm run by the system manager. Algorithm Setup takes security parameter k as the input, and outputs public parameter π.
- KeyGen(π) $\rightarrow (sk, pk)$: It is a probabilistic algorithm run by a signer. Algorithm KeyGen takes public parameter π as the input, and outputs secret key sk and public key pk.
- Sign(π, sk, pk, m) $\rightarrow \sigma$: It is a deterministic algorithm run by a signer. Algorithm Sign takes public parameter π, secret key sk, public key pk, and message m as inputs, and outputs signature σ.
- Verify(π, pk, m, σ) $\rightarrow \{$Yes, No$\}$: It is a deterministic algorithm run by a verifier. Algorithm Verify takes public parameter π, public key pk, message m, and signature σ as inputs, and outputs the validity of (m, σ) under pk.

These algorithms must satisfy the following requirements:

- **Consistency:** For every public parameter π produced by algorithm Setup, every key pair (sk, pk) produced by algorithm KeyGen, and every message m, we have that Verify($\pi, pk, m,$ Sign(π, sk, pk, m)) = Yes.
- **Uniqueness:** For every public parameter π produced by algorithm Setup, every key pair (sk, pk) produced by algorithm KeyGen, every message m, and every pair of signatures σ_1 and σ_2, if we have Verify(π, pk, m, σ_1) = Verify(π, pk, m, σ_2) = Yes, then it must imply $\sigma_1 = \sigma_2$.

Strongly Existential Unforgeability. Security for a unique signature scheme is defined as the security against strongly existential forgery under an adaptive chosen message attack. Strongly existential unforgeability is a stronger security property, comparing with existentially unforgeable signature schemes. In both cases, an adversary who is given a signature for some message of his choice might not be able to produce a valid signature for a new message. Nevertheless, the

---

[2] Goldwasser and Ostrovsky called it invariant signature.

strongly existential unforgeability property ensures that the adversary cannot even produce a valid signature for a previously signed message. This notion is defined by the unforgeability game $\mathsf{Game}^{\mathsf{UF}}$ between a challenger C and an adversary $\mathcal{A}$:

- **Setup.** Challenger C runs algorithm $\mathsf{Setup}(1^k)$ to generate public parameter π. Then, C runs algorithm $\mathsf{KeyGen}(\pi)$ to generate secret-public key pair (sk, pk). C holds sk and gives (π, pk) to adversary $\mathcal{A}$.
- **Query.** Adversary $\mathcal{A}$ queries q messages $(m_1, m_2, \ldots, m_q)$ of his choice. Challenger C returns q signatures $(\sigma_1, \sigma_2, \ldots, \sigma_q)$ to answer the queries. These queries are issued adaptively, namely, $\mathcal{A}$ can choose m_i after seeing the signatures $(\sigma_1, \ldots, \sigma_{i-1})$.
- **Forgery.** Adversary $\mathcal{A}$ outputs a message-signature pair (m^*, σ^*), where m^* has not been queried in the query phase.

Adversary $\mathcal{A}$ wins the game if $m^* \notin \{m_1, m_2, \ldots, m_q\}$ and $\mathsf{Verify}(\pi, pk, m^*, \sigma^*)$ $= \mathsf{Yes}$. The advantage $\mathsf{Adv}_{\mathcal{A}}^{\mathsf{UF}}$ is defined as the probability that $\mathcal{A}$ wins the game.

Definition 1. *A signature scheme achieves (t, q, ϵ) strongly existential unforgeability against adaptive chosen message attack if no adversary, who runs in time t and queries at most q messages, can win the unforgeability game with advantage over ϵ.*

Malicious Signer Resistance. Besides strongly existential unforgeability, we study another important security property which is called *malicious signer resistance*. A malicious signer will try to find a specific setting of his secret key so that he can sign two different messages with the same signature. The signer obtains some benefit from this collision. He can sign a message first and then claim that the signature is for another message instead. The malicious signer resistance property ensures that an adversary cannot sign two distinct messages to the same signature even if the secret key is on his choice. This notion is defined by the malicious signer game $\mathsf{Game}^{\mathsf{MS}}$ between a challenger C and an adversary $\mathcal{A}$:

- **Setup.** Challenger C runs algorithm $\mathsf{Setup}(1^k)$ to generate public parameter π. Then, C gives π to adversary $\mathcal{A}$.
- **Answer.** Adversary $\mathcal{A}$ outputs a public key pk, two messages (m_1, m_2), and a signature σ, where m_1 and m_2 are distinct.

Adversary $\mathcal{A}$ wins the game if $m_1 \neq m_2$ and $\mathsf{Verify}(\pi, pk, m_1, \sigma) = \mathsf{Yes} = \mathsf{Verify}(\pi, pk, m_2, \sigma)$. The advantage $\mathsf{Adv}_{\mathcal{A}}^{\mathsf{MS}}$ is defined as the probability that $\mathcal{A}$ wins the game.

Definition 2. *A signature scheme achieves (t, ϵ) malicious signer resistance if no adversary, who runs in time t, can win the malicious signer game with advantage over ϵ.*

3.2   Cryptographic Primitive

One-Way Permutation. Let $\mathcal{X}$ be a space of exponent size. A owe-way permutation $F : \mathcal{X} \to \mathcal{X}$ is a bijective one-way function. Specifically, F should satisfy the following properties:

- Computability. For all input $x \in \mathcal{X}$, there is a (deterministic) polynomial-time algorithm $A(\cdot)$ who can output $F(x)$. That is, we have $A(x) = F(x)$ for every input x.
- One-Wayness. For a random message $x \in_R \mathcal{X}$, there is no probabilistic polynomial-time adversary $\mathcal{A}$ who can output an inverse of $F(x)$ with non-negligible probability. That is, for every probabilistic polynomial-time adversary $\mathcal{A}$, every positive polynomial $P(\cdot)$, and all sufficiently large k, we have

$$\Pr_{x \in_R \mathcal{X}} \left[x' \in F^{-1}(F(x)) : A(F(x)) = x' \right] < \frac{1}{P(k)}.$$

Definition 3. *We say that a one-way permutation F is (t, ϵ) one-way if no adversary can break the one-wayness of F in time t with probability over ϵ.*

Cryptographic Hash Function. Let $\mathcal{M}$ be a message space of exponent size, and $\mathcal{D}$ be a digest space of exponent size. A cryptographic hash function $H : \mathcal{M} \to \mathcal{D}$ is a one-way function. Specifically, H should satisfy the following properties:

- Computability. For all messages $m \in \mathcal{M}$, there is a (deterministic) polynomial-time algorithm $A(\cdot)$ who can output $H(m)$. That is, we have $A(m) = H(m)$ for every input m.
- Pre-image Resistance. For a random message $m \in_R \mathcal{M}$, there is no probabilistic polynomial-time adversary $\mathcal{A}$ who can output an inverse of $H(m)$ with non-negligible probability. That is, for every probabilistic polynomial-time adversary $\mathcal{A}$, every positive polynomial $P(\cdot)$, and all sufficiently large k, we have

$$\Pr_{m \in_R \mathcal{M}} \left[m' \in H^{-1}(H(m)) : A(H(m)) = m' \right] < \frac{1}{P(k)}.$$

- Second Pre-image Resistance. Given a random message $m \in_R \mathcal{M}$, there is no probabilistic polynomial-time adversary $\mathcal{A}$ who can output another inverse $m' \in \mathcal{M}$ of $H(m)$ with non-negligible probability. That is, for every probabilistic polynomial-time adversary $\mathcal{A}$, every positive polynomial $P(\cdot)$, and all sufficiently large k, we have

$$\Pr_{m \in_R \mathcal{M}} \left[m' \in H^{-1}(H(m)) \wedge m \neq m' : A(H, m) = m' \right] < \frac{1}{P(k)}.$$

- Collision Resistance. There is no probabilistic polynomial-time adversary $\mathcal{A}$ who can output two distinct messages $m \in \mathcal{M}$ and $m' \in \mathcal{M}$ such that $H(m) = H(m')$ with non-negligible probability. That is, for every probabilistic polynomial-time adversary $\mathcal{A}$, every positive polynomial $P(\cdot)$, and all sufficiently large k, we have

$$\Pr \left[H(m) = H(m') \wedge m \neq m' : A(H) = (m, m') \right] < \frac{1}{P(k)}.$$

Definition 4. *We say that a cryptographic hash function H is (t, ϵ) collision resistant if no adversary can break the collision resistance of H in time t with probability over ϵ.*

Bilinear Map. Let $\mathbb{G}$ and $\mathbb{G}_T$ be two multiplicative cyclic groups of prime order q. Let g be a generator of $\mathbb{G}$. A map $\hat{e} : \mathbb{G} \times \mathbb{G} \to \mathbb{G}_T$ is called an admissible bilinear map if it satisfies the following properties:

- Bilinearity: for all $u, v \in \mathbb{G}$ and $x, y \in \mathbb{Z}_q$, we have $\hat{e}(u^x, v^y) = \hat{e}(u, v)^{xy}$.
- Non-degeneracy: we have $\hat{e}(g, g) \neq \mathbf{1}$, where $\mathbf{1}$ is the identity element of $\mathbb{G}_T$.
- Computability: there is a polynomial-time algorithm to compute $\hat{e}(u, v) \forall$ $u, v \in \mathbb{G}$.

3.3   Hardness Assumption

The security of our unique signature scheme will be reduced to hardness of the *computational Diffie-Hellman* (CDH) problem.

Definition 5. *Let $\mathbb{G}$ be a multiplicative cyclic group of prime order q. Let g be a generator of $\mathbb{G}$. The CDH problem is to compute g^{ab} when given $g, g^a, g^b \in \mathbb{G}$, where $a, b \in_R \mathbb{Z}_q$.*

Definition 6. *We say that the (t, ϵ)-CDH assumption holds in the group $\mathbb{G}$ if no adversary can solve the CDH problem in $\mathbb{G}$ in time t with probability over ϵ.*

4   Unique Signature Scheme

In this section, we give a simple construction for unique signatures. Our construction is based on a result due to Lysyanskaya [14], where the signature on an n_0-bit message consists of $\theta(n_0)$ group elements. We show that our solution gives rise to a signature of a single group element on an n_0-bit message.

4.1   Construction

We use the cryptographic hash function, one-way permutation, and bilinear map to build our unique signature scheme. The construction is described as follows:

- Setup$(1^k) \to \pi$. Let k be the security parameter, and n_0 be the message length, where $n_0 = \mathsf{poly}(k)$. Let n be $2^t + 1$, and $[x]$ denote $[x]_n = x \mod n$, where $t \in \mathbb{N}$ and $n = \theta(n_0)$. Let q be a k-bit prime, $\mathbb{G}$ and $\mathbb{G}_T$ be two multiplicative cyclic groups of prime order q, and g be a generator of $\mathbb{G}$. Let $\hat{e} : \mathbb{G} \times \mathbb{G} \to \mathbb{G}_T$ be an admissible bilinear map, $H : \{0,1\}^* \to \{0,1\}^{n+t-1}$ be a cryptographic hash function, and $F : \{0,1\}^{n+t-1+n_0} \to \{0,1\}^{n+t-1+n_0}$ be a one-way permutation. The system manager publishes the public parameter

$$\pi = (k, n_0, n, q, \mathbb{G}, \mathbb{G}_T, g, \hat{e}, H, F).$$

- KeyGen$(\pi) \rightarrow (sk, pk)$. A signer randomly chooses $2n$ exponents $a_{i,j} \in_R \mathbb{Z}_q^*$ and computes $A_{i,j} = g^{a_{i,j}}$, where $i \in \mathbb{Z}_n$ and $j \in \mathbb{Z}_2$. These exponents have to satisfy the two requirements:
  1. For every $i, i' \in \mathbb{Z}_n$ and every $j, j' \in \mathbb{Z}_2$, we have $a_{i,j} = a_{i',j'}$ iff. $(i, j) = (i', j')$. It can be verified without knowing the exponents by checking whether every $A_{i,j}$ is unique.
  2. For every $h \in \{1, 2, \ldots, \frac{n-1}{2}\}$, every $i \in \mathbb{Z}_n$, and every $j, j' \in \mathbb{Z}_2$, we have $a_{i,j} + a_{[i+2h],j'} \neq 0$. It can be verified without knowing the exponents by checking whether every $A_{i,j} \times A_{[i+2h],j'} \neq 1$.

  The signer stores his secret key
  $$sk = \{(a_{0,0}, a_{0,1}), (a_{1,0}, a_{1,1}), \ldots, (a_{n-1,0}, a_{n-1,1})\}$$
  and publishes his public key
  $$pk = \{(A_{0,0}, A_{0,1}), (A_{1,0}, A_{1,1}), \ldots, (A_{n-1,0}, A_{n-1,1})\}.$$

- Sign$(\pi, sk, pk, m) \rightarrow \sigma$. To sign a message $m \in \{0,1\}^{n_0}$ of n_0 bits[3], a signer generates the signature σ as follows:
  1. Use his public key pk and the cryptographic hash function $H : \{0,1\}^* \rightarrow \{0,1\}^{n+t-1}$ to compute $x = H(pk\|m)$.
  2. Use the one-way permutation $F : \{0,1\}^{n+t-1+n_0} \rightarrow \{0,1\}^{n+t-1+n_0}$ to compute $y = F(x\|m)$.
  3. Use the cryptographic hash function $H : \{0,1\}^* \rightarrow \{0,1\}^{n+t-1}$ to compute $z = H(y)$.
  4. Let $h = \mathsf{LSB}_{t-1}(z) + 1$, where $\mathsf{LSB}_{t-1}(z)$ is the least $t-1$ significant bits of z. Use his secret key $sk = \{(a_{0,0}, a_{0,1}), (a_{1,0}, a_{1,1}), \ldots, (a_{n-1,0}, a_{n-1,1})\}$ to compute signature
  $$\sigma = \prod_{i=0}^{n-1} g^{a_{i,z(i)} a_{[i+h], z([i+h])}}.$$

- Verify$(\pi, pk, m, \sigma) \rightarrow \{\mathsf{Yes}, \mathsf{No}\}$. Suppose that the signer's public key pk is well-formed. A verifier verifies a message-signature pair (m, σ) of the signer as follows:
  1. Use the cryptographic hash function $H : \{0,1\}^* \rightarrow \{0,1\}^{n+t-1}$ and the signer's public key pk to compute $x = H(pk\|m)$.
  2. Use the one-way permutation $F : \{0,1\}^{n+t-1+n_0} \rightarrow \{0,1\}^{n+t-1+n_0}$ to compute $y = F(x\|m)$.
  3. Use the cryptographic hash function $H : \{0,1\}^* \rightarrow \{0,1\}^{n+t-1}$ to compute $z = H(y)$.
  4. Let $h = \mathsf{LSB}_{t-1}(z) + 1$, where $\mathsf{LSB}_{t-1}(z)$ is the least $t-1$ significant bits of z. Use the bilinear map $\hat{e} : \mathbb{G} \times \mathbb{G} \rightarrow \mathbb{G}_\mathbb{T}$ and the signer's public key $pk = \{(A_{0,0}, A_{0,1}), (A_{1,0}, A_{1,1}), \ldots, (A_{n-1,0}, A_{n-1,1})\}$ to check whether
  $$\hat{e}(\sigma, g) = \prod_{i=0}^{n-1} \hat{e}\left(A_{i,z(i)}, A_{[i+h], z([i+h])}\right).$$

---

[3] A cryptographic hash function $H' : \{0,1\}^* \rightarrow \{0,1\}^{n_0}$ can be used to expand the message space.

Consistency. If the signature σ is well-formed, then we have

$$
\hat{e}(\sigma, g) = \hat{e}\left(\prod_{i=0}^{n-1} g^{a_{i,z(i)} a_{[i+h],z([i+h])}}, g \right)
$$

$$
= \prod_{i=0}^{n-1} \hat{e}\left(g^{a_{i,z(i)}}, g^{a_{[i+h],z([i+h])}} \right)
$$

$$
= \prod_{i=0}^{n-1} \hat{e}\left(A_{i,z(i)}, A_{[i+h],z([i+h])} \right)
$$

Uniqueness. If there are two signatures (σ_1, σ_2) for the same message m under a secret-public key pair (sk, pk), then we have

$$
\hat{e}(\sigma_1, g) = \prod_{i=0}^{n-1} \hat{e}\left(A_{i,z(i)}, A_{[i+h],z([i+h])} \right) = \hat{e}(\sigma_2, g)
$$

because σ_1 and σ_2 share the same $x = H(pk\|m)$, $y = F(x\|m)$, $z = H(y)$, and $h = \mathsf{LSB}_{t-1}(z) + 1$. Thus, it must be $\sigma_1 = \sigma_2$ unless g is not a generator.

4.2 Efficiency

Let Hash be an execution of hash function H, Perm be an execution of one-way permutation F, and Pair be an execution of bilinear map $\hat{e}$. Let $\mathsf{Add}_{\mathbb{Z}_q}$ be the operation of addition in $\mathbb{Z}_q$, $\mathsf{Mul}_{\mathbb{Z}_q}$ be the operation of multiplication in $\mathbb{Z}_q$, $\mathsf{Exp}_{\mathbb{G}}$ be the operation of scalar exponentiation in $\mathbb{G}$, and $\mathsf{Mul}_{\mathbb{G}_T}$ be the operation of multiplication in $\mathbb{G}_T$. The computational complexity of algorithm Sign is $2\mathsf{Hash} + \mathsf{Perm} + (n-1)\mathsf{Add}_{\mathbb{Z}_q} + n\mathsf{Mul}_{\mathbb{Z}_q} + \mathsf{Exp}_{\mathbb{G}}$. The computational complexity of algorithm Verify is $2\mathsf{Hash} + \mathsf{Perm} + (n+1)\mathsf{Pair} + (n-1)\mathsf{Mul}_{\mathbb{G}_T}$.

We now compare our construction with the related works in Table 1. The schemes [6,11] are verifiable random functions, and the others are verifiable unpredictable functions (unique signatures). Our unique signature scheme is based on the standard CDH assumption. Our key size is the same as [14], but our signature consists of only one group element instead of n elements. This differs from that of Micali et al. [15], in the size of signature as discussed in [7]. For the RSA assumption to have the same security level as DDH-based assumptions for the same input size, the signature size will grow in the order of a few hundred kilobytes. There are number of important differences between our construction and Jager [12] in both signature size and underlying hard assumption. The BLS signature [4] enjoys shorter key size besides signature size. It is also based on the standard CDH assumption. As we mentioned earlier, its group size is dominated by the output length of the employed hash function.

4.3 Applications

Our scheme produces a signature of only one group element. When such a signature scheme is used with arbitrary input message length, a better bandwidth is obtained, as a shorter signature needs to be transferred.

Table 1. Comparison with related work

Scheme	Type	Assumption	Secret Key (bits)	Public Key (bits)	Output (bits)
[6]	VRF	SF-l-DDH	lk	$l\ell$	$l\ell$
[11]	VRF	l-DDHE	$(n+1)k + 2\ell$	$(n+3)\ell$	$(n+1)\ell + \ell_T$
[15]	VUF	RSA	k	$(2k^2+1)k + t$	k
[12]	VUF	l-CDH	$2nk$	$(2n+2)\ell$	$n\ell$
[14]	VUF	l-CDH	$2nk$	$2n\ell$	$n\ell$
[7]	VUF	l-DHI	k	ℓ	ℓ
[4]	VUF	CDH	k	ℓ	ℓ
Ours	VUF	CDH	$2nk$	$2n\ell$	ℓ

- k is the security parameter
- ℓ is the size of an element in $\mathbb{G}$
- ℓ_T is the size of an element in $\mathbb{G}_T$
- l is the parameter of complexity assumption
- t is the size of random coin
- n is the equivalent size of a message
- VUF stands for verifiable unpredictable function
- VRF stands for verifiable random function

In addition to explicit applications of unique signatures for authenticity, integrity and non-repudiation of a message, there is a natural transformation from unique signatures to VRFs by an early work of Goldreich and Levin [9]. VRFs behave similarly to pseudorandom functions, namely, giving the adversary the oracle access of the VRF function to evaluate for some input of his choice. Eventually, the adversary should not be able to distinguish the output of a VRF function from a random source. Besides, the VRF has another additional property that, given the output of the VRF function to the verifier, it is easy for the prover to non-interactively convince the verifier that the given commitment is correct with respect to prover's public key. Due to these properties, VRFs found some significant applications such as resettable zero-knowledge proofs, adaptive oblivious transfer protocols, and verifiable transaction escrow schemes.

Unique signatures have also found an important application for building a secure cryptosystem. Boneh et al. [2] proposed a conversion from a selective-identity CPA-secure IBE cryptosystem to an adaptive CCA-secure IBE cryptosystem. In this conversion, they manipulate the selective-identity CPA-secure IBE encryption function to sign the ciphertext by a one-time strongly unforgeable signature scheme. Therefore, the sender of a message m, first evokes $\mathsf{KeyGen}(\pi)$ to obtain verification key vk and secret key sk. The sender then encrypts the message m using recipient pk and also computes $\mathsf{Sign}_{sk}(\pi, sk, vk, C)$. The final ciphertext is $\langle vk, C, \sigma_c \rangle$. The recipient, after receiving $\langle vk, C, \sigma_c \rangle$, checks if $\mathsf{Verify}(\pi, vk, C, \sigma_c) = \mathsf{Yes}$ holds and then decrypts the ciphertext to obtain the message m.

5   Security Proof

The unique signature scheme is provable to achieve strongly existential unforge-ability and malicious signer resistance against any probabilistic polynomial-time adversary. Due to page limitation all proofs are omitted and can be found in the full version [16].

5.1   Strongly Existential Unfogeability

Theorem 1 states that if the CDH assumption holds, the unique signature scheme achieves strongly existential unforgeability in the random oracle model.

Theorem 1. *Let k be the security parameter. Let $\mathcal{O}_S$ be the signing oracle of the unique signature scheme. Suppose that an adversary queries at most q_s messages to $\mathcal{O}_S$, and each query is handled in time t_s. Let $\mathcal{O}_H$ be the random oracle of hash function $H : \{0,1\}^* \rightarrow \{0,1\}^{n+t-1}$, where $n = 2^t + 1 \in \mathsf{poly}(k)$ and $n \geq \frac{q_s+3}{2}$. Suppose that an adversary queries at most q_h messages to $\mathcal{O}_H$, and each query is handled in time t_h. If the (t, ϵ)-CDH assumption holds, the unique signature scheme achieves $(t - q_h t_h - q_s t_s, q_s, 2e(n-1)\epsilon)$ strongly existential unforgeability, where e is the Euler's number.*

5.2   Malicious Signer Resistance

We define the equivalent set of a signature to prove malicious signer resistance. Given a secret key $sk = \{(a_{0,0}, a_{0,1}), ((a_{1,0}, a_{1,1}), \ldots, ((a_{n-1,0}, a_{n-1,1})\}$ and a signature σ of the unique signature scheme, the equivalent set $E_\sigma^{(sk)}$ of the sig-nature σ under the secret key sk is the collection of hash outputs which result in the signature σ. That is,

$$E_\sigma^{(sk)} = \left\{ z \in \{0,1\}^{n+t-1} \ \middle| \ \begin{matrix} h = \mathsf{LSB}_{t-1}(z) + 1 \\ \prod_{i=0}^{n-1} g^{a_{i,z(i)} a_{[i+h], z([i+h])}} = \sigma \end{matrix} \right\}.$$

We can partition the equivalent set $E_\sigma^{(sk)} = \bigcup_{h=1}^{(n-1)/2} E_{\sigma,h}^{(sk)}$, where

$$E_{\sigma,h}^{(sk)} = \left\{ z \in \{0,1\}^{n+t-1} \ \middle| \ \begin{matrix} \mathsf{LSB}_{t-1}(z) + 1 = h \\ \prod_{i=0}^{n-1} g^{a_{i,z(i)} a_{[i+h], z([i+h])}} = \sigma \end{matrix} \right\}.$$

A malicious signer intends to choose a secret key sk which maximizes the size of an equivalent set $E_\sigma^{(sk)}$. Thus, the malicious signer has the largest chance to find two messages which result in the same signature σ. We give an upper bound for the size of an equivalent set $E_\sigma^{(sk)}$ by analyzing the size of each partition $E_{\sigma,h}^{(sk)}$. Lemma 1 states the upper bound for the size of an equivalent set.

Lemma 1. *Suppose that secret key sk consists of $2n$ secret exponents. The size of an equivalent set $E_\sigma^{(sk)}$ is at most $2^{n/3+t-1}$.*

The unique signature scheme is provable to achieve malicious signer resistance in the random oracle model. Lemma 2 states the result of malicious signer resistance.

Lemma 2. *Let k be the security parameter. Let $\mathcal{O}_H$ be the random oracle of hash function $H : \{0,1\}^* \to \{0,1\}^{n+t-1}$, where $n = 2^t + 1 \in \mathsf{poly}(k)$. If malicious signer S runs in time t_S and queries at most q_h messages to $\mathcal{O}_H$, then the unique signature scheme achieves $\left(t_S, \frac{q_h(q_h-1)}{2}\left(2^{-n-t+1} + 2^{-2n/3}\right) + 3q_h \times 2^{-n-t+1}\right)$ malicious signer resistance.*

We provide a proof of malicious signer resistance under a more relaxed condition. Theorem 2 states that if the hash function is collision resistant and the one-way permutation is indeed one-way, then the unique signature achieves malicious signer resistance.

Theorem 2. *Let k be the security parameter. Let c be a positive real number, where $1/3 < c < 1$. Let t_S be the execution time of a malicious signer S, where $t_S \in \mathsf{poly}(k)$. Suppose that hash function $H : \{0,1\}^* \to \{0,1\}^{n+t-1}$ is (t_H, ϵ_H) collision resistant, where $n = 2^t + 1 \in \mathsf{poly}(k)$. Suppose that one-way permutation $F : \{0,1\}^{n+t-1+n_0} \to \{0,1\}^{n+t-1+n_0}$ is (t_F, ϵ_F) one-way. If we choose $\epsilon_H \le 1 - e^{-\frac{t_S(t_S-1)}{2} \times 2^{-cn-t+1}}$, the unique signature scheme achieves $\left(t_S, \epsilon_H + \frac{t_S(t_S-1)}{2} \times 2^{(1/3-c)n} + 2\epsilon_F + t_S \times 2^{-cn-t+1}\right)$ malicious signer resistance.*

6   Conclusion

We propose a unique signature scheme on groups equipped with bilinear map. The key feature of this study is its efficiency and signature size. Our unique signature scheme produces a signature of only one group element. The security of the proposed scheme is based on the computational Diffie-Hellman assumption in the random oracle model.

References

1. Abdalla, M., Catalano, D., Fiore, D.: Verifiable random functions: Relations to identity-based key encapsulation and new constructions. J. Cryptol. **27**(3), 544–593 (2014). http://dx.doi.org/10.1007/s00145-013-9153-x
2. Boneh, D., Canetti, R., Halevi, S., Katz, J.: Chosen-ciphertext security from identity-based encryption. SIAM J. Comput. **36**(5), 1301–1328 (2006). http://dx.doi.org/10.1137/S009753970544713X
3. Boneh, D., Franklin, M.: Identity-based encryption from the weil pairing. In: Kilian, J. (ed.) CRYPTO 2001. LNCS, vol. 2139, pp. 213–229. Springer, Heidelberg (2001)
4. Boneh, D., Lynn, B., Shacham, H.: Short signatures from the weil pairing. J. Cryptol. **17**(4), 297–319 (2004). http://dx.doi.org/10.1007/s00145-004-0314-9

5. Boneh, D., Shen, E., Waters, B.: Strongly unforgeable signatures based on computational Diffie-Hellman. In: Yung, M., Dodis, Y., Kiayias, A., Malkin, T. (eds.) PKC 2006. LNCS, vol. 3958, pp. 229–240. Springer, Heidelberg (2006)
6. Dodis, Y.: Efficient construction of (distributed) verifiable random functions. In: Desmedt, Y.G. (ed.) Public Key Cryptography – PKC 2003. LNCS, vol. 2567, pp. 1–17. Springer, Heidelberg (2003)
7. Dodis, Y., Yampolskiy, A.: A verifiable random function with short proofs and keys. In: Vaudenay, S. (ed.) PKC 2005. LNCS, vol. 3386, pp. 416–431. Springer, Heidelberg (2005)
8. NIST Report on Cryptographic Key Length and Cryptoperiod. In: Recommendation for Key Management, Special Publication 800-57 Part 1 Rev. 3. NIST, July 2012
9. Goldreich, O., Levin, L.A.: A hard-core predicate for all one-way functions. In: Proceedings of the Twenty-first Annual ACM Symposium on Theory of Computing. STOC '89, pp. 25–32. ACM, New York, NY, USA (1989). http://doi.acm.org/10.1145/73007.73010
10. Goldwasser, S., Ostrovsky, R.: Invariant signatures and non-interactive zero-knowledge proofs are equivalent. In: Brickell, E.F. (ed.) CRYPTO 1992. LNCS, vol. 740, pp. 228–245. Springer, Heidelberg (1993)
11. Hohenberger, S., Waters, B.: Constructing verifiable random functions with large input spaces. In: Gilbert, H. (ed.) EUROCRYPT 2010. LNCS, vol. 6110, pp. 656–672. Springer, Heidelberg (2010)
12. Jager, T.: Verifiable random functions from weaker assumptions. In: Dodis, Y., Nielsen, J.B. (eds.) TCC 2015, Part II. LNCS, vol. 9015, pp. 121–143. Springer, Heidelberg (2015)
13. Kuchta, V., Manulis, M.: Unique aggregate signatures with applications to distributed verifiable random functions. In: Abdalla, M., Nita-Rotaru, C., Dahab, R. (eds.) CANS 2013. LNCS, vol. 8257, pp. 251–270. Springer, Heidelberg (2013)
14. Lysyanskaya, A.: Unique signatures and verifiable random functions from the DH-DDH separation. In: Yung, M. (ed.) CRYPTO 2002. LNCS, vol. 2442, pp. 597–612. Springer, Heidelberg (2002)
15. Micali, S., Rabin, M., Vadhan, S.: Verifiable random functions. In: Proceedings of the 40th Annual Symposium on Foundations of Computer Science. FOCS '99, p. 120. IEEE Computer Society, Washington, DC, USA (1999). http://dl.acm.org/citation.cfm?id=795665.796482
16. Shen, S.T., Rezapour, A., Tzeng, W.G.: Unique signature with short output from cdh assumption. Cryptology ePrint Archive, Report 2015/830 (2015). http://eprint.iacr.org/

Constructions of Unconditionally Secure Broadcast Encryption from Key Predistribution Systems with Trade-Offs Between Communication and Storage

Yohei Watanabe[1](✉) and Junji Shikata[1,2]

[1] Graduate School of Environment and Information Sciences,
Yokohama National University, Yokohama, Japan
watanabe-yohei-xs@ynu.jp
[2] Institute of Advanced Sciences, Yokohama National University,
Yokohama, Japan
shikata@ynu.ac.jp

Abstract. An $(\leq n, \leq \omega)$-one-time secure broadcast encryption schemes (BESs) allows a sender to specify *any* subset of receivers so that only the specified recievers can decrypt a ciphertext. In this paper, we first show an efficient construction of a BES with general ciphertext sizes. Specifically, we propose a generic construction of a BES from key predistribution systems (KPSs) when its ciphertext size is equal to integer multiple of the plaintext size, and our construction includes all known constructions. However, there are many possible combinations of the KPSs to realize the BES in our construction methodology, and therefore, we show that which combination is the best one in the sense that secret-key size can be minimized.

Deriving a tight bound on the secret-key size required for $(\leq n, \leq \omega)$-one-time secure BES with any ciphertext size still remains an open problem. Our result also means that we first show an upper bound on the size of secret keys for general ciphertext sizes.

1 Introduction

Berkovitz [1] introduced a concept of a *broadcast encryption scheme* (BES) [9] which allows multiple receivers to decrypt a logically single ciphertext, and later, Fiat and Naor [9] developed a formal and systematic approach to the construction of BESs. Since then, BESs have been investigated both in the computational security setting [6,8,11,15,18] and the unconditional security setting [1,3,4,7,9,10,12,13,16,17], and used in various situations such as copyright protection in the real world.

Roughly speaking, in the unconditional security setting, there are two types of BESs, a $(t, \leq \omega)$-one-time secure BES [3,4,12,13,16] and an $(\leq n, \leq \omega)$-one-time secure BES [3,9]. In the former BES, a sender encrypts a plaintext for some subset $\mathcal{S}$ of users such that the cardinality of the subset $\mathcal{S}$ is exactly t

© Springer International Publishing Switzerland 2015
M.-H. Au and A. Miyaji (Eds.): ProvSec 2015, LNCS 9451, pp. 489–502, 2015.
DOI: 10.1007/978-3-319-26059-4_27

(i.e. $|\mathcal{S}| = t$). On the other hand, in the latter BES a sender can encrypt a plaintext for *any* subset of users. The latter can be applied to more flexible applications than the former, however, Blundo and Cresti [3] showed the secret-key size of the latter BES is significantly larger than that of the former BES by deriving tight lower bounds on the sizes of secret keys of both BESs in the context of *zero-message broadcast encryption schemes*, which is the same as *key predistribution systems* (KPSs) [2,14]. In other words, their lower bound holds only when the ciphertext size is equal to the plaintext size, and therefore, deriving a tight lower bound on the secret-key size for any ciphertext size still remains an open problem.[1]

Blundo et al. [4] showed that there is a trade-off between the secret-key size and the ciphertext size in $(t, \leq \omega)$-one-time secure BESs. Namely, they derived lower bounds on the secret-key size of $(t, \leq \omega)$-one-time secure BESs when the ciphertext size is equal to an integer multiple of the plaintext size. Later, a trade-off between sizes of ciphertexts and secret keys in $(t, \leq \omega)$-one-time secure BESs was improved by Padró et al. [16]. There is no doubt that such a trade-off in $(\leq n, \leq \omega)$-one-time secure BESs exists, however there is no concrete analysis of the trade-off as mentioned above.

Our Contribution. As explained above, an $(\leq n, \leq \omega)$-one-time secure BES provides more flexible functionality than a $(t, \leq \omega)$-one-time secure BES. However, only two constructions of an $(\leq n, \leq \omega)$-one-time secure BES are known so far: One is the Fiat–Naor construction [9] when the ciphertext size is equal to the plaintext size; and another is a trivial construction from the one-time pad when the maximum ciphertext size is n times larger than the plaintext size. In this paper, we propose a generic construction of an $(\leq n, \leq \omega)$-BES from KPSs with more general ciphertext sizes. Our generic construction includes them, namely, it can be regarded as a natural extension of the two above constructions. Specifically, we show that, if the maximum ciphertext size is δ times larger than the plaintext size, an $(\leq n, \leq \omega)$-one-time secure BES can be constructed from δ KPSs. However, for fixed n, ω, and δ, there are many possible combinations of the KPSs to realize the $(\leq n, \leq \omega)$-one-time secure BES in our construction methodology. In addition, we analyze parameters of all possible combinations in our construction methodology, and we show which combination is the best one in the sense that secret-key size can be minimized. Our (optimized) construction provides a *flexible* parameter setup (i.e. we can adjust the secret-key sizes) by arbitrarily choosing δ based on channel capacity, etc.

As explained above, deriving a tight bound[2] on the secret-key size required for $(\leq n, \leq \omega)$-one-time secure BESs for any ciphertext size is an open problem. As the first step for solving the problem, our work shows an upper bound on the size of secret keys required for $(\leq n, \leq \omega)$-one-time secure BESs for general

---

[1] Unconditionally secure protocols usually require long secret keys, and therefore it is important to show the minimal key size (i.e. derive a tight lower bound on the secret-key size).

[2] In general, for deriving a tight bound, it is necessary to show upper/lower bounds with tightness.

ciphertext sizes by means of natural extension of the existing constructions for the BESs.

Notations. For $n \in \mathbb{N}$, let $[n] := \{1, 2, \ldots, n\}$. The calligraphy $\mathcal{X}$ indicates a set, in particular, let $\mathcal{U} := \{U_1, U_2, \ldots, U_n\}$ be a set of users. Except for a user U_i and a set of colluders W, the roman capital X indicates a random variable which takes values in $\mathcal{X}$ (e.g., A, B, and C are random variables which take values in $\mathcal{A}, \mathcal{B}$, and $\mathcal{C}$, respectively). For a random variable X, $H(X)$ denotes the Shannon entropy of X.

2   Broadcast Encryption and Key Predistribution

In this section, we describe the mathematical models of unconditionally secure broadcast encryption and key predistribution systems.

2.1   One-Time Secure Broadcast Encryption Scheme

As explained in the introduction, we deal with a BES where *any* subset of $\mathcal{U}$ can be specified as a privileged set, and we call such a BES simply "BES".

Formally, the definition of a BES is as follows. Let $\mathcal{M}$ be a set of possible plaintexts. For any subset $\mathcal{J} := \{U_{i_1}, \ldots, U_{i_j}\} \subset \mathcal{U}$, let $\mathcal{C}_{\mathcal{J}}$ be a set of all possible ciphertexts for the privileged set $\mathcal{J}$, and let $\mathcal{C} := \bigcup_{\mathcal{J} \subset \mathcal{U}} \mathcal{C}_{\mathcal{J}}$. Let $\mathcal{EK}$ be a set of possible encryption keys, and let $\mathcal{DK}_i$ be a set of possible decryption keys for U_i. Let $\mathcal{DK} := \bigcup_{i=1}^{n} \mathcal{DK}_i$.

Definition 1 (BES). *A broadcast encryption scheme (BES for short) Π involves $n + 1$ entities, a sender E and n users $\mathcal{U}$, and consists of the following three-tuple of algorithms (Setup, Enc, Dec) with four spaces, $\mathcal{M}, \mathcal{C}, \mathcal{EK}$, and $\mathcal{DK}$, where all of the above algorithms except Setup are deterministic and all of the above spaces are finite.*

1. *$(ek, dk_1, \ldots, dk_n) \leftarrow Setup(n)$: It takes the number of users n as input, and outputs an encryption key $ek \in \mathcal{EK}$, and n decryption keys $(dk_1, \ldots, dk_n) \in \prod_{i=1}^{n} \mathcal{DK}_i$.*
2. *$c_{\mathcal{S}} \leftarrow Enc(ek, m, \mathcal{S})$: It takes an encryption key ek, a plaintext $m \in \mathcal{M}$, and a privileged set $\mathcal{S} \subset \mathcal{U}$ as input, and outputs a ciphertext $c_{\mathcal{S}}$.*
3. *m or $\perp \leftarrow Dec(dk_i, c_{\mathcal{S}}, \mathcal{S}, U_i)$: It takes a decryption key dk_i of a user U_i, the ciphertext $c_{\mathcal{S}}$, the privileged set $\mathcal{S}$, and the identity U_i as input, and outputs m if $U_i \in \mathcal{S}$ or $\perp$ if $U_i \notin \mathcal{S}$.*

In the above model, there is the following correctness requirement: For all $n \in \mathbb{N}$, all $(ek, dk_1, \ldots, dk_n) \leftarrow Setup(n)$, all $m \in \mathcal{M}$, all $\mathcal{S} \subset \mathcal{U}$, and all $U_i \in \mathcal{S}$, $m \leftarrow Dec(dk_i, Enc(ek, m, \mathcal{S}), \mathcal{S}, U_i)$, or equivalently it holds $H(M \mid DK_i, C_{\mathcal{S}}) = 0$ for any $U_i \in \mathcal{S}$.

In a BES, we assume the one-time model where it is allowed for the sender to encrypt a plaintext and broadcast a ciphertext only once.

We consider perfect secrecy against at most ω colluders. Namely, at most ω colluders who are not included in the privileged set cannot get any information on the underlying plaintext from the ciphertext. For any $\mathcal{J} := \{U_{i_1}, \ldots, U_{i_j}\} \subset \mathcal{U}$, let $\mathcal{DK}_{\mathcal{J}} := \mathcal{DK}_{i_1} \times \cdots \times \mathcal{DK}_{i_j}$ be a set of possible secret keys of $\mathcal{J}$. Formally, security of a BES is defined as follows.

Definition 2 (Security of BES). *Let Π be a BES. Π is said to be $(\le n, \le \omega)$-one-time secure if the following conditions are satisfied: For any privileged set $\mathcal{S} \subset \mathcal{U}$, and any set of colluders $W \subset \mathcal{U}$ such that $\mathcal{S} \cap W = \emptyset$ and $|W| \le \omega$, it holds that $H(M \mid C_{\mathcal{S}}, DK_W) = H(M)$.*

In this paper, we focus on an $(\le n, \le \omega)$-one-time secure BES when the maximum ciphertext size is an integer multiple of the plaintext size, whereas ciphertexts in most of the previous $(\le n, \le \omega)$-one-time secure BESs were assumed to be the same size as plaintexts.

Definition 3. *For an $(\le n, \le \omega)$-one-time secure BES Π, we define*

$$\delta := \frac{\max_{\mathcal{S} \subset \mathcal{U}} \log |C_{\mathcal{S}}|}{\log |\mathcal{M}|}.$$

Then, Π is said to be $(\le n, \le \omega; \delta)$-one-time secure.

2.2 Key Predistribution System

Formally, the definition of KPS is given as follows. For any subset $\mathcal{J} := \{U_{i_1}, \ldots, U_{i_j}\} \subset \mathcal{U}$, let $\mathcal{K}_{\mathcal{J}}$ be a set of all possible session keys for the privileged set $\mathcal{J}$, and let $\mathcal{K} := \bigcup_{\mathcal{J} \subset \mathcal{U}} \mathcal{K}_{\mathcal{J}}$. Let $\mathcal{UK}_i$ be a set of possible secret keys for U_i, and $\mathcal{UK} := \bigcup_{i=1}^n \mathcal{UK}_i$.

Definition 4 (KPS). *A key predistribution system (KPS for short) Φ involves $n+1$ entities, a trusted initializer TA and n users $\mathcal{U}$, and consists of the following two-tuple of algorithms (Init, Der) with two spaces, $\mathcal{K}$ and $\mathcal{UK}$, where all of the above algorithms except Init are deterministic and all of the above spaces are finite.*

1. *$(uk_1, \ldots, uk_n) \leftarrow Init(n)$: It takes the number of users n as input, and outputs n secret keys $(uk_1, \ldots, uk_n) \in \prod_{i=1}^n \mathcal{UK}_i$. Here, we also define uk, which is called a master key, as a randomness required for determining $uk_1, \ldots, uk_n$.[3]*
2. *$k_{\mathcal{S}} \leftarrow Der(uk_i, \mathcal{S})$: It takes a secret key uk_i of a user U_i, and a privileged set $\mathcal{S} \subset \mathcal{U}$ as input, and outputs a session key $k_{\mathcal{S}}$ for $\mathcal{S}$.*

---

[3] Although uk is not explicitly described in several papers on KPSs [2,4,5,12,14], we introduce uk for measuring actual sizes of secret keys which TA has to generate. It is reasonable to consider uk since Blundo and Cresti [3] also dealt with uk in another context. We note that uk is actually not used in the scheme, and hence we do not explicitly describe it in output. We can also see uk as a deterministic function for deriving secret keys $uk_1, \ldots uk_n$.

In the above model, there is the following correctness requirement: For all $n \in \mathbb{N}$, all $(uk_1, \ldots, uk_n) \leftarrow Init(n)$, and all $\mathcal{S} := \{U_{i_1}, \ldots, U_{i_j}\} \subset \mathcal{U}$, $Der(uk_{i_1}, \mathcal{S}) = \cdots = Der(uk_{i_j}, \mathcal{S})$, or equivalently it holds $H(K_{\mathcal{S}} \mid UK_i) = 0$ for any $U_i \in \mathcal{S}$.

As in a BES, we consider perfect secrecy against at most ω colluders. Namely, a set W of at most ω colluders cannot obtain any information on a session key for any set $\mathcal{S}$ such that $\mathcal{S} \cap W = \emptyset$ from their secret keys. For any $\mathcal{J} := \{U_{i_1}, \ldots, U_{i_j}\} \subset \mathcal{U}$, let $UK_{\mathcal{J}} := UK_{i_1} \times \cdots \times UK_{i_j}$ be a set of possible secret keys of $\mathcal{J}$. Formally, security of a KPS is defined as follows.

Definition 5 (Security of KPS). *Let Φ be a KPS. Φ is said to be an $(\leq n, \leq \omega)$-KPS if the following conditions are satisfied: For any privileged set $\mathcal{S} \subset \mathcal{U}$, and any set of colluders $W \subset \mathcal{U}$ such that $\mathcal{S} \cap W = \emptyset$ and $|W| \leq \omega$, it holds that $H(K_{\mathcal{S}} \mid UK_W) = H(K_{\mathcal{S}})$.*

We describe some known results on $(\leq n, \leq \omega)$-KPSs. First, we describe tight lower bounds on the secret-key size required for $(\leq n, \leq \omega)$-KPSs. In [3], these bound were first derived in the context of *zero-message broadcast encryption schemes*, which is the same as KPSs. In the following proposition, for all $\mathcal{S}, \mathcal{S}' \subset \mathcal{U}$ it is assumed that $H(K_{\mathcal{S}}) = H(K_{\mathcal{S}'})$ for simplicity. This common entropy is denoted by $H(K)$.

Proposition 1 ([3]). *Let Φ be an $(\leq n, \leq \omega)$-KPS. Then, the following lower bounds hold:*

$$(i)\ H(UK) \geq \sum_{j=0}^{\omega} \binom{n}{j} H(K),$$

$$(ii)\ H(UK_i) \geq \sum_{j=0}^{\omega} \binom{n-1}{j} H(K)\ \text{for any } i \in [n].$$

Next, we define some notations before describing a construction of an $(\leq n, \leq \omega)$-KPS. We define the following families of sets:

$$\mathcal{W} := \{W \subset \mathcal{U} \mid |W| \leq \omega\},$$
$$\mathcal{W}^{(i)} := \{W \subset \mathcal{U} \setminus \{U_i\} \mid |W| \leq \omega\},$$
$$\mathcal{W}(\mathcal{S}) := \{W \in \mathcal{W} \mid W \cap \mathcal{S} = \emptyset \wedge |W| = \min(\omega, n - |\mathcal{S}|)\}.$$

An optimal construction of an $(\leq n, \leq \omega)$-KPS is as follows. This construction can be easily obtained from an $(\leq n, \leq \omega)$-one-time secure BES proposed by Fiat and Naor [9]. This *optimal* means the construction attains the lower bounds, which were described in Proposition 1, with equalities.

1. $(uk_1, \ldots, uk_n) \leftarrow Init(n)$: Let q be a prime power such that $q > n$, and $\mathbb{F}_q$ be a finite field with q elements. For every $W \in \mathcal{W}$, it chooses $r_W \in \mathbb{F}_q$ uniformly at random. Then, it outputs $uk_i := \{r_W \mid W \in \mathcal{W}^{(i)}\}$ $(1 \leq i \leq n)$. Also, $uk := \{r_W \mid W \in \mathcal{W}\}$.
2. $k_{\mathcal{S}} \leftarrow Der(uk_i, \mathcal{S})$: For any privileged set $\mathcal{S}$, it computes and outputs a session key $k_{\mathcal{S}} := \sum_{W \in \mathcal{W}(\mathcal{S})} r_W,$

As seen above, the above construction is optimal since the size of secret keys is $\log|\mathcal{UK}_i| = \sum_{j=0}^{\omega} \binom{n-1}{j} \log q$. Moreover, the size of master keys uk (i.e. the number of random bits that TA has to generate) is $\log|\mathcal{UK}| = \sum_{j=0}^{\omega} \binom{n}{j} \log q$.

2.3 Known Constructions of $(\leq N, \leq \omega)$-One-Time Secure BES from KPS

We briefly describe two known constructions of $(\leq n, \leq \omega)$-one-time secure BESs from KPSs when $\delta = 1$ and $\delta = n$, respectively.

First, for the case $\delta = 1$ we describe an $(\leq n, \leq \omega; 1)$-one-time secure BES, which is proposed by Fiat and Naor [9], from the $(\leq n, \leq \omega)$-KPS described in the previous subsection and the one-time pad. Specifically, a sender obtains a secret key for a privileged set from the $(\leq n, \leq \omega)$-KPS, and then encrypts a plaintext with the secret key by the one-time pad. Blundo and Cresti [3] showed this Fiat–Naor construction is *optimal* when $\delta = 1$.

The second one is an $(\leq n, \leq \omega; n)$-one-time secure BES from n $(\leq 1, \leq 0)$-KPSs (i.e. from n one-time pads), which we call the trivial construction, for the case $\delta = n$. Namely, a sender generates n independent secret keys of the one-time pad, and each decryption key is one of the secret keys. The sender encrypts a plaintext with secret keys of the users in a privileged set by using the one-time pad, and an entire ciphertext is a concatenation of the resulting ciphertexts. This trivial construction is obviously optimal.

As can be seen in related works [3,9,12], it is meaningful to consider the case $\delta \geq 1$, and the case $\delta > n$ is not interesting since secret-key sizes cannot become shorter than those in the case $\delta = n$ due to a tight lower bound on secret-key sizes required for the one-time pad. Therefore, in the next section we propose a generic construction of an $(\leq n, \leq \omega; \delta)$-one-time secure BES, which is an intermediate construction between the above two constructions, for arbitrary $\delta \in [n]$.

3 Generic Construction of $(\leq N, \leq \omega; \delta)$-One-Time Secure BES

We propose a generic construction of an $(\leq n, \leq \omega; \delta)$-one-time secure BES from KPSs. Then, we show its instantiation such that the secret-key size can be minimized in it.

3.1 Simple Construction from KPSs

A basic idea is simple. First, we split a user set $\mathcal{U}$ into δ disjoint subsets $\mathcal{U}_1, \ldots, \mathcal{U}_\delta$ of $\mathcal{U}$. Then, we assign an $(\leq|\mathcal{U}_i|, \leq \omega_i)$-KPS with each subset $\mathcal{U}_i$, where $\omega_i := \min\{\omega, |\mathcal{U}_i| - 1\}$ since an $(\leq|\mathcal{U}_i|, \leq \omega)$-KPS such that $\omega \geq |\mathcal{U}|$ is meaningless. For a privileged set $\mathcal{S}$, let $\mathcal{S}_i := \mathcal{U}_i \cap \mathcal{S}$. Then, a session key $k_{\mathcal{S}_i}$ is generated by $(\leq|\mathcal{U}_i|, \leq \omega)$-KPS, and an entire ciphertext $c_{\mathcal{S}}$ is $c_{\mathcal{S}} := (m \oplus k_{\mathcal{S}_1}, \ldots, m \oplus k_{\mathcal{S}_\delta})$.

However, there are various combinations of δ natural numbers such that the sum of the numbers is n. Formally, for any natural number $n \in \mathbb{N}$ and $\delta \in [n]$, we define the following set:

$$\mathcal{L}(n,\delta) := \left\{ \boldsymbol{L} := (\ell_1, \ell_2, \ldots, \ell_\delta) \in \mathbb{N}^\delta \middle| (\ell_1 \geq \ell_2 \geq \cdots \geq \ell_\delta) \wedge \sum_{i=1}^{\delta} \ell_i = n \right\}.$$

$\mathcal{L}(n,\delta)$ means a set of δ natural numbers such that the sum of the numbers is n, therefore we have to choose $\boldsymbol{L}$ such that secret-key sizes are minimized for fixed n, ω, and δ. Hence, we will clarify such an optimal condition for minimizing secret-key sizes in the next subsection.

Formally, our generic construction of a BES $\Pi = \{Setup, Enc, Dec\}$ from KPSs $\Phi_i = \{Init_i, Der_i\}$ ($1 \leq i \leq \delta$) is given as follows.

- $(ek, dk_1, \ldots, dk_n) \leftarrow Setup(n)$: Choose $\boldsymbol{L} \in \mathcal{L}(n,\delta)$. Without loss of generality, let $\mathcal{U}_i := \{U_{\sum_{j=1}^{i-1} \ell_j + 1}, \ldots, U_{\sum_{j=1}^{i} \ell_j}\}$.[4] Run $Init_i(\ell_i) \to (uk_{\sum_{j=1}^{i-1} \ell_j + 1}, \ldots, uk_{\sum_{j=1}^{i} \ell_j})$ ($1 \leq i \leq \delta$), and let $uk^{(i)}$ be the corresponding master key. Set $ek := (uk^{(1)}, \ldots, uk^{(\delta)})$ and $dk_i := uk_i$.
- $c_{\mathcal{S}} \leftarrow Enc(ek, m, \mathcal{S})$: Choose $\mathcal{S} \subset \mathcal{U}$ and let $\mathcal{S}_i := \mathcal{S} \cap \mathcal{U}_i$ ($1 \leq i \leq \delta$). If $\mathcal{S}_i \neq \emptyset$, then for some $U_j \in \mathcal{S}_i$, run $Der_i(uk_j, \mathcal{S}_i) \to k_{\mathcal{S}_i}$ ($1 \leq i \leq \delta$). Note that any uk_j can be derived from $uk^{(i)}$. Set $c_{\mathcal{S}} := (m \oplus k_{\mathcal{S}_i})_{\mathcal{S}_i \neq \emptyset}$.
- m or $\perp \leftarrow Dec(dk_i, c_{\mathcal{S}}, \mathcal{S}, U_i)$: Parse $c_{\mathcal{S}}$ as $(c_{\mathcal{S}_1}, \ldots, c_{\mathcal{S}_k})$ and suppose $U_i \in \mathcal{U}_j$. If $U_i \in \mathcal{S}_j$, compute $k_{\mathcal{S}_j} \leftarrow Der(uk_i, \mathcal{S}_j)$ and then obtain $m = c_{\mathcal{S}_j} \oplus k_{\mathcal{S}_j}$.

Theorem 1. *The above construction of Π given by $(\leq \ell_i, \leq \omega_i)$-one-time secure KPSs Φ_i ($1 \leq i \leq \delta$) is $(\leq n, \leq \omega; \delta)$-one-time secure.*

Proof. It is not difficult to see the above scheme is $(\leq n, \leq \omega; \delta)$-one-time secure. The maximum ciphertext size of the above scheme is obviously $\delta \log |\mathcal{M}|$ since if each $\mathcal{S}_i \neq \emptyset$, then a ciphertext size is δ times longer than the underlying plaintext size.

We show the above scheme is $(\leq n, \leq \omega; \delta)$-one-time secure. Without loss of generality, suppose $\mathcal{S}$ such that $|\mathcal{S}| = n - \omega$.

We first consider the case that $\mathcal{S}$ contains at least one user from $\mathcal{U}_i$ (i.e., each $\mathcal{S}_i \neq \emptyset$ and $c_{\mathcal{S}} = (c_{\mathcal{S}_1}, \ldots, c_{\mathcal{S}_\delta})$). Let $W := \mathcal{U} \setminus \mathcal{S}$ and $W_i := \mathcal{U}_i \setminus \mathcal{S}_i$. Then, we have

$$H(M \mid C_{\mathcal{S}}, DK_W) = H(M \mid M \oplus K_{\mathcal{S}_1}, \ldots, M \oplus K_{\mathcal{S}_\delta}, DK_W).$$

However, in each $(\leq \ell_i, \leq \omega_i)$-KPS, W_i ($|W_i| \leq \omega_i$) cannot get any information on a session key $k_{\mathcal{S}_i}$ from security definition of the KPS (Definition 5). In addition, W_i cannot obtain any information on session keys $k_{\mathcal{S}_1}, \ldots, k_{\mathcal{S}_{i-1}}, k_{\mathcal{S}_{i+1}}, \ldots, k_{\mathcal{S}_\delta}$ since W_i's secret keys are independent of them. Namely, for $i \in [\delta]$, we have

---

[4] For example, when $n = 9$, $\delta = 3$, and $\ell_i = 3$ ($i = 1, 2, 3$), then $\mathcal{U}_1 := \{U_1, U_2, U_3\}$, $\mathcal{U}_2 := \{U_4, U_5, U_6\}$, and $\mathcal{U}_3 := \{U_7, U_8, U_9\}$.

$$H(K_{\mathcal{S}_i} \mid DK_{W_1}, \ldots, DK_{W_\delta}) = H(K_{\mathcal{S}_i}). \tag{1}$$

Therefore, we have $H(M \mid C_{\mathcal{S}}, DK_W) = H(M \mid C_{\mathcal{S}})$ since DK_W is independent of M and $\{M \oplus K_{\mathcal{S}_i}\}_{1 \le i \le \delta}$ from (1). Moreover, from security of the one-time pad, we have $H(M \mid C_{\mathcal{S}}) = H(M)$.

Next, we prove the case $\mathcal{S}$ such that at least one $\mathcal{S}_i = \emptyset$. Suppose $\mathcal{S}$ such that $\mathcal{S}_{i_1}, \ldots, \mathcal{S}_{i_j}$ are empty sets (then each $W_{i_k} = \mathcal{U}_{i_k}$ $(1 \le k \le j)$), and let $\widetilde{W} := \bigcup_{k=1}^{j} \mathcal{U}_{i_k}$ and $\widehat{W} := W \setminus \widetilde{W}$. Then, $\widetilde{W}$ cannot obtain any information on the underlying plaintext from $c_{\mathcal{S}} = (c_{\mathcal{S}_{i_{j+1}}}, \ldots, c_{\mathcal{S}_{i_\delta}})$ due to security of the one-time pad. Further, $\widehat{W}$ cannot also get any information on the plaintext as in the former case (the case of $\mathcal{S}$ such that every $\mathcal{S}_i \ne \emptyset$). □

3.2   Optimal Parameters for Minimal Keys

To obtain the most efficient scheme in terms of the secret-key size, we have to carefully choose a combination of $(\le \ell_i, \le \omega)$-KPSs. We obtain the following theorem.

Theorem 2. *When we apply an optimal construction of each KPS Φ_i $(1 \le i \le \delta)$ to the resulting $(\le n, \le \omega; \delta)$-one-time secure BES Π, then sizes of the secret keys required in the above construction are given by*

$$(i) \ \log |\mathcal{EK}| = \sum_{i=1}^{\delta} \sum_{j=0}^{\omega_i} \binom{\ell_i}{j} \log q,$$

$$(ii) \ \sum_{i=1}^{n} \log |\mathcal{DK}_i| = \sum_{i=1}^{\delta} \left(\ell_i \sum_{j=0}^{\omega_i} \binom{\ell_i - 1}{j} \right) \log q.$$

Moreover, $L \in \mathcal{L}(n, \delta)$ minimizes the sizes of the encryption keys if it satisfies the following conditions:

$$\begin{cases} \text{arbitrary } L & \text{if } \omega = 0, \\ L = (n - (\delta - 1), 1, \ldots, 1) & \text{if } \omega = 1, \\ \ell_1 - \ell_\delta = 0 & \text{if } \omega \ge 2 \land n/\delta \in \mathbb{N}, \\ \ell_1 - \ell_\delta = 1 & \text{otherwise.} \end{cases}$$

On the other hand, $L \in \mathcal{L}(n, \delta)$ minimizes the sizes of the decryption keys if it satisfies the following conditions:

$$\begin{cases} \text{arbitrary } L & \text{if } \omega = 0, \\ \ell_1 - \ell_\delta = 0 & \text{if } \omega \ge 1 \land n/\delta \in \mathbb{N}, \\ \ell_1 - \ell_\delta = 1 & \text{otherwise.} \end{cases}$$

We prove the above theorem by solving a certain type of optimization problems through the following approach. To prove that *even*[5] L minimizes secret-key sizes, we change how to sum terms as follows: For the encryption-key size, we have

---

[5] L is said to be *even* when $\ell_1 - \ell_\delta = 0$ if $n/\delta \in \mathbb{N}$ or $\ell_1 - \ell_\delta = 1$ if $n/\delta \notin \mathbb{N}$.

$$\sum_{i=1}^{\delta}\sum_{j=0}^{\omega_i}\binom{\ell_i}{j} = \sum_{j=1}^{\widetilde{\omega}}\sum_{i=1}^{k_j}\binom{\ell_i}{\widetilde{\omega}-(j-1)} + \sum_{i=1}^{\delta}\binom{\ell_i}{0}$$

$$= \sum_{i=1}^{k_1}\binom{\ell_i}{\widetilde{\omega}} + \sum_{i=1}^{k_2}\binom{\ell_i}{\widetilde{\omega}-1} + \cdots + \sum_{i=1}^{k_{\widetilde{\omega}}}\binom{\ell_i}{1} + \sum_{i=1}^{\delta}\binom{\ell_i}{0},$$

where $\widetilde{\omega} := \min\{\omega, \ell_1 - 1(= \omega_1)\}$ and $k_\alpha := \beta$ such that $\ell_\beta > \widetilde{\omega} - (\alpha - 1) \geq \ell_{\beta+1}$ $(1 \leq \alpha \leq \widetilde{\omega})$. Then, we prove a lower bound for each $\sum_{i=1}^{k_j}\binom{\ell_i}{\widetilde{\omega}-(j-1)}$ $(1 \leq j \leq \widetilde{\omega})$ in the case $k_j = \delta$ (Lemma 1) and in the case $k_j < \delta$ (Lemma 2), respectively. Specifically, in proofs of these lemmas we show that $\sum_{i=1}^{k_j}\binom{\ell_i}{\widetilde{\omega}-(j-1)}$ given by any "not even" L is always larger than or equal to that given by "even" L. (To be precise, except for the case $k_1 < \delta$ (Corollary 1).) We also prove the case of the decryption-key sizes in a similar way (Lemma 3). The formal proof is as follows.

Proof (Theorem 2). For $L \in \mathcal{L}(n, \delta)$, we define

$$F(L, \omega) := \sum_{i=1}^{\delta}\sum_{j=0}^{\omega_i}\binom{\ell_i}{j} \quad \text{and} \quad G(L, \omega) := \sum_{i=1}^{\delta}\left(\ell_i \sum_{j=0}^{\omega_i}\binom{\ell_i - 1}{j}\right).$$

Obviously, $F(L, 0) = \delta$ and $G(L, 0) = n$ for any $L \in \mathcal{L}(n, \delta)$.

First, we show the case of $F(L, \omega)$ when $\omega > 0$ and $n/\delta \in \mathbb{N}$. To prove this, we show the following lemma. Due to space limitation, we omit proofs of lemmas which will appear in this proof. The full proofs will appear in the full version of this paper.

Lemma 1. *For any $a, j \in \mathbb{N}$ and any $r \in \{0, 1, \ldots, a\}$, choose any $b_i \in \mathbb{Z}$ $(1 \leq i \leq j)$ such that $b_1 \geq \cdots \geq b_j \geq -(a - r)$, and $\sum_{i=1}^{j} b_i = 0$. Then, it holds that*

$$j\binom{a}{r} \leq \binom{a + b_1}{r} + \binom{a + b_2}{r} + \cdots + \binom{a + b_j}{r}.$$

The equality holds if and only if $r = 0$ or $r = 1$.

We have the following corollary.

Corollary 1. *For any $a, j \in \mathbb{N}$, choose any $b_i \in \mathbb{Z}$ such that $b_1 \geq \cdots \geq b_k > -(a - 1) = b_{k+1} = \cdots = b_j$ and $\sum_{i=1}^{j} b_i = 0$. Then, it holds that*

$$j\binom{a}{1} > \binom{a + b_1}{1} + \binom{a + b_2}{1} + \cdots + \binom{a + b_k}{1}.$$

Obviously, the value is minimized when $k = 1$, namely it holds

$$j\binom{a}{1} > \binom{a + b_1}{1} = \binom{ja - (j - 1)}{1}.$$

This corollary means that if $r = 1$ and some terms are removed from the right side in Lemma 1, then the inequality sign is reversed.

Then, we can prove the case $\omega = 1$ from Corollary 1. Specifically, if $\omega = 1$, then we have

$$F(\boldsymbol{L}, 1) = \sum_{i=1}^{k} \binom{\ell_i}{1} + \sum_{i=0}^{\delta} \binom{\ell_i}{0} = \sum_{i=1}^{k} \binom{\ell_i}{1} + \delta,$$

where $\ell_1 \geq \cdots \geq \ell_k > 1 = \ell_{k+1} = \cdots = \ell_\delta$. Therefore, the minimum value of $F(\boldsymbol{L}, 1)$ is given when $\boldsymbol{L} = (n - (\delta - 1), 1, \ldots, 1)$ by setting $j := \delta$ and $a := n/\delta$ in Corollary 1.

Next, we show the following lemma, which is a variant of Corollary 1. The lemma gives a contrary result to Corollary 1 when $r \geq 2$.

Lemma 2. *For any $a, j \in \mathbb{N}$ and any $r \in \{2, \ldots, a\}$, choose any $b_i \in \mathbb{Z}$ such that $b_1 \geq \cdots \geq b_k > -(a - r) \geq b_{k+1} \geq \cdots \geq b_j > -a$ and $\sum_{i=1}^{j} b_i = 0$. Then, it holds that*

$$j \binom{a}{r} < \binom{a + b_1}{r} + \binom{a + b_2}{r} + \cdots + \binom{a + b_k}{r}.$$

Further, it holds that

$$\binom{a + b_1}{r} + \binom{a + b_2}{r} + \cdots + \binom{a + b_k}{r} - j \binom{a}{r} > \sum_{m=1}^{\lambda} \binom{a + \alpha_m}{r - 1},$$

where $\lambda := \sum_{i=1}^{k} b_i - (j - k)(a - r)$, and $\alpha_m \in \mathbb{N}$ $(1 \leq m \leq \lambda)$ such that $1 \leq \alpha_m \leq b_1$.

We then prove the case $\omega \geq 2$ and $n/\delta \in \mathbb{N}$. Now, let $a := n/\delta$. Then, for $\widehat{\boldsymbol{L}} = (a, \ldots, a)$, we express $F(\widehat{\boldsymbol{L}}, \omega)$ as

$$F(\widehat{\boldsymbol{L}}, \omega) = \delta \binom{a}{\hat{\omega}} + \delta \binom{a}{\hat{\omega} - 1} + \cdots + \delta \binom{a}{1} + \delta \binom{a}{0},$$

where $\hat{\omega} := \min\{\omega, a - 1\}$.

In the same manner, for any $\widetilde{\boldsymbol{L}} \in \mathcal{L}(n, \delta) \setminus \{\widehat{\boldsymbol{L}}\}$, $F(\widetilde{\boldsymbol{L}}, \omega)$ can be expressed as

$$F(\widetilde{\boldsymbol{L}}, \omega) = \sum_{i=1}^{k_1} \binom{\ell_i}{\tilde{\omega}} + \sum_{i=1}^{k_2} \binom{\ell_i}{\tilde{\omega} - 1} + \cdots + \sum_{i=1}^{k_{\tilde{\omega}}} \binom{\ell_i}{1} + \sum_{i=1}^{\delta} \binom{\ell_i}{0},$$

where $\tilde{\omega} := \min\{\omega, \ell_1 - 1\}$, $k_m := i$ such that $\ell_i > \tilde{\omega} - (m - 1) \geq \ell_{i+1}$ $(1 \leq m \leq \tilde{\omega})$. Note that $k_1 \leq \cdots \leq k_{\tilde{\omega}}$.

Then, we consider the following two cases: (i) $\hat{\omega} = \tilde{\omega}$; and (ii) $\hat{\omega} < \tilde{\omega}$. Note that the case $\hat{\omega} > \tilde{\omega}$ would never occur since $\ell_1 > a$.

We first prove the case (i). Then, we have

$$F(\widetilde{\boldsymbol{L}}, \omega) - F(\widehat{\boldsymbol{L}}, \omega)$$

$$= \left(\sum_{i=1}^{k_1} \binom{\ell_i}{\hat{\omega}} - \delta \binom{a}{\hat{\omega}} \right) + \cdots$$

$$+ \left(\sum_{i=1}^{k_{\hat{\omega}-1}} \binom{\ell_i}{2} - \delta \binom{a}{2} \right) + \left(\sum_{i=1}^{k_{\hat{\omega}}} \binom{\ell_i}{1} - \delta \binom{a}{1} \right)$$

$$= \left(\sum_{i=1}^{k_1} \binom{\ell_i}{\hat{\omega}} - \delta \binom{a}{\hat{\omega}} \right) + \cdots$$

$$+ \left(\sum_{i=1}^{k_{\hat{\omega}-1}} \binom{\ell_i}{2} - \delta \binom{a}{2} \right) + \left(\sum_{i=1}^{k_{\hat{\omega}}} \binom{\ell_i}{1} - \sum_{i=1}^{\delta} \binom{\ell_i}{1} \right) \quad (2)$$

$$> \sum_{m=1}^{\lambda_1} \binom{a + \alpha_m^{(1)}}{\hat{\omega} - 1} + \cdots + \sum_{m=1}^{\lambda_{\hat{\omega}-1}} \binom{a + \alpha_m^{(\hat{\omega}-1)}}{1} + \left(\sum_{i=1}^{k_{\hat{\omega}}} \binom{\ell_i}{1} - \sum_{i=1}^{\delta} \binom{\ell_i}{1} \right) \quad (3)$$

$$> 0,$$

where $\lambda_i := \sum_{j=1}^{k_i} \ell_j - (\delta - k_i)(a - (\hat{\omega} - i))$, and $\alpha_m^{(k)} \in \mathbb{N}$ ($1 \le k \le \hat{\omega} - 1$) such that $1 \le \alpha_m^{(k)} \le \ell_1 - a$, (2) follows from Lemma 1, and (3) follows from Lemma 2.

In the case (ii), we have

$$F(\widetilde{\boldsymbol{L}}, \omega) - F(\widehat{\boldsymbol{L}}, \omega)$$

$$= \sum_{i=1}^{k_1} \binom{\ell_i}{\tilde{\omega}} + \cdots + \left(\sum_{i=1}^{k_{\tilde{\omega}-\hat{\omega}+1}} \binom{\ell_i}{\hat{\omega}} - \delta \binom{a}{\hat{\omega}} \right) + \cdots$$

$$+ \left(\sum_{i=1}^{k_{\tilde{\omega}-1}} \binom{\ell_i}{2} - \delta \binom{a}{2} \right) + \left(\sum_{i=1}^{k_{\tilde{\omega}}} \binom{\ell_i}{1} - \delta \binom{a}{1} \right).$$

Therefore, we can also prove $F(\widetilde{\boldsymbol{L}}, \omega) - F(\widehat{\boldsymbol{L}}, \omega) > 0$ in a similar way to the case (i). Hence, if $\omega \ge 2 \wedge n/\delta \in \mathbb{N}$, the minimum value of $F(\boldsymbol{L}, \omega)$ is given when $\ell_1 - \ell_\delta = 0$.

Similarly, we can prove the case $\omega = 1 \wedge n/\delta \notin \mathbb{N}$ and $\omega \ge 2 \wedge n/\delta \notin \mathbb{N}$, and then the minimum value of $F(\boldsymbol{L}, \omega)$ is given when $\boldsymbol{L} = (n - (\delta - 1), 1, \ldots, 1)$ and $\ell_1 - \ell_\delta = 1$, respectively, since we can express $n = \delta a + \delta_1 = \delta_1(a + 1) + \delta_2 a$ for $a := \lfloor n/\delta \rfloor$, $\delta_1 := n \mod \delta$, and $\delta_2 := \delta - \delta_1$.

We can show the case of $G(\boldsymbol{L}, \omega)$ in a similar way to the case of $F(\boldsymbol{L}, \omega)$ by the following lemma.

Lemma 3. *For any $a, j \in \mathbb{N}$ and any $r \in [a]$, choose any $b_i \in \mathbb{Z}$ such that $b_1 \ge \cdots \ge b_k > -(a - r) \ge b_{k+1} \ge \cdots \ge b_j > -a$ and $\sum_{i=1}^{j} b_i = 0$. Then, it holds that*

$$aj \binom{a-1}{r}$$

$$< (a+b_1)\binom{a+b_1-1}{r} + (a+b_2)\binom{a+b_2-1}{r} + \cdots + (a+b_k)\binom{a+b_k-1}{r}.$$

Note that the above lemma holds even if $r = 1$, whereas Lemma 2 holds if $r \geq 2$. Hence, we can prove that if $\omega \geq 1 \wedge n/\delta \in \mathbb{N}$, then the minimum value of $G(\boldsymbol{L}, \omega)$ is given when $\ell_1 - \ell_\delta = 0$. Similarly, we can prove that if $\omega \geq 1 \wedge n/\delta \notin \mathbb{N}$, then the minimum value of $G(\boldsymbol{L}, \omega)$ is given when $\ell_1 - \ell_\delta = 1$.

Thus, the proof of Theorem 2 is completed.   □

Hence, we can obtain the following minimal sizes of secret keys by applying the optimal parameter obtained from Theorem 2 to our generic construction.

Corollary 2. *Let Π be an $(\leq n, \leq \omega; \delta)$-one-time secure BES from our generic construction. Let $a := \lfloor n/\delta \rfloor$, $\delta_1 := n \mod \delta$, and $\delta_2 := \delta - \delta_1$. Then, the sizes of the secret keys (in particular, decryption keys) can be minimized when we apply δ_1 $(\leq a+1, \leq \omega_1)$-KPSs Φ_i $(1 \leq i \leq \delta_1)$ and δ_2 $(\leq a, \leq \omega_2)$-KPSs Φ_i $(\delta_1 + 1 \leq i \leq \delta)$ to Π, where $\omega_1 := \min\{a, \omega\}$ and $\omega_2 := \min\{a-1, \omega\}$. Namely, we have*

$$(i)\ \log|\mathcal{EK}| = \left(\delta_1 \sum_{j=0}^{\omega_1} \binom{a+1}{j} + \delta_2 \sum_{j=0}^{\omega_2} \binom{a}{j}\right) \log q,$$

$$(ii)\ \sum_{i=1}^{n} \log|\mathcal{DK}_i| = \left(\delta_1(a+1) \sum_{j=0}^{\omega_1} \binom{a}{j} + \delta_2 a \sum_{j=0}^{\omega_2} \binom{a-1}{j}\right) \log q.$$

As the result, the above is an upper bound on sizes of secret keys required for $(\leq n, \leq \omega; \delta)$-one-time secure BESs for any $\delta \in [n]$.

Remark 1. As can be seen in Theorem 2, we cannot always minimize both of the encryption-key size and the decryption-key size for any n, ω, and δ. Specifically, the above size of encryption keys is not minimal one if $\omega = 1$, however in that case, the overhead of the encryption key is small. Therefore, in Corollary 2, we chose a parameter to always minimize the decryption-key size and to make the encryption-key size as small as possible. The reason why we focus specifically on the decryption-key size is that it is generally considered that the decryption-key size is more important than the encryption-key size in the context of BESs. Actually, most of previous works (e.g., [3,4,12,13,16]) dealt with only a lower bound on the decryption-key size.

Remark 2. The $(\leq n, \leq \omega; \delta)$-one-time secure BES with the above optimal parameter includes known two constructions described in Sect. 2.3: When $\delta = 1$, then the above key size is equal to that of the Fiat–Naor construction; and when $\delta = n$, then the above key size is equal to that of the trivial construction. Therefore, we can say our construction is a natural extension of these known constructions.

4   Concluding Remarks

In this paper, we proposed a generic construction of an $(\leq n, \leq \omega; \delta)$-BES from KPSs, which can be regarded as a natural extension of the two existing constructions. However, there are many possible combinations of KPSs to realize the $(\leq n, \leq \omega; \delta)$-one-time secure BES in our construction methodology. Therefore, we found the best parameters among all possible combinations of KPSs in the sense that secret-key size can be minimized. Our construction is the first construction of an $(\leq n, \leq \omega; \delta)$-one-time secure BES for arbitrary $\delta \in [n]$, and therefore this work is the first concrete analysis of trade-offs between the secret-key size and the ciphertext size in $(\leq n, \leq \omega; \delta)$-one-time secure BESs for arbitrary $\delta \in [n]$.

Deriving a tight bound on the size of secret keys required for $(\leq n, \leq \omega; \delta)$-one-time secure BESs for arbitrary $\delta \in [n]$ is an open problem which is not easy to solve in general, whereas such a tight bound has been well studied and known in the case $\delta = 1$ in the literature. In this paper, as the first step for solving the problem, we showed an upper bound on the size of secret keys required for $(\leq n, \leq \omega; \delta)$-one-time secure BESs by means of natural extension of the existing constructions for the BESs.

Acknowledgments. We would like to thank anonymous referees for their helpful comments. We would also like to thank Shota Yamada and Goichiro Hanaoka for their valuable comments for the preliminary version of this paper. The first author is supported by JSPS Research Fellowships for Young Scientists. This work (Yohei Watanabe) was supported by Grant-in-Aid for JSPS Fellows Grant Number 25·3998. This work (Junji Shikata) was supported by JSPS KAKENHI Grant Number 15H02710, and it was partially conducted under the auspices of the MEXT Program for Promoting the Reform of National Universities.

References

1. Berkovits, S.: How to broadcast a secret. In: Davies, D.W. (ed.) EUROCRYPT 1991. LNCS, vol. 547, pp. 535–541. Springer, Heidelberg (1991)
2. Blom, R.: An optimal class of symmetric key generation systems. In: Beth, T., Cot, N., Ingemarsson, I. (eds.) EUROCRYPT 1984. LNCS, vol. 209, pp. 335–338. Springer, Heidelberg (1985)
3. Blundo, C., Cresti, A.: Space requirements for broadcast encryption. In: De Santis, A. (ed.) EUROCRYPT 1994. LNCS, vol. 950, pp. 287–298. Springer, Heidelberg (1995)
4. Blundo, C., Frota Mattos, L.A., Stinson, D.R.: Trade-offs between communication and storage in unconditionally secure schemes for broadcast encryption and interactive key distribution. In: Koblitz, N. (ed.) CRYPTO 1996. LNCS, vol. 1109, pp. 387–400. Springer, Heidelberg (1996)
5. Blundo, C., De Santis, A., Herzberg, A., Kutten, S., Vaccaro, U., Yung, M.: Perfectly-secure key distribution for dynamic conferences. In: Brickell, E.F. (ed.) CRYPTO 1992. LNCS, vol. 740, pp. 471–486. Springer, Heidelberg (1993)

6. Boneh, D., Gentry, C., Waters, B.: Collusion resistant broadcast encryption with short ciphertexts and private keys. In: Shoup, V. (ed.) CRYPTO 2005. LNCS, vol. 3621, pp. 258–275. Springer, Heidelberg (2005)
7. Chen, H., Ling, S., Padró, C., Wang, H., Xing, C.: Key predistribution schemes and one-time broadcast encryption schemes from algebraic geometry codes. In: Parker, M.G. (ed.) Cryptography and Coding 2009. LNCS, vol. 5921, pp. 263–277. Springer, Heidelberg (2009)
8. Dodis, Y., Fazio, N.: Public key broadcast encryption for stateless receivers. In: Feigenbaum, J. (ed.) DRM 2002. LNCS, vol. 2696, pp. 61–80. Springer, Heidelberg (2003)
9. Fiat, A., Naor, M.: Broadcast Encryption. In: Stinson, D.R. (ed.) CRYPTO 1993. LNCS, vol. 773, pp. 480–491. Springer, Heidelberg (1994)
10. Garay, J.A., Staddon, J., Wool, A.: Long-lived broadcast encryption. In: Bellare, M. (ed.) CRYPTO 2000. LNCS, vol. 1880, p. 333. Springer, Heidelberg (2000)
11. Gentry, C., Waters, B.: Adaptive security in broadcast encryption systems (with short ciphertexts). In: Joux, A. (ed.) EUROCRYPT 2009. LNCS, vol. 5479, pp. 171–188. Springer, Heidelberg (2009)
12. Kurosawa, K., Yoshida, T., Desmedt, Y.G., Burmester, M.: Some bounds and a construction for secure broadcast encryption. In: Ohta, K., Pei, D. (eds.) ASIACRYPT 1998. LNCS, vol. 1514, pp. 420–433. Springer, Heidelberg (1998)
13. Luby, M., Staddon, J.: Combinatorial bounds for broadcast encryption. In: Nyberg, K. (ed.) EUROCRYPT 1998. LNCS, vol. 1403, pp. 512–526. Springer, Heidelberg (1998)
14. Matsumoto, T., Imai, H.: On the key predistribution system: a practical solution to the key distribution problem. In: Pomerance, C. (ed.) CRYPTO 1987. LNCS, vol. 293, pp. 185–193. Springer, Heidelberg (1988)
15. Naor, D., Naor, M., Lotspiech, J.: Revocation and tracing schemes for stateless receivers. In: Kilian, J. (ed.) CRYPTO 2001. LNCS, vol. 2139, pp. 41–62. Springer, Heidelberg (2001)
16. Padró, C., Gracia, I., Martín, S.: Improving the trade-off between storage and communication in broadcast encryption schemes. Discrete Appl. Math. **143**(1–3), 213–220 (2004)
17. Padró, C., Gracia, I., Martín, S., Morillo, P.: Linear broadcast encryption schemes. Discrete Appl. Math. **128**(1), 223–238 (2003)
18. Phan, D.H., Pointcheval, D., Strefler, M.: Security notions for broadcast encryption. In: Lopez, J., Tsudik, G. (eds.) ACNS 2011. LNCS, vol. 6715, pp. 377–394. Springer, Heidelberg (2011)

Author Index

Printed in the United States
By Bookmasters